The Life & Times of Swansea R.F.C.

THE
ALL WHITES

The Life & Times of Swansea R.F.C.

THE ALL WHITES

DAVID FARMER

with contributions by

David Price & Vernon Rees Davies

FOR IVOR WATKINS

Christian, Carpenter, Teacher, Gentleman

and 'All Whites' season ticket holder from 1919 until his death in December 1993

Published by

DFPS Ltd
Beaufort House, Beaufort Road
Plas-Marl, Swansea, SA6 8JG

Published in conjunction with the

BJ GROUP plc
sponsors of Swansea R.F.C.

ISBN 0 9525680 0 4

Printed in Wales by
Dinefwr Press
Rawlings Road, Llandybïe
Dyfed, SA18 3YD

Cover Photographs:
Front: Top (left to right): Billy Bancroft, Billy Trew, Dickie Owen.
Bottom (left to right): Dewi Bebb, Mervyn Davies, Robert Jones.
Back: Top: 'Genny' Gordon's Invincibles.
Bottom (left to right): Dick Jones, Clem Thomas, David Richards, Richard Moriarty.

CONTENTS

FOREWORD

Sir Glanmôr Williams

IT IS IMPOSSIBLE TO THINK of any town or city in Wales that has a stronger awareness of local patriotism than Swansea. All those born in the city, or even associated with it by long habitation, cherish this sense of pride and affection for it. One of the most powerful strands within that feeling, for the past one hundred years or more, has been Swansea's ecstatic delight in its 'All-Whites'. The unique conjunction of playing first-class rugby and first-class cricket on the same delightful St. Helen's field has only added still further to that emotion. Its characteristics are unmistakable: intense devotion – usually life-long – to the club; inextinguishable belief in its unquenchable spirit; and the burning conviction that there has always been a superior style of open, flowing, inventive rugby played in Swansea which, at its best, is unsurpassed in the world. There is a confidence that, on their day, the 'All-Whites' have been able to take on any team from anywhere and prove more than a match for them. Yet, running through it all, too, is the typical South Wales humour, nowhere to be found more pointed than in Swansea. Those mischievous, light-hearted, and good-natured observations on players (especially opponents!), and fellow-spectators (with some of the more barbed shafts being reserved for visitors from Llanelli, Cardiff, and Neath!). Underlying it all, like some constant ground-bass, is that note of laconic satire and realism that always keeps Swansea feet firmly on the ground, never allowing them to become too levitated in their raptures. One of the healthiest instincts of the club throughout its history has been its capacity to shrug off defeat and disappointment and start again with renewed hope. The jinx of inconsistency or under-performance has never been allowed to cast too long a shadow; behind the passing clouds, bright sunshine has invariably lit up Swansea Bay.

It takes a Swansea man, born and bred, to inherit this legacy to the full and be able to convey it to others. It needs an even rarer being to recapture the whole flavour of the collective mentality of players, officials and the 'faithful' over a century or more. By remarkable good fortune, the club found just such a person in David Farmer. Born, brought up, and educated in Swansea, he absorbed the city's sporting tradition with the very air he breathed. The many years he spent away from Swansea putting a fine edge on his skills as scholar, business expert, and author, served only to intensify his affection for his native 'square mile'. Now, back among his own, he has returned to write an enthralling history of the Swansea Rugby Football Club. He has not only with incredible diligence combed the formal printed and written sources of its history but has succeeded in restoring to life something much more elusive – its personality, mind and spirit. He has gone to immense pains to set down for the present generation and posterity the euphoria of the many successes and triumphs and, also, the breathless anxiety and the occasional despair; these conflicting moods that are an essential part of the saga of a club's history. He has done it with a sureness and readability of style, and enlightened his whole narrative with a guiding sense of serious purpose lit up by charming touches of humour.

No wonder, then, that in a club of such peerless achievement and tumultuous emotions, there should have been so many heroes and demi-gods down the generations; men whose names are mentioned with bated breath wherever the game of rugby is played. To name any one of these Olympian figures would be invidious. If rugby is anything, it is a team game; every team is more than its stars, it performs only as well as all its members play. Behind the players themselves, stand a host of others: coaches, bottle-carriers, programme-sellers, officials, and the thousands down the years 'on the tanner bank'. They also serve who only stand and shout.

PREFACE

David Price, J.P.

WHEN READING Professor David Farmer's 'Magnum Opus' on the *Life and Times of Swansea R.F.C.* it would be difficult not to be impressed by the quantity and quality of detail within the book. David Farmer has produced what surely must be the definitive history of the 'All Whites'; a work which will be appreciated by all who have been entranced by the rugby game at St. Helens.

It is manifest that behind the finished text lies an extensive programme of painstaking research in both local and national archives, followed by assiduous drafting and re-drafting. As the reader will perceive, the author brings to his work a lifetime of experience as a businessman, academic, management consultant, sportsman, and writer, and, as will be obvious, a special feeling for Swansea.

The book fills a long-felt need for a full, interesting and accurate account of the history of Swansea Rugby Club, following, as it does, the laudable first attempt, by Brinley E. Matthews, which was published almost thirty years ago.

The concept of the book arose as a result of a conversation at St. Helens between the author, myself and several committee members. We agreed at that time that there was a need for a definitive history of the Club, and, like all those who have great affection for the 'All Whites', we are extremely grateful to Professor Farmer for using his time and talents over such a long period in order to satisfy that need.

In order to give the reader some idea of the extent of the research which has been necessary, it would be helpful to point out that extremely few records exist at the Club for the period from 1874 up to the start of the second World War. The major exception is a General Committee minute book for the period 1903-10 which has only recently come into my possession. It has always been a mystery to me that this is so, for it is difficult to accept that no records were kept by the administrators during that period. The commonly held belief is that they were destroyed in the Blitz during the early nineteen forties; but that is something I have not been able to prove or disprove.

It follows, that the book fills an extensive gap in our archives at St. Helens, and provides a fascinating record of the happenings at the Cricket Field interwoven with the fabric of Swansea society as it has developed in parallel with the life of our club. In that respect, it is a valuable social document which describes the part which the 'All Whites' played in the nascent industrial town of Swansea. The descriptions of the Victorian and Edwardian town are vivid, particularly those of the early torch-lit processions, when Swansea men returned home after league and cup victories, and were met at the railway station by hundreds of supporters, who transported them through the streets of the town in triumph. The players of that era became legendary figures within the town and were held up as exemplars to the youth of the old borough. Meanwhile, the club developed into an institution which represented Swansea itself at home or abroad, wherever it played.

Another notable feature of the book is the section containing the appendices. In the first of these, the author has listed over two thousand men, some famous, some not so famous, and, probably, even some who were infamous, who have represented the Club at first team level since its inception. All these men, whether they played on one occasion or on several hundred, are part of the Club's history, as indeed are the trainers, committeemen, club officials, supporters and ladies' committees, and others who are mentioned in the book. These lists will provide each reader with memories of times, occasions, places and people which will be of singular fascination. As, indeed, will the extensive photographic content of the book. The stalwart men in those wonderful early photographs would be proud to see their faces contained within the covers of this book, and to read about the part which they played in the life of this great club.

This book will take its place on the shelves of the most discerning rugby enthusiast, but is unlikely to remain there unread. Apart from anything else, it is an extensive book of reference, one which will settle many arguments now and in the future. It is a book which will be read and re- read over the years ahead.

It is my view that,as a result of completing this work, David Farmer is assured of his place in the Valhalla of rugby writers and historians. Could there be a greater accolade?

AUTHOR'S INTRODUCTION

IT IS INEVITABLE THAT ANY BOOK project which has necessitated extensive research, and which has taken over two years to complete, will have involved many people other than the author. Consequently, in this introduction, it is appropriate for me to thank all those who have helped me over the last thirty months. Whilst space does not allow me to name every person who has been of assistance, I wish to place on record my appreciation of *all* the help which I have been given. Taken together, that assistance has made a significant contribution to the writing of the book which you have in your hands. I am grateful for that support.

In making this statement, I feel it to be important to record my thanks, not only for the support which related to the the content of the book, but also that which helped to sustain my enthusiasm throughout the project. I believe that it was J. B. Priestley who said, 'I only write when I feel like it, and I make sure that I feel like it at nine o clock every morning.' As far as the present author is concerned, the motivational support which I received over the two and a half years made a major contribution to supporting my own inner-drive in 'making sure that I felt like it.' As will be seen from the following section, certain individuals were of immense help to me in that regard. Nonetheless, each cheery 'How's the book going, David?', also played its part.

One important motivator as far as I was concerned, was the enthusiasm for the project shown by everyone at St. Helens. Everyone from EDDIE BURNS on the door of the officials entrance, through to Presidents, VIVIAN DAVIES and DAVID PRICE, from Chairman MIKE JAMES and his board to PAUL CULLEN and his staff retained interest in the progress of the work throughout the life of the project. Whenever I asked for assistance it was readily forthcoming, and invariably was provided in a manner which demonstrated interested enthusiasm.

In particular, I received significant encouragement first from VIVIAN DAVIES and subsequently from DAVID PRICE, as a result of their agreement to read each of the twenty-eight chapters (in draft form) as they became available. Their task was to consider the accuracy of the content from the standpoint of their vast experience of all things St. Helens. Not only did their work prove to be helpful to me as regards the content, but their comments and obvious pleasure in undertaking the task had a positive impact on me in motivational terms. It is important to point out however, that from the outset we agreed that it was my prerogative to interpret the information which I had, and to present it according to my own perceptions. It follows that it is my view of the history of Swansea Rugby Club which is contained within these pages. Thus any errors of interpretation are mine, as, indeed are any errors of fact. Nonetheless, if it should ensue, my St. Helens 'Readers' are entitled to a share in any positive reaction. Thank you gentlemen!

I wish to thank DAVID PRICE, too, for allowing me to use the extensive records which he has maintained since becoming secretary of the Club. These data were of immense benefit to me, not only with the regard to the appendices which appear at the back of the book, but with respect to the discussion in the various chapters. David's memories of people and events at St. Helens over the last half century were also extremely helpful.

Earlier I mentioned the importance to me of motivational feedback. In that regard I have been extremely fortunate in having had, throughout the project, the ready guidance, support and warm friendship of PROFESSOR SIR GLANMOR WILLIAMS. When I undertook the initial planning for the book, I wanted to ensure that the work, as it developed, was of a standard which would make a useful contribution, not only to Swansea Rugby Club, but to the history of Swansea itself. Having, previously had the benefit of the advice of Professor Williams in that regard, I was delighted when he agreed to read each draft chapter with that need in mind. Typically, not only did he read the material and make helpful suggestions, but each of the twenty-eight chapters which landed on his doormat was returned to me with some comment in the covering note which helped to motivate me. Given the scholarship and standing of Professor Williams as an historian, this was of particular benefit to me, an amateur intruder into the field. What a delight it must have been to have sat at Sir Glanmor's feet as a student! If my experience is anything to go by, to have done so must have been the height of privilege. Thank you Sir! *Diolch yn fawr!*

At this point I should like to thank my wife, PAT, for her forbearance. Apart from anything else, during the last months of the project, my study spread into lounge, dining room, and on occasions even kitchen. Not surprisingly, my single-minded dedication to my 'production schedule' resulted, shall we say, in times of frustration. One result of all this is that, 'now that the book is finished', there are numerous tasks which are set to be completed in and around the house, and a variety of places which are to be visited. Yet, despite it all, as has happened on a score of previous occasions, she has given me her full support. I am extremely grateful for that. Usual message!

Given the scarcity of material available, particularly concerning the early days of the Club, in the initial stages of the project I appealed for anything which would be of assistance to me. Among those who responded to my request were the following :

TONY JENKINS of Gowerton loaned me two scrapbooks which had been compiled by Glanddu, youngest son of Morgan Jenkins, the old Swansea wholesale draper. BARRY GRIFFITHS of Dunvant let me borrow a copy of the programme for the 1905 New Zealand match. BOBBY WHITE, an old cricketing colleague, loaned me many items, including a copy of the rare book by Rev. Marshall, *Football-The Rugby Union game* (1892). JEFF TOWNS, of Dylans Book Store, was also of considerable assistance to me in loaning books and photographs which proved to be of considerable benefit to me; BILLY TREW (Jnr) let me have several photographs relating to his father's period at St. Helens, as well as an insight into his modest disposition. Another former player, CURTIS GROVE, sent me a photograph of a 1950's Sevens side, whilst LEN BLYTH, also a St. Helens stalwart, gave me numerous photographs from his playing days, as did DIL. JOHNSON. Other former 'Whites' who were helpful with respect to the photographic section of the book, were TEIFION WILLIAMS, FRANK WILLIAMS, JEFF HERDMAN, HAROLD POWELL, GEORGE TAYLOR, STUART PARKER, DEWI BEBB, HARRY PAYNE, CLIFF BANCROFT, ROGER BLYTH, HUW DAVIES, DAVID RICHARDS AND CLEM THOMAS, who, not having kept many photographs, searched high and low to assist me. In addition, MRS. J. IDWAL REES loaned me several items of interest, including photographs of her late husband. IVOR MORGAN let me borrow several books, including the history of the Barbarians. BRIAN SIMPSON entrusted me with the original letter from the

E.R.F.U. relating to the reinstatement of the James brothers. TUDOR DAVIES of Pennard let me borrow an 1890's team photograph which included his grandfather, Livingstone, and JILL FORWARD loaned me the photograph of the Uplands Hotel. MRS. MARCIA THOMAS found the photograph of 'St. Helens around 1910' and let me borrow it, and MRS. ANN PORTSMOUTH, daughter of Bruce Barter, let me have a great deal of material from her father's files. In addition, Mrs. Portsmouth loaned me an historic 'almanack' of matches played by the 'Whites' in the 1880's, which was published by the Swansea Finance Company of Goat Street. CHRIS THOMAS, was also extremely helpful. Current players, RICHARD MORIARTY and PAUL ARNOLD, also found photographs for me, and MRS. PAT MALLETT, niece of former secretary, Cliff Prosser, let me borrow a scrapbook which had been kept by her uncle. I am grateful to them all.

My thanks, too, to HUGH BERLYN, Editor of the *South Wales Evening Post*, who gave permission for all the *Post* photographs which are included in this book to be reproduced without cost as far as the paper is concerned. BARBARA POWELL, photographic archivist on the paper's Sports Desk was extremely helpful in finding appropriate illustrations for me, and I am grateful for that willing assistance. I appreciated, too, the ready collaboration, which has always been available to me, of Sports Editor, DAVID EVANS and his colleagues. My thanks, too, to JOHN HARRIS, photographer, of Dunvant who gave permission to reproduce some of his action-shots.

At the research stage, I was well served by the staff at Swansea Museum, Swansea City Archives and at the Central Reference Library at Alexandra Road. The cheerful response of the staff at each of these establishments to what must have appeared to be my never-ending requests, was greatly appreciated, as indeed was that of the staff at Collendale, the Newspaper Library.

Further, as has always been the case, BRIAN LILE, a diligent collaborator of mine with respect to a previous project, opened up the resources of the Library at Aberystwyth for my benefit. That, too, was appreciated, as was the interest of JOHN JENKINS of Aberystwyth. I am grateful, too, for the information provided for me by PETER OWENS of the W.R.U., and my namesake, STUART FARMER, author of *The Tiger's Tale: The official history of Leicester Football Club*, for helpful information on 'Tigers' versus 'Whites' matches. In addition, BILL GREEN, that walking repository of 'Whites' history, was of considerable help to me on several occasions and I am grateful for his assistance.

As regards converting my inexpert typing into disks ready for the printer, I have to thank my daughter, JILL ISAAC, who did an outstanding job for me. As, indeed, did the team at Dinefwr Press, who, ever ready to apply their expertise to the production of a rugby book, were enthusiastic about the project from the outset (even though the history concerned a team other than those which they followed). Donald, Eddie and Emyr, in particular, 'nursed' the project with interest and enthusiasm!

Finally, I record my gratitude for the support given me by my colleagues at the B.J. Group plc; TERRY FRANCIS, MIKE JAMES, and ROBERT DAVIES. As will be seen from the dust cover of this book, the Group gave significant financial support to rugby at St. Helens, through sponsorship, over four seasons. Now, through the generosity of the directors, it has been possible to produce an 'All Whites' history of significant size. Had that support not been available, a slimmer volume would have ensued and at, proportionately, greater cost.

In that regard, too, I am grateful for all those who subscribed to the Limited Edition, which given the economics of publishing, particularly of a single book, was an essential element in the business plan concerned with the production of this history. Thank you, ladies and gentlemen.

The book

It could be argued that it was an impossible task to attempt to chronicle over one hundred and twenty years of the history of Swansea Rugby Club, and to compress it into 200,000 words. Yet, given the commercial realities of the market-place, whatever the difficulties involved, if a book was to be produced, then there was no option other than to make an honest attempt to satisfy the criteria, whilst accepting the constraints.

Nonetheless, in so doing, it will be obvious to the reader that I have been obliged to omit a vast amount of material from the main body of the text. Among other things, in the narrative. I have not been able to include the names of many players who have worn the white jersey, and I have had to omit accounts of countless matches which have been played over the years. As a result, it is inevitable that my account will disappoint many who may have deserved to have been mentioned, or mentioned more frequently,or others, where friends and loved ones believe them to have been so deserving. In response I can only ask all concerned to have in mind what I have tried to do.

The story which you are about to read is, as far as I have been able to make it, an accurate account of the life and times of Swansea Rugby Club. In writing it, whilst recording the 'facts' of its life, I have attempted to capture the ethos and the 'personality' of that great institution as it has evolved over more than a century. In addition, I have done my best to reflect the vision, the ambition, the humour and the character, not only of the individuals involved, but of the institution itself. Furthermore, I have attempted to meet these objectives whilst producing a book which will be attractive to read and to look at.

Whatever the shortcomings of the finished product – and I accept full responsibility for them all – I offer it as an honest, objective attempt to present a complex story in a form which reflects its subject in the most appropriate way. If, perchance, what is written provides the reader with a pleasurable insight into the many facets of the story of the 'Whites', then I shall be delighted! Whilst acknowledging that the finished book is the outcome of hundreds of hours of quite exacting work, I should own to the fact that, if the reader enjoys reading it, such benefit must stem from the pleasure which I have derived from writing the book. In my days as a management teacher I argued, frequently, that the 'Nonconformist work ethic' was more powerful that the Protestant variety. Whilst, at the time, my tongue might have been embedded in my cheek, my experience of life suggests that, at least as far as my generation is concerned, there is more than an element of truth in the hypothesis. Certainly,it appears that I may be imbued with the version which stems from the Congregational denomination. For me, work has proved to be a source of enjoyment and satisfaction on numerous occasions.

In closing, I wish to record my gratitude to Swansea Rugby Club for aligning themselves with me and with this project, and for the accidents of life which led to me being selected as the chronicler of the history of such a famous Swansea institution.

DAVID FARMER
Swansea, July 1995

P.S. *A point of explanation*

In the text which follows, Llanelli is spelt in the current way. However, where the name of the town is contained within a quotation, then the original form is retained.

LEN BLYTH

Literally, just a matter of hours before this book was to 'go to press', came the news that Len Blyth had died in South Africa. He had been there to see the World Cup, and had passed away during the morning following the final of that competition. Len will be sadly missed, not only by his loved ones, but by his many friends, both at St. Helens and in the wider context of world rugby football.

For more than 50 years, Len had been involved with cricket and football at St. Helens. As far as Swansea Rugby Club is concerned, he was initially a player, subsequently became chairman of selectors, chairman of the club, and President, and was, finally, a Life Patron. In each of those roles, Len served the club which he loved with that special fervour which made him the man he was.

Len Blyth made his début for the 'Whites' during the 1946-47 season, was Club Captain for the 1951-52 campaign and was 'capped' during the same period against South Africa, England and Scotland. As the reader of the story which follows will perceive, the name Blyth is etched deeply into the very fabric of Swansea Rugby Club, thus it is fitting that this brief tribute to a special man should be included in this book.

ILLUSTRATION ACKNOWLEDGEMENTS

THE FOLLOWING LIST SHOWS THE ORIGIN of each illustration which is included in this book. Reasonable care has been taken to ensure that proper reference has been made to the originator of the photograph or drawing. Where it has not been possible to identify a source, the person who loaned the item to the author is cited. Once again, the author wishes to thank all concerned for their assistance in helping to ensure that this book is well illustrated.

Chapter 10

Chapter 11

Chapter 12

Chapter 13

Chapter 14

Chapter 15

Chapter One

THE EARLY DAYS

IT WAS AT A MEETING held at the Tenby Hotel on 12th October 1874 that a momentous proposal was put to the members of the Swansea Football Club. It was then, according to James Livingstone, writing in 1910, that it was proposed that the Club should adopt Rugby Union rules rather than those of Association Football, which had been its code since inception. However, the meeting could not come to a conclusion, and F. F. Meager, who had put the proposal, ensured that it was not defeated by arranging for an adjournment to be moved. Meager, who was to play an important part in the development of the Club, then used his considerable political skills to convene a further meeting at the Club's ground five days later. At that meeting, with a quorum weighted in his favour, he and his supporters carried the day. From that day forward, Rugby Football became the adopted code of the Swansea Football Club.

The combination of factors which, probably, resulted in Meager's motion are discussed in some detail in that excellent book, *Fields of Praise*. Suffice it to say here that, as a result of that change, Swansea men were destined to play a significant part in the development, not only of the Swansea club, but of the rugby game in south Wales.

It was in 1872 that the Swansea Football Club had first been formed, with a view to ensuring that the town had a credible representative body to play the game. The Club decided to adopt Association Football rules, though, despite the codification of the laws of that game and of Rugby Football, the games played in those days took various forms. For example, in 1871, a match was played on the Swansea Grammar School ground between twelve of the schoolboys and a dozen gentlemen from the Town. Interestingly, in view of what was to happen three years later, the Town side had been 'got together' by Mr F. F. Meager. The brief report in the *Cambrian* stated that the School 'kicked a goal' from which we might assume that some form of rugby had been played, had we not known that during 1871 this was the *Cambrian's* sole reference to football of any kind. In consequence, the reporter might have been as confused as the handful of spectators.

Notwithstanding the emergence of a football club in the town, up until that time, and, indeed, for several years to come, the major sporting pastime in Swansea was cricket. And it is proper in the present context to recognise the significant role which the Swansea Cricket Club played in the early development of Swansea rugby. Apart from anything else, the early leaders in the development of the winter game were also active cricketers. Included among them were C. C. Chambers, W. H. Gwynn, F. F. Meager, E. M. Jones, H. R. Knill and H. A. Richardson.

In this context it is interesting to note the subordinate position occupied by football *vis-a-vis* cricket around that time, at least if we are to accept a statement in the *Cambrian* of June 1876 as evidence:

The Uplands Hotel.
This photograph was taken long after the 'Whites' had gone to St. Helens. However, the building shown is substantially as it was when Swansea C & F Club used it as an unofficial clubhouse.

> ... the truest representatives of the 'old village green' will be found on the modern cricket field. At any rate, up to the present, this is so in Swansea. Most of the subordinate games and the proudest associations of the players cling around the leading pastime of cricket ... cricket deserves its national pre-eminence because of its moderation. It is free from the abuses, the rough play and the cruelty of ruder games.

Nonetheless, the fact that many of the town's cricketers were also its footballers suggests that, short of some form of metamorphosis, the participants gained great enjoyment from both games. Indeed, it would seem that, because of their enjoyment of the winter game, the cricketers of that period were prepared to put at risk the wickets on which they played during the summer. The point being that the two games often shared the same ground for much of the early period and, in winter, rugby was played over the cricket square. For lovers of cricket, especially if they aspired to be batsmen, that called for a long suffering tolerance above and beyond the call of duty. As cricketer of the period, E. M. Jones put it:

> In those days (the last decades of the century) football was played over the cricket pitch and consequently the wickets began to get in decent condition about the end of August, if we were favoured with wet weather ... given fine weather they were never, at any time, fit to play on.

But tolerate the situation they did, firstly at the old Bryn-y-Môr field, then at the Primrose

Field, and subsequently at St. Helens, though it is fair to say that, as time went on, the tolerance of those early cricketers was tempered by economic necessity.

At the time when the Swansea Football Club was first formed its games, like those of the Cricket Club were played on the picturesque Bryn-y-Môr field, (opposite the Uplands Hotel) which was encircled by mature trees. One problem with this venue was that the ground was inclined to hold water which, even in those days, at times fell rather too liberally on Swansea. As a consequence, on several occasions the ground was too marshy to allow football to be played and games were transferred to Swansea sands. These matches as the reporter 'Free-lance' observed, 'were not confined to Saturday afternoons, and advantage was taken of the moonlight nights to play in the vicinity of the Slip'.

When the Cricket Club was given notice to leave the Bryn-y-Môr field so that houses might be built there, the footballers also found themselves without a home. Their solution was to play their matches on the ground which was to become that of the Workingmen's Club. Known as the Primrose Field, this arena sloped from one goal to the other, which added an extra hazard to all matches played there. Since the pitch was off Constitution Hill (where Chaddersley Terrace and Cromwell Street now stand) it was centrally convenient. However, that advantage was more than offset by the disadvantages of the slope and the lack of other facilities. Not surprisingly, when the footballers followed the cricketers to St. Helens at the end of the 1874/75 season, it was not with any great reluctance.

The significant role of the Cricket Club in obtaining and developing St. Helens will be discussed in greater depth in the next chapter. At this point, the part played by The Swansea Workingmen's Club and Institute in the destiny of the footballers should also be noted, since, because many of the rugby men were members of this institute, it was used by them for some time as an unofficial club house.

To understand what, at this distance, may seem to be an unusual liaison, the reader should consider the background to the Institute's establishment. Writing in 1878, a *Cambrian* reporter pointed out that 'The club affords a common platform upon which the magistrate, county gentleman, merchant and higher class trades people may meet and mingle with their artisan brethren to the mutual advantage of all concerned.'

Marx might have been tempted to interpret such a situation as providing, like religion, another opiate for the working classes, but, at the time in question there was real concern to promote healthy activities among working people. That apart, as far as the footballers were concerned, this was the place where 'officers' and 'men' might meet on common ground. Indeed, it was to the Institute, in High Street, that the human cavalcade of the Swansea team and its supporters proceeded on returning from Carmarthen in March 1880, having won the South Wales Football Cup for the first time. As the press reported, 'Captain Richardson and the other players were carried through the town in triumph.'

When they arrived at the Institute they would have found the familiar surroundings, so lyrically described a year later by another reporter on the occasion of the fourth Anniversary of the worthy organisation:

> The place, though rough, had an eminently comfortable appearance ... a cheerful blazing fire ... at a long table sat a company of notable gentlemen ready to speak ... in front, many ... benches well tenanted by smartly dressed young women and more soberly

James Livingstone – patriarch; campaigner for healthy activity for the working man; senior figure in the fight to save St. Helens. This photograph was taken around 1900.

> attired matrons, together with working men and youths ... It may be mere sentimentality, but to our mind there is a kind of luxury there, walking on a well saw-dusted floor, the little yellow grains of wood impressing you with an idea of freshness, and sending up to your nostrils that sometimes sweet woody odour.

Whatever its attractions, it was to be the haunt of many Swansea footballers for several years to come.

Early games

James Livingstone suggests that the first match played by the Swansea club under rugby rules was that against Llandovery College, though a September edition of the *Cambrian* listed four prospective fixtures for the Swansea Football Club with the Llandovery game being a 'return'. This is intriguing, for those fixtures which were listed must have been arranged when the Club favoured Association. Yet, as David Smith and Gareth Williams point out, there were influences at the College which favoured the oval ball game. Was this the influence which reached Swansea and F. F. Meager in particular? Whatever the reason, the fact that the fixture was played under rugby rules suggests that the College officials were more than willing partners in the venture. If that is the case, and noting the date of the original fixture, it is probable that the first match under rugby rules took place on 28 November 1874. Livingstone, a man who was intimately involved in Swansea sport throughout this period, lists the historic side as:

C. C. Chambers (Capt.), A. Richardson, F. F. Meager, H. Sutton. Jeffreys, C. Tuckfield, A. Williams, M. T. Jones, P. O. Ingram, A. Ingram, H. Head, L. L. Green, H. R. Knill, P. Warren, and C. Sutton.

It is interesting to note that the list does not indicate the positions occupied by these players. However, the *Cambrian* and the *Swansea Journal*, the contemporary papers, began to specify players' positions in their (infrequent) reports from January 1875. For example, the Swansea team which played Glamorgan (Cardiff) F.C. at Arms Park that month designated one position in the team listed. It was E. M. Jones (Goalkeeper). By the end of that season 'Half-backs' and 'Quarter-backs' were being listed, and, in due course a pattern emerged where eight forwards, two half-backs, three quarter-backs and two backs were specified. Though, as late as 1878 the Swansea side which played Cardiff at the Sophia Gardens Field included a goalkeeper, two half-backs, and eight forwards (only fourteen players were listed). Then, just when the public must have been coming to terms with the terminology of the game, the paper listed, on two occasions, nine forwards, two half-backs, two three-quarters and two backs, a team structure which was repeated in the report of a game versus Newport in 1881, whilst twice in 1882 three half-backs were named in the side.

Another feature of the games played during this period was the paucity of opposing sides, and therefore of the number of fixtures. For example, at the end of the 1875-76 season, only eleven games were listed as having been played by the Club, and five of those were against Llandovery College. Only three other clubs were involved, Glamorgan (Cardiff), Llanelli and Newport.

Furthermore, administrative aspects of the fixtures which were played at this time hardly measured up to the levels of efficiency which nowadays would be expected. The duration of matches, for example, varied from an hour to one and a half hours, whilst kick-off times were rarely the same, with starts being noted as differently as '3.15 p.m.', 'About 3.40 p.m.', 'Shortly after 3 p.m.', '3.25 p.m.' and even '4.30 p.m.' Meanwhile, despite, or because of, the few games which were being played and the lack of central organisation, 'difficulties' occurred.

For example, in February 1879, the press noted that: 'The Swansea men were on the ground by 3 o'clock, the time selected for the commencement of the match, and waited until nearly four, but the Llanelli men had not put in an appearance'. On another occasion the referee did not turn up for a game against Neath on their ground and, when he did arrive, there was not a ball available to play with. As a result, someone had to go into the town to get one.

Violence was another concern during this period, partly, one suspects, as a result of the style of the game which was in vogue at the time. There was little passing and progress, what there was of it, was often made as a result of one-to-one confrontation. For example, a 'Maul-in-goal' was described by one scribe as 'a death like struggle for the ball, for the player who succeeded in wresting it from an opponent and touching it down was credited with a try. The struggle often lasted for several minutes.'

Whatever the reason, there were those who adopted dubious approaches which the sportsmen of the time deplored. As one writer put it: 'Some players are proverbially more or less brutal in their play ... two or three can be found in almost any team ... Foul play is all too common and ... attacks are often deliberately made on prominent players to incapacitate them'. Another wrote, following the seventh game played between Neath and Swansea in an attempt to find a winner in the cup competition of that period:

> 'It is to be regretted that some personal violence was used towards the end of the game by some members of each team ...'

Without trying to justify whatever went on in this instance, some might have cited frustration as the root cause of this trouble. Not only had the teams played six previous games without gaining a result, the match in question involved a total of two and a half hours play before a result was achieved.

Then, as now, rugby was a physical game and, from this distance, it is reasonable to make allowances for spectators brought up to watch cricket. It is hardly surprising that the football of that period should have appeared to them to be a rough, brutal and barbaric game. Certainly H. E. Sutton would have agreed with them after a game against Llanelli in 1876, when he became the first Swansea player to break his leg in a match. Fortunately, there was a Dr. Samuel on the ground and Sutton's leg was attended to immediately prior to the player being taken home to Neath. It is interesting to note that the game was brought to 'an abrupt end' as a result of the injury. Not so, however, the cup tie played against Newport at Bridgend in December 1879. The *Cambrian* reported (on the game played on a ground partly covered with ice) that: 'Fortunately only one severe accident took place, Loane of Newport broke his leg ...' On that occasion the game continued and resulted in a win for Swansea. This was the game, according to Fred Meager, in which the Swansea players wore their stockings over their boots in order to improve their grip on the icy surface. It was also the game following which Newport appealed against the result, arguing that the Swansea players were guilty of sharp practice in scoring their winning try. Nothing was to come of that appeal.

The dangers of the football field at the time were not confined to Welsh football, at least if we are to interpret with humorous imagination an item printed in the *Cambrian* in December 1876 with no comment except a minute acknowledgement to the comic journal, *Punch*, at its foot.

NEW FOOTBALL RULES

1. No match to be played without a surgeon being in attendance
2. Should there be a hospital within a convenient distance, notice to be given before hand that the services of the staff may be called into requisition.
3. An ample supply of bandages, lint, splints and other appliances to be kept always in readiness.
4. An ambulance to be in waiting to convey anyone who may receive an injury to his home or to the hospital.
5. If an ambulance cannot be procured, then a sufficient number of cabs to be within immediate call.
6. Proper attendants and nurses to be engaged to wait upon the sufferers.
7. Brandy and other stimulants to be kept on the grounds.
8. Crutches and sticks to be supplied for the use of those whose injuries may be slight, but who require some artificial support to enable them to return to their homes
9. No game to be played except on a ground within easy reach of a telegraph office.

The humour of this item would not have been lost on the football players of that period, nor would another item which appeared in the *Cambrian* soon after. It was entitled 'How to rule a tartar wife', and the present author, having found it and claiming copyright, is prepared to send full details to any contemporary sufferer in return for stand tickets for the next two internationals at Cardiff.

As the game developed so the importance of fitness and new skills emerged. A report on a game in 1877 included the comment that Swansea were so much on top that the backs had nothing to do. Subsequently, as we shall see, the most skilful teams which the club was to meet played as a unit, passed with dexterity and backed each other up. The lessons from those games were not lost on the fledgling club.

Certainly, whether the concerns about rough play were justifiable or not, there were those in the game who were thinking about more successful ways to play. Again it was Fred Meager who led the way in promoting change at Swansea. He had taken a weakened side to Newport and the Swansea men had sustained a crushing defeat. In Meager's view there were two key factors which gave Newport the edge over other sides at that time. They passed the ball 'in a rapid and dexterous way' and they were fitter than the Swansea men. Consequently, Meager came back to Swansea determined to have his men practise the art of passing whilst improving their level of fitness. As the *Cambrian* noted at the beginning of the following season, 'The Swansea men this year have gone in for judicious training, denying themselves the so-called luxuries of life and backing this up with spirited practises. The policy has borne fruit as on Saturday they defeated the once invincible Newport.'

Judging by one or two results during the following season, the decision to make the change could have been vested with greater resolve, at least in terms of longevity. For, reporting on another Newport game in 1881 the *Cambrian* noted that 'the home team (Swansea) played seven new men, and it ought to be stated that the Swansea men had only had one practise this season.'

Nonetheless, the seeds had been planted. Skill, which was to become the hallmark of Swansea success in the not-too-distant future, had been identified as one of the corner stones upon which Swansea rugby was to be built.

Following the visit to St. Helens of the English team to play Wales (1883) those lessons were re-emphasised. The Saxon invaders had shown the Welsh team and all those who watched the first International on Welsh soil, what successful rugby was all about. Spectators, officials and players alike applauded the English play. 'The superb passing of the backs, the most unselfish and uniform way in which each man played – never for himself but for his side,' as the *Cambrian* reporter put it. There were other comments from the paper's reporter, too, aimed, it seemed, at the younger men who were playing the game at that time in the Swansea area. 'Those youngsters who take an exaggerated view of their prowess ... could do well to imitate these skilled players.' No doubt, the two Swansea players who were in the historic Welsh side that day would also have enthused to their clubmates about the play of the victorious English. The men concerned, G. L. Morris and D. Gwynn, were to play their part in establishing the base from which the outstanding Swansea sides of the new century were to emerge.

Swansea F.C. absorbed the Bryn-y-Môr Club in 1886, and the Dan-y-Graig Club in 1894.

The colours first adopted by the Swansea Club were blue and white horizontal stripes. Then, for one season the players wore a vivid scarlet. The white jersey was adopted after that, and retained.

Chapter Two

THE CLUB DEVELOPS

IN 1877, WITH 'RESIDENTIAL' SWANSEA spreading towards the west of the town away from the industrial pollution of its eastern side, would-be developers eyed the new cricket field at St. Helens with considerable interest. Not surprisingly, the members of the Swansea Cricket Club and those of its sister Football Club, were less than enamoured with the possibility. Having lost their former ground to the builders only three years before, and having spent a considerable sum of money and a great deal of effort in levelling and improving their new home, they wished to stay where they were.

Following a concerted effort over a very short period, the New Cricket Field was officially opened on Whit Monday 1875 with the traditional athletics meeting run by the Cricket club. Whilst all the preparatory work had not been completed by the appointed day, '... a sufficient smooth grassy surface was secured in time for the Sports.' That day, between six and seven thousand people were reported as having come to the ground to enjoy the events and, in the process, to help defray the expenses of the Cricket Club. It was said that the site had been transformed from 'hillocks and sand dunes to billiard table surface.' John Tucker, the man who laid the turf over the sandy soil and who, later, tended it for more than a quarter of a century, deserves a special mention at this point. After all, he it was who provided the foundation for what was to become a world-renowned surface. Yet, all Tucker's efforts would have come to nought if the 'Build on St. Helens' lobby had had its way.

Fortunately for those who wished to preserve their open space, they had two champions in their midst. One was William Thomas of Lan, 'The pioneer of open spaces'; the other was the highly influential J. T. D. Llewellyn, the son of a wealthy Swansea industrialist, who was an extremely keen cricketer and a patron of the game in south Wales. In due course, Llewellyn was to become President of the W.F.U. and also a patron of rugby, but, at the time in question, it was his passion for cricket which was to be the decisive factor in saving St. Helens 'from the encroachment of unromantic lines of bricks and mortar which puts to flight all rural sweets and compels the weary denizen of the town to seek them from afar ...' as the *Cambrian* put it.

Sir J. T. D. Llewellyn, Bart.
Cricketer, Patron & President SC & FC.

Llewellyn and Thomas had collaborated on a previous occasion. Thomas had persuaded the landowner to give to the Borough what was to become Parc Llewellyn, and

The Cricket Field – St. Helens as it was circa 1910.

Llewellyn, a keen advocate of healthy sport for working people, was more than willing to collaborate with 'Lan' with regard to St. Helens. Apart from anything else, Llewellyn was a regular member of the Swansea cricket XI and it was he who brought W. G. Grace and Lillywhite, among others, to play on the new ground which many regarded as the best in Wales. In due course J.T.D. was also instrumental in arranging for his relative, Lewis Dillwyn Llewellyn, to provide a £500.00 donation to help save the ground. Whilst the campaign for open spaces, so popular at the time, was the overt reason for Llewellyn's interest, one is left with the impression that his most powerful personal motive was his love for cricket. Nonetheless, before the day when William Thomas and his allies could claim victory in the St. Helens Field question, much turbulent water was to flow beneath the bridge.

In 1878, after the controversy regarding the future of the ground had rumbled on for some time, the Mayor made a public statement. He said that the executors of the (late) Colonel Morgan were prepared to surrender their leasehold interest for the sum of £10,000. Such an offer seemed distinctly unfair, when it was the cricketers who had enhanced the value of the property at St. Helens as a direct result of their own efforts. This now seemed to work to their detriment.

As far as the Corporation was concerned, its officers argued that it did not have the money to buy the lease, nor did it wish to borrow the money involved, since that would result in an additional burden being put on the ratepayers. Nevertheless, since considerable public interest had been shown in the matter (the columns of the *Cambrian* had been filled with letters on the topic for several weeks), the Mayor decided to call a public meeting.

At that meeting, Llewellyn and Thomas marshalled their troops with great skill. Many spoke in favour of retaining the field, whilst letters from other (absent) influential gentlemen, also supporting the cause, were read to the assembled throng. Among other things Llewellyn stated that he deplored the absence of the Mayor, which indicated, he declared, that the First Citizen was partisan in the matter. After a lengthy debate, the chairman for the day concluded that a further meeting of the Council should be called to consider the views which had been so forcefully expressed.

However, by May 1880 the energetic Thomas of Lan had gathered together a 'memorial' recommending that the Cricket Field should be preserved. The press enthusiastically reported that 800 signatures were appended. To emphasise his own commitment, Thomas offered to give £500.00 towards a fund. Yet again a final decision was deferred, though a statement made at the time did give the sportsmen an assurance of safe tenancy for a number of years. At the end of that period, it was announced, 'upon mature reflection', a decision would be made. Whilst they were relieved, there were those among the sportsmen who wondered whether the pro-development party was hoping that in five years time the matter would be less fraught with public emotion. They were wise to be concerned.

During the years which were to follow several ploys were devised by the pro-developers. In 1883, for example, a part of the St. Helens Field was used as a temporary Fever Hospital and a lobby developed to make the establishment permanent. However, accompanied by much correspondence in the Press about the implications of prevailing winds and fever, that proposal was defeated. Finally, as late as April 1885, there was an attempt by the Town's 'Gallant Volunteer Corps' to secure a portion of the field at St. Helens (with a gravel surface) as a drill ground. On these and other occasions, like a true champion of his cause Thomas of Lan defeated 'the enemy'.

At long last, in the Christmas Eve edition for 1885, the *Cambrian* was able to announce:

> 'Alderman Thomas is to be congratulated ... having fought the prolonged fight and fairly won the battle in favour of retaining the St. Helens Field as an open space for the use of the public.'

St. Helens was safe, though since it was necessary to enter the ground through turnstiles, in its truest sense it was hardly an 'open space'. The sportsmen who used the ground, however, were little concerned with the niceties of language. They could drink a toast to an assured home at St. Helens, and a handsome one at that.

The Welsh Football Union

Whilst the St. Helens controversy was rumbling on, the key men at St. Helens were promoting the development of the game in Wales as well as at their own club. In September 1875 C.C. Chambers, the Club's captain, joined with colleagues from other south Wales clubs to establish the South Wales Football Club. Two other men, both of whom were to captain the 'All Whites', A. H. Richardson and F. F. Meager, were also prominent in the new organisation. These pioneers of the game saw the need for this new club as a vehicle for arranging representatives games and selecting appropriate sides. The new club's first game was against Hereford, and it was Richardson who scored the only try of the game, another unique first for the Swansea club.

Three years later, in recognition of the need to govern the game more effectively in south Wales, the new club became the South Wales Football Union, and in 1881 this body, in turn, became the Welsh Football Union. Throughout this period Swansea men played a key part in the process of development. C. C. (Charlie) Chambers was elected the Union's first President, another accolade for the Swansea club, whilst F. F. Meager, H. R. Knill and A. H. Richardson were members of the committee.

The influence of these men may be gauged by what happened after the famous meeting at the Castle Hotel, Neath. The initial County game (Glamorgan versus Monmouthshire) took place in November 1881 at Swansea's New Cricket Ground. The first Rugby International on Welsh soil – against England – was also played on the Swansea ground in December of the following year. Whilst representatives of other clubs in south Wales might have suggested that the Swansea men wielded undue influence in the matter of venues for these matches, Chambers and his colleagues held a trump card. Was there another ground to compare with the New Cricket Field? There was only one answer to that question. Not in south Wales.

W. H. Gwynn – player, coach, administrator SC & FC, first paid secretary Welsh Union.

Whilst Charlie Chambers was to bring great honour to the Swansea club by becoming the W.F.U's inaugural President, a decade later a colleague, W. H. Gwynn, was to become the Union's first paid secretary. Gwynn had played with Chambers on the cricket and football fields and had served with him on the committee of the Swansea club. Gwynn, a former soccer player of note, had been an outstanding half-back at rugby and a talented 'all rounder' on the cricket field before he took up the Welsh post. He brought vigour and honesty to his new role and was a successful secretary until illness forced him to resign his post.

The Club grows

In many respects the decade of the 1880's saw the Swansea Football Club take its greatest step forward from being a fledgling to becoming a major force in Welsh football. Building upon the foundation so skillfully laid by Chambers and his colleagues, the Club's management throughout this period is to be commended for its vision, enthusiasm and dedication to the game. Developments on the field were to catch the eye, particularly towards the end of the decade, but without effective management off it, many of the opportunities which presented themselves might have been spurned. Whilst, thanks to Meager and Chambers, Swansea Football Club started its life as a leading organisation in Welsh football, the administrators which were to follow were to ensure that that position was strengthened as the game developed in the Principality.

In 1876 the *Cambrian* was congratulating the club on being able to field two sides on the same day, and by the A.G.M of 1880 that development was formalised as a result of the appointment of a Second XV captain. During the 1875-76 season the Club played eleven games, by 1888-89 its fixture-list had increased to twenty-nine matches. Whilst, it is true that this change reflected the growth in the popularity of the game over that period, the quality of the opposition from henceforth reflected the standing of the Swansea club in the rugby football world. The hard work of the Club's administrators was a significant factor in that regard and, whereas in 1875-

76 Newport was the geographical limit of Swansea's travels, by 1888–89, Halifax, Gloucester, Bristol and Oldham were among the opposing clubs. In addition, in December 1888 new ground was broken in that the Club entertained its first touring side, Warbrick's native-born New Zealand team, then known as the *Maoris*.

The developments at the Club were also reflected in the 'Gates' throughout this period, whilst significant numbers of supporters travelled to away games on special trains. As early as 1881, the Great Western Railway ran an excursion to Neath in response to this interest and such special trains became the norm. For example, five years later the press carried the following advertisement:

> GRAND FOOTBALL MATCH
>
> Swansea v. Llanelly
> at Neath
>
> Saturday 19th February
>
> Train leaves High Street 1.35 p.m.

In 1886 2,000 people were reported to have taken the train to Llanelli to watch the 'Whites' play the 'Scarlet Runners' at the Stradey Grounds. The attendance for a game with Cardiff at St. Helens in December of the same year was noted as 5,000, whilst 3,000 more, representing the largest 'gate' of the season, saw the same sides clash at St. Helens. The gate-money from that match was reported to be the' largest known at our football matches – £113.0*s*.0*d*, though, since the adult price to watch a match at that time was 6*d* (2.5*p*), with ladies free, an auditor might have inquired why the figure was so low? Nonetheless, the income from the match was significant, as were the numbers attending, and this suggested that the 1897–88 season would see an even better return for the Football Club than that reported for the previous season. Then, at the first A.G.M. of the newly amalgamated Swansea Cricket and Football Club, it was announced that £729.8*s*.7*d* had been taken at the gate during the previous season. In contrast, and as if to demonstrate the phenomenal growth of football in terms of public interest over the previous favourite, the Cricket Club was stated to be £98.13*s*.11*d* in debt.

Developments on the field also reflected the committees' sound judgment, for new faces were beginning to appear on a regular basis. Unearthing new talent was an important objective of the Club's committee and they used various methods in that quest. For example, in November 1879 a First XV versus 'The Rest' match was played. The Rest, numbering twenty-five, was made up of players from junior clubs in the Borough and the papers reported that 'some of the opposite side played so well that they will soon be aspirants for a place in the first XV'. Useful players emerged from that process and from word of mouth recommendation, but it was to be almost a decade later before three giants of the Swansea rugby stage were to make their first appearances in the Club's colours. Whilst Swansea had had its heroes before this trio emerged,

Swansea Rugby Giants 1886.
Included in the photograph are: A. Wolff, E. M. Jones, D. Burnie, A. Whapham, T. Russell, G. Bowen, W. Bowen, D. Williams, W. Smith, J. Samuel, H. Bevan, G. James, W. Wilcocks, T. Roberts, C. Coke, E. Thorogood, A. Lewis, S. Rice, D. Samuel, J. Meredith, W. J. Bancroft, A. Lewis, W. Williams, P. Jones, W. H. Gwynn, J. Morgan, J. Thomas, J. Davies, T. Blackmore, D. Morgan, T. Deacon, T. Williams.

it is fair to say that they were to become the first major stars of the Swansea club. Though it ought to be noted that, outstanding as they were, they did have the good fortune to begin their careers following the rule changes which helped to open up the game, increased its pace and give individual talent the stage upon which skills could flourish. That trio, W. J. Bancroft and David and Evan James were to become known throughout the rugby world. Bancroft was to grace the Swansea team for many years, whilst the 'Brothers James' were to enjoy a relatively short but dramatic career akin to a pair of meteors flashing across the night sky. Others were to follow in the years to come as Swansea Football Club continued to establish itself as a major institution in the town and as a leading club in the rugby world.

There is little doubt that the changes made to the rules of rugby late in 1888 greatly benefited the game. In its early days the game must have been incredibly boring to watch. The ball was lost for long periods in 'scrimmages', whilst it was rarely, if ever, passed. Indeed the picture suggested by descriptions of games of that early period is of a mass wrestling match with numerous players on both sides being unemployed for much of the time. That image is reinforced by a painting by the South African artist, Landsberg, which shows such a maul in progress, whilst the backs of both sides stand and chat as they await developments. Whilst Swansea had done well under those conditions, they were to derive great benefit from exploiting the possibilities offered by the new rules. 'Old Hand', writing his critique of the first match played under the new laws, was enthusiastic about some aspects. He wrote, 'When a player is collared he puts the ball down at once ... this making the game much quicker than formerly.' It was also, he believed, less dangerous with fewer of the 'objectionable tight scrums'. He was appreciative, too, of the opportunities given to the backs who had '... sufficient fair play to get in their kicks.' The Swansea men were a quick to grasp the benefits of the changes in the laws as they were with comparable changes a hundred years later. Their awareness of the opportunities which presented themselves was thus reflected both in the developing skill of individuals and in the Club's results on the field of play.

At this distance it is interesting to note how, over time, the game of rugby took on a form which would be reasonably familiar to the game's supporters today. The emerging structure of teams has been mentioned before, though it was not until the mid 1880s that the four three-quarter system was adopted by the Club. Even then, as late as the end of 1889, the single full-back was still being referred to on occasions as 'the goalkeeper'. By that time, however, the two half-backs had clear roles as linkmen between the forwards and the backs, though there was continuing reference in reports of games to their 'dribbling'. As far as the forwards were concerned the skills of dribbling were an accepted part of their play for sometime thereafter. Examples from contemporary match reports illustrate the point: 'Swansea forwards, by a good rush and some all round dribbling, invaded their opponents 'ground'. and 'The Swansea Ups (forwards) showed good dribbling'. Those who watched Scottish international sides before and immediately after the Second World War would have recognised the part which 'feet' appeared to play at the time.

Whilst that aspect of the game has, largely, disappeared, modern followers of rugby will immediately relate to other developments which were being reported. David Gwynn, one of the stars of the Swansea side of the mid-eighties, was renowned, it seems, for his 'screw kick' out of his hands into touch; the Whites forwards were reported as 'wheeling the scrimmages to good advantage', whilst the 'Brothers James', W. H. Gwynn, W. H. Jones and E. Bishop were all credited by the press with remarkable skills as they attacked the opposing line. Bishop, it seems, was a specialist in 'corkscrew runs', whilst, even in their initial season, it was said of Evan and David James that 'It was a positive treat to watch the brilliant play of the 'Swansea Gems' ... the way they baffled their opponents was marvellous.' The 'Gems', too were ever ready to mix it with men who were far bigger than they were since, on account of their level of skill and understanding, they frequently became targets for over-robust opponents. For example, in a December 1889 match against Llanelli they 'took hard knocks (and) ... did not shine as usual (being) well watched by 'Gitto' Griffiths and Richards, but they stood firm in defence and stopped several ugly rushes ... the wonder is they could stand it at all.'

Meanwhile, in his report of that same game, W. J. Bancroft was being congratulated by 'Argus' on his deadly tackling. 'Banky', as the scribe called the full-back, had suffered criticism at the hands of the same journalist earlier in that season, so it would appear that he had made efforts to improve that aspect of his game. Yet there were always those who chose to criticise the great man's tackling throughout his distinguished career.

A young W. J. Bancroft in Welsh jersey v. Scotland 1892.

Whilst the arrival of 'Argus' did not signal the emergence of the specialist football journalist *per se*, at least he and his ilk could have claimed to have been in at the start of that development. Then, as now, the press reported matters which they believed would be of interest to their readers. Thus, throughout the first decade of its existence, Swansea Football Club's exploits were sparsely recorded in local papers. Conversely, the happenings in the Chapels and Churches and the development of the Blue Ribbon (temperance) movement were reported in detail. Given that many English-speaking chapels were built in Swansea during this period, there is little doubt that religion was a major focus of the population at that time. That was not to diminish until after the Second World War; but the growing interest throughout the town in the fortunes of the Football Club was to be reflected in increasing coverage being given to rugby. In effect, notwithstanding the religious fervour in the town, the press at that time was heralding the emergence of the first pastime to command mass interest in the old place.

One early sign of this interest was reflected in an edition of the *Cambrian* in February 1886 when, for the first time, it devoted a whole column to a report of the South Wales Challenge Cup match against Llanelli. By the following December the paper was reporting the departure of the Swansea Club party (twenty-two picked players, with E. S. Richards as captain of the team) for their first tour. Swinton and Dewsbury were among the scheduled opponents. By then, too, the newspaper was trumpeting '... the well earned reputation ... the Swansea Club has acquired this season throughout the football world.' Clearly, association with the Club's success was not to be sneezed at either.

When they reported on the personal standards of fitness set by certain football players, the papers were also indirectly commenting on the normal behaviour of their readership. E. S. Richards was referred to as 'an inspirational captain who leads by example.' And, in discussing the Swansea Club's win over Llanelli at Newport (described as one of the hardest fought game of football ever witnessed in south Wales) the *Cambrian* reported:

> Days prior to the match our men went into rigid training ...they disdained alcoholic beverages and met at the field every evening ... ran like hares around the field ... smoking was partially prohibited ... no wonder they looked in the pink of condition.

No doubt, the more imaginative of the many outstanding pulpit orators of the day may well have seized upon some of the inferences to be drawn from that report in order to inspire emulation among the younger men in their congregations. Given his exploits, Richards would have been an ideal role model for the young men to copy.

The Club's great win over Llanelli provoked another journalistic emotion, too. Pride and joy were to the fore as a *Cambrian* journalist reported on the return of the victorious Swansea team from Newport:

> As early as nine o clock a large throng gathered outside the High Street Railway Station. Between that hour and ten the throng increased until, at length, the square and portions of High Street and Alexandra Road were completed blocked ...

The writer then went on to describe the scene as E. S. Richards, the captain, and his men were hoisted on to the shoulders of willing supporters who carried them, in a torch-lit procession, down High Street, into Castle Street, down Temple Street into Oxford Street, and then via Union Street back to Alexandra Road. Their destination was the handsome new building, designed by Bucknall, the Swansea architect, which was the new home of the Workingmen's Club and Institute, the unofficial clubhouse of the 'All Whites'.

As he thanked the huge crowd for the enthusiasm of their reception, E. S. Richards must have realised, perhaps for the first time, that Swansea Football Club had become a vastly popular institution in the town. If for no other reason, in reporting that reception, the newspaper's proprietors must also have recognised the popular interest of the game in Swansea. Nonetheless, it took the *Cambrian* a further eighteen months before that awareness was reflected in the editorial policy.

It was in December 1888 that the newspaper announced that 'Football has become so popular ... we have decided to give a weekly record of principal matches ...' For the purpose, they stated that they had 'secured the services of an old football player of experience and repute'. thus it was that 'Old Hand' made his first appearance, commenting on the game against Bristol at St. Helens. His most important criticism concerned service to the half-backs. 'It is impossible', he wrote' for the half-back to pass the ball out until he receives it properly from the forward ... Until the ball is heeled out quicker it is impossible to have that combination which is so necessary for the success of the team.' His other criticism concerned the selection of Jones at centre. 'Jones is,' he argued, 'a wing player ... speed in a centre three-quarter is almost useless.' Whilst no modern coach would agree with this last sentiment, the comment ought to be borne in mind when considering the way the game was played during that period. Many fast centres were to play with distinction for Swansea in the years ahead.

Since no further mention was made of 'Old Hand' in the editions of the paper which were to follow, we can only assume that the former player's contract was not renewed; criticism, however, continued. Following a game just before Christmas 1888, an unnamed scribe wanted to know why a particular player had been selected. 'X,' he thundered, 'made several mistakes ... the team could have done better without him ... whatever possessed the committee to select him?'

Papers further afield were also featuring the 'All Whites' in their columns. *The Athletic News*, the leading sports paper of the day in England, commented in January 1889 that there was : 'Considerable uncertainty ... as to which of the Welsh clubs has the strongest claim to be the "Boss" team ...' With the support of a comparative table of results of the four leading Welsh sides, however, they concluded that 'Swansea is from every point of view well ahead of its formidable rivals.'

So the local Swansea press had professional confirmation from one of the leading organs of the day, if it were needed, that Swansea had a rugby side of which the town could feel proud. Whether that was the most telling stimulus or not we may never know. Nonetheless, from then on, the editor of the *Cambrian* devoted a regular section of this paper to matters concerning the 'All Whites'. The man entrusted with that task sheltered behind the *nom de plume* 'Argus'. Whether he was a watchful guardian or not, he seems to have been on familiar terms with certain of the players. As we noted earlier, the Club's new full-back star, W. J. Bancroft, was 'Banky' to him.

'Argus' was also a man who was prepared to innovate. Poetry was a regular feature in the *Cambrian*, but the football writer introduced items of doggerel into his column as the season progressed and the team was carrying all before it. His first effort hardly tripped off the tongue, but there was little doubt as to the sincerity of his sentiments:

> Hurrah for the 'All Whites' of Swansea
> We owe them of thanks a large debt
> The Champion team of the season
> Unbeaten as yet.

Then, after the side had won eight and drawn two if this first ten games, his muse took fire again:

> Once again, Hurrah for Swansea
> On the football field
> Every team that dares attack her
> Has to yield.

Whilst the results did not, perhaps, quite match the poetic sentiment, the team was unbeaten and most of its opponents had had to yield, for when the 1889-90 season came to a close, the Club had lost only four matches out of the twenty-nine played. Having won twenty-two matches out of twenty-nine, the season was the Club's most successful up to that time. One thing was certain; the Swansea press and its Rugby Club had forged a relationship which would sell many papers in the years to come. As far as S. C. Gamwell, Editor and Managing Director of the *Cambrian* at that time, was concerned, the exploits of the men in the white shirts provided the inspiration for him to write a poem in praise of the Swansea 'All Whites' which was published by the newspaper following his death.

The third verse of the poem entitled 'The "Good Old" game of Football' and subtitled 'The recantation of a somewhat crusty critic' suggests that he might have been a convert to the cause:

> How they kick! How they run! How they stop!
> How they dribble! How they pass! How they punt!
> How they save! How they score!
> And the crowds who look on –
> How they breathlessly follow the play!
> How they hiss! How they groan! How they roar!
> As a public recorder of modern days' doings
> I have heard many stories and seen many sights,
> But few things more brave than a football encounter
> With the Swansea 'All Whites'.

The first 'Caps'

Finally, in this chapter, it is right and proper to mention those men from the Swansea club who gained international recognition with Wales during the Whites' first fifteen seasons. Whilst, as Smith and Williams show, the Welsh Football Union was not officially formed until the meeting in the Castle Hotel, Neath on 12 March 1881, Wales's first recorded international was played against England at Blackheath a month before that date. It seems that no Swansea or

Llanelli players were considered for that infamous Mullock selection, for the two clubs were playing a semi-final cup-tie at Neath that same afternoon. However, with Messrs. Meager, Chambers and Richardson, all Swansea men, in key positions in the new organisation, it would have been surprising had Swansea players not been given due consideration for the next game against Ireland. In the event, G. L. Morris, a mobile forward and the Swansea captain at that time, had the honour of being selected as the first player from the Club to be 'capped'. Morris was to gain a total of five 'caps' in a relatively brief career. In 1883, David Gwynn, a classy half-back, gained recognition, and the following year his brother, W. H. Gwynn, another Swansea Club captain, joined F. G. Andrews and Morris in being selected for the matches against England and Scotland, whilst S. Goldsworthy and W. H. Gwynn played against Ireland. Between then and the last year of the decade, E. S. Richards, another great Club captain, D. Morgan, G. E. Bowen, W. H. Towers, and T. Williams were also 'capped', as were J. Meredith, W. H. Howells and E. Bishop. Thus it was that in its earliest years Swansea Football Club provided thirteen players for the National XV. In the years which were to follow many other names were to be added to the list. The above mentioned, however, were the first, a distinction which no one can ever emulate.

Chapter Three

THE BEST YET

1889-90

SUCH WAS THE FORM of the team throughout the new campaign that it was not until near the end of the 1889/90 season that the 'All Whites' lost their unbeaten record. On that day, in February 1890, 1,500 Swansea supporters had taken a G.W.R. excursion to Newport to back their team. Sadly, after 'a grand fight worthy of both contestants ... (with the) ball continually on the move and the spectators kept in a state of "fever" excitement', the Monmouthshire men emerged the victors. The 'Invincibles' could not longer lay claim to that title.

Swansea R.F.C. 1889-90.

'Argus', in his report of the game, claimed that the 'All Whites' were 'beaten by the Newport mud', conditions which, he argued, were 'foreign to the Swansea boys, so used to playing on the fast-drying St. Helens Field surface'. Yet the unbiased reader might have pointed out that, by the nature of things, only fifty percent of Swansea's games were played in that arena. Nevertheless, whether the excuse was valid or not, the Club had not sustained its unbeaten record.

Nonetheless, the Newport defeat had come after a remarkable run during which the side had won twenty-one of the two dozen games which it had played and had drawn the others. Such success had generated confidence among the Club's supporters to such an extent that they believed that their team could remain unbeaten throughout the season. It was not to be so. Indeed, following the defeat by Newport, Cardiff was to claim victory (although the 'Whites' were reduced to fourteen men for most of the game) and so did Swinton. Finally, in an extra match, played in aid of the Morfa Explosion Fund, the team were defeated by Llanelli.

Notwithstanding the disappointment of the final games, congratulations were showered on Swansea Football Club from many quarters. *The Athletic News*, the most influential sports paper of its day, stated that 'No other conclusion could be drawn other than that Swansea are entitled to whatever honours appertain to the premier team'. 'Argus', in his end-of-the-season review, bemoaned the fact that it would be six months before football was seen at St. Helens again. He congratulated the Club on its 'unparalleled and brilliant record'. The season had commenced, he wrote 'with harmony and good feeling among the players ... the result, success in so many matches'.

There were, of course, many factors which had contributed to the Club's success in that campaign. Several commentators mentioned *esprit de corps*, and most had put that down to the qualities of the Club captain, William Bowen. Bowen, described as a 'dashing, genial colleague' had not missed a match all season, despite 'leading from the front'. He had led by example, being 'always in the thick of the fray, ordering and encouraging his men on', as one scribe put it. 'Argus' wrote that he was 'an honest scrummager, a splendid dribbler, a deadly tackler, and one of the fastest in the pack.' And added, as if to emphasise Bowen's qualities of leadership, 'He is liked and admired by the whole team'.

Of course, *esprit de corps* is far easier to generate when things are going well, and Bowen was fortunate in that regard. Nonetheless, success in such matters is similar to the conundrum, which came first – the chicken or the egg? Since Bowen had set out to develop and nurture team spirit, there is little doubt that his efforts were crucial to the success which his team had enjoyed. In addition, the captain had been influential in introducing into the side embryonic folk heroes of a stature which Swansea supporters had not experienced before.

In the town, so great was the excitement which accompanied the team's success that, when a special dinner was arranged at the Mackworth Hotel, 'the room could have been filled a dozen times over'. At that celebration, James Livingstone, who was for many years a significant figure in the administration, not only of the Swansea Club but the Welsh Union, spoke in glowing terms of the team and its 'unparalleled captain'. Speaking later, Bryant, the Club secretary, emphasised the commitment of the players. They had, he said, 'trained hard, and excess in all things had been carefully avoided'. Bryant also observed that ' whilst the standard of play had been raised, so had the standard of feeling between players and spectators'. Clearly, the love affair between the Swansea public and its football heroes had begun in earnest.

Prior to the Club's A.G.M. during the following September, rumours were circulating to the effect that the Club captain wished to stand down. It seemed that Bowen, who had worked hard for his success during the previous season, was uncertain as to whether he could give as much time to the task again. However, the strength of his resolve was to be severely tested at the A.G.M. 'Amidst a scene of wild enthusiasm, Walter Evans proposed Bowen's re-election.' When that proposal was seconded, the whole meeting 'cheered to the rafters'. The captain, caught up in the enthusiasm, 'felt compelled to give way'. It was reported that all present were delighted. Whilst Bowen, as he made his way home may have contemplated his fate somewhat ruefully, in the coming season he was to be sustained by further glory. In addition, there was an added salve. At the meeting, he and his colleagues each went home with a gold medal inscribed: 'The best team in Wales', some comfort, if only in retrospect.

1890-91

Even better

Notwithstanding the success of the previous season, as the beginning of the new campaign approached, a groundswell of pessimism appeared among the Club's supporters. That peculiar quirk of the collective Welsh personality which, often, seems to focus on the negative, resulted in 'gloomy talk' around Swansea. The 'All Whites', so it was said, 'were going to collapse'. As the rumours proliferated, the supporters became more down-in-the-mouth. The overall effect of this wave of depression was demonstrated early in October. At that time, 'Argus' conducted a 'straw poll' on High Street Station prior to the departure of an excursion train bound for Neath. Not one man to whom the journalist spoke predicted a Swansea victory. It was said that 'Dr. Pegge and his Black Boys had been training all the week'. Not for the first time did a champion club find that every team it played was eager to lower its colours. Neath, according to the travelling Swansea supporters, were likely to do just that.

As it turned out, Swansea pessimists were proven to be dismal forecasters. 'Digging deep', the 'All Whites' won a bruising encounter by a goal and a minor to a minor. It is interesting to note here that whilst a minor did not result in any points being earned by the attacking side, they were always recorded when a result was announced. Amongst other things, the number of minors awarded to each side gave some indication of the pressure which had been exerted on the opposing team's line. Thus, a drawn game with one side gaining more minors that the other could be claimed by the former as a moral victory. In the Neath game, however, it was the goal which won the game proper, though, given the fact that the minors cancelled themselves out, it must have been a very tight game.

By the middle of October, as a result of further success, Swansea supporters were beginning to believe in their side again. Indeed, prior to the match against Llanelli, for which there were 9,000 people at St. Helens Field for the 'most important fixture of the day in south Wales', the home supporters were buoyant. For its part the *Cambrian* might have claimed some credit for that change in mood. On the Friday before the match, the *Cambrian* published a table of results of games between the clubs which had taken place over the four previous seasons. The statistics were telling:

Results of matches between Swansea and Llanelly

Season	P	W	D	L	For G	For T	Agst G	Agst T
1886-87	5	4	0	1	8	4	0	1
1887-88	5	2	3	0	3	4	1	3
1888-89	4	1	2	1	4	2	3	4
1889-90	2	2	0	0	3	2	1	0
Total	16	9	5	2	18	12	5	8

On the day, despite the best efforts of marauders like 'Bonser' Williams and 'Gitto' Griffiths to 'mark the Brothers James out of the game', the men in white controlled matters to win comfortably. Indeed, the press, commenting on the victory, thought that Swansea should have scored many more points. There was criticism, too. The three-quarters, in particular, were accused of over-elaborating, whilst Thorogood was blamed for being 'more anxious to "fetch the gallery" than play well for the team'. Yet, for Swansea supporters, the decisive victory – by 3 goals, a try and 2 minors to nil – was significantly better than they would have believed possible a few short weeks before.

David and Evan James – the Swansea 'Gems'.

Newport was the next club to have its colours lowered. 'Argus', (by now, hardly a model of neutral objectivity) in his report, let his enthusiasm run away with him as he described a Swansea try.

'D. James's little figure,' he wrote, 'is seen to spring on the ball ... his opponents rush him. He springs aside, but hardly out of danger ... watch out Evan, or you are caught ... a nimble fellow ... regains his balance and, with the whole team on him, he literally throws himself over the line and scores the winning point.'

It must have been all the journalist could do to stop himself cheering as he wrote. Yet, then, he may well have caught the mood of the Swansea supporters in the crowd of 7,000 which watched the game. 'Free-lance' described them as 'delirious'. It seemed that the doubting Thomas's had been banished. Pessimists had become optimists. The mighty Newport team had been defeated and in the process the previous season's loss was avenged.

The next hurdle which was to test both the team and its supporters, was a match against Cardiff on the Arms Park pitch. At that time the Cardiff club's ground was even more inclined to resemble a mud bath when it rained than it was when Dewi Bebb scored those international tries there many years later. On the occasion in question, the severity of the rain was such that the teams ran out into a veritable quagmire. However, the spectators who could afford to sit in the stand could feel reasonably pleased with themselves. Whilst the sixpenny supporters stood in the open and the players waded through mud and water, at least the privileged onlookers were dry. Such was their contentment that the Swansea element among them wanted to know why they could not have a similar structure at St. Helens. 'We've got the wood,' they said, 'we've got the men, and more important still, we've got the money'. They were rather taken, too with the 'string band' which stood in the mud in front of the grandstand an provided the entertainment before the game. Clearly, there was a segment of rugby supporters who wished to enjoy their football from a vantage point more akin to the creature comforts to which they were accustomed. The message was not lost on the Swansea committee. Furthermore, with the 'All Whites' forwards 'carting their opponents around the field', their favourites were victorious on the day. It followed that, on their way home, they could contemplate the comforts which might be theirs at St. Helens which, of course, would befit 'The Premiers', which they were now convinced they supported.

Meanwhile, the extent to which the Swansea supporters were beginning to idolise their heroes was illustrated by a report regarding the unavailability of David James for that game at Cardiff. James had had an accident at work and, when it was announced that he could not play, The *Cambrian* reported that 'little boys cried'. The bigger boys, however, seemed to have no reason to exercise their tear-ducts, they were all confirmed optimists.

Another Swansea v. Llanelli match in November produced a further victory for the 'All Whites' in a game in which 'Free-lance' reported that 'Llanelly played like Kilkenny Cats'. Yet again, the fact that Swansea was the side to beat was illustrated by the effort and determination shown by 'The Scarlet Runners'. Clearly, if Swansea wished to retain its position as the premier side in Wales, the team had to rise above all attempts to disrupt its play. Furthermore, it had to be able to perform effectively in conditions of any kind, and not only on the 'quick-drying St. Helens surface'. At Llanelli on that winter Saturday, the rain lashed down and the surface of the ground was churned up into a veritable morass. Despite that, the performance of their team enabled those Swansea supporters who stood in the open to go home with an inner glow which must have compensated in some part for their soaking wet clothes.

After the excitement of the games up to Christmas, those which were played over the holiday failed to impress. The *Post* complained about the ineffectiveness of the London-based opposition (The Civil Service, and St. Thomas's Hospital). Such opponents, so the argument went, were of unsatisfactory quality to 'place before honest supporters who braved fierce conditions in an open field'. Though, after the rigours of the first months of the season, one suspects that the players may not have objected to an 'easier passage'. There was, too, the opportunity to try out new players. Among them for the Civil Service game was 'Davies, Pontardawe', who, according to the *Post* was in 'fine fettle'.

In the New Year the team began where it left off, only to lose its unbeaten record to 'The Cathedral Boys' (Gloucester) and they followed that defeat by losing to Cardiff. Thus, when the Taffsiders came to St. Helens in February to play the return game, it was hailed as being for the 'Premiership of Wales', for at that stage in the season, Cardiff, themselves remained unbeaten.

One result of the considerable interest which developed was that a large number of 'Blue and Black' supporters travelled to Swansea by train. So confident was this east Wales contingent that the *Post* commented on their 'swaggering gait' and the 'arrogant cries of good old KERDIFF' (*sic*). The paper did not comment on their demeanour on leaving the town. They simply reported that, in front of a crowd of 14,000, a magnificent game was played 'at tremendous pace and we saw Cardiff hopelessly beaten'.

By March, as the Swansea team continued its majestic progress, it won yet another return, this time at Newport. Though, by this time, 'Argus' was developing a conspiracy theory. He noted that 'after a hard and unpleasant game (against) ... opponents who set out to win at any cost' they had won by the only goal of the game. It had been, he wrote 'a scrambling and bashing match on a pitch which was soaked with water'. It was his final sentence which betrayed his doubts. 'I suppose,' he pondered, 'the pitch could have been soaked by the rains of the previous day, although the roads were as dry as a bone!'

Between that Newport game and the final match of an eventful season, the Swansea men were victorious on every occasion. Given that they were by then undisputed Champions of Welsh football – 'The Premiers', as the contemporary jargon had it – there was another hurdle to negotiate. Were they the best in Wales AND England? That question was to be answered on the Easter Monday at St. Helens Field when Blackheath were the visitors.

Both local newspapers built up the game as being for the Championship of Great Britain. They argued that 'every football follower from Lands End to John O'Groats had heard of Blackheath' and, 'because the "All Whites" were also known throughout the length and breadth of the land ... the whole of England, Scotland and Ireland would have their minds on Swansea on ... Monday'. The uninvolved reader must have felt that the Swansea journalists had invented the concept associated with hyperbole! Nonetheless, there was no doubt that the match created immense interest in rugby circles. In many respects it was the biggest game that the Swansea club had ever played. Not surprisingly, it caught the imagination of the public, and 18,000 spectators, most of whom had been determined pessimists at the beginning of the season, crammed into the ground.

'Argus' wrote of that day 'I shall never forget the squeezing as I pushed myself through the top gate'. The scribe went on to complain about the arrangements which had been made for managing such a large crowd. Yet the committee might have argued that they did not expect such an attendance. As far as the match was concerned, despite the fact that 'The Heathens' physique was much admired, and 'they fielded many internationals', it was the Swansea men who triumphed. Whether the game was for the Championship of Great Britain or not, by winning, Swansea Football Club had further enhanced its reputation in the football world. They defeated the English Champions by 1 goal, 1 try and 5 minors to 1 try. A magnificent victory!

Given that it was a milestone in the history of the Club, it is only right to list here the team which claimed the 'scalp' of The Heathens.

Swansea v. Blackheath; St. Helens Field; Easter Monday 1891

W. J. Bancroft; E. T. Thorogood, C. Coke, J. Davies, J. Longden; Evan and David James; W. Bowen (Capt.), D. Samuel, J. Samuel, E. Charles, T. Deacon, T. Williams, W. Williams, H. Bevan.

That historic game brought down the curtain on the 1890/91 season. It followed that, not only could the Club boast that it was the premier side in Wales, unofficially at least, it could also claim the Championship of England and Wales. As far as the supporters were concerned, even if someone at the time might have coined the title 'World Champions', it would hardly have been enough.

Not surprisingly, the Club's great success resulted in much discussion in the Press. Having won 26 of its 29 matches, drawn one other and scored 55 goals and 48 tries in the process, it was certainly newsworthy. The *Athletic News* pointed to the leadership of Bill Bowen as a major factor in the Club's success. 'Argus' in the *Cambrian* agreed, though he tempered his remarks by stating that the Captain was 'somewhat reserved and not the kind of man that a reporter would like to interview'. Presumably, the Pembrokeshire man ... (who had) lived in Swansea since boyhood 'was somewhat taciturn', thus his success as captain must have been built on qualities other than the ability to use words well. 'Free-lance', too, praised the popular Bowen, and, like his contemporary in the *Cambrian*, emphasised that captaining a first-class side was no sinecure. Bowen had found that to be true during his first season, and despite the great success during his second, the pressures had remained. The truth was that over the two campaigns, Bowen had faced many difficulties on and off the field. He had risen above most of them, but there remained others which still needed to be resolved.

One point about that Championship season which would be of interest to modern readers was the size of the 'Big Men' of the day. The brothers Samuel, for example, key forwards in the Swansea pack, tipped the scales at 12st. 9lbs and 12st. 4lbs respectively. Harry Bevan, another forward was only 11st. 10lbs, whilst only two players weighed as much as 13 stones, and, then, with just a few pounds over. Nevertheless, at the time they were giants, both metaphorically and physically.

1891-92

The ground and finances

During the 1891 close season, significant efforts were made to improve the ground. Among other things, a large quantity of earth was removed from the south side of Bryn Road and taken to other parts of the field. A new 'handsome pavilion' was erected and the 'grandstand on the south side was improved and rearranged'. The cottage in which the Bancroft family had lived was removed, whilst the wall along the Mumbles Road and running into Gorse Lane was raised several feet. Clearly, some people had been seeing the games for nothing and the Committee was not going to allow *that* to happen during the coming season.

Despite the best efforts of the Committee, the new arrangements for the standing supporters were not well received. 'Free-lance' wrote, in his report of one of the early games of the new season, 'There was much uncomfortable crowding on the Brynmill side and unpleasant neck craning at the Gorse Lane end, where the necessity of the bank had been absolutely destroyed'.

As far as the Club's finances were concerned, despite the 'heavy expenses relating to ground improvements, the additional costs stemming from the renewal of the lease for the ground, plus the tour expenses', at the start of the season the Football Club still had a credit balance of £682.0*s*.7*d*. At the A.G.M. it was announced that more than £700 had been received from football gate receipts. Not only was the Swansea Club doing well on the field, in a business sense it was not doing so badly either.

Professionalism was the great concern throughout rugby as the new season approached. In south Wales there was a great deal of muttering about guineas in pockets and job offers, and there was animated discussion about broken-time payments. The debates at that time, formal and informal, were to be the precursors of a discussion which still continues to this day. At that time, however, it was a relatively new concern and, whilst they were not decisive in their actions, the Welsh Union was to be forced to become more overtly involved as time passed. In the meantime, the Match Committee – which included two former Swansea captains, W. H. Gwynn and E. S. Richards – announced revised scoring arrangements for the 1891/92 season. Two points only were to be awarded for a try, 3 points for a penalty, whilst other goals were to merit four points. The fact that the decision regarding tries was to be reversed at the end of the campaign is indicative that it was found to be detrimental. At this distance, the least knowledgeable rugby follower would realise that the game would have suffered as a result of reducing the emphasis on try scoring. However, taking a charitable view of the administrators of the day, presumably they held strong views as to why such a decision should be made, and legislated accordingly. One thing may be said, however, and that is that they were fortunate that they did not have to interact with today's media.

When the new campaign commenced, William Bowen was still a somewhat reluctant captain. He had not wished to continue, but with the euphoria of the previous season in everybody's mind he found himself obliged to retain the leadership. Furthermore, he was to have to lead the Club without the support of certain key players from the previous season, though precisely why this was the case is not clear from the data available to the present writer. Yet, being the man he was, Bowen accepted the challenge, and throughout what in many respects was to be a difficult season, he gave his all. As the reader will have perceived, there is no doubt that Bill Bowen deserves a special place in the history of Swansea Rugby Football Club.

The 'Cambrian' offices in Wind Street from which 'Argus' emerged. Whilst this illustration is of Wind Street forty years before, it is probable that the scene would be little changed by the 1890's.

The early matches of the season provided Bowen, his team and the supporters with considerable encouragement. In October, against Dr. Pegge's 'Black Boys', the brothers James 'had a field day and earned rounds of applause time after time'. The 'All Whites' won comfortably, though Dr. Pegge introduced a feature of sartorial novelty. The Neath captain cut the sleeves off his jersey and played 'with bare arms'. Those Heineken League forwards who took similar steps a century later should, thus, reflect on the old adage about there being 'nothing new under the sun'.

There was innovation, too, in the newspaper world. At the end of the first month of the season the Swansea club went to Lancashire to play two matches. This development resulted in 'Argus' being summoned to his Editor's office, where he was told that he was being sent to 'cover the tour'. He described the experience in his column. 'I invariably obey his (the editor's) orders to 'do' the police, or an inquest, or a missionary meeting, with an unmistakable reluctance ... On hearing the news, I left the office in a state of high glee'. Passers-by in Wind Street, where the offices of the *Cambrian* stood, must have witnessed a very happy man that day. Whilst this occurrence hardly represented the birth of the specialist sporting journalist in Swansea, it was a step in that direction. Darwin might have adapted his ideas to meet the case had he been aware of the development. As it was, 'Argus', with his glee wrapped around him, left Swansea Victoria Station at midnight in the company of 500 other enthusiasts, and arrived at the 'Cottonpolis' at 8.00 a.m. the following morning. No doubt there were missionaries and corpses in Manchester, but the scribe could joyfully focus upon the football which he loved.

On that tour, the side lost to Swinton but beat Oldham – for whom the former Swansea man, and brother of W. H. Gwynn, David Gwynn, was still playing. When the team returned to

Welsh competition, they 'completely routed' Cardiff in a game in which the James brothers were in impressive form. In November, the English cupholders, Coventry, came to challenge the men in white. The *Cambrian* report of the match showed 'Argus' at his patriotic and lyrical best.

'When a Welsh club does battle on English soil it invariably creates a sensation ... how different when the Saesnich clubs come here ... with big sounding reputations and a flourish of trumpets they cross the border animated with the exuberance of their prowess, and they go home with a lesson'. The 'lesson' provided for the Saxons on that occasion amounted to an 'All Whites' victory by 3 goals and 2 tries to a single try.

David Gwynn when with Oldham.

Problems for Bowen

Notwithstanding the relatively successful start which the side had made to the new campaign, many were concerned by the problems being faced by captain Bowen. 'It was known', the *Post* reported, 'that a few players had resigned and the captain had to go begging for men on Friday' That was not what was expected of the 'premier side in Wales'. At this distance, it is difficult to understand what was going on. Why had he been let down at the last minute? Why had the key players resigned? After all, in analysing Bowen's success in the previous seasons, many commentators had pointed to his leadership qualities and the *esprit de corps* which he had fostered. One possibility is that Bowen was expecting all his players to keep to the athletic standards by which he lived. Did some balk at his demands? Were others too complacent? Whatever the cause, something was wrong.

In December, for example, it was reported that the Swansea players 'walked from the pavilion (to face Penarth) with remarkable indifference ... an indifference (which) I fear kept them from training for every match'. At one stage, too, the supporters seem to have been caught up in the malaise. The press reported that they deprecated the conduct of their number whose remarks 'were offensive and showed that they cannot stand defeat'.

It was a defeat at St. Helens at the end of the season which resulted in Newport winning 'The Premiership', whilst the 'Whites' had to be content with being runners-up. As a result, there was disappointment in the town, though finishing a 'good second' was something of a triumph for the noble Bowen. In their subsequent analysis, the press came to the conclusion that, coupled with the resignation of key players, it was injuries, and the unavailability of others at important times which resulted in the relative decline of the Club. As they said, 'The committee was forced to chop and change throughout the season'. Even so, apart from that final match at St. Helens, when Newport won by a single dropped goal, the side had been extremely successful – after Christmas. Remarkably, they did not concede a single point for two months prior to the final game.

Sadly, in April 1892, Bill Bowen not only resigned the captaincy; he retired from the game altogether. James Livingstone, another important figure in the early history of the Club, was to say that Bowen had 'given his all for the Club'. Despite the many difficulties which he faced in his third term at the helm, his side had lost only five of its thirty-one games. Indeed, during his term as Captain, they had won 70 and drawn 9 of the 90 matches played. It was to take a decade before the quality of that record was challenged effectively.

Northern allure

By April 1892 the Brothers James had gained a new sobriquet. An English journalist, in his report of the Wales versus England match in which the James's played, likened their antics to a particular breed of monkey. He referred to 'The curly headed marmosets' and this amusing reference was taken up by press and supporters alike. The 'Gems' had a new identity.

A month later they were up to some monkey business of their own. A rumour swept the town that they had gone to play in the north of England, and on 6 May they confirmed that they had played a game for West Hartlepool. However, they said, 'despite the tempting offer made to us we prefer to stay in Swansea'. Whilst that incident was regarded as closed at the time, it was to prove to be the precursor of a long running saga in which the brothers were embroiled in the developing web of the 'professionalism' arguments. Indeed, even at that time they were enmeshed in controversy. It was established that the brothers had left for Hartlepool immediately after the 'All Whites' Easter Monday game and had played for the Teeside club on the Wednesday. As had been implied, the brothers had been offered an incentive to travel north and to join the West Hartlepool club.

According to the *Post* this was 'a clear case of professionalism'. Whilst the players, the Club and supporters preferred to play down the matter, the James's had been alerted to the possibility of gaining financially from doing what they enjoyed. For two young men, who had probably never left Swansea before, the long journey to Hartlepool might have put them off. Yet, they had tasted 'freedom' and smelled money. As a result, the matter was not to end there.

At the A.G.M. in May, the Treasurer reported that £1,724.12*s*.0*d* and been received at the gate from football matches. It was a significant sum, which was just as well, for the Club had spent more than £2,000 in developing 'The Field', whilst the grandstand had cost a further £1,400.* Whilst the conservative caution of the treasurer's subsequent remarks may be thought of as typical of the dedicated men who perform such tasks, his warning was prudent. 'Unless the record receipts are equalled in the coming season, the Club will have an adverse balance for some time'. The balance in hand was reported as £65.5*s*.7*d* and, for once, the Cricket Club must have felt that it was not such a poor relation after all. Meanwhile, the players must have looked with envy at the announcement in *Pearson's Weekly*. The 'Team of the Season' award had been made to Newport. The prize was £90, which the *Post* suggested 'will run to £5.00 each'. No one commented about the implications of professionalism which the award might suggest.

In July 1892 the English Union refused to sanction the proposal that a League should be established in Lancashire and an Alliance in Yorkshire. At this distance it seems reasonable to suggest that, had the proposal been accepted, there might never have been a thirteen-a-side code. However, it is necessary to recognise that the proposal was made at a time when there were real concerns about professionalism in the union game, and when professional soccer (with leagues) was establishing itself. As a result, leagues smacked of professionalism. In consequence, the Union administrators might have felt that to agree to a league system might encourage a trend parallel to soccer.

* To put these figures into perspective, a respectable dwelling house could have been purchased at the time for £200.

W. McCutcheon, 'Capped' in 1891.

As far as Swansea was concerned, the controversy and subsequent developments resulted in the Club losing matches which were at that time regularly played against northern clubs such as Swinton and Oldham. And that was the case despite the announcement by the northern administrators that they intended to stay in the English Union and '... make (southern) officials come round to the modern way of thinking'. It was to take almost a hundred years before the southerners were so converted.

Meanwhile, prior to the 1892/93 season there was an air of lethargy in the town and around St. Helens. The press complained about the lack of activity. As 'Free-lance' put it: 'Whilst others are putting their house in order, Swansea is allowing the grass to grow under its feet'. Local grammarians might have frowned at this mixing of metaphors, but the journalist's readers knew exactly what he meant.

Certainly, all was not well at the Club, and the new captain Charlie Coke, had a major job on his hands. A report in the *Cambrian* illustrated one aspect of his problems., It was stated that the new captain had gone to the home of the Brothers James to find out why they had not been in touch. He was, it was said, taken aback to be told that they would not play for Swansea during the coming season. The town was aghast. The talk was about 'accommodating the players' and of using 'a little persuasion in the right quarters'. Yet, it is probable that the poorly-educated brothers had now been given a financial indication of what they were worth. As ill-paid labourers, the sums involved must have appeared to be extremely attractive. If that was the case, a popular argument went, it was not a question of if, but when, they would go.

The general lethargy surrounding the Club affected the A.G.M. too. It was held behind closed doors. Only members were admitted and 'With most of the First XV absent, only 45 people were present'. James Livingstone, in the Chair, did his best to rally the meeting. He reminded his listeners of the Club's record at the end of the previous season. 136 goals and 128 tries had been scored whilst opponents could only boast 22 goals and 38 tries and – 'some of those clubs were said to be the best in the land.' It was, he continued, 'a record not equalled by any club in England'. Readers of the report must have imagined that they could hear Livingstone's ringing tones. It was as though the Chairman was saying 'come on lads. We can't throw all this away!'

Yet 'all that' was history. All was not well at Swansea Football Club. In some respects the problems may have been personified by the appointment of Charlie Coke as captain. By implication, at least, it appeared that the appointment was one which 'would cause less friction than any other'. Coke, a skillful and popular player and an honest and sincere man, was thus to start his task at a disadvantage. At the same time, in a short acceptance speech, he stated that he was 'fully aware of the high honour ... and all the heavy responsibilities which would ... devolve on him'. Coke was to find that the Club's problems plus an unfortunate personal injury record during the coming season, were to add to his burden of office. At least there was some good news for the new leader. Before the Club's 'opener', the Brothers James denied that they had said that they would not play for Swansea again. Their version carried a caveat. 'But we will if we stay in Swansea'.

Chapter Four

THE JAMES SAGA CONTINUES

1892–93

PRIOR TO THE GAME AGAINST Barnstaple at St. Helens at the end of September 1892, it was announced that the James brothers had 'refused to don the All Whites jersey again'. 'Argus' was indignant: '... if the brothers are under the impression that they can have everything their own way, the sooner they dispel the illusion the better for themselves'. The scribe continued, in haughty tone, to inform the recalcitrants that 'fame is a weak and fickle thing'.

Since this was also the line taken by the contemporary *Post*, it is reasonable to assume that the general feeling in Swansea was that enough was enough. Time was to show that such resolution was also weak and fickle, though, in the meantime, the Club 'got on with things'. However, without the James brothers and several other regulars from previous seasons, the 'Starter' against the men from Devon turned out to be a 'scrambling affair'. Furthermore, the journalists on both Swansea papers were of the opinion that, if that was to be the standard of play offered by the team, they would have an 'awful hiding at Newport'.

Clearly, the journalists were reflecting the sentiment in the town, whilst, at the Club, the situation was thought to be serious enough to merit urgent action. A special training session was called, and because it was 'too wet to train on The Field', there was a new development. The Club's first indoor training sessions were held in the Agricultural Hall. W. H. Gwynn, described by 'Argus' as a 'good coacher' was there to organise things.

One thing which Gwynn would have impressed upon his charges was the importance of scoring tries. During the close season, the Welsh Union had reversed its decision regarding the number of points which were to be awarded for a try. Henceforth, three points were to be given for such a score. Another change in the laws was announced, too. The starting or reopening of play could no longer be made by means of a dribble. The new law stated: 'At the kick off the ball must reach ten yards'.

Not that either change seemed to make a big difference to the level of entertainment provided by the next game. Whilst Cardiff were defeated, the match itself was described as 'flat and unprofitable'. Furthermore, only 3,000 people turned up to see it, whereas games against the 'Blue and blacks' usually attracted 'three times that amount'.

It was difficult to account for the depression. Was it their dismal showing, or the more general malaise which had gripped the town earlier? In any event, when the G.W.R. ran an excursion for the game at Newport, only 300 supporters took advantage of the facility. Without the James brothers and some others, and with the prospect of facing an experienced and successful Newport team, the 'All Whites' chances were not held to be bright. The result confirmed the fears of the pessimists.

Frank Mills.

Despite the 'heroic efforts of Frank Mills and his comrades', Newport won. However, there was something of a silver lining in the cloud. Swansea had played for much of the game with 14 men, and, overall, the Press argued, Coke's men had done well against a strong Newport side. That news must have stirred the interest of Swansea supporters, for, at the next game against Llanelli at St. Helens, there were 7,000 present. As the *Post* had it: 'Even the would-be deserters turned out'. Furthermore, they must have returned to their homes in high glee after the 'Scarlet Runners' had suffered defeat.

The next phase in the Club's fixtures (including a short tour of Lancashire) was overshadowed by dramatic news about the Brothers James. After a meeting of the English Football Union – behind closed doors – it was announced that Evan and David James were debarred from playing for any English team in the future. It appeared that captain Coke, secretary Bryant and former skipper, Bowen of the Swansea club, plus the brothers themselves, were among the witnesses called in the case. It was said that 'contradictory evidence' was given by several parties, though the press could not 'authenticate what had gone on'. One wonders what modern tabloids would make of such restraint?

The fact concerning the case which was generally agreed was that the James brothers had joined Broughton Rangers rather than stay in Swansea. Whilst the Manchester club and the Jameses contended that the brothers had not been induced to go there, no one in Swansea believed that to be true. As Argus put it, 'No man would leave his work without a moment's notice to be in Manchester playing for another team unless ...'

Nevertheless, and notwithstanding the feeling which the 'desertion' of the Jameses had generated in Swansea, there were those who noted that the brothers were only banned from playing for *English* clubs. Presumably, this meant that the matter was back with the Welsh Union as far as Swansea was concerned. Could the matter, some Swansea supporters pondered, be resolved in the favour of the Swansea club? Whether any moves were made with such a reconciliation in mind, is not clear. However, the residual haughtiness of the Club officials, coupled with the stubborn attitude of the Brothers, resulted in an impasse. As a result, many more games were to be played on the St. Helens Field before 'The Gems' were seen again in the white shirt.

Life without the Jameses

'Because of the desertion of the Brothers James, the forwards and three-quarters had much more work to do'. This statement, in a report of a game against a combined London Hospitals side, said a great deal about the contribution to the Swansea team of the banned East-side brothers. To borrow a modern soccer term, in addition to their rare skills, they must have had a phenomenal 'work rate'. The situation was, however, that, whatever the problems which their absence caused, the Club and its supporters were going to have to learn to live without David and Evan James.

Perhaps it was the resultant 'bottled up disappointment' which contributed to an unfortunate incident later that month. Sadly, there were unpleasant scenes at St. Helens, provoked, so the

Press had it, by poor refereeing. The *Cambrian* reported that, after the game against Cardiff, there was 'a great rush of spectators across the field', and 'The referee was escorted by Sir John Llewellyn and Captain Colquohon to the dressing room'. Immediately afterwards, Sir John mounted the grandstand steps and appealed to the crowd to disperse. 'For the honour of the Swansea Club,' he said, 'put an end to a scene such as this (loud cheers)'. The crowd dispersed at once.

Later, the referee agreed that he had been distracted when reversing a decision which he had made, thus disallowing a winning score by a Swansea player. Since the laws, at the time, stated that a referee could not alter a decision once made, the Swansea club appealed to the Welsh Union. At a meeting on the following Friday, the Union dealt with that matter and with another which concerned the 'All Whites'. The *Cambrian* published the Union's decisions :

1. They recommended to the English Union that the transference of the Brothers James should not be sanctioned.
2. They ruled that, according to the laws of the game, the referee of the Swansea-Cardiff match had no right to alter a decision once made. As a result, the score (and the game) was awarded to Swansea.
3. They strongly disapproved of the conduct of some spectators towards the referee, and warned that the slightest repetition would result in the ground being closed.

For their part, the Cardiff club was incensed by the ruling, and there was talk about them threatening to secede from the Union. Whilst that was something of an empty threat, the ruling concerning the possible closure of St. Helens was real. Protestations by the Swansea press that the demonstration had not involved mobbing – 'Say what the Cardiff papers like' – did not carry weight. Consequently, the St. Helens authorities would need to ensure that nothing like it ever happened again.

Problems for Coke

On the field, at that time, the side's successes of previous seasons were but memories as its performances lacked lustre. After losing to Neath, the team could only draw with Abercarn. There was little doubt that the 'Stars' were being missed, and the Press was urging Coke to try to persuade some of the veterans to return. The captain, heeding the suggestions, went to see the Samuels brothers in Manselton. David said that he would play if John would, but, at that point agreement could not be reached. As a result, and having failed to persuade others, Coke was forced to do his best with the players at his disposal, though even that pool of talent was diminishing. Jere Edwards, Mainwaring and R. G. Edwards all left the Club at the same time.

Coke must have been dispirited, though he received some encouragement when the Samuels brothers agreed to play against Llanelli. Whilst that news was not sufficient to encourage many supporters to travel to the Tinopolis – only 200 took advantage of the excursion – the match report suggests that the side played with renewed zest. Despite having to play up the Llanelli slope in the second half, the 'All Whites' held out for a draw. Whilst in previous seasons that result would have been regarded as a failure, in the circumstances in which Coke found himself, it must have seemed like a ray of hope.

Meantime, interest in the fate of the James brothers persisted. Contrary to the tough talking at the time of their defection, there was now a distinct softening in attitudes. It was almost as though the whole of Swansea was trying to find a way to welcome home the prodigals. The fatted calf may not have been prepared, but there was little doubt that it had been picked out of the herd in readiness.

In the January of 1893, the Swansea committee showed initiative when icy conditions threatened a St. Helens match. They protected the field from the elements by laying down a 'blanket of straw'. As a result, the Swansea v. Gloucester game was played, whereas most of the others due to be played in south Wales were postponed. In bitterly cold conditions, 4,000 spectators huddled together on the banks. Indeed, such was the cold that, at half-time the Swansea players 'sought refuge ... in the straw which lined the touch line'. No doubt, at that time, a cup of tea would have been more welcome than the ubiquitous lemon, but, in the second-half they warmed up enough to beat 'The Cathedral Boys' by three tries to one. Coke was delighted.

On the following Saturday, those Swansea supporters who were at Cardiff to see Wales gain an historic victory over England, must have been warmed by the performance of Billy Bancroft. The *Pall Mall Gazette* reported that 'Bancroft, at full-back, was outstanding and dropped an extraordinary goal from a penalty kick'. Bancroft, who had been playing in the centre for Swansea, had found a stage in keeping with his glorious skills.

At club level, the full-back supported Coke on and off the field as the captain tried to revive Swansea's fortunes. Unfortunately, at the end of the season he could only reflect on what had been a disappointing campaign. The team had lost twelve of its thirty-one games, whilst drawing another three. Everyone agreed that Charlie Coke had worked extremely hard to try to develop his team, but he had been handicapped by injuries (including himself for long periods) and by 'defections'. As has ever been the case Coke had his critics. However, he started in most difficult circumstances and never recovered. Nevertheless, it was Coke who brought the Samuels brothers back to the Club, even for a short period. Furthermore, despite his frequent absences through injury, he finished top try scorer with seven to his credit.

At the May A.G.M., a new captain was elected. He was W. J. Bancroft. This time the appointment was not a compromise. Bancroft, although a young man, was an international, and he had gained the respect of his colleagues by the manner in which he had supported Coke. Whilst his first tenure was brief, the experience was to stand him in good stead for the future, when he was to lead the Club for five seasons in succession.

Meantime, despite the disappointment of the previous season, there were those who were longing for the return of the football season. Among them was 'Argus' of the *Cambrian*. Whilst, no doubt alienating one section of the sporting community, he nailed his colours firmly to the mast:

> 'I'm glad,' he wrote, 'that the football season is now at hand. I am sick and tired of cricket – weak, effeminate and lisping cricket ... I want to see football defy the elements and chase the ball across the snow, or in the rain, or in the face of free and biting winds.'

Had such an organisation existed, it is probable that the secretary of Ascetics Anonymous would have been in touch with the scribe on reading that item.

Professionalism again

As is the case today, there was much discussion in the press regarding professionalism as the new season approached. In Swansea, the matter had been brought to the fore by the case of the James brothers, but there was concern throughout the Principality. W. H. Gwynn, the former Swansea captain and secretary of the Welsh Union, was in no doubt as to where he stood on the matter. In general, he expressed himself in favour of professionalism which, he argued, was inevitable. He claimed that the departure of Welsh players for the north of England was 'the forerunner of the adoption of professionalism'. Gwynn went on to forecast that the 'North clubs will make a big attempt to influence the E.R.U. to legalise it and, failing that, they will secede and act upon their own responsibility'. Whilst the secretary was somewhat premature, his forecast was to prove uncannily correct.

Elsewhere, a writer in the influential *Athletic News* urged the Lancashire and Yorkshire clubs to 'seize the initiative'. The writer quoted Gwynn's concept of payment which was: 'A player should be paid a weekly sum which would compel him to work for a livelihood ... a player should be insured to get his weekly wage and no more ... clubs should not be allowed to offer players belonging to other clubs more than they were getting already. That would put an end to poaching'. Whilst some of Gwynn's ideas may have been flawed, there is no doubt that he had a vision of future developments which, though unattractive to the purists, proved to be the basis of the Northern Union approach.

Meanwhile, there were some signs of renewed spirit at St. Helens, stemming largely from Bancroft's appointment. After all, he had been 'capped' for Wales – 'as custodian when but a youth'. Even the English papers had showered him with praise following his first game against their national side and, of course, all of Swansea knew of his prowess. Yet, as the young man was to find, captaincy involves much more than having playing skills. Restoring the fortunes of the All Whites was a far from an easy task. Not unnaturally, the captain would have been delighted to have players of the calibre of the James brothers in his side. However, as was reported in the *Post*, 'The temper of the committee is not favourable to such a procedure just now'. Though, as time was to show, 'just now' was to extend for several years. 'Banky' would have to manage without the brothers.

1893–94

A reconciliation

Since the season started with several lacklustre displays, the Press, presumably reflecting public opinion, expressed its concerns. 'Argus' wrote : 'There is no denying that the Swansea team is not what it was ... if things do not alter materially, Swansea's reputation in the football world will be a thing of the past'. In the weeks that followed, 'Free-lance' in the *Post* joined his contemporary in continuing to express dissatisfaction, whilst the groundswell of public opinion regarding the Brothers James became something of a clamour. Yet there was a great deal more behind the concern than the matter of the James brothers. The team was not working 'as a combination', and with the memory of Bill Bowen's successful sides still fresh in the minds of supporters, it was not surprising that there was general dissatisfaction abroad.

Such were the concerns at St. Helens that, for a match with Cardiff 'Quins, the 'stalwart Frank Mills turned out with "flu"'. Mills, it transpired, appeared in response to a telegram which was sent to his home, though he must have wished that he had stayed in bed. During the game he was 'thrown heavily into touch' and broke his collarbone. As a result, he did not play again until Christmas. In addition, Bancroft's woes were deepened when W. Griffiths, a centre, damaged his nose so severely that he had to join Mills in the dressing room. The remaining thirteen hung on to win, which, at least, illustrated the existence of a lively team spirit which seemed to have been missing in previous games.

Nevertheless, despite all his difficulties, the captain rallied his remaining troops and, to the surprise of many, Llanelli were defeated at St. Helens. After that, whilst they lost the next game to Newport, the team 'played their hearts out against the giants'. As has always been the case, when a side gives of its best supporters tend to rally around the players. Given that this renaissance in support coincided with the visit of Cardiff to St. Helens, there was a larger attendance for that game. Part of the reason for this renewed interest could have been that it was the Taff-side club's only visit to Swansea that season. As a result of the dispute during the previous campaign, the Cardiff committee had 'only agreed to two matches this season'. As a result, there was much regret throughout south Wales'. Among those who experienced keen disappointment would have been the treasurers of the two clubs. The traditional rivalry between Cardiff and Swansea always resulted in thousands of supporters travelling to swell the home 'gate'. On this occasion a total of ten thousand people were in St. Helens as the game started. At the end, the Swansea portion of that crowd went home delighted as Swansea gained a narrow win over the 'Blue and Black Boys'. A victory of any kind would have lifted Swansea spirits. Since it was at the expense of Cardiff it had an enhanced effect.

Immediately prior to the kick-off in that match there was a victory for inter-club relations. 'Before hostilities commenced, both sets of players came out with "hospital boxes" ... and made a raid on the generosity of the occupants of the grandstand'. Someone, it seemed had been taking lessons in diplomacy with great effect! Arrangements for the next season ensured that four matches between the clubs were to be played again. Both treasurers were delighted.

The effort at Newport and the victory over Cardiff had renewed enthusiasm in the town, but by December it seemed that the clouds were gathering again. Both the *Post* and the *Cambrian* were critical of the performances of the team. 'Free-lance' felt that there was a 'lack of combination and *esprit de corps*', while the *Cambrian* scribe was of the opinion that 'the time has come for the committee and players to put their house in order'. In general, the views of both journalists reflected the belief that, after the Cardiff victory, the form of the team had deteriorated. As the *Cambrian* put it, 'disaffection has spread and deepened to such an extent that the outside world know it'.

That malaise was present throughout the remainder of the season, and the mood in Swansea was not improved by the news that the English Union had refused to reinstate the Brothers James. Since, in the eyes of the supporters, at least, the demise of the Club had coincided with the departure of 'The Gems', they became a veritable icon for all their loyal followers. Even those who had muttered, darkly that the Club was bigger than any individual, were now modifying their positions.

In February 1894, after a poor performance at Bristol, the *Cambrian* opined: '... unless the "All Whites" rouse themselves out of their lethargy ... unless Captain Bancroft insists upon their training ... there is every prospect that this season may be more disastrous ... than ever before'. Whilst the language may indeed have been colourful, the sad truth was that by the end of the

Swansea R.F.C. 1894-95.
A. M. Jenkin, C. Coke, T. Jackson, W. Bowen (Umpire).
W. J. Bancroft, R. S. Jenkin, R. Messer, T. Chegwidden, E. Thorogood, F. Gordon.
W. Grey, S. Rice, R. Thomas, J. Williams.
R. Oldham, J. Prescott, T. Blackmore.

season, the side had in fact lost eleven games and drawn eight others. To supporters weaned on the success of the Bowen era, this reflected dismal failure. It was as if the honour of the town was at stake. Something had to be done!

1894–95

Thorogood I. C.
There was general agreement at the Club that Billy Bancroft had worked hard in his season as captain. He was 'to be congratulated on his efforts', but there was a significant 'however'. He

had not been able to elicit a satisfactory response from his team, though, at this distance, it is clear that he had not inherited a strong 'squad'. Furthermore, given that the origins of the problems which he faced appeared to stem from the final year of Bill Bowen's captaincy, the Committee should have accepted a significant proportion of the blame. Yet, the offering of an appropriate sacrifice in such circumstances can act as a palliative. Bancroft was chosen as the lamb for the slaughter. For the 1894-95 season, Teddy Thorogood would be the Club captain.

When Thorogood spoke at a 'packed' A.G.M. at the Albert Minor Hall, he commented on the importance of the task and of the responsibilities which went with it. Since he had been at the Club since 1886, Thorogood must have enjoyed being part of the successful Bowen era. All Swansea hoped that he would benefit from that experience. In welcoming the new leader, secretary, Bryant stressed that the team would need to work very hard to support the new man. 'W. H. Gwynn,' he said, 'was to be asked to do coaching again'. Bryant, also reported that a letter had been written to Mr Rowland Hill* of the English Union requesting that favourable consideration be given to the reinstatement of the Brothers James – 'at the earliest'. The Secretary declined to say any more than that, other than that the matter would be 'pursued with vigour'. A problem, however, was that Hill and his committee were judge and jury in the matter. Swansea's vigour was wrecked on the rocks of that submerged reef.

Notwithstanding substantial defeats at the hands of Newport and Cardiff in November of the new season and a disappointing draw at Llanelli in the same month, there were some encouraging signs for the new captain and supporters alike. Among them was the emergence of a strong running winger called Frank Gordon, who was to make a significant contribution to Swansea football in the years ahead. Following the Llanelli game, he was described as being a 'ferocious tackler 'and 'having judgment and coolness.' Since his namesake, General Charles Gordon, was still a folk hero a decade after his death, it was hardly surprising that the young man attracted the nickname of 'The General'. Whilst, in due course he was to become captain of the Swansea Club for four successful seasons, he was forever 'General' or 'Genny' as far as the players and supporters were concerned. He was, also an effective talisman.

The results in the second-half of the season gave supporters further encouragement, and, at the close, only seven games had been lost throughout the campaign. In addition, the Treasurer must have been delighted with some large 'gates' for high profile matches. 7,000 people were at St. Helens to see Oldham (for whom former 'All Whites' David Gwynn and McCutcheon were playing), whilst 20,000 saw the Llanelli game. On that day, such was the crush at the Gorse Lane entrance that the gates burst open and 'upwards of a thousand people gained access "on the nod" '. Both the 'Nodders' and those who paid, saw an exciting game which ended in a draw. At the time, Swansea supporters were happy to settle for that. At least, they felt, there was room for cautious optimism.

Had there been a mathematician about it is doubtful whether any of those who entered the *South Wales Daily Post's* 'Forecasting Competition' would have been optimistic. The paper announced that £5.5*s*.0*d* was to be awarded for the 'Correct Tip', whilst £1.1*s*.0*d* was the prize for the nearest forecast. As will be seen from the panel on page 40, the probability of any forecaster obtaining the five guineas was, to put it mildly, extremely slim. Nonetheless, the competition must have attracted a high level of entries, for it ran for several weeks.

---

* Grandson of the originator of the penny postal system.

Forecasting Competition – England versus Wales

(a) The English score at half-time
(b) The Welsh score at half-time
(c) The English score at full time
(d) The Welsh score at full time
(e) The English try getters
(f) The Welsh try getters

During the period when the competition was running, the supporters had certain other things to forecast. The town was said to be 'awash' with the news that Billy Bancroft was 'going', so it was said 'for monetary benefit'. The *Post* reported local doggerel which reflected the feeling in the town.

And shall our Bancroft fly?
And shall our Bancroft fly?
Then thirty thousand Swansea boys
Will know the reason why.

So great was the concern in the town, and at the Club, that a special meeting was called at the Longlands Hotel. One suggestion was that the Cricket Club should offer the player professional terms, to counter those which had been proposed by the Chippenham club. However, it was pointed out that that would defeat the objective of keeping the full-back in Swansea colours.

A Welsh Union law effectively banned anyone from playing rugby under its jurisdiction if the person concerned was a professional in any other sport. Later, so as to defuse the situation, Bancroft was to make a personal statement denying that he had signed for the Wiltshire County Cricket Club. At least for the moment, the 'Bancroft is going' issue could be put aside.

Meanwhile there was further news regarding the Jameses. The *Post* reported that the English Union had decided not to re-open the case. Such was the situation that the paper ran the item under the headline 'Banned for ever'. Whilst the caption proved to be inaccurate, it did not appear to be so for Swansea supporters at the time. Nonetheless, they were able to put the matter into context when they heard the news that Dick Burrows had died. Dick, a tenacious young forward, had badly injured his spine in a match against Newport. The player, who was paralysed as a result, was rushed to Swansea Hospital and detained there. Such was the real concern among Swansea supporters that, throughout his illness, the hospital posted a daily bulletin which reported on the player's condition. Sadly, there was no happy ending. Burrows did not recover and Swansea lost a popular young man.

Before the start of the new season Burrows was remembered at the Club's A.G.M. James Livingstone stated that 'To Swansea-ites, the season 1894-95 will long be remembered with deep regret ... one of our most dashing and promising forwards died of injuries received whilst playing for the Club'. The meeting remembered the player in silence.

1895-96

A brighter outlook

A. M. Jenkin, 'All Whites' captain, 1895-96.

In the summer of 1895, with the encouragement of the results achieved during the latter part of the previous season in their minds, the assurance that 'Banky' was staying, and new rumours circulating that the James brothers might, yet, be reprieved, Swansea supporters were a great deal more positive about the season to come. 'Free-lance', reflecting new optimism, thought that 'there is enough material in our midst to produce another excellent side'. Indeed, so bullish was the man from the *Post*, that he went on to say that the players could develop into a team '... equal to that which won the Premiership for two successive seasons under W. Bowen'.

It is interesting, here, to note the title used to designate the Champions of Welsh Football. In due course, the breakaway Northern Union was to adopt the term, whilst, almost a century later, some highly paid marketing man proposed the same name for England's top soccer competition.

For the 1895-96 season, Teddy Thorogood stood aside as captain and one Albert Mortimer Jenkin, a student of Mining, was elected to succeed him. An Uplands boy, who was 'capped' at 22 years of age, his was an outstanding talent. Frequently matched with men two stones heavier than he was (he tipped the scales at 11st. 6lbs), he performed exceedingly well. That, however, said little about his ability to captain the Club. Unfortunately, his term of office only lasted until November when he resigned 'because of professional duties'. Probably, this was an example of a man finding that the task of captain was onerous, and involved many hours of activity each week. Modern readers should remember that, without telephones, the task of maintaining contact with other members of the team, alone, was extremely time consuming, whilst the role of captain had a much wider scope than it does today.

Whilst losing Jenkin from the captaincy, the Club lost another key figure at that same time. W. Bryant, who had filled the role of secretary for thirteen years, resigned. Bryant, who took up a new post in the West Country, was presented with a 'handsome writing desk and a purse of gold' as a measure of the appreciation of the Swansea club. The secretary, who was to maintain links with St. Helens, said that he would 'greatly miss his work at the Club'.

Strangely, despite the more positive outlook of everyone concerned with the club before the new season began, matters on the field did not live up to the promise so confidently held out. By the turn of the year there was little doubt that Swansea football needed a stimulus. January of 1896 provided one which the most romantic story-teller would have been delighted to invent. The English Union announced that they were to re-open the case of the Brothers James. Whilst the brothers had not played for the Swansea club for almost three years, they were still folk heroes. Indeed, their absence had embellished their skills in the minds of supporters. Had the St. Helens surface allowed water to form into a pool, there were those who did not doubt that these men would walk over it.

For some reason, the English Union decided to hold the meeting which included consideration of the James case late on a Friday evening. Thus it was that, on the evening of 31st January 1896, the whole of Swansea held its breath as it awaited news of the decision. Indeed, there is

Swansea R.F.C. 1895-96.
R. S. Jenkin, R. Grey, D. Williams, T. Jackson, W. Smith, G. Evans, W. Bowen.
G. Gordon, R. Croker, R. Oldham, A. M. Jenkin (Capt.), S. Rice, S. Croker,
R. Thomas, R. Messer, W. Prescott.

little doubt that certain unofficial prayer meetings were held throughout Swansea as many eyes turned to the night sky. Whilst some were undoubtedly praying for Heavenly intervention, a more compelling earthly reason for this unusual stargazing could be traced to an item in the *Post* earlier that week. 'As a service to our readers,' the newspaper confided, 'we have arranged with J. S. Brown, the enterprising Swansea ironmonger, to use his flashlight to announce the decision of the English Union'. That 'flashlight' was, in fact an embryonic searchlight, which was to become familiar to the citizens of Swansea many years later. Three contingencies were provided for in the code which was published in the paper:

1. If the brothers were reinstated an upward shining light would revolve in the sky.
2. If the application was refused, a single light would shineupwards
3. In the event of an adjournment, a double stationary beam would be seen shining upwards.

With the 'whole of Swansea gazing up into the night sky', the light swung around in gay abandon. The James boys were back !

On the 1st February 1896, 'amidst extraordinary scenes' the 'All Whites' ran out onto St. Helens field. As the James brothers emerged, 'everyone in the grandstand rose to their feet and cheered. Hats, umbrellas, and handkerchiefs were waved in a tremendous tribute of delight'. Little wonder that the brothers were said to have 'grinned with pleasure'. The prodigals were home! Since they had last played at St. Helens in the Spring of 1893, it was asking a great deal to expect them to pick up where they had left off. Apart from the fact that, to use a boxing term, they were ring rusty, they could hardly have been fit. The game had developed, and teams were better organised whilst there were new star players with whom the brothers had to compete. None of that, however, counted for much in the minds of the expectant Swansea crowd. Were they not gods ?

Not surprisingly, in their early games, the brothers did not dominate as they had done. Yet, as the weeks passed and they regained fitness and developed better understanding with their team mates, there were flashes of their old form. For example, in its report of a game against Llanelli, which Swansea won comfortably, the *Post* included a diagram which, through the use of arrows, illustrated how the 'All Whites' had scored one of their tries. The accompanying commentary read:

(a) David James scooped up the ball from behind the scrummage and passed to his brother ...
(b) Who, after covering a few yards sent it out to ...
(c) Richards, who, shaking off the Llanelly backs, turned sharply ... and fell under the crossbar.

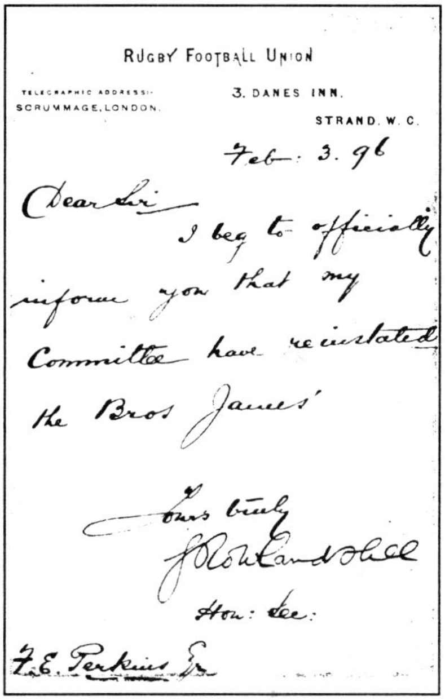

RUGBY FOOTBALL UNION

TELEGRAPHIC ADDRESS: SCRUMMAGE, LONDON.

3. DANES INN. STRAND. W. C.

Feb. 3. 96

Dear Sir

I beg to officially inform you that my Committee have reinstated the Bros James'

Yours truly
G Rowland Hill
Hon: Sec:

F. E. Perkins Esq

Photograph of the original letter from the Rugby Football Union confirming the reinstatement of the James Brothers, 3rd Feb. 1896.

In a match against Gloucester, described as 'the best result since W. Bowen was captain', it was stated that the brothers 'orchestrated the game'. Whilst the team was far from being a two-man affair, there was no doubt that the very presence of the James brothers had a positive effect on the remainder of the side. As so often happens when influential players are introduced to a team, the others begin to have greater belief in themselves.

And, of course, at the time the team had other outstanding players. Among them were Gordon, and Bancroft, though, in that respect, it is interesting to note that even 'gods' have their off days. In its report of the game against Gloucester, the *Athletic News* had to admit: 'Bancroft scored one try but failed with all five kicks at goal'.

Whilst the season was wound up with two magnificent victories – Llanelli, and Old Merchant Taylors being the victims – the overall record showed that the side had been defeated on the same number of occasions as during the previous campaign. Nonetheless, without doubt, there was a brighter spirit in the air, greater *esprit de corps* among the team ... and the James brothers were back. Their saga was at an end; or was it?

Chapter Five

BANCROFT TO THE FORE

1896-97

AT THE 1896 A.G.M., Billy Bancroft who, in fact, had acted as captain for the greater part of the previous season, was formally elected to the post. Bancroft was now a more mature person than he had been when first made captain, and was an experienced international. Furthermore, he had 'learnt his trade' during the previous season, as well as in his first campaign as captain. Whilst his side was to lose eight games during the coming campaign, such was his appeal as leader that he was to retain the captaincy for five seasons in succession. Whilst that record was to be equalled by Billy Trew, it still stands proud today.

Before the new season started, most observers were of the opinion that things would go well for the Club during the 1896-97 campaign. Whilst the outcome was slightly poorer than the previous season as far as results were concerned, there were encouraging signs for the future. Bancroft did well, the three-quarters excelled in many games, as did the Brothers James, whilst Messer and Gordon, in particular, caught the eye. Unfortunately, some of the eyes concerned belonged to 'Northern poachers'. 'Argus' reported that 'emissaries from the north had been in Swansea'. Mentioning one such 'fiend' by name and quoting his home address, the scribe complained that the man had tried to tempt the Swansea men to leave the town and go to Lancashire. 'Shall we never be free of these sneaking poachers?' asked the *Cambrian* man. The answer was to be 'no'.

W. J. Bancroft, captain Swansea R.F.C. 1893-94 and 1896-1901. International and extraordinary player.

At the beginning of October the 'All Whites' were to play at Barnstaple, and the 'powers that be' decided that they would cross to the Devonshire town by Messrs Pockett's 'popular pleasure boat'. Whilst it must have seemed like a good idea at the time when the arrangements were made, on a murky Swansea October day the prospect seemed less inviting. As it transpired, *The Brighton*, which was the Pockett vessel, was 'tossed about in a savagely roaring sea and a fierce wind'. As a result, 'the majority of the Swansea players were victims of *mal de mer*'. Not Billy Bancroft, though. Such was the captain's dislike of the sea that he had elected to travel by train. Thus it was that he was one of the few Swansea men who 'felt up to playing' when the party arrived at the Barnstaple ground. Yet play they all had to, and in conditions which could only further have

Swansea R.F.C. 1896-97.
W. Messer, W. Hill, J. Evans, Geo. Davies, Hopkin Davies, S. Rice, W. J. Williams, D. Mainwaring, W. Grey, H. W. Morgan. A. Jones, W. J. Bancroft (Capt.), F. J. Gordon. D. James, Dan Davies, E. James, Robt. Thomas.

dampened their spirits. On a ' sodden, heavy field, with the rain lashing down' they could only achieve a 'miserable, irritating draw'. Happily, they recovered in time for the following match at Devonport. This time the party joined captain Bancroft in travelling by train. *Terra Firma* was never so inviting. In its report of that match the *Western Independent* declared that 'Albion were thoroughly routed at every point by better trained, heavier, more active and more skillful opponents'. Clearly, the men who, several days before, were contemplating joining their Maker, had been restored to full health.

Not only did the players enjoy the game on the new Devonport ground, they were also involved in a happy reunion. Mr. Bryant, the Club's former Secretary, accompanied the party to the game at Devonport and to their next match versus Cornwall County.

When October ended, Bancroft's men remained unbeaten. Whilst their form up to that point had not been attractive enough to bring supporters back in numbers to match the crowds of previous seasons, 'several hundred' travelled to Neath to see their favourites play 'Captain Powell's Black Brigade'. When they arrived at Neath there was some reason for concern – the referee had not 'turned up'. As a consequence, the new secretary of the Welsh Union, Walter Rees, 'took up the whistle'. When the Neath man blew to end the match he had recorded that the 'All Whites' had been victorious by four tries to nil. As if inspired by that result, the team continued to be successful for several weeks, and it was not until mid-November that the 'All Whites' were first defeated.

Llanelli were the victors by two tries to one, though there were extenuating circumstances. David James had been badly injured and had to leave the field. He did not play again for several weeks.

In the period that followed, with further injuries to key forward Fred Scrine and to Evan James, matters 'took a turn for the worse'. 'Argus' in trying to pin-point the reasons for the decline, complained that the captain was 'interfering too much'.

As an example he cited the case of the James brothers, whose judgment, he argued 'was being puzzled by the captain shouting orders'. Whether that criticism was justified or not, there was evidence to suggest that Bancroft had a strong yearning for greater personal involvement in games than the 'Custodian' role of that period allowed. Many years were to pass before the 'attacking full-back' became fashionable. Billy Bancroft was, clearly such a man before his time.

In January an announcement was made which indicated the level of concern the Swansea club had for its members. As a result of ill health, W. H. Gwynn had had to resign from his post as Secretary of the Welsh Rugby Union. The condition of the former Swansea captain deteriorated rapidly, and an announcement was made from St. Helens to the effect that he had been 'seized with an attack of paralysis ... (and) at length, his mind being damaged (he was) taken to Bridgend Asylum'. The statement went on to explain that Gwynn would be maintained there as a private patient at the expense of the Swansea Club. Sadly, Gwynn died within a relatively short time. The action of the Club's administrators in supporting Gwynn was applauded as reflecting its caring and considerate policies with respect to its members. As time was to illustrate, apart from the human aspects of these policies, they were, also, valuable with regard to the 'Northern Threat'.

As far as W. H. Gwynn is concerned, it is proper in a book of this nature to emphasise the contribution which he made to Swansea Football Club. Only 37 years of age when he died, he had been Club captain twice, an influential figure in its administration, served as coach on several occasions, in particular when the fortunes of the Club had been at low ebb, had represented his country, and was the first paid secretary of the Welsh Union. Not only had he been a great servant to the St. Helens Club, but Welsh Football had also benefited greatly from his contribution to the game.

Whether the passing of Gwynn was a factor in the equation or not, his death seemed to add to a 'developing gloom' which appeared to be affecting Swansea football at the time. 'Argus' summed it up when he wrote:

> 'There is no denying that ... for the last two months the Swansea team was distinctly on the downgrade ... even the James brothers frequently fell below expectations, while an unmistakable "rot" set in among the three-quarters'.

The public seemed to agree. 'Only a couple of hundred turned up' to see one of the end of the season games against Birkenhead Wanderers. Whilst in his end of term report, Bancroft could point to an improvement in overall results as compared with the previous campaign, all was not well. Apart from anything else, the collective memory of supporters is often extremely short lived. Thus, much was made in the Town of the poor end-of-season form. The doubting Thomases thrived again.

1897-98

Bancroft re-elected

During the close season, the 'gloom mongers' warmed themselves with further rumours about Bancroft leaving. However, his re-election as Club captain put such misgivings to rest; at least for another season. Meantime, as a result of his finding employment at the Mannesmann Works, a new centre joined the Club. He was Tom Davies (Treherbert). Evan James, now said to be fully fit, was elected vice-captain.

On the broader front there was continuing concern in the game about 'the encroachments of the Northern Union'. The *Times* thundered that the four Unions should work more closely together, and, for example, 'unify' the laws of the game. (At that time each union had slightly different laws). However, the paper's greatest concern related to the clubs in the north 'which offer pecuniary inducement to less wealthy players to secede'. Meanwhile, the *St. James' Gazette* argued that, 'If Rugby Union Football is to be retained as played by amateurs, they may have to condescend a little, and regularise professionalism, as has been done in cricket'. Clearly, many in the amateur game were concerned that monetary inducement would denude their game of its better players.

At St. Helens, the team was forced to manage without its captain's contribution until the game against Devonport Albion in late October. Business and fitness were the reasons behind his absence, and the results were to show what a contribution the player made to the side. Whilst Devonport was defeated on the captain's return, 'Free-lance' felt that 'unless Swansea considerably improve, Cardiff will be all over them'. He thought that the 'forwards were at sixes and sevens', whilst the attempts of the three-quarters to pass the ball were 'ludicrous'. Yet, when the game against the Taffsiders was played, both Swansea papers claimed that the 'Whites' had achieved a brilliant victory.

Fourteen thousand people were at St. Helens to see the game which, 'Argus' stated 'bristled with exciting incidents and revealed in surprising manner the true form of the 'All Whites'.' Given that, at the time, Cardiff was generally considered to be the strongest side in south Wales, whilst Swansea's start had been less than propitious, this was praise indeed!

Unfortunately, the fine form shown in the game against Cardiff was not replicated in the next game against old rivals, Newport. 'Argus' reported that the game was 'slow and uninteresting', whilst the Swansea play was 'disappointing'. Consistency, a key factor in the make up of any successful side, was, clearly, not a feature at Swansea at that time. Yet Bancroft had an excellent opportunity to do something about that. The Club was about to embark upon its annual tour of the Midlands, where they were to play Leicester and Northampton. Since the tour meant that the party would be together for several days in succession, there was an excellent opportunity to contribute to an improvement in *esprit de corps*. Despite dreadful weather, the first match was confined to 20 minutes each way, that aspect of the tour was extremely profitable. The fact that both games were won, proved to be a bonus. The party travelled home at the end of the tour undefeated and in good spirits.

There was a further boost to the morale of all at St. Helens when the Welsh Trial teams were announced. Despite the fact that they had stated that they did not wish to be considered, the James brothers were selected. Furthermore, in an interesting match, which was played at St. Helens, the brothers were outstanding. After the game there was a groundswell of opinion which suggested that they had done enough to be selected 'as a pair' for the National side. Unfortunately, there was some bad news, too. In a game against Neath at the beginning of December, Bancroft was badly injured and, as a result, did not play until the Christmas Day game against Watsonians. In his absence, Evan James led the side.

The young W. J. Trew.

A new star

By early January, with Bancroft back to full fitness and the James brothers 'turning it on', the team looked to be more cohesive. 'Argus', showing his usual, heavily biased, desire to see Swansea winning, and winning well, wrote of the game against Old Merchant Taylors: 'The Swansea three-quarters have never passed so prettily and with so much profit ... the ball was handled with a skill and precision which delighted the spectators and perplexed the Londoners'. One player who, that day, helped to perplex Old Merchant Taylors, was 'Young Trew (who) ran, passed, dodged, and took his passes with much skill'. As the future was to show, the young man's performance that day was but a harbinger of things to come. Swansea supporters had seen a new hero for the first time.

As the second-half of the season unfolded, the supporters were in much better humour. Young Trew continued to impress, Bancroft was at his best, whilst the James brothers, according to 'Argus', were in such form that 'take them together and there is not a better pair of halves playing in Wales today. They are as tricky now as when they first astonished the football world.' The good humour of the supporters was nurtured further, as Gloucester's unbeaten record was taken in front of a crowd of 13,000, whilst Bristol were 'swamped by 3 goals and 5 tries to nil'. A feature of that Bristol match was the entertainment provided for the spectators before the kick-off. 'The crowd', according to the *Cambrian*, 'were highly amused at the antics of Trumpeter Murray (4 ft. tall) his dog and donkey'. The said 'antics' resulted in the spectators giving 'freely and generously' to the Hospital Fund.

In the meantime, matters were coming to a head in the north. Most observers now accepted the inevitability of professional rugby in Lancashire and Yorkshire. The *Times* published a report of a meeting in Manchester at which a Northern Union sub committee had recommended to its parent body that professionalism be adopted. Another recommendation was that players should have legitimate employment, which echoed, in part, the suggestions made much earlier by Swansea's W. H. Gwynn.

As far as Swansea's form was concerned, after the encouraging mid-season period, the side was unable to maintain its consistency and, in the process, lost games against Llanelli at Stradey, and an impressive Newport XV at St. Helens. In his report of that game against the 'Mustard and Blackings', 'Argus' complained about the treatment of Bancroft by some spectators. He wrote: 'The great majority of people in this country are as fickle as the sea. They are favoured with the most uncharitable dispositions and wonderfully short memories'. The scribe went on to argue that Bancroft had been the 'god' of supporters for the previous seven years, yet 'on Saturday', when the full-back was reported to be off colour, the '"Cheap" hooted and jeered at him. They scoffed at his kicking, laughed derisively when he attempted to run, and shouted joyously when he was tackled'. 'Argus' did not indicate on that occasion whether those who had 'perpetrated the outrage' were home or visiting supporters. However, in a report of a later game, he identified those of the Cardiff club as 'jeering and laughing at Bancroft and the Brothers James to try to put them off their game'. From this it will be clear to any reader like the author, brought up with the concepts of 'fair play' and 'sportsmanship' as the bases of athletic competition that it was not always thus.

Nevertheless, despite or because of the behaviour of those mindless supporters, matters on the field improved for Swansea in the latter third of the season. The side seemed to regain its consistency and, with it, the ability to play the attractive football for which its followers yearned. In March the 'Metallurgical Capital of the World beat the Tin-plate Capital'. That match against Llanelli was thought by 'Argus' to be 'one of the prettiest played between the two rivals'. Whilst the language would hardly fit a game between 'Sospan' and 'The Whites' today, given 'Argus's' penchant for using colourful phrases, it is likely that he intended to convey the idea that he saw a fast, flowing, skillful game. However the team performed, it stood them in good stead when they went to Cardiff for the next match. On that occasion, when 16,000 people were said to be in the ground, the Swansea backs were outstanding. As a result, the Cardiff entrepreneurs who had prepared black-edged 'Mourning Cards' for sale after the game (In memory of poor Swansea), were obliged to consign them to the fire.

Playing brilliantly now, the 'All Whites' won both their Easter games (against Rockcliffe, and Leicester) and thus wound up their season on a positive note. Overall, only six matches had been lost whilst there were 22 victories, which meant that Bancroft could look back on a record which bore positive comparison with the previous season. Most observers now felt that there was room for optimism about the future of the Swansea club. The Brothers James had had a fine season, Bancroft, when fit, had been on top of his game for most of the campaign, whilst Gordon, Trew and Rees had been effective in what was thought to be the best three-quarter line which the Club had had for many years. 'The General', Gordon ended as top try scorer with seventeen, whilst Bancroft had converted fifty per cent of the tries which had been scored. Given the number of games which he missed that performance was highly satisfactory. Then, of course, there was 'Young Trew'. Could Bill Bowen's achievements be bettered? They were thinking such things in Swansea at that time.

1898–99

Welsh Champions again

Whilst Billy Bancroft was elected captain for the third season in succession, Evan James was replaced as vice-captain by 'Genny' Gordon. Whether James's disappointment at losing the post had anything to do with what was to happen later, is not clear. However, it is fair to say that it would not have helped. On the other hand, had Gordon not had the opportunity to 'learn the trade of captain', he might not have been as successful as he was when he gained the captaincy for himself. Without doubt, therefore, those decisions, taken at the 1898 A.G.M., had a significant bearing on the future fortunes of the Club.

As far as Bancroft was concerned, prior to the new season, he stated that he was 'quietly confident'. His sole concern related to developments in Manchester and Leeds. 'Providing that the

Swansea R.F.C. 1898-99.
H. Ball, J. L. Davies, T. Harries, (G. E. Bowen), T. Jackson, (W. T. Farr, Treas.), D. Harries, B. Thomas, (F. E. Perkins, Sec.), W. Parker, W. Bowen, J. Prescott.
D. James, F. J. Gordon, S. Rice, W. J. Bancroft (Capt.), A. Jones, F. Scrine, E. James.
H. Davies, W. J. Trew, G. Davies, D. Rees.

Northern poachers are kept away,' he argued, 'we should be able to muster a very strong XV'. After referring to the 'sermon' preached by James Livingstone on 'The snares, dangers and disappointments of professionalism under the Northern Union' he reinforced his confidence when he said that he did not believe that Swansea would lose any more of its leading players. On a happier note, he applauded Mr. Livingstone's efforts in arranging a match in Paris. He said that the Club was agog with excitement at the possibility that Swansea would become the first Welsh club to play in France. It was hardly surprising that Livingstone's initiative had created such interest among the players. In those days, ordinary working men hardly ever travelled outside the boundaries of their own home towns. It was true that rugby players and some supporters were used to journeying 'up England way', to places like Leicester, Northampton, Oldham and Swinton; but France; that was another matter altogether.

With professionalism now inevitable in the north, there were those who viewed matters through business eyes. In their world, the emotion felt in the Union camp about professionalism was not an issue. The concern of financiers related to the potential viability of the clubs as businesses. The *Shareholder* for August 1898 carried an article which related to this concern under the heading 'Football Finances'. Whilst the football being discussed was professional soccer in England, the principles were the same. From the report, the implications of professionalism for clubs which were, currently, amateur were clear to see. Among the examples given in the article was the case of Aston Villa Ltd. At that time, the Birmingham club had the biggest income in football. During the previous season it had received £11,077, and had paid its players

£5,124 whilst making a profit of £735. Those amateur clubs which were following the developments now had a yardstick against which to measure business potential. From the investor's point of view, however, football did not appear to be an attractive option.

Nevertheless, in early September, 'Argus' reported that, despite the unattractive economics of their adventure, and Mr. Livingstone's sermon to Swansea players, the 'Northern poachers' were still active. Danny Rees and George Davies, two of Swansea's key three-quarters, had 'caved in' to the inducements of representatives of the Oldham club. Both players had travelled to Manchester to discuss terms and it looked as though each of them was 'deserting'. Happily, nothing came of the discussions and both players returned to Swansea. It seemed that Oldham wanted Rees and Davies to take part in a trial match before contracts could be signed. 'Rees, very wisely, declined', reported the *Cambrian*. 'Had he played ... he would have made himself a professional in the eyes of the English and Welsh Unions'. The lines were now firmly drawn. Amateurs and professionals now knew where they stood.

Given that the Club was to win the Premiership in the season ahead, it is interesting to note that the Swansea captain, Billy Bancroft, stated on the Wednesday before the first game that he 'had not seen the James brothers'. Whilst during the period in question, and for many years afterwards, there was a Corinthian attitude towards training, it is surprising that two of the Club's key players had not had any contact with their captain up to the week before the season started. Yet, this might have been something to do with Bancroft's own approach. He felt that he was fit enough from playing cricket, whilst, 'the rest of the chaps have been practising'. Presumably, 'Genny' Gordon had led any training sessions which had taken place. However, it was clear that the pre-season training approach which had been pioneered by E. S. Richards fifteen years before had given way to a much more casual regime.

Perhaps it was the lack of attention which had been paid to pre-season work which resulted in the *Cambrian* complaining about lack of cohesion in the first match against Bridgend. 'Argus', even castigated Bancroft for 'trying to play like a fifth three-quarter ... if he were not the captain he would not be allowed to indulge in such tactics', the scribe argued. It was an old concern of the *Cambrian* man, but was, also, echoed by 'Free-lance' in the *Post*.

Further criticism, however, was muted, not only by a number of victories in October, but by the manner in which the games were won. Both local papers commented on the *esprit de corps* of the side, while 'Free-lance' wrote of 'perfect understanding between all departments'. Ben Evans's store would have been delighted with such a report. The prevailing view of both papers was that the 1898-99 campaign promised to be most successful. As ever, comparisons with Bill Bowen's successful sides were drawn, whilst the collective hope which beat in the hearts of Swansea supporters was stronger than it had been for many years.

The élan with which the side was playing was greatly appreciated during the Club's winter tour to Devonport and Bristol. Prior to the match against the 'Albion', and after the final whistle sounded, 'the "All Whites" were applauded and cheered'. During the Bristol game 'the home supporters showed their appreciation of skillful handling'. Clearly, the reputation of the men in white was well established in the West Country, whilst it had been enhanced by the manner in which the team played its games. 'Young' Trew, for his part was the hero of the tour. He had come of age. As the year drew to a close, Bancroft must have felt that everything was in place to continue the 'profitable' campaign into the new year.

Old Merchant Taylors provided the first opposition for 1899, in a match played in 'very adverse climatic conditions'. After heavy morning rain, even the St. Helens Field was sodden, and with a 'steady downpour being blown from goalpost to goalpost' during the game, it was surprising that the spectators saw a fairly open match. Indeed, such was the pattern of play of the 'All Whites' that 'Argus' declared it to be 'a performance of which any team might be proud in the conditions which prevailed'. Trew, George Davies, Gordon and Rees were in fine form, and the visitors were beaten by two goals and six tries to nil. Such was the growing reputation of Billy Trew, that the *Cambrian* scribe was moved to write: 'The match could not, of course, be finished without Trew crossing the Rubicon'. It seemed that, by implication at least, Caesar was being drawn into comparison with Swansea's new sporting hero.

Exit the Jameses

On 1st January 1899 St. Helens was the venue for the Wales versus England international. With Bancroft as captain and the Brothers James at half-back, the Swansea club was represented in key positions in the side which gained a decisive victory. 'Free-lance' reported that 'every coign of advantage was taken up; every inch of ground utilised ...' as 30,000 people crammed into St. Helens Field. 'Argus' reported that the brothers (James) distinguished themselves above any two players on the field. Evan, it transpired also distinguished himself by his bravery. Despite the fact that he 'damaged his shoulder early in the game' (afterwards it was discovered that he had fractured his collarbone) and, subsequently damaged his hand, he played throughout the match. Whilst Wales benefited from his tenacity, Swansea did not. A post-match announcement stated that it was 'unlikely that Evan will play again this season'. Whilst there is no evidence to confirm the assumption, it is reasonable to suppose that the injury might have triggered thoughts in James's mind about taking 'the northern silver'. Certainly, not many weeks were to pass before the east-side lad took the irrevocable step. Powerful as it was, James Livingstone's 'sermon' was to prove to be less than a match for Broughton's bribe.

Without Evan James, the Swansea committee turned to a third James brother, Sam, to fill the International's position for a game against Aberavon. This decision provided the James family with another record, in that they were the first to have three brothers turn out for Swansea's senior XV in a single season. Whilst Sam could not match Evan for skill, the team, also without Trew and David James, did enough to beat Aberavon and retain their unbeaten record. 'Free-lance' reported, 'The precious record remains intact. The escutcheon, so proudly borne by captain Bancroft and his men, is still unsmudged. It is as lily-white as ever.'

Later in January, with the 'execrable' weather continuing, even St. Helens Field was being affected. 'Argus', reporting on the home game against Devonport Albion, recorded that '... (it) was in woefully bad condition, what the Cardiff Arms Park and other such grounds were like (at the time) is better imagined than described'. On the following Monday, after George Davies had announced that he was not 'going north', the curtain finally came down on the James brothers saga. The *Cambrian* announced the news to all Swansea:

> 'On Monday, the Brothers James left for Broughton. They have thrown in their lot with Broughton Rangers – the latter have, in fact, taken the whole family, father and mother, sons and grandchildren, under their accommodating wing.'

'Argus' wished the Jameses good luck, for he and his contemporary 'Free-lance' had been of the opinion that 'defection' was inevitable. Swansea, they thought would 'manage without them.' Nonetheless, behind the brave faces which the journalists put on for their readers, was a natural concern that the unbeaten 'All Whites' were going to miss the talent and instinctive genius of the half-back brothers. They were to be proved right in that regard, but not for long.

Yet, there was little evidence that the departure of the Jameses affected the team's performance at all in the next match at St. Helens. The opponents were Lampeter College, a side which had lost only narrowly to Llanelli earlier in the season. This time, however, the Collegians were swept aside by an avalanche of scoring. In all the 'All Whites' registered 83 points (121 points today) in scoring 13 goals and six tries to set a new Club record. The visitors did not score a single point. That result, however, flattered to deceive. At the beginning of February, Gloucester, the same club which had taken Bill Bowen's unbeaten record, lowered Swansea's colours for the first time during that campaign. The partial 'Argus' complained about poor refereeing, referring to 'English decisions' and of a Gloucester side which set out to 'win at any cost'. On the other hand, he felt that the 'tension of maintaining the record had been removed, and perhaps none lament the fact less than captain Bancroft's men themselves'. However, in the context of that report, this conclusion sounded rather hollow, akin to the apologia of a spokesman for a losing party at a Parliamentary election. Apart from anything else, Gloucester had won narrowly (a dropped goal to a try), and Billy Bancroft did not convert the Swansea try which was scored late in the game. Whilst the Swansea supporters who made their way home that October evening would have been disappointed, their spirits would have been lifted had they known that they had witnessed the début of a new star-to-be. His name was Dick Jones.

As had happened in previous seasons, having lost its unbeaten record the Club quickly sustained a second defeat, this time against Newport. In that match, which was played at St. Helens, the 'Usk-siders' won by a penalty goal and a try to a try, though the match was 'finely balanced throughout'. There was another new name in the Swansea team that day. Partnering Reynolds at half-back was Dick Owen. 'Free-lance' described him as 'the diminutive Hafod and Morriston boy'. Unbeknown to the Swansea supporters who saw that match, a jigsaw with several new pieces was falling into place. The James brothers were being missed, but, in their absence, the selectors were being forced to experiment with new faces. The old saw, 'Cometh the hour, cometh the man' might not quite fit the circumstances which applied at the time. In retrospect, however, it seems appropriate to amend the saying to include 'boys' instead of 'man'.

At the end of February, reporting on the 'All Whites' tour match against 'The Tigers', the *Leicester Daily Mercury* stated that the visitors 'gave one of the finest exhibitions of football ever seen on the Welford Road Ground'. The side was outstanding, too, against Northampton, and the *Cambrian* stated that 'the tour ranks among the most successful and enjoyable in the history of the Club ... the players arrived home in the best of spirits'. Inexplicably, when the domestic schedule was resumed, the sparkling form of the tour could not be sustained. Whilst Llanelli were beaten by 3 goals to nil, it was a poor game. A draw with Cardiff was described as 'uninteresting', whilst, even a 47-point victory over Penarth was reported by 'Argus' as 'having excited very little interest'. Furthermore, in dreadful weather, a return match with 'Scarlet Runners' ended in an even more depressing way. 'Free-lance' reflected that 'a man who travels over a dozen miles to witness a football match in weather like that which prevailed on Saturday, must be football mad'. So bad was the weather, and the standard of play, that the referee stopped the game three minutes into the second-half and awarded the match to Swansea.

At this stage, with injuries to Bancroft and Trew not assisting matters, the side seemed to have lost its rhythm. Indeed, until the Easter Monday return game with Northampton, they struggled even when winning. But the spark was re-ignited for the Northampton game, when the supporters saw a mature performance from the Club's new half-back pairing. 'Argus' reported that the new pair, Owen and Jones, 'clicked'. He wrote, 'they did remarkably well. The latter is a showy and effective player. He rarely loses his head. Owen is very nippy, and although he is exceedingly diminutive, he does not shirk heavy work'. In that match the team scored 5 goals and 3 tries without conceding a point. It was one of the best performances of the season and a significant improvement on the matches played in the preceding period. Was the improvement 'down to the new boys'? At least the young men gave the supporters something to talk about. What a side they would have, they must have thought, when Bancroft and Trew were fit again.

Once again, at the end of March, the Swansea committee was to show its concern for the game in the Principality. They discussed how they might help Llanelli. The 'Scarlets', who had lost several players to the Northern Union, had found that their 'gates' had diminished and they were in a parlous financial position. They had expected a large income from a game against the 'All Whites', but dreadful weather on that day had kept many people away. As a result, the Llanelli Secretary had written to St. Helens to ask for an additional fixture. Following their deliberations, the committee announced that 'in order to assist Llanelly they were to offer them an extra game at St. Helens. They would be given half the gate'. The match was to be played at the end of the season after Swansea returned from Paris.

It was the game in Paris, however, which caught the imagination of the supporters. By that time, notwithstanding the departure of the Jameses, injuries to key players, and a period during which the side lost its rhythm, the 'All Whites' had been declared Welsh Champions. When fit, Bancroft had had a fine season, George Davies, Danny Rees, Billy Trew and 'Genny' Gordon had 'played the passing game to perfection', whilst 'R. Jones and R. Owen now look as though they will be permanent features'. As ever, in the end-of-season comments in the Swansea papers it was the backs who claimed the attention. The forwards were given little glory. However, they had provided the platform from which the backs could 'work their magic'. The speed, trickery and adroitness of the Swansea backs – so beloved by Swansea supporters throughout the Club's history – would have come to nought without the efforts of the 'doughty front eight'.

There was another interesting development in the week prior to the game in Paris. Clearly, Swansea's reputation in the football world extended across the Channel. A 'communication' was received from the French asking the Swansea club if they would play a combined side rather than Stade Francaise *per se*. They felt that a representative team from the chief French clubs would provide more appropriate opposition. Thus it was that, given that the 'All Whites' secretary, F. E. Perkins 'cabled his agreement', Swansea was to play what 'Free-lance' called 'All France'. On the day, in a downpour reminiscent of Swansea weather, the men in white were victorious by 30 points to 3. Later, it was announced that the trip had cost the Club £200, yet everyone agreed that that was a small price to pay for the experience, and the glory of being the first Welsh side to play in Paris. The fact that 'All France' had been defeated in the process added another dimension to the matter.

In his end of the season comments, captain Bancroft stated that he had been pleased with the

Club's performances overall. His side had scored 732 points whilst conceding only 47 in 35 games; truly amazing statistics. Danny Rees had scored 32 tries, Frank Gordon and Billy Trew 31 each, whilst the captain had converted 73 tries, dropped 4 goals and converted 3 penalties. The mediocrity of the beginning of the last quarter of the campaign was forgotten.

In June, a Welsh Union sub-committee met with a view to discussing the development of 'two grounds suitable for the vast crowds which are considered likely to attend International matches'. There were those in the east who were unhappy that St. Helens stood, as 'Argus' had it 'head and shoulders above the rest'. They put forward the perfectly reasonable argument that there should be one centre in the east and one in the west. The thin end of the wedge was being driven home.

Chapter Six

PROMOTING RUGBY

DURING THE PREVIOUS SEASON, there had been two Association Football matches played at St. Helens, courtesy of the Swansea committee. A schools match between Swansea and Cardiff was played, as was a match in which West Bromwich Albion competed against a selected Swansea side. Furthermore, the extent of interest in the round ball game in Swansea was such that the local schools were beginning to become involved with it. This was a concern for the Swansea committee, for, apart from any implications concerning professionalism, and the growth of the senior soccer game, the schools in the town were a 'training ground for future players'. Furthermore, it would not have escaped the notice of the Treasurer that the schoolboy population represented future supporters of the rugby game.

As a consequence of their deliberations about the matter, James Livingstone announced that the Club had offered a valuable cup to the Swansea schools for a rugby competition. He was pleased to announce that 'the School Board had been good enough to accept the cup and had endorsed the Club's action'. The Committee had another card up its sleeve, too. St. Helens, they felt, was the 'only good football field in Swansea'. They thought it 'unwise and useless to encourage both games'. Consequently, they said that they would, in the future 'think carefully before allowing more Soccer to be played on St. Helens'.

Meanwhile, as the players prepared for the coming season – once again with Bancroft as captain – there were further 'Northern Poacher' rumours. According to the gossip, Trew, Gordon, and Rees had been approached by men from the north. By this time, the image of these emissaries was firmly established in the minds of the Swansea public. They were scheming, devious, untrustworthy 'bribers'. The fact that the mission of these men was to try and 'steal our boys from their homes' made them doubly despicable. So, whilst the rumours were relayed, the hope in the hearts of the Swansea supporters was that they would go away and leave the Swansea stars to their adoring public. Whilst none were reported, given the extent of chapel-going in the town at the time, there is every likelihood that many unofficial prayer meetings were held in order to protect Swansea players from the northern snares. Surely, the argument might have run, God is an amateur Union man ... and Welsh at that!

In his pre-season interview, now a feature in the *Cambrian*, Billy Bancroft, 'from his St. Helens Avenue residence', declared that he did not believe that any of the boys' would succumb to 'Northern Poachers'. With respect to Fuller, however, who had played the previous season, there were a different set of influences. The player would not turn out for the Club again, because 'his people ... are averse to him playing'.

With Trew having 'filled out' and having 'won several prizes on the running path', now fully fit, with the previous season's three-quarters available, the promising Owen and Jones combination at half-back, and a pack of reliable forwards, the new season could be approached with confidence. Yet, despite substantial early victories, by the middle of October, 'Argus' was reporting that the form of the side was 'bewildering'. He went on to say that '... the majority of supporters ... fear that all is not well'. And that was after a 36-0 victory over Penarth, in which Trew was 'irresistible'. It seemed that the Club had the same problem as the previous season; there was 'a lack of cohesion and combination.' Perhaps the supporters, and the press, were expecting too much, too soon from the younger players, particularly Jones and Owen at half-back. A problem with many young players is that, early in their careers, they tend not to be consistent, and those who nurture them have to take that fact into consideration. The 'Two Dicks' together represented the fulcrum around which the team operated. As a consequence, they needed to be effective as a pair if the team was going to be able to perform at optimum level. In October, 'Free-lance' referred to Owen as being 'plucky', whilst Jones was too methodical and not quick enough. A month later he reported that 'the half-back pairing did exceedingly well'. Apart from becoming more consistent, the two young men had to learn their trades and develop that sixth sense level of understanding which only comes from playing together frequently.

Late in October there was a controversy in the Club regarding the conditions imposed upon members who had seats in the grandstand. 'Argus', reporting on the feeling among these members, argued that a new entrance should be opened on the Mumbles Road. 'At present', he wrote, 'hundreds of people are compelled to walk from the Mumbles Road to the top entrance opposite Gorse Lane and then back to the grandstand'. Subsequently, the *Cambrian* published several letters agreeing with the scribe. The author of one of these letters stated that unless something was done about the matter 'I shall drop my membership ... clear loss of 15 shillings per annum to the Club.' The request seemed reasonable, and something was done about the matter soon after.

1899-1900

Newport again

It was the game against Newport in November which many thought would be the real test of the Swansea side. Indeed, at the Club, the match was thought to be important enough to warrant special training twice during the previous week. No doubt, by modern standards, the intensity of these training sessions would be considered mild. However, in the light of the Corinthian approach to sport which prevailed at the time, they were noteworthy. Furthermore, in the case in question they seemed to have contributed to another success. In front of a crowd of 10,000 people, the men in white won by 21 points to 6. A significant victory in the annals of Swansea/Newport clashes. This time the report in the Press gave full credit to the play of the forwards. 'Argus' reported that the home Ups (forwards) played magnificently. 'They rushed, dribbled, tackled and scrummaged in a way that must have surprised their opponents'. Playing into 'the teeth of a gale' in the second-half, 'Scrine, Parker, Hopkin Davies, and Bob Thomas were outstanding'. However, 'Free-lance', in his report felt that the half-backs were disappointing, though, given the conditions described by the *Cambrian* reporter, it is probable that the forwards controlled the game and 'nursed' the young halves. As far as the *Western Mail* was concerned, their reporter saw enough in the game to declare: 'After Saturday's win over Newport,

Swansea R.F.C. 1899-1900.

there does not seem to be any doubt as to Swansea being the Season's Champions'. And that was a Cardiff paper! No doubt that appraisal was based upon the overall Swansea record at that time. Nine games had been played, all of which had been won, whilst 184 points had been scored and only six conceded. Whatever the Swansea followers desired in terms of flowing football, they could hardly complain about the results.

There followed a 'Great Victory' at Cardiff, enjoyed immensely by 1,200 Swansea supporters who took a G.W.R. excursion. Because Lockman was suspended and Bancroft injured J. Davies (Llandeilo), brother of George, played at full-back. After that match the Swansea press felt that 'the inclusion of Trew and George Davies in the Welsh side is now a practical certainty'. The halves were singled out for praise, too. Owen was 'as plucky as he was dashing and tackled with fine effort', whilst Jones 'played the correct game'. Jones was also mentioned following the game against Leicester during the Club's annual Midlands tour. His play was now 'more accurate'. The *Athletic News* was greatly impressed by the performance of the team. At the time, Leicester were Midlands Cup holders and had not been beaten that season before the game against the 'All Whites'. Yet, 'they left the field having gone down before a better team'. The paper was equally complementary about the win over Northampton on the same tour. As far as the Swansea club was concerned, though, that victory was achieved at a cost; Billy Trew was injured.

On returning to domestic competition, the side continued winning until a match at Llanelli, which took place just before Christmas. Then, the 'Scarlet Runners' surprised the football world by taking Swansea's unbeaten record. There were those in Swansea who blamed the defeat on 'staleness'. Others complained that Billy Trew and George Davies (chosen to play for Wales against England) 'held back for fear of injury'. Nonetheless, whilst the defeat was a disappointment, in the games which followed the side played with greater freedom. Owen and Jones, now firmly established, were beginning to dominate games. Owen was described as

Danny Rees.

Billy Bancroft.

'ubiquitous' which said something about his growing confidence; the young man was 'looking for the ball'.

George Davies, who was twenty-five on Christmas Day 1899, enjoyed himself hugely in the Yule-tide game against Watsonians, and he followed that success by playing 'outstandingly' in the International match against England at Gloucester. Five Swansea men wore the red shirt that day. Apart from Davies, they were Danny Rees, Billy Trew, Billy Bancroft and H. Thomas. To add to Swansea's pride, Billy Trew scored a fine try.

Trew was on target in the next Swansea match, too; in the final stages of the game, he beat the Gloucester defence with a 'dazzling run'. It was a referee who was to perform the next piece of dazzling. Late in January, Aberavon came to St. Helens for a game which the 'All Whites' were expected to win comfortably. The referee for the match was the much respected Harry Bowen of Llanelli. Bowen was a skillful official, but the game 'stopped and started', whilst the whistle sounded too frequently for the liking of the home supporters. They had come to see 'the finest three-quarter line in the land' cutting through the opposing defence. Instead, they saw a 'scrambling affair, with the forwards dominant'. Notwithstanding Bowen's reputation, 'the 6*d.* crowd ... expressed strong disapproval of (his) decisions ... There was no wind ... the least noise carried ... some of them used disgusting language. How the ladies present would have been shocked ... Bowen, however, would have none of that. He stopped the game and indicated that it would not be continued... The grandstandites applauded approvingly ... Mr. Bowen won ... His conduct had a sobering effect on the rowdies.'

In mid-February, the Owen-Jones partnership 'completely nonplussed their Cardiff opponents' in a game in which the 'Blue and Blacks' were defeated by 16 points to nil. The Jameses were forgotten, the Swansea supporters now had a pair of halves to compare with the best. That game was also noteworthy for another reason. 'In view of the importance of the match, neutral umpires (touch judges) were appointed.' 'Argus', who, clearly, greatly enjoyed the victory, could not resist a 'dig' at one of his Cardiff contemporaries. 'Welsh Athlete' had, confidently, predicted that the Taffsiders would win comfortably. The Swansea man, hardly renowned for objectivity himself, and referring to the Cardiffian's prediction, wrote: 'so argued the superior "Welsh Athlete", whose contempt for anything outside Cardiff makes most people smile'.

By the end of February, the *Cambrian* man, echoing the *Athletic News*, could write: 'The "All Whites" have now established beyond all cavil and doubt their claims to the Championship of Wales'. Newport had been beaten on their own ground by two goals to a try. Furthermore, the *Newport Daily Star* reported that the game had been the best seen on the Newport ground that season. Whilst the Swansea supporters enjoyed not only the victory but the manner in which it had been achieved, they were dispirited by some other news. Buller had been defeated at Colenso. Given the feelings which the South African War had generated among the population at large, this was indeed a psychological setback. The *Cambrian* reported: 'For the moment, the spirit was knocked out of most of us. Many enthusiastic followers of the Swansea team failed to fix their minds on the game'.

Nevertheless, when the supporters could focus, again, on rugby, they could consider a record in which the 'All Whites' had been defeated just once in 27 games. Furthermore, the team had scored 399 points and had conceded only 46. To say the least, it made 'handsome' reading.

A recherché banquet

In March, the supporters had a further diversion. The Stade Francaise representative side (All France) came to St. Helens for a return match. Before the match, Mr. Chapman photographed the sides, whilst the national anthems were played as the teams stood to attention. James Livingstone, who had arranged the fixture, looked on proudly. He was even more proud at the end of the game, the 'All Whites' had won a decisive victory by 41 points to nil. Furthermore, at the *recherché banquet* held after the game at the Hotel Metropole, there was a 'wonderful atmosphere' at which the relationship between the two clubs was cemented. *Entente cordiale* indeed.

On the return to domestic competition, there was a 'sensational opening' to the match against Llanelli. After just one minute of the game, Bancroft collected a 'hack on' and from a position ten yards inside his own half, coolly dropped a goal. Despite that goal and the fact that Llanelli were defeated, the 'Scarlets' gave the 'strangely lethargic Swansea side' something of a fright. Whatever was said following that match, things improved for a visit to Neath. The 'Black Boys' fought, grimly, for every inch of ground, but, as the *Athletic News* had it, 'Even when Trew went off (injured) and Swansea had a seven man pack, their scrummaging was superior to that of the Neath men'. And, the paper concluded, 'Against Neath on their own ground that was remarkable'.

Other English journalists were equally flattering. The *Plymouth Herald*, reporting on Swansea's annual West Country tour match against Devonport, was of the opinion that 'Swansea's exhibition of all round football was as near to perfection as the Rectory spectators have ever seen'. In April, following further handsome victories, the local press was equally complimentary. 'Argus', in his report of the match in which Northampton had been 'crushed' by 35 points to 3, reminded his readers that, prior to that game the visitors had 'lost only one game out of thirty'. Danny Rees and 'The General' were outstanding in that win, as was Billy Trew. Indeed, the *Cambrian* man thought that Trew was 'the most dashing try getter in Wales'; he had scored 28 times at that point in the season. Bancroft, meanwhile, had converted 40 goals, dropped 4 and kicked 5 penalties. Scrine was acknowledged as the 'cleverest forward in Wales', whilst Smith, Bevan, Joseph, Arthur Jones and Hopkin Davies had all done well.

As far as the young half-backs were concerned, the 'end of term report' was encouraging. 'Free-lance' wrote 'Jones is, perhaps, a more polished player than Owen, but the two are so good that one is loathe to individualise'. It was the combination that mattered.

Having won 31 of their 32 games, the 'All Whites' greatly enjoyed a further *recherché banquet.* On this occasion the host was Sir John Llewellyn M.P. One of the toasts at the dinner reminded all concerned that there was a war going on. It was to 'Our boys at the Front'. This time, however, whatever concern was felt about the war in South Africa, it was submerged in the glow of the evening. At the banquet the members of the First XV collected gold medals, whilst the successful second string were given silver medals to celebrate their record. They, too, had lost only one match. Whilst the players 're-lived their glory', those behind the scenes were not forgotten. Harry Ball, who had been the 'Trainer' of the First XV for several years was retiring, and was presented with 'a very handsome pipe in case and pouch'. James Livingstone, the chairman for the evening, proposed a toast to Sir John Llewellyn, declaring that he was 'a President without precedent'. Llewellyn, who was reported to have enjoyed the 'play on words' had had a very long association with the Club. There was a poem, too, to help round off the evening, which emphasised the close association which the Club enjoyed with the town of Swansea. One verse read:

Three cheers for the brave 'All Whites'
who fight for Swansea's fame,
To them we give on football fields
the honour which true prowess yields
Our Town's good name.

Au revoir, Paris

During the close season, friends of Billy Bancroft were doing all they could to support the player's latest business venture. He had decided to form a company, W. J. Bancroft Ltd. and the *Cambrian* reported that there had been a good demand for shares in the new venture. The implication in the statement which followed was, also clear: 'We have no doubt that Mr. Bancroft's many friends will not fail to patronise him'. Swansea, as well as the Club, should show its appreciation of the outstanding service which had been given by one of its foremost sporting heroes.

As far as the player himself was concerned, in accepting the captaincy for the fifth consecutive season – a Club record – he said that he did so reluctantly. However, reported the *Post*, 'Since it was their wish, he would do his best'. The captain left his team-mates with a clear message about fitness, however, 'he hoped that the players would give every attention to training'. Frank Gordon, again vice-captain, was described by Bancroft as 'the best fellow in the team'.

There was, however, one controversial matter raised at the A.G.M. Bancroft, in his remarks, emphasised that the players wanted to play in Paris again. Whilst understanding the players' position, James Livingstone had to report that the Welsh Union had passed a resolution prohibiting fixtures either at home or abroad on Sundays. Though a Churchman himself, the chairman stated that the resolution was based upon a 'good deal of nonsense (which had been) talked about the last match played in Paris'. Whether this was Nonconformist Wales defending the Sabbath, or other clubs jealously spoiling Swansea's initiative, is not clear. However, the result was that the fixture was not renewed for the season to come.

1900-01

A hat-trick?

Fred Scrine.

In facing up to the first full season of the new century, captain Bancroft and his men had a significant task in hand. The Club had been Welsh 'Premiers' at the end of each of the preceding two seasons and had lost only four games over both campaigns. Furthermore, they had scored 1,085 points during that time, whilst conceding only 129. Was it fair to expect the team to emulate this achievement? That was the question which exercised the minds of the journalists who followed the fortunes of the Club. Both 'Free-lance' and 'Argus' were cautious. The *Cambrian* man said 'we will have the answer about Christmas time'.'Free-lance' in the *Post*, believed that it was a great deal to ask of the team. Yet, he found comfort in certain facts. The young half-backs had 'put on some flesh during the summer', whilst all the players from the previous season were available. Though, had Broughton Rangers had their way, that would not have been the case. These 'poachers' had offered Billy Trew £100 down and a tobacconists shop, whilst Fred Scrine's 'bribe' had been £75 down and £8 per week. Happily, for Swansea, both men declined. Their reported, 'we don't intend to go north', was sweet music in the ears of the supporters.

When speculation came to be reality, whilst the season started reasonably, the Club's unbeaten record was soon lost. Those old adversaries, Newport, were the victors, winning what had been a tight match, in the last twenty minutes on a 'gloomy November day'. Whilst only one other match was lost during the whole campaign, that defeat had a strangely depressing effect on the Club's supporters. At the time, however, the captain, taking on the defeated politician mantle, declared that: 'It is a good thing that our record has been smudged, it takes the pressure off'.

Nonetheless, if the next game was anything to go by, Bancroft was right. Leicester 'Tigers' were beaten by 16 points to four, with Billy Trew scoring a 'hat-trick' of tries. Then, during the team's annual West Country tour, 14,000 people saw Devonport Albion 'strive in vain to retain their unbeaten record', whilst Plymouth were beaten 13 points to 0. Back in Swansea, Neath became the club's next victims, whilst Llanelli succumbed by 22 points to nil. That victory, however, was gained at a cost. Frank Gordon, tackled by the Llanelli full-back, 'broke his arm on falling'. Since 'The General' had broken the same limb earlier in the season and had 'only been back for three weeks', it was a blow for the player as well as the team. 'Free-lance' reported that 'chloroform and morphia were used by Drs. Reid and Elseworth', which, presumably, meant that the popular winger had been in great pain.

Since Bancroft and Trew, as well as Gordon, were absent for several weeks during the season, it would not have been surprising had the rhythm of the side been affected. However, such was the strength of the the Club's second string that new men were introduced without adverse effect. The Christmas games provided further encouragement for the Club and its supporters. Tudhoe (a County Durham side) was defeated by 32 points to nil, while, on Christmas Day, when a 'high wind blew and heavy rain fell', Watsonians were the victims following a dour game in which only a single try was scored. The Boxing Day fixture against Edinburgh University, however, 'allowed the homesters free rein', which resulted in a fine win. That winning run continued into the new year, so 'Argus' must have felt confident in predicting that the 'All Whites' were going to ' do the trick again'. Other encouragement for Swansea supporters came in the announcement of the Welsh team to play England. Bancroft, again, captained the national side, whilst George Davies, Billy Trew and Bob Thomas were other Swansea men to wear the red jersey that day.

'Argus' was now brimming with confidence. He was bullish. 'Despite the absences and injuries, things are going well and the future looks good.' In mid-January, however, he was misquoting another Celt as the return match against Devonport Albions at St. Helens petered out into a draw. 'But alas,' he wrote, 'the "schemes o' men aft gang agley" and those sanguine hearts were disappointed'. Yet, not too disappointed, presumably. After all, the team had not lost. Furthermore, in terms of life in general, the 'mood of the nation' reflected matters other than football. 'Victoria, The Good' had died. The Victorian era was at an end, and the whole country was in mourning. Swansea followed suit. Rugby did not feature in the *Cambrian* for two weeks. Yet the season continued, and the side, often without several key players, continued to make positive progress.

At the end of February, Newport came to St. Helens and were beaten by two tries to nothing in front of what was said to be 'the largest crowd since Blackheath'. Furthermore, the victory was even sweeter than would usually have been the case. Prior to the match, Newport had held an unbeaten record. Scrine and Joseph were both in great form, whilst the pack as a whole had 'done well in the tight and in the loose'. However, 'they did not shine in the line-out'. Owen and Jones, meanwhile, 'fairly beat the Newport couple', which suggested that the pair were maturing nicely. Swansea and Wales would see the benefits of this development as they became an outstanding duo in the seasons ahead. Another young star of the side added to an unfortunate list of injuries when he damaged a knee on the Club's Midlands tour. Billy Trew, so the popular Swansea rumour had it, was the target of opposing sides. Whether, as the *Post* suggested 'other sides set out to stop the flying winger by whatever means', or not, the young man had had his share of injuries. At Leicester, for example, he was forced to leave the field early in the match, leaving fourteen men to play out the bulk of the contest. From the Club's point of view, in such circumstances, against 'one of the best sides in England', to have earned a scoreless draw was no mean achievement.

'Oval' in the *Morning Leader*, enthused: 'There is always temptation to exaggerate ... but I shall be well within the mark in classing the Leicester/Swansea game ... amongst the half dozen contests which ... will always live in my memory.' The correspondent went on to say that 'Owen and Jones, the young players whom Swansea are running for the International against Ireland ... outplayed the Leicester pair'. Clearly, the duo *were* maturing fast. On 15th March, the *Cambrian* confirmed that the Welsh selectors thought so, too. Jones and Owen were selected as a pair to play against the Irish.

When the Irish game was played, 35,000 people were packed into St. Helens (a Welsh record at the time) to see the young men, Bancroft, George Davies, Scrine and Hopkin Davies, represent Swansea in Welsh colours. The *Daily Express* reported that 'at half-back, the Swansea pair played well'. 'Argus', for his part, proclaimed that 'had Trew not been injured, the Swansea contingent would have been increased to seven.' Clearly, in the opinion of the *Cambrian* man, the Welsh selectors should look more closely at the rest of the Swansea team. And why not? The

Hopkin Davies.

Frank 'Genny' Gordon.

side was continuing its majestic progress. They won by 19 points to 3 against Llanelli. Gordon, back from injury, scored a fine try in that game. Bancroft, however, was absent on that occasion. Indeed, 'Free-lance' reported that the player had 'retired from active football for the present season'. It appeared that the veteran had strained 'tendons in one of his legs'.

On a day in which 'a gale blew and heavy rain fell', the next victory was at Cardiff, where 'the usual heavy and sodden ground did little to assist good football'. Despite the conditions, Swansea won by 14 points to 8. The Cardiff supporters, however, were not at all happy with the referee, a Mr. Alderson of Yorkshire. The Cardiff Club had to provide an escort for the official at the end of the game 'in the face of hostile baying and jostling'. In the game, Danny Rees dropped a superb goal whilst Owen and Jones 'eclipsed the Cardiff pair'.

At Easter, Rockcliffe, Belfast College and The Barbarians ('The pick of the English Rugby Union team') were all beaten, and whilst Gloucester won the final game of the season by two tries to one, the 'All Whites' were, once more, the Premier side in Wales. For the third time in succession they had gained the championship of the Principality. Danny Rees 20, Billy Trew 19 and Jowett 17 were the leading try scorers, whilst Bancroft had converted 36 tries. The committee must have wondered what might have been achieved had the Club been free from injury and international calls.

As it was, the annual 'post mortem' in the Press was encouraging for all concerned. The 'All Whites' 'highly creditable record' had only been possible as a result of 'all round brilliant play ... judicious and constant training, and *esprit de corps*'. Bancroft was congratulated, not only for the fact that he was a 'remarkable player', but also for his excellent generalship. 'Few men,' 'Argus' argued, 'know how to win the respect and confidence of his comrades better than he does ... (he) deserves the thanks of the whole football world for his services to the game'. The *Cambrian* man was preparing his readers for the possible retirement of the veteran. Meantime, however, he had a related axe to grind. Bob Thomas, who had been 'an honest Swansea scrummager for several seasons', had announced his retirement from the game. The Club wished to present Mr. Thomas with 'badges' to the value of £10, but the Welsh Union would not sanction the presentation. 'Argus' was incensed. 'The Welsh Rugby Union is not endowed with a superabundance of common sense', he wrote, 'Its decisions are often bewildering, such as "no fellah can understand". Last week the Union declined to allow ... a presentation (to Thomas) out of Club funds to the value of £10 ... The W.R.U. is a weak, pitiable and floundering organisation and it is time it was taught a lesson'. No doubt, were he pressed, the journalist might have suggested that there was insufficient Swansea representation on the Union committee. Not like, he might have suggested, the 'old days'.

1901-02

Four on the trot

The question on the minds of Swansea supporters as the new season approached was, 'Could they do it for the fourth time in succession?' The answer was to be YES, though, this time, 50% more games were lost. However, since that meant that the team suffered only three defeats, there were few who grumbled.

As the new campaign got under way, there was little room for concern in the Swansea camp. Bancroft had 'retired', but would assist the side whenever possible, otherwise, only Bob Thomas was missing from the group of players used during the previous season. Trew, and Gordon, who had missed several games in the previous campaign, were, now, said to be 'fully fit', whilst Owen and Jones were internationals, which, most people believed, made them into 'finished players'. Then, there was the captain, Frank Gordon – 'The General'. The argument here was that he had completed his 'apprenticeship' and could now 'take the helm with confidence'.

Whilst Trew was carried off in the 'Opener', the momentum began to build almost at once. By this time 'Argus' had extended his vocabulary; for 'half' his readers had 'moiety' to ponder. The effect, however, was the same. After the match against Bridgend, the *Cambrian* man, and 'Free-lance' could both glow as they wrote their reports. The side scored 10 goals and three tries without reply (59 points to nil) and, in their first three matches the 'All Whites' notched up 161 points. Surely, this was championship form! Yet, in modern parlance, championships are won by clubs with strong 'squads'. As a result of a catalogue of injuries in the season ahead, that from which the Club drew its reserves, was to be severely tested.

In a game against Mountain Ash at St. Helens, George Davies had to retire with a serious injury to his face, whilst Dick Jones had 'a nasty shaking'. Yet again, the side was finding that every team they met 'raised its game to beat the champions'. And, where they could not match the Swansea men for skill, they tried to do it with vigour and ' low cunning'. Given that injuries to key players seemed to be the end product of such contests, it was important that capable people should be available to replace them. For that reason, the committee was delighted to introduce a new face for the game against Llanelli in mid-October. A. E. Freer, an Irish international, had taken up an appointment in the town and was 'available for selection'. The Irishman, a fleet-footed winger, played a useful part in the defeat of the 'Scarlets' and was involved, again, when Neath were defeated by 41 points to nil.

Given the results achieved and the form of the team, when the 'All Whites' journeyed to Cardiff for their next game they did so with confidence. The 2,000 Swansea supporters who accompanied them were no less unfearing. This time, however, the game was scoreless, neither team was able to achieve mastery over the other.

The match was significant, however, for another reason, the 'gate' 'was a record for a rugby match taken at Cardiff.' The Llanelli club, which hosted the following game, also had a delighted treasurer when the final whistle blew. Ten thousand people were in the ground, and 'Free-lance' stated that he was delighted to note that 'Saturday's takings will go a long way towards liquidating the debt under which the Llanelli club have been labouring.' Jack Davies (Llandeilo) was at full-back for Swansea on that occasion, who played with fourteen men for 'all but a few minutes of the game'. In the *Post* report of the match Dickie Owen's nickname was used for the first time. 'The way in which "Bullet" Owen dribbled the ball past the opposing three-quarters was a treat ... (he is) one of the smartest halves in the Kingdom.'

In the meantime, Billy Trew had gone to Cardiff to see a specialist. Wales, as well as the whole of Swansea trusted that the medicos would be able to restore the 'flying winger' to full fitness. Because of his injury, the popular threequarter was not in the Welsh side to play England at Blackheath, nor was George Davies. On this occasion, the Swansea contingent was to consist of Jones and Owen at half-back and W. Joseph in the pack.

Despite the fact that they were said ' not to be up to scratch', throughout November and into December, the 'All Whites' continued to win. 'Argus', however, had it that they were 'still below the high water mark of last season's form'. Furthermore, they were 'lumpy'. Indeed, so 'lumpy' were they that in a game at Aberavon, 'the homesters did all the attacking ... and pinned Swansea in their own half from start to finish'. Whilst the side still managed to win, 'Free-lance' as well as his contemporary were less than impressed. Given the old rugby adage that good sides keep on winning, even when they are playing badly, as the year ended, the 'All Whites' appeared to be on course for their fourth consecutive championship title. The top of the table showing the records of the leading Welsh clubs at the year end told its own story.

Whilst they could admire this table, there were other things which the Swansea supporters

Welsh club records at year end 1901

	P	W	L	D	For			Agst.		
					G	T	Pts	G	T	Pts
Swansea	14	11	0	3	40	29	283	3	2	19
Cardiff	13	11	1	1	19	15	137	4	8	35
Newport	13	7	2	3	16	16	124	5	4	33

could contemplate as they read their papers over the Christmas period. 'Scotch Critic' in the *Athletic News* paid handsome homage to a Swansea boy. Referring to the retirement of Billy Bancroft from international rugby, the Scot wrote:

> 'His piquant personality added a charm to many a hard fought game. He was an attraction all by himself; and one who went to see wonders was never disappointed. What remains most vividly is one's memory of his colossal self assurance ... He seemed to love to get

into difficulties for the sheer pleasure of finding an exit. His tremendous kick with either foot was his great strength.'

A fitting postscript to the piece might have been – *Le Roi est mort. Vive le Roi*!

Despite the appalling weather, there was one of the largest attendances of the season to see Watsonians play on Christmas Day. On Boxing Day, a Dublin side, Old Wesley, 'had scarcely a ghost of a chance', and on the Saturday, Pontypridd, the previous season's champions of the Glamorgan League, were 'trounced'.

As the 'All Whites' contemplated the new year, unbeaten, captain Gordon was cautiously confident. 'I should like to express the hope,' he said, 'that we will go through the remaining half of the season in as brilliant a fashion as we have gone through the initial moiety'. Clearly, the 'General' had been reading the *Cambrian*.

In January, the side had to work hard for every point in beating Leicester, though they did so with the disadvantage of playing with fourteen men. Indeed, at one point they had a six-man pack; Scrine had been kicked on the head and had to leave the field. The edition of the *Cambrian* which contained the report from Leicester, also included a letter from America. A Mr. Edward Davies had written from Newcastle, Pennsylvania, to say that his team had beaten Pittsburgh and were now English rugby champions of the state. Four Swansea-born men were in the winning side. Was there no end to the fame brought to the old town by its footballing sons?

In the January International against England, the Swansea halves 'outclassed the English pair'. Swansea was pleased on that account, too. Furthermore, the English Press was impressed. A correspondent in the *Daily Mail* wrote: 'They reminded me of the Brothers James.' To most observers, however, there was something of a strange look about the Welsh XV which won that game; Billy Bancroft was missing. Whilst the Swansea idol had retired, there were those who were campaigning to bring him back. In reporting on a vintage display by the full-back in a match against Llanelli, 'Old Stager' wrote: 'The attitude of the Union is not strictly logical.' As far as 'Argus' was concerned their viewpoint was 'absurd'. Yet Bancroft had retired of his own free will, injuries and *anno domini* had provided the veteran with good reason to retire whilst he was at the top.

Late in January Frank Gordon had to declare himself disappointed. The 'All Whites' lost their treasured unbeaten record to Newport. It was true that there were extenuating circumstances; four key players were absent, whilst George Davies had been concussed during the game. Gordon made it clear, however, that Newport had played well in 'taking our colours' in a three-point victory. Among the absent that day was Billy Trew, who was struggling to regain full fitness.

In the next match, against Neath, it was the turn of a forward to capture the headlines. Joseph, the Swansea international, gathered a kick ahead on the home twenty-five near the touch line: 'he made his mark from which he dropped a goal'. The Forwards Union must have been delighted with that. But there was no such glory in the following game, which Llanelli won with something to spare. Again, there were several key absentees, but Gordon declined to 'hide behind that excuse'. 'Sospan Fach' had been in great evidence, and his side had been well beaten.

Nonetheless, whilst two matches had been lost with several weeks of the season to come, there was no talk of crisis, nor was there an increase in pessimism among the supporters. The

'General' would have none of that anyway, and marshalled his troops to beat Aberavon, draw with Newport, and gain a 'glorious victory' over Cardiff. 'Argus' called that win 'an annihilation – as good a word as any that may be used'. Owen and Jones had a 'day out', whilst the team combined well, despite the fact that Lockman at full-back had played for three-quarters of the game with a dislocated jaw. It was a fine victory, for, as the *Athletic News* noted, Cardiff had been beaten only once before that match against the 'All Whites'. There were smiles, once again, on Swansea faces. Whilst on the Club's usual West Country tour Devonport Albions won narrowly, after that the side scored five consecutive victories, including a fine win over the Barbarians by 1 goal and 4 tries to nil. As the *Post* put it, 'the "All Whites" outstanding record against the crack teams of England, Scotland, Wales and Ireland is worthy of note'. And so it was. Whilst their line had been crossed only sixteen times throughout the season, the team had amassed 503 points. Furthermore, they were Welsh champions yet again! No doubt there would be more poetry to chronicle the feat and yet another *recherché banquet*.

Chapter Seven

AT LAST ... UNBEATEN

1902-03

IT WAS EXPECTED THAT 'Gennie' Gordon would be re-elected as captain for the 1902/3 season, for, in some respects, he had been a more successful leader than his predecessor, Billy Bancroft. 'Free-lance', certainly thought that he would, and stated that 'the success of the side had been due to the cohesion of the team. Every man having the good of the team at heart, and not his own self-glorification.' Picking out 'The Bullet' Owen, the *Post* man thought him 'so unselfish that he did not score himself'. 'Argus' added that much of the team's success could be traced to the captain's 'geniality and kindly disposition'. Yet no one, both journalists agreed, would dream of taking advantage of this 'strong determined player'. Clearly, there was steel behind the bonhomie. Neither journalist was disappointed, Gordon was re-elected.

Whilst Billy Bancroft declared that, during the coming season, he would only play in emergencies, he did agree to be 'back stop' in the event of the captain and his vice, George Davies, being unavailable. However, the cricketers who were present at that meeting, might have pointed out that in his summer game, he never fielded in such a modest position. Other discussion at the meeting centred around the renewed presence of 'northern poachers'. Oldham, it was reported, had appointed former Swansea player, McCutcheon, to come to the town to recruit key players.In response to that news, the chairman, a key figure in the Anglican Church in Wales, displayed most un-Christian principles when he said that 'they ought to be thrown in the North Dock, tarred and feathered, put in a trunk and sent back home'. But then, there were plenty of Nonconformists who would have agreed with him. For his part, James Livingstone had a telling parable to enliven his 'sermon'. 'Take the James brothers,' he said, 'one was engaged, one fell ill ... they were both discarded and came back to Swansea ... It was a good job that the Club helped ... otherwise the widow of Evan James would have died of starvation'.

On a happier note, the meeting noted that Billy Trew was now fully fit. Will Joseph, on the other hand, said that he was retiring; 'Five seasons in the pack is enough for any man', but, he reckoned without the persuasive powers of 'The General'. Joseph did play.

After a rather lack lustre start to the season, the side began to run into form, though, by now there was no 'Argus' lovingly to chronicle their doings. A colourless 'Observer' took his place, and noted that Bridgend had been beaten by 44 points to nil, and Llanelli by 17 points without reply (during which game Dickie Owen scored his first try for two years). Gloucester was the next club to fall, before Cardiff were 'crushingly beaten' at St. Helens. 'Free-lance' thought that the score on that occasion, two goals and four tries to nil 'no way over-represents their (the 'All Whites') superiority'. The fourth try in that match was outstanding. 'Trew, receiving on the Gorse Lane side of the Field ... travelled across with Rees and Gordon in attendance. When with the centre, he feinted to pass, swerved between Nicholas and Winfield, and, in a flash, was over under the posts. The applause ... was simply deafening'. That, they said , was 'a real Swansea try'.

In mid-November, a game took place which many regarded as likely to settle the Welsh championship race. Thus, given that Swansea were the victors (by ten points), confidence in the Town was high. Whilst it had not been 'a day for passing', the forwards had come into their own. What a team! Surely it was good enough to take its fifth premiership in succession. That, at least, was the popular feeling in the old Borough.

'Observer', certainly, thought so after Llanelli had succumbed. He wrote ... 'it looks as if it is beyond the power of any Welsh club to put a stop to their all conquering season.' However, he did caution the bullish 'Whites' supporters. 'People expect too much of them (the team)', he wrote. It was as well that he issued his warning, for, in the first game of their West Country tour, the side was beaten by a single try to nil. This time there were no excuses about absentees and injuries, the 'All Whites' were at full strength. Furthermore, they had 'trained all the week' before leaving for the tour, whilst 'Mr Perkins had got them all to bed as early as possible the night before'. Yet, it was all to no avail. During the game, Dickie Owen suffered a bad cut over his eye which necessitated 'the surgical abilities of Harry Ball'. Since Ball had retired eighteen months before, presumably he had been persuaded to 'come back'. If there was consolation in the defeat by Devonport, it was that the team had been 'all over' Albions for most of the game. The fact was, though, that they had been unable to score.

Harry Ball.
Trainer Swansea Rugby Club.

As the season progressed, the Irishman, Freer, and the local man Jowett, on the Swansea wings, were winning many friends in the town, whilst Owen and Jones, at half-back, were revelling in their 'stardom'. Not surprisingly, the diminutive halves were subjected to 'heavy handling' as their skills became more widely known, and, in the game against Newport, it was the turn of 'little Owen' to sustain a deep cut over his eye. Typically, he came back after 'attention' (including stitches), and played on with his head swathed in bandages.

During the Christmas period the side played what the *Post* described as an 'Exhibition game against Cork Constitutional'. The Irishmen had come with a good reputation, but, as 'Freelance' put it, 'they must have left it on the boat'. The 'All Whites' scored 42 points without reply.

At the beginning of January there appeared an item in the *Bristol Evening News* which the Swansea players found to be rather flattering. The writer, unable to list the Swansea team for a forthcoming game in the City, wrote:

> However arranged it will be a good XV, for, in Swansea they grow footballers, and when one man of ability falls, another immediately takes his place. If you live in Swansea and do not play football, and play it well, too, the girls will cut you dead.

The 'All Whites' at Parkmill, circa 1901/02.

Turning to Billy Bancroft, and implying that the veteran would play, he referred to him as 'William the great – who was playing first-class football when many of his opponents were babes lisping at their mother's knee. Rumour has it that he dodged around his cradle and handed off his nurse in fine style.' He concluded, 'ten stone of fencing wire filled with the electricity of life is a description that may be applied to Bancroft'. Whilst the only nurse in the Bancroft family was 'Mam', the journalist was right in several respects. The Swansea plant was turning out footballers of note long before Max Boyce discovered the outside-half factory.

Runners-up

As a result of producing skillful footballers, and because of the flowing style of game which it played, the team attracted large 'gates' wherever it went. When the 'All Whites' travelled to Gloucester early in that campaign, the attendance was said to be a record for the season, whilst at Plymouth, Devonport, Bristol, Leicester and Northampton, the attendances for Swansea games were always significantly higher than the norm. Whilst the Club's reputation went before it in stimulating such attendances, more importantly, when they left the field at the end of a particular game, usually, they did so with that reputation enhanced.

In mid-January, the Club played host to the touring Canadians (who played with five three-quarters). Once again, the Swansea administrators rose to the challenge. Because of severe frost, the St. Helens match was the only one played on the day. The 'miracle' had been achieved by protecting the hallowed turf with tons of straw. The 'Colonials', whilst, presumably, being more used to such cold weather, had no such luck. They were beaten by six tries to nil. On that occasion, however, Bancroft's kicking was 'off'. The great man missed even in front of the posts. No try was 'majorised'.

Perhaps Bancroft had his mind on other things, for, shortly afterwards, he began to write a column in the *Post*. Commenting on a game at Neath, in one of his pieces, he castigated the referee for keeping the players waiting. It seemed that the official, A. J. Gould, did not arrive until half an hour after the game was supposed to start, and when he was ready, there was a further delay. 'There was no ball available ... and the players had to stand around the ropes like sheep until someone ran back to town for the oval'. When the match did start, Swansea were in complete control, winning by 26 points to nil. That, at least, improved Bancroft's humour.

By the end of February, with Newport having won a 'cracker of a game' on their own ground by a dropped goal to nil, the Premiership was said to be a 'very open question'. Nonetheless, following the Club's short Midlands tour, during which Jowett had been in sparkling form, the 'All Whites' were showered with praise. Then, following 'crushing wins' over London Welsh and Bristol, the confidence of Swansea supporters grew. However, that confidence proved to be ill-founded. Whilst the 'Whites' failed to beat Cardiff, Newport kept on winning, and the season ended with the Club in second place, though there was some consolation for Swansea supporters when, in the final game of the season , the new champions were defeated. There was, too, the season's record to contemplate. The 'Whites' had scored 619 points whilst their opponents had registered only 68. Jowett had scored 42 tries and had been 'capped', Danny Rees had crossed 21 times and was said to have 'made' many tries for the 'flyer', whilst Trew and Gordon weighed in with 18 and 12 respectively. Whilst there was disappointment in the town, the collective philosophy was bullish. 'We're only lending the crown to Newport'. The 'Whites', they were sure, would soon reclaim it!

1903-4

A salute to Parker

A talking point at the A.G.M. for 1903 was the nomination of W. Parker for the captaincy. 'The General' was said to have 'stood down in favour of the veteran forward', and the first forward for ten years to be elected to the post took office. However, the appointment was not without controversy. There were those who thought that Danny Rees should have been chosen, but the centre defused the situation by saying that he was not ready for the responsibility. Parker, Rees pointed out, was a far more experienced player and, given his service to the Club, deserved the appointment. Not that sentiment was the issue. As Parker was to show, he made an excellent captain. Whilst his reign was brief, the results achieved by his sides were outstanding. Only one match was lost and another drawn out of thirty one played. Whilst another captain was to lead the club during its 'invincible' season, it should be noted that Parker's side won a greater percentage of its games than the unbeaten side.

W. Parker, captain 1903/04.

When October ended, Swansea supporters were veritably 'licking their lips'. Neath had been beaten in the month by 30 points to nil, Llanelli by 20 points without reply, as were Cardiff in the 'dreadful conditions of the Arms Park mud'. After the sixth game of the season, the side's record stood at a remarkable: P6, W6, D0, L0, F166 points, Agst. 0. Furthermore, and this was important for the supporters, all six games had been won 'in style'. It was being argued that as far as Swansea Football Club was concerned, the best defence was attack. Yet, what a defence the team must have had!

The *Athletic News* in its account of a game at Gloucester which the 'Whites' won by 25 points to nil, crossing for seven tries, reported: 'Swansea were represented by a powerful team ... including ten internationals ... the cleverness and pace of the Welshmen proved altogether too much for the home team ... at the close the Swansea men were heartily cheered for their brilliant exhibition'. And that was an English paper!

As the first of the season's games against the champions, Newport, approached, it seemed that the whole town was awash with confidence. On the day of the game, with the weather being 'Summerlike', a Club record of £400 was taken at the gate. 20,000 spectators poured into St. Helens. The official total should have been greater, but it was estimated that 2,000 entered the ground without paying when 'a last minute rush broke through the big doors opposite the Avenue'. In the match, which supporters who paid and those who didn't, enjoyed immensely, Newport became the first side to score against the 'All Whites' that season. Swansea, however, scored one more than their opponents to win their eighth game in succession. 'Old Athlete', writing in the *Cambrian*, noted that the side had, by then, scored 184 points whilst only 5 had been conceded.

Neath, Cardiff and Leicester were then beaten to take the team into December with its record 'unbesmirched', though the Taffsiders had only been beaten after a hard fight. The Leicester game also provided frustration. The *Post* reported:

> The 'All Whites' were continually pulled up for infringements which existed only in the referee's imagination. The game was ... stopped twice because Danny Rees feinted to pass. Unfortunately, he diddled not only his opponents but the ref. as well. 'Toot' went the whistle for a forward pass, and Mr. Bell looked quite annoyed when he saw that there had been no pass at all.

After the Cardiff match, the *Post* proudly printed the 'Table' positions of the Welsh clubs. The three at the top were:

	P	W	D	L	F	A
Swansea	11	11	0	0	222	8
Cardiff	11	8	0	3	138	26
Newport	11	8	0	3	136	47

Whilst the Swansea supporters would have enjoyed contemplating that table, it might have been wiser not to tempt fate. The return game against Newport was not on the all conquering agenda, and the 'Amber and Blackings' won a dour game by a dropped goal to nil. Not only was this the first defeat of the season for the Swansea club, but 'Newport's magnificent defence' had prevented them from scoring for the first time during that campaign. The disappointment felt in Swansea was real. There had been a growing belief that the side would remain unbeaten throughout the season and set a new record for the Club. That hope had been shattered.

Perhaps that was the reason why 'only 5,000' came to see Devonport Albions on the Saturday before Christmas. Yet, clearly, D. H. Bowen, writing in the *Daily Express*, had no doubts about the team. In his report on the Christmas Day win over Watsonians, he wrote: 'Swansea's display ... dispelled the idea that the loss of their record would mean a loss of heart ... Nothing can exemplify the character of their work more than the words of a Watsonians forward: "I'm never coming to Swansea again. I've been over six years chasing those Swansea backs and I've had quite enough".'

The Swansea supporters would have enjoyed reading that, as they would have done when they learnt that among those invited to put their names forward to go on the English Rugby Union tour to New Zealand were R. M. Owen, R. Jones and W. Trew. All three said that they were willing to go, though, in due course, each of them withdrew, leaving Syd. Bevan and Fred Jowett to represent the Swansea club in the 'England' party. Since it had recently been announced that the Wright brothers had made the first powered flight at Kittyhawk, it was entirely appropriate that a Swansea flyer should travel with the England party.

For a match against Aberavon early in January, Dickie Owen was absent and Rhys Rees, brother of Danny, was brought into the side. In freezing conditions when 'hands were numbed with cold', the newcomer did well. In the next game, against Llanelli, it was the turn of Billy Joseph to shine. In a closely fought game the forward was 'outstanding'. Whilst the Llanelli supporters were disappointed, their treasurer could afford to smile. 8,000 people had paid to see the match and, given Llanelli's financial position at that time, the revenue was very welcome.

When Newport were beaten in the third meeting between the clubs that season, Swansea supporters felt that honour had been satisfied, at least in part. After that match, the outstanding Swansea record read P17, W16, D0, L1, F305, A27. This meant that the side had scored an average of 18 points per game whilst conceding 2. Not surprisingly, the spirit in the team was at an extremely high level. 'Free-lance' commented on this with regard to some criticism which had been levelled at Dickie Owen (it had been said that he was too selfish in the Newport game). However, the journalist pointed out that Dick Jones was only 'half fit in that game and should not have been playing'. As a result, Dickie Owen spent the afternoon protecting his partner from the ravages of the Newport forwards. 'Free-lance' also pointed out that it had been a hard match in which the forwards dominated. Those Swansea supporters who 'longed for brilliant open play' had to be satisfied with an exhilarating Jowett try. During a Newport attack, the flyer had intercepted near his own line and had 'run the whole length of the field to touch down'.

In February there was a diversion from the Premiership chase. Wales played Scotland at St. Helens. The Welsh won by 21 points to 3 and Dick Jones scored a try 'after cutting through a tight Scottish defence'. The game necessitated another form of defence, too. Swansea's Chief Constable used the local press to appeal to the Town's citizens. 'Do not leave your houses unsecured and unattended during the great football match tomorrow', he advised. Clearly, on occasion,the 'open door' policy followed by Swansea householders at the time, required modification. Not that it was the presence of the Scots which necessitated such change. As the policeman pointed out, 'Wherever there are big crowds there are thieves about'.

As was usual at the time, the match reports of the international illustrated the partisan nature of south Wales rugby. 'Old Athlete' wrote: 'It will be interesting to read what the Eastern critics who tried to keep Dick Jones out of the team will now say about the outside-half. A better game ... has not been seen by a Welsh outside-half for many years.' Meanwhile, 'Free-lance', showing his love for all things Swansea, was campaigning on another front. He wanted someone to investigate a 'public testimonial' for Billy Bancroft. Within weeks, others were doing the same thing for the 6' 2", eighteen-stone journalist.

In mid February, the 'All Whites' went 'mudlarking', which was 'Free-lance's' way of describing a visit to Cardiff Arms Park. Despite the best efforts of the Cardiff committee, their ground held water to such an extent that, following heavy rain it quickly turned into a quagmire. As a result, as the *Post* man put it, 'on a wet day Science is shelved'. On the wet day in question, he reported that 'the ground was in a fearful state, and was like a ploughed field in front of the grandstand'. With Fred Scrine injured for much of the game, the 'Whites' had to play with seven forwards. The depleted pack had, as a result, a 'gruelling fight in the mud'. Happily for Swansea, they held their own, and when Dickie Owen 'romped over for a try', the game was won for Abertawe.

Such a testing match was hardly the best preparation for the side's next game. That was against 'All France' (Stade Francaise) at the 'Princes Park Ground'. However, the team rose to the occasion, and on a lovely surface, 'akin to St. Helens', the men in white won by 24 points to nil. In the process they 'won fresh laurels' and many friends in France.

On their return home, there were further wins, over Gloucester and Llanelli, the latter being by 6 goals and 5 tries (45 points to nil), with George Davies in fine form. There followed the toughest test in the remaining schedule. The side was to play Newport in the final meeting of the season between the old adversaries. With Dick Jones absent, Billy Trew showed his versatility by playing at outside-half. Happily, for Swansea supporters, despite poor weather and a difficult playing surface, another fine victory was won. Whilst the supporters were overjoyed, it was not a happy day for 'Free-lance'. The journalist was obliged to use the new telephone system to transmit his report of the match from Newport. Unfortunately, the report which was printed in the paper as a result of this process contained several errors. During the following week, 'Free-lance' apologised for the mistakes and declared that he was 'deeply thankful that it will not be necessary to use the machine again this season'. Was the response to new technology ever thus?

Bristol (away), Cardiff, who had not won at St. Helens since 1897, Rockliffe, Bristol (home), the Barbarians, and London Welsh were all defeated in a marathon spell during which the Club played five games in eight days. Not surprisingly, this schedule took its toll of the players. Whilst Rockliffe were beaten 40-0, and Bristol 15 points to 3, there were those who were criticising the team. It was said that the 'Whites' were not 'playing to their best form', though 'Free-lance' responded by arguing that 'you cannot keep them to concert pitch week after week for seven months'.

Yet the season was not over. There was the matter of a match against the powerful Devonport Albions side at their Rectory Field. Consequently, the team had to 'dig deep' again, as they faced the challenge of the 'crack Cornish side'. A record attendance of 16,000 people saw the struggle which ensued. No points were scored and honours were even.

On returning from their tour, the players must have been looking forward to putting their feet up, but there was one more match to play before their 'togs' could be stored away. Captain

Parker had promised to take a side to Aberavon to 'give them a helping hand towards clearing off the deficit they have experienced on the season's working'. Yet again, Swansea Football Club was demonstrating its caring policies. The Aberavon club was 'extremely grateful'.

When the dust had settled, all Swansea could look with satisfaction at another tremendous record 29 games had been won out of the 31 played, and only one was lost. Captain Parker expressed himself delighted, and, for a man of few words, that said it all. He was particularly pleased that opponents had managed to score only 46 points throughout the season, whilst his own side had amassed 550. George Davies had had an outstanding season at full-back,and the forwards had done extremely well. 'Free-lance' was of the view that 'were it possible to obtain the opinion of the thousands of followers of the Town's football side, they would acclaim Dickie Owen as the smartest inside-half in the four countries'. Billy Trew, Dick Jones and Gordon were also picked out for praise by the *Post* man, as were Bill Joseph and Dai Davies among the forwards. As far as the captain was concerned, 'Free-lance' thought that 'he had led the side as well as it ever was'. Parker, according to the journalist, was not only a capable skipper, he was the 'cleverest forward of the eight'. Billy Bancroft was not forgotten either, in the journalist's summary, he had trained the players every week.

Whilst Swansea football supporters were remembering the season which had passed, the citizens of the town witnessed another act of remembrance. The South African War memorial was unveiled. The two field guns either side of the plinth and statue were thought to be a fitting memorial for those who had given their lives in the conflict.

In mid-May, Jowett, who had finished as joint top try scorer (with Billy Trew), and forward Syd Bevan, left for New Zealand with the English team. It was a further honour for the Swansea club, though, it was said that three other 'All Whites' could have taken the trip had it been possible for them to do so. Meantime, in the local papers, another Bevan was advertising. Bevan and Company, Wind Street offered a satin walnut bedroom suite for £6.17*s*.6*d*. cash. T. C. Palmer, The Cash Tailors, however, were involved in a different kind of advertising. They declared that they had been 'made tailors for the Swansea Football Team'. The 'All Whites' were respectfully requested to call and get measured for their suits.

1904–5

The Invincibles

Notwithstanding the extremely successful season which had been enjoyed by the Club, other matters were on the minds of Swansea's citizens in July 1904. The new king was to visit Swansea. In days when security for the prominent was far less intrusive than it is today, the route which was to be taken by the Royal party as they processed through Swansea was published in the local papers in advance. Among those who took advantage of this information were the authorities at Swansea Hospital. Noticing the proximity of their grounds to the published route, they offered reserved seats at 5 shillings and two shillings and sixpence, with 'excellent views of the procession'. The Market Economy was alive and well in 1904. With the Royal yacht, two cruisers and a torpedo boat in Swansea Bay, the Royal party proved to be an even bigger draw than the 'All Whites'. 100,000 people poured into the town to welcome the Monarch. The King responded to the hospitality by knighting the Town's mayor. From then on he would be Sir Griffith Thomas.

The 'Invincibles'.
D. Davies, A. E. Freer, D. J. Thomas, Aubrey Smith, H. Hunt, Sydney Bevan, George Davies, Frank Gordon (Capt.), Dan Rees, F. J. Scrine, W. Joseph, W. Coles, W. J. Bancroft, R. M. Owen, R. Jones, W. J. Parker, W. J. Trew. Swansea played 32 matches, won 28 and drew four.

A month later, the Town's football followers rallied around 'Free-lance' (J. T. Gwynn). The giant reporter had been 'struck by a serious and painful illness'. His many friends arranged a 'bumper benefit' at the Empire Theatre, as a result of which, £300 was given to the Gwynns. Sadly, the man who 'loved Swansea Football Club' deteriorated quickly and died within weeks. He was only 32 years of age. With 'Argus' gone, and now 'Free-lance', Swansea football had lost its two most passionate journalistic supporters. It was to be some time before others were to establish themselves in their place.

Comeback Gordon

Frank, 'The General' Gordon, by now classified as a veteran, found himself elected as captain at the 1904 A.G.M. It was his third season in the post, and his election reflected the warmth of feeling for the man within the club. Had he not stood aside for W. Parker at the beginning of the previous campaign, it is probable that Gordon would have equalled Billy Bancroft's record for successive captaincies. As it was, the winger was to have the honour of leading the Swansea club during its first invincible season.

At the beginning of September, Gordon found that he was likely to lose two key players. Parker, the captain for the previous campaign had announced his retirement, while Willie Arnold indicated that he wished to play for Llanelli. Both men reckoned without the persuasiveness of 'The General'.

Prior to the start of the season, 'Atticus', one of several journalists who were to write about rugby in the *Post* , was extremely confident. He believed that the general opinion in Swansea was that the club was likely to 'stand on a plane of their own in Welsh football this year'. With the *Cambrian* broadly in agreement, the whole town must have viewed the coming campaign with equanimity. Yet, could the side better the outstanding results which had been achieved during the previous season? It was, as was reported, 'asking a lot'.

When the campaign began, the side found that little had changed from the previous season. Every team they met wanted to beat 'The Premiers'. Gordon was of the opinion that this meant that other clubs played at a 'higher level' than was normally the case. Certainly, Gloucester did in a St. Helens match in early October. The home side won by a single try to nil in a hard fought match, with Danny Rees being the hero of the day. The *Post* reported that '... he diddled his *vis-a-vis* and transferred to Arnold , who raced for the line and threw back for Dan to get over'. George Davies, who had spent 'many hours working on his kicking', was unsuccessful with the conversion attempt. George, however, was to benefit from his practice later in the season when his form resulted in him being selected by Wales at full-back.

The next game was an historic one for the 'Scarlet Runners', in that they opened their new ground with a match against the 'All Whites'. No longer would sides needs to plan their game in accordance with whether they were playing up or down the Stradey slope. The new ground was 'as flat as St. Helens'. On the day, sadly for 'Sospan', the new stadium did not provide sufficient incentive for the homesters. In a match which was started by J. T. D. Llewellyn kicking off, the 'Whites' won an 'interesting game' by a goal and a try to nil.

Cardiff provided the next opposition, but, despite working hard, the 'Blue and Blacks' failed to score, whilst the 'Whites' registered eight points. Most observers, however, felt that the Swansea boys should have scored more. 'Felix', in the *Post*, noted that 'Trew, that versatile and extraordinary artiste, was outstanding', whilst 'Jones is entitled to almost as many encomiums for his capable and finished exhibition at outside-half'. 'Old Stager', in providing his analysis, felt that he could put his finger on the reason for Swansea's continuing success. 'The players,' he wrote, 'have long association, and through periodic rehearsal know the idiosyncrasies of individual colleagues'. To put the matter into local vernacular, they could pass to each other blindfold.

By early November there was another defection from St. Helens, though not to the North. It was reported that Willie Arnold had found a well-paid job in London, but that he would come down (to Newport) to take part in the match against the 'Usksiders' on the following Saturday. Arnold did not wish to miss that match, which was just as well, for the only other experienced wing three-quarter available was Fred Jowett, and he was 'only half fit'.

The G.W.R excursion to the Monmouthshire town cost each of the two thousand who went on it, 3*s*.3*d*. 'Felix' thought that there was some 'lingering doubt' among the supporters as to the outcome of the game, but such thoughts were quickly dispelled when the Usksiders found that they 'could not match the skill and tenacity of the "Premiers" '. 'Atticus', growing into the mantle of his predecessors, stated, 'On Saturday's form there is no club in Wales – or out of it – which can defeat the 'All Whites', and I say it all with *sang froid*, which, as you know, is the French equivalent of "let them all come" '. 'Old Stager' wrote of the team being a 'happy family', that description, he argued summed up the spirit in the side, which, together with skill and confidence, oozed out of the XV. The third of the tries which were scored by Swansea during that game exemplified it all. 'About ten players handled the ball in its flight, the opponents were bewildered'. Not only were opponents bewildered by the 'All Whites' attacking machine. At that stage in the season, with eight games having been played, no opposing side had managed to score a single point.

An English club, Devonport Albions, were the next to tilt at the windmill. Albions, the leading Saxon side of the period,with their own ground advantage, made Swansea fight all the way. Indeed, they led at half-time, but the fates would not be bested and the men in white recovered to share the spoils. The *Post*'s 'Plymouth Correspondent', covering the second game of the club's West Country tour waxed lyrical about the 'Whites' performance there. He thought that every time the Swansea backs had the ball the Plymouth line was always in danger. He was particularly impressed with George Davies, stating that 'his kicking was excellent and immense'. Whilst George Davies's name is not etched into the collective Swansea Rugby Football memory as are players like Trew, Bancroft, Jones and Owen, in considering his tremendous contribution to the Club as a player, one is left with the impression that he is worthy of far greater recognition. A fine three-quarter, he converted to full-back on Billy Bancroft's retirement and made the position his own. Always reliable, and a great club man, he, probably suffered from having a ubiquitous Welsh surname.

After the West Country tour, and on returning to 'domestic' competition, the side seemed to suffer from something of a negative reaction. Whilst winning at Neath, for example, they were accused by the press of being over-confident. The *Cambrian* reported that 'there was a bit of a disturbance among spectators ... and that comprised nearly all the excitement of the afternoon'. 'Felix', perhaps reflecting his *nom de plume*, wrote 'a sort of lassitude was conveyed to the spectators by the forwards'. He warned, too ' Another game like that ... and a certain benevolent tailor ... will be found endeavouring to dispose of fifteen new suits'. Nor were the journalists alone in their criticism. Several letters in the *Post* complained about 'swelled heads'. Among these correspondents was 'Disgusted Swansea', though whether this was from a single writer or the population as a whole was not made clear.

A different kind of controversy surrounded the late postponement of the next fixture. The Cardiff club had called off the game against the 'All Whites' on the Saturday morning, but did not inform Swansea of their action. As a consequence, the team and supporters travelled up to Cardiff, only to be told the news on their arrival at the ground. To say that the Swansea folk were disgruntled would be an understatement, and much was made of the situation, by both parties, in the weeks ahead. However, the 'Whites' had to put all that behind them as they continued their campaign. A return with Newport was the next challenge, and, perhaps, it was a week's rest from competition which acted as a tonic for the Swansea players.

Willie Arnold had managed to get home for the weekend, again, and was included in the side against the 'Amber and Blackings', though it proved to be an ill-starred day for him. Early in the game, the little Morristonian, who had recently taken up a new post in London, fractured his leg in two places. Drs. Gabe and Williams set the fractures 'on the field' and sent the winger home to Morriston by horse ambulance. Dr. Reid announced that the injury was serious, that the player would be confined to his home for six weeks, and would be 'off work' for twelve. After Arnold left the field, Scrine was withdrawn from the pack, and the seven remaining men 'played their hearts out' to contain the Monmouthshire eight. At the end of the game, the crowd, presumably including 'Disgusted Swansea', rose to the victors. The fourteen men had won by three tries to one.

In mid December, Neath, who were about to play the 'Premiers', found that they had a defection. With the Evan Roberts revival gathering momentum, D. J. Rosser, one of the 'Black

Boys' best forwards, was 'captured by the Valley Revivalists', and gave up the game. It was not the kind of conversion relished by the Neath club.

On the Monday following that match there was a new feature in the *Post*. The paper published a 'League' table in which the results of the '15 leading clubs in England and Wales' were compared. The table reflected the position of the clubs up to and including the previous Saturday. Forgetting their grouses, the Swansea supporters basked in the glory of what they read. The 'All Whites' stood proudly at the top of the table.

Results of the 15 leading clubs

	P	W	L	D	Pts	Proportion of pts to finished games
Swansea	13	12	0	1	12	100%
Devonport	13	10	1	2	9	81%
Blackheath	13	10	2	1	8	66%

The other Welsh clubs in the table were Cardiff, Llanelli and Newport.

At Christmas, Watsonians came to Swansea for their annual fixture and were preceded along St. Helens Road by two pipers. The *Cambrian* noted that 'the piobroche screeched as they drove down to St. Helens'. Sadly for the Scots, who, according to the *Post* 'played their National game of Rush, Rush, Rush', the enemy were not disturbed by the pipes. Swansea were triumphant again. It is interesting to note that in the *Post* report of that game the press box is mentioned. Presumably, by that time, the Swansea club was aware of the power of the press and its influence on income and, as a consequence, provided 'facilities'.

After Christmas, as if to reflect the Evan Roberts crusade, the 'Whites' did some missionary work of their own. The club sent a side to play Pontypridd (the Rhondda capital) on a Tuesday afternoon. The intention was to support the Rhondda club's development, and the locals, according to the *Post* 'turned out in numbers, for they held the "All Whites" in high regard'. Pontypridd netted £116 from the game and the club's committee stated that they were 'most grateful for the kind gesture'. An interesting feature of the second-half of that match was the fact that Bill Parker played at outside-half, which, for the long-serving forward, had been a 'life long ambition'. Such are the dreams of hard working forwards.

At the turn of the year, Swansea still stood proudly at the top of the 'Anglo-Welsh League Table'. Positions two and three were as at December, with Richmond and Leicester being in fourth and fifth position. For their part, Leicester, who were to play a scoreless game at St. Helens later in the season, were at the centre of a dispute with the 'All Whites' regarding a game at Welford Road in mid-November. In that match, according to the *Athletic News*, the referee had awarded a scrum on the goal line (instead of five yards out) and Leicester claimed that a try had been scored from it. This was not allowed at the time. Subsequently, after a Leicester appeal and a great deal of discussion, the try was awarded to the 'Tigers', which had the effect of turning a Swansea victory into a draw. Subsequently, the controversy gathered momentum, and there was even talk about a special arrangement being made for a Leicester player to travel to Swansea to attempt the conversion. In the end, common sense prevailed, though not before

'McJenkins' in the *Post* had written about the Welsh Union's involvement. 'The War Office and the Welsh Union may be classed together. Both are mindless'. Nonetheless, whatever the merits of the appeal decision, had Leicester converted the try on the day, the 'All Whites' would not have achieved their longed-for unbeaten record.

In January there was a boost for the club. George Davies was selected at full-back for Wales, a fitting accolade for a great clubman and a popular player. Danny Rees and the 'Two Dicks' were also picked, while Billy Trew was 'reserve'. Both Swansea papers complained about the omission of Trew, but the selection of George Davies acted as a balm. Billy's day was to come.

Meanwhile, notwithstanding his 'retirement' statement, Bill Parker was continuing to make a significant contribution to the Swansea pack. Whatever it was that 'Gennie' Gordon said to him must have acted as an elixir. Against Bristol, he, Fred Scrine, 'Mumbles' Davies, Will Joseph and Aubrey Smith excelled as the 'City' side was routed. The Swansea backs were provided with a superb platform to 'weave their spells' and the side won by 47 points to 3. With Llanelli beaten in the next game, Cardiff came to St. Helens to try their luck. At this point in the season the 'Taffsiders' were playing well and a tough game was expected. And so it turned out. 'Felix' reported on a 'great struggle at St. Helens', and a 'momentous victory'. Captain Gordon was the hero of the day, scoring an opportunist try with 'half the Cardiff side in pursuit'.

World Champions?

At the end of February, 25,000 people packed St. Helens for the return match with Devonport Albions. Throughout the season, the Albions had been lying second in the Anglo-Welsh table, and were, in effect, English champions at that stage. Thus, the game was built up as being between the English and Welsh 'Premiers'. With Dick Jones absent, a Neath three-quarter, Lewis Jenkins, was drafted into the Swansea side at half-back, and the former 'Black Boy' did well on his début. The 'All Whites' won by 11 points to nil and the try of the match was scored by Fred Jowett after a 'classy movement' when the ball was switched from right to left. Surely, the supporters must have argued, no one can stop them now! Yet all opponents were trying to do that.

After a scoreless game with Cardiff and a return against Stade Francaise, (when the Swansea players romped around the field), Gloucester, Bristol and the Barbarians ('The *Crème de la Crème* of the principal clubs in the four countries') were beaten. Thus it was that an Irish side, Belfast Collegians, came to St. Helens for the final game of the season. The rugby world expected the 'All Whites' to win, and whilst the Swansea supporters did their best not to be over confident, they were bullish as they gathered to watch the match. In the event, if there were lingering concerns, they were not justified, and Swansea Football Club completed its first undefeated season. Remarkably, in twenty-one of the matches which had been played by the club the opposing side had failed to score a single point.

At the end of the season the Anglo-Welsh table reflected the position of the Swansea club, at least in the 'European' world. The 'All Whites' were top of the 'League' with a record which read: P28, W24, L0, D4, Pts 24, 100%. Furthermore, the table illustrated the extent of their supremacy, for second placed Devonport Albions had lost four times and could only boast 71%. Consequently, having beaten English, Scottish, Irish, French and Welsh sides, the supporters could be forgiven for wishing to append the accolade 'World Champions' to their favourites. In the not too distant future, however, rugby followers were to learn that a concept of 'the World' which ended in Paris was flawed.

Chapter Eight

NORTHERN POACHERS AGAIN

1905–06

IN SEPTEMBER 1905, THE *Cambrian* informed its readers that Fred Jowett was 'in negotiation with Hull Kingston Rovers'. The story was that the offer made to Jowett was the highest which had been submitted to a Welsh player. Jowett, who was a schoolmaster in St. Thomas, was astute enough to put the matter in the hands of a Swansea solicitor, 'in order that he might be fully protected'. If nothing else, the James Livingstone 'sermons' had made Swansea players more aware of the need for commercial prudence in dealing with 'the poachers'. Furthermore, with respect to the negotiations which he was undertaking, the astute Jowett had a 'fall back' position. If Hull K.R. would not meet his demands, the neighbouring Hull club would be more than interested. Furthermore, there were two ex-Swansea-ites playing there, Freer and Burchell.

Since it appeared to be inevitable that the flyer would leave, the rumour mongers, quickly, added other names to the Northern 'shopping list'. Danny Rees, Jack Bancroft and Billy Trew were 'certain to go'. As the rumours intensified the Swansea committee was concerned; the supporters were distraught.

A major factor in the success of the Swansea club during the previous decade had been the continuity provided by the use of a relatively small group of players. The pack, for example, had remained largely unchanged for several campaigns, with stars like Scrine, Bevan, Aubrey Smith, Joseph, Parker and 'Mumbles' Davies, turning out season after season. In the backs, whilst new men had been introduced, Danny Rees, the two Bancrofts, Billy Trew, 'Gennie' Gordon, and George Davies had provided the backbone for several seasons. As 'defections' and *anno domini* took their toll, the seasons ahead were to challenge that security.

As the new campaign unfolded, supporters and the Press reflected on the old adage, 'After the Lord Mayor's show ...', for the side struggled to find its form. It was almost as if they had taken too much out of themselves during the previous season. Bridgend did well to contain 'a sluggish "All Whites" side to only nine points'. In the following match, against Neath, the pack was 'beaten all ends up by the home eight'. Furthermore, in his comments on that match, Billy Bancroft, now writing in a London paper, felt that 'Swansea are playing 50% below last season's form'. Yet, many of the players in the side had been members of the Invincible team of the previous season. The supporters were confused.

In October they were further depressed by the news that Oldham had offered Dickie Owen £150.00 to go north. Whilst he had refused, the *Post* believed that 'another £25 would have found him'. To supporters and the Swansea committee alike the preciseness of that statement made it sound as if it were authentic. Clearly, there were those who wished to rip the heart out of the Swansea side for their own benefit.

Dickie Owen: 'The Bullet'.

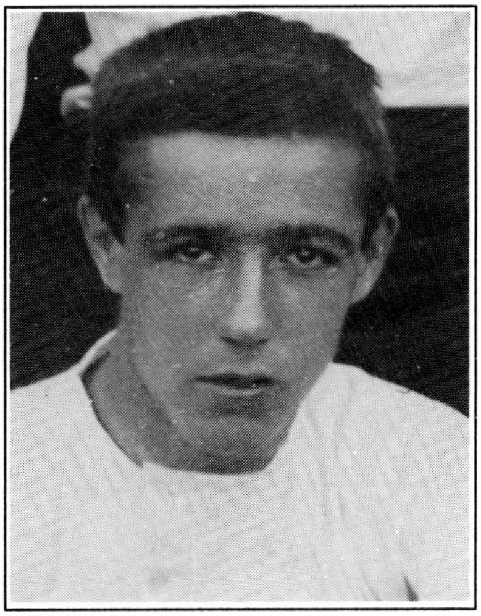

Billy Trew: 'The One and Only'.

Meantime, Billy Trew, who was 'covered from head to foot in bruises' following one match, was unavailable due to a bad ankle injury. Dick Jones had been sent to London to undergo special treatment for his injured foot, whilst there were recurring rumours that Danny Rees was about to defect. Coupled with the team's indifferent form, this resulted in a pall of gloom settling over football followers in Swansea. Furthermore, others were commenting on the change in fortunes.

In its report of a 'bruising game' against Gloucester, which the 'Whites' won by a single try to nil, the *Daily Mail* pronounced that 'Swansea are not the team of old, their smart back play being entirely absent'. After a match against Llanelli, won by 'just two points', the *Western Mail* noted 'the three-quarters were not on song and the forwards have not found their legs'. Furthermore, some advertising executive must have felt that the team's demise presented a sales opportunity. As a result, an advertisement had been placed in the middle of the *Cambrian's* report on the game at Stradey, which asked: 'Are you weak and thin? If so, try Veno's Seaweed Tonic'. Irony indeed!

Whilst Dick Jones was undergoing his treatment in London, he took the opportunity to go to Stamford Bridge to see Middlesex play the touring New Zealanders. Given that the 'Whites' were to play host to the 'All Blacks' for the final game of their tour, this was useful intelligence. Jones reported that he was 'Thunderstruck with their all-round exhibition ... the three-quarters are all Billy Trews'. He also reported a new feature in the match. All the players were numbered so that 'by looking up the programme, each man can be identified'. In Swansea it was felt that the all conquering team of the previous season might 'have New Zealand's "number" ', but what would the current side make of a line of Billy Trews?

Late in October, rumour became reality, Danny Rees left to join Jowett at Hull K.R., whilst Swansea were beaten by 14 point to 3 at Cardiff. Not, according to the *Post*, by the home side's brilliant play, but by 'an indifferent exposition rendered by the Swansea backs'. Whilst there was, then, some encouragement following a win over Bristol, the absence of key players was exacerbating the problems faced by captain Gordon. Indeed, so short was the Club of three-

The earliest action photograph of a match between the Barbarians and Swansea, 22nd April, 1905.

quarters, that in one game, stalwart forward 'Mumbles' Davies was selected on the wing. As a result, many permutations were tried in the attempt to arrest the decline in the form of the team. After a 'scrambling three point win over Newport at St. Helens', the *Cambrian*, bemoaning the poor form, the defections and the continued absence of Dick Jones and Billy Trew, demonstrated the effect on the side by quoting its playing record to that date. 'Swansea have not displayed the prolific scoring accomplished during the past 3 or 4 years. So far they have 74 points to their credit as against their opponents' 21. Seven matches have been played'. Indeed, these bald statistics provided a vivid picture of the Club's poorer form, though, in all fairness to the beleaguered Gordon and his men, the results to the middle of November would have satisfied supporters not spoiled by 'outstanding brilliant play'. At that point the record read: P10, W9, L1, D0, F93, A 21, though, as the coming weeks were to show, it flattered to deceive.

All Blacks beaten

In December, whilst Swansea lost to both Newport and Cardiff, at least there was some encouragement for the Welsh nation. Its team, including Owen and Joseph of Swansea, defeated the 'All Blacks'. The match was said to be 'universally recognised as the "Game of the Century"', and, since the New Zealanders had started the match with a perfect record (P27, W27, F801, A22), the men in red had a 'formidable enemy to contain'. Swansea supporters were, particularly cheered by the fact that Dickie Owen played an outstanding part, not only in the game, but in the preparation for it. As Smith and Williams record, 'thirteen of the selected Welsh XV met in Cardiff (on the Thursday before the match) to practise various manoeuvres ... under the direction of R. M. Owen'. After the game some 'All Blacks' argued that Owen had had a 'hand' in the disallowed try incident, but this was dismissed in Swansea. Dickie Owen

was a sportsman, they argued. In any event, there was another game to play in which the diminutive 'Bullet' would test his skills against those of the 'All Blacks'. That, they said, would put the record straight.

Despite the fact that Swansea Football Club was not at its pinnacle at the time the New Zealanders came to play at St. Helens, the fixture aroused interest in many quarters. After all, had not Swansea won the 'World Championship' at the end of the previous campaign? Those who were not following the current situation at St. Helens were still assuming that the old abilities were extant. As a result, people came to see the game from the Midlands, the West Country, London and from all over Wales. In addition, a special excursion had been arranged by the Stade Francaise club, to add a French element. Clearly, whatever their current form, the 'All Whites' had a significant reputation to uphold.

It was at the end of December 1905 that Swansea was to host the final match of the New Zealand tour. Apart from the defeat by Wales, which they disputed, the 'All Blacks' had an outstanding record. They had won 29 of the 30 matches which they had played and were keen to ensure that the Welsh champions did not mar that record. Because of this reputation, the *Cambrian*, in its preamble to the match, was cautious. 'Because of defections to the Northern Union, Swansea is not the club its was ... (it) is hardly expected to win when others have failed'. Nevertheless, the paper found some hope with which to help bolster the confidence of the supporters. 'Yet,' they noted, 'there is an air of quiet confidence existent in the ability of the Swansea players to rise to the occasion'. Such a statement could hardly be contradicted, but it was a straw to cling to.

Swansea v. New Zealand, 1905.

On the appointed day, the 'Whites' lined up with seven forwards and with Scrine at 'Extra Back', or 'Rover'. With Dick Jones still unavailable, Hopkins partnered Trew at half-back. In their pre-match comments the English press, in particular, went to great lengths to point out that the New Zealanders were tired, could not field their strongest team, and, after a rigorous fixture list which necessitated them playing two matches a week over several months, they were 'stale'. Should the 'All Whites' win, the explanation had been prepared in advance.

In the event, that explanation proved to be unnecessary. Despite a brave Swansea effort, the New Zealanders won by a dropped goal (4 points) to a try. Fred Scrine crossed for the Swansea score whilst Wallace dropped the goal for the visitors, which, thirty years later, Billy Bancroft was to say was one of the finest kicks he had ever seen. Yet, in defeat, Swansea could hold its head up high. The 'All Blacks' had not crossed the home line and had won by an opportunist effort when Swansea were on top. As the *Post* noted, it had been 'exceedingly hard lines'.

The team which did battle with the mighty New Zealanders on that December day was:
Geo. Davies, Trew, Arnold, Gordon, Scale, Scrine, Owen, Hopkins, Morgan, Thomas, Cole, Hunt, Parker, Smith and Joseph.

Given the less than scintillating form of the side during the first-half of the season, the performance against New Zealand served as a tonic for Swansea supporters. They preened themselves, too, when reading the words of the 'All Black', Duncan McGregor, who said that 'although Stamford Bridge was a good one, Swansea was the best ground I have played on'.

After the New Zealanders departed, the next Swansea match was against the Welsh 'All Blacks'. Neath, at that point in the season, had an unbeaten home record, thus a struggle was expected. Nevertheless, whilst both their half-backs were injured during the game, the 'struggle' was won for Swansea by a single goal to nil. There followed a drawn game against the 'Scarlets' in which Billy Trew was the 'light in a dark game'. Newport were beaten at St. Helens in a 'dull and uninteresting game' and Gloucester defeated again in a 'scrambling affair' by 5 points without reply.

As he considered his side's progress, captain Gordon, the triumphant 'General' of the previous invincible campaign, must have pondered on the delicate margin which exists between success and failure. How he must have longed for the players who had 'taken the bribe', and for Dick Jones, who provided some comfort when he said that 'my foot is improving every day'. Nonetheless, it was to be many 'days' before the outside-half appeared again in a white jersey.

Late in February, Leicester were entertained at St. Helens, and 'In the fastest match played this season ... the "All Whites" came out of their shell'. Such was the unexpected form of the team that day that twenty points were scored, in some style, without reply. That was significant, for it was the 'Tigers' biggest defeat of the season. However, just as one swallow does not make a summer, so one exciting win did not make a successful season. In a mud bath, Cardiff won the next match, 15 pts to 3; Newport fought a 'dour draw', then, after several other 'middling games', the Taffsiders were victorious at St. Helens , as were Bristol and Devonport Albions. The effect on supporters, not only of the defeats, but also 'the lack of Swansea form' was demonstrated when, for the penultimate game of the season at St. Helens, only 1,500 spectators turned up.

In the context of the history of Swansea Rugby Club, it is a pity that Frank Gordon could not have retired from his captaincy on a high note. He had been a fine servant of the club on the field, and was to be off it, yet, who could have forecast such a loss of form? Thus it was that Gordon retired with some disappointment.

As the season was drawing to a close, there was another disappointing departure. James Livingstone, the Club's long-time vice-president and *de facto* leader for so many years, was in dispute with the General Committee. As one of two trustees, he held the lease for the ground. The committee wanted him to 'hand it over to the club'. They argued that it should be in their possession, and, even, threatened legal action in order to retrieve it. At the threat, Livingstone dug his heels in, and stated that he would not part with the lease. Livingstone's position in the long running dispute related not to the lease, that was a symbol of his position, but rather to his views on how St. Helens should be used. 'I am going to fight,' he declared, 'for the Swansea Schools' League and the Amateur Athletic clubs ... why should they not be allowed the use of the field on the same conditions as the Cricket and Football Clubs?' Since Livingstone had been closely involved with Llewellyn and Thomas of Lan in obtaining the field, presumably he was defending the original 'open space' ideals upon which St. Helens was established. The General Committee, however, jealous of their world-famous facility, wanted to preserve it from over-use. Whatever the rights and wrongs of the case, it was extremely sad that a man who had done so much for the club should depart from the scene in this way. There is no doubt that James Livingstone is a major figure in the history of Swansea Football Club. As such, he should be remembered for the significant contribution which he made to its establishment, early development and to the vision which sustained it through its most successful period. Such men are rare.

1906–07

A brighter season

The concern of the Swansea club for its players was demonstrated, again, at the 1906 A.G.M., when it was announced that special treatment travelling expenses amounting to £39.10*s*.6*d* had been paid to Dick Jones during the previous year. The chairman followed the statement with the comment that 'no doubt everyone here thinks the expenditure justified'. A lusty 'Yes' put the matter into perspective. Swansea needed Dick Jones and the sooner he was fit the better. Certainly, Billy Trew, who, at the meeting, was appointed captain for the coming season, thought so, for he had a great deal to think about. He was clear about one thing he wanted to do,which was to get back to playing 'flowing football'. The supporters would have applauded. That, however, was easier said than done.

Whilst the 'opener' was won, the next game, against Bridgend did not suggest a renaissance. 'The Kelt' in the *Cambrian*, reported that 'against the 'Asylum Men', as they are, perhaps, not too euphoniously described, the '"Whites" played a listless game'. However, he and his contemporary were better pleased following the next match. 'In a most encouraging game in which the side shaped like winners from the kick-off', Plymouth were defeated by 18 points to nil. That *was* more like it. There followed wins at Kingsholm, where Gloucester were bettered in the mud to the tune of 13-nil, and at Llanelli. However, it was the next match which gave all concerned in Swansea genuine reason to feel that things were improving.

Cardiff were beaten. Not only did the 'Whites' win, but 'The Kelt' felt that 'a more thorough beating in a match between two first-class teams is not conceivable'. Then, perhaps reflecting the adventure literature which was popular at the time, he added, 'the "All Whites" have reached the highest point with one bound'. After that match, R. T. Gabe, the Cardiff legend, stated, 'We were badly beaten'. The Swansea fraternity, understanding the context in which the statement was made, might have added 'but brilliantly'. There was now a new spring in the step of Swansea players and supporters , but could the new 'form' be maintained?

With Dick Jones still absent, Harry Toft was partnering 'The Bullet' at outside-half, and doing well. Whilst Toft did not have the presence and range of skills of a Dick Jones, he was a competent footballer and, as time was to show, was prepared to play in a variety of positions in the interests of the club. Certainly, Billy Trew appreciated the player's qualities. Toft did well as Bristol, Gloucester ('The Cheesemongers'), Aberavon and Newport were beaten. Whilst, it was true, the scores were not as conclusive as in previous campaigns,the style with which the victories were achieved gave everyone the feeling that Swansea football was 'on the up'.

In December, Swansea supporters had a chance to see another Colonial side, as South Africa played, and defeated, Wales at St. Helens. Such was the size of the crowd that day, that many were said to have had difficulty in seeing the game. 'The Kelt' reported on a conversation which he had overheard:

> 'Man in red muffler (with studied politeness) ...
> 'Scuse me, boss, but if you can gimme 'arf an inch I'll be able to see Dickie Owen's ear'ole'.

Whilst the item was meant to amuse, it was indicative of a long-standing difficulty at St. Helens relating to the ability of spectators to see the game from some parts of the ground. Eventually, this was to result in Swansea losing its international games, and one wonders whether, if someone had taken the initiative, then, to rectify the problem, whether St. Helens would be hosting Internationals to this day?

As if affected by the Welsh defeat, in their next matches the 'All Whites' reverted to the mediocre. In a 'poor display of the handling code', the side played a pointless draw with Newport. The *Post* reported that not only had the match been pointless in its result, 'it might as well not have been played'. The team could point to vile weather as a reason for their poor performance, but Mrs Odo Vivian, who was amongst the spectators, was said 'not to have enjoyed the game'. Whilst rain and mud persisted, there was an improvement for the next game, against Llanelli, which the side won by 5 points to nil. 'The Kelt' enthused in his report about the form of Harry Toft who, 'on today's work is as good as the best of his side, which includes Trew and Owen'. Praise, indeed.

Just before Christmas, the 'Whites' welcomed to St. Helens, Pontypridd, the 'Rhondda Metropolitans'. Whilst the visitors lost by 12 points to 5, they gained many friends. A spokesman for the Swansea committee said that 'Pontypridd are very welcome again at St. Helens. They played a good clean game of football and should go far'. Since Ponty were, at that time, playing in the Glamorgan League, 'Old Moore' could not have done better with his forecasting.

After further 'drab' games, Dickie Owen and Billy Trew took a break from domestic football to contribute to a significant Welsh victory over England. Owen, who was captain for the match, was said to have been 'outstanding'. Perhaps the couple brought back a touch of inspiration from that win, for, in their next match, the 'Whites' found 'some form' in a clash with Llanelli. The *Post* reported that it had been a 'grand game, occasionally revealing the best of the rugby code'. Trew was said to have been 'in a higher class', whilst Toft, who dropped a goal during the game, played well.

The weather affected several games thereafter, including one at Rodney Parade, where the 'All Whites' emerged from a victory 'so plentifully daubed with the generous Uskside mud, that they were unrecognisable'. Despite the weather, 8,000 saw that match, during which Fred Scrine ran 'fifty yards, tricking all opposition' before passing to newcomer Lew Davies, who dived over for a try. Unfortunately, the team left that form behind them when they travelled to Leicester for the first game of their Midlands tour. The *Cambrian* reported that there was 'a crowd of 9,000, which was very good considering that Leicester Fosse and Clapton Orient were playing "Association" over the way'. That 'crowd' saw the home team win by 12 points to 3 in a game which 'Recorder' felt was won by the better side. However, in the second game of the Midlands tour, Northampton could not emulate their neighbours. The 'Whites' won by 10 points to 3, though the Swansea halves were said to have been 'bothered by the home side's flying forward'. Clearly, rugby tacticians were finding effective ways of stifling the creative play of opponents.

On returning to Swansea, the 'Whites' supporters had to suffer another disappointing defeat. The *Cambrian* headline summed it up, 'Whites Whacked'. Whilst the score hardly bore out the caption, (Swansea 3 points, Neath 5), the defeat, when victory had been expected, was hard to swallow. As a result, captain Trew, still clinging to his pre-season policy of trying to play attractive football, was delighted when the next match, against Newport, was won with a little of the old style. The *Post*, however, had a criticism: 'The whole art of taking the ball from the line out is being neglected by Swansea. This is a mistake!'

Threats on the horizon

A letter to the *Cambrian*, which was, clearly, important enough in the eyes of the paper's editor to warrant a full column, was indicative of some of the concerns of the rugby fraternity at the time. Ostensibly concerning the lack of Swansea players in the next Welsh side, it focused on other matters. 'If things do not improve, Swansea will be compelled ... to provide the Association game with that first footing in south Wales which will lead to the disappearance of rugby'. Whilst the correspondent was overstating his case, with the relative demise of Swansea football, particularly in entertainment terms, those who clung to the oval ball must have been concerned.

The 'Whites' replied in the best way they knew, by beating Devonport Albions convincingly. Despite 'fielding a weakened side', they beat their Saxon adversaries by 18 points to 3. Furthermore, Trew kept his word; despite a strong wind, they won with a 'bit of the old style'. By the end of March, something of the old enthusiasm gripped the Swansea supporters as a record 3,500 people took the numerous excursions to Cardiff. Together with 27,000 Cardiff followers, the Swansea contingent saw a vital match. The *Post* had it that 'everything conspired to make the fixture of supreme importance to both sides ... the Welsh Championship was at stake'. When the final whistle sounded, Cardiff were the victors by a single try to nil. 'Recorder' in the *Cambrian*, however, anxious to placate the Swansea followers, opined that: 'We have not lost the

Championship outright, although Cardiff will claim it. Each side has lost two matches ... and they tie for position at the top of the ladder'. For his part, 'The Kelt' felt that Swansea had lost because Scrine was played as a 'Rover' and 'stood waiting for work'. In addition, there was the fact that Dickie Owen had been injured and the side played with fourteen men for most of the game. From the historical point of view, that game resulted in a 'first' in Swansea journalism. The *Cambrian* published its first rugby 'action' photograph. The indistinct images showed that the 'All Whites' were, still wearing dark shorts.

As the season drew to a close, the club's results were more encouraging. Despite being a man short, again, Northampton were beaten, as were Bristol and Bridgend. In several of these games there was the added encouragement that the win had been achieved with a 'patchwork side'. However, as far as Welsh competition was concerned, the *Post* reported that 'the "All Whites" ceased from troubling about Championships and watched the hauling down of the posts with equanimity'. Nonetheless, as Billy Trew looked back on his first season as captain, he must have done so with some satisfaction. Defections apart, absences for a variety of reasons had forced him to introduce many new players to the side, yet his team had lost only three games during the campaign, whilst winning twenty-four. He knew, too, that he had done his best with respect to the style of play. However measured, it was a considerable improvement on the outcome of the previous season.

1907-08

Class distinction?

The 1907 A.G.M. was enlivened by an 'earnest discussion' in which Fred Scrine was to the fore. Scrine wanted to know why the nomination of a player for the club's Committee had been rejected? He was told that a club rule only allowed 'Class A' members (who paid a guinea a year), to hold office. Scrine argued that this was class distinction. 'Speaking for men who gave ten or eleven years service on the football field,' he stated, 'and who are not allowed to stand for the Committee ... If I had known six or seven years ago my resignation would have gone in!' Secretary Perkins did his best to placate Scrine, but pointed out that he had to abide by the rules. There was a suggestion from the floor that that first team players should be eligible, but the matter could not be resolved 'there and then'. Scrine was not appeased and left the meeting with the clarion call, 'Where would the moneyed people be without labour?' The players, it seemed, had found a shop steward.

There was a different distinction apparent at the beginning of the 1907-08 campaign. The Merthyr and Ebbw Vale clubs had joined the Northern Union, and, in September 1907, the first games under the aegis of that organisation took place in south Wales. Professionalism was on the march. At the same time, the Welsh Union's sub-committee on professionalism – which was said to be 'rampant among south Wales clubs' – reported on its work. Whilst the committee's major finding was that the allegations were not proven, decisions were taken which resulted in six Welsh players, including Fred Scrine, being suspended for six months. The charge was that the players had received expenses 'in excess of the amount actually disbursed'. T. Arnold, another Swansea player, was permanently suspended for playing under an assumed name whilst banned. Subsequently, the Aberdare, Barry, Mid Rhondda and Treherbert clubs were expelled for embracing professionalism, as the Welsh Union took its stand against that threat. From the point of view of the Swansea club, at that time, professionalism in the rugby game seemed to be focused on the soft coal areas in the east (where professional soccer was also starting). At least, there was nothing nearer home.

Nonetheless, there were threats of another kind. Despite Trew's efforts to play attractive football, Swansea supporters, sated by the successes of previous years, were difficult to please. As a result, with the exception of a limited number of matches, 'gate' income was, frequently, far smaller than it had been. At this distance, two factors seemed to have influenced this trend. The first was the defection of outstanding, exciting, backs like Fred Jowett and Danny Rees. The other was the development, by opponents, of negative tactics which were designed to disrupt the flowing kind of football which the Swansea supporters had enjoyed. As will always be the case in competitive team games,the teams of that time evolved methods which were intended to negate the attacking threats of their opponents. Primarily, the focus was upon winning rather than entertaining. Naturally, from the point of view of spectators, this made the game less enjoyable to watch, and fewer came.

This was reflected in a game at the end of September, when the 'Whites' played Plymouth at home. At the kick-off, only 2,000 people were said to be in the field for what was an attractive fixture. On the day, the Plymouth defence was outstanding and the men in white won by the narrow margin of 11 points to 6. There, were, of course, those clubs which tried to play Swansea at their own game. One such club was Bridgend, but the 'Asylum men' could not match the class which was shown by their opponents. As a consequence, the 'Whites' won convincingly, 37 points to 4, even though they lost Jack Bancroft and Ivor Morgan, both injured. Aubrey Smith led the side for that match, for Billy Trew had been injured in training. The Swansea list of injured was growing, and, as in the previous season, this resulted in 'patchwork' sides representing the club in many games. Nevertheless, results, if not the old excitement, were most frequently in Swansea's favour.

Jack Bancroft.

Jones returns

Billy Trew must have been delighted to learn that, for the match against Newport at St. Helens, Dick Jones was to make his comeback. As they had done with the returning James brothers, the supporters turned out in force to welcome the outside half. 20,000 people were said to be in the ground as Trew, fit once more, led out the 'All Whites'. However, when Dick Jones emerged, 'strolling on in his own way with his hands in his pockets', there was, according to the *Cambrian* 'a shout the volume of which has not been heard at St. Helens for some time'. Jones, a veritable artist with the ball, signalled his return in the best way possible. The *Post* reported: '... thence it flashed to Jones. It was then that the genius of the famous outside-half was demonstrated. He was absolutely surrounded by opponents, but, by feinting and dodging he beat the opposition and went under the posts for a try; which sent the spectators into transports of delight ... the

Dick Jones.

shouting and screaming of the crowd will live in my memory for ever.' That, they must have thought, was the way to beat defensive ploys.

With Toft back at centre, Billy Trew on the wing and Jones and Owen at half-back,was 'Swansea football' going to be seen again? 'Watchman' thought that there were signs to suggest that the answer was 'yes', when Leicester were beaten on the Midlands tour. Certainly, when fit, Owen and Jones, now christened 'The Dancing Dicks', were a remarkable pair of footballers. Billy Bancroft, in later years, argued that, had not Jones suffered a serious ankle injury he would have rivalled Dick Owen for the greatest number of Welsh 'caps'. When coupled with Owen's famed standing reverse pass, a dip of Jones's shoulder often confused the opposition far more than a dozen prearranged moves. When Owen, Jones, and Billy Trew were available, and with an emerging Toft, there was enough exciting potential in the side to provide hope that Swansea Football Club might recapture something of its old grandeur.

Whilst Cardiff won at St. Helens in November, it was an extremely close game, and might have gone either way. However, the match demonstrated the importance of forwards. Flair behind the scrum could only be released if the forwards won the ball. On that occasion, the Cardiff eight outplayed the home pack, and thus the game was lost and won. Swansea had a lot of work to do in that area.

Nonetheless, at that stage in the club's programme, the 'All Whites' record was 'not to be sneezed at'. Twelve games had been played, nine won and three lost, 173 points scored and only 32 conceded. As significant for Trew, his team and the supporters was the fact that the games which had been lost had all been by relatively small margins. Gloucester won 8-3, and Cardiff 4-0, and 7-5. The general feeling was that if the committee could find a settled and effective front eight to complement the backs, not only would professionalism and the rise of 'Association' be overcome, the grumbling contingent would forget that they had ever uttered a word of criticism.

Yet, that was not to happen overnight. In an edition which reported a motoring accident involving Lloyd George, the *Cambrian* also noted that, whilst Devonport Albions had been beaten at St. Helens, 'people left the field before the end. Interest had quite gone'. Trew must have been frustrated as a string of dour games ensued. Indeed, in three successive matches the 'Whites' scored a total of nine points whilst winning twice and drawing once. It was not the football to 'bring back the crowds'. Yet, there were those who were beginning to think that it might win the championship.

In analysing the situation, Trew and his cohorts must have recognised that there were extenuating circumstances which were affecting the way in which the team was playing. For example, in a bid to find a winning combination, no less than seventeen new men had appeared in the white shirt during the year 1907 alone. It was a far cry from the balmy days when continuity was recognised as being a major factor in the team's success.

Performances into the New Year brought little change as far as gate income was concerned.

Even for a February match against major rivals, Newport, only 5,000 people turned up to see the game, whilst a match against the popular Leicester side did not show much improvement, even though the 'All Whites' fielded a new star. Dr. Teddy Morgan, a Welsh international winger of some note, made his début. Nonetheless, it was Morgan's presence which was said to have given the side a psychological boost on that day and for the next match. Two thousand Swansea-ites took the excursions to Cardiff to see the new man play against the Blue and Blacks. They were not disappointed. The *Post* reported on a 'brilliant victory', even though, yet again, the team was obliged to play the bulk of the game with fourteen men. The stalwart forward, Aubrey Smith was kicked on the head and had to leave the field. In his report of the game 'The Kelt' included the comparative statistics of the two clubs following the match. Whilst, admittedly premature the scribe argued that the data illustrated that the 'Whites' were 'Champions of Wales'.

Swansea	P 24	W 20	L3	D1	F 285	A 49
Cardiff	P 22	W 19	L3	D0	F 247	A 79

With Newport beaten at Rodney Parade in a 'return', 'Dr Teddy' scored in that game, and Penarth were defeated in a 'rough house match in which Dick Jones was laid out, and Fred Scrine played on with a broken collarbone', no one could complain about the fortitude of the Swansea men. Furthermore, there was room for encouragement following the next match, in which the flair behind the scrum was released as the 'Scarlets' were beaten 22-nil. The *Post* report suggested that it had been 'the most pleasant game of the season ... the leather had been given air' and Llanelli's ambition to beat the leaders in the championship race, thwarted.

Swansea optimism was also enhanced when Wales won the 'Triple Crown', with the Swansea half-backs restored and with Trew and Hayward in the side. Then the 'Caps' came back to assist Swansea in the next game against Cardiff at St. Helens. This match was said to be 'the decider 'for the Welsh Championship, though most people felt that the crown was safely in 'All White' hands. 30,000 people were in the ground as the teams took the field, demonstrating, yet again, the fickleness of the football following public. The Swansea treasurer, however, could afford to smile as he surveyed the scene. Not surprisingly, the match was keenly fought. The *Cambrian* reported 'heated exchanges during which Owen and Jones were laid out'. This time, though, the Swansea pack was inspired and dominated their opponents. According to 'The Kelt' they were irresistible. As a result, the 'Whites' won by two converted goals (10 points) to a dropped goal (4 points); the championship was secure.

The remainder of the season provided the opportunity for the team to show that traditional Swansea football was alive and well. At least, the Plymouth papers thought so when they previewed the game against Devonport Albions with the assertion that 'Swansea are the Champions of the World'. The team must have felt good about that piece of hyperbole. Certainly they did about the arrangements which were made to transport them to Plymouth. For the first time they travelled there 'without any break in the journey'. It was reported that they left Swansea at 11.40, took luncheon on the train, and reached Plymouth by 6.30. Secretary F. E. Perkins was in charge of the party, aided by Frank Gordon. 'All were in bed by 11 o clock.'

The highlight of the last quarter of the season, though, was the victory over 'The Barbarians'. It was reported that the visitors included twelve internationals and 'tried all they knew to make a game of it'. However, on a beautiful afternoon, the 'Whites' scored four tries without reply. 'The Kelt' reported that it was the best game of the season. The first try set the scene:

> In the first minute, Owen completely upset the Barbarians defence by a reverse pass to Jones. Almost without moving the latter passed out wide to Toft who, missing Trew ... and with a feint went over for a splendid try.

Why, oh why, the Swansea supporters may have thought, don't other sides play the game like the Barbarians? What they enjoyed, of course, was an exhibition which depended upon both sides being prepared to 'give the leather air'. The Barbarian philosophy, clearly, was complementary to Swansea's traditional style. The reality was, however, that other sides, frequently, set out to strangle 'flair'; entertainment was a secondary factor among their objectives.

Chapter Nine

A FAMOUS VICTORY

1908–09

IN SEPTEMBER 1908, the traditional opening match, against the League, resulted in the 'Whites' scoring twenty-six points without reply. However, the praise in the press for the victors was muted; the display had 'lacked spark'. Bridgend, who were to provide the opposition for the first game proper, might have taken comfort from that statement. If they did, they were misguided. When the match was played, Swansea 'turned it on'. With Trew and Jones absent, Tom Bateman played at outside-half, and proved to be 'a capable deputy', while Fred Scrine had 'one of his best games for Swansea'. Bridgend conceded 33 points without reply, and the St. Helens faithful were alerted, once again, to the possibility of a season of thrilling rugby.

When Plymouth, strengthened by two 'Wallabies', were beaten 16 points to 6 in the next match, the promise was underlined, as it was when Gloucester visited St. Helens in mid-October. Then, due to some extraordinary weather, the crowd, dressed in 'straw hats and summer raiment', watched Swansea beat the English side by eight clear points. Whilst the victory was not as conclusive as the optimists would have liked, the Gloucestermen (then called the 'Citizens') had played a 'spoiling game which had disrupted the flow of the home play'. Clearly, rugby tacticians were continuing their search for effective defensive ploys, and, as a result, in the future, those who loved the 'open game' would find themselves frustrated.

The impact of such frustration was apparent at the end of the month, after 'dour games' had been played against Cardiff and Bristol. In the eyes of 'Watchman', at least, a rot had set in. With an eye on the expected incursion of 'Association', he wrote:

> If Swansea players have been desirous of supplying to the argument that rugby is less attractive than the game of soccer, they could not have been more successful than they were this afternoon. The game was positively painful.

Whilst the journalist took no account of Swansea absences through injury, the early season euphoria had, clearly, evaporated. Yet, the underlying skill and spirit were still there, and the same writer, two weeks later, was delighted to report that 'The "Whites" are themselves again'. By that he meant that, in a game against Leicester, four fine tries had been scored, whilst 'the crowd was warmed by the excellence of the passing'. Then came a victory which lifted the collective Swansea morale even further. Before a crowd of 40,000 people at the Arms Park, Cardiff were defeated by a dropped goal and four tries to a dropped goal. The *Leader* reported that it was 'Swansea's greatest win of the season', even though 'the usual Cardiff mud' had not favoured the men in white. Toft was outstanding in that match, scoring twice, and, at the end of the game, Cardiff's Percy Bush said, 'We were beaten to the world'. As they 'walked, cheering, through the streets after the game', the two thousand Swansea supporters who attended the match were happy to endorse that view. No Cardiff vendor was reported as being there to offer mourning cards to the Swansea men.

At that stage of the season, notwithstanding 'Watchman's' remarks during the period of 'gloomy football', the Swansea record was impressive. Of the twelve games played, ten had been won and only one lost, whilst 151 points had been scored and only 30 conceded. Captain, Billy Trew must have felt pleased with his charges. As far as the supporters were concerned, with vivid memories of recent victories plus the tasty scalp of the 'Blue and Blacks' to consider, they were in no mood to remember the dour games which had, so recently, worried 'Watchman'. Once again, Swansea was sitting at the top of the Welsh Table; all was good with the world.

There followed a successful, short, Devon tour when both games were won and, a week later, with fourteen men, a disappointing defeat at St. Helens, when Newport took the honours in a close-fought match. Given that several players had been injured in that match and during the Devon tour, there was concern at St. Helens. As it was put, 'the "Wallabies" have arrived before we are ready'.

Nonetheless, given the reputation which the visiting 'Colonials' brought with them, and the memories of the game against New Zealand, three years earlier, as Christmas approached, there was tremendous excitement in the town. The match against the Australians was to be played on Boxing Day, and, at the appointed time, 'very nearly forty thousand people' packed into St. Helens. Apart from anything else, the treasurer was delighted; £2,100 had been taken at the gate, a new record for Wales. And there was another record for Swansea, too; the 'All Whites', despite tremendous Australian pressure in the latter half of the game, were victorious. Furthermore, the much-vaunted 'Colonials' failed to score, whilst Swansea registered six points – from a Jack Bancroft penalty and an Edgar Morgan try.

After the match, the 'Wallabies' complained that they did not know what Dick Jones was going to do with the ball. 'When he commences a run,' they said, 'not a muscle on his face moves'. Whilst their heroes had not been able to play flowing football, even the most diminutive Swansea supporter who made his way home that day, strode six feet tall. Indeed, there were those among the happy throng who were harbouring thoughts about the 'Whites' being champions of the world. It was heady stuff!

Those who gained the first Swansea victory over a major touring team on that memorable day were:

J. Bancroft; W. J. Trew (Capt.), P. Hopkins, H. Toft, H. Thomas; R. M. Owen, R. Jones; D. J. Thomas, H. Hunt, I. Morgan, E. Morgan, G. Hayward, I. Williams, D. Griffiths, D. Davies.

Invincible skipper, F. J. Gordon, was the Swansea touch-judge that day, whilst R. W. Dowdle was the trainer. Others in the indistinct team photograph published in the press following that game, were Aubrey Smith and F. E. Perkins.

'Genny' Gordon as touch-judge.

Without exception, all the papers in England, Scotland, Ireland and Wales - and probably the press of other countries- were unanimous in selecting Jack Bancroft as the outstanding success of last week's international match. He has certainly added lustre to a famous name.

A cartoon which appeared in the 'South Wales Daily Post', 13th February, 1909.

Since Wales had also beaten the Australians, largely as a result of inspiring play by Billy Trew, the *Athletic News* published a poem in honour of the Swansea man, the last verse of which read :

Wallabies came hopping,
Mandible and Co.
Thought they'd take some stopping,
And would make Wales woe.
They, themselves deceiving,
Met their Waterloo,
And,alas, they're grieving,
Thanks to Swansea's Trew.

Given that that Welsh side had included six other Swansea men: Jack Bancroft, Phil Hopkins, Dickie Owen and Dick Jones, George Hayward, and Ivor Morgan, 'Whites' followers were ecstatic. Swansea, they assured themselves, was the home of the 'World Champions'. Let them all come!

Unfortunately, the players had taken a great deal out of themselves in the matches against the Australians, and, by the end of February, the team had been displaced, by Cardiff, from the head of the Welsh table. The reason for this, according to the *Post*, was the spate of injuries to key players and the demanding schedule which the Swansea team had been set. There was, in addition, the fact that, in domestic competition, other sides were prepared to try to lower the Swansea colours by any means available to them. In one local derby, for example, the 'Whites' ended the game with twelve men. Among those injured was Billy Trew, who chipped a bone in his shoulder following a 'blatantly late tackle'. Harry Hunt and Harry Toft were both concussed in the same match. The *Leader*, in its report of the event commented that 'little could be said about the game, other than it was not football'. Apart from anything else, after the glamour of the 'Wallabies' victory, such domestic 'warfare' held little appeal for the Swansea supporters. Furthermore, they had to contemplate the near future without the mercurial Billy Trew.

Nonetheless, the team fought hard to maintain its supremacy, and, at the end of the campaign, the 'Whites' found themselves runners-up in the Welsh championship. Whilst the team had failed to gain yet another 'Premiership', at least the club and its supporters could bask in the glory of the Australian result. It was a powerful salve for any disappointment felt.

1909-10

Despair and delight

As he came off the field after damaging his shoulder in the match at the end of the previous season, Billy Trew had said that he was 'finished with football'. At the time, that statement caused much concern in the Swansea camp, but, happily, not only did the footballing genius start the 1909-10 season, he did so as captain. And such were his inspirational abilities, that, on hearing the news of his acceptance of the post, all Swansea exuded a sigh of relief. There was, after all, only one Billy Trew!

Unfortunately, hardly had the new season started than the captain was injured again. In a match against Plymouth, it was reported that he had 'twisted his bad knee'. The knee had been damaged at Leicester during the previous season and, now, there was speculation that not only might Trew not be able to play again, he might not be able to run. 'Freelance' put the prospect of losing the captain into perspective when he wrote: 'If anyone required an ocular demonstration that Trew is indispensable to Swansea, he received it on Saturday. Swansea, just now, are a one man team ...'

Then, as if to underscore that opinion, after a defeat by Gloucester, the *Western Mail* noted that 'Swansea have descended to the level of most other sides'. In the eyes of supporters who had been sated with exciting success during the previous decade, that was a frightening judgment.

The *Post*, following the same theme, argued that the decline in standards at Swansea had been gradual, and that 'there is not, now, the same anxiety to keep in good trim'. Yet, whilst the criticism in the papers was hardly groundless, there was sufficient *hwyl* left in the Swansea camp to ensure that 'Whites' supporters would be able to smile again. In the games which followed, Llanelli were beaten and Cardiff held to a draw. Perhaps, argued the *Leader*, seeing hope on the horizon, the short Midlands tour might help to cement the improvement through better team spirit and confidence. In the event, on that trip, the 'Whites' had all their work cut out to avoid defeat at Leicester, where they drew, and, 'only scraped a win' (via a penalty) against Cambridge University. It was hardly the form of 'World Champions', however one looked at it.

Nevertheless, as Christmas approached the supporters looked to the traditional Yule-tide games to give them a lift. With visiting teams prepared to 'give the leather the air', there seemed to be better prospects in view. That, after all, was 'Swansea football'.

The holiday schedule started with the defeat of a strong Watsonians side, and when that was followed by 'a brilliant display of Swansea football' against London Irish, the optimists were massing again. In that match, the returned Billy Trew, Dickie Owen, Phil Hopkins and Harry Toft were all outstanding, as was the exciting Toft in the next match. Toft, popular opinion suggested at the time, 'may well replace Billy Trew when the latter retires'. Unfortunately, though, that was not to be. Harry Toft was unemployed, and a strong rumour began to circulate that he was about to take the northern silver. Thus it was that the renewed elation of the supporters was tempered by their gloomy premonition that they were about to lose yet another young star. The *Post*, evidently aware of the position, was campaigning for the club to find a job for the young man. They argued that 'one can hardly expect him (Toft) to stay ... without work when he has a tempting offer from elsewhere'.

Toft must have appreciated the paper's concern, for, at the end of January, bowing to the inevitable, he sent a telegram to the *Post* 'Signed for Hunslet. Playing today. Toft'. The pieces of silver amounted to £160 cash, and a job. Once again, Swansea had lost a talented player to the Northern Union. The lessons from previous seasons had not been learnt. Apart from the Toft case, it was clear that the haemorrhaging could not go on for ever without damaging the quality of the Swansea side. As far as Toft was concerned, not only would the club miss his playing skills, the Danygraig boy had been a 'hugely popular member of the team, who made friends wherever he went'. Not only had the club lost his abilities on the field, it would miss his contribution to the nurturing of *esprit* de corps at St. Helens.

By the end of February, after being beaten by Newport, the 'Whites' were third in the Welsh Table. Despite everything, the club's record at the time would have more than satisfied the supporters of lesser clubs; seventeen games had been won out of twenty-four played. The truth was, though that the club's position was, in part, a reflection of the poor quality of football being played in the Principality at the time. But all that was forgotten at the end of the next match, for Cardiff were defeated. Indeed, the *Leader*, demonstrating a rare appreciation of hyperbole, reported that the 'Taffsiders' were 'hopelessly beaten', when 'the eastern papers had predicted a victory for the 'Blue and Blacks"'. Billy Trew restored again, and the 'Dancing Dicks' were scintillating in that victory, and the Cardiff defence could not contain them.

Next, the Barbarians were 'beaten at their own game', which prompted 'Freelance' to write, 'It is a pity that Swansea did not start the season in the same manner as they are finishing it'. Every 'Whites' supporter would have said 'Amen' to that.

To finish the campaign, the colours of both Northampton and Bristol were lowered 'in some style', which was just as well. Given the club's drab start to the season, the Swansea public was beginning to drift away, and gates, overall, were lower than they had been for several years.

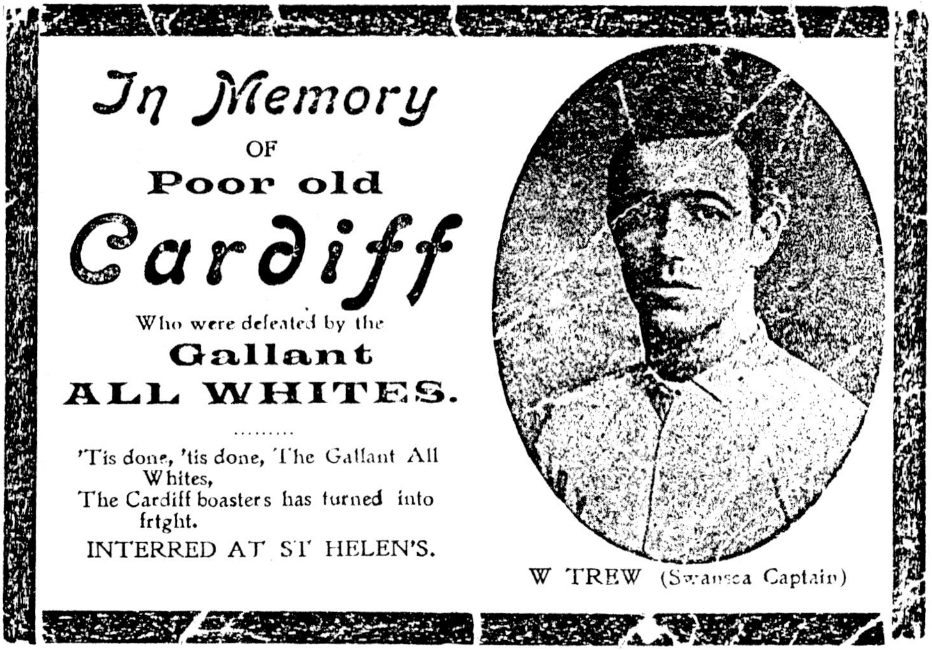

'In Memoriam' card.

Not surprisingly, this concerned the St. Helens authorities, for there was a vibrant new threat on the horizon. Professional soccer was being played in Cardiff and was attracting large crowds, while the Association authorities were making representations to interested parties in Swansea to establish a club in the Borough. Whilst the diehards wanted to shrug off this challenge from 'the upstart game', the more objective were not slow to realise that, to retain support at St. Helens, attractive, winning football would need to be played. They were cognizant, too, of the effects of *anno domini* and injuries on the key players in the current team. As a result, many shoulders were looked over, as the cricketers oiled their bats for the beginning of the summer season. There was disappointment, too. Ivor Morgan had been selected to go to South Africa with the British team but had been unable to accept the invitation. Few working men, at the time, were in a position to be absent from their jobs for three months. Ivor was no exception.

1910-11

A landmark for Trew

At the start of the new season, several key players were unavailable and, Billy Trew, captain for the fifth successive season (thus equalling Billy Bancroft's record), had problems fielding a strong side. Nevertheless, there was early encouragement for him when Plymouth were defeated by 14 points to 5. 'Freelance' wrote of that match, 'Trew and his merry men are improving every match, and the side is bound to have a successful season'. It was a bold prediction by one who, only months before, had lamented the poor standard of play. Yet, the games which fol-

The Rev. Alban Davies.
One of Swansea's rugby-playing clergy who was to become part of Wales's 'Terrible Eight' (1914).

lowed seemed to underscore his optimism. Against Bridgend, 'Swansea, in pleasing form, romped home'. Indeed, so 'pleasing' was the team's form on that day that eight tries were scored by the men in white, six of them 'resulting from exciting combination between half-backs and three-quarters'. Newcomer, Oswald Jenkins, scored twice on his début, whilst Howell Lewis, Billy Trew and Tom and Ivor Morgan were other scorers. The only negative note in the *Post* report was the news that Haydn Evans had chipped a bone in his shoulder. Yet, for the happy supporters, the positives outweighed the negatives. The match had been won in true Swansea style. If they kept playing like that, the popular feeling had it, 'the Soccerites could go and whistle!'

When October began, the *Leader* noted that the games played up to that point had all ended in conclusive victories for the 'Whites'. Indeed, the paper crowed that 'points had been rattled up in the old sweet style'. Not surprisingly, at that time the points record was reminiscent of the 'good old days'; the side was ninety points in credit. Yet there were underlying difficulties facing Trew and the selection committee which hung over from the early days of the season and had been exacerbated by injuries since. As a result, in the matches which followed, injuries and absences affected the cohesion of the side's play. Whilst Gloucester were defeated, their men 'disrupted the flow of the home game'. In the process, several other Swansea players suffered injuries. Nonetheless, that Gloucester match drew warm praise for the Swansea pack from both the *Post* and the *Leader*. Despite being two short at one point, the Swansea eight were magnificent, with D. J. Thomas, Rev. Alban Davies, Tom Morgan, and Ben and Dai Davies being picked out for particular praise. Of the backs, who spent much of the match 'on defensive duties', Jack Bancroft received an accolade for his 'magnificent kicking'.

During the whole of this period, Billy Trew was driving his men in training. As the *Post* noted, he 'sets a fine example to his men in working at his fitness'. He did so, too, on the field. After the 'Whites' had beaten Llanelli, and Swansea became the only unbeaten side in Wales, the *Leader*, reporting on the Stradey game, was effusive in its praise of the captain. 'Trew is one of the brainiest and most skilled players who ever handled a football', they wrote. They had praise, too, for Dick Jones, and Ivor Morgan – a roving forward in a class by himself. According to the *Post*, the quality of Swansea play 'was down to practices on the field with the ball early in the week'. No one referred to the gloomy period of the previous campaign. The 'Whites' were back playing 'Swansea football'. Let the whole world note that fact. Unfortunately, those who were encamped on the banks of the Taff had other ideas.

Given what had gone before, when Cardiff came to play at St. Helens, there was an air of confidence about the home side. Indeed, after the match, it was a widely-held opinion that there had been over-confidence. Prior to the game, the 'Taffsiders' had been in poor form, whilst the 'Whites' had been exciting the crowds with significant wins – in style. Unhappily for the home supporters, early in the match, Jack Bancroft, assuming that the whistle had blown, kicked the ball over his own goal line and did not bother to follow up to minor. Unfortunately for him, a

Cardiff player sprinted over the line to claim a try. The decision seemed to 'knock the stuffing' out of the home men, and they were not able to recover.

'Freelance', commenting on the loss of Swansea's unbeaten record, wrote of the influence of the state of mind of players on the outcome of matches. Cardiff, he stated, 'wanted to win more than the Swansea men'. Whilst Billy Trew and his team might have disagreed with that, they would have had to agree that they had been beaten by a less skillful side. Had the phrase 'the inner game' been invented at that time, it might have provoked much discussion in the St. Helens clubhouse.

As the trial of Dr. Crippen was probably focusing the mind of that infamous killer on his approaching nemesis, *anno domini* was stalking the Swansea camp. Some, however, if we are to judge by the Limerick form of a contemporary piece of doggerel, were unaffected by it.

Though you really can't say that he's growing,
To time's stern decree he's not bowing,
There's this about Dick,
He can make others sick,
But quite well all the time's R. M. Owen.

Yet Owen, Jones and Trew, to name but three, were all getting older; some, it seems faster than the others. Not that such a conclusion could be drawn from the next two matches. Aberavon were 'well beaten', as Swansea 'returned to form', and Newport, even though Billy Trew was absent from the Swansea side, surrendered their ground record to 'a rampaging Swansea eight'. 'Freelance', though, was somewhat muted in his reactions to that victory. He thought that the standard of rugby seen that day was 'much lower than a couple of seasons ago'. Nonetheless, since the 'Amber and Blackings' ground record had lasted more than eighteen months, the victory was notable.

Meanwhile, Dick Jones let it be known that he was 'not as keen as he had been, and was only waiting for a capable reserve to be found to retire'. Not surprisingly, *anno domini* apart, the outside-half was feeling the effects of the various injuries which he had sustained over the years, Furthermore, because he was who he was, lesser players, and the young Turks of the day were all anxious to stop him playing his magical game. In the process, as his reactions slowed, and the methods used by opponents became more 'liberal', his body was beginning to complain.

Nonetheless, on the Saturday following the Newport victory, the *South Wales Argus* reported that Swansea had removed another scalp. 'Pontypool's proud record' had been taken. Swansea, it seemed, had set a 'furious pace', and had scored three tries, one from 'a beautiful flowing movement'. Howell Lewis crossed for two of them, and was cited as a young player with considerable potential. Then, when Leicester were beaten by a 'Whites' team, forced into several late changes, Swansea looked down, proudly, from the top of the Welsh Table. Of the eleven games which had been played, ten had been won whilst one hundred and eighty points had been scored against a mere thirty. At the time, the sun was shining in Swansea even when it rained.

There followed the Devon tour, which, whilst it was enjoyed by the players, put further pressure on them. Devonport Albions, in particular, were doughty, traditional opponents. Subsequently, 'Watchman' argued that it would have been better to have played Plymouth first (the weaker of the two opposing sides on the tour), rather than Devonport. 'The long and tiresome journey,' he wrote, 'had taken the steam out of the players'. He also complained about the antiquated coach which the railway company had provided. Whilst the 'Whites' rose to the challenge, the *Plymouth Herald* reported that the visitors were now 'without their traditional sting'.

On their return home, the 'Whites' had to face Newport at St. Helens. It would have been a tough enough fixture in any circumstances, but, on this occasion, with the Swansea players 'jaded', the 'Usksiders' gained a 13 points to 8 victory. Whilst both Swansea papers reported that Newport had been 'lucky', they had to agree, grudgingly, that Swansea teams of yesteryear would have won – despite the rub of the green, and some peculiar refereeing decisions. The defeat was only the second suffered by the St. Helens men in fourteen matches, yet those whose task it was to chronicle the affairs of the 'Whites', were plunged into a bout of pessimism. The *Post*, for example, reported that 'the "Whites" are not maintaining their reputation for consistency'. What, one wonders, would they have made of the club's reputation for inconsistency which was to become established in the years to come?

As Christmas approached, the citizens of Swansea were given the opportunity to see one of the marvels of the age. A firm of motor engineers advertised in the *Post* urging Swansea people to come to see the first aeroplane in Wales. In large type the advertisement stated that THE MACHINE IS THE ONE IN WHICH MON. BLERIOT FLEW THE CHANNEL. However, the careful reader would have noticed the tiny line of type between 'The machine is' and 'the one ...', which stated 'identical with'. Whilst, no doubt, the advertisers were honourable men, there was something of a Dick Jones sleight of hand in the way they were enticing people to spend their 3*d.* pieces.

Meantime, the 'Whites', as if responding to press criticism, were doing some flying of their own. In scoring thirty-one points without reply, they inflicted 'the heaviest defeat Bristol had had on their own ground'. Given what had gone before, it was a remarkable performance, particularly since, at one stage in the game, the 'Whites' had just thirteen men on the pitch. Owen and Trew were 'champion' in that match, Tom Williams and Ivor Morgan were in 'immense form', whilst the three-quarters, Howel Lewis, Phil Hopkins, Frank Williams and Haydn Evans, 'ran like the athletes they are'. It was an encouraging win for 'Whites' followers.

At Christmas those same supporters had further encouragement – Dick Jones returned after a six-week layoff. Furthermore, all three matches were won over the holiday period, with fifty-one points being scored and only three conceded. The optimists, at the time, must have been asking what all the fuss was about. Even the pessimists, full of Christmas spirit, were rather off guard, and, if they needed further encouragement, it came with the news that five of their favourites had been picked to play for Wales, against England, at St. Helens. Among them was Ivor Morgan, who played a great game. The *Leader*, in commenting on that performance wrote that 'journalists had used up all the stock of adjectives in eulogising him'. Since Ivor was playing in the same team as gods like Billy Trew and Dickie Owen, that was praise, indeed.

In January, Haydn Evans ran in five tries in a second runaway victory over Bristol, and it was not until the last day of January that the team tasted defeat again. Once more, Newport were the villains in a 'roughhouse at Rodney Parade' Whilst the 'Usksiders' won by six points, the *Western Mail* opined that 'they hardly deserved the victory'. Whether that was the case or not, the 'Whites' had lost what 'Freelance' called 'one of the poorest games I have seen'. Furthermore, they were deposed from the top place in the Welsh Table in the process.

In February, there was an even greater blow to the club's prestige. They lost to Northampton. 'Watchman' claimed that the defeat was 'unparalleled in the annals of the St. Helens club'. Since Northampton had won by 18 points to 3 whilst the club had lost, for example, by 21 points to 3 in 1888, presumably 'unparalleled' was not intended to convey a numerical precedence. Rather, we must suppose, it implied a qualitative one. At the time, Northampton were not among the strongest sides in the Swansea fixture list. It must have been a famous victory for them.

Before the season ended, there were further losses, with Gloucester and Bridgend being among the victors, and, at the final count, the 'Whites' finished third in the Welsh championship. Twenty-eight games had been won and six lost. Once again, that would have been an acceptable return for most clubs. Not for Swansea, however, where the Club's pedigree lifted it above the common herd. At least, that was the assumption, and the supporters were disappointed.

There was further, more worrying, disappointment, too. Billy Trew fractured his collarbone, and was talking about 'definitely retiring from the game', as was the reliable Ike Williams. Ike was greatly admired as an outstanding club man and would be missed. The loss of Trew, however, was on a different plane altogether. 'Freelance', in contemplating the unthinkable, wrote: 'If a vote was taken to find the most popular player of the present team ... Trew (would win it) with an outstanding majority ... his clean play, splendid sportsmanship, and his rugby genius have combined to win the hearts of rugby followers everywhere'. Given that Jack Bancroft also fractured his shoulder near the end of the campaign, it was just as well that the season had come to an end. At least, the respite would enable bones to heal and spirits to be recharged. Perhaps, every 'Whites' supporter hoped, the boys might be tempted to come back.

During the final weeks of the season an item appeared in the *Post*, which demonstrated that Trew-like sportsmanship was not necessarily the norm in Welsh rugby at that time. A writer hiding behind the pen-name, 'A Welshman', was, clearly, not happy with what he had seen on rugby fields of the Principality during the season. He wrote :

> The word sportsmanship ... denotes the ability to take a licking, or a victory in the proper spirit; it denotes the ability to be chivalrous towards opponents; also the ability to recognise and acclaim merit, even when that merit has been our undoing. The true sportsman is he who bears no malice when defeated in a fair fight; neither does he gloat over his own success.

Modern players and followers of the great old game might benefit from following the old teacher's direction regarding this piece; read and inwardly digest.

Meantime, in 1911, the Barbers' Federation was complaining that fewer men were coming to their shops each morning for a shave. It seemed that they were 'performing the operation themselves'. Clearly, at the time, the market being served by the tonsorial artistes was changing. Change was a word, too which would impact itself upon St. Helens in the not-too-distant future. Indeed, with the benefit of hindsight, it is possible to see in those changes, the beginnings of a decline in the majestic standards which had been enjoyed for so long by Swansea-ites. Yet, there were still some days of glory to enjoy before those changes really manifest themselves.

Chapter 10

AN INDIFFERENT SEASON

1911–12

THE SUMMER-LIKE WEATHER which enveloped Swansea at the beginning of September 1911 was hardly conducive to the playing of rugby football. At the time, there was much debate about the season starting too soon, with the forceful opinion being expressed in the press that 'the end of September was soon enough'. Gone, it seemed, were the days when 'Argus' and his cohorts could hardly wait for the season to start.

Nonetheless, as the new season approached, 'Freelance', who followed the fortunes of the 'Whites' on behalf of the *Post*, clearly felt the need to write an 'open letter' to the members of the Swansea team. In his letter he commented on the rumours which were circulating in the town to the effect that the 'Whites' were going to have a lean season.

Then, he urged them on:

> ... remember your recuperative powers and your inexhaustible supply of 'never say die spirit' ... in Dickie Owen, you have a skipper second only to Trew ... Now, boys, you have several home matches in succession before you meet the Cardiffians, and you must lose no time in settling down ...

Dickie Owen: the new captain.

It was a powerful message, clearly, written by someone who wore a 'White' heart on his sleeve. Criticise he might, but he did that with affection, whilst taking every opportunity to promote the Swansea cause *vis-a-vis* the eastern press. In that respect, at least, he was fiercely partisan.

In 'blazing weather', the opening match, against the League, finished, predictably, in a 'handsome victory' for the 'Whites'. However, Billy Trew did not appear in the game, and it was his absence which provoked a number of items in the press which focused upon the possible retirement of the great man. One, by 'An English Writer', put Trew's absence into perspective. He wrote:

> It was a pleasure to watch Trew play, and even when he was the chief cause of 'the side of your heart' being badly beaten, he compelled admiration for his quickness of conception and his supreme skill in execution ... Moreover, he is a splendid moral example ... He is a cunning player, but his cunning is of the intellectual order ... his guile is instinct with the spirit of the game.

Whilst, as the future was to show, Billy Trew had not, yet, played his final game for Swansea, comments like this reminded 'Whites' followers of the exceptional talent which they had had in their midst. They must have recognised, with some concern, that the time would come when the genius would finish playing. Meantime, the best that could be done would be to try to put off the evil day for as long as possible.

Meantime, 'Association' was growing in popularity, so much so, indeed, that the Welsh Rugby Union felt sufficiently threatened to issue a circular to its member clubs, to the effect that grants would be disallowed to those which permitted soccer to be played on their ground. At Swansea, since 4,000 people had watched a soccer match at Morriston, while 800 were at St. Helens, concern about the damage which the growth of soccer might do to rugby was very real. Apart from anything else, Billy Trew was needed in that respect, for, as yet, the 'Soccerites' had no such personality to grace their playing fields.

At St. Helens, whilst Bridgend and Aberavon were beaten in successive matches, the press, *en masse*, declared that Billy Trew was being badly missed; the Swansea team was not functioning as it had been when the former captain was at the helm. Not that this reflected badly on the new skipper, Dickie Owen. Yet, as the diminutive 'scrum worker' had said at the time of his appointment, 'I am no Billy Trew, but I shall do my level best'.

Frank Holbrook might have said the same thing, for he was picked in Trew's place for the early games. Whilst Holbrook strove hard, the general opinion was that he was more of a winger than an outside-half. At the end of the season his total of eighteen tries bore witness to the accuracy of that judgment. Nevertheless, the 'Whites' won their fifth match to record a perfect record up to that point in the season. Having in mind the pre-season gloom and doom, it was an encouraging start, yet, by the end of October, the depression had returned. Three matches had been lost in succession, and the club had dropped to fourth place in the Welsh Championship table.

At this news, the *Leader* expressed the feelings of all Swansea pessimists, when it reported: 'With veterans getting older and "star articles" dropping out, Swansea football is in the doldrums'. If that was true, and fewer people were inspired to pay their entrance fee to matches, then the club could face financial difficulties. As it was, there were a variety of other attractions which were emerging to claim what the economists call the 'disposable income' of the Swansea population. Nor was Soccer the only competitor for the entrance money to St. Helens. The Oxford Electric Theatre opened its doors in Union Street. It was, according to the advertisement in the press, 'The most luxurious and up-to-date picture theatre in the provinces'. Furthermore, two other cinemas which would be opened in Swansea in the near future, were planned. Together with the 'live' theatres in the town, these picture houses provided the citizens with a wide variety of entertainment possibilities.

When the Swansea players left all this behind to travel to the Midlands for their usual short tour, they did so with the club placed sixth out of eight in the Welsh Championship table. As they left Victoria Station of the London and North Western Railway, it was generally agreed that the party was at a 'low ebb'. Recognising this, F. E. Perkins must have done everything possible to help lift the spirits of the tourists. 'Several special compartments and a dining saloon', were made available for the party. Those who stood on the station platform as the Swansea men boarded the train would have noted the presence of certain luminaries in the party. Aubrey Smith, 'Gennie' Gordon and Billy Trew accompanied the players. Given what was to happen later, one wonders whether Billy Trew, a captive 'audience' for many hours for the prominent former-'Whites', found himself being persuaded to 'get his togs out again'?

Whatever was said to Trew during that journey, the players who represented Swansea in the opening match astounded the 'score or so' of supporters who accompanied them. In front of the largest Leicester 'gate' of the season, the men in white, playing their best football of the campaign, won by 16 points to 8. Dickie Owen was 'outstanding', whilst Jack Bancroft was 'on top of his game'. Given that Cambridge University were also beaten in the second match, the *Post* declared that the tour had been highly successful.

Jack Bancroft – a full-back 'on top of his game'.

On the return of the players to St. Helens, a strong Devonport side was the next to be beaten, though play in that game was confined almost entirely to the forwards. The Rev. Alban Davies was prominent throughout. After several defeats in succession, this victory, and the two which had preceded it, were welcomed, warmly, by the St. Helens faithful. They had cause for further celebration a few days later, when it was announced that Billy Trew would return to the side to face Cardiff. In the event, though, the former captain could only 'ease himself back into the game', in what proved to be a dull, pointless draw.

By the time Christmas came around, 'Whites' supporters needed further comfort. Games against Gloucester, Newport and Aberavon were described as 'dull' or 'dreary', whilst the press was of the opinion that the Swansea club was 'in a rut'. Injuries, absences, loss of form, and the fact that 'the skill is not there', were, all put forward as reasons for the problems which faced the club. Yet, as ever, the Christmas games provided cheer for the supporters. London Irish were beaten by 31 points to nil in a match refereed by Tom Harry (the appointed official did not turn up), and, on their annual visit, Watsonians were 'vanquished'. But then, in line with a developing theme of inconsistency, the side lost at Bristol.

Perhaps, as much as anything, the defeat at Bristol put the matter of Swansea's form into perspective. In two matches during the previous season, the West Country men had been soundly beaten, conceding sixty-four points in the process. Consequently, it seemed little wonder that, by the end of January, the 'Whites' found themselves bottom-but-one in the Welsh Championship table, whereupon the *Post* ceased to publish these placings. Yet, Billy Trew and Dickie Owen were, still, the half-backs in the Welsh international team versus Scotland, and Jack Bancroft and Ivor Morgan were also in the side. Whilst four men do not make a team, it was something of an enigma that a Swansea side which included four such giants should be playing so indifferently.

Meanwhile, reflecting his mercurial spirit, 'Freelance' was lamenting the fact that the 'Whites' had won only fifty per cent of the matches which they had played. Whether he was getting at the Swansea players or Welsh rugby men in general is not clear, but, then, he added:

> Footballers nowadays think but little about spectators, and their only set purpose appears to be to win games – whatever happens.

But, two weeks later, the *Post*-scribe was on top of the world again, for he could report on a 'delightful exhibition' by the Swansea team in a match against Leicester. The 'Tigers', always popular at St. Helens, attracted 6,000 spectators, who were treated to football 'as it was played in the old days'. The 'Whites' scored eight tries whilst conceding just one. In 'Freelance's' opinion, Cardiff, who were the next side to play the 'Whites', 'must be trembling in their boots'. In particular, he boasted, 'they would need to watch Trew, who had a hand in half the tries which were scored'.

Sadly, the Cardiff game, and that at Newport, were reported in most papers as being 'disagreeable'. The reports of both matches were littered with descriptions of 'fouling, hacking, and obstruction'. In one game 'fisticuffs were resorted to and, then, without interference from the referee'. Unhappily, in both matches, Swansea men were carried from the field, and in one game the 'Whites' were left with six forwards. It was hardly the rugby to bring the crowds back, and the W.R.U was concerned. As a result of frequent reports of a similar nature, the Union had set up a committee to investigate:

(i) how to purge the game of undesirable players?
(ii) how to abolish time-wasting? and
(iii) why clubs failed to deal adequately with violent players?

Present-day readers will recognise the agenda.

As the investigation continued, so did Swansea's indifferent season. At the beginning of March, only Abertillery and Penarth were below the 'Whites' in the Welsh table. Furthermore, while Llanelli had been beaten, the team lost to Devonport on the usual West Country tour. Morale was hardly at a high point as the 'Whites' travelled to Cardiff to play the first domestic match after their tour. Indeed, before the game, Swansea chins were on the ground, for the 'Blue and Blacks' had been in fine form during the period when the 'Whites' had been struggling. On the day of that match, the few Swansea supporters who took the train to the eastern port would, probably, have been rehearsing their excuses for defeat. Their favourites were, after all, tired after their tour. In the event, they need not have been concerned. With Billy Trew 'outstanding', the 'Taffsiders' were beaten by 11 points to 3. The result was a shot in the arm for the whole of Swansea, and the *Post*, in joining in the celebrations, argued that Trew had 'responded to criticism in a Cardiff paper that he was now "a back number" '. Not only had the great man shown his critics that that was not the case, the Swansea eight had dominated matters 'up front'.

Thereafter, the side seemed to take on a new lease of life. The Harlequins were beaten in a 'breathless' game in which Trew outplayed the exalted Adrian Stoop; the Barbarians were defeated by 12 points to 8 – and 'it should have been more', whilst young Jerram, at outside-half, had made 'a most auspicious débût'. Nonetheless, as the news of the demise of the 'Unsinkable' *Titanic* was carried in the papers (two Pontardawe men and a musician from Swansea were aboard), 'Freelance' had a sinking feeling about the 'All Whites'. He wrote:

> Few supporters will be sorry that rugby is practically at an end, for the form of the 'All Whites', generally speaking, has been much below what it should have been ... Football interest locally is practically dead.

Given that the formation of a professional soccer team in the town was now a practical certainty, the St. Helens administrators who read those words must have been filled with alarm. The 'Soccerites' argued that 'there was no reason why the two codes could not exist side-by-side'. However, football receipts at St. Helens that season had been lower than in recent years, and the club had lost £300 on its season's workings. Whatever the soccer men said, those at St. Helens recognised that the desertion of supporters to Association would exacerbate the problems which they faced. Picture theatres were not going to help either!

1912-13

A remarkable turn-around

For the sixth time in seven seasons, Billy Trew agreed to become captain. At the time he declared himself reluctant to undertake the responsibilities, but his colleagues must have persuaded him that only he could reverse the downward trend which was affecting the club. They needed Trew 'the Leader'.

Billy Trew – captain for the sixth time.

In addition to Trew, Edgar Morgan – who did not play during the previous campaign – agreed to come back. There were new men, too. Among them were Alf Thomas (Llandeilo), 'Dodger' Owen, and a winger called Waters. Furthermore, there was a pleasant surprise for the St. Helens officials when, during the month before the new season started, '£100 worth of season tickets were sold in a single day'. Given that Swansea Town professional soccer club had attracted a 'gate' of 8,000 (£153) at its opening game, that was encouraging news , indeed.

As far as the *Post* was concerned, its new 'Football Edition' set out to cater for both codes, and, in mid-September, carried action photographs from games at both grounds. The indistinct rugby scene was said to depict Oswald Jenkins carrying the ball away from a tackle, though his mother would have had some difficulty in recognising him.

At the end of the same month, the rugby men were bullish. Ten tries had been scored by the side in a match with Aberavon,and 'old time enthusiasm had gripped the crowd'. In particular, a movement started by A. L. Thomas and finished by Howel Lewis, had 'brought the house down'. Alf Thomas, who had 'demonstrated great skill during the game, scored twice and had a hand in three others'. Newcomer, Bob Shepherd, also scored a brace of tries.

The euphoria, however, was short-lived. Whilst the 'Whites' beat Gloucester by 15 points to 0, the *Leader* reported that 'none of the spectators went away pleased'. For its part, the *Post* felt that the supporters would have left the ground 'without hope of a victory over Cardiff next Saturday'.

At this distance, it would appear that, at the time, there were two recurring themes which illustrated the major concerns of 'Whites' watchers; the demand for open, running rugby (*viz.*, Swansea football), and the need to beat Cardiff. It seems that the very virility of the old borough was impaired or enhanced depending upon the results of games against the 'Taffsiders', whilst, only when 'the ball was given the air', were supporters really satisfied.

When the game against Cardiff was played, the 'Whites', even though they had seventy-five per cent of the play, 'scraped home' by a Jack Bancroft penalty. Nonetheless, it *was* a victory and, furthermore, Billy Trew had played his first match after illness. It seemed that the captain always dragged himself off his sick-bed to play in the east-west tussles. Had he appeared on one leg, it is likely that his mere presence would have inspired his men.

Newport was the next club to be beaten, in a match played in 'heavy fog and continuous rain'. Despite what were described as 'wretched conditions', the 'Whites' won through a dropped goal, scored in the last minute. Whilst the margin was narrow, given that the 'Usksiders' had defeated the South African tourists, the result was put into perspective for the St. Helens faithful. In that Rodney Parade match, the 'Whites' had adapted their game to the conditions far more effectively than the home side. Hollingdale, Alban Davies and Edgar Morgan were all prominent in what was described as a 'hard fight'.

Whilst that match was reported as having been played in fine spirit, the next game suffered by comparison. With the W.R.U. committee still talking about the 'rough play' problem, Swansea, at one stage, were reduced to twelve men. Indeed, during the match, four different outside-halves were used. First, after five minutes, W. J. Lewis was 'knocked out', before half-time, both Billy Trew and Tom Williams suffered the same fate, and, then, Alf Thomas played out the second period of the match in an unaccustomed role. Nevertheless, in keeping with the colour code familiar to all those who watched the early cowboy films in south Wales cinemas, the 'white hats' won by six points to nil. In doing so they had 'done the double over the Taffsiders'.

Prominent in the Swansea side that day was centre, W. A. Davies, a former Plymouth player. Davies, who had been a student at Exeter had received expenses whilst playing for Plymouth to the extent of 5*s*.6*d*. for train fare and 2*s*.6*d*. for meals. However, the English Union charged the player, along with a number of others, with 'receiving expenses in excess of the sum spent'. As a result, Willie Davies was suspended by that union, but appealed. The charge was puzzling, for Davies had retained documentation which established his innocence, yet the paranoia of the authorities needs to be considered in the context of events of the day. Willie's former club had gone out of existence because of financial difficulties, and 'certain irregularities' were said to have been uncovered. Given that a professional soccer club had been established in Plymouth nine years earlier, one can only assume that the English Union was hypersensitive about people being paid to play. W. A. Davies was but a pawn in that game.

Meanwhile, a letter was received at St. Helens from the secretary of the newly-formed Swansea Town Association club, requesting that St. Helens might be used for a soccer match (against Northampton). The 'Soccerites' were concerned that, since they did not have a grandstand of their own, if it rained, they might not be able to cover the guarantee required by the visiting club. Not surprisingly, if only because of the W.R.U. directive about the matter, the request was refused. No doubt, in the eyes of the committee, there was a much more practical reason for the refusal. Why support a potential competitor? What happened, of course, was that the response was seen by the soccer lobby as a 'negative reaction to a reasonable request'. Subsequently, there were hints that there were those who wished to make some capital out of the matter. Something of this came through in the report of the Vetch Field match by a writer called 'Ajax'. He wrote: 'If Swansea is to witness more games like this, rugby's decline will be more rapid than it is'.

Yet the 'Whites' could still demonstrate flair. In a match against United Services the side was in 'terrific form', with Owen and Trew 'controlling matters'. Unfortunately, Billy Trew hurt a leg in that match, and he, Owen, and three others were obliged to 'stand down' for the next game, which was against Llanelli. Thereafter, despite the fact that the selectors were forced to make numerous changes, the side remained unbeaten. Against Newport, for example, 'a glorious victory was won against tremendous odds'. It was, according to 'Freelance', 'the most magnificent performance for several seasons'. New outside-half, S. Jerram, was said to be a 'real find', and it was he who 'made the decisive break to open the Swansea scoring after a pointless first-half'. Billy Trew, who was back at centre, said that the youngster showed great promise.

By that stage in the season, remarkably, given their form of the previous campaign, the 'Whites' stood proudly at the top of the Welsh table. Their record read : P16, W13, L0, D3, F224, A53. That, the optimists argued, should give the upstart 'Soccerites' something to think about. And then, there was the matter of the touring South Africans – who were due to play at St. Helens on Boxing Day. Surely, the 'Whites' would beat them, too! Such was the restored confidence in the Swansea camp that, had they existed, banners declaring that the 'Whites' were champions of the world would have been brought out and dusted. As it was, such 'spring cleaning' took place in the minds of the optimists who loyally followed the rugby men in white. Even some of the pessimists were beginning to believe that a victory over the 'Colonials' was possible. After all, hadn't the Australians suffered such a fate four years earlier?

Came the day, and, once again, the Swansea team 'rose to the great occasion'. The South Africans, 'of grand physique and exceptional speed' were beaten by 3 points to nil. The winning try was scored by D. J. Thomas, who had a magnificent match. Trew was said to have been 'the general', whilst Tom and Frank Williams, and Howel Lewis were 'prominent throughout'. At half-back, Oswald Jenkins and Jerram underlined their potential by 'outplaying their counterparts'. 'Freelance', no doubt with one eye on the soccer lobby, declared that 'All Swansea should be proud of the fact that we beat the South Africans'. In fact, it wasn't only Swansea-ites who enjoyed the victory. According to the *Leader*, spectators came to St. Helens 'from all parts to see the game'. No doubt, 'all parts' were just as proud of the men in white as were the residents of the old Borough. And pride, was, indeed, a relevant emotion, for the 'Whites' had played for twenty minutes of the match with fourteen men, thus embellishing a memorable result with an overlay of heroism.

The heroes who represented Swansea that day were:

D. Williams; H. Lewis, W. J. Trew (Capt.), T. Williams and F. Williams; S. Jerram and O. Jenkins; D. J. Thomas, T. Morgan, E. Morgan, B. Williams, B. Hollingdale, G. Hayward, H. Moulton and G. Evans.

It is interesting to note that, whilst there were four men called Williams in the Swansea side and two Morgans', the tourists team contained four players named Morkel and three called Luyt. At least two sets of parents must have had great pride in that fact, particularly the Morkels. Indeed, between 1903 and 1928, ten members of that family gained Springbok colours, a record unlikely to be equalled.

Early in January, no doubt tired after their exertions before and after the Christmas period, the 'Whites' drew 'a disappointing match' with Aberavon. Nonetheless, in twelve days, the side had beaten Newport, Watsonians, South Africa, and Neath and had drawn with the Port Talbot side. In the process, they had scored thirty-five points without conceding one. As a result, the word 'invincible' began to creep into the vocabulary of supporters, and committeeman, 'Gennie' Gordon, must have wondered whether the record set by his famous side was going to be equalled during the present campaign. Sadly, those who harboured such thoughts were to be disappointed.

In mid-January the unbeaten 'Whites' were forced to take a break from competitive football. Rain was the culprit. Even Swansea, traditionally imbued with an intimate familiarity with water from the sky, was astounded as an inch of rain fell on the town in one night. One result of this, was to flood the normally fast-drying St. Helens playing area. A match had to be postponed, and the committee called in a surveyor to establish whether the drains below the playing surface had become blocked.

Whether it was because of that enforced rest, or the effects of a gruelling first-half season programme, when they resumed, the 'Whites' lost their unbeaten record in the first match they played. According to the Swansea press, Swansea 'played their poorest game of the season', and 'performed like a second-class side'. Newport , who were the opponents, 'raised their game' to win in convincing fashion. 'Freelance', no doubt expressing rehearsed sentiment, wrote: 'Personally, I don't think that the Swansea players are sorry to see the back of the record ... (they were) tired of the continual strain'. The *Western Mail*, however, presumably reflecting eastern sentiment, opined that 'The wonder is not that they (Swansea) lost the record, but how they were able to keep the precious thing so long with a comparatively ordinary team'. Whilst Swansea lips would have curled at such a comment, the truth was that a combination of Billy Trew's remarkable qualities of leadership plus the fact that Welsh football as a whole was at a low ebb, had resulted in the 'Whites' being the best of an indifferent lot. Qualitative comparisons drawn with Swansea sides of old would have resulted in the conclusion that there was some truth in the eastern barb. Nonetheless, say what they might, any team can only beat those of its contemporaries. It was not the fault of the Swansea players that the game at the time was 'in the doldrums'. Furthermore, the 'Whites', still led the Championship table, *and* South Africa had been defeated. It was also true, in quantitative terms, that when the season ended, the club had lost fewer games during the campaign than in all but three of the previous seasons in its history. Given the position from which Trew and his men started, that was a remarkable record!

As far as the supporters were concerned, they could, also, point to the fact that in twenty-four of the matches played over the season, the opposition had failed to score a single point. In addition, the potential of the new half-back pairing of 'Dodger' Owen and Jerram was to be relished. So confident were they about these young men that they were being compared with gods like the Brothers James, and the 'Dancing Dicks'. Then, Billy Trew, Alban Davies, Jack Bancroft, Howel Lewis, Tom Williams, Bryn Lewis and Bert Hollingdale, had all been 'capped' during the recent season. Which other club, they might have asked, could boast such representation?

On the commercial front, whilst some opponents had attracted large 'gates' at St. Helens, considering that the Championship had been won by the 'Whites', the crowds drawn to the 'Cricket Field' had not been as large as of yore. Numbers attending soccer games at the Vetch had risen in line with the success of the soccer side. Ten thousand, for example, were there to see an Easter game, equalling the number at St. Helens. Since the 'Swans' had won the Welsh Cup in the first season of their existence, interest in the town in the round ball game had been further stimulated. One reaction to this was exemplified by a comment from 'Freelance'. 'What Welsh rugby needs is its own cup competition (last won by the 'Whites' in 1887), to keep up interest right to the end of the season'. If the coverage of the soccer cup games in the local press was anything to go by, there was a great deal to be said for the *Post*-man's argument!

Meantime, at the Caernarvon Hotel, Swansea Football Club held a 'Swansea Rugby Smoker', to celebrate the winning of the Welsh Championship. An unnamed Swansea jeweller must have been delighted with one aspect of that 'enjoyable function', for twenty-two players were each presented with a 'handsome black marble and bronze clock and two equestrian ornaments to match'. Whilst all this was a far cry from the recherché banquets of the 'Golden Years', D. J. Thomas, the captain for the season ahead, must have wondered how he was going to follow such success. He, as much as anyone, would have recognised the wonders which had been performed, with limited resources, by Billy Trew. But, D.J. was not one to shirk a challenge. The new captain, like his predecessor, was keen on 'all matters to do with physical fitness', and, among other things, he was an advocate of a good night's sleep. For that reason, he must have hoped that none of his new charges saw a 'small ad' which appeared in the *Post* around the time of that Smoker. 'For sale', it announced 'a box mattress and a good banjo'. In certain cases, he might have thought, the temptation to play the banjo might have outweighed the desire to sleep.

1913–14

The curtain comes down

Before the 'opener' with the League, Billy Trew stated that he had 'definitely retired'. Injuries and *anno domini* had combined, he said, to 'bring him to the decision'. There was another factor, too, though unspoken at the time. Trew felt that, in young Jerram, the 'Whites' had an outside-half of unusual promise. Sadly, towards the end of September, Trew and the St. Helens club were both rocked by the rumour that Jerram and his partner, 'Dodger' Owen, were going north. On the 28th of the month, rumour became reality. A Wigan representative met the pair at the Bush Hotel and, after they had agreed to sign, a draft was wired to a Swansea bank. In turn, that draft was exchanged for gold sovereigns to the value of £180 for each player, whilst each was given a job, £2 per week, cash, and bonuses for wins and draws. At 11.30 they were Wigan men, and left soon after for the Lancashire town.

There followed a run of three 'lacklustre' matches before United Services were beaten by 'rugby at its best'. Then, with Billy Trew answering the call yet again, Devonport Albions were 'overwhelmed' by 18 points to 3. That day, when Trew appeared, the crowd gave him a warm welcome, and, whatever doubts he might have had about reversing his 'retirement' decision must have been submerged beneath the euphoria of the day. 'Freelance' spotted another factor in the chemistry of the two wins: 'There is no team,' he stated, 'which sticks together with splendid camaraderie as much as Swansea'.

Two weeks later, when the 'Whites' had lost their unbeaten record at Gloucester, the *Post* man was arguing that the team needed to be strengthened. Whilst he conceded that the 'Whites' had had to play the bulk of the match with fourteen men, he thought that the performance had been poor. Seven days later he was congratulating the team on a 'splendid victory' over Llanelli; it was, he stated, a performance which was one hundred per cent better than the previous match. By mid-November, the gloom had descended again. 'Not once,' he complained, 'during the last three games have the "Whites" crossed the opponents' try line!' The ringing tone of his report was little short of an indictment. Furthermore, Billy Trew had been injured again.

By the end of November, when the 'Taffsiders' came to play at St. Helens, gloominess had permeated both Swansea papers. For its part, the *Western Mail* stated that it 'would be most surprised if Cardiff failed to beat the very moderate Swansea side'. Unhappily for the 'Taffsiders', the jibe resulted in the fifteen Swansea men being highly motivated. The pack was outstanding. Indeed, such was their domination of the Cardiff eight, that the *Leader* was carried away to the extent of stating that they were, probably, the best pack in Wales. The upshot was that Swansea beat their eastern rivals by 8 points to nil. In the process, another young inside-half came to the fore. He was 'Tit' Davies. Davies was joined by his namesake, John, who hailed from Pontarddulais, and who played a 'fine game at full-back'. 'Freelance' in heralding the victory, noted that it was 'surprising how a period of adversity makes us appreciate our success even more when it comes along'.

In the interim, Sir J. T. D. Llewellyn had been to the Vetch Field to see an English Cup game against Cardiff City. Whilst he stated that he had enjoyed the match 'immensely', he confirmed that he was still a rugby man at heart. Nonetheless, no doubt with an eye to diplomatic *entente* between the two codes, he said that he would be glad to see soccer played at St. Helens for the more important games. Llewellyn was, of course, a Trustee of the St. Helens lease, and thus, had influence with the club there. However, given the position of the W.R.U. with regard to soccer, if his invitation was genuine, then it would not be unreasonable to assume that he had influence in the corridors of rugby power as well.

In December there was a further defection to the north. George Hayward – the heaviest footballer in Wales (15 stones, 2lbs) signed for Wigan, thus joining Jerram and Owen. The player received £150 in gold, together with a job and the usual bonuses. When he signed it was another blow for the 'Whites'. Not only was Hayward a key member of the side, he also served on the selection committee. 'Freelance' was in despair. The Northern Union was the biggest culprit in damaging the chances of the 'Whites', though it appeared that Oxford University wasn't much better. They had 'taken' Oswald Jenkins. With 15,000 at the Vetch Field for a cup match and 'gates' dwindling at St. Helens, 'Freelance' was in a trough of despond. Unless a miracle happened, he could foresee disaster for the club. Fortunately, it did not take a miracle to lift his spirits; the Christmas matches came along with their traditional running rugby and appropriate excitement. London Irish conceded twenty-four points, with Owen Jenkins, Tom Parker and Alf Thomas in 'fine fettle', and Neath were beaten. Nevertheless, at the turn of the year, the 'Whites' were still sixth in the Welsh Championship table. Only Cardiff and Llanelli were below them. Amazingly, given this position, only five matches had been lost by the club out of nineteen played; nonetheless, morale at the club was at a low ebb. It was damaged further, when the men from the north struck again: 'Tit' Davies joined Dewsbury for £100. Whilst Davies (10 stones and 5'4") had not established himself as a regular in the first team, he was thought ~~to~~ have genuine promise. Now, that promise was gone.

As the gloom settled upon St. Helens, so interest increased at the Vetch Field. For the second season in succession, the soccer men were making progress in the English Cup. Such was the interest which this aroused in the town, that 'Ajax', the *Post*'s soccer correspondent, felt moved to draw comparison with the 'Whites' greatest years. He wrote: 'As Swansea men we are proud to think that we once possessed the finest rugby club in the world, and we are equally proud of the Swans'. As far as the 'Whites' were concerned, it was something of a left-handed compliment. Whilst they wished the local soccer club well in a sporting sense, to speak of the rugby club in the past tense as far as greatness was concerned, was hardly welcome.

Stung by this and other criticism – 'Ajax' was not the only journalist who was being less than complimentary to the St. Helens men – the 'Whites' went to Llanelli with a 'weak side' and won a 'thrilling match'. As it happened, two men played in that game who had, or would have, a connection with Swansea soccer. The Rev. W. T. Havard had played as an amateur for Swansea Town reserves in the club's first-ever game. Consequently, there was controversy about his inclusion in the Llanelli side, for the W.R.U. ruling stated that: 'Anyone who turns out for a professional soccer team cannot afterwards play for an amateur rugby club'. Somehow, Havard, who was later to be 'capped' by Wales at rugby, and become the Bishop of St. Asaph, was allowed to play in contravention of that rule. The other versatile ball player who was involved in that game, was Swansea's outside-half, Ben Beynon, who was making his début for the 'Whites'. Beynon, it was, who was to play for Swansea Town during the 1914-15 season following the cessation of rugby at the outbreak of the Great War. He, too, was to become a Welsh international rugby player.

Late in January 1914 when Newport came to play at St. Helens, there were 8,000 people present. It was a mark of the decline in rugby attendances that, when the two sides competed for the Welsh Championship season after season, 20,000 would find their way to the Cricket Ground. However, according to the *Leader*, those who came 'saw rugby at its best'. 'Freelance', no doubt stung by the language of his colleague 'Ajax', was delighted to be able to write: '... if only teams would play like that, soccer would have to take a back seat'. Whilst the 'Whites' had won by the relatively small margin of 12 points to nil, what had thrilled the crowd was the fact that the match was played 'in the old-time way'. Ben Beynon, the young Manselton boy, was a revelation at outside-half. According to the *Post*, 'he beat all the Newport backs (to score the first try), without a finger being laid on him'. Jim Rapsey, too, was reported as having had a great game at the base of the scrum, whilst Tom Williams and Jack Bancroft 'also excelled'.

After a 'sweeping victory' over Leicester, 'Freelance' was moved to poetic prose: 'The clouds are rolling away and the silver lining is showing', was hardly the language of an objective commentator. Yet, as far as the loyal Swansea rugby supporters were concerned, it more than filled the bill. The name Ben Beynon was on many lips, and the inevitable comparisons were being drawn with the gods of old. But thoughtless burdens are placed on the shoulders of promising players by anxious supporters who long for a virtual reincarnation of some former playing genius. Their memories of players of the past are of brilliant consistency in every match. Apart from the fact that even the greatest gods had indifferent days, young players tend to be inconsistent as they begin to 'learn their trade'. Beynon was no different.

There followed 'dull matches' in the mud at both Cardiff and Newport, plus the annual tour to the West Country. Since the Devonport Albions match was lost on that tour, 'Freelance' searched for reasons. The men, he thought, were feeling the effects of too much touring. Furthermore, whilst the club had been travelling to Devon for many years, at the time he was writing, circumstances were somewhat different. Some of the players, it seemed, were finding it difficult to get time off from work to go on the tours. As a result, he noted that more than half the Swansea party could not leave Swansea until early evening on the Friday, and arrived at Plymouth in the early hours of Saturday morning. It was hardly the best preparation for an important match. Unhappily, there was also a casualty in that first game; Jack Bancroft broke a rib after five minutes, and was said to be unlikely to play again that season.

When the 'Whites' returned to play domestic football, it was as though 'Freelance's' analogy about clouds and silver linings was being enacted. Gloucester were 'swamped', Cardiff 'outplayed', and the Scarlets 'well-beaten', by a Swansea side playing flowing football. With Ben Beynon feeding his back line superbly, two other young men came to the fore during that period. Bryn Lewis scored eight tries in three consecutive matches, whilst C. B. Davies showed himself to be a 'player with a future'. Billy Trew, if we are to accept the atmosphere generated by the Swansea rugby press as a guide , could now hang up his 'togs' with equanimity.

As far as 'Freelance' was concerned, he was euphoric. After Cardiff had been beaten (by 'the biggest margin for six years'), he wrote: 'Swansea rugby enthusiasts are very sorry that the season is drawing so rapidly to a close ... the "All Whites" are playing really clever football'. Two weeks later, he was arguing that 'Swansea rugby cannot be in a bad state when two totally different fifteens can be fielded, strong enough to score wins over sides like Harlequins and Northampton'. Whilst acknowledging that those wins had been 'achieved by hard and determined football rather than by flair and skill'; no Swansea supporter was prepared to argue with his conclusion. As ever, hope beats eternal in the breast of the ardent football fan.

Notwithstanding 'Freelance's' euphoria, when the curtain came down on the campaign, captain D. J. Thomas must have been reasonably pleased with the season's outcome. Apart from anything else, rugby supporters have relatively short memories, and in the forefront of their minds would have been the fine performances of the last month of the campaign. Furthermore, they had new, young stars to contemplate, in the process enhancing their skills and ignoring their weaknesses. All in all, for those who loved the 'Whites', things must have looked promising for the future.

Unhappily, the arrival of that future for rugby football, was postponed by an event which happened in a place called Sarajevo. An Archduke, called Ferdinand, was assassinated, and thus was sparked off what British politicians called, 'The War to end wars'. Whilst it did not do that, it did end rugby, 'for the duration'. St. Helens supporters were to have to wait for five years before the club resumed its activities. By then, much would have changed. Apart from anything else, the umbilical cord which connected the Swansea rugby team to its eminent predecessors would have been all but severed.

Chapter 11

OVERTURE AND BEGINNERS

1919-20

WITH KAISER BILL DEFEATED, and the Great War ended, the people of Swansea could turn, once more, to matters sporting. They now had two football codes to follow. Professional soccer had established itself as a mass interest sport during the first year of the war, so the St. Helens authorities recognised that they had competition. Thus it was that, in August 1919, they advertised a 'Great Victory Football Match' against the District League. This match, according to the *Leader*, would be different from those of previous years. In the first-half the 'Whites' would play the selected League side, but in the second period the Swansea backs would play behind the League pack, and *vice versa*.

In the event, the match proved to be something of a damp squib, for, even though the 'Whites' won comfortably, the *Post* reported that there was 'nothing superlative about the football'. Furthermore, there were other concerns. The match had been sparsely attended, whilst ten thousand were said to have been at the Vetch Field. With strong rumours circulating that the town's 'Soccerites' were to become members of the English League, the rugby men knew that the Vetch Field counter-attraction might well become even more of a problem for the St. Helens treasury.

Nevertheless, a rugby man through-and-through, the new captain, Howell Lewis, was 'quietly confident' about the season ahead. Lewis, who had been wounded in France, must have viewed whatever problems he faced with an equanimity forged in the killing fields of Ypres and Passchendaele. In that light, important as it was, rugby *was* only a game. Nonetheless, as time went on, in their fervent desire to recapture the great footballing days of the Golden Era, Swansea rugby supporters were to forget the horrors of war. Indeed, at the time, had Lord Haig been available to assist the Swansea committee in its recruiting drive for new players, the famous pointing finger and full moustache might have been immortalised in a different setting.

However, the general opinion was that some of the footballers who donned the white jersey in those early months after the War, would not have been out of place in teams populated by the giants of earlier years. Among them were Billy Bowen, Benny Beynon (back from his sojourn with soccer), A. E. Jenkins, and D. J. Grey, and these men did well in the 'missionary' at Treherbert. On that occasion, four Swansea tries were scored in what the *Post* called a 'smart programme'. The game had produced, announced the paper, 'the kind of play to bring the crowds back'. When Bridgend were 'trounced' in the next match, it appeared that the Swansea club had the raw material upon which to build a successful season, and St. Helens smiles were beginning to re-appear. The brothers Parker were among the stars of that game, though, in the press, the backs were given most of the glory. The *Western Mail*, however, felt that the team as a whole 'was beginning to strike the right note'.

A week later, a sad note was struck in Swansea. The town's beloved Madame Patti had died at her 'Craig-y-Nos' home. In the not too distant future, her death was to result in a new landmark being erected adjacent to St. Helens: the Patti Pavilion.

As the first month of the season came to an end, the worst fears of the rugby fraternity seemed to have been ill-founded. Ten thousand people were 'thrilled by end-to-end football' at Stradey, and whilst the 'Scarlets' were the victors, as a result of a try three minutes from the end of the game, excitement had been the order of the day. The *Post*, figuratively smacking its lips, reported , 'the man who said that rugby was a dead letter would have had an eye-opener had he seen this contest'. During that game, Benny Beynon scored a 'dashing try' for the 'Whites', whilst fellow pre-war Swansea player, Jack Bancroft converted it.

In the following week the club's fixture list was disrupted as a result of a rail strike. Instead of travelling to Pontypool, the side met Briton Ferry in a match in which 'Freelance' thought the 'Whites' took things too easily. By mid-October, with a match against Cardiff scheduled, the *Post* felt that there was 'an air of undue optimism about the Swansea camp'. If that was true, then that confidence proved to be unfounded, as the 'Blue and Blacks' won a 'dour game'. Since only six thousand people attended the match, the defeat gave the St. Helens men plenty to think about. For example, in pre-war days, at least twice the 'Gate' would have been expected. Then, those who came 'saw a dull and lifeless display by the 'Whites' ... (they) played as if they had never seen each other before'. Only Benny Beynon, Joe Rees, and Tom Parker were singled out as being above criticism.

When the 'Scarlets' took the next match at St. Helens – their first victory there for twenty-three years – the 'Whites' found themselves in the lower regions of the 'Unofficial Table'. The confidence which had preceded the Cardiff match had all but evaporated, and Swansea supporters must have wondered what lay ahead?

But then, in keeping with its developing character of inconsistency, the team took Gloucester's unbeaten record in what the *Leader* called 'its best display of the season'. Benny Beynon was outstanding that day, whilst the forwards were said to have been 'in charge throughout'. Thereafter, matters improved somewhat, and, after ten matches had been played, Swansea stood in fourth position in the 'Table'. The popular Leicester club, who were paying their first visit to St. Helens since the outbreak of war, were the next visitors, and were warmly welcomed. The *Post* reported that the '"Tigers" had played a fine open game, and that it was a great pity that we have to see an English club opposed to a Welsh one before we can get a game played in such a sporting fashion'. At one stage, during this exciting match, it looked as though Leicester were going to become the first English club to win at St. Helens for two decades. Benny Beynon, however, had other ideas. With just ten minutes to go, the outside-half dropped a fine goal to clinch the match for the homesters. This was the kind of football which 'Whites' – watchers were longing to see!

By the end of November, with Beynon, Joe Rees, Trevor Davies and the Parker brothers in fine form, the 'Whites' had moved up to third position in the 'Table', and things looked much brighter for the St. Helens faithful. Then came December, which provided them with a veritable curate's egg of performances. The lowest point in this series of games came on Christmas Day, when the traditional Scottish visitors, Watsonians, 'licked Swansea'. Never before had the

Scots won the Yule-tide fixture, and, before the end of the game, 'hundreds of spectators left the ground disgusted with the feeble play of the "All Whites"'. Given that the Watsonians game had traditionally involved the homesters playing bright, open (winning) football, the defeat and its manner were particularly damaging to the Swansea rugby cause.

Whilst Neath were beaten in the next match, the 'Whites' had missed a golden opportunity to woo the marginal supporters, who, by then, were alternating between St. Helens and the Vetch. Furthermore, the position was further exacerbated when defeats were suffered in the next two games. According to the *Post*, the second of those defeats was 'one of the worst performances in the history of the club'.

Notwithstanding the club's indifferent results, when Wales played England at St. Helens, Joe Rees, Benny Beynon and Tom Parker wore the red jersey. It was a welcome boost to the club's morale. Conversely, captain, Howell Lewis was finding the game to be physically taxing. It was said that, when he played, he gave his all in every game. However, his war wounds were affecting him adversely, and this had resulted in the popular skipper missing many matches.

Whilst one star was missing from the St. Helens firmament, the papers carried the news that an astronomer believed that 'certain phenomena in the heavens are due to efforts to convey messages from Mars'. Whilst this was dismissed by a 'Swansea astronomical student' as 'a lot of rot', St. Helens officials would have been delighted to learn that the distant planet could offer them big, athletic forwards and tricky, speedy backs. Meanwhile, the man on the Mumbles train was of the opinion that those heavenly disturbances, including, storms, clouds, and heavy rain, could be attributed to the firing of guns in the Great War.

At St. Helens, at this time, a different storm was brewing. Faced with injuries and indifferent form, the Swansea selectors had turned to clubs in the District League for new recruits. The League officials, however, were 'up in arms' about the manner in which the junior clubs had been approached. It seemed that, on one occasion, the 'Whites' had taken three players from one club 'only hours before a game was due to be played'. Not surprisingly, this left the donor club in some difficulty with regard to its own fixture. As a result of this and other experiences, the League men wanted to agree a system whereby the 'Whites' would give a junior club at least three days' notice of their need for a player. Furthermore, that they would not take more than one player from a particular club. Whilst the St. Helens men could only agree that the requests were reasonable, the actions which had given rise to the controversy had, on one occasion at least, arisen out of virtual desperation.

In February, with the west Wales members of the Welsh selection committee unable to get to the meeting to choose the side to play France, Benny Beynon was dropped. Since the consensus of opinion following the previous international had been that the player was the best half-back on view, there was a feeling in the west that he had been left out of the side as a result of eastern bias. It was reported that Beynon was very disappointed by the news, and that he had confided in 'Freelance' that he was going to give up rugby and rejoin Swansea Town as a professional. 'Pendragon' denied this story, and reported that Beynon had told him 'It is absolute lies'. Two days later, Beynon left St. Helens and signed for the Vetch men. He'd gone east rather than north and, then, by little more than a mile. Given that the player was a key figure in the 'Whites' team at that time, it was a blow which the rugby men could have done without. There was irony, too. A *Post* photograph showed Dick Jones sitting in the Vetch Field stand watching Beynon's professional début. Was nothing sacred?

Paradoxically, Beynon's defection seemed to act as a spur to the rest of the side. Neath were beaten, with Tom Parker 'in *excelsis*' for the 'Whites', Cardiff lost at St. Helens, and the team gained a ' sensational win' over Newport. Since the 'Amber and Blackings' had been undefeated prior to that match, the *Post* declared that 'the result was a surprise to the Swansea team as well as its supporters'. Yet , other than the treasurer, no Swansea man was concerned about that. As the money man counted the day's takings he would have reflected on the fact that, at the kick-off, there were 'only about a thousand standing on the cheapside'.

Yet, the St. Helens authorities would have recognised that it takes time to win back back-sliders. And, at least, there was some encouragement in that regard, when Dick Huxtable, Joe Rees, and Tom Parker were included in the side to play for Wales against France. All Swansea would have recognised that the Welsh selectors had confirmed the quality which remained in the St. Helens side. As it happened, each of the three 'capped' on that occasion was to become captain of the Swansea club during the seasons immediately ahead. A decade later, Rowe Harding was to pay homage to two of them when he wrote:

> The leader of the (Welsh) pack was Tom Parker, of Swansea, a great personality with the countenance and figure of a knight of the Crusades ... representing the best type of Welsh athletic manhood. He captained Wales seven times without defeat, a fine record in a lean period.

Tom Parker.

And ...

> Joe Rees is, I think, unquestionably the best post-war full-back. His kicking was never of great length, but it was accurate, and that ... was particularly noticeable under bad conditions ... His defence was little short of miraculous ... Best of all his tackling. Until he damaged his knee, I did not see him being beaten more than once in as many seasons.

This was praise, indeed, for two outstanding 'All Whites'.

A highlight of the last weeks of that first post-war season, was the defeat on their own pitch of what was described by the *Times* as a 'poor Richmond side'. Apart from the extent of the victory (twenty-five points to six), the match was remarkable in that the home side included two Japanese players in their line-up, each of whom was 'given a soft try'. At the time, no one could have contemplated a Japanese international XV playing Wales in a full international. When that happened, the giving of soft tries to the men from the east was not on the agenda.

As Swansea supporters considered the campaign which had finished, and contemplated the season which was to follow, they must have wondered how they would fare without the two leading scorers from the 1919-20 season. Howell Lewis retired on health grounds, whilst Benny Beynon was beyond the pale. Indeed, such was the bigotry of the Welsh Union with respect to

Beynon, that they refused to present him with his caps for the two matches which he had played for his country. And, at that time, he had never played a game of Rugby League. His crime was to play professional soccer before being presented with the caps which he had won.

1920-21

An open commitment

The new Swansea skipper for the 1920-21 campaign was, already the captain of his country's XV. Tom Parker, so eloquently described by Rowe Harding, was a man who led by example. At the end of his season as Swansea captain, he could point to the fact that his men had improved upon the performance of the previous campaign. Much of that improvement could be put down to his leadership. However, according to the *Leader*, at the end of July, when the club held its annual picnic at Llangennith, the 'question of the captaincy had not been discussed'. Nonetheless, when the announcement was made, no one was surprised. Parker's selection had been an open secret.

Despite the competition from Association, before the season started, the club was delighted to announce that it had enrolled more than a thousand members. With stand seasons at £1 (10*s*. for ladies), and 3*s*. for boys, the income provided a welcome boost for club funds. Furthermore, it did no harm to the rugby cause to let the town (and the 'Soccerites') know that 'the old game' was attracting considerable support. In addition, a spokesman for the club let it be known that 'Swansea rugby team intend leaving nothing to chance this season ... it is the intention of the players and the committee to see that spectators at St. Helens are treated to really excellent football'. Unequivocal it might have been, yet, with Swansea Town now ensconced in the English League, and the soccer game attracting much interest, it was essential that the rugby men should use every weapon in their armoury to maintain the game's position in the footballing hierarchy. Whilst the term P.R. had not been coined at the time, the announcement was an example of that 'art'. Nonetheless, as the rugby men would have realised, making the statement was not without its risks. As modern Marketing theorists have it, to maintain or improve your market position it is necessary to *deliver your promises*. Swansea rugby team would need to do just that in the season ahead.

After the 'opener' against the League, confidence was high at St. Helens. In his comments on that game 'Freelance' pinned his colours to the mast. 'Two things were very evident to all spectators', he wrote, 'the team is going to be a power in Welsh football this season ... and (there is) magnificent reserve material in the Swansea and District League'.

When Treherbert were beaten in the next match, the *Post* man's statements seemed to have substance. The *Leader* in its report, stated that the 'Whites' were 'brilliant against mediocre opposition'. Among the brilliant were Joe Rees, Billy Bowen, Willie Griffiths and Tom Williams, Yet in the first games against senior opposition that brilliance was somewhat tarnished. Cross Keys and Bridgend both beat the 'Whites', following which, the *Post*, no doubt swallowing hard, announced, 'Swansea have flattered to deceive'. Furthermore, the telling statistic that Bridgend had never before won at St. Helens, rather rubbed salt into the wound. In that match it seemed that 'the 'Whites' had never shaped like winning'. Tom Parker must have wondered what was going wrong?

By the beginning of October, 'Freelance' was subdued. Whilst Bath had been beaten at St. Helens, the *Post*-man wrote of 'scraping home by a single point', and, no doubt with the pre-season promise in mind, 'the manner of the victory did not at all please supporters'. It was as well that the 'Soccerites' were also finding life to be challenging. Then, in following a pattern which was to become familiar to 'Whites' followers in seasons to come, the Swansea men surprised the pundits. The *Post*, seizing the opportunity to be positive, trumpeted, '"All Whites" glorious victory at Cardiff'. Bert Palmer scored a fine try that day, whilst Billy Bowen 'dropped two outstanding goals'. For their part, the 'Taffsiders' only managed to score a penalty, though 'a tremendous Joe Rees tackle on a Cardiff man twice his size', ensured that the Swansea try line was not crossed.

In the week before that Cardiff victory, a property changed hands in Swansea which had historic connections with the St. Helens club. The Tenby Hotel, where F. F. Meager had first hatched his plot to make the 'All Whites' a rugby rather than a soccer club, was purchased by Swansea's Conservatives as their headquarters. No one, it seemed, enquired whether the new owners would erect a plaque to record the momentous event.

Back at St. Helens, the visit of Plymouth Albion provided the next fillip for 'Whites'-watchers. In a match which was won by 24 points to 3, it was reported that 'Swansea swung the ball about with delightful abandon'. Accompanying that *Post* report was a photograph entitled 'Hero Worship'. It showed Swansea players going out onto the field through a crowd of spectators. Small boys and old men alike, gazed with admiration at their favourites. Those feelings must have been enhanced when the teams left the field. Tudor Williams and Billy Bowen were reported as having had a 'day out' during that match. Once again, the lively half-back pairing evoked comparison with the famous 'Whites' halves of old. But, like many before and after them, the young men were to find that such comparisons were onerous.

In January, outside-half Billy Bowen joined Tom Parker and Joe Rees in the Welsh side to play Scotland, and the 'Whites' came very near to taking Newport's unbeaten record. After that match, a Newport player told the *Daily Chronicle* that 'Newport had a desperate struggle against Swansea ... (who) were constantly putting pressure on the 'Black and Ambers'. If they are kept together, they should, before long, reach the old Swansea standard'. On reading that, skipper Parker might have allowed himself a godlike smile. Indeed, since the 'Whites' had not been beaten in the previous eight matches, few would have criticised him had he beamed with delight. But then, Parker was aware of the inconsistency which had bedevilled the side earlier in the season. Just in case he had forgotten, his team lost the next match at Aberavon.

As new houses were being built for the 'Garden City' of Townhill, Wales took on Scotland at St. Helens. Unfortunately, the arrangements made by the W.R.U. for dealing with the crowd at that game proved to be inadequate. The Welsh Secretary, Walter Rees, had assumed that there would be a 'gate' of 35,000 people at the match, and his arrangements were made with that number in mind. In the event, more than 60,000 turned up and were packed into every corner of the ground. Inevitably, as the game progressed, the crowd surged, and, in the second half, hundreds spilled onto the pitch and play was suspended. Furthermore, the *South Wales Daily News*, among others, reported 'discreditable features', which included drunken behaviour and foul language by 'a minority'. The game, according to the *Post*, 'was absolutely spoiled'. Wales lost. Whilst the St. Helens authorities could not be blamed for what had happened – the W.R.U.

were in charge of the arrangements – the events were to prove to be an early nail in the coffin of the Cricket Field as an international venue. Although gate receipts of £4,800 taken that day beat an earlier Cardiff record by £800, the eastern press was reported to be 'bowling for all international rugby to be played at Cardiff in the future'. Eastern hammers were, once more, driving at the wedge which had been placed beneath the door marked, 'equal allocation for east and west'.

Back at St. Helens, the club, once again, showed its concern for the community when the committee resolved to give the whole of the proceeds of a match with Bristol to the Mayor's Unemployment Fund. Club members were asked to pay for admission to that match in order 'to swell the fund to help relieve the distress brought about by the depression in trade'. The public response was tremendous, and twelve thousand people attended the match, where they saw both teams playing open rugby. The 'Whites' won an exciting game by thirteen points to nil and the Mayor's fund and the image of rugby in the town were boosted by the event.

In March, despite the fact that, early in the match, W. Hopkins broke his leg in two places, Neath were 'well-beaten', then, in 'terrible conditions, Cardiff were trounced'. A feature of that match with the 'Taffsiders' was Trevor Davies's 'braininess'. The 'Whites' won by seventeen points to nil. Before the end of the campaign, Gloucester 'lost to marauding Swansea', and the St. Helens men won their first match 'on the new Bath enclosure'. At that stage unbeaten in thirteen games, the side travelled to Newport to take on the most powerful side of the day. After that game, a Newport official was reported as having said:

> Swansea were near to a brilliant win today ... their display stamped them as a really clever fifteen ... a side which, next season, if they continue to improve, ... should sweep the whole of Wales. They are the best all round side to visit Newport this season.

Since the 'Whites' played with just fourteen men for three-quarters of that match, that was praise, indeed. Tom Parker, the Swansea committee, and their loyal supporters must have felt more confident than they had dared hope they might be at the beginning of the campaign. Certainly, despite early inconsistency, the team had served the rugby cause in Swansea extremely well.

For his part, Bob Dowdle was 'bemused'. It seemed that there had been 'complaints from certain quarters' about him leaving the Field before games ended. Yet, as he explained, he had to go to the baths to 'make preparations for the players' after-match soak'. Not only was Dowdle responsible for physical fitness training, and for carrying the 'magic sponge', he had to tend fires and lay out towels as well. Swansea, like many other clubs, has always relied on such dedicated service.

The season's statistics demonstrated more evident signs of service. Tom Parker had captained Wales as well as Swansea, Tudor Williams and Billy Bowen were the Welsh halves versus France, and Joe Rees played against all four 'home' countries. Together with the side's performance in the second-half of the season, the 'caps' provided the St. Helens men with a warm glow. Thus it was that another season beckoned with hope and excitement, and with the possibility of a return to winning Swansea football; the kind which would bring back the crowds and restore the smiles to Swansea faces.

1921-22

Huxtable at the helm

The captain for the 1921-22 season was Dick Huxtable, who had been 'capped' by Wales in 1920 for the matches against France and Ireland. Dick let it be known that he regarded it as an honour, both to captain Swansea, and to follow such a great leader as Tom Parker.

As far as St. Helens Field was concerned, matters were not left to chance. After the problems which had occurred during the previous season's international, certain work was to be undertaken. The Welsh Union had accepted a tender from Mr. Henry Billings 'for the reconstruction of the Swansea ground'. Since the successful tender was priced at only £500, the reconstruction must have been on a limited scale. Indeed, the feature most detailed in the press reports of the award was the fact that 'iron railings were to be fixed around the enclosure and the pitch'. The implication that this barrier was intended for crowd control at big matches was not lost on those who read the report.

On the field of play, after 'missionary' games at Bryncethin, and Ystalyfera (where Trevor Davies 'scored a dazzling try'), the 'Whites' 'turned it on' against the League, winning by 53 points to 3. 'It was,' the Leader reported, 'just like the old days'. 'Planet', writing in the *Post* described the side as having 'played brilliant open football'. According to the journalist, the side 'looked formidable'.

When Pontypool were beaten in the first senior match, the confidence which many people had had in the side at the end of the previous season appeared to be more than justified. And when Bridgend were 'well beaten' in the next game, 'Planet' was ecstatic. He wrote, 'Those who argue that there is little or no excitement in rugby football should have been at St. Helens on Saturday ... the game was a revelation'. Given the growing popularity of soccer in the old Borough, these were the kind of sentiments which the rugby fraternity was delighted to endorse. The 'Whites', it seemed, were 'on the march' again!

Llanelli were the next side to succumb to the 'Whites', in a match in which 'speed and skill told'. In its report of that game, the *Leader* pointed out that 'the clever back play of the Swansea men resulted in Llanelly's biggest defeat before their own crowd for many years'. Joe Rees, Rowe Harding, and Dick Huxtable were picked out for special praise in most reports of the game, though the *Post* opined that 'it was a victory for team work'.

By this time, there was an air of confidence around St. Helens, and the approaching match with Cardiff was thought to be 'something which the "Whites" will be able to handle with ease'. Sadly, the lessons from the previous season had not been learnt, and the 'Blue and Blacks' won an exciting match by 8 points to nil. Despite the fact that the game took place in mid-October, the weather was described as 'sweltering'. The truth was that the Cardiff men 'lasted the course better', and the Swansea element in the encouraging 20,000 crowd was disappointed. Nevertheless, the spectators had been treated to 'the most thrilling match seen at St. Helens for many years'. Furthermore, since Joe Rees and Rowe Harding were passengers for the bulk of the match, 'Whites'-watchers could console themselves with the thought that, with all fifteen Swansea men fit, their heroes would have won.

Then the malaise which was personified by the side's inconsistency struck again. There followed three consecutive draws, the last of which was described as 'dismal'. 'Planet', by now showing his disappointment, wrote: 'could some philosopher tell us why it is that the larger the

Swansea Rugby Football Club, 1921-22.
A. Davies, W. Tanner, P. Evans, J. H. John, T. Parker.
J. Bancroft, W. Griffiths (Sec.), D. D. Evans, W. Lewis, L. Jones, J. John, G. Michael, R. Dowdle, F. Rees.
D. Hopkins, J. E. Evans, Bruce Barter, R. Huxtable (Capt.), I. Evans, Rowe Harding, F. C. Palmer.
Joe Rees, Trevor Davies, T. Williams, R. Smitham.

gathering at St. Helens, the poorer the game from the spectacular standpoint?' Warming to his theme, he warned, 'Unless form is consistently displayed, the revival we have spoken about will not materialise'. As far as the supporters on the 'cheap' side were concerned, they found it difficult to understand how the team could play like old time Swansea in one game, and like a disorganised set of individuals in the next?

Unfortunately, the depression at St. Helens was mirrored in the economy of the town. Ninety-four tinplate mills were said to be idle, and the numbers of men out of work increased sharply. As far as the 'Whites' were concerned, leaving aside the human misery involved in the situation, the disposable income among the unemployed was even less disposable. But, then, as if they were taking their cue from some capricious director, the side returned to form in the grand manner.

A 'brilliant victory' was gained at Leicester, when Smitham, 'a versatile young player ... absolutely dazzled the opposition ... swerved and twisted effectively'. Among the forwards, according to the *Post*, 'no one shirked his duty, with Dick Huxtable, Tom Parker, and Phil Evans outstanding'. Tudor Williams was another success in that match. Northampton were, then, soundly beaten, with the 'Whites' 'superior in all phases'. Their performance, according to the *Post*, was a 'distinct tribute to Welsh Rugby'. When Llanelli were beaten in the next St. Helens match (by 25 points to 6), 'Planet' was in orbit. It had been a 'brilliant spectacle', and an 'outstanding exhibition of football of the best kind'. In modern football-speak, it might be said that 'Planet' was 'over the moon'. The Swansea player who was mentioned in most reports of that Stradey game as being the outstanding figure on the field was Billy Bowen. The *Leader* reported that he was 'back to his baffling brilliance ... each of his three tries was the work of a master-mind'. Clearly, the *Post* did not have a monopoly in superlatives.

It is interesting to note that in the match against Leicester, the 'Whites' had adopted the home side's five three-quarter formation, and in the matches which followed they persisted with this form of organisation. And it was successful, again, when Cardiff came to play at St. Helens, for the 'Whites' avenged, what was at that time, their only defeat of the season. The *Times*, in its report, noted that 'Cardiff did four-fifths of the attacking, and yet were soundly beaten'. Whilst Swansea supporters would have enjoyed reading that, they literally relished what the 'Thunderer' went on to declare: '"Swansea" are a great side this season ... probably the best club in Great Britain'. The man in the Mumbles Train would have said 'Amen' to that. However, Anglican church-goers among 'Whites' followers, might have pointed to another factor which may have had an influence on the outcome of the match. At the beginning of the encounter, Dr. Harrington-Lees, the retiring Vicar of Swansea, had kicked off. Whilst few doubted that God was Welsh, there may have been a growing conviction that he was also a Swansea boy.

Yet, after the Lord Mayor's Show ... Between the end of November and the turn of the year there were some surprising results. A 'surprise defeat' was suffered at the hands of Guy's Hospital; a 'big victory over Cambridge University attracted only five thousand people', and the 'Whites' were beaten by 'little Skewen'. In its report of that defeat, the *Leader* stated that 'the whole of the Swansea side played like tired men'. No one could explain what had gone wrong.

Meantime, on the national front, the Depression deepened. More people were unemployed; the Railwaymen took a 'cut' in wages equal to 4*s*. per week; a company in the Midlands announced that it was making two million 'Put and Take' spinners, as gambling fever swept the country; the pound could be exchanged for four U.S. dollars; and, at St. Helens, the road building programme which was being promoted by Lloyd George – to help to alleviate unemployment – had an impact upon the club. The Mumbles Road was being widened, which necessitated the wall between the town end of the grandstand and Gorse Lane being demolished, and rebuilt on a new boundary line. Unfortunately, that rebuilding work had to be paid for by the members of the Swansea club, and an appeal was made to all eleven hundred. Whilst the objectives of the Lloyd George scheme attracted widespread acclaim, the impact of the Mumbles Road contract upon the treasury of the Swansea club was less than welcome.

Another matter exerted an impact upon the St. Helens administration, too. After 'extensive discussions', henceforth, the Swansea Seconds side was to be run by the League and not by the club itself. At the time, everyone agreed that this arrangement would ensure better results for the second string, whilst liaison between St. Helens and the District League would be improved.

During the remainder of the season the fortunes of the 'Whites' fluctuated. Among the highlights was a magnificent victory at Newport – the 'Usksiders' first defeat for twenty-five games; twenty-four points were scored against Devonport Services, when Tudor Williams was 'in his element', Phil Evans scored a brace of tries and Islwyn Evans and Trevor Davies were the pick of the 'third line'; and the side drew with Stade Francaise in Paris in front of a crowd of twenty thousand people. One modern 'All White' will be interested to know that the French side's full-back was called Clement. At the inevitable banquet after the match, the Swansea players sat proudly as they listened to the remarks of the president of the French Rugby Federation. He said that it had been because of the skill shown by the early Swansea sides which had toured France that his country began to take the game seriously. It was a fine tribute to the Swansea club.

Whilst the 1921-22 season was not the most successful in the club's history, there were factors which warmed the hearts of the optimists. Five Swansea men, Tom Parker, Islwyn Evans, Frank Palmer, Billy Bowen and Joe Rees had worn the Welsh jersey during the season; twenty-seven of the forty-six matches played had been won; and Islwyn Evans and Rowe Harding, with fifteen each, shared top place in the list of try-scorers. All in all, Dick Huxtable must have felt that reasonable progress had been made Yet the inconsistency of the side continued to be a nagging worry. In the season ahead, if the 'Whites' were going to win back the 'soccer absconders', they would need to be more consistent, and play more attractive (winning) football.

In April, as a blizzard covered Swansea with a freak fall of snow, secretary, W. Griffiths, resigned. He explained that he had been promoted to be headmaster of a new school, and, as a result, did not have the time to devote to the important task at St. Helens. In thanking Griffiths for his 'stalwart work', the club's chairman announced that Mr. E. C. Perkins, who had acted as assistant to the previous secretary, had been appointed in his place.

Chapter Twelve

HOPE AND DISAPPOINTMENT

1922-23

WHEN JOE REES ACCEPTED the captaincy of the 'All Whites', he must have done so with hope which was justified. Whilst the club's playing record for the previous two seasons might have left something to be desired, the positive signs far outweighed the negative. Apart from anything else, during each of the two previous campaigns, knowledgeable commentators had expressed the belief that the 'Whites' were not far off the old Swansea standard. It was little wonder that, as the new season approached, the optimists among the 'Whites'-watchers were blooming. The *Leader*, reflecting this optimism, declared that there was 'an air of eager anticipation among the town's rugby men', whilst the *Post* was 'looking forward to an exciting season'.

Rowe Harding.

In the event, that confidence proved to be misplaced, for, when the season ended, the club's record was the poorest in its history. Faced with this outcome, the Swansea rugby community was bemused. After all, many of the men who had done so well in the seasons since the war played during the ill-fated campaign, and four of them – Gwilym Michael, Tom Parker, Rowe Harding, and Joe Rees – had been 'capped' during that period. Furthermore, there were other individuals in the side who were believed to be on the fringe of the Welsh team. In addition, Albert Jenkins, the outstanding Llanelli player, was so impressed with the potential of the St. Helens club, that he was interested in joining it. At the time, he was reported as having said that he had 'long cherished the hope to assist the "All Whites"', but in the end, he remained a 'Scarlet'. Perhaps, like the prophets of old, he had been warned in a dream.

Among the pre-season photographs which were published in the local press, was one which bore the caption: '"All Whites" in training'. Though, in keeping with the Corinthian spirit of the day, the 'training' which was illustrated involved a dozen men playing leap frog. Days after that photograph appeared, another 'All White' 'went north'. Not that, on this occasion, it affected the St. Helens club. Benny Beynon turned his back on professional soccer and joined Oldham's Rugby League team. In so doing, he became the first 'All White' to play Union, League and Soccer at a senior level.

When the season got under way, after a pointless draw against Llanelli. The *Post* reported that 'Swansea had one of their "off days" at Cross Keys, and were well beaten'. Next, the 'Scarlets' won the first return at Stradey, and, when 'seven changes in the side did not help team work', the *Leader* reported that the 'Whites' had been lucky at Neath. At least there was a victory in the match which followed, and a new 'hero', Owen Rees (Llangennech), who had made his début at Neath, kicked two penalties and a conversion to win the match against Aberavon. Yet, the purists would have noted the relative lack of tries, and 'Pendragon' was unhappy about the quality of the Welsh game in general. He wrote, 'Innumerable free kicks are making Welsh Rugby a monotonous spectacle'. It was hardly the kind of football which the Swansea committee had promised its supporters two seasons earlier. And the situation was worrying, if only because, at the time, the 'threat of Soccer' was nowhere more evident than in Swansea. The town's professional club was attracting ever larger 'gates'.

After a dozen matches had been played, the pessimists were gathering strength – six games had been lost. However, the team had performed creditably at Cardiff, where they were only narrowly beaten, despite losing Joe Rees early in the second-half, (Eddie Williams and Tom Parker were outstanding that day). However, despite that performance, and the fact that the St. Helens ground record was still intact, whilst only one try had been scored there by opponents, frustration, born of inflated expectancy, was beginning to affect the team and its supporters.

At the end of November, that frustration 'boiled over'. Former 'All White', Mr. H. Fuller, was the referee for a match against Devonport Services, which the Swansea men were expected to win comfortably. During previous seasons, both teams had contrived to play open football, and the Swansea crowd, in need of a match to lift their spirits, were relishing the prospect of such a spectacle. In the event, the *Post* reported that the 'Whites' display had been 'wretched', and that 'much-changed Swansea had played like a bunch of individuals'. To the chagrin of the Swansea supporters, during the match, the Services had the audacity to score three tries, which, with minutes to go, gave them the lead. There followed a movement which resulted in Dai Burns being in a position to drop a 'goal', which, had it been allowed, would have won the match for Swansea. Unfortunately for the home crowd, the referee disallowed the kick and, moments later, blew for no side. At that point a group of about a hundred Swansea supporters spilled onto the field and surrounded the referee. Some papers stated that he was 'jostled' as he made his way to the dressing room. Whether that was true, or not, it was not the kind of scene which anyone wished to see at St. Helens. The *Post*, speaking for all who loved the game, scolded the unruly malcontents with the words, 'Swansea-ites must learn to take defeat as well as victory'. Before the season ended the supporters were going to get further practice in that regard.

Between mid-December and the end of January, the 'Whites' won only two matches, though the team's record perplexed the supporters of Bridgend, who were 'run off their feet' by a 'rampant Swansea side'. The highlight of that match was a try by Rowe Harding, which the *Post* reported with undisguised pleasure. 'Harding, on his own ten yard line, intercepted high in the air and went full stride for the line. Man after man tried to stop him ... faced with the full-back, Harding pretended to go right, but darted left to leave his man with mouth open ... and grounded the ball between the posts ... even Bridgend players clapped.'

However, in Swansea, as the season wore on, the mouths which were open were expressing disapproval of the way in which the Swansea team was playing its rugby. In fairness, at the time, Welsh rugby as a whole was going through an indifferent period, but this was small consolation for the Swansea faithful. As a result, Swansea chins were on the floor, though, not to the same extent as the German mark, which, at the time, was being exchanged for the pound

David and Tom Parker – Internationals.

at a rate of 75,500. The Swansea Parks Committee was none too pleased, either. They were informed that the town's new Patti Pavillion was losing £38 per week.

March brought with it unwelcome news for the Committee at St. Helens. Despite being selected by Wales, Tom Parker announced his retirement. He wanted, he said, to let younger players have their opportunity. 'Whites' followers, though, would have recognised that such players could not bring with them the wealth of experience which the former Welsh captain could offer. Nonetheless, Parker's mind was made up, and Swansea would have to manage without his skills.

When the Barbarians 'romped home' in the Easter fixture 'doing what they liked as they scored twenty-three points without reply', advice, most of it unsolicited was heaped upon the Swansea committee. Among the advisers was 'Freelance', who noted, after a home defeat by Bridgend, that 'Smitham was the only player in the Swansea side (that day) who was included in the "All Whites" team at the beginning of the season'. The *Post*-man went on to develop his argument, in the process, complaining about 'constant chopping and changing'. He finished with the telling comment, 'It is a case of too many cooks ... Three people pick the English team, in Swansea it takes twelve to select the local side.'

Joe Rees, who had suffered several injuries during the season, had seen his right-hand man retire, had had other key players injured for long periods, and whose team had suffered from the inexplicable loss of form of others, retired at the end of the campaign. As was his nature, he had given his all during the season, though, if contemporary press comments are to be believed, not all the Swansea players had been as diligent about keeping fit. Perhaps that said something about their motivation, and about the way in which they perceived themselves as being treated by the selectors. Yet, when institutions like Swansea Rugby Club face prolonged difficulties, in the common mind, rumour and innuendo are converted with alacrity into fact.

Nonetheless, there *were* concerns which had to be faced by the club's administrators, and which were unquestionably factual. After the stand had been extended, the club was £5,367 in debt. Given that, since the war, it had not been possible to create 'reserve finances', this necessitated a large overdraft. Happily, 'influential gentlemen' had agreed to act as guarantors, and the matter was not pressing. Nonetheless, the loan had to be repaid, and the principal way of achieving that was through 'gate' income. Since, at the time, an increase in the cost of admission was out of the question, improvement in this revenue could be achieved only by attracting more people to St. Helens. In turn, that would only happen when the side was playing open, winning, 'Swansea' rugby.

Thus it was that, as they contemplated the season ahead, the St. Helens administrators must have been well aware of the size of their task. The impoverished form of the 1922-23 campaign would need to be forgotten.

1923-24

A better showing

Whether the Borough authorities felt that Lloyd George's presence would boost the performance of the 'All Whites' is not known, but in September 1923, the great man was given the Freedom of Swansea. However, there might have been some among those who had invited him, who had heard the silver-tongued orator weave his spell over countless audiences as he urged young men to join Kitchener's Army. Such men might have harboured ideas about using the former Prime Minister in a recruiting capacity at St. Helens. Rugby, however, seems not to have been mentioned during the historic day.

Still, Swansea now had a war hero in charge of its rugby team. Capt. Frank Palmer M.C. was a popular figure in the Town, and brought with him to the job of captain a certain panache. He was, too, something of a charismatic figure, the kind, as one press comment had it, 'who soldiers would follow "over the top"'. Given the low spirits in the Swansea camp, the analogy was not without its relevance. There were other new faces at St. Helens, too, and in the first senior match, against Bridgend, there were eight débutants in the side which beat the visitors. The *Leader* reported that the win had been a 'fitting illustration of the wealth of talent available'. Then, when the side won its next match by 7 points to 6, with 'eleven men who are fresh to the side this season', the *Post*, quite forgetting its 'chopping and changing' criticism, purred. 'People who thought that Rugby was a spent force in Swansea would have had a rude awakening had they seen the Neath game at St. Helens.' The paper reported that the match had been 'intensely interesting', which, whilst hardly the language to bring to mind the flowing Swansea rugby of old, was, at least, indicative of a more positive attitude in the Swansea camp. Furthermore, in reporting that there were eight thousand people present to watch the match, the *Post* could point to significant interest in the 'old game'. Perhaps the 'gate' was nothing like those attracted to such a derby fixture in days of yore, yet, given the previous season's outcome, and competition from Soccer, the treasurer must have been encouraged. Among the new Swansea players that day were Bryn Peters, Dai Parker, and Ivor Jeremiah – who, in due course, was to 'go north'.

When, in the next game, Cardiff were held to a draw on their own ground, the St. Helens optimists were to the fore again. Such was the dominance of the 'All Whites' pack in that match, that the *Western Mail* reported that the home side 'were so busy defending that they rarely had any chance to become aggressive'. Of the Swansea players, Bryn Peters, Tom Jones, and Rowe Harding were singled out for praise in most reports of that match. As a result of that encouraging performance at Cardiff, Frank Palmer must have gathered his troops for the next game with some confidence. As yet unbeaten, the men in white were beginning to believe in themselves, but, sadly, according to the *Post*, 'Grass six inches long at Aberavon was too much of a handicap for the Swansea men'. 'Bravon won by 8 points to 3, and the Swansea club's unbeaten record was gone for another season.

There followed a 'dour, scrappy game' against Pontypool, and a defeat at Stradey, though, in that instance, whilst Llanelli were said to have been the better side, the 'Whites' played with fourteen men for most of the match. P.C. Joe Grey broke his collar bone. The optimists must have taken some encouragement from that fact, from the form of Bob Smitham, who was said to have 'played an excellent game', and from the performance of W. J. Davies who was 'brilliant in defence'. Whilst the next match was also lost, once again the team was disrupted by an injury early in the match. This time, the dependable Joe Rees was 'carried off'.

At this time, there was a new scribe reporting on Swansea's matches. He used the pseudonym, 'Old Forward', though his ability to manipulate the English language cast doubt upon those who referred to the front eight by the collective term 'Donkeys'. For example, in his report of a match at St. Helens against Leicester, he drew upon his cultural background to write: 'The "Tigers" are the Cubists of the Rugby world'. Of a game at Neath, he wrote of 'thirty, valiant, earnest individuals who splashed through a sea of mud'. In commenting upon Bob Smitham, he advised his readers that: 'In every sense, the fact of his inspiration becomes more deeply impressed upon the team'. Reporting on a London Welsh, Yule-tide match at St. Helens, he stated that: 'Rugby Football is essentially a young man's game. Occasionally ... someone defies the ravages of time ... Hippocrates gave thirty-five as the limit of youth ... some can go on, but, in every case, there is a limit from which vitality and ability to take knocks begins to wane.' And Hippocrates never played rugby.

As Lord Montague's company was lobbying for the construction of a motorway from Birmingham to Manchester, to help to alleviate unemployment, the 'Whites' were recovering their form They were 'unlucky to lose' in the second game of the season at Cardiff, when Smitham was again 'the star article'; Cross Keys were defeated on their own ground, when Tommy Lewis and Albert Owen were outstanding; Cambridge University were beaten by a comfortable margin, as 'the virile young Swansea pack showed amazing vitality about the field', and Watsonians, Maesteg, and Bristol all lost to the men in white. As the *Leader* had it, 'it is just what the doctor ordered'.

Along with this success came increased gates, which made the treasurer smile. And, as far as 'Old Forward' was concerned, at the end of the year he felt confident enough to suggest that, 'At this rate the ground record will be retained until the end of the season'. He should have known better than to tempt fate.

As the *Post* had it in its report on a match with Llanelli which followed the *Post*-man's pronouncement, 'Scarlets red letter day at St. Helens'. The report below this headline concluded that 'it was a scrambling game, and Llanelly were the better scramblers'. Given that the 'Scarlets' took the St. Helens ground record, and Rowe Harding broke his collar bone after five minutes, it was not an auspicious game from the point of view of the Swansea men. Nonetheless, as Swansea supporters nursed their disappointment, they could, at least, have consoled themselves

'Whites' v. 'Quins.
Note: Stand before extension; the old L.M.S. Station.

with the thought that they might have won with a full side. In any event, they were not miserable for long. In the first match of the annual Midlands tour, the youngsters beat a strong Leicester side, including W. W. Wakefield, in a match in which Joe Rees was outstanding. Whilst the second tour match was drawn, the team was, once again, depleted, and, as the *Leader* put it, 'earned a share of the spoils by a great team effort'. That was more like it Swansea!

Meanwhile, new technology was making an impact on the old borough. There was a proposal to electrify the Mumbles Railway, and the British Broadcasting Company was considering the possibility of establishing a 'wireless relay station' in Swansea. In addition, the futurists in the media were discussing the feasibility of something called Television. Not that there was any reference in the discussion about the future impact of such an invention on disposable income and the Swansea Rugby Club. As far as the club was concerned, the treasurer preferred not to think about the implications of such a device.

Three Swansea men were chosen to play in the international against England, and many people felt that they should have been joined by the in-form Bob Smitham. However, that was not to be, and Joe Rees was joined by two new 'caps', Albert Owen and Ivor Morris. Once again, the Swansea club had shown its ability to develop talent to international class. Furthermore, at that stage of the season, the side had a record which confounded those who had criticised the club during the previous campaign. No wonder the optimists were smiling.

In February, 'Old Forward' was delighted to report on a victory at Bristol. He wrote of 'a sparkling exhibition of football ... and brilliant passing of the backs'. The match saw the welcome return of Frank Palmer, who had been unwell for some twelve weeks, and a fine performance from the elusive Smitham who 'directed proceedings'. In addition, as the *Post*-scribe noted, the 'Whites' were the first side that season to beat the Bristolians 'on their own patch', and the first to win on the new Avonside ground.

At the end of February, the young men won 'a turbulent game at Cardiff' to take another ground record, which pleased 'Old Forward' a great deal. The Welsh selectors were also impressed, and another two 'Whites', Dai Parker and Tom Evans, were chosen to make their international débuts against Ireland. Since the Welsh team had Rowe Harding as captain, it was another accolade for the burgeoning talent of the young side. When, later in the season, Joe Jones was selected to play against France, the Swansea committee could point to the fact that five of their youngsters had gained their first 'caps' during the campaign.

Once again, at this distance, it is difficult to explain why the St. Helens authorities could not have retained the bulk of a successful side from one season to the next. On many occasions throughout its history, the club appeared to consider the start of one season almost as if it were beginning afresh. Effective combinations from one season were broken up, and even successful players were not heard of again. Unfortunately, club records and minute books were lost during the air raids of the second World War, thus it is not possible to establish the reasons responsible for this behaviour. whatever they were, however, the policies which were followed during this period in the club's history can be seen to have had a detrimental effect on its success on and off the field.

As far as the 1923-24 season was concerned, as the campaign wore on the young legs could not 'stay the pace'. Between mid-March and the end of the season, the side had little success, and finished having lost fifteen of the forty games which it had played. Nonetheless, the young turks could point to the fact that they had won six more games than the team had done during the previous campaign, and had provided seven men for the national side, thus lessening the potential of the Swansea team. Furthermore, when the 'Centenary' game had been played at Rugby School, two Swansea men were in the combined England/Wales XV – Gwilym Michael and Rowe Harding. That was a further indication of the standing of the Swansea club in the eyes of the rugby fraternity.

1924–25

True 'All Whites'

Since the club's inception, despite having been given the sobriquet, the 'All Whites' Swansea men had played in white jerseys and dark (usually) blue shorts. No one questioned the apparent anomaly, presumably because the team's shirts were only white – uncluttered by hoops, stripes or quarters in other colours. However, on January 10th. 1925, for the St. Helens match against the popular Leicester club, fifteen Swansea men ran out of the dressing room dressed, for the first time, in white shirts and white shorts. Since the original intention had been to have the players wear the new strip in a match a week earlier, it would appear that 'the powers that be' had decided to greet the new year with the change. From that day forward, at least until the incursions of the marketing men resulted in kit being decorated, Swansea teams were genuinely all white.

The captain who led the team on that historic day was J. H. John, who had been appointed at the beginning of the '24/'25 campaign. John, a very capable footballer, was to win 'caps' during the two seasons which were to follow, and was to say that his period as club captain had been beneficial in improving his game. On his appointment, he stated that to captain a Swansea side containing several internationals – whilst he was uncapped – was a great honour which he appreciated.

Among those internationals was a Scot, Dr. D. M. Bertram, a big forward with a reputation as a goal kicker. Bertram had been recruited by Dr. Teddy Morgan to join him at his Sketty practice. No one asked whether Morgan was acting as an agent for the 'Whites'. Most assumed that the former Watsonian forward had enjoyed his Christmas visits to St. Helens so much that he wished to play there regularly. No doubt, too, those 'All Whites' supporters who were patients of Morgan's practice, would have enjoyed the thought of a second rugby international looking after them when they were unwell. Several other new faces joined the doctor in the Swansea side for the traditional game against the League. Among them were Elvet Rees and D. Jenkins, both of whom 'caught the eye in a match when the team as a whole looked efficient'.

Towards the end of September, that efficiency was augmented by flair, as the side played 'brilliant football to beat Neath'. Dr. Bertram, George White, Bob Smitham and P. C. Ivor Thomas were said to have been 'outstanding in a fine side'. According to the reports of that game, despite heavy rain and thick mud, the team played 'as though they will give the New Zealanders a tough time next Saturday'. And the St. Helens men also believed that to be true. The general view was that, given the club's record against major touring sides, the 'Whites' had a good chance of doing well.

On the day of the match, Porter, the 'huge captain of the New Zealanders', sniffed the St. Helens air, noted the superb playing surface, and declared: 'It's a fine day, it's an excellent ground, so it will be a good game.' Later, Swansea supporters would have given some thought to what he meant by 'good'? In his account of the tour match, Reed Masters recounts how the 'All Blacks' were impressed by the singing of the crowd, and the billiard table-like turf. Masters, who did not play in the match, like the 45,000 crowd, must have been impressed, too, by the superb play of his colleagues. The 'Whites', outstanding in their previous match more than held their own for the first twenty minutes, but, thereafter, fell away as the 'All Blacks' took command. In the final quarter, troubled by a low sun in their eyes, the Swansea backs seemed to lose their composure, and were over-run. Only Dai Parker who 'kicked a magnificent goal from an awkward angle on half way', scored for the 'Whites'. In so doing, he became the first player to score against the New Zealanders on that tour. That, at least, was some consolation for the 39 points to 3 defeat.

> The Swansea team on that occasion was:
> P. Lloyd, J. E. Watkins, T. Evans, M. Evans, D. Jenkins, Elvet Rees and R. Smitham, J. H. John (Capt.), Dr. Bertram, G. White, Ivor Morris, D. Parker, L. Thomas, H. Rees, and Ivor Thomas.

Subsequent to that match, the scale and manner of the defeat which had been suffered by the 'Whites' had a detrimental effect on the confidence of the Swansea men. During this period, such was the diminished level of their self-belief that they lost five consecutive games. The selectors responded by 'shuffling the pack'. Bruce Barter, Ivor Jeremiah, E. A. H. Jones,

A. L. Perkins, T. Mabbett and Stanley Walters, were among the players selected during this period. Yet, until the side visited London at the end of October, it seemed to make little difference to the results. The turning point came at Winchmore Hill, the ground of the Barts. Hospital club. There, 'in wretched conditions', the Swansea pack was magnificent. Dai Parker, Dr. Bertram and Ivor Morris 'seemed to be everywhere', but it was not until a few minutes from the end of the match that the winning try was scored. Tom Mabbett 'dribbled some twenty yards on his own and dived over to score'. Covered with mud, soaked by the continuing downpour, their kit grey rather than white, the Swansea men trooped off the pitch exuding a collective sigh of relief. As the *Post* put it, 'They have stopped the rot!'

As it happened, whilst the team lost its next two matches, the psychological burden on them had been lightened. In addition, newcomer E. A. H. Jones, had scored tries in three consecutive matches, whilst Tom Evans had added his name to those being noted by the press. Then came the victory which lifted St. Helens spirits to pre-tourist match levels. The *Post* used the headline 'A famous victory'. According to the report in the paper, 'In a game full of finesse and brilliant, spectacular movements, the 'All Whites' filled the Leicester spectators with amazement'. 'Old Forward', demonstrating his delight at the way the team had played, added 'If the "Whites" can reproduce this form in a few home games, the future of rugby in Swansea is assured'. His next sentence betrayed his concerns, dreams and hopes, '... and St. Helens will again be thronged by thousands as before the advent of soccer in the town'. This was the kind of football to bring the crowds back. Yet, both Swansea and Leicester had played with five three-quarters. Few other sides would wish to compete in such an open fashion.

Meanwhile, the 'Great Trade Slump' deepened, and thousands in Swansea were unemployed. As a result, humour was used in many ways to try to bring some cheer to drab lives. For example, the *Post*'s 'Wireless beginners' column was being written by someone calling himself 'Yves Dropper'. At the time, his was a popular feature, for, around Swansea, hundreds of wireless enthusiasts were building crystal sets, and tuning into broadcasts provided by the British Broadcasting Company. Like sport, it was another diversion from a testing world.

Sport, of course, was amongst the most powerful of diversions, and the 'Whites' and Wales provided such a focus for Swansea's rugby fraternity, who had two Swansea men to cheer as the red shirts of Wales took the field for the match against New Zealand. They saw Dai Parker and Rowe Harding, like their colleagues, give of their best, but, once again, the 'All Blacks' were victorious. According to the *Western Mail*, the Welshmen were 'outclassed in speed and combination'.

In December, there was new excitement in the town as the Swansea Wireless Relay Station was opened. Despite the slump, hundreds of licences were sold throughout Swansea, a 110 foot aerial was erected 'On Townhill', and Britain had the privilege of tuning in to 5 SX to listen to the Mayor of Swansea giving the first broadcast from what he called, 'the capital of west Wales'. Swansea was on the wireless map.

Meantime, on the football field, the 'Whites' were going through a 'dismal patch'. Continuing rain throughout the month had resulted in pitches turning into quagmires. In such conditions, 'scientific football', beloved of the Swansea supporters, was said to be impossible, and 'scrambling matches' resulted. During this period, two games were drawn, and the 'Whites' Christmas Day fixture with Watsonians was lost. Certainly, this was *not* what the doctor ordered, particularly since the town's soccer men were top of their division, and the reducing disposable income available to sports followers was being attracted in greater proportion to the Vetch Field. Yet, as the New Zealand games had shown, there was, still, a strong demand for first-class rugby in the town. 'Old Forward' believed that, 'If the St. Helens men can provide the fare, they will get the following'. Sadly, it was unfortunate that, at the time, the side was playing more attractive football 'with greater heart *away* from St. Helens'. No one could explain the phenomenon, for the, usually, fast-drying surface of the Cricket Field was more conducive to the playing of 'Swansea football' than most other grounds.

At the beginning of January, however, even St. Helens succumbed. The continuing rain, which had brought floods to many parts of Swansea, resulted in the famous surface being 'drowned in water'. Thus it was that, despite the best efforts of Swansea's Fire Brigade, the first match at St. Helens to be postponed because of flooding, was reported in the press. Swansea's rugby men must have hoped that this was not some kind of omen. They had enough problems as it was.

As the rain continued to fall, the Swansea Rugby Supporters Club gave a dinner at Thomas' Café in honour of Rowe Harding. By then the Cambridge 'Blue' had been 'capped' by Wales, captained the Welsh side, was a Lion, and had been chosen to play in the Rugby Centenary Match at Rugby School. At the dinner, Harding emphasised that the future of Swansea Rugby Club was 'very dear to him', but, because of career commitments he did not expect to be in Swansea again for several seasons. The player, who had come to St. Helens after being rejected by Llanelli, had had a meteoric rise to the top flight. He was first 'capped' just two years after making his Swansea début, and was to be made captain of the national side in 1926. The young man's chief assets were his outstanding speed, 'gutsy' determination in defence and attack, and an ability to read the game well. Unfortunately a spate of injuries disrupted his rugby career, and most commentators felt that he did not achieve his true potential because of these problems. Later in his life he was to be a key figure in the administration of the club which he loved, thereby demonstrating that his declaration of commitment that night in Thomas' café was not an idle statement.

Towards the end of January, football matches across the country were affected by an eclipse of the sun, and prior to the event, the newspapers printed diagrams which indicated when the eclipse was going to take place. In Swansea, given a 3 p.m. start, it was scheduled to happen at half-time. In the event, reports indicated that, even the total eclipse had not had much of an effect on the game. Not surprisingly, given the reputation of Swansea 'wags', there was much banter at half-time, with the local Oscar Wildes uttering their 'impromptu' witticisms (carefully constructed the night before). As might be expected, most of them were to do with the referee not being able to see what was going on.

A few days later, as the New Zealanders left the U.K., they lit up Swansea faces with the comment that Dai Parker had been 'the best forward they had played against during their British tour'. Swansea, and Wales might have been eclipsed, but not, it seemed, the burly Parker.

As far as the 'Whites' were concerned, the eclipse match provided the team with its third consecutive victory. It had been, according to the *Leader*, 'A convincing win over the "Scarlets"'. The *Post*, meanwhile, opined that 'After Saturday's display ... it can safely be said that the "All Whites" are now out of the wood'. Edgar Price, 'a centre of great resource', and Dr. Bertram, were singled out for special mention. Unfortunately the 'Whites' must have stumbled upon a clearing, rather than the edge of the wood. The team lost its next game in such a manner that 'Old Forward' was exasperated. 'Yet again', he wrote, 'the fickle "All Whites" blighted the hopes of a large number of supporters, and lost the opportunity of winning back to rugby the thousands who, of late, have been watching the Swans.' The *Post*-man wrote as though he had been jilted by a lover. In his exasperation, he declared, 'Swansea have become as fickle as a woman. I would not be surprised if the team wins at Newport'. Perhaps it was a good thing for 'Old Forward' that the feminist movement, at the time, was more concerned with representation than with male attitudes. Meantime, the men knew exactly what he meant.

Unfortunately, Newport were not in the mood to prove his point. They won the match by 15 points to 5. Of the Swansea men, only Eddie Beynon, who had been chosen to play for Wales against France, and J. E. Watkins came out of the match with credit. Thereafter, only a fine win over Cardiff at St. Helens lifted the spirits of the Swansea rugbyites. By this time, the *Post*, clutching at straws in its loyal attempt to support rugby in the old borough, was 'delighted to report that all but one of the tries was the result of exhilarating movements', and 'it was excitement from first to last'. The paper's sole complaint concerned the 'gate'. 'It was a great pity', 'Old Forward' reported, 'that the seven or eight thousand spectators at St. Helens were not doubled or trebled.' Yet, one swallow ... Such was the state of Welsh rugby at the time that Dr. Teddy Morgan, now broadcasting each week from B.B.C. Swansea, was decidedly critical. 'The game', he declared, 'has developed into a kick and rush business ... matches between neighbouring clubs are likened to a dog fight ... players have become excellent at kicking the ball into touch.' Obviously, the game at that time was not what *that* doctor ordered.

Morgan could not have grumbled, however, had he been at St. Helens for the Easter matches. Then 'the leather was given air' by the Barbarians, the Harlequins and the homesters. Several tremendous tries were scored in the two matches. Among them were two Rowe Harding specials, and a forty yard dash by Dai Burns, which had the crowd 'on its feet roaring'. Sid Davies and Albert Owen were said to have been a 'superb combination' at half-back, and, as if to show the 'glamour boys ' that forwards could 'play a bit', too, Alf Parker scored an excellent try, which his brother, Dai, converted. 'Whites' supporters were, also delighted to see Tom Parker come out of retirement for the Easter games. Tom, however, whilst agreeing that he had been tempted to make a 'come-back', let it be known that he did not intend to play again. Whilst Swansea-ites were delighted to have seen Tom play once more, they respected his decision, for all else apart, the Parker family had made a huge contribution to St. Helens rugby. Four brothers, Alf, Sid, Tom and Dai had all worn the white jersey with distinction; Tom and Dai were 'capped', and Tom had led Wales during one of its most successful periods. In addition, George Taylor, a cousin, was to play for the 'Whites'. Had any other family contributed as much to the Swansea cause? At the time, no one could provide an example.

With Easter past and domestic games resumed, the *Post* reported that 'teams were just going through the motions ... It was end-of-season fare' Worse still, the *Leader* reported that, in one of these drab games, there 'was a total lack of interest among spectators'. Consequently, when the St. Helens authorities sent a congratulatory telegram to the Vetch Field – the town's Soccerites had become champions of their division, and had gained promotion to the Second Division of the English League -they must have wished for a rugby competition of a similar kind, to help sustain interest to the end. Dr. Teddy Morgan, however, argued that by 'playing Swansea rugby' constantly (and winning, of course) the 'Whites' would retain their faithful. The trouble was, as 'Old Forward' had put it, the side 'was as fickle as a woman'. The players, however, could have said the same thing about Swansea supporters.

1925-26

Enigma Abertawe

The season started with another act of St. Helens goodwill. Prior to the match with the League, the 'Whites' 'opened the Killay ground of the Swansea Harbour club'. An added attraction of that match was Tom Parker, who came out of retirement to help the local cause. Having won that game comfortably, the side faced the District League with confidence, but were surprised by the 'wealth of talent' in the combined XV. In his report of the match, 'Freelance' suggested a 'motto for the "Whites"'. It was, 'Support the man with the ball'. That, he argued was the policy which had made 'Swansea rugby a household word'. Since the League had been beaten by the narrow margin of fourteen points to eight, on the day,it was clear that he felt the team had forgotten that basic principle.

After the side had lost against Skewen in the next match, the *Post*-man was exasperated. 'The side was too bad to be true', he wrote, and 'if things do not improve, then Swansea rugby will be fighting for its very existence.' The *Leader* echoed this concern, whilst the supporters wondered, yet again, about the policies which were being followed by the St. Helens authorities.

When the season ended, the supporters were no wiser, for, despite the presence of several internationals in the side and the best efforts of captain J. E. Watkins, the 'Whites' lost twenty of the forty-three matches played. That was the greatest number of defeats ever suffered by the club. The *Leader* in searching for reasons for this poor outcome, suggested that the 'Whites'

Swansea R.F.C. 1925-26.
Top Row: W. H. Evans (Hon. Gen. Sec.), E. C. Perkins (Asst.-Sec.), W. Faull, J. H. John, W. Burgess, B. Jones, M. Rice, D. Parker, T. Hopkins, G. Grimshaw, R. Dowdle (Trainer), W. R. Arnold (Committee).
Second Row: D. R. Jenkins, E. Hopkins, B. Barter, J. E. Watkins (Capt.), R. Jones, D. Hopkins, L. Shipton.
Front Row: S. Davies, J. Jones, E. A. H. Jones, A. L. B. Perkins.

were something of an enigma – brilliant one week and 'hopeless the next'. Though in their endeavour to find an answer to their conundrum, there was no record of them having consulted a certain Dr. Daniell. The doctor, on being made a freeman of Llanelli, had stated that he had found a flaw in Einstein's theory. Given such erudition,the St. Helens men might have approached him to solve their problem.

By the second month of the campaign, even the optimists at St. Helens were losing faith in their favourites. Furthermore, their mood was not enhanced when Dick Davies, a promising young full-back, took the northern silver and joined Halifax. Davies said that he had made his decision because he could not find work locally. In Swansea, that was a familiar statement, one which had been made by many other Swansea boys who had taken the train north.

Then, as if to add to the gloom which was settling over St. Helens, Bill Bowen, successful captain of the 'Whites' for three seasons in the 1890's, died at his Gwydr Crescent home. Bill, who had served on the match committee at St. Helens following his retirement, had won twelve 'caps' and had been a member of the first Welsh side to beat England. He was to be missed.

Meantime, as the Archbishop of Canterbury was arguing that 'poor sermons are the cause of empty churches', there were those among 'Whites'-watchers who might have wondered whether the statement that 'poor play resulted in empty grounds', was just as valid? Then, out of the gloom, came a shaft of light.

Given the disappointing results of matches played up to that point, for a match at Aberavon, the selectors made eight changes from the side which had played in the previous game. Those changes seemed to have the necessary effect, for the 'Whites' surprised every one with an exhilarating display. According to the *Leader*, it had been 'a game in which the "All Whites" found their feet'. Since it was 'Bravon's first defeat of the season, the win must have given the Swansea faithful new heart. Stan Walters was the hero of the day, scoring all Swansea's points, whilst the pack had played 'a momentous game'.

There followed another victory at Pontypool, following which, 'Freelance' placing his optimist's hat firmly on his head, declared that 'the win showed that the defeat of Aberavon was no flash-in-the-pan'. Furthermore, the *Post*-scribe was able to report that the Swansea tries that day were 'both made in the approved Abertawe style, with the wing men going over after thrilling movements'. Even the pessimists must have smiled at that. Sadly, those smiles would have frozen as the 'Whites' lost the next two matches in succession.

Nonetheless, both the *Post* and the *Leader* detected positive signs in each of the defeats.In the first, against Llanelli, 'half a gale was blowing into Swansea faces throughout the first half', yet, when the teams changed around it died down. At Neath, invincible at home at the time, the 'Whites' had three 'tries' disallowed. Furthermore, Dai Parker was said to have had his best match of the season, and the young side to be 'gaining in experience'. Whilst this may have been poor consolation for 'Whites' supporters, at least it gave the optimists something to hang onto. Whilst the pessimists would have taken a different view, both sets of supporters were united in their sorrow at the news of the death of Captain Frank Palmer M.C. Frank, who had been captain of the 'Whites' two seasons earlier, had been 'capped' three times in 1922, and was only twenty-nine when he died, but had been in poor health for some time. The black crêpe bands worn by the 'Whites' for their game against the 'Scarlets', were but one mark of respect for the popular Palmer.

Then, as if to honour the 'Captain' and confound their critics, the 'Whites' gave a 'really

Bruce Barter, who played a good game on his 'All Whites' début.

encouraging display at Gloucester'. There, despite the fact that they lost the match, 'they almost took the homesters' ground record. Indeed, had not Dai Parker's kick been charged down a minute before time, sweet victory would have been in the mouth of each 'All White'. Prominent for Swansea that day were D. B. Evans who 'won golden opinions', and captain Elwyn Watkins, who 'scored a clever try'. By then the positive thinkers were showing signs of revival, and that opinion was reinforced when Leicester were 'outclassed at St. Helens'. Indeed, such was the side's superiority that they won that match by 17 points to 3 despite missing 'four relatively easy penalties'. As ever with 'Whites' versus 'Tigers' matches, it was the play of the backs which caught the imagination of the spectators. 'All four Swansea tries were capitally engineered', the *Leader* reported, whilst the *Post* had it that 'Barter was the life and soul of the Swansea side'. It seemed that the player 'brought the crowd to its feet' as he sold 'a "dummy" to both opposing centres, and side-stepped the full-back to run over for a dazzling try'. The St. Helens crowd was ecstatic. The boys were back.

When Cardiff came to St. Helens on the following Saturday most neutral observers were of the opinion that the Whites would have a hard fight. In the event the 'Blue and Blacks' were well beaten. The *Post*, no doubt taking its lead from Billy Bunter, reported that 'Cardiff were soundly Whacked'. Sid Phillips and Barter were said to have had 'day out', and the *Leader* was of the opinion that 'Swansea's supremacy was so pronounced that Cardiff looked like a second-class organisation'. In the euphoria, which followed that Cricket Field match, Swansea supporters must have shaken their heads in wonder. 'Dreadful in one game, and brilliant in the next', exasperating and enthralling in turn; they were enigmas in white.

By the end of the year, the supporters were becoming used to the side's inconsistency; not that they appreciated it! Reporting on a match with Neath, the *Athletic News* put the matter into perspective. The previous week the paper had described, enthusiastically, the performance of the 'Whites' against Cardiff. Now, it argued that 'Until half-time Swansea played like a team without a plan'. Yet, the players involved in the second match were, largely, those who played against Cardiff.

Whilst, at this distance, it is not difficult to make a case to the effect that there was little tactical planning in the team's training sessions, the 'Whites' were typical of most rugby sides at the time. They were imbued with the Corinthian spirit: too much preparation smacked of professionalism, and was unfair. The whole ethos of the game was built around natural ability to combine with colleagues and take advantage of opportunities as they arose. And this, of course, bred the worship of demi-gods who had flair and precocious talent. The giants of the past, like Trew and Dick Jones, were role models, and, at the time, Bruce Barter was filling that need for Swansea supporters. Yet, such genius is frequently inconsistent. Not that that made them any less attractive to supporters and to the press.

The *Post* demonstrated this in its report of a match at the Gnoll. 'Barter ... realising that a

The opening of the new stand extension at St. Helens.
Architect Sidney Crocker hands the keys to Horace Line (W.R.U.).

superhuman effort was needed ... zigzagged his way through the Neath defence ... beating three or four men ... and sent Sid Phillips over for a try.' As far as the paper was concerned, Flash Gordon and Bulldog Drummond had nothing on the Swansea centre, though unlike the heroes of the emerging world of cinema, Barter and his ilk did not have a script and planned events to star in. Theirs was the stage of numberless options, of the need to take decisions in a fraction of a second, and of men trying to stop you doing what you intended.

In its report of the same match, the *Leader*, in addition to eulogising about Barter, focused upon a forward. Tom Hopkins, the paper argued, 'is the best forward in Wales at the present time'. Like their contemporaries in other Welsh towns, when the occasion demanded, the Swansea papers were not loath to indulge in a spot of hyperbole.

The traditional Swansea Christmas games gave 'Whites' supporters the opportunity to see one of their old favourites (and another demi-god) in action. The player was Rowe Harding, who was particularly prominent in the side's third successive victory, whilst Elwyn Watkins scored a brace of tries. There was promise, too, in the play of Eddie Beynon (Pontarddulais) at full-back, and Johnny Jones, who was described by the *Post* as the outstanding Swansea player. Indeed, the description of Johnny's try in the *Post* match report, was almost a carbon copy of Barter's effort in an earlier game. With a good set of Christmas results behind them, the side, and the supporters, looked forward to the new year with greater confidence. Inconsistency? What inconsistency?

Happily for the St. Helens treasurer, the exciting form of the side over the Christmas period resulted in larger crowds. Furthermore, once again, there was greater interest in the 'Old Game' in the town. Thus it was that about five hundred supporters travelled to Leicester for the club's annual match with the 'Tigers'. Then, the Leicester press, reporting on the match, stated, 'Not content with hymn singing, and climbing the goal posts, they (the Swansea supporters), kept up the enthusiasm throughout the match with the aid of a ukulele within the sacred precincts of the committee box'. The man who perpetrated this ghastly deed, hugely appreciated by the Leicester folk, was probably A. L. Perkins. The circumstantial evidence upon which this assumption is based is provided by a photograph in the *Post* of the Swansea party about to depart from High Street station. In the middle of the party stands Perkins, playing his instrument, whilst in the foreground is Bruce Barter 'as Harold Lloyd'. The smiling faces in the photograph suggest that the spirit was good in the Swansea camp. And the talent of Barter in playing the role of the great cinema comedian, suggests that he was the team 'jokester'.

Whilst the Welford Road match ended in a draw, the boisterous supporters would have made their way home with a spring in their collective step. The 'Tigers' line had been 'charmed', and, importantly for the supporters, the 'Whites' had played the game with panache.

There was additional joy for all associated with the St. Helens, club when the Welsh team was announced to play England. D. B. Evans, Tom Hopkins and J. H. John were to make their international débuts. With Rowe Harding retained in the side, Swansea Rugby Club had once again made a significant contribution to the Welsh cause despite the fact that, earlier in the season, it had struggled to find consistent form. Because of their improved form, the 'Whites', at that stage in the season, were attracting much better 'gates'. In the light of the news that the 'Swans' were to play in the semi-final of the English Cup, and were attracting huge support, this was encouraging. The 'Whites' had proved that, given better form, and flowing play, the rugby loyalists would return to St. Helens.

The Borough Engineer was one of those who returned. His objective, at the request of the club, was to investigate the reasons for the flooding which had occurred. The report of that

The 'Whites' at Leicester – complete with chrysanthemums and ukulele.

work recommended that new drains, at a cost of £1,000, should be installed. The problem was, where was the money to come from? There was still the bulk of the 'stand loan' to be repaid. Gates would have to improve, even more, if that amount of cash was going to become available.

On the field, the momentum of the 'winning streak' had been disrupted, and the side reverted to its old inconsistent form. Consequently, during the last quarter of the season, results were as mixed as they had been in the first. It was true that International calls had weakened the side, whilst a spate of injuries to other key players exacerbated the problem. However, whatever was its root cause, Enigma Abertawe was, once more, alive and well. As a result, enthusiasm waned, and in their reports, the Swansea journalists wrote of 'Kick and rush football', and 'end-of-the-season staleness'. Indeed, after the 'Whites' had lost at the Arms Park, 'Observer' in the *Post* stated that 'he had the impression that the players were not sorry that the curtain is about to drop'. Unlike in the theatre, no exciting finale to precede the fall of the curtain was forthcoming. Thus, Swansea supporters were left to reflect on the hugely successful spell in the middle of the season, as they sought some solace from the results of a mediocre campaign.

At least, in their search for consolation,they could focus upon the gifted players in the side. Bruce Barter, Elwyn Watkins and Johnny Jones had done well in the backs, whilst Dai Parker, then an established international, was leading points scorer with sixty-three. Nonetheless, it must have been difficult to ignore the fact that, for the second season in succession opponents had scored more points than the 'Whites'. *That* had never happened before! As Elwyn Watkins took on the captaincy for a second season, he must have wished for greater consistency, and the emergence of outstanding players to augment the skills of his sides. Indeed, since he was a chapel-boy, he might have succumbed to the temptation to pray for his needs.

Chapter Thirteen

A GIANT DEPARTS

1926–27

WHILST THE DEATH OF FILM STAR, Rudolph Valentino, was said to have caused half the women in the world to wail and weep, within days of that event, another passing had a far greater impact upon the people of Swansea. On 20 August 1926, the 'immortal' Billy Trew passed from this life.

It seemed that the whole of Swansea stood, bareheaded, along the route from the Brooklands Hotel in Oxford Street to Danygraig cemetery. Hundreds of floral tributes were carried in the procession, and men who had played with Swansea's 'greatest player', were prominent among the mourners. 'Genny' Gordon, Fred Scrine, Ivor Morgan, Dick Jones, Dickie Owen, Dai Davies (Port Tennant), and Bob Dowdle were there, but so were numberless supporters. Even the 'absconders' to Soccer were there. Each mourner had his personal memory of some incident in the playing life of the great man. There was only *one* Billy Trew! A veritable giant of the game. A player without equal. A god who had chosen Swansea to live among men.

Many tributes were paid to Trew in the press at that time, but none more fitting than that written by D. R. Gent* in the *Sunday Times*: 'The term "genius" is applied nowadays with little discrimination, but, in my own mind, I am quite convinced that Trew *was* a football genius ... the finest all-rounder behind the scrummage that Rugby Union has produced ... whatever position he played, class was writ large ... He leaves me with a memory of a brilliant footballer, a wonderful tactician, a splendid example of the superiority of mind over body ... a magnificent sportsman ... and the most modest and retiring of men.'

And this, it should be noted, was an English international, a writer, well-known for presenting objective analysis of players and games. Sentiment and hyperbole played no part in his writing. Yet his words, and the strength of feeling underlying them, left the reader with no room to doubt the god-like stature of Swansea's Billy Trew.

At the now deprived St. Helens, J. Elwyn Watkins, captain for the second season in succession, as he gathered his men together for pre-season training, must have looked heavenward for inspiration – he was in need of it! The words on the previous season's end of campaign report were etched on his mind: Must do better!

Whilst the 'opener' against the League provided the 'Whites' with numerical encouragement – they won by 38 points to 3 – 'Observer' in the *Post*, felt that the standard of play had 'rarely risen above the mediocre'. There followed a disappointing display against Pontardawe, and a defeat at Neath, though the team's second-half performance at the Gnoll gave supporters some encouragement.

---

* D. R. Gent was an English International, 'capped', whilst with Gloucester. In one of those matches, against Wales, his opposite number was Dickie Owen. Since Gent was educated at Swansea Grammar School, this Swansea 'double' is noteworthy.

The funeral of a legend – W. J. Trew, August 26, 1926.

Meantime, certain petty officials in Unemployment Exchanges in south Wales were beginning to flex their muscles. One such bureaucrat announced that 'a man who accepted an engagement as a referee for rugby union matches was not available for work that day, even if it were offered to him'. As a result, the argument continued, technically, the referee who was 'pegging', was in breach of regulation and should lose his dole money. Happily, common sense prevailed, as the W.R.U. pointed out, at the time, hundreds of players were unemployed, and they, like the referees only received expenses whilst playing. Nothing further was heard of the matter.

At the end of September a new-old name appeared on the Swansea team sheet; Billy Trew junior was chosen to play against Cardiff. Trew the younger, was to say that he was proud to follow his father, but naturally, he would have liked him to be present on his first team début. Obviously, Billy must have meant 'physically', for, surely, the spirit of the great man must have looked down with pride as his son and the 'Whites' rose to the occasion.

The *Post* headline on that occasion screamed. 'Whites spring a surprise', whilst a secondary headline trumpeted, 'promise of a rugby revival'. Seven thousand spectators were at the match to see the 'Whites' pack 'beat the Cardiff octet in every phase of the game'. As for the backs, 'Observer' noted that, 'people gasped with astonishment'. No D. R. Gent, he, but, after a disappointing start to the new campaign, the *Post*-man could be forgiven for eulogising.

And he did. 'Hearts were filled with joy at the sight of the Swansea forwards heeling. ... nine times out of ten ... and the backs played the proper Swansea game, passing and interpassing, and only kicking when the movement was in danger of being held up' Bruce Barter, who scored all the points for Swansea, was cited as having had an outstanding match, whilst 'Young Trew was a huge success'.

Sadly, in his joy and excitement, and in implying that that performance was the beginning of another revival in the club's fortunes, 'Observer' had overstated his case. The next match must have reminded him of the old adage about swallows and summers. The 'Wizards' played a spoiling game, which resulted in there being 'too much tension'. A three-points-all draw resulted, and the spectators were frustrated. 'Wing Three', no doubt summoned by his editor to provide a more considered view of Swansea matches, was unimpressed. 'There has been a decline in quality', he wrote, though in fairness to the 'Whites', in the match which was the subject of the journalist's report, Swansea had played with fourteen men for the bulk of the game. There were two newcomers in that match, C. F. Walters, who was to make his name on the cricket field, and Fred Rees made their débuts.

As far as the St. Helens faithful were concerned, according to the *Leader*, they were 'gloomy'. The joy, excitement, the skill and movement of the Cardiff match were but a memory, and play in two successive games had been 'prosaic'. But then, as if to underline the team's mercurial inconsistency, Llanelli were beaten in a match during which a remarkable try was scored by the men in white. Judging by the inference of his report, 'Wing Three', would have loved to have been the Swansea winger who touched down to finish the move. At any rate, his prose was breathless; 'The ball came loose in the home twenty-five ... Dan Hopkins, Watkins, and Walters

'Whites' v. 'Maoris'. St. Helens, 23 October 1926.

Swansea R.F.C. 1926-27.
Back Row: Joe Grey, Jack Rees, Roger Ling, J. H. John, D. R. Jenkins, Dai Parker.
Second Row: Lewis Jones (Treas.), Ben Jones, Bert Palmer (Sec.), E. A. H. Jones, G. Grimshaw, M. Rice, W. Clement, Rees Evans, E. Long, Bob Dowdle (Trainer), Tom Harry (Com.).
Sitting: R. H. R. Lloyd (Com.), D. P. Manley, Bruce Barter, W. Faull, J. E. Watkins (Capt.), D. B. Evans, D. Hopkins, W. Roberts, W. H. Evans (Com.). On Ground: Sid Davies, Roy Jones (Vice-Capt.), W. J. Trew.
Inset: L. Perkins, G. White.

made the running across the field. Forwards became 'on side', and there followed short, swift passing which was carried on by Roy Jones and Tom Hopkins, until the wing-man, who had handled four or five times, touched down amidst the wildest excitement.'

That was a real Swansea try! Such was the euphoria which followed that match that both Swansea papers predicted that the team would be inspired against the touring Maoris. But, on that occasion, after the 'Whites' had made the running for the first quarter, it was the visiting team which ran out winners by eleven points to six. For the 'Whites', Dan Hopkins scored all his side's points, while Ivor Matthews did well at scrum-half.

The Swansea side on that occasion was:

D. Hopkins, C. F. Walters, J. E. Watkins (Capt.), B. Barter and Roy Jones, Billy Trew, Ivor Matthews, J. H. John, D. Parker, T. Hopkins, D. R. Jenkins, W. Faull, E. Long, P. C. M. Rice, and J. Rees.

When the 'Whites' went to Cardiff for the next domestic match, 'Wing Three's' mood had swung from euphoria to depression. 'Only the incurable optimist', he wrote, 'dared to hope for a Swansea victory.' Clearly, the journalist's moods were as mercurial as the team's form. Unfortunately, though, his realism proved to have a sound foundation; Cardiff won by 16 points to 6. Then, after another defeat in midweek, in commenting on a match against Gloucester,'Wing Three's' muse burst into flame. Against all expectations, the 'Whites' routed the 'Citizens', and inspired the *Post*-man to write; 'The dolours of Thursday and the megrims of Friday vanished like magic ... The foible to feel the slings and arrows more sensitively than the common run of men is a sign of vitality ... and a Celtic trait.' After having looked up one or two of the journalist's words in a dictionary, the man on the Mumbles Train, must have wondered what more there was to say? Every bemused 'Whites' supporter must have felt like he did. Even if they did not, the style of the victory over the 'Citizens' must have lifted many hearts, and the *Post* report must have reflected their joy. Danny Hopkins was 'the D'Artagnan of the backs', Matthews and Trew 'sparkled at half-back', whilst Roy Jones, A. L. Perkins and Evan Hopkins 'played with dash and skill'. According to 'Wing Three', it was the manner of the win which 'will give heart to the team, for it came when despondency threatened to envelop everybody'. Whilst the journalist had demonstrated that he was prone to overstate his case, the tone of Swansea's other paper confirmed that, prior to the Gloucester match, things *had* been at a low ebb at St. Helens.

When the next match was won, and victories over Leicester, and Cambridge followed, Swansea smiles were more assured. Dai Parker, Danny Hopkins, Cyril Walters and the captain were prominent during that spell, and, by mid-December, the *Leader* was arguing that 'Swansea are able to play more attractive football than any side in Wales'. Cynics, however, might have asked 'Ah., but can they do so consistently?' As the British Broadcasting Commission took over broadcasting duties from the Company, the outcome of 'Whites' matches demonstrated that the answer to that question was in the negative.

During that period, 'Wing Three' wrote of 'tackling to make a schoolboy blush', and of a side 'playing like men in a state of bewilderment'. By February, after 'little Maesteg' had won a 'dour match' at St. Helens, the *Post*-scribe was citing the Gloucester match programme as advice for 'temperamental Swansea supporters'. As a spectacle, the Maesteg match had been 'an utter failure', and the sparse crowd had given voice to its disappointment. 'Wing Three', in responding to the clamour, referred the supporters to the Gloucester philosophy. 'Hope is anticipation with the possibility of realisation ... Hope is an antidote to misery, a cordial for the despondent.' Sadly, as the season drew towards its close, had that cordial been bottled, it would have been a best-seller among the Swansea faithful. For a match against Bristol 'the Tanner Bank was deserted', and, whilst the team recovered something of its mid-season form to beat the Harlequins and Cardiff, on balance, another disappointing campaign was concluded with twenty matches having been lost. However, for the optimists, there was one new figure to pin their hopes upon. A 'speedster', D. P. Manley, had shown 'great promise' in scoring several 'classical tries'.

Yet, Manley aside, as Malcolm Campbell sought to set a new land speed record at Pendine, and the Vetch authorities were to build a double-decker stand to 'increase their capacity to fifty thousand', the St. Helens committee must have looked in on itself anxiously. Had they employed a soothsayer, they might have drawn some comfort from the arrival of a new goalkeeper at the Vetch called Ferguson. In years to come the big-man's issue would have an influence on rugby matters in the town. At that time, however, the despondency which was evident at the home of Swansea rugby necessitated a 'cordial' of more immediate potency. The future was the territory of the soothsayer. The need at St. Helens for the campaign ahead, was to find the means to make the side consistent. It went without saying that such consistency would need to be of the winning variety.

1927/28

A better performance

Having lost twenty matches in each of the two previous seasons, there was a determination at St. Helens to do better in the new campaign. Welsh international, Dai Parker, was the man at the helm, thus emulating his brother by being appointed to the Swansea captaincy. He recognised that his was a tough task, but surely, the popular opinion had it, the side 'would do better this time'. After the 'opener' against the League, that view was reinforced.

Indeed, 'Wing Three', writing in the *Post*, was carried away to the extent that he posed the question, 'A vintage Year?' Given the extent of the rain which had fallen on Swansea during the previous season, the analogy which could be taken as relating rugby to the cultivation of grapes was somewhat ironic. Yet, the journalist's account of the match with the League, must have given heart to the loyal supporters (particularly those who had not been present at the game). 'Wing Three's' buoyancy was such that he was of the opinion that the 'Whites', 'could hope for a great season'. Not surprisingly, that hope was grasped to the collective bosom of Swansea supporters with alacrity.

When the side inflicted a heavy defeat on Pontardawe in the next match, the *Post*-man reported that, 'the Swansea passing was delightful to watch'. Everything seemed to be falling into place. All in all, the 'warm-up' games, and, particularly the manner in which victories were achieved in them, were considered to be most satisfactory. The real test, however, would come when the side played its first 'proper' game. That match was to be at Llanelli against the 'Scarlets'.

Presumably as a result of the encouragement which supporters had gained from the two 'openers', more Swansea folk travelled by train to Llanelli to see the game with the 'Scarlets' than had been the case for many years. They went to the Tinopolis with hope wrapped around them like their mother's shawl. In the event, that hope was dashed, as Llanelli won by virtue of a late penalty. Nevertheless, as it made its way home,the Swansea contingent was not downhearted. According to the *Leader*, they had seen,' an exciting and enjoyable match ... played in chivalrous spirit'. In addition, the best try of the match had been scored by a Swansea man. Roy Jones, 'spying a vestige of an opening, sprang at it like a terrier ... he was clear away with several Llanelly men in pursuit ... then dived over for a capital try'.

During the week prior to that Llanelli match, overtures had been made to the Swansea Council and to the Cricket and Football Club, by a 'consortium of businessmen'. These men wished to use St. Helens for greyhound racing, but they reckoned without both the St. Helens sportsmen, and the council members. The members of the club were unanimous in wishing to reject the concept, and they were delighted when the Borough Council turned down the proposal (by forty votes to eight). A spokesman for the Council stated that members were against dog racing, not only at St. Helens, but on any council-owned property. The major reason for their stance, they said, was related to the 'moral aspect of the greyhound racing business'.

Meantime, at St. Helens, the only rabbits involved were those which the 'Whites' were pulling out of the hat. In successive matches, Aberavon, Neath, and Cross Keys were all soundly beaten. 'Wing Three', however, let it be known that he was not enamoured with the style of play in two of the games. He felt that the 'Whites' backs were 'too fond of kicking', and he was critical of the referee who had officiated in the Neath match, on the grounds that he was 'whistle happy'. Indeed, in describing the game in which there was 'a plethora of penalties', the journalist likened the referee to 'a bosun who was determined to remind the crew that he was the big noise'. Nonetheless, 'Wing Three' picked out Bruce Barter and Roy Jones as being the outstanding men in the match, as they were, with Syd Davies, in the game with Cross Keys. However, the *Post*-scribe was happier on that occasion, reporting that the victory was 'the most significant of the season'. At least, the Swansea supporters were able to enjoy some open rugby in that match. Furthermore, in Manley they had on the wing, a new 'flyer' to satisfy their thirst for spectacular tries.

Whilst Newport were the victors in the next match – at Rodney Parade – the supporters accepted defeat with greater equanimity than they might have done had another club been the victor. The 'Whites' had not won at Newport since 1912, consequently,the supporters had travelled with little expectation of victory. Thus it was, that, when the Swansea youngsters performed so well, their followers took pride from the defeat. 'Wing Three' reported that the young Swansea players were 'acutely disappointed at the narrow defeat, but had played well.' Billy Trew Jnr. was said to have been a 'complete success on the wing'. Evan Harries was 'the pick of the Swansea pack', and D. W. Evans made 'some magnificent bursts'. At no side, the Newport crowd applauded both sides and 'gave particular emphasis to clapping the Swansea men from the field'.

By the end of October, both the *Leader* and the *Post* were expressing themselves delighted with the progress which was being made by the young side. D. P. Manley, D. W. Evans, Dai Parker, Billy Trew, and Bruce Barter were mentioned frequently, and, when Gloucester were defeated at St. Helens, Swansea smiles were becoming less diffident. Not surprisingly, sometimes 'on the big occasion', the young side lost its composure. On one such occasion, in a match against Llanelli, the young men 'froze'. Nonetheless, by and large, in the games up to Christmas, the youngsters did very well. In one match, despite the fact that 'conditions were awful', they contrived to 'play football of the exciting variety in the grand style'. One try, when 'twelve pairs of hands handled the leather', brought 'waves of applause from the grandstand and the cheap side'. And, on that day, that maritime analogy was not without its relevance. 'Rain fell like stair rods' and trainer, Bob Dowdle, was 'clad in sou'wester and an army surplus waterproof cape'.

Another 'big occasion', was the match against the touring 'Waratahs', which was lost in the first quarter, when the youngsters were, were still, 'feeling their feet'. The Australian side scored three tries during that first period, but, in the remainder of the game, because of the determination of the Swansea men, they did not score again. The *Leader* reported that the 'Whites' pack was magnificent, whilst the backs, 'tackled everything in sight'. Dai Parker scored the Swansea points with a penalty, which, in itself, was noteworthy. His points were the first scored against the Australians up to that stage in their tour.

The side which represented Swansea that day was:

H. C. Perry, D. P. Manley, D. W. Evans, Bruce Barter, J. E.Watkins, Syd Davies, Roy Jones, D. Parker, J. H. John, D. R. Jenkins, E. Harries, T. Hopkins, T. Mabbett, E. Long and W. Clement.

Before snow, frost, and ice caused several matches to be postponed, there was another 'landmark' match which tested the young Swansea side. Neath were beaten at the Gnoll; whilst the home side played with fourteen men for the bulk of the second-half, press reports suggest that the Swansea team was in control throughout. And that was despite the referee, who wore a white shirt and blue shorts, which 'often confused the Swansea players'. The Swansea wags suggested that either the official was colour blind, or he was of the school which likes to melt into the background.

From that stage in the season until the posts were 'hauled down', the young men won some fine victories; none more impressive than the final game of the campaign. On that day, in 'ideal rugby weather', Bristol were beaten by 13 points to 8. During the match, Danny Hopkins carried his aggregate of points scored past the 500 mark, whilst two of the team's tries 'brought those in the stand to their feet'. The first was a real 'crowd pleaser'. Dennis Manley, nearer his own goal line than his twenty-five, took a pass one-handed, and 'flew along the right flank to score one of the best tries of the season'. Then, in the second-half, Dan Hopkins ran in from thirty yards after fine inter-passing between Rowe Harding and J. E. Watkins. Those tries, and the manner in which the side 'played the Swansea game' that day, gave the home supporters a rare fillip to carry them through the summer in readiness for the next campaign. No one mentioned 'end-of-season' staleness that day!

1928–29

Further improvement

D. P. Manley, who scored 23 tries during the previous season, was one of a strong nucleus of players on whom the new captain, Rowe Harding, could rely for the campaign ahead. For the first time for several years, the 'Whites' were to set out into the new season with the bulk of the side which had played during the previous campaign. As experience was to show, the benefits which came from this 'familiar combination', were among the factors which resulted in an improved outcome. Such benefits were immediately apparent when the 'Whites' played the first 'opener' against the District League. The District side was beaten by 55 points to 5, which was the highest Swansea score in the fixture since the War.

Following that match, 'Wing Three' was of the opinion that the 'Whites' were 'going to be a formidable side this season'. With no newcomers in the team, the men in white 'played as if they had never stopped'. According to the *Post*-man, the passing was 'of the kind which delights every rugger man's heart'. For its part, the *Leader* believed that the Swansea three quarter line was the fastest in Wales. As the *Post* had it, 'Rowe Harding – the "Cantab" – was the driving force in the centre', whilst the wing men were 'of the stuff which thrills the loyal supporter'.

When 'similar fluency' was evident in the second 'opener', against Pontardawe, 'Wing Three' waxed lyrical. He wrote, 'Football ironsides have been throttling rugby in Wales by their unimaginative methods. Thousands have been driven from rugby grounds by sheer boredom at the continual spectacle of pure forward slams.' Swansea, the *Post*-scribe implied, had the antidote to that malaise, and he, and, no doubt the whole of the Town's rugby community, looked forward to administering that theriac during the season ahead.

Unfortunately, the first 'proper' match was lost without the Swansea men scoring a point. Coventry, the victors, were organised more effectively, and gained their fourteen points as a result of only attacking when they were in the last quarter of the field. Conversely, the Swansea expansionist game, built on flair and understanding, with attacks being launched whenever the mood dictated, was shown to be flawed. It was a timely lesson for the young men to learn.

By early October, the side had undergone some change, and, whilst a further match was lost, there were exciting wins against Bridgend, Penarth, and Aberavon. Elfryn Bowen, Billy Trew, Phil Beynon, and Aubrey Hill were among those cited in the press as having done well in those matches, whilst Dai Parker's boot was responsible for most of the points in the game against ''Bravon'.

As it happened, the Aberavon match was historic in that it was the first Swansea game in which both sides wore numbers. Presumably with a nod towards the superstitious in both camps, neither side included a number 13 jersey. Winger, D. P. Manley, who wore number 2, scored a thrilling try, after number 6, outside-half Trew, had made the opening as a result of 'neat work, which is the hall-mark of a born footballer'.

As 'Robots' replaced policemen at busy traffic junctions in Swansea, the team's form fluctuated like the lights. Fine wins (green) were followed by close matches (amber) or defeats (red). The side won at Pontypool for the first time for seven years, with Elfryn Bowen at his brilliant best, and Rowe Harding 'having his finest match for Swansea'. Neath, 'just preserved their unbeaten record', and Cardiff, playing with 'dashing, debonair confidence' put twenty-one points on the scoreboard to beat the 'Whites'.

Yet, supporters had to remember that the side was relatively young and inexperienced. Consequently each game, win, lose, or draw, provided further opportunities for its development. When the side travelled to Gloucester in November, they looked as if they had learnt a lot since the season started. J. H. John was outstanding at hooker, Watcyn Thomas and W. Davies 'excelled in the pack', Roy Jones and Elfryn Bowen 'controlled matters' at half-back, whilst wingers, Bruce Barter and Dennis Manley, were 'exceptionally good'. So dominant were the 'Whites' in that match that, whilst they only scored eight points, they might well have doubled that total. Gloucester meanwhile, failed to register a single point.

In the next match, at Stradey, whilst the M.C.C. were scoring 734 for 7 in Australia, three 'Whites' were carried off in a fractious match. Then, with mud, gusting winds and heavy rain to contend with, 'dribbling dominated', as did 'physical contact of the less attractive kind'. The play up front, according to 'Rambler', was 'highly provocative', and, having lost Harry Rees early in the game, and two other players early in the second-half, the 'Whites' finished with twelve men. Given that fact, when the final whistle blew, the drawn match was a greater testimony to the tenacity of the 'All Whites' than to that of the 'Scarlets'. Furthermore, according to both Swansea papers, the scoring of the Swansea points provided the pinnacle of the excitement in the match. Elfryn Bowen, 'with a characteristic interception', paved the way for Dennis Manley to 'tear through the mud' to touch down.

Dai Parker about to convert v. Llanelli.

The force of the wind during that match was remarkable, but, later that night it increased in intensity, and, as a result, part of the Stradey stand was 'blown the length of the pitch', whilst a house in Danygraig lost its roof, and trees were blown across the Mumbles road. Perhaps the gods were showing their displeasure at the Stradey battle?

As far as football was concerned, for Swansea supporters,the high point of that windy month was the victory over Newport. Whilst the result (8 points to 5) suggested a much closer match, the men in white were dominant throughout. In particular, the young pack played 'above themselves', with Tom Day, who had made his début in the previous match, prominent. The game was, according to the *Leader*, one of the most exciting seen at St. Helens for many years. Not only was it exciting, Swansea won the match in some style. Elfryn Bowen was 'the star article', and he and Rowe Harding combined to great advantage. Seymour Hicks, who, at that time, was appearing in a play at the Grand Theatre, would have been delighted to have left an audience so satisfied at the end of a performance.

When the 'Scarlets' were well-beaten in the return at St. Helens, the 'gate' was recorded at 8,000 people. However, the *Post* cartoonist believed that that was not the true total. According to the artist, 'Swansea's Scotsman's stand' (a footbridge over the Mumbles Road and L.M.S. railway) was 'well packed'. Besides the cartoon, the *Post* included a feature which had been conspicuous by its absence for some time. The 'unofficial' Welsh Rugby Table showed the 'Whites' in fourth position. Eleven matches had been won out of eighteen played. Presumably the editor felt that things at St. Helens were going to improve.

Injuries to Rowe Harding and Dennis Manley did little to assist in this cause, but in their absence two young men were drafted into the side who were going to play important roles in the Swansea story. Claude Davey and Denver Rees made their débuts against Skewen. Davey, according to the *Post* 'was rather too prone to try to get through on his own'. That was a trait which the young man was to turn to advantage in the seasons ahead.

At least one man at St. Helens was happy over the Christmas period. The treasurer was delighted with Yuletide 'gates'. The 'biggest Christmas Day attendance since the War' saw the Watsonians being beaten, whilst the Boxing Day attendance and that of the following Saturday were both larger than they had been for some time. The results of the games involved were also encouraging. Watsonians and Cross Keys were both well-beaten, whilst there was 'an exciting draw in difficult conditions' with London Welsh. That game, according to the *Post's* report, was a 'ski-ing, curling and species of soccer' match. As the rain poured down, the mud was churned up, and the 'lump of soap' (the ball) was 'impossible to handle'. Windsor Lewis and Guy Morgan played in that match, but it was Aubrey Hill who 'plunged into a pond' ten seconds before no side to register the points for the 'Whites'.

At the turn of the year the weather changed, bringing with it snow and ice, which, in turn resulted in many matches being postponed. As a result, a number of 'Whites' found themselves at a New Year's Eve dance in a Swansea hotel, where, according to the *Post*, a sensation occurred. It seems that the hotel's cat chased a rat into the ballroom. The first protection which offered itself to the rodent was the leg of a man's trousers. To the horror of the unfortunate wearer, the creature scrambled up his trouser leg. The story continued; 'The cat clawed at the outside of the trousers where the form of the prospective meal was bulging. The episode ended when a friend crushed the intruder, this being impossible for the wearer of the trousers, whose hands were engaged in preventing further progress up his leg.' No doubt, the man's ally was a wing-forward.

The second day of the new year brought with it sad news for Swansea rugby followers. David James (62 years of age) died at his Bonymaen home. A tribute in the *Post* by 'Old Rugbyite' exemplified the legendary image of the old star 'So supple were they, and gifted with such elasticity, that they were difficult to tackle, and still more difficult to hold. If thrown to the ground, they would bounce about like rubber balls and be up and off again in a twinkling.' No one stopped to ask if the writer was over-stating his case. Forty years after they had held centre stage, *that* was how the Brothers were remembered!

At St. Helens, whilst rugby was 'in cold storage', the authorities were not idle. A 'welcome initiative' resulted in powerful arc lamps being erected at the ground 'to enable the players to train during the hours of twilight'. Unfortunately, though, that initiative was not sufficient to prevent a further 'desertion' to the Northern Union. D. R. Jenkins, who had been 'capped' by Wales for the match against the 'Waratahs', signed for Leeds in return for the sum of £370. An ever-present in the Swansea pack that season, D.R. was to be missed.

When the weather changed and football resumed, results were mixed, though, in a February match at St. Helens, the young men 'ran riot'. Claude Davey and Denver Rees were 'in great form', J. H. John 'hooked like a machine', and, as for Roy Jones, 'there is no more pertinacious man in attack'. Despite the fact that the 'Whites' lost a player after eleven minutes of the match,they ran out winners over Bristol by 22 points to 5. The depleted pack attracted much praise, with Jack John, Watcyn Thomas and E. Day being described as 'indefatigable'.

And so was the Mumbles Railway. At the end of February 'without public acclamation or ceremony ... steam gave way to modern electric traction'. Thus another era began which, among other things, in years to come would add colour to the commentaries of Arlott and

Swanton. Furthermore, the 'upstairs' passengers in the electric train were afforded a fleeting view, at least, of St. Helens cricket, as the vehicle slipped past the ground. It might not have been another 'Scotsman's stand', but it whetted the appetite.

As March came towards its end, the citizens of the old borough were experiencing atypical Swansea weather. No rain had fallen for thirty days. The weather-watchers said that that had not happened for twenty years, and, given the status of the 'Whites' in '08, there may have been those who wished to see this coincidence as an omen. Thus, when Llanelli were beaten in a match in which Tom Hopkins, Watcyn Thomas, Edryd Jones, Claude Davey and Roy Jones excelled, and the Harlequins conceded 22 points to the 'Whites', the wishful thinking seemed to have gained some credence. And that euphoria was reinforced when the Barbarians, Aberavon, and the Combined Universities sides succumbed to the Swansea men. In the last three of those matches, Swansea scored seventy points whilst conceding just six. This was the form which the supporters longed for! This was the form to bring back the 'backsliders' from the Vetch. And, with the town's soccer team not doing as well as it had, there was some evidence that this was happening.

When the season's final whistle blew, there was a feeling of satisfaction at St. Helens. Twenty-nine matches had been won and only ten lost, whilst Dennis Manley had scored twenty-five tries. That was more like the old Swansea! Thus, when Roy Jones, 'one of the most modest and unassuming of footballers', was elected to the captaincy for the season ahead, he must have felt that the foundations which had been built during the campaign which had just ended, would stand him in good stead. In general, both papers felt that there was an air of confidence about the place. After all, the comparison with 1908 might not be as far fetched as all that.

1929–30

The best since the War

The summer-like weather which greeted the start of the new rugby season, was such that 'Wing Three' felt moved to write, 'The strength and splendour of the autumn sunshine was enough to invest the idea of football with a touch of fantasy'. Yet, despite the 'broiling sun', the 'Whites' played in both 'openers' as if such a climate suited them admirably. The District conceded 37 points, and Pontardawe were beaten by 43 points to 7. The *Leader* reported that, in the first of these games, 'the "Whites" sprang to the attack from the kick-off'. Though, for his part, 'Wing Three', having learnt something from his experience of the previous season, urged his readers not to get carried away by the results. 'Even though sparkling football has been played, the real test will come in the proper matches.'

As it transpired, the *Post*-man need not have been concerned. Apart from a narrow defeat at Newport, the side played fine football to defeat Coventry, Bath, and Cross Keys. In his report of the first of those matches, 'Wing Three' compared the persistent Swansea attacks to waves breaking on a sea wall. He and 'Pendragon' were much impressed by the quality of the Swansea play and combination. Bryn Evans and Roy Jones, at half-back, were singled out for particular praise, for, as has ever been the case, the pivotal positions are an essential ingredient of successful rugby sides. Happily, though, no one attempted to compare the pair with the 'Dancing Dicks', or the 'Swansea Gems'.

Swansea R.F.C. 1929-30.
Back Row: R. Dowdle, D. B. Jones, Lewis Jones, G. Davies, J. Rees, C. Davey, T. A. Hill, D. F. Thomas, T. B. Day, E. Jones, J. H. John, D. Thomas, R. S. Palmer (Secretary), Bruce Barter. Second Row: J. P. Tyler, Ben Jones, J. Evans, W. Davies, D. P. Manley, Roy Jones (Capt.), E. Howell Jones, E. Long, D. Parker, Councillor W. Owen, W. Griffiths. Front Row: W. J. Trew, Idwal Rees, Bryn Evans.

Behind the half-backs, Claude Davey was doing well in the centre, whilst Dennis Manley's potential on the wing was undiminished. At full-back, Edryd Jones 'started as if he had never stopped playing', whilst, in the power-house, Watcyn Thomas, Tom Day, Dai Parker and D. F. Thomas were said to have been 'prominent throughout '.

As the airship R.101 was successfully launched at Cardington, and Jays were offering the public a solid oak bedroom suite for 18 guineas, the *Post* report on the match with the Monmouthshire side, carried the headline 'Whites put Keys in their pocket'. They did that, according to the report, despite losing skipper, Roy Jones with a dislocated shoulder early in the match. Furthermore, such was the style and purpose with which the 'Whites' played on that occasion, that 'Wing Three' felt moved to write, 'With the "Whites" playing as they are, the coming game with Neath should bring back all the rugby backsliders who have been temporarily attracted to another place'. Whilst the *Post*-man did not mention the words 'Vetch' or 'soccer', there was little doubt as to where the journalist's sentiments lay. In consequence, on the day of the Neath match, 'Wing Three' must have been delighted to see 'a crowd of old time dimensions', at St. Helens to see the 'Whites' play the 'Blacks'.

On that day, despite the fact that Swansea supporters had to agree that their favourites had been second best, the excitement and incident in the match compensated in no small measure for their disappointment. The Swansea pack had 'played themselves to a standstill', whilst every 'White' 'had given his all'. As for scrum-half, Bryn Evans, he was described as being 'as ubiquitous and persistent as a mosquito'. Clearly, though,his sting was not potent enough to affect the Neath men adversely.

As the season progressed, and the side went from strength to strength, both Swansea papers sought to identify the reasons for this success. When the 'Wizards' and Gloucester were well-beaten, apart from commending Billy Trew ('the Master-mind') on his play and leadership – he was acting as captain in the absence of Roy Jones – and congratulating Bryn Evans on his fast and accurate service, the conclusion of both papers was that 'teamwork is making the difference'. Clearly, the supporters were enjoying the experience, too. The size of the 'gates' at St. Helens was steadily increasing, which reflected the attractive play of the side and, of course, its success. As fickle as ever, many Swansea folk only wanted to see a winning side, and one that won with style. Commercial minds, too, were noting the phenomenon. The L.M.S. railway, seeing profit in the increased traffic to St. Helens, announced that a special train would be run from Victoria Station to Swansea Bay at a fare of a penny-halfpenny.

By Christmas time, Swansea supporters were beginning to believe that the 'Whites' were developing into a side which would achieve 'old-time success'. Against Llanelli, Dennis Manley scored a hat-trick of tries to 'thrill the crowd'. The first of these started with the winger taking a one-handed catch 'high above his head',and sprinting the length of the pitch to score. How Swansea fans loved such scores! In the same match, Dai Parker 'had his kicking boots on', and Bryn Evans, W. J. Trew, Claude Davey and J. P. Tyler were 'thrilling the crowds with their play'. For his part, Davey was developing what was to become known as 'the crash tackle'. Swansea-ites, in years to come, were to argue that the University man invented the concept.

Unfortunately, amidst the euphoria, came the news that another key Swansea player was 'going north', though, in this case, not to join a Northern Union side. Watcyn Thomas, the man in question, moved to Lancashire to take up a teaching post in St. Helens. A Welsh international and a powerful scrummager, he would be missed. On the other hand, the club was delighted to welcome Howie Jones into its fold. The ex-Neath man was also an international, though, in his case, a three-quarter. On his arrival, Jones said that 'Swansea's style of play will suit me well'.

Subsequently, results on the field followed the early pattern of success. Cambridge University, Penarth, Cross Keys, Watsonians, and Bristol were all beaten, as were the popular Leicester side. In that match with the 'Tigers', Billy Trew was outstanding, Davey and Roy Jones, thrustful, Manley, Snipper and Howie Jones 'took their chances well', and the pack 'played its part'. Prominent in the front eight were Will Davies, Eddie Long, and Dai Thomas. The smiles at St. Helens radiated confidence. The 'Whites' were ' on the march', again!

In February, the short Midlands tour also proved to be a success. Coventry were beaten 'decisively', with Bryn Evans and Trew again outstanding, whilst Derby were 'outclassed' in a match in which the 'Whites' played with 'verve and vigour'. In the Derby match, W. D. P. Hopkins was at scrum-half, and did well enough to allow 'Young Trew' to have a hand in all the Swansea tries.

On returning to St. Helens, the vivacity of the team remained undiminished. Skewen – the 'Oilville men' – were beaten by a massive 57 points to nil. As far as the 'Whites' supporters were concerned, that win 'put the gilt on the gingerbread'. During that match, no less than thirteen tries were scored by the men in white, Howie Jones 'went nap', whilst the forwards joined in the passing movements. Indeed, Jack Rees, Tom Day and Will Davies were said to have been 'in their element'. Quite right, too. Why should the backs have all the glory?

On 17 March 1930, Swansea ceased to have two evening papers. The *Leader*, in the language of business diplomacy, 'merged' with the *Daily Post*. In effect, the former paper had been taken over by a financially stronger company. The trade depression had claimed another victim. Nonetheless, as far as the 'All Whites' were concerned, the 'merger' resulted in one 'Pendragon' becoming the sole journalistic 'Whites'-watcher in Swansea. It was the start of a relationship between club and the journalist which was to last for many years. 'Wing Three', he of the extravagant prose, disappeared.

In its first edition, the new paper printed a drawing of the town's handsome new civic centre to be. Appropriately, as far as the rugby men were concerned, it was to be sited nearer to St. Helens than to the Vetch. There were, however, those who wanted to know what Thomas of Lan, pioneer of Swansea's 'open spaces', would have said about another portion of Swansea being built upon. Other developments were reported, too. On Townhill, a large water tower was being erected which, in years to come, was to prove to be a landmark, whilst, at St. Helens, the old cricket pavilion was to be demolished and a new one built.

At the end of March, as Al Jolson was making his Swansea début in the 'Jazz Singer', the local wags were not slow to replace 'Swanee' with the name of the old borough. As far as 'Whites' supporters were concerned, they could have joined in the chorus, 'How I love yer, my dear old Swansea', as the 'Scarlets' were 'thrashed' by 29 points to nil. According to 'Pendragon' that victory 'could be put down to effective teamwork', and an outstanding triangle of Claude Davey, Billy Trew, and Roy Jones. Fittingly, after that match, Swansea stood proudly at the top of the 'Unofficial' Welsh table. *That* was more like it!

Neath were the next to feel the edge of the keen-edged Swansea sword, as they conceded 16 points without scoring themselves. The 'triangle' was again in evidence, though, this time, they were fed by a new inside-half. Swansea University man, and Welsh captain to be, Idwal Rees, made his début.

Thereafter, during that season, the 'Whites' lost only two matches, and one of those, against the Barbarians, only by a single point. Thus it was that, when the curtain fell, the new *Post*-scribe was able to argue that the season had been 'the most successful for many years'! In point of fact, it was necessary to go back to the last campaign before the War to find a season during which fewer games were lost. Furthermore, the percentage of games won in relation to those played had not been bettered since the 1912-13 season, when the side had won the 'Premiership'. Interestingly, the captain of that side had been W. J. Trew, Senior. The great man's son, having acted as captain for part of the season which had just finished (in Roy Jones's absence) could feel proud of such comparison. Clearly, his team-mates thought that to be the case, for W. J. Trew junior, was elected as captain, unanimously, for the 1930-31 campaign. It was the first time that a father and son had captained the club.

As he looked forward to the coming season, Trew 'the younger', in keeping with his reserved nature, must have felt quietly confident. In Dennis Manley (29 tries), and Claude Davey (22) he had attacking players of top quality. Howie Jones, and his namesake, Roy, were men of considerable rugby stature, whilst Dai Parker, who had kicked 18 penalties and converted 22 tries during the previous season, provided the necessary place-kicking skills. Furthermore, the pack had welded itself into a potent unit. All in all, Trew, his team-mates, the officials at St. Helens, and all who supported Swansea rugby, would have been justified in expecting even greater success in the season ahead. Given that the team had finished runners-up to Abertillery in the 'Unofficial Welsh Table', the question was, could they win the Premiership next season? If they did, thought the oval ball men, *that* would make Swansea a rugby town again!

Chapter Fourteen

THE 'PUBLIC SCHOOLBOYS'

'PENDRAGON' WAS OF THE OPINION that the season of 1930/31 had been 'one of the worst on record'. Seventeen games had been lost, and, for a variety of reasons, the club had struggled to find a settled side. During the season 45 players had appeared in the white shirt, including several seventeen-year-olds. In his end-of-the-season analysis, the *Post* man, whilst searching for something positive to say, could only ponder on the root cause of the club's problems. 'Thirty years ago', he wrote, 'Swansea was the most successful club side in the world ... even when it is allowed that the game has changed since those days, it has to be confessed that the "All Whites" have neither maintained the old standards nor advanced with the times'.

In searching for reasons as to why the side had been relatively unsuccessful, there was a hint of despair in the journalist's writing. 'Opportunities for practice were not so numerous as they used to be, there were smaller crowds and less enthusiasm.' Furthermore, and this seemed to be a corner-stone of 'Pendragon's' argument, unlike their artisan predecessors, the new breed of player, 'the Public Schoolboys', could not be relied upon to stay with the club. He concluded his analysis with the thought that 'the present season has been a mixture of satisfaction and depression ... a period of never-ending experiment'. No doubt, on reading those words,any member of the beleaguered British Government of the time, would have been able to nod sagely in agreement, as he considered them in the light of the nation's economy.

As far as the 'Whites' season was concerned, one can understand at this distance the loyal scribe's concern. The man had grown up with the *fact* of a Swansea team which was a collective living legend. His lot was to report on the doings of what he saw as mere mortals. Looking back on the happenings at that time it is, perhaps, fairer to see the season which so disturbed 'Pendragon', in the context of the post Great War period. Statistically, the campaign had not been the worst in that era. At the end of three other seasons during the period in question, more games had been lost, including two campaigns during which opponents won a score of games. Furthermore, there were positive aspects to be considered. Some exceptional talent had been unearthed, with the University club providing players of the calibre of Watcyn Thomas, Claude Davey and Idwal Rees, whilst Dai Thomas was regarded in 'high quarters' as one of the best all-round forwards in the country. In addition, Davey, Watcyn Thomas and Tom Day had all been 'capped' during the season. Dai Parker had led the side well in the absence through injury of W. J.Trew Jnr., while the play of R. R. Morris, a seventeen-year old Carmarthen Grammar School boy, had been likened to that of the great Dick Jones, and, when he had played, the captain, Billy Trew had had some fine games.There were, too, unexpected victories over Bristol, and Gloucester and, in April, over a Cardiff team 'packed with internationals', who were 'swamped in all phases' by an experimental Swansea side in which three of the backs were under eighteen.

Thus, underlying 'Pendragon's' gloom there were many positive factors to consider, though, no doubt, the reality of the economic situation at the start of the third decade of the century was hardly conducive to outright optimism. For that reason, the point which the journalist made about 'public school boys', was particularly valid. It was probable rather than possible that once a university man graduated he would leave Swansea to follow his career. Conversely the likes of Fred Scrine and Dick Jones, both of whom were stonemasons and Ivor Morgan, who was a coal trimmer, followed their trade in the old borough. In due course,as if to prove the point, Watcyn Thomas took a post in St. Helens, Lancashire, whilst Claude Davey moved to the Midlands, Meanwhile, the artisans in the club were still being tempted by the 'Northern Poachers', and soccer was increasing in popularity in the town, thus diverting potential rugby talent and support to the round ball game.

Nevertheless, whatever was happening on or off the field, the club was still upholding its caring policies. A colourful figure on the 'Tanner bank' for many years after the Great War, was John Derricott. In April 1931, the club arranged for a match to be played between sides from Swansea Corporation, and its Chamber of Trade in aid of the popular character. John, of the basso profundo voice, who wore white moleskin trousers to all Swansea matches in order to signal his allegiance, was given the 'entire income from the game'. He had had to have an arm amputated.

There was something of a diversion, too, regarding the venue for international football in Wales. It had been proposed that a 'Welsh Twickenham' be developed at Bridgend. The idea caused an uproar in both east and west Wales. Influential people in both parts of the Principality joined together in their opposition. Were the proposal adopted, the partial men argued, it would sound the death knell of rugby in Wales. Unbeknown to those in the west, however, there were those in the east who, perhaps triggered by the proposal, had their own ideas about a monopoly of international games.

1931/32

A better outcome

In contrast to their form during the previous season, the 'All Whites' started the 1931-32 campaign with a flourish. By the end of September the team's record read something like that of Gordon's 'Invincibles'. They had played six games, won them all, and their points record stood at 113 for, 41 against. Eyebrows were raised in Swansea, for there had been no indication during the close season that such a start would be made. Yet, before each season starts, hope beats eternal in the hearts of the supporters of a rugby club; those who followed Swansea were no different from any others.

Nonetheless, prior to the start of the campaign, that hope had been somewhat clouded by controversy. It was reported that the club's financial committee had 'stirred up a hornets nest' by arranging for a resolution to be put to the A.G.M. to disband the Second XV. It was, they argued, necessary to do so because 'of the need for an economy campaign'. Opponents of the proposal were vehement. Their position was summed up by a spokesman who stated, 'if this measure is enacted then the status of the club will be affected'. The 'opposers' carried the day, and the finance committee was obliged to look elsewhere for savings. Sir Oswald Mosley, who had been speaking in the town that day, could not have been more eloquent in stating a case.

Swansea R.F.C. 1931-32.
Back Row: J. W. Faull, Ernest Davies, J.P., Lewis Jones, M.P., R. S. Palmer (Secretary), P.C. Rhys L. Evans, Dennis Hunt, J. Gwilliam, D. Edgar Thomas, Glyn Davies, Gwynfor Lewis, Eddie Long, T. A. Hill, Clifford Cowling, M. Bowen, Trevor Davies, Tom Harry, Bruce Barter.
Second Row: Tom Day, W. Davies, C. Davies, I. Davies, Idwal Rees, Jack Rees (Capt.), Bryn Evans, L. V. Michael, I. Herbert, Glyn Jones, Joe White, R. W. Dowdle.
Front Row: Dudley Folland, D. Emlyn Davies.

The Springboks

Since the team had started so well, there were those who argued that the winning side should be retained *en bloc* to oppose the visiting South Africans. However,the selectors felt that they should call upon famous 'outsiders', like Claude Davey, Watcyn Thomas, and D. P. Manley, all former Swansea players (domiciled at the time in England), to oppose the tourists. The arguments about retaining team spirit, giving the existing team members their chance, and it being unfair to drop players for the big day when they had done so well in early games, fell on deaf ears. In the event, the temptation to include the 'stars' was too great. Whether the 'Whites' would have done better if a different decision had been taken can only be a matter of conjecture. However it is possible to argue that, in the long run, it might have been better for the club if the 'normal' side had been selected. On the other hand, on the day, 40,000 people, said to be a Swansea club record, packed St. Helens for the game, thus giving the tacit approval, at least, of supporters to the selection of Davey and the others.

On the day of the match , whilst the South Africans won by 10 points to 3, it was reported that the 'Whites' had a fair measure of the play. Indeed, 'Pendragon' felt that the side was 'glorious in defeat', whilst Bryn Evans had the distinction of being 'the better of the two inside-halves'. Swansea's try was scored by Claude Davey who 'followed up at top speed' to ground the ball after a Will Davies 'tactful kick'. Unaccountably, the conversion was missed, which, according to the *Post* and the *Western Mail*, would have resulted in a score more in keeping with the run of play.

The Swansea side which did so well that day was:

I. Herbert, D. P. Manley, C. Davey, J. Dark, Rhys Evans, Bryn Evans, Idwal Rees, Jack Rees (Capt.), D. Thomas, T. Day, Glyn Jones, Gwynfor Lewis, Joe White, E. Long and Will Davies.

At the post-match dinner at the Hotel Metropole, the Tourists' manager endeared himself to all Swansea when he said 'We were run close'. The ghosts of the founders of the Swansea club must have smiled down at that happy scene, no doubt, nodding in approval.

Domestic football again

After the excitement of the Springboks game, the next visitors to St. Helens were Neath. Given that their favourites had done so well in domestic football and had run the tourists so close, Swansea supporters viewed the game against their neighbours with some confidence. Indeed, prior to the kick off it was quite like old times at St. Helens, 9,000 people were said to be in the ground. In the event, despite the fact that their side dominated the game, it was the Swansea supporters who left the ground disappointed. Neath had taken the club's unbeaten record 'on the break'. Furthermore, the Neath side included W. J. Trew, who had moved to the Gnoll club during the close season. Thus the defeat was doubly hard to take. Surely, the argument went, it was wrong for such a famous Swansea name to be included in the line-up of an opposing side which won at St. Helens. The Neath followers had no such sentiment in their minds.

Happily, whilst the Swansea supporters were bemused by that defeat, they did not have long to dwell on such matters. Following the next match, the *Post's* headline declared 'Rugby history made at Newport'. The fact behind the headline was that, prior to that Saturday, Swansea had not won a game at Newport in the period since the War ended. Thus it was that Swansea smiles were well in evidence. Dudley Folland, a well-built wing, had scored on his début, whilst centre Cowling, and T. J. Jenkins were reported as being outstanding in a 'magnificent Swansea side'. Cardiff, who included the Glamorgan cricketer, Maurice Turnbull in their team, were the next to be overcome. Indeed, according to the *Western Mail*, they were 'well beaten'. Even though several chances were spurned by the men in white, the Swansea team-work and spirit were superb. Outstanding among the Swansea backs that day was Cliff Cowling, whilst Will Davies 'a clever skirmisher', was said to have been the pick of the forwards. However, the generally held view was that the secret of the team's success was that it was a 'side without stars'.

Three further victories followed, and 'Pendragon', basking in these successes, felt that the younger players who had come into the side had 'gone a long way to justifying the reversing of the decision to scrap the Seconds'. At that stage in the season the finance committee would have agreed, for, the South Africa game apart, the club's successes had resulted in improved 'gates'. Furthermore, the 'coin counters' were reminded that budgets should be concerned with income as well as expenditure. Not that the matter rested there. These men would reintroduce their proposal on another occasion and, then, win the day.

It was in December that the winning run was interrupted. The 'Whites' were beaten away from home for the first time that season, Bridgend being the victors. Yet, could that have been a mere accident? The next match was to answer that question. Llanelli visited St. Helens having previously beaten the men in white on four out of five occasions.

J. Idwal Rees in his 'Blues' rugby rig-out.

Given the importance of the game the selectors had hoped to include Watcyn Thomas and Idwal Rees, both of whom were home for Christmas, but in the event they were not available. With the famous W. W. Wakefield as referee – one of the few officials to have been cheered before a match at St. Helens – the Scarlets and the Whites fought a dour battle and shared the spoils, 11 points each. Honours were even.

Half-term report

As if to measure the progress of their favourites near the half-way stage in the season, prior to the Christmas Day game, the *Post* published the 'Unofficial Welsh Table'. It showed the 'Whites' lying fourth, having won 13 of the 17 games they had played. It was a more encouraging position for the success – starved supporters, who now hoped that even better things were to come.

For the Boxing Day match, Reggie Bateman came home from Barnstaple, and Watcyn Thomas and D. P. Manley were also available on that occasion. Whilst their presence did little to affect the quality of that game (against Cross Keys), in that against London Welsh the whole team flourished. For once, the 'Whites' piled up the points and the 'Exiles' were beaten by 26 points to 3.

In the matches which followed, several other newcomers were introduced to the side in what appears, at this distance, to have been a rash of *ad hoc* selections, though there were extenuating circumstances. Against Llanelli, Will Davies, an international break-away forward had to play at inside-half, whilst Tyler was played in the centre even though he was a forward with the Seconds. Other introductions were more orthodox, including restoring the schoolboy outside-half, R. R. Morris to the side.

Thereafter, against a backcloth of falling gates, the team was unpredictable, whilst matches were described in less than flattering terms by the press; 'dour', 'scrappy', and 'unimaginative' being among the adjectives used. Nevertheless, whilst George Eyston was breaking the land speed record for baby cars (on Pendine sands), the 'Whites' did some record breaking of their own. Llanelli's two year home ground record was taken with what 'Pendragon' called a 'substitute side'.

By February an optimistic 'Sentinel' was putting forward the view that 'the "All Whites" will go through the remainder of the season in a blaze of glory', sadly it was not to be. In a week in which Dickie Owen was found dead in his home, Llanelli avenged their earlier defeat. Thereafter, apart from the Easter holiday games, results were inconsistent and games uninteresting, though Cardiff were defeated by a side which played most of the game with fourteen men.

In April, 'Sentinel', in his column, discussed why rugby was so much less attractive than it had been in the past. His conclusion was simple; it was the fault of the wing forwards. They were, he argued, 'obstructionists' in their play, and their negative approach stifled creativity. Whilst he did not mention Fred Scrine, who many believed had invented the 'Rover', Dick Jones, in discussing the same issue at a later date, was to point out that the old Swansea forward had been primarily constructive. Presumably, the implication was that the lesser mortals of the day found it easier to destroy than to create.

It was at the end of that month that the Swansea club again showed its compassion. It arranged a special match between Glamorgan Police and South Wales for the benefit of Dickie Owen's dependents. The touch judges were Frank Gordon and Dick Jones, and the 'brilliant and carefree game in which joyful rugby was played' enthralled 10,000 spectators. No one wanted it to end, not even the referee, who let the second-half run for 45 minutes. No mention was made in the report of wing-forwards.

'Pendragon's' final words on the season were that, whilst only 8 games had been lost, the club's record was 'not one to look back on with exceptional pride'. Nonetheless, 440 points had been scored, though the top try getter, Reg Bateman, had only crossed eight times. Furthermore, the 46 players who had been used during the season hardly suggested that there was a core of a settled side waiting for the new campaign to begin.

1932/33

Double figures again

When the '32-3 campaign' came to an end, 'Pendragon's' concerns at the end of the previous season proved to have been well-founded. Having lost just eight matches in the previous season, the 'Whites' submitted fourteen times during the new campaign. Whilst it was the twelfth time since the War that losses had run into double figures , after the relative success of the previous term, it was nonetheless disappointing.

In the October of that season the *Post*'s front page featured a Swansea man, Captain Spencer Freeman, who, the paper suggested, was 'the brains behind the Irish Sweep'. Given the U.K. law at the time, this lottery always created considerable interest in the town. Thousands of tickets were sold, and even those who simply drew horses were fêted. At the time, those who ran Swansea Rugby Club must have wished that some of the luck involved in such ventures would rub off on them.

In the second month of the season, despite an outstanding display by young Willie Davies, Llanelli came out on top at the end of a St. Helens encounter. Yet, a week later, Cardiff, who, at that point in the season had an unbeaten record, could only draw with the 'Whites' on their own ground. According to the *Post*, Joe White was the best forward on the field in that game, and as the report had it, he 'even impressed the Cardiff crowd'. Faced with what he felt was going to be another mediocre season, 'Pendragon' sought further reasons why the 'Whites' were not performing 'as they used to in the old days'. Then, according to the scribe, employers allowed players to take Thursday afternoons off for training. Indeed, he reported that, in those days, thousands would watch and enjoy the practice sessions. 'Now, with thousands seeking jobs in vain, there is a reluctance to release people'. In addition the article went on to restate the arguments about 'spoiling' wing-forwards, and the need for the pack to do more than push in the scrum. However, no ideas were put forward to circumvent the 'spoilers'. The article simply seemed to reflect a yearning for the old order.

Meanwhile, on the field, the 'Whites' continued to please and frustrate game by game. Maesteg were 'thrashed', Neath won a match in which Swansea dominated the play, Newport, with the St. Helens men reduced to 13 for much of the game, were 'outplayed', with young Ronnie Morris, Bryn Evans and Trew outstanding, and three further games were lost when victory was expected. No one used the word enigma, but it might well have been applied to the Swansea side of the period.

In November, whilst the *Post* carried the report on the 'Whites' match in a corner of the back page, its front page was dedicated to the English cricket tour to Australia. Jardine's men were 634 for 9 wickets. Whilst 'Bodyline' was not yet a phrase in common use, a short item on the back page of the paper gave Swansea rugby lovers great satisfaction regarding two of their bodies. Reggie Bateman and Ronnie Morris had refused 'northern offers'. On the same page a revelation regarding the origins of some of the Swansea team seemed designed to give readers a warm glow. Five of the, then, current pack, Edgar Long, Dai Thomas, Joe White, Jack Rees, and Dennis Hunt were all Swansea-born, whilst three of the backs were sons of former Swansea players – Billy Trew, Reggie Bateman (father, Tom) and Ronnie Williams (son of Ike).

Later in the month a tiny item on the front page of the *Post* announced that Germany had selected a new man as 'pack leader'. Herr Hitler had been offered the Chancellorship of Germany. Since the little man was not a rugby player, and no one could see into the future, the appointment aroused little interest at St. Helens. Nevertheless, the future was to show that the activities of the 'housepainter' were to force Swansea Football Club to do something which no one could have envisaged at that time; close the club and surrender the lease of St. Helens to the council.

On the field, results for the remainder of the season followed the same inconsistent pattern. At the turn of the year, 'Pendragon' thought that the 'Whites' team was 'in a melting pot'. Yet, once again, there were encouraging aspects. Youatt and J. P. Tyler were both thought to be 'promising'. Bryn Evans, an Edinburgh M.A., Ronnie Morris and Dai Thomas were all selected to play for Wales, whilst Gloucester, Watsonians and Leicester were all 'put to the sword' at St. Helens when other results might have been expected.

Furthermore, had Swansea rugby lovers been able to see into the future they would have beamed at an item in the *Post* in early January 1934. It announced that two Gowerton boys had been selected to play for Glamorgan Schools against the West of England. The two boys, W. T. H. Davies and H. Tanner, were cousins, whilst Tanner's father, Will, had been a Swansea forward. Two young gods were preparing themselves to appear on the hallowed turf at St. Helens; gods who would receive almost as much acclaim as the James brothers and the 'Dancing Dicks'.

In March a familiar St. Helens figure was fêted in the local press. Bob Dowdle, 'the popular trainer', was about to enter upon his thirtieth year as first team trainer. However, as Dowdle was quick to point out, he had been involved at St. Helens for 35 years in all, for he had worked with the second team prior to his 'elevation'. The trainer, who had been a long-distance competitive walker, thought nothing of walking from St. Helens to his home in Parkmill after a match.

As far as the season's record was concerned, nineteen games had been won and fifteen lost. Dudley Folland (13) and Ronnie Morris (13) led the try scorers, whilst the outside-half also dropped eight goals. 'Pendragon' felt that the side had been 'altered so frequently (that) ... they were always at a disadvantage'. He was disappointed, as were the supporters. Another disappointment was the retirement of Bryn Evans from first-class rugby. Bryn, a popular, if not very assertive captain was 'one of the best-liked players in the country'.

1933/34

More defections

With unemployment a continuing problem the attitude of Swansea supporters to further incursions from the Rugby League was now fatalistic. Most families had one or more of their number without work, and, consequently they could understand the lure of the north. Lump sum payments were appealing, but the real attraction was the guaranteed job. Nevertheless, the club was less than enamoured. Once again it was Broughton Rangers who darkened the doors of St. Helens. Reggie Bateman was the player involved, and to cross the line he took £250, a match fee arrangement and a job. He told the press that, had he been offered a job in Swansea he would have remained an amateur.

Despite the 'defection' and the previous season's track record, there was an air of optimism about at St. Helens when the new campaign began. Apart from anything else, Billy Trew was back from Neath to replace Bateman (and quite right, too, the supporters said). Unfortunately this optimism was not translated into the form of the team for the opening fixture proper. Bath won 5-3 on their own ground in a game in which 'both sides made numerous mistakes'. Whilst, in the next game, Bristol, playing in their lettered jerseys, were beaten on a bone-hard St. Helens the old pattern continued. Cardiff came to St. Helens and took the 'Whites' ground record, and as the supporters and the selection committee braced themselves for another season of hope and disappointment, the 'Northerners' struck again. This time Broughton Rangers took Glyn Jones. Once again, the hooker had been unemployed, and, whilst the Manchester club could arrange for jobs for its new players, there were no such benefits at Swansea. Whilst Bateman had been a loss, 'Pendragon' felt that the impact of Jones leaving would be much harder-felt. Indeed, the scribe thought that 'Swansea will not recover from his loss (Glyn Jones's) for a long while'. Certainly, given the frequent changes which were being made to the side, the team would miss one of the few players who appeared regularly in the 'Whites' XV. Sadly, Jones was not the last to leave at that time. D. Edgar Thomas also joined the Broughton club.

Drought

With a lack of rain affecting Swansea's water supply, the grounds were hard for the early season games. There was something of a drought, too, regarding winning Swansea performances. In early October, Llanelli held the upper hand throughout the game and beat the homesters for the third time in succession. Such were the expectations of the press at this stage in the campaign that it was reported that 'there was some consolation that the deficit was as small as it was'.

A fortnight later, when it was announced that Billy Trew was also going north, the Swansea club and its supporters were downcast. Even the strongest club would have reeled at losing four senior players in such a short time. In Swansea's case the blows were even more damaging. 'Rover', in attempting to analyse the position in which Welsh rugby found itself at the time, expressed understanding of the action of players who 'went north'. He castigated the Welsh Union for not doing more to alleviate the problem, and argued that 'Rugby should provide a career for its top performers'. Many south Wales clubs, he asserted, were 'steeped in debt', and every one of them would have to 'put its house in order and its methods would have to be modernised'. Those who administered Swansea Football Club were no different. For example, 'Pendragon' argued that 'they should pay more attention to the welfare of their players'. Ronnie Morris, he pointed out, had been 'capped' at outside-half and, in the following game for Swansea the selectors had moved him to centre The scribe felt that the young man was being 'messed about'. As far as Billy Trew was concerned, 'Pendragon' believed that Trew Senior would have 'given his son his benediction' about going north. Furthermore, he thought that the great man would have said that 'his boy had not been given a square deal in his native town, because (he) ... was moved about in the side in a way which must have discouraged him'. Whatever the

The 'Whites' on a picnic at Llangennech, circa 1934. Included among the party were: 'Pendragon', J. Edgar Watkins, Wilf Harris, Jimmy Wilde (boxer), Cliff Bancroft and Willie Davies.

rights and wrongs of these viewpoints, it was clear that the strength of Swansea Football Club was being sapped at an alarming rate. The arrival of fifteen footballing messiahs would solve the problem. Presumably in the meantime, experimentation would continue as the order of the day. And continue it did, though, paradoxically a 'patchwork side' did remarkably well at Cardiff, with Eddie Long the outstanding forward on the field, and newcomer Wilfred Harris doing well among the backs.

Perhaps it was civic pride engendered by the announcement in October 1933 that the Brangwyn Panels were to be housed in Swansea's new Civic Centre which provided the fillip. Whatever it was, the 'Whites' confounded the critics by beating Llanelli for the first time in two years. According to the *Post*, the pack were 'glorious', with Norman Pugh, Tom Day and Edgar Long 'amazing in open play'. E. Youatt, the young inside-half also had a fine game, making a 'corkscrew run to assist with the try'.

In November there was fresh controversy in Welsh rugby. The Welsh Union was to erect a 'colossal stand at Arms Park'. 'Pendragon' and, clearly, those who administered the sport in the west, read more into the development than might have been apparent. 'Judging by the portents, the members of the Welsh Union are concentrating on the centralisation of international games at Cardiff. This is a sad blow for the west.' Despite Llanelli's initiative in calling a meeting of west Wales clubs to protest, the easterners were continuing to drive in the wedge designed to result in an eastern monopoly.

In December, as if the 'Whites' had not had enough problems to deal with, there was a further defection. This time it was W. G. Beynon, who left Swansea for a job in Bristol. Nevertheless, at Christmas time the *Post* could report an old style victory at St. Helens. With Claude Davey (home on holiday) in the side, and Bryn Evans back from Penclawdd, the 'Whites' indulged in an 'orgy of scoring'. Idwal Rees was the dominant figure in a match which was recorded as the biggest defeat handed out to the 'Exiles' by the Swansea club. But, hardly had the smiles settled on Swansea faces than there were two further defections. Dudley Folland signed for Swansea Town A.F.C., and Wilfred Harris also said that he was interested in changing codes.

Paradoxically, there followed victories over the Universities Athletic Union, Leicester, and Cross Keys, and, as a result of a fine Ronnie Williams try, Cardiff were defeated on 'their own mud patch'. Cliff Ball at full-back did well in that match, whilst forward Eddie Long gave a fine performance at centre. Such were the climatic conditions for that game that Swansea touch judge, Jack Watkins, was reported as having been dressed in oilskins and a sou'wester. During this period, H. M. Powell, who had joined Swansea from Neath, was making his mark. Indeed, when the final whistle of the season blew he was the club's leading try scorer.

In his end-of-the-season comments, 'Pendragon' was as forthright as ever. 'The apathy of followers can be traced to the poor quality of rugby we have been seeing recently.' However, he was pleased to record that, on occasions, the side had reached exceptional heights. One example which he quoted was the game against Harlequins. In that game the 'Whites' 'had given a sparkling exhibition of the finest attributes of rugby'. Both sides, the scribe recorded had thrown the ball about with 'delightful freedom'. It was no surprise to his readers that he went on to advise that 'the spoilers should be warned off'. Sadly, winning was becoming more important than entertaining. Only in holiday games did teams perform in the 'old way'.

United

At the 1934 A.G.M., Dai Thomas succeeded Tom Day as captain. Day, who had been a popular skipper was generally regarded as having been unlucky not to have been 'capped' during the previous campaign. Presumably that meant that, given the defections and enforced experimentation in Swansea team selection, Day had had an outstanding campaign as a player as well as captain. For his part, Dai Thomas, regarded by 'Pendragon' as Swansea's best all-round forward, was delighted to have the opportunity to lead the side.The club treasurer, however, was far from delighted. 'Gate' takings were lower than in previous seasons, and, as the *Post* man put it, 'football of the kick and rush order is reflected in Swansea's unfavourable balance sheet'.

The meeting also gave its blessing to a change in selection policy. 'Lively discussion' had resulted in positive steps being taken with regard to another matter – the Second Team. In future this would be known as Swansea United. The name 'Athletic' had been considered, but most preferred the name which had been adopted. It was the new 'rule' which was agreed which satisfied the change agents. In future, anyone who wished to play for the first team would need to serve for a period with the United. This policy was generally agreed to be a good one, though, for a variety of reasons it was not implemented.

1934/35

The gods arrive

Prior to the start of the new campaign proper, Swansea Football Club played another 'missionary' game. A team was sent to Merthyr to play the first match there for 26 years. The five thousand strong Merthyr crowd were said to have 'greatly enjoyed a brilliant exhibition'. However, it was after a mediocre performance against the League that reports of a win at Bristol resulted in superlatives beginning to flow. In their reports, rugby journalists of national as well as local papers used words such as 'astounding'. 'exceptional talent' and 'brilliant'. Their focus was a pair of 'schoolboy' half-backs – W. T. H. Davies and H. Tanner. Had 'Argus' been writing about the Bristol game he would, surely, have drawn comparison between the play of the two youngsters and the vivid flashes of lightning and thunder which provided the backcloth to that match. The more restrained 'Pendragon' reported that the Penclawdd halves had had a splendid match. Willie Davies, the latest in the line to be compared with Billy Trew, was said to have 'perplexed the Bristol defence with his variation of pace and stride.' Both he and Tanner, who scored a 'classy try', were thought to have the temperament as well as the technique to go 'right to the top'. Since both young men were still at Gowerton Grammar School the accolades were appealing. For once the initial assessment was not misplaced; two young gods had arrived.

With Wilfred Harris back from his flirtation with soccer, Claude Davey home because of his wife's illness, and no further defections to the north, as the season developed there was renewed spirit at St. Helens.This was enhanced by a victory over Cardiff in which the young half-backs again excelled, despite heavy rain and a greasy ball. As ever, however, the pessimists reared their heads. The youngsters would not stay. The optimists, however, set out to enjoy the youthful brilliance. Apart from anything else, there was always hope that the young men would make their careers in south west Wales. In those days, though, there were no paternalistic employers who would sponsor careers for young giants. The lads would need to make their own way in life, and, in the process, Swansea Football Club would need to take every chance to utilise the precocious talent whilst it was available, for there were other complications; the boys were required to play for their school, and, furthermore, their master did not want them to be over-exposed. Whilst thinking-Swansea would have agreed with these principles, the results were, to say the least, inconvenient.

Since on occasions Tanner and Davies were not available, other players had to be selected for some matches, and then, be prepared to stand down when the youngsters were available. Later in the season, 'Pendragon' was to pay particular homage to Ron Richards of Brynamman, 'who stands down when Tanner is available ... (and shows) wonderful loyalty to the club in circumstances which would discourage most players'. Truly great clubs are peopled by such men.

In October 1934 there were two historic occasions in Swansea. The Duke of Kent opened the town's new Guildhall, whilst the 'All Whites' played Blackheath for the first time for forty years; that old hatchet had, at last, been buried. Whilst they were not reported as being at the Guild-hall, once again, Tanner and Davies revelled in the challenge which the match with the Englishmen provided. Sixty years later another T and D pairing were to capture the nation's attention by their performances on ice. At the time, no one could remember a young pair who so enthralled those who watched them wherever they played a game of rugby. Had television been available to record their performances for posterity we should be able to relive those magic moments today. Instead, we can only rely on memory and press comment. However, many believe that the *Western Mail* put it into context when it reported that 'the young men have had a psychological effect in each of the games they have played'. As far as Swansea football was concerned, the unfortunate thing was that the youngsters were not available more often to influence games in that manner. By the middle of November, with Swansea United doing well there was some controversy at St. Helens regarding the stated policy that new players were required to 'graduate through the United ranks'. They cited an example, W. T. Griffiths of

J. Idwal Rees stands in at scrum-half v. England.

Ystalyfera, who had not followed that route; not that he was the only one. Those who complained said that the players were not to blame, but that the committee was ignoring the agreed policy. Not surprisingly, for a while there was some dissatisfaction in the camp. However, as has always been the case, victories on the field of play provided an effective balm. The controversy was soon forgotten.

As the year drew to a close with the 'Whites' 'undefeated in a Saturday match', the team scored 19 points against Aberavon without reply, despite having only six forwards for the last quarter of the game. The team's play was described as being 'faultless' in gaining a further 'handsome victory' over Cambridge University. In its report of that match the *Post* had it that the team played 'brilliant football in all departments'. Following two further victories, the smiles at St. Helens would have lifted the densest fog. R. S. Palmer, the club Secretary, speaking at a Round Table meeting, was, certainly buoyed up. 'We are now entering a period of rugby which reminded many of the greatest days ... Certainly, the two young halves have already induced comparison with the finest players of the past.' Yet, as ever, there were lingering doubts to sustain the pessimists; was the team flattering to deceive? Despite an outstanding performance by Griffiths at full-back, the 'Whites' lost their unbeaten record to the 'Scarlets', but the smiles were restored in the following match, Bridgend were beaten. Whilst Tanner was not available, Willie Davies, watched by the 'Big Five', showed 'positive genius ... his try was a masterpiece. It can almost be said that he beat the whole Bridgend side ... in a most bewildering fashion.'

And so the encouraging pattern developed.In the next match (at Cross Keys), 'Pendragon' reported that the outside-half had 'reached heights of brilliance and was the inspiration behind every movement'. Among those so inspired was full-back Griffiths, who 'from a position forty yards out dropped a magnificent goal'. By mid-December the *Post* scribe was claiming that the 'Whites' were enjoying their best season for twenty years. He was perplexed, though, that the club's 'gates' had been unworthy of the quality of rugby which was being played; sports followers, even then, were the most fickle of creatures.

Scotland play 'feet' v. Wales at St. Helens. Dai Parker lurks.

In January, Tanner and Davies played in one of the Welsh trials and 'Pendragon', among others, fairly drooled about the quality of their play. The scribe even went so far as to suggest that Davies was 'even better, in some respects, than the great Billy Trew'. Whilst some of those who watched that trial may have agreed with the selectors that it was too soon to risk the young men in the international arena, there was little disagreement that another pairing of Swansea gods had been seen. As fate would have it, the pair were not to play in Swansea colours for long. However, if any omens were evident then, unlike their acknowledgement of the Belisha Beacons which were being erected in the town at the time, Swansea supporters chose to ignore them.

With Tanner and Davies unavailable for many games, several half-back 'deputies' were tried. There was little doubt, though, that when they turned out the pair brought an extra dimension to Swansea play. Furthermore,when they did, more money was taken at the gate. Yet Swansea was not a two-man team. W. J. Griffiths was developing a fine reputation as a full-back, Powell on the wing was capturing the attention of the Press, Tom Day, Dai and Joe White, Edgar Long, Dai Thomas, Harry Payne and D. J. Tarr all gave noteworthy performances, Wilf Harris, by now converted to a forward had 'excelled as a goal kicker', and Tom Day and Dai Thomas were 'capped'. Over the season 26 matches had been won and 11 lost. Harold Powell was the top try scorer with 24, whilst Wilfred Harris had converted twenty tries and kicked 11 penalties. For his part, Eddie Long had completed 10 seasons in the side and, as he said, 'I'm still a young man'. Judging by the atmosphere at St. Helens as the posts were hauled down, the *esprit de corps* at the club was of the highest order.

Chapter Fifteen

THE ALL BLACKS ARE BEATEN

1935-36

GIVEN THAT THE CLUB had found another pair of half-back gods, there was a degree of optimism among Swansea supporters as the season approached. Together with players like Edryd Jones, Harry Payne and D. J. Tarr, the 'Schoolboys' were thought to represent the nucleus of a fine side. There was, too, the New Zealand visit to look forward to, with the possibility that the home team would be motivated to raise its game. Furthermore, there was early encouragement when the League were defeated 45-0, Bristol 8-0 and Bath were beaten by nine points to nothing. Thus, in the first three games, 62 points had been scored without reply. Those who kept records would have drawn comparison with the halcyon days of Bill Bowen and 'Genny' Gordon. Not only were the results encouraging, but the manner of the victories gave additional cause for optimism. For example, the Bath pack, 'second only in size to that of the New Zealand tourists', had been well beaten, whilst Tanner and Davies had been outstanding. In that match, the outside-half had scored an 'exhilarating try', whilst Tanner had dropped an 'amazing goal, striking the ball whilst he was in the process of falling'.

Even though Cardiff took the 'Whites' unbeaten record soon after that match, there were extenuating circumstances; three Swansea men had been injured and had to leave the field, whilst Cardiff's try was 'questionable'. Whilst there was disappointment in the Swansea camp at that defeat, the biggest concern was whether the three players would be fit to face the All Blacks. Sadly, the unfortunate Tom Day and Colin Davies were both unable to recover in time.

As far as the tourist match was concerned, the selectors followed the policy of bringing 'exiled' players into the side. Edryd Jones, selected at full-back was an officer in the Metropolitan Police, and he was joined by Claude Davey in a side which fielded as follows:

Edryd Jones; Gwyn Griffiths, Ronnie Williams, Claude Davey, Granville Davies, Willie Davies, Hadyn Tanner; Geo. Taylor, D. J. Tarr, Harry Payne, Joe White, D. Hunt, Edgar Long (Capt.), Wilf Harris and D. White.

Prior to the great day, the press let it be known that there was a 'clear call in the Swansea camp for going low to stop the Commonwealth players'. It seemed that as the Abyssinian Emperor was signing a mobilisation order for the defence of his country, Swansea was enacting a version of its own. And 'low' the Swansea guardians went. Yet, not only was the Swansea 'thin white line majestic', as one paper put it, but the team's attacking play left the cheering supporters hoarse with excitement. Swansea scored three tries on that memorable day, two of them result-

Line-out 'Whites' v. New Zealand.
Donald Tarr, Harry Payne, George Taylor and Dennis Hunt take on the 'All Blacks'.

ing from Claude Davey's searing pace. Edgar Long played a captain's part, D. J. Tarr, 'the Navy Schoolmaster', was prominent, Tanner completely outplayed his opposite number, and Davies 'did some bewildering running to pave the way for two of the tries'. Not only had St. Helens witnessed another famous victory, but Swansea had gained the distinction of being the first club side ever to defeat a full New Zealand touring team.

On that famous day, the 'Whites' won a hard-fought match as a result of effective all-round play. The side showed superb spirit, brilliance at half-back, tenacity, combination and purpose in the pack, and magnificent defensive and offensive play, particularly by Claude Davey in the centre. Whilst, quite rightly, much has been made of the tries which Davey scored that day, it was his generalship which impressed knowledgeable onlookers. With Davey at the back and Eddie Long performing a similar role 'up front', and the 'Schoolboys' investing the match with innocent flair, the New Zealanders found the Swansea combination to be irresistible.

Despite being much lighter than their opponents, the Swansea pack on that tension-filled afternoon refused to submit to the 'All Black' power. To the amazement of the watching press corps, the home eight won more ball from the set pieces, and, as a result of their vigour, athleticism and mobility in the loose, quickly stamped their authority on the proceedings. Not surprisingly, this provided the home backs with opportunities, and, as the game wore on, the 'Schoolboys' at half-back began to believe that they could 'play their normal game'. It was as a result of this growing confidence that the 'Whites' drew first blood.

Following a line-out, a forward rush took the ball towards the New Zealand line and, in the mêlee which followed, Dennis Hunt 'grabbed the ball and forced himself over'. Whilst Wilf Harris missed the conversion, that seemed to have little effect on the Swansea men, and within minutes the rapturous crowd had a further score to cheer.

E. C. Davey.

The ball came back to Tanner from a loose maul and, for a moment, the inside-half seemed to freeze, but, spying Willie Davies lurking to his left, his body pivoted and he sent out a pass of such pace and distance that Davies, taking the ball in mid-stride, found himself with space to work his magic. The outside-half swerved beyond the grasp of a would-be tackler and found himself with only the full-back to beat. As the New Zealand defender came to meet the youngster, a 'dip of the shoulder and a change of angle' resulted in the full-back taking the wrong option. With Claude Davey at his shoulder, Davies released a lovely pass to the centre who powered over the 'All Black' line to

During a training session at St. Helens.
The group includes: W. D. Williams, Gwyn Griffiths, Harold Powell, Ronnie Williams and Jack Littlejohns.

Internationals and Reserves at High Street Station.
Eddie Long, Willie Davies, Haydn Tanner, Jim Lang and Harry Payne.

score a memorable try. Between cheering what had been a 'Swansea' try of the first order, the general opinion of the crowd on the Tanner Bank was that even the buffers at High Street Station would have failed to stop the powerful Davey in full flow. The wags, too, were not slow with their comments about the 'All Black' full-back. Given that his name was Solomon, they said that they were less than impressed by his judgement. Yet, surely, even his illustrious namesake would have expected to have been out-thought by a god?

Despite the tremendous efforts of the visitors to get back into the match, the Swansea defence, orchestrated by Davey, held firm. Furthermore, as the New Zealand attacks became more frantic, openings appeared which were exploited by the 'Schoolboys' and by the 'Whites' three-quarter line. In due course, following another fine move, Claude Davey powered his way through to register his second try and Swansea's third. When the whistle went for no side, the indefatigable Eddie Long, the Swansea captain, was surrounded by cheering Swansea supporters, as were the fourteen other men in white. None were more proud, however, that the relatives of the two schoolboys, who, in the cauldron which was St. Helens that day, had performed with the aplomb and panache of seasoned internationals.

After the match, the New Zealanders were generous in their comments about the Swansea XV. In particular, J. E. Manchester, the captain of the defeated tourists, was unstinting in his praise. He did, however, add a postscript to his comments. 'Please,' he said, 'don't tell them at home that we were beaten by pair of schoolboys!' The remark was appreciated for its wry humour by all who were there. Some said that, in making the comment Manchester had his tongue 'ever so slightly' in his cheek. However, as far as Swansea, Wales and the whole of 'Greater Gowerton' were concerned it was purely proper recognition of outstanding talent. For them, the boy-gods had arrived!

After the Lord Mayor's show arrived came defeat by the Welsh 'All Blacks', although Tanner and Davies were absent, as were the 'guests'. Thereafter results reverted to the irritating norm, though a defeat by Llanelli and a pointless draw with Cardiff seemed of less importance whilst the afterglow of the New Zealand victory was still entrancing. There was, too, the balm of potential 'caps' for several of the Swansea men who had vanquished the tourists. Whilst, in the event, Willie Davies was overlooked in the first Welsh selection, Tanner, Tarr, and Payne were picked, whilst the 'exiles', Davey and Idwal Rees were also considered to be representing the old borough. Since that Welsh side emulated the 'Whites' by beating the 'All Blacks', the whole of Swansea was able to bask in that glory. However, it was not until the Home Championships started that Edgar Long received his first 'cap', which, according to the *Post*, was five years later than the popular captain's play had merited.

During the remainder of the season the young half-backs, Davies and Tanner, were lionised. In its report of a decisive victory over Leicester, the *Daily Express* opined that the match had been 'a personal triumph for W. T. H. Davies. He was the dominating figure from beginning to end ... his try must be regarded as the finest ever seen at St. Helens.' According to the *Post*'s report of that game, Davies ran forty yards to score that try, 'wriggling and dodging in bewildering fashion, beating half the Leicester side in the process'. In a match against Bristol, Tanner was reported as having 'dropped two excellent goals and controlled the game in a manner which belied his years'. Whilst Tanner's place in the Welsh side was assured, such were Davies's performances that the national selectors could no longer ignore him. Whilst retaining Cliff Jones at outside-half, for the game against Ireland they awarded Davies his first 'cap' in the centre.

Since Davies was unavailable for a number of games thereafter, the 'Whites' selectors had to look elsewhere for an outside-half. Thus it was that, for a match against Newport, another schoolboy, Glyn Samuel, made his début. As it transpired, the young man was privileged to play a part in what 'Pendragon' called 'a match of champagne rugby'. Swansea beat Newport on that day by 15 points to 13, and the *Post* man reported that the game had produced 'Rugby of the kind we have all been longing for!' Behind his joyful statement was something of a hidden agenda. Clearly, he was not in favour of league tables. He wrote, 'I am afraid that this so-called unofficial championship has a lot to answer for. It causes the public to form an entirely wrong estimate of values.'

By mid-April, as the team's performances gave cause for concern, the scribe was discussing 'Swansea's problems'. The burden of his argument was that fixture list congestion had resulted in the club having to play as many as three games in a week, whilst injuries, absences, staleness and selectorial whims had also taken their toll.

The end of the season coincided with a government announcement that income tax was to be increased (up 3*d.* at once) in order to pay for defence costs. As far as Swansea R.F.C. was concerned, the 'cost' of its loss of form in the final quarter of the campaign had been that it had forfeited its place at the head of the unofficial Welsh table. Even though 'Pendragon' had stated that he did not like this arrangement, the discerning reader of the comments in his season's summary would have noted the implication that he would have been delighted had the 'Whites' maintained their 'senior position'. The situation was that five weeks before the end of the campaign there was every hope that Swansea would emerge as champions. Nonetheless, despite the disappointment, 'Pendragon' found many positive points to raise. Edgar Long, 'light-haired son of Mumbles', had had a particularly good term of office; Harry Payne had been a 'consistent scrummager without pretensions', whilst Ronnie Williams, Joe White and George Taylor had all made valuable contributions during the season. As far as the young half-backs were concerned, it was the general view that Swansea was 'a different side' when they were playing. There was some excellent news, too about young Tanner. University College, Cardiff had offered him a place for the following term. However, 'yielding to the persuasion of his relatives' he had made up his mind to enter the University College at Swansea. Temporarily, at least, he was still a Swansea man.

Whatever disappointment was felt in Swansea at the season's outcome, no one could take away the tremendous pleasure which the victory over New Zealand had given to everyone associated with Swansea rugby. On that day, at least, the Swansea XV had been a truly great team, and their feat had been etched on the collective memory of all who loved 'All White' rugby.

1936–37

A new King and war in Spain

September 1936 saw the issue of the new King Edward stamps, and provided the news that fierce fighting had taken place near Madrid. Both matters were to take a significant place in history, but the performances of Swansea R.F.C. were destined to be less than newsworthy during another mediocre season.

After the usual gambol against the League, in a game in which Gwyn Griffiths scored five tries, (including three in succession), the 'Whites', down to fourteen men for much of the game, were too good for Bristol. Tanner and Davies were in brilliant form in that game, leading the Bristol defence 'a rare dance'. In his report of the match, 'Pendragon' declared that 'Tanner stands alone'. He was 'alone', too, for the next game when, with Davies unavailable, Neath won by the only try of the match. That defeat was compounded by the fact that the Neath scorer was ex-'All White', Harold Powell.

Despite the fact that the performance of the side in that game was reported as having 'left a great deal to be desired', the next fixture showed something of the potential of the Swansea team. Cross Keys, who had won the unofficial title at the end of the previous campaign, were beaten in convincing fashion. The 'Whites' registered 24 points against 8, and had opened in 'a most amazing fashion with two quick scores'. Having beaten the Champions, the next challenge for the St. Helens men came from Llanelli. After that game, at Stradey, even the Llanelli papers reported that the 'Whites' had played with 'unexpected dash'. The men in white won 8-3, and it was the first Swansea victory over the 'Scarlets' since 1932. In the process, the home side lost its unbeaten record, despite the fact that Tanner was injured for much of the game.

Another unbeaten record was claimed the following Saturday, when the English club,

Wilf Harris and Cliff Bancroft 'play soccer' v. Cardiff.

Richmond, fielding four internationals, were well beaten. The score – 15 points to 8 – according to the *Western Mail*, 'hardly reflected Swansea's superiority'. In that match, Swansea's 'Varsity men, Gwili Jenkins, Tanner, Davies, and Gwyn Griffiths 'shone', whilst captain, Ronnie Williams, another man with Swansea University connections, 'led by magnificent example'.

At that point in the season, 'Pendragon', relishing his role as observer of all things White, could scarcely subdue his purr. He wrote, 'a few more of that variety will bring back the crowds'. The next match, however, was to result in the converse and in the cessation of Swansea-Llanelli matches. In a fiercely fought match with the 'Scarlets' at St. Helens, the *Post* reported that 'many discreditable happenings took place'. What was reported as an 'unpalatable climax' resulted in a player from each side being sent off. Club officials moved swiftly to defuse the situation. Swansea and Llanelli spokesmen made a joint statement immediately after the match to the effect that the remaining two games of the season, and all those scheduled for 1937-38 would not now take place. The seriousness of the steps which were taken was not lost on either club, but it was agreed that 'the worst exhibition of bad feeling ... between the sides in living memory', justified the action taken. It was a sad day for both clubs.

Thereafter, as if affected by the happenings at St. Helens, results were disappointing. Blackheath became the first English side during the season to beat the 'Whites', and Penarth held a weakened Swansea side to a draw. There was disappointment, too, in the knowledge that Glyn Samuel, Willie Davies's stand-in, was going to London to study and would not be available other than at vacation time. In November, Cardiff 'completely outplayed' the homesters in a match in which Hadyn Tanner captained the 'Whites'. Then, whilst the country was reeling at the news that the King had abdicated, Swansea supporters were doing some reeling of their own as Penarth beat their favourites 6 points to 4. December, however, brought with it better news, for the side gained three victories and a draw. In the process 55 points were scored whilst only 17 were conceded. That, the Swansea supporters must have felt, was more like it.

Whilst it was clear that with Tanner and Davies in harness, Swansea was a far superior side, it was not always the case. Gwili Jenkins, for example, scored in four consecutive games, and there was a remarkable performance by the forwards in the Christmas match against Watsonians. Even with three men injured, the six-man pack still outplayed the Scots. Not surprisingly, though, that effort affected the performance of the eight on the following day. Then, according to the *Post*, the Swansea men were well beaten 'by one of the best packs seen at St. Helens'. Nevertheless, Tanner varied his game to compensate, while Willie Davies, 'largely subdued', flashed through the visiting defence 'in bewildering fashion', to score the try of the match.

On the last Saturday of 1936 there was further joy for Swansea followers, as, with Idwal Rees in the side, the 'Whites' gave a 'gratifying performance' to beat London Welsh – scoring 21 points without reply. Since neither Davies nor Tanner played on that occasion, there were those who rejoiced in the fact that Swansea was not a two-man team. Whilst this was patently true, there were few supporters to be found who would not liked to have seen the 'schoolboys' playing every week.With the new year approaching the topic of conversation around the club was whether the improved form displayed by the team at the end of the old year might be carried forward into 1937? The optimists were beginning to gird their loins, the pessimists required further comfort.

Some of that comfort was made available following the New Year's Day game at St. Helens. Leicester were the visitors and became the victims of a Swansea side in which Phil. Davies and W. E. Jones played at half-back in lieu of Tanner and Davies, who were playing in a Welsh trial. The Swansea pack dominated that day, with Bancroft, Matthews and Payne prominent as the home eight 'wore down their opponents'.

Off the field, the Mayor of Swansea took it upon himself to initiate 'peace moves' on behalf of the Swansea and Llanelli clubs. With Herr Ribbentrop and Mr Chamberlain soon to be attempting the same thing on a larger canvas, this news was welcomed by all parties. For his part, the Llanelli Mayor declared himself ready to 'help in any way I can'. Whilst the mayors were unsuccessful in the short term, at least they did better than the British Prime Minister. Meantime, A. E. Daniel (Pendragon), speaking at a dinner, declared that 'he knew of a number of people who will no longer go to a needle match between two of the leading Welsh clubs'. If he was to believed, the Llanelli-Swansea rift was but indicative of a more widespread malaise in Welsh football.

In February, Phil Davies, Tanner's deputy, 'went north'. Since Ron Richards and Steve Morgan had followed that path during the previous two years, 'Pendragon' could point out that, since Tanner had made his début, three of his seven stand-ins had gone to play League football. Whilst the attraction of the signing-on fee and regular employment was the overt reason for each of these players 'taking the silver', it was hardly surprising that those who waited in the wings, seeing Tanner's genius, must have recognised that their opportunities were limited.

However, there was one man at St. Helens who had 'come south'. He was groundsman Harry Creber, who, after the Wales-Scotland international at Swansea, could bask in the glory of a remark made by one of the Caledonian officials. 'St.Helens', said the official, 'was the best pitch in the country.'

The highlights of the remainder of the season were fine wins over Leicester, on their own pitch, when the 'Whites' scored 23 points, and over Harlequins at St. Helens, when 'typical Swansea rugby' was played. Whilst, following indifferent performances several other matches were lost, the two victories were greeted warmly by the press. The Leicester game was described as 'a great tonic', during which the forwards and Tanner and Davies excelled. The Harlequins match, on the other hand was a 'triumph for Claude Davey and Glyn Samuel'. Samuel was home on vacation from St. Mary's Hospital and, in Willie Davies's absence, was heartily welcomed at St. Helens.

Summarising yet another season, 'Pendragon' sought for reasons which might explain the inconsistency of the side. Amongst other things he restated his continuing criticism that the club had never put out a settled side. Part of that problem, he argued, could be put down to the fact that the club had to rely on university players. He pointed out that these men were obliged to turn out for the University and the U.A.U., and, in some cases for invitation XV's, in Welsh trials, and even in internationals. Whilst he recognised that these calls vested the Swansea club with a degree of glory, the effect on the Swansea team selection left a great deal to be desired. The university men apart, the *Post* scribe chastised the Swansea selectors for their *ad hoc* policies. He believed that a record number of players had been used during the season. Whilst that was incorrect, there was little doubt that constant changes hardly assisted understanding between players. What was difficult to figure out was the fact that ten out of the club's fourteen defeats had occurred during 'bad patches'. 'Pendragon' was at a loss to explain why that should have been. For their part, the selectors must have looked at their leading scorers and recognised the significant contribution of the men from Swansea University College. Gwyn Griffiths was top try scorer (10), whilst Gwili Jenkins (73) had scored most points. Perhaps, in the face of such criticism, they felt like inviting the *Post* scribe to join their committee. What sort of team would they have without these young men?

1937-38

Black to white to black

During the close season, W. E. Jones, who was to make his mark as a Glamorgan cricketer, transferred to the Gnoll. He said that he wanted to play at outside-half and believed that his prospects at St. Helens were limited. Vernon Friend joined him. In order to balance the books, as it were, after a few weeks of the season had passed, Harold Powell, the flying winger, left Neath to come back to St. Helens. Powell, who had scored 24 tries for the 'Whites' during the '34-35 campaign', was of the opinion that his game was more suited to St. Helens than to the Gnoll. Judging by his try-scoring performances for both clubs, there was little doubt that that was the case.

The captain for the new campaign was a most popular choice. Harry Payne, who had been a member of the Welsh side which had beaten New Zealand, had 'led the pack admirably' during the previous season. Harry felt that, given the talent available – when there was a full compliment to choose from – he was to lead one of the best teams in the country. Harry's problems, however, included the fact that that was rarely possible.

Early indications

Since the opposition had found it to be extremely difficult to raise a side, the opener against the League provided a poor measure of the club's potential. Thus, whilst 43 points were scored without reply, no one at St. Helens became excited. Nonetheless, the match provided the

Swansea Round Table Rugger Night – March 1938.
Among those present were: W. J. Bancroft, W. Rowe Harding, Dick Jones, Fred Scrine and boxer, Jack Peterson.

opportunity to practise, and Gwili Jenkins started where he left off by scoring 3 tries and converting four. He continued too against Bristol, when his tally consisted of a try and two penalties. Haydn Tanner also scored in that game, but he aroused concern among Swansea supporters when he was injured and had to leave the field for twenty-five minutes. Nevertheless, following his return, his service to Davies was as impeccable as ever, whilst the outside-half was reported as being 'magnificent'. Notwithstanding that victory over the west of England side, 'Pendragon' expressed himself concerned about the 'makeshift three-quarter line'.

When the selectors met to pick the side to play Neath, captain Payne and the others must have been frustrated. After such a sound start, Tanner was unavailable as were three other men, and they did not have a recognised full-back. Their solution to the last problem was to borrow Dai Morgan from Morriston. Having used 22 players in just three games, it was hardly surprising that the side selected to meet the 'All Blacks' lacked cohesion. Neath took advantage of that situation and, despite the best efforts of the Swansea forwards, won a scrappy game.

Since the United had been disbanded to save costs, whenever they were in need of a replacement, the selectors had to ask junior clubs in the region to release players. Thus, for the next game, with Tanner absent, Frank John (Brynamman) was chosen to play against Cross Keys, along with four other new men. 'Pendragon' was exasperated, and wrote of 'the deterioration of Swansea rugby'. He said that he deplored the decision to disband the second string, pointed out that Ronnie Williams, the previous season's captain, was out of the side because he objected to being moved from position to position, and rehearsed again his argument about the availability of the university men. Tentatively he suggested that there should be a debate within the club around the theme – should the club sacrifice the stars who appear irregularly? As a parting shot, he commented that the sporting public in Swansea was 'getting fed up with poor rugby'. However, even if that statement had substance, it would have taken a very brave selection committee to implement an 'only regular players policy'. Even so, the next game demonstrated that the concerns of the *Post* scribe were justified. With Richmond as opponents, three further new players were drafted into the side, five of the Swansea backs were under twenty, and, whilst he had not intended to play, Tanner had to turn out on the wing because the side was short.

Nonetheless, seemingly in keeping with the side's inconsistency, after a dismal period, the 'sun' shone again. If a newspaper report can smile, that written by 'Pendragon' about a match with Cardiff certainly did. It appears that the visitors had four internationals in their side and were expected to win easily. However, Swansea shocked the 'Taffsiders' through a 'virile pack and a plucky three-quarter line', though the objective reader would have noticed that the 'stars' played a significant part in the victory. 'Tanner and Davies were a great inspiration',wrote the *Post* man. Given his joy he must have been glad that no one had taken him up on the 'no stars debate'. On that day, too, there were further newcomers. Howard Davies, a Burry Port boy, came in at full-back, while his namesake Idwal turned out in the centre. Overall, 'Pendragon's' report can best be summed-up by his final statement that 'it was easily the best display of rugby seen at St. Helens this season'.

Perhaps inspired by that display, by the next match, Harold Powell, who had been the most prolific try scorer since Dennis Manley and Fred Jowett, secured his transfer from Neath. Powell's first match back in the white shirt was against Newport at Rodney Parade, and, although he did not score, he was part of the side which 'shocked the Usksiders'. Gwili Jenkins scored a try in the first minute of that game after a 'bewildering run' by Willie Davies. With Blackheath and Penarth succumbing to 'Swansea flair outside the scrum', a visiting Martian might have wondered about the validity of 'Pendragon's' earlier concern. But, just as the run of success had come about without warning, a negative pattern re-emerged. Bridgend, Neath, Cardiff and Aberavon all defeated the 'Whites'. Writing about the defeat by Cardiff, the *Post* scribe was even more severe than the eastern press. He wrote, 'on no occasion have the "Whites" been so badly beaten'. Whilst the score, 21 points to 3, hardly confirmed that pronouncement, there was little doubt that happenings on the field had wiped the smile from 'Pendragon's' report. He wrote of 'unpalatable lessons learnt during the last three weeks'. In addition, he had picked up indications of some dissension at St. Helens. The selectors, perhaps responding to the *Post* man's criticisms had stated that 'men who do not practise cannot complain if their claims to a place in the side are ignored'. Certainly, the committee was finding it to be increasingly difficult to recruit players from district clubs. Not unnaturally, these teams wished to retain their best players and enhance their own position. Yet, without the United, and with seemingly ever increasing calls on their 'star' players, the selectors, as 'Pendragon' put it, were having to beg junior clubs to release players. Apart from anything else, Pendragon felt that this was hardly the position in which a famous club like Swansea should find itself.

Paradoxically, the three games over the Christmas period all provided Swansea followers with something to shout about. Watsonians were defeated by 28 points to 6, 20 points were scored against U.A.U. without reply, whilst London Welsh succumbed 28-10. Whilst it was true that the usual number of 'on vacation' men strengthened the sides, the wins were no less welcomed by all at St. Helens.

Unfortunately, on returning to 'domestic' football the team ran into yet another unsuccessful spell. Losses against Llanelli, Aberavon and Cardiff did little to brighten a grey January. Whilst the next two matches were won, it was not until mid-February, when Leicester were the visitors to St. Helens, that the side recovered something like its potential form. In the same edition of the *Post* which featured the 'Anti-air raid plan for Swansea', 'Pendragon' was able to report on a fine Swansea victory. In his opinion, superior Swansea teamwork and the outstanding form of Tanner and Davies 'demoralised the Tigers'.

In March the Swansea club was informed by the Welsh Union that their proposed development scheme for St. Helens had been rejected. The Union argued that they did not have the money to proceed with the scheme because such large sums had been spent on the Arms Park development. Given that the St. Helens club had a 'heavy overdraft' itself, the matter was shelved. Swansea's mayor, however, speaking at a Park Hall 'Rugger Night', warned the W.R.U. that, by turning down Swansea's approach they were 'committing Hara Kiri'.

On the playing field, despite the team's inconsistent form, Harold Powell crossed for his twenty-first try of the season as the 'Whites' recovered from a poor start to defeat Pontypool. The side did well, too, in an evenly balanced game against Cardiff, and whilst Wilfred Wooller dropped a goal two minutes from the end to give Cambridge University the spoils, most observers felt that the 'Whites' had done enough to win that game. And win they did in the next match, Newport being the victims by a 'significant 18 points to 3'.

Sandwiched between the last two of these games came the news which was to cause concern in high places. 'Hitler's Austrian Conquest' the headline screamed. Whilst the rugby fraternity in Swansea may not have seen any significance in the report, they were soon to find that the 'Corporal's' ideas of conquest were not confined to his German-speaking neighbour. However, at that time the thoughts of those who ran Swansea Football Club were focused on other matters. According to the *Post*, so serious was the club's financial position that its very existence might be threatened. Stimulated by this concern, the club's committee announced that they were significantly to improve the quality of the team's fixture list for the '38-39 campaign. Presumably this was intended as a means of increasing gates. However, it would not have been lost on anyone at St. Helens that, in order to attract more people to home matches, it would be necessary to develop a winning side in order to capitalise on the benefits provided by an improved fixture list.

In April there were signs that the club had found the nucleus of such a side, if only it could keep the players together on a continuing basis. United Services Portsmouth were 'thoroughly beaten' in a game in which Harold Powell scored six tries and equalled Dennis Manley's post-war record (28). Since the ex-Neath man did not join the 'Whites' until the middle of October, his was an outstanding feat. Next, Newport and the Harlequins were beaten, with the pack in fine form and with Tanner and Davies 'weaving their magic spells'. Whilst the last game of the season was lost by a single point, when the curtain fell on the campaign there was a greater atmosphere of confidence at the club than there had been for many years. In truth, though, it had been a season of fluctuating fortunes. There had been spells when, as 'Pendragon' put it, 'the side had touched real greatness', including a period during which seven consecutive games had been won. At this distance it would appear that the *Post*-man's conclusion was valid that 'much more would have been achieved with a settled side' (60 players were used during the season).

Among the encouraging features of the season had been the number of new men who had come into the side and established themselves as quality players. Howard Davies had developed into 'one of the finest full-backs in the country', while Idwal Davies, in the centre, had been much lauded, and the lightning winger, Harold Powell had set a new post war record of 34 tries* Over the season, the side had won 24 of its 37 games and 440 points had been scored, which was the highest total for seven seasons. However, careful consideration of the season's record showed that on the whole, without Tanner and Davies the side was less effective. Those who supported and administered Swansea Football Club could only hope that the pair would appear more frequently during the season ahead.

Certainly, the club's treasurer hoped so. At the May A.G.M. he reported that rugby 'gates' were £1,400 lower than for the previous campaign, whilst there had been a loss of £542 on the year's working. His earnest hope was that, with a better fixture list, and Tanner and Davies in harness more often, he would be able to put away his red pen. Meanwhile, with rumours still circulating to the effect that St. Helens was to lose its international matches to the Taffside faction, Walter Rees had written to the Swansea Chamber of Trade. 'I am directed to inform you', he wrote, that this union has not at any time decided that no further international matches shall be played in Swansea.' The statement might have been written by a politician. Those who received the letter may be forgiven for thinking that there was more to the statement than first met the eye. The President of the Chamber put his concerns succinctly: 'the sting is in the tail.'

1938-39

The shut down approaches

During the close season, rugby followers in Swansea had their interest in the game maintained through following the fortunes of the Great Britain side in South Africa. There were two 'Whites' in the party, Hadyn Tanner and Eddie Morgan. Sadly, they also learnt that Willie Davies was going north, not at that time to play Rugby League, but to study at Leeds University. Not surprisingly, the news came as a disappointment to all at St. Helens. Yet, having lost 'stars' before they could always hope that another gem would be unearthed. And, at least, they still had Tanner; *pro tem.*

The traditional 'opener' against the League proved to be something of a romp. Notwithstanding the fact that the 'Whites' scored 41 points – Harold Powell crossed for six tries – there were many who questioned the value of the match. They argued that the weakness of the League XV hardly provided the kind of contest which would give the selectors reliable indication of the strength of the group of players available to them. Those who disagreed pointed to the opportunity which the match provided for the team to 'bed down'. And, for his part, Harold Powell, quite rightly, could cling to his record; six tries by an individual in any game is a remarkable achievement.

When the first match 'proper' was played, those in favour of the 'opener' could point to some benefit. Powell had resumed where he left off, scoring twice in the defeat of Bristol (then in their Jubilee season). Full-back Howard Davies was outstanding in that game, too, and given that the side was without Tanner and Davies, the selectors would have been extremely pleased.

* There is evidence to suggest that Harold Powell scored a further five tries in matches against Junior sides. His six tries against Penarth and the District League are a remarkable testimony to his speed and skill.

In mid-September, as the British Premier travelled to see Hitler, negotiations between the Swansea and Llanelli clubs were coming to fruition. One innovative arrangement in the 'Whites'-'Scarlets' peace movement involved the rugby supporters organisations of each club staging a 'Reconciliation Dinner' It was, it was reported, 'an occasion of mutual congratulation'.

On the field, Willie Davies played his last game prior to travelling to Leeds, and Llanelli-Swansea matches were resumed with a fixture at Stradey which attracted a 5,000 crowd. Overall, though, results were patchy. In the absence of both Tanner and Davies, the key half-back positions were proving to be difficult to fill and, not surprisingly, the performances of the team reflected that fact, as did the 'gates'. In that regard, 'Pendragon' reported that there was 'grass growing on the Tanner Bank, a sure sign of the decline of rugby'.

Despite the rumblings of war, discussions about a government of national unity, and economic strictures which affected most families, the Earls Court Motor Show was indicative of the fact that people hoped for better things, (a Morris Eight could be obtained for £138). At St. Helens that hope burned fiercely among the optimists. Tanner was due back soon, *then* the previous season's promise could be fulfilled. Furthermore, despite the team's inconsistency, there were positive factors to help sustain the optimists. Captain, Wilfred Harris was leading the side with some dash, Powell was scoring consistently, Howard Davies was 'immense' at full-back, whilst Joe White and Harry Payne excelled in the pack. The pessimists, however, had a worrying bone to chew. The Rugby League threat still remained.

Quite apart from the problems caused by the recruiting activities of the men from the north, the games which they staged on Welsh soil were attracting significant crowds. For example the third Rugby League international in Wales that season drew a crowd of 15,000 to Stebonheath, 'despite heavy rain'. It was little wonder that the union camp was beginning to look over its collective shoulder, and a St. Helens concern was that Howard Davies had been approached by two northern clubs.

Meantime, the Swansea club's supporters were being treated to infrequent, but thrilling matches in which 'Swansea football' was the order of the day. A young side 'dispatched' Newport in a match in which new outside-half, Douglas Williams, scored on his début; Cardiff were beaten by 'a side of real tryers', Williams dropping a 'perfect goal', and unofficial champions, Penarth, were 'thrashed' 21 points to nil in a match which saw the return of Hadyn Tanner.

With Paul Robeson appearing in concert at the Plaza Cinema, the hope which his spirituals exuded must have rubbed off on those who followed the 'Whites'. And they needed that comfort, for between the successes, 'Pendragon' could only report on mediocrity, and on matches in which 'long and dreary scrummages in monotonous succession dominated games'. If only those who changed the laws prior to the 1993/94 season had been *au fait* with the *Post* man's comments, the 'long and dreary' mauls which the rugby spectator was to witness during that campaign might have been avoided. In 1938, however, the purists had some respite over the Christmas period. Then, 'typical Swansea football' was played. And with Willie Davies, home on vacation, orchestrating the play, the games, as 'Pendragon' put it, were 'lit up'. One game which exemplified this description was that in which the U.A.U. were defeated. Such was the extent of the fog on that occasion – coal fires had a lot to answer for – that visibility was reported as being 'less than twenty yards'. Willie Davies, however, was seen because 'his subtle moves brought him near to us'. Perhaps it was warmer nearer the stand! If only Carnegie College, where Willie was studying, was nearer!

Harold Powell hacks on v. Neath (his old team).

In the east, ex-'All White', Dudley Folland, was banned from assisting Ebbw Vale R.F.C. because of his association with Swansea Town Football Club. 'Pendragon' wanted to know whether anyone knew of 'a more absurd, narrow view as that taken by the Welsh Union?'

Late in March, with the 'All Whites' still searching for an outside-half, they lost someone who had been 'near and dear to the club'. Harry Creber, who had been attached to Swansea Cricket and Football Club for forty years, died at his home. Harry, whose prowess at cricket had been his initial reason for coming to Swansea from his native Liverpool, was renowned for his stoicism. He never wore an overcoat, even in the coldest weather, whilst his shirt was always open at the neck. He had tended the St. Helens turf with loving care.

When the campaign ended, captain Wilfred Harris, whilst publicly thanking all the players for their support, looked back on a season of mixed fortune. The club's playing record was inferior to that of the previous campaign, with five fewer matches being won and almost 130 less points being scored. Nevertheless, Harold Powell had crossed on 26 occasions, to register a quarter of all points scored by the team, and on one occasion, the club had provided five men for the Welsh side. The men concerned were Howard, Leslie and Willie Davies, Eddie Long, and Haydn Tanner. Whilst all Swansea was delighted with this selection, there were drawbacks. As had happened during the previous campaign, Haydn Tanner had been embarrassed by the scale of the invitations which he received. Apart from the 'Lions', Welsh trials and internationals, he was selected for the University, university representative sides plus *ad hoc* teams such as Crawshay's. Not surprisingly, as a result, the Swansea club saw less of the great player than they would have liked.

On the financial front, the treasurer reported that there was 'cause for real concern', the Club had lost £1,000 over two seasons. Furthermore, had it not been for the generosity of the Club's landlords, and the work of R. S. Palmer (he had raised £650 for the club), they 'would not have been able to carry on'.

There was much debate at the A.G.M. about reduced attendances, which, 'Pendragon', writing later, put down not only to indifferent form, but to a new 'threat', which was 'the broadcasting of important games.' The B.B.C., however, did not have to carry all the blame; other reasons enumerated by the scribe included, 'the demands of the Welsh Union trial games ... lack of star players and open football' and, even, 'the damaging effects of rain'. Was that a hardy annual in Swansea? Rain apart, there was the interest in the thirteen-a-side game, and a growing support for soccer. In May 1938, 25,000 packed the Vetch Field to see Swansea Schoolboys challenge for the English Schools' Trophy. All in all, the hope which had been expressed at the start of the campaign had all but evaporated.

Yet, in electing Eddie Morgan as captain for the 1939–40 season, all concerned believed that, in facing up to the challenge of the situation, they were to be led by the right man. Because of the intervention of Adolf Hitler, Eddie did not have the opportunity to put into practice the many ideas which he had in mind. No sooner had he been given the news that Willie Davies had joined Bradford Northern, than Germany invaded Poland, and 'Peace in our time' was but a hollow phrase. With the declaration of war, conscription and with no means of honouring the terms of their lease, Swansea Cricket and Football Club surrendered its tenure of St. Helens Field to the Borough Council. In effect, Swansea Rugby Football Club had ceased to exist.

United Services Wales v. England at St. Helens (circa 1942).
The Welsh side includes H. Tanner, Gus Risman, Willie Davies, Tom Sullivan and Harry Payne.

Chapter Sixteen

AFTER THE WAR

1945–46

GIVEN THAT THE CLUB HAD surrendered its lease at the beginning of hostilities, as the 1945–46 season approached new arrangements had to be made regarding the availability of St. Helens. As a consequence, in June 1945 R. S. Palmer wrote to the Town Clerk asking for clarification of the club's position. In due course a 'deputation' went to see the Estates Committee of the Borough, and, following the meeting the new secretary elect at St. Helens, Cliff Prosser, received a letter which pleased all concerned.

'I have to inform you that the Council has agreed to the use by your club of St. Helens ground for the playing of Rugby Football matches during the season 1945/46.'

The letter went on to outline the terms of the agreement, and Prosser, in delighted mood, acknowledged the offer and thanked the Council for their generosity.

Having secured tenure, at least for a season, those who administered the club had to face up to a number of challenges. The club's financial position had to be improved, and players had to be

'Whites' v. 'Scarlets', February 1946.
The side included Harry Payne (Capt.), D. J. Davies, Elvet Jones, Elved Phillips, Guy Addenbrooke, Percy White and John Hopkins.

found. There was the challenge, too, to improve facilities, including renovating the pavilion, which had been used for Civil Defence purposes during the war.

Yet problems are a fact of life and, as far as Swansea was concerned, so were the 'All Whites'. Thus, whatever difficulties needed to be overcome would pale into insignificance in the minds of the sporting public if they had a successful team to follow. Such a team, of course, would attract larger crowds and thus greater income at the 'gate'. Fortunately there were certain factors which were to prove to be beneficial to the club. Young men were coming home following service in the armed forces probably fitter than they had ever been. In some cases their rugby skills had been honed as a result of playing with top class footballers during their service. As a consequence, in their search for talent, the pool available to the Swansea selectors was larger than it had been for many years. In addition, those who were spectators rather than players returned home with appetites whetted to watch sport in their home town. Often more 'Welsh' than when they went away, these young people were fiercely loyal to the home town which had been in their minds for five long years. Post-war austerity might not have measured up to their images of the joy of homecoming, but for many, the 'All Whites' provided a focus which allowed their dreams to live.

In January 1946, with a gap in the fixture list, Secretary Prosser advertised for potential players to turn out in a trial match. They were requested to write giving details of their playing experience with a view to taking part in the match. Probably as a result of space limitations (the *Post* was limited to four pages because of paper shortages) no report appeared of that match. However, later that month the paper carried an account of a game against Bristol which the 'Whites' 'dominated'. As it happened, the match provided supporters with two links with pre-war Swansea football. Harry Payne was the Swansea pack leader, whilst Ronnie Morris turned out for Bristol.

February saw a 'hat-trick' of wins for the 'Whites', including one over Llanelli during which Gwyn Griffiths dropped 'a remarkable goal from over thirty yards'. In the next game the winning run was extended when an enthusiastic crowd saw the home team, in brilliant form, 'overwhelm Leicester'. Whilst the score, 19 points to 6 suggests a degree of journalistic hyperbole in this statement, there was no doubting that the win was achieved in Swansea style. The description of one of the tries is indicative. 'Gwyn Griffiths ... feinted to pass to Addenbrooke, then, swerving sharply ... like a flash he ran down the middle carving a way between defenders, then eluding the full-back scored one of the most spectacular tries seen at St. Helens. Full-back Elvet Phillips made a safe conversion.'

If the editor of the *Post* was concerned with saving paper, from this distance, his judgement in not using his 'blue pencil' with respect to this piece of 'Pendragon's' prose appears to be more than justified. Apart from anything else, the contrast between the excitement of the description of the try and that of the relative quiet of the conversion attempt demonstrated the skill of the journalist.

For the Welsh international match against Scotland at Cardiff, Haydn Tanner, who scored the winning try, was partnered at half-back by the Cardiff man W. B. Cleaver. Reports of the game declared that the pairing had been a considerable success. Sadly, for Swansea followers, that partnership was to be resumed at club level at the Arms Park in the not too distant future.

Meanwhile the 'Whites' continued their successful run. Griffiths and Addenbrooke were outstanding among the backs, whilst D. J. Davies and Elvet Jones were said to be the pick of the forwards. Such was its success that, by the end of March the side had lost only one match out of seven played during 1946. Among those victories was one over Aberavon. The score, 3 points to nil gives some indication of the closeness of the match. However, the game deserves its place in the history of Swansea R.F.C. in that the kick off ceremony was performed by the British Foreign Secretary of the day. Ernest Bevin was guest of honour at the match after receiving the freedom of Port Talbot.

Unfortunately, thereafter, as Swansea searched for a replacement for Tanner, results were disappointing. Nevertheless, there was a degree of encouragement in the way in which the team performed in several games. That against a talented Barbarians side typified this effort. With the New Zealand captain, C. K. Saxton leading the 'Whites', the home side were said to have been unlucky to lose by 11 points to six. As ever, the Swansea public greatly enjoyed worshipping a flying winger. During that season Guy Addenbrooke had filled that need. Not only did he 'run with his knees up making it difficult to tackle him', but his name might have been coined by an author of popular adventure novels. During the campaign he had crossed for sixteen tries.

1946/47

A new dawn?

The first post-war season had provided the kind of fare to whet the appetites of Swansea followers as they contemplated another campaign. Furthermore, there was a buoyant spirit at the club, because, as 'Pendragon' reported, the selectors were embarrassed by the riches at their disposal. However, there was a negative side to that embarrassment. The club did not have a second fifteen and, thus, could not accommodate all the players who wished to don the white shirt. There was another difficulty, too. Because Swansea Corporation had entered into certain commitments regarding the availability of St. Helens, the club was obliged to play its first six fixtures away from home. One of these, a 'missionary' game against Carmarthen 'Quins was lost, though the selectors felt that some of their experiments in that match had been worthwhile. One of them was to introduce a new wing-forward, W. D. Johnson.

W. D. Johnson.

In September, veteran trainer Bob Dowdle completed fifty years with the club; a reminder, if one was needed, of the tradition of loyal service which Swansea football club had enjoyed from its earliest days. Happily that enviable tradition has been preserved up to the time of writing. Like many facets of an organism which is an institution such as Swansea Rugby Club, that tradition is based upon role models which have developed in the past and which have been replicated as time has passed. Dowdle was such a role model.

In boxing, Pontardawe's Ronnie James was defeated, it was said, by the 'bolo' punch of Ike Williams, thus, with one local sporting hero having been beaten, the Swansea public's thirst for success needed to be quenched elsewhere. For those who followed the 'Whites' that meant on the rugby field. And, as tradition was followed, in Swansea's case those fields were away from the town.

The club embarked on its annual tour of Cornwall, where all three matches were won in the space of four days. In the match against Redruth in which full-back Elvet Phillips scored all the Swansea points, the Cornish papers reported on a 'delightful exhibition of all round rugby'. Penzance were defeated in front of a crowd of 5,000 with Addenbrooke scoring a 'hat-trick' of tries, and Falmouth were well beaten by 25 points to 5. Thus it was that the tourists returned to Swansea thoroughly satisfied.

Nonetheless, there was continuing concern within the club regarding keeping 'the abundance of talent happy when only fifteen could play'. 'Pendragon's' forecast that some players would drift away to other clubs in order to get a game, was difficult to refute. Yet, as the committee pointed out, the club could not run a second team because of problems with the availability of the ground. The simple fact was that St. Helens was booked for a number of Saturdays for other activities. For example, three Rugby League internationals were to be played there during the coming season. Furthermore, the first team was scheduled to play only two home games during the period September to October. Whilst the ghosts from the club's past must have writhed in pain at the thought of St. Helens hosting the thirteen-a-side game, the cash flow difficulties which arose as a result of the unfortunate fixture schedule must have endangered the already fragile financial condition of the club.

Yet, faced with these problems the club's supporters wished to indicate their support for their parent body. Frank Johns called the first meeting of the Swansea and District Rugby Supporters Club which had been held since 1938. All at St. Helens were appreciative.

As it transpired, by the middle of October those supporters could smile with satisfaction. 'Missionary' games apart, the 'Whites' were undefeated. Only Newport had looked capable of lowering Swansea's colours, but with Rees Williams and Tom Briggs prominent in the pack and Tanner controlling matters at the base of the scrum, in that match honours were even at no side. Even more encouragingly, in the next fixture a 'star-studded Cardiff side were taught a lesson'. Bleddyn Williams, Jack Matthews, *et al* were beaten by D. J. Davies and his men following a 'titanic struggle'. By that time Haydn Tanner was teaching at Bristol Grammar school, and Swansea were forced to introduce new men in the crucial inside-half position. In the Cardiff game, stand-in D. Jennings wrote his own piece of history when he 'dropped a goal in a flash'. Meantime Swansea old boy, Willie Davies, was playing outstanding football for Bradford Northern. Whilst reluctant to appear to be encouraging the professional code, Swansea supporters could not help enjoying that news.

Meanwhile, Secretary Prosser declared himself delighted with the demand for membership tickets. There was, he stated, something like the old time atmosphere at St. Helens. Even the cynics had to agree with his comment that the grass which was growing on the Tanner Bank would soon be obliterated. But, as if supporters were re-living an old Swansea script, just as they were enjoying success the team ran into a bad patch. The unbeaten record was lost following a 'grim' game against Llanelli; a depleted side surrendered its ground record to Pontypool, whilst Bristol, Newbridge and Leicester all proved to be too good for the 'Whites'.

At the turn of the year 'Pendragon's' review of the first part of the campaign had a familiar ring about it. There was, he argued 'too much chopping and changing ... the Cardiff side should have been kept together ... there was no line out specialist to replace Trevor Lewis ... and the selectors arrive at too hasty verdicts'. Whilst at this distance these comments seem to have substance, given the lack of a second string, the selectors were doing their best to operate a rota system in a bid to retain their players. One who was not retained was Haydn Tanner. Now the 'Schoolmaster', the Welsh international scrum-half had thrown in his lot with Cardiff, and, as the *Western Mail* reported, 'he was the difference' when Cardiff took their revenge in the return. Yet, amidst the gloom surrounding the Tanner transfer there was some good news; Dai Jones was selected to play for Wales.

In February, as heavy snow made Swansea look like an alpine town and power cuts were in force as fuel supplies were short, the Swansea players turned their backs on the shivering scene and headed for France. Two games were to be played there, against the Bayonne and the CA Beglais-Bordeaux clubs. The *Post* carried a photograph of some of the players as they were about to depart from High Street station. The caption indicated the origins of the players by district. It read Tom Rees (Morriston), Bryn Evans (Uplands), W. D. Johnson (Swansea), Tom Briggs (St. Thomas), Graham Morse (Felinfoel) and Len Davies (Brynmill). It seemed that the old concept of Swansea being a cluster of villages was alive and well.

Meanwhile, discussions about the development of St. Helens continued. The Borough Estate Agent, D. Ivor Saunders, presented a 'voluminous report' one recommendation of which was to reject a request which had been made to establish a greyhound track on the field. Saunders and his team were of the opinion that an 'ideal stadium' could be developed at the ground for an estimated £250,000, with parking on the 'Rec' and a sectional steel stand at the Mumbles Road end. The document also set out the terms for a fourteen year licence for Swansea Cricket and Football Club.

In France the 'Whites' found that French Rugby had developed significantly since men in Swansea jerseys first did battle with 'All France'. Whilst Bayonne were well beaten in the next game, against Bordeaux, the home side outlasted the visitors to win by 12 points to 3.

Back in Swansea the weather was taking its toll of rugby fixtures. Matches were abandoned for a record five Saturdays in succession as snow and ice affected south Wales. During this period, when the *Post* printed a photograph of a snowbound St. Helens, one freak game took place at the famous ground. Blackheath, having travelled from London, were keen to play a match of some sort despite 'half a gale and a snow storm'. Whilst no lines were visible, the referee agreed to play 25 minutes each way. Two hundred hardy supporters, probably the smallest crowd to attend a Swansea first XV fixture, 'froze' as they watched the home side win by 11 points to nil.

As a result of the many postponements, the end of the season became something of a lottery, with, at one stage, the side playing four games in five days. During that period Gilbert Parkhouse, home from Palestine, made his début, whilst Tom Briggs, who had been moved from front-row to flanker, showed remarkable pace and constructive skill. However, in the final analysis the season's results were rather like the curate's egg. Nineteen games had been won and thirteen lost. 'Pendragon' argued yet again that the performance of the team had been adversely affected by constant changes. His telling point that 'many men who contributed to beating Cardiff are no longer with us', was irrefutable.

Yet, as was ever the case, there was some encouragement. D. Glyn Davies at full-back was felt to be an outstanding talent, Howard Jones, the University hooker, had done well, and, 'despite poor service', Guy Addenbrooke had scored 13 tries in first-class games, whilst centres Graham Morse and George Beynon had shown much promise. In addition, the Swansea club's tradition of helping others continued to be followed. At the end of the season 'missionary' games were played against Waunarlwydd, Pontarddulais, and Amman United to assist those clubs, and in one case to help Bert Hollingdale, who had played for the 'Whites' before the first world war.

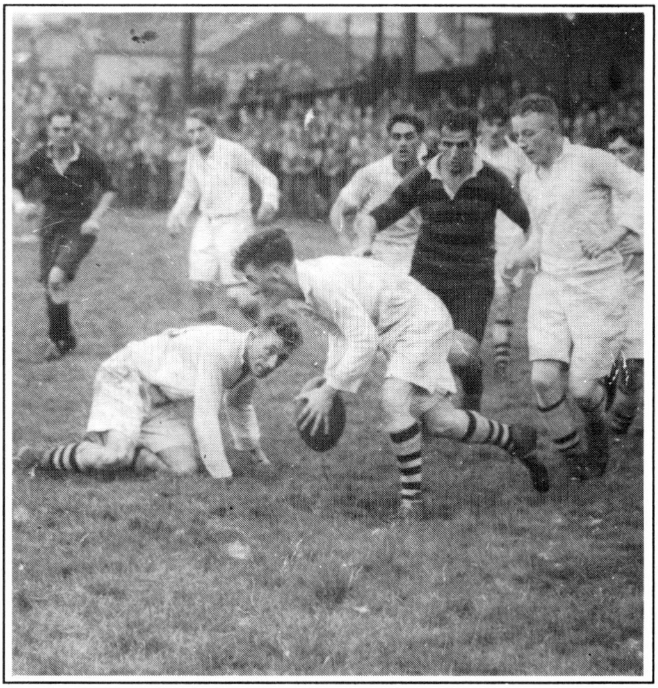

Swansea v. Aberavon. Frank Williams makes a break. Also in the photograph: Tom Gange, Len Blyth, D. J. Davies, D. Swain and J. Rowland.

1947/48

A busy season

The 1947–48 season was one during which the 'Whites' sustained many injuries which affected performance in some games and team selection in others. Nevertheless, only Cardiff were able to 'do the double' over the club and the 'Taffsiders' were the only team to win at St. Helens. With 27 matches being won and the 'Wallabies' run close, at the end of the campaign the Swansea committee could look back with satisfaction on the best outcome for many years.

After a promising start there was disappointment at St. Helens when club captain, Rees Williams, signed for Batley Rugby League club. Furthermore this loss was compounded by a series of injuries to key players, and, for a match against Rosslyn Park, all five first team backs were unavailable. Nonetheless, the 'stand-ins' did well and the 'Whites' won by 24 points to 11 with Norman Sparrow and W. D. Johnson each scoring a fine try. The side was, also, triumphant at Richmond in the next game in which Alun Thomas kicked an 'impossible penalty from 45 yards', and a 'clever solo try' was scored by Frank Williams at scrum-half. But in the next match Haydn Tanner came back to torment his old club. Cardiff dominated proceedings and scored 32 points, whilst Newport went one better in the following match. 'Pendragon' felt that these defeats would have been alarming had not the side suffered so many injuries. Nonetheless, he emphasised the need to tighten the defence particularly since the Australians were due to play the 'Whites' at St. Helens in December.

Given that temporary shops were being built in Oxford Street to help fill the gap left by the Blitz, the Swansea committee must have wished that the team's defence could be shored up with the alacrity with which the prefabricated buildings were being erected. In the event, in typical Swansea fashion, two fine victories were gained in succession as Swansea prepared itself for the 'Wallabies'. The previously invincible Neath side was 'vanquished' by 12 point to nil, with the Swansea pack outstanding, and a strong Bristol side defeated despite the fact that Tom Briggs had been off the field for thirty minutes. Denzil Jones (Amman United) played at outside-half that day and D. Glyn Davies, the new captain, led by example from full-back. With Tom Gange injured for most of the next match, Swansea contemplated the coming Australians from

'Whites' v. Australia. 13 December 1947.
Players, back row: D. Jones, T. Gange, Doug Jones, T. Briggs, D. Swain, A. Thomas.
Seated: L. Shaw, L. Davies, B. Evans, D. G. Davies (Capt.), W. D. Johnson, J. Rowland, J. W. Jenkins.
Floor: Denzil Jones, F. Williams.

the top of a long injury list. In the event most of the 'wounded' were available for selection 'on the day', when 30,000 people were at St. Helens to see the 'Colonials'. And how that crowd cheered when the 'Whites' led Australia at half-time as a result of a Len Davies penalty! Could this be another famous victory? In the second-half, when Dil Johnson ran the length of the field to score, it looked like that and St Helens was awash with noise. Sadly for the partisan crowd, with just five minutes to go, following a line-out, the Australian forward Shehadie threw himself over the line to score. When that try was converted the game was won and lost, though, in defeat, the men in white could feel proud of their performance.

The Swansea side that day was:

D. Glyn Davies (Capt.), L. J. Shaw, Alun Thomas, Len Davies, J. W. Jenkins, Denzil Jones, Frank Williams, Doug Jones, J. Rowlands, Dai Jones, D. G. Swain, Tom Gange, W. D. Johnson, Bryn Evans and Tom Briggs.

The remainder of the season saw victories over Aberavon, Leicester – when sixty German prisoners of war cleared snow from the pitch – Bristol and the 'Quins, with defeats by Llanelli, Coventry and Cardiff. New faces seen in the white shirt around that time included Danny Lewis, Graham Jeffries, Gwilym Bowen and a seventeen-year-old wing-forward listed as R. C. Thomas. Whilst Don Bradman had disappointed Swansea cricket lovers by announcing that he would not play at St. Helens, those who followed the 'Whites' were far less disappointed than they had been at the end of the previous campaign. Meanwhile the club's administrators promised a 'far stronger' fixture list for the Athletic for the coming season. This change, they hoped, would result in a superior flow of players than could be obtained by the *ad hoc* methods which had previously been pursued.

1948/49

More new faces

According to the *Post*, the trial match prior to the beginning of the new season showed that 'the club had a glut of good players for all positions'. Danny Lewis, partnered by another Vardre man, Roy Sutton, made it clear that theirs was going to be a serious challenge to the established pair Denzil Jones and Frank Williams. Len Davies, the new captain, was to show that he was in sound kicking form from the outset, whilst there was strong competition for the three back-row positions. It was true that D. Glyn Davies had not returned to Swansea, thus leaving a gap at full-back, but the committee felt that they would be able to find a satisfactory replacement. The general view, however, was that the 'Whites' needed more weight in their pack.

Nevertheless, early results were encouraging. Bath were beaten by 14 points to nil, while the match against Llanelli, described as 'the most spectacular game seen at St. Helens for many years', was won by eight points without reply. Newport were the next to be beaten, with Bryn Evans dominating the lines-out, by which time 'Pendragon' was claiming that 'with the pack reassembled, Swansea have all the equipment for the best side for many years.'

When Neath came to St. Helens in October the 'Blacks' included Frank Williams in their side, which was unusual in that the player had worn the Swansea shirt in the previous game. Williams, however, found himself on the losing side. Len Blyth and Dil Johnson had 'stifled Neath's attacks at source', whilst Roy Sutton, at scrum-half, had set the 'Whites' backs in motion time and again. Whilst the optimists were beginning to hail a new dawn, the pessimists were looking for signs of what had almost become a traditional poor spell. Nonetheless the prevailing view was that the club was building a side which could be a genuine force in Welsh rugby. Thus it was that, when Guy Addenbrooke left to join Bristol, instead of bemoaning the fact, the selectors saw it as a means of giving a game to another of the several promising players which they had at their disposal. Such was the confidence at the club at that time that the mighty Cardiff side of the period were thought to be 'beatable'. In the event, the 'Taffsiders' took the 'Whites' unbeaten home record, but only after they had been 'fully extended' in a match in which Tom Briggs, Len Blyth, Bryn Evans and Trevor Lewis were outstanding. The *Post* felt it to be noteworthy that the spectators on the Tanner Bank had had a far better view of that game as a direct result of the terracing improvements which had been carried out.

Prior to a match at the end of October the Llanelli and Swansea sides stood in silence to remember Bob Dowdle who had passed away. For the Swansea players the traditional black arm bands were not enough to mark the occasion. They won for the 'old sergeant major', scoring all their points in a three minute spell after the interval. In November Dicky Dobbs found himself playing against Swansea. Richmond had arrived a man short and the young forward donned the Londoners' jersey for the day. Trevor Lewis controlled the lines-out in that match, while Len Blyth scored a fine try from a Richmond heel near their own line.

With the young R. C. C. Thomas home on vacation from Cambridge in their line up, Swansea played the traditional game against Watsonians in front of an enthusiastic holiday crowd. It was the fifty-first consecutive Christmas game against the Scots and eight tries were scored in the match. Without doubt the most exciting of these was that registered by Curtis Grove, who, using both strength and speed tore through the Watsonian defence to touch down. Another young 'Varsity man from Swansea appeared on the Boxing Day. Dai Price, described by 'Pen-

Roy Sutton makes a typical break, with Len Blyth in support.

dragon' as a 'lively winging forward' was in the U.A.U. side beaten by the 'Whites'. Whilst, on graduation, the young man was to revert to the white shirt of his home town club, his major contribution to Swansea rugby was to be as Secretary, serving for an unprecedented 37 years before becoming President in 1992.

In 1949 the success of the side was underlined in the new year when powerful Coventry and Gloucester sides were well beaten and Roy Sutton, now established at scrum-half, was being hailed as the new Tanner. In February Dai Jones was the only Swansea player in the Welsh side which took on Scotland at Murrayfield. Yet, as the *Western Mail* pointed out, Swansea was a young team with great potential. Indeed. such was the enthusiasm for the young turks at the club that 'those splendid old timers D. J. Davies and Tom Briggs dropped out of the pack to make room for the youngsters'. There was, clearly, a Corinthian attitude at St. Helens which was bolstered by a strong Athletic side. The pre-season planning had borne fruit.

By the end of the campaign there were many smiling faces at Swansea Football Club. Some of the football which had been played during the season had been outstanding, whilst a fine crop of players was available for selection. Roy Sutton, Len Davies, Dil Johnson, Bryn Evans ('unaccountably overlooked by the Welsh selectors'), Graham Jeffries, Len Blyth, Trevor Lewis, Leslie Pearce, W. D. Johnson and J. W. Jenkins were among those who had excelled. Jenkins, a native of Penclawdd, ended as top try scorer, even though he had missed many games through injury, and captain Len Davies, leading by example, was top scorer for the season with 88 points. Despite a 'heavy casualty list' the club achieved its best record for almost two decades, winning 29 of its 42 games and scoring 439 points. 'Pendragon' felt so strongly about the improved form that he announced that 'Swansea Rugby is reclaiming its former glory'. With the club's 75th anniversary season in prospect that could not have come about at a more appropriate time.

1949/50

The 75th anniversary season

Whilst Wales had failed to recognise Bryn Evans, Swansea Rugby Club did not make the same mistake; he was elected captain for the 1949-50 season. Evans, who was also pack leader, had a new young man in his eight for the first games of the season. He was 'W. Williams', who played in the second row. Williams, who had replaced Les Pearce,* made an early impression on the supporters of the day. Soon they would add an 'O' after the initial 'W' and enjoy many seasons of outstanding service from the big Gowerton man. Another newcomer to catch the eye in the early season games was A. B. Daniel, who, later in the season also attracted the attention of the Welsh selectors and featured in one of the trial matches.

With Ken Williams playing impressively at full-back, Roy Sutton and Alun Thomas performing well at half-back and many players fighting for places in the pack, the side began the new campaign with some panache. Abertillery, Pembroke, Bayonne and Bristol were defeated in quick succession. Bristol, whose pack was said to he the heaviest in first class football (it weighed over 100 stones) were well beaten by the speed and constructive skill of the Swansea eight, and that was followed by another win, over Newport at Rodney Parade. There Daniel scored early in the match, while Dai Jones crossed for a try under the posts. After that game the *Western Mail* reported that 'Swansea have been the most impressive of the leading Welsh teams'. And that despite the fact that several key players had been injured and were not available. When a strong Rosslyn Park side was 'swept away' by forceful Swansea rugby, the 'Whites' supporters must have felt that the 'old days' had returned. Six victories in succession represented the kind of form which appealed to those who followed the club. Since the season was the club's 75th anniversary that superior form fitted the bill particularly well. 'Pendragon' fairly glowed. He argued that the Swansea club was not only winning games, but was subscribing to the Welsh Union's appeal for brighter football. The breakaways, he argued, were focusing on linking with the backs. Attack, it seemed, was the best form of defence.

From the point of view of the Union game, the upturn in Swansea's form could not have been better timed. Because the Rugby League game was being heavily promoted in the Principality at the time, the Welsh Union had appealed to clubs to play brighter football. This appeal was felt to be important, for, apart from the internationals which were being played in Wales under League laws, several thirteen-a-side clubs existed in south Wales at that point. Neath, Ystradgynlais, Bridgend, Abercrave and Amman Valley were among them. Thus, Swansea, with its tradition of playing open rugby, was ideally placed to challenge this bridgehead. At St. Helens, the club had in Bryn Evans an 'inspiring leader who believed that he had a clear duty to the public that rugby should be spectacular'. Of course, such exciting spectacles could only occur when the forwards provided the platform from which expansive attacks might be launched. The captain saw it as his personal task that that base was laid down.

* Les Pearce left to join Halifax in the Rugby League.

Since Swansea Rugby Club had been formed on 17 October 1874, the nearest match to its 75th birthday was that to be played at the Arms Park against Cardiff on the 15 October 1949. With the 'Whites' in such form, that game, against a Cardiff side which had not lost at home to a Welsh club for two years was anticipated with great eagerness. Before that, however, there was a game against 'Ranji' Walker's XV which, traditionally, involved a great deal of running rugby. In the event it proved to be otherwise with neither side giving an inch in a hard-fought match. Whilst the 'Whites' spent most of the game in the visitors' half, determined defence kept them out and, intercepting a Swansea pass near his own line, M. J. Turner ran the length of the field to win the game for the visitors.

Paradoxically, the defeat gave an extra spur to the Swansea preparation for the Cardiff match. The players felt that they had been somewhat complacent in their approach to the R.A.F. game. Against Cardiff, a side with eight internationals, there could be no room for such an attitude. On the day, 35,000 people were said to have packed into the Cardiff ground and, despite fine work by the Swansea pack, they saw the home side take the lead. If the Welsh public wanted exciting rugby then this was it. All thirty players gave of their best and the play switched from end to end. There was no doubt, though, that the 'Taffsiders' were in the ascendancy when the half-time whistle blew. At 'lemon time', Bryn Evans gathered his Swansea men around him and exhorted them to greater effort. No mention was made of the ghosts of the past, but some would argue that many former Swansea giants added their spiritual blessing to the captain's rallying cry. In any event, though they were nine points down, the 'Whites' became transformed in the second period. At half-back, Sutton and Thomas outplayed their opposite numbers whilst

Bryn Evans is 'chaired' off the field after taking Cardiff's unbeaten record. The policeman looks anxious.

the rest of the Swansea side rose to greater heights. When the final whistle blew the 'All Whites' had gained a memorable victory by 18 points to 12. Bryn Evans was 'chaired' off the field by his victorious team, who had saluted the heroes of the St. Helens past by taking the 'Taffsiders'' scalp. One wonders what 'Argus' and 'Free-Lance' would have made of the great day?

A 75th anniversary dinner was to be held at the Brangwyn Hall on 17 November – the month in which the club played its first game under rugby rules – but there were several games to be played before that event. It would have been appropriate had all those games been won, but, in the event, while Leicester were well beaten, both Llanelli and Coventry won by small margins slightly to mar any concept of a fairy tale. There were, however, extenuating circumstances relating to the Coventry match. The Midland side faced a Swansea XV stripped of nine of its regular players. The 'Whites' were said to have been embarrassed by the calls of the Welsh trial which was held on the same day. 'Pendragon' was not amused. He felt that it was time to revive the argument that trial matches should be held on week days.

Nothing, however, could spoil the 75th celebrations. At the Brangwyn event, giants of the past mixed with the players of the day. Among the former players were Fred Scrine, Billy Bancroft, Will Joseph, Bill Parker, 'Genny' Gordon and Joe Rees. These men not only represented the period in which they played, between them they could remember most of the characters who had strode across the Swansea Football Club stage from its inception. Any exponent of oral history attending (that event) that evening would have had a proverbial field day. As it was, all the Swansea men who were there must have sat up with pride as Eric Evans, Secretary of the Welsh Union, declared that 'Swansea's contribution to rugby has been immeasurable'. It was a sentiment with which no one was prepared to quarrel.

In the *Post* soon after the Brangwyn event there was a photograph of 'Barrow Boys' plying their trade on a bomb site near Castle Street, and an announcement that the sweet ration was to be increased. Overall there was much to remind the citizens of Swansea that austerity was still the order of the day. Nonetheless another special event in the Diamond Anniversary calendar provided those who followed Swansea rugby with riches beyond compare. At a reunion at the clubhouse a special plaque was unveiled accompanied by 'firm handshakes between Billy Bancroft and Bryn Evans who, between them, spanned fifty years of Swansea rugby'. Also there were Bill Bowen, and the 'Invincible' captain, 'Genny' Gordon. For Swansea lovers of the oval ball game it was a magical night!

When 'Pendragon' came to write his half term report he enthused. Without doubt, he wrote 'the "Whites" were the outstanding Welsh rugby club of 1949'. Len Blyth and W. D. Johnson had scored tries 'with refreshing freedom ... the displays of Alun Thomas and Roy Sutton had touched the highest pinnacle'. He went on to argue that without the long list of injuries and absences the side would have done even better. Even those problems provided the *Post* scribe with room to enthuse. He was delighted to note that the performance of players coming through from the Athletic in emergencies 'spoke volumes for the second string'.

Late in January, with Sir Thomas Beecham at the Brangwyn Hall (tickets 12*s*.6*d* to 3*s*.6*d*), the 'Whites' did some orchestrating of their own. In order to ensure that the return match with Cardiff was played, dozens of braziers were burned throughout the night in an attempt to defeat the effects of frost which, at that time, was affecting Swansea. This one had to be played! In the star-studded Cardiff side W. B. Cleaver was replaced by a new young player, Cliff Morgan, but internationals like Matthews, Bleddyn Williams and Trott packed a Cardiff team out to avenge the defeat earlier in the season. However, as 'Pendragon' put it, the 'Cardiff stars did not twinkle'. Continuing with his heavenly metaphor, the *Post* man claimed that Roy Sutton had 'totally eclipsed' Rex Willis in the battle of the scrum halves. Once again, however, all fifteen Swansea men played their part in that 'double' victory, though Len Blyth, W. D. Johnson, Dai Jones and Len Davies were singled out for special praise. When the final whistle was blown, the fact that Cardiff had failed to score put the gilt on the gingerbread as far as the excited Swansea supporters were concerned. That day in Swansea homes, tea was graced by many smiling faces.

As if inspired by that win, the team came into its own in the final quarter of the campaign. In beating Newbridge with a side which included only seven regular first team players, the 'Whites' won their eighth consecutive game. That day, Douglas Jones was said to have done the work of three men. Overall the Roy Sutton, Alun Thomas, Len Davies triangle was thought to be the key factor behind the side's cohesion. Herbert and Abel Thomas, Len Blyth, J. W. Jenkins and W. D. Johnson were players of unusual versatility, whilst Douglas Jones, well supported by Dai Jones, G. J. Rees, Billy Williams, Graham Jeffries and Dicky Dobbs had 'led the forwards like a lion'. Bryn Evans's captaincy was thought to have been of the highest order, thus it was a considerable disappointment when he broke his ankle and was unable to lead the side for the last games of the campaign.

At that time Len Blyth, featured in the *Post*, illustrated new found talents as a soothsayer. Readers were told that he had a two-week-old son who was 'a potential "All White"'. Prior to his making that statement no one at St. Helens had an inkling that the popular back-row forward had pretensions to be another 'Old Moore'.

Meanwhile there was a significant change at the *Post*. 'Pendragon' retired and was replaced by John Christopher, thus severing a line of observers with intriguing *noms de plume* who had written about things 'All White' since the earliest days of the club. Somehow, the trend to modernise journalism by eradicating picturesque pseudonyms robbed the reporting of something of its mystique. In any event, the language, the colour and the vehemence associated with such reporting was to become but a memory.

Chapter Seventeen

UNCERTAIN SELECTION

1950–51

WITH MOST OF THE PREVIOUS season's successful side available, supporters of Swansea Rugby Club looked forward to the new campaign with excited anticipation. In the event, with the exception of a good win at Bristol, early results were disappointing. Indeed, half way through the opening month, John Christopher, the new *Post* scribe, was arguing that there was the need to develop better team work. It was almost as if the previous season had not been played. Bryn Evans, elected captain for a second season, could not put his finger on the problem. Nor could the selectors.

Such was their uncertainty that, in October when the 'Whites' went to London to play Rosslyn Park, the selectors took seventeen players with them. The side was selected prior to the match. Whilst this unusual procedure is hardly to be recommended, it happened that, on the day, the selected XV outplayed the London side. The captain, Bryn Evans, W. J. Francis, H. Griffiths (Cross Keys) and Wynn Bratton all shone in that match. Alun Thomas scored a magnificent try straight from a restart, whilst Len Davies, 'with a 35 yard kick-ahead and chase', also scored to win the match for the 'Whites'. That win did a great deal for morale at St. Helens.

In a column adjacent to his comments on that Rosslyn Park game, John Christopher reported on a survey which he had undertaken of Swansea players who had won international 'caps'. In October 1950 he calculated that 90 Swansea players had been honoured over a 68-year period and 542 'caps' had been won in the process. Those, statistics, of course, represented just one measure of the contribution which the Swansea club had made to rugby football during that period. No wonder Eric Evans felt that the club's contribution had been immeasurable. On the other hand, the Town Council was concerned with things measurable. They promised that plans for the development of a 70,000 capacity St. Helens would be available by 1952.

Horace Phillips.

Whilst the Council was certain about its pronouncement, at the time the press thought that Swansea's selectoral policy was 'uncertain'. For example, in the middle of November the *Post* pointed out that thirty-one players had been used up to that point in just nine matches, and less than half of the games had been won. In discussing the situation, one of "Pendragon's" old scripts might easily have been recycled. Yet, as ever in the continuing Swansea panorama, amidst the gloom there were encouraging signs. Alun Thomas, who was being watched by the

'Whites' v. 'Scarlets' – Dai Howells, Tom Griffiths dribble.

Welsh selectors, was playing well at outside-half, Billy Williams, Dicky Dobbs and Doug Jones had been conspicuous in the pack, whilst the new 'flyer', Horace Phillips was exciting the crowds. In due course, the winger, along with Arwyn Morris, Billy Williams and Alun Thomas, was selected to play in a Welsh trial match. Horace scored a try in that game.

However, problems behind the scenes at St. Helens were beginning to erupt. The *Post* referred to 'the distant rumblings of an approaching row at St. Helens'. From this distance it is reasonable to argue that, given the continuing changes which were being made to the side, it was not surprising that some players were discontented with their lot. Among that group was Alun Thomas, who resigned from the club and threw in his lot with Cardiff. Thomas argued that he wanted to play at outside-half and not be required to play in other positions at the whim of the selectors. Whatever the rights and wrongs of the case, the Swansea club could ill afford to lose a player of Thomas's quality. In commenting on the departure of the player, John Christopher pointed out that, during the current campaign, some of the men from the previous season's successful side had played on only two or three occasions. He declared that he and 'many supporters' were bemused by the selectoral policy.

Nonetheless, whatever the problems at the club, the players continued to give of their best. Paradoxically, after the departure of Thomas and a defeat by Coventry, Richmond were well beaten, as were Abertillery and Coventry (in the return match at St. Helens). By this time Clem Thomas was in tremendous form and was being tipped for a Welsh 'cap', as were Horace Phillips and Billy Williams. However, as if to demonstrate the vagaries of their policy, for a Christmas match against U.A.U., the selectors chose Clem Thomas as a centre. The Yule-tide, of course, allowed the 'Whites' to open up the game and play traditional Swansea rugby. Thus it was that, despite or because of the decisions of the selectors, Watsonians and London Welsh were submerged under an avalanche of scoring. 58 points were scored whilst only six were conceded. Len Davies and Herbert Thomas sated themselves in the process, and, yet again, criticisms were diverted by success on the field.

Burnt ash

Meantime, St. Helens was being prepared for the coming England v. Wales international. 12,000 tons of burnt ash were deposited on the bank at the town end, whilst the playing pitch was moved 25 yards in the same direction. Later, D. Ivor Saunders, the Borough Estate Agent, showed the end product of the development to representatives of the Welsh Union. He told the press that the comments of the men from the Union were 'highly complimentary'. 75,000, it was said, could now be 'comfortably accommodated at St. Helens'. Sadly, as the near future was to show, the men from the east would shortly be administering the *coup de grace*. Despite the efforts of the Swansea Borough, international football at St. Helens was about to become a thing of the past.

In January an eighteen-year-old full-back made his début for Swansea. He was Terry Davies and, in the match – against Ebbw Vale – he was 'several times applauded for his fielding and kicking'. The lad from Bynea was believed to be a 'real find', and, 'when he filled out' it was felt that he would be a formidable player. Not that the newcomer would have been able to add bulk to his young body from eating. As a result of shortages, at the time when he made his début the meat ration was reduced to 8*d* worth per week.

Nonetheless, by the middle of February, the full-back had established himself in the side, and, in a victory over Bristol played in heavy rain and sleet, he was declared 'man of the match'. By this time, too, Len Davies was showing his versatility by playing at outside-half and linking well with Roy Sutton.

Notwithstanding the inconsistency of the side, when the season ended Bryn Evans could look back on some fine performances. Blackheath had been outplayed, whilst Leicester were beaten at Welford Road on what the *Western Mail* described as a 'black swamp'. John Christopher thought that on that occasion the side had played better than it had throughout the season. Terry Davies excelled that day, too. According to the *Post* he was 'applauded by the home crowd for his immaculate performance', whilst Brian Edwards received an accolade for scoring a try after a 'twenty-five yard dribble'. Billy Williams was selected to play for Wales, though in an unaccustomed front-row position, whilst the Swansea back-row – Thomas, Blyth and Johnson were lauded wherever the 'Whites' played. Among the backs Brian Edwards, Herbert Thomas and Horace Phillips had had encouraging seasons, with Thomas heading the try scorers. Len Davies had claimed most points. Whilst the club had ended its sixth post-war season with a slightly poorer record than that of the previous campaign, 24 matches had been won and there was plenty of fuel to warm the optimists. For their part the pessimists were strangely quiet.

1951-52

A new captain

One of the most consistent players from the previous season found himself elected club captain for the 1951-52 campaign. Len Blyth, popular with the players and supporters, said that he had a great deal to live up to in following Bryn Evans. Whilst, at the end of the new skipper's first

'Whites' v. South Africans. 15 December 1951.

term of office the season's results were poorer than those of the previous campaign, no one could fault the effort made by the big forward to weld the team into a unit. He led from the front in more ways than one. According to the *Post* in its end-of-season review he had 'set a fine example and was the fastest back-row forward in the country'.

Unfortunately, Blyth's period of office started poorly, with defeats by Cardiff and Newport in successive games. However, both these sides were said to have had far heavier packs than the 'Whites', whilst, in the Newport game, both Tom Griffiths and Billy Williams had to leave the field at a time when the men in white were holding their own. But then, as if to illustrate that the early losses did not represent the strength of the side, Bristol were 'thoroughly beaten' in an exciting match at St. Helens. In that game both backs and forwards were in fine form, whilst Horace Phillips scored what the *Post* described as 'an historic try'. Intercepting near his own line, the wing man ran 'at tremendous pace down the middle of the field ... tackled, he lost the ball but kicked on ... and gathered to score under the posts.' Whilst, unlike the modern soccer player, the winger did not perform back flips or kiss his shirt, the Old Dy'vorian, according to the *Post*, 'was seen to smile'.

The Bristol game apart, by mid-October, John Christopher was urging the selectors to take remedial action, 'or they will find themselves at the bottom of the Unofficial Welsh Table'. Despite his previous arguments about 'chopping and changing', the *Post* man wanted to play both Clem Thomas and Dil Johnson in the centre. In particular, Christopher was concerned about the pending visit of the Springboks. 'It is essential', he wrote, 'that they should be given a good run for their money.' It would have been surprising if those sentiments were not echoed by the beleaguered selectors. As far as they were concerned, they were striving to find their best side, and in the same month that Handel Greville was brought in at scrum-half, Teifion Williams

Dil Johnson's try v. Springboks.

was introduced as his partner. The new arrangement seemed to benefit the team, and Llanelli, Aberavon, Penarth and Pontypool were all defeated in what was a relatively purple patch.

However, it was a November game against Coventry which really lifted Swansea spirits. At that time the Midlands club was the only undefeated side in the country, and they came to St. Helens in 'confident mood'. The reports of the game, though, illustrated that it was the Swansea men who excelled. National and local press wrote of 'tremendous Swansea defence', as the home side negated Coventry's attacking ambitions. Len Blyth and Clem Thomas then 'inspired a late Swansea rally', and, when winger Horace Phillips threw in an accurate line-out ball, newcomer Hitchings wrote his name in the Swansea record books by diving over for a try. Then, as if inspired by his involvement in that score, the winger sprinted over in the corner to double Swansea's total. It was the side's eighth consecutive victory. Swansea smiles were back in place.

In the next match, away to Richmond, Ieuan Evans and Horace Phillips both scored, whilst Terry Davies had 'his best game of the season' and Len Blyth 'didn't put a foot wrong'. As early season blues were banished, it looked as though the 'Whites' were striking form at the right time. With Plymouth Albion becoming the club's tenth successive victims in a match in which the 'Whites' scored 28 points, that view was reinforced with some flair.

By mid December all John Christopher had to complain about was the foolishness of the Welsh selectors. They kept picking Billy Williams as a front-row forward 'when that was not his position'. In fairness, at the time, 'W.O.' himself felt that to be true, yet he was to make the front rank position his own, not only for Swansea and Wales, but also for the Lions. For the Welsh match against the Springboks, Williams was joined by his club captain Len Blyth, a fact which delighted all Swansea supporters.

In the meantime there was the matter of Swansea's own game with the Springboks to stage and to celebrate. One of the aspects of the celebration involved bringing together surviving members of the club's 1912 side which had gained a memorable victory over the men in green. As a result, Dai Williams, Harry Moulton, Edgar Morgan and Howell Lewis all attended the game as a kind of collective talisman. Whilst there was no fairy tale victory to lift their spirits, the old-timers saw Swansea take the lead as Dil Johnson 'leaped like a tiger and dived on the ball for a try'. 'Playing like demons', the 'Whites' kept their line intact right up to the half time whistle, the only South African score coming from a penalty by Geffin. Even then the tourists had a piece of good fortune, for, from the penalty kick, the ball hit the upright and, as if in slow motion, rolled along the bar to drop behind.

At the end of the game the general opinion was that the 'Whites' had done enough to have earned a draw. The *News Chronicle* had it that 'no team has fought with such valour', but the reality of the scoreboard showed that the South Africans had won by eleven points to three. The Springboks were genuine in their praise. They had been warned about the strength of Swansea football; now, they said, they knew for themselves.

The Swansea team which earned those plaudits fielded as follows:

Terry Davies, Horace Phillips, Brian Edwards, Roy Sutton, Peris James, Teifion Williams, Handel Greville, Doug Jones, Ken James, Tom Griffiths, W. O. Williams, Harry Payne (Skewen), Len Blyth (Capt.), Clem Thomas and Dil Johnson.

By mid-February, when the King died in his sleep and a new Elizabethan age began, Swansea football had gone through yet another period of inconsistency. It seemed as though the team had 'peaked' in time to meet the Springboks, for, thereafter, the 'Whites' had some disappointing results. The U.A.U. romped home by 24 points to 8, Neath were victors by a single point, Cardiff by two, whilst Gloucester and Bristol played out draws. On the first day of March a new writer covered the Swansea game with Blackheath. Ron Griffiths normally reported on Neath games, but on this occasion was allocated to St. Helens. Happily for the *Post* scribe, he saw a fine display of rugby and reported that it had been 'a free-scoring, delightful thriller'. The final score – 23 points to 16 – spoke for itself, and Griffiths had seen Dil Johnson, J. R. Davies and Clem Thomas in fine form. Whilst some weeks were to pass before Ron Griffiths began to cover Swansea games on a full time basis, that match, against Blackheath, was to be the beginning of the journalist's long association with the St. Helens club.

In the next match, young Haydn Mainwaring scored soon after the start, but opponents Bath were in no mood to follow Blackheath, and fought 'tooth and nail' to contain the 'Whites'. The match was said to have been a poor spectacle, but, thanks to a second try by Brian Edwards, the home side did enough to win. In addition they had maintained their unbeaten record against English clubs, though they were to lose that when they were beaten at Leicester in the next game.

In April, faced with a logjam of fixtures, as the 'Whites' played ten games in a three week period, John Christopher was arguing for a shorter rugby season. Partly as a result of that and a spate of injuries, results were not good. All that apart, the *Post* journalist believed that the team had 'steadily declined since the Springboks match'. There was little doubt that the team had missed the influence of Len Blyth, who was out of the game for a month. Furthermore, whilst the men from the north were no longer active in Swansea, another acquisitive organisation spirited away two key players. Billy Williams and Terry Davies were both called up by the Royal Navy to undertake their National Service. From that time on Williams, by then an established international, was to be known by the sobriquet 'Stoker'.

Whilst these men left, other names were added to the large number used during the season. Among them was a Secondary Schools International by the name of Onllwyn Brace. Brace, it was said, was a born footballer, and, in a game against Harlequins, he and Roy Sutton struck up a fine partnership. That partnership, however, was not destined to flourish at St. Helens. Overall, during the season, fifty per cent of the matches played had been won, Wilf Jones (66) was top points scorer, whilst Horace Phillips had crossed for 11 tries and gained his 'cap' in the match against France at St. Helens.

1952-53

Rebuilding again

The impact upon the Swansea club of losing Williams and Davies, both international players, was significant. Given that the pair had been part of the backbone of the side during the previous campaign, the selectors had to find replacements of calibre. As usual, the pre-season trials and games were one means of spotting such talent. As far as John Christopher was concerned some of the newcomers who played in those early season matches were extremely promising. J. R. Davies was thought to be an ideal replacement for Clem Thomas, whilst Haydn Mainwaring and John Leleu looked to be 'first team material'. Nonetheless, for all Christopher's optimism, it was asking a lot for the young men to take the place of those who had left. Happily, Len Blyth was fit again, whilst Vivian Davies, who had been playing with Gloucester, looked to be a capable scrum-half. Another trialist, Ken Richards, had the distinction of being picked by the County before playing his initial first class game. All in all, therefore, the mood in the Swansea camp was far more optimistic than might have been expected. The new captain, Roy Sutton, echoed that sentiment when he said that he was looking forward to the season with quiet confidence.

In September, the 'Whites' revived a tradition associated with the club's earliest days when they met Halifax at St. Helens. The Yorkshire men, perhaps showing the influence of the League game on their play, were 'great crash tacklers'. However, tackling alone does not win games and Viv Davies, deputising for the absent captain, orchestrated things from the base of the scrum as the tourists were outplayed. At full-back for Swansea on that occasion was Glamorgan cricketer, Bernard Hedges. By the middle of the month, Arwyn Morris, who had worked hard at his kicking during the close season, had scored half the points registered by the side. During that period, Bristol were beaten in a match in which the 'Whites' did some crash tackling of their own, Llanelli, superbly led by Lewis Jones, took the St. Helens ground record against the run of play, and 'Ranji' Walker's XV were held to a draw.

In the next match undefeated Newport scraped a win, converting the winning try with the last kick of the game, thus negating a magnificent individual try by Dil Johnson which had given Swansea the lead. Throughout this period Bernard Hedges was playing soundly at full-back, but there was some debate about the scrum-half position. Roy Sutton's detractors felt that he was 'too individualistic', but many more believed that his experience was invaluable in what was a young side. Thus it was that John Christopher rehearsed his own predilections when he commented on the fact that two scrum-halves had been selected for a match against Rosslyn Park. In the event neither man played, instead, a third man, Handel Greville, was at inside-half in a game which the 'Whites' won comfortably.

When Llanelli were beaten in the next match – Dil Johnson stood in as captain for the injured Sutton – the Swansea supporters must have wondered whether they were about to witness a revival in fortune. Arwyn Morris won the match with a last minute penalty, Greville was 'brilliant', Brian Jenkins crossed for a fine try, whilst that scored by Horace Phillips was said to have brought the crowd to its feet. Penarth and Blackheath were then defeated in succession, with Billy Williams, home on leave, being given the chance to play as a result of a gesture by Doug Jones, who stood down.

In November, gale force winds uprooted trees in the Uplands, and Llanelli lost Lewis Jones to Rugby League for a record fee. Both events caused consternation in west Wales, for, whilst Swansea supporters were not directly affected, they knew how their Llanelli counterparts felt. Another Welsh hero of the rugby field had also been uprooted.

In a match at St. Helens the 'Wizards', including Onllwyn Brace, were trounced, as were Coventry, for whom another former Swansea player, Clem Thomas, was making his début. By that time, in the wake of the successful run, Ken Richards, Bryan Jenkins, Arwyn Morris and Bernard Hedges were being singled out for praise, though the 'young side' as a whole was being much lauded. Then, just as the press was beginning to believe that Swansea was once more a formidable presence in the land, the side crashed by 20 points to 6 at Richmond, and followed that with a defeat at St. Helens at the hands of a West Wales Rugby Union side. To rub salt into the wound, John Christopher's account of the latter match, emphasised that the west Wales combination had been the more skilful on the day. Since Handel Greville was outstanding for the visitors, a man from Mars might have been inclined to question the club's selectoral policy. As it was, this was left to the man from the *Post*. John Christopher opined that 'the selectors are at a turning point ... they are putting players out of position ... Teifion Williams is no wing three-quarter ... others were allowed to drift away'.

But, undaunted, the selectors continued to experiment. Meanwhile, Roy Sutton had 'stepped down' reflecting, 'his loss of form', Viv Davies was selected for a Welsh trial, and in matches against Cardiff and Newport Len Blyth, Des Bater, Horace Phillips and Bryan Jenkins were reported as having 'given their all'. For a game at the Gnoll, Swansea rested Teifion Williams, but found themselves opposing their team mate as he turned out for Neath. Since the 'Blacks' took Swansea's unbeaten away record on that day, the irony of the situation was not lost on the Abertawe supporters. Then, when Cardiff 'overwhelmed Swansea's pluck' to win at the Arms Park, those same supporters must have looked in wonder as Alun Thomas, another former 'All White', controlled the game for the 'Taffsiders'.

By March the press was reflecting concern in the Principality regarding the quality of the Rugby which was being played in the home internationals. 'Full-Back', clearly a throw-back to more colourful times, wrote:

> 'If inter-club rugby ever reaches the all-time low of international clashes, then there will

> be plenty of room in the grandstands for those who choose this form of torture for their ... sports leisure.'

Yet, at St. Helens, as if to illustrate the mercurial form of the Swansea team, they won a 'spanking game' against Leicester, scoring two 'classical' tries in the process. Leicester, who had not won at St. Helens for thirty years, were 'outplayed in every department'. In that match, Viv Davies and Des Bater played well at half-back, as did the Swansea back-row. After several false dawns, the win heralded a mini revival and as a result, until the end of the season, attendances at St. Helens were 'on the upward trend', which reflected the style of football being played as well as the victories which were gained. With the Bater-Davies pairing flourishing, Bernard Hedges having a fine season at full-back and two new young forwards catching the eye – Dudley Thomas and John Leleu, the club enjoyed welcome success.

Overall, whilst the season as a whole had been disappointing in terms of results, there was more than enough to sustain the optimists. Apart from the young talent which had developed, Terry Davies and Ken James were both due to be demobbed in the following December and would be available thereafter. At least the press was enthusiastic. Ron Griffiths, who had been switched from covering Neath's games to write about the 'Whites', was in no doubt as to the immediate future. 'When other clubs are expressing concern about end-of-the-season staleness', he wrote, 'Swansea are in the happy position of being able to boast of ... far better football than has been seen at St. Helens for some time.' Supporters who read those words might well have asked, what might have been achieved had there been a settled side from the beginning of the season?

Certainly, the man from Mars, contemplating the seasons since the war, must have wondered why successful sides from one season were systematically dismantled at the beginning of the next? Notwithstanding the enforced departures of men like Billy Williams and Terry Davies, it was a reasonable question for the neutral observer to ask. Yet, there was no doubting the ambition of those who ran the club. At the A.G.M., Judge Rowe Harding declared that he had two ambitions. 'First, that he should attain a seat on the Judicial Bench, and second, that the Swansea club should be "right on top of the world".' Leaving aside the judge's legal ambitions, at the end of the season which was to follow, the jury would be out on his attempts to achieve the latter goal. Nonetheless, at that same meeting, treasurer T. G. Grimshaw was able to report that the club had posted a small surplus (£347) for the previous season. At least, some progress was being made.

1953–54

The 'All Blacks' cometh

Given that the New Zealand tourists were to play in south Wales during the season ahead, there was much discussion about the possibility of the duration of matches being extended to forty minutes each way. In general the change was welcomed and, in due course, was enacted. At St. Helens, the selectors felt that they were in a better position to contemplate the visit of the New Zealanders' than they had been for some recent touring sides. Apart from the encouragement which results at the end of the previous season had given them, Clem Thomas had returned from Coventry to resume his partnership with Len Blyth and Dil Johnson. For his part,

Teifion Williams goes low v. 'All Blacks'. 12 December 1953.
Other Swansea men in the photograph: Trevor Petherbridge, Jim Rees, Len Blyth and Goronwy Morgan.

Johnson, now club captain, was looking forward to the challenge. He, also, declared himself flattered when Sir Lewis Jones presented him with a framed photograph of himself 'to commemorate his selection for Wales'. Not to be outdone, the Supporters' Club gave the popular flanker a blazer to mark the same occasion. With Billy Williams reported as expecting to gain earlier release than had been envisaged, and Terry Davies hoping for more leave, St. Helens had a smile on its face.

Unfortunately, Dame Fortune did not add her smile to that early confidence. Early season injuries were numerous – for one match eleven players were stated to be unavailable through injury – and it was not possible to select a settled side during the first six weeks of the campaign. As a consequence, additional newcomers had to be brought into the team, whilst there was, at least, one returnee. John Faull made his début at full-back against Pontypool, whilst Handel Greville played at inside-half versus Llanelli. The Llanelli match was won by the 'Whites', and, after the game, it was announced that the scrum-half 'had been made a life member of the Swansea club in recognition of his services and sportsmanship'.

In a November match against Coventry, Greville found himself being replaced by Clem Thomas, though not as an aspect of selection policy. Early in the second half the scrum-half sustained an injury which necessitated his leaving the field.The flanker took over. Then, at the same time as Sir Edmund Hilary was signing the Visitors' Book at the Guildhall, the 'Whites' were climbing an Everest of their own. Cardiff, including players like Bleddyn Williams and Cliff Morgan, were defeated in a match in which the Swansea pack took the honours. In particular, Ron Griffiths picked out the home 'All International' back-row for special praise. Nevertheless, in general, the club's results were disappointingly inconsistent. Immediately prior to the Kiwi match, the side lost to Harlequins, Neath and Richmond, whilst beating Blackheath and Coventry.

Perhaps it was the gesture of Mr W. G. Watts of Cherry Grove which activated the spirit of players past to inspire the 'Whites' of the day. Mr Watts presented the club with the jersey which had been worn by Deans during the 1905 tour, in which the influence of Swansea men was quite large. Whatever it was, a Swansea side, said to be weakened by injuries and absences, lifted its collective game to hold the mighty New Zealanders to a draw. Among those absent was Terry Davies who had dislocated a shoulder whilst digging a trench at the Royal Marine School. Given that Gwyn Lawrence and Ken Richards were 'doubtful' and did not play, whilst Handel Greville had broken an ankle, it was hardly surprising that there was concern at St. Helens immediately before the match with the tourists.

Because of the length of the injury list, the selectors had no option other than to take chances with the team which they picked. Among them was the selection of young John Faull for only his second match in first-class football. It was asking a lot of the young man, who, nevertheless, rose to the occasion, and kicked two long-distance penalties. Had it not been for the 'All Black' Elsom, who scored two tries, Swansea might have won another historic victory over a touring side. As it was, the men in white were magnificent, particularly the front eight, who 'gave as good as they got'. When the final whistle blew, the 40,000 crowd roared its approval of the fifteen local heroes who had fought the New Zealanders 'tooth and nail'. No grey men played that day; only black and white.

The Swansea team for that match was:

W. Bratton, T. Williams, B. Jenkins, J. Faull, H. D. Phillips; J. Marker, G. Morgan, W. O. Williams, T. Petherbridge, D. Jones, E. J. Rees, D. Bruce-Thomas, R. C. C. Thomas, L. Blyth and W. D. Johnson.

After the New Zealand game, there were the traditional Christmas matches, much enjoyed by lovers of 'Swansea football'. For the Watsonians game, Swansea supporters welcomed back one of their former favourites. Alun Thomas, then working in west Wales, turned out at outside-half and 'ran the match'. According to the *Western Mail*, the player was directly responsible for three of Swansea's tries and was 'applauded, warmly as he left the field'. With no Clapham Omnibus in Swansea, the man on the Mumbles Train wanted to know if the international was going to revert to the white shirt on a more permanent basis? Unfortunately, there was to be no happy ending to satisfy the desires of that average man in the Swansea street.

In January, snow and ice in Wales resulted in many games being postponed. However, just prior to that spell of bad weather, the 'Whites' had broken further new ground with their 'missionary' work. They met a north Wales representative side at Wrexham to become the first senior club from south Wales to play in the north. According to the Wrexham press, 'the huge crowd enjoyed a fine game full of incident'. The 'Whites' won the game (31 points to 10) with something in hand and, in the process, also won the appreciation of the north Wales rugby fraternity.

In the edition of the *Post* which carried John Christopher's end-of-the-season review, the paper published a photograph of a group of 150 people standing, ghoul-like, outside Swansea prison, where an execution had taken place. Whilst there were no executioners at St. Helens, there were those who viewed the corpse of the season past with strong views about the longevity of the tenure of the selectors. Once again, it had been a disappointing season. Fifteen matches had been lost of the forty-two played and only on rare occasions had 'Swansea football' been played. Without doubt, the highlight of the season had been the draw with New Zealand,though there had been fine victories such as those over Blackheath, Coventry, Watsonians and the Wasps. Teifion Williams (17) led the try scorers, with Horace Phillips (13) second. Christopher felt that these totals were commendable since 'the wingers had received poor service'. The *Post* writer believed that Len Blyth had been missed, whilst John Faull, who had converted 17 tries, was 'the find of the season'.

As Roger Bannister broke the four-minute-mile barrier on an Oxford track, those who administered Swansea rugby must have wished that for the season which had just ended, the team could have set performance records which at least, approached the best in the club's history. Instead the statistics confirmed that it had been another mediocre campaign. Thus it was that, at the A.G.M., Clem Thomas, elected captain for the season to come, declared it to be his intention to play open rugby from the outset. He wanted to put Swansea rugby back on the map. It was a laudable ambition which was applauded by all concerned.

Meanwhile, at the A.G.M. of the Welsh Union, the men from the east finally drove home their wedge. Their arguments from fifty years before, when they campaigned for an equal and fair share of games for east and west, were forgotten. A proposal put forward by a man who was said at the time to have been a 'Cardiff placeman', was passed at the meeting. In future, all international matches in Wales would take place in Cardiff. St. Helens, where the first had been played, would host no more.

1954–55

Downhill via Bucharest

Prior to the start of the 1954–55 campaign special permission was given to the 'Whites' to play two matches during August behind the 'Iron Curtain'. The Swansea club had been invited by the Romanian Rugby Federation to play the matches there because of its 'fame and tradition'. Thus it was that the Swansea party set out from High Street station and eventually arrived in Prague. From there they flew in three planes to Bucharest. However, such was the weather that two of the aircraft were forced to land at another airport off their flight plan. Horace Phillips, the senior man in the plane which got through, found himself having to make impromptu speeches whilst his colleagues at the other airport were held for a time under guard. When, eventually, the party was re-united in the capital, they were fêted with a round of receptions and dinners. It was hardly the right preparation for the first match, which was played in a ground capable of holding 80,000 people. Nor was the temperature in which the game was played helpful to rugby footballers from Swansea. As Clem Thomas led his men onto the field the thermometer read 90°. Not surprisingly, the 'Whites' melted in the second quarter of the game, during which the home side scored 15 points. In the second-half, when the temperature dropped somewhat, the men in white came back into the game, but were unable to close the gap. Consequently, Locomotive were the victors in the first game between a Romanian side and a British XV. They won by 23 points to 12. Happily, there was a favourable result at the end of the second match. That was played in the relative cool of the evening, and the 'Whites' beat the Constructors club by 16 points to 5.

'The young "General" inspires his troops'.
Clem Thomas talks to some of the touring party before leaving for Bucharest.

On the party's return, Bruce Barter, then the chairman of the selectors at St. Helens, was delighted to report that the Romanian Minister of Sport had said that the Swansea men had made a wonderful impression on all who had met them. They were, the minister said, a credit to their club and country. Whilst that accolade was appreciated, from the Swansea point of view, the visit to Romania had been costly. During one match, Horace Phillips was concussed and broke his hand, whilst Terry Davies dislocated his shoulder. In view of what was to happen during the approaching season, the selectors may have wished that the pair had stayed at home.

Because of the absence of Terry Davies and Horace Phillips changes had to be made in the back division. The full-back position was given to Wyn Bratton again, whilst in a pre-season match at Glais, Peris James caught the eye with a hat-trick of tries. After that game there was an air of confidence about the club. Sadly, that evaporated rather quickly once the season proper began.

Having lost two players, the next thing to be mislaid was the kit hamper. Since this was the third thing to be lost, as it were, the superstitious might have thought it to have been an omen. For the initial game of the season – at Newport – the team's kit was put in the guard's van at High Street station. Unfortunately, when the team changed trains at Cardiff the hamper was not taken off. Consequently, when the 'Whites' arrived at Newport, they had to play in borrowed kit. There was further misfortune, too; E. J. Rees and W. D. Johnson had to cry off at the last minute. As a result, an urgent message was sent to Viv Davies, captain of the Athletic, to go to Newport and play. Unfortunately, the 'patched-up' Swansea side was no match for the 'Usk-siders' who were in fine form (Onllwyn Brace appeared for them at outside-half). Despite the 'inspirational display' of captain, Clem Thomas, Newport won comfortably by 20 points to 5. The *Post* report of the game spoke of gaps in the Swansea defence which Newport exploited, and 'a disheartening start for a young and inexperienced side'. A photograph in the same edition of the paper showing the gap between the two halves of the new Briton Ferry bridge might have been symbolic. 'Gaps' had to be bridged in the Swansea defence, too. For the next match young Graham Tregidon, the Secondary Schools outside-half was brought into the side, and with Wyn Bratton playing for the police, Howard John wore the number one jersey. Nonetheless, Group Captain Walker's XV, who were the visitors, won a closely contested game by two points.

Billy Williams jumps in a line-out – 'Whites' v. Romania.

Whilst boxer Dai Dower was registering his 20th successive victory, the 'Whites' found themselves with an unwanted sequence of losses. After being beaten by Neath, the club's record read Played 3 lost 3, though the display of the team in the Gnoll game had given 'Whites' watchers hope for better things. Raymond Jones (Brynamman) had enjoyed a first-class début, Teifion Williams had scored a superb try, and the *Western Mail* thought that Clem Thomas was the most enthusiastic captain in the game. However the side had not enjoyed the 'rub of the green'. The team had misfortune, too, in the next match, when Bristol scored two tries within the last two minutes of the game to gain a win which was hardly deserved. Yet, as any team which has struck a bad patch will confirm, when you are down the fates seem to conspire against you. In turn that tends to engender a loss of confidence and the 'slippery slope' becomes ever more precarious. If, at that time, the season had been represented as a game of snakes and ladders, there would have been no rungs where the 'Whites' found themselves.

Not surprisingly, whilst Clem Thomas was sticking to his principles and attempting to play open rugby, the pundits among the press, on the terraces and in the stands were theorising about the situation. Most people did not wish to disagree with the Thomas philosophy, but there was a groundswell of opinion which called for a modified approach. Ron Griffiths argued that 'modern tactics should be employed'. By that he meant, closing up the game and only launching attacks from inside the opposing half. There were, too, those who argued that Clem Thomas was the victim of his own policy, in that sides, being aware of his intentions, set out to negate Swansea's open play and strike 'on the counter'.

Whatever the validity of these arguments, by early October, when the captain was absent with a suspected broken ankle, the 'Whites' had lost seven matches in succession. Not that anyone could complain about the lack of effort on the part of the players. The *Post* called a game against Llanelli 'a stirring, fast moving affair', and was of the opinion that the 'Scarlets' won because of their superior team work. However, Llanelli did have Carwyn James at outside-half.

With Alun Thomas joining Llanelli before the next game, and Alan Prosser-Harries coming to St. Helens, there was another new name at full-back in the Swansea side. However, Ron Griffiths felt that the side needed 'an experienced campaigner to guide, advise and dictate matters behind the scrum'. His readers must have wondered whether that was newspaper speak for Alun Thomas, and why the player had chosen to go to Stradey instead of coming back to St. Helens?

On 30th October the front page of the *Post* had the headline 'Dock strike – the end in sight'. Omen seekers at St. Helens must have wished that the second part of the headline had some bearing on their travail. But with nine successive defeats behind them, the 'Whites' entertained Neath at St. Helens, and, according to the *Western Mail*, they were 'a side riddled with self doubt'. Sadly, a tenth defeat resulted and, in the following Saturday's *Football Post*, Ron Griffiths was taking his lead from Job. The headline of his discussion column read 'Future of Swansea rugby in balance'. Whilst the level headed reader would have seen this as being a rather extreme view, there were extenuating circumstances. At the time, with the 'Swans' at the top of the Second Division, the crowds were flocking to the Vetch Field, where Tom Kiley and his colleagues were playing their version of flowing Swansea football. Conversely, the 'gates' at St. Helens were diminishing by the week. Nonetheless, prophets of doom had forecast the demise of Swansea Rugby Club forty years earlier. They were proved to be wrong then as they were to be again. The headline writer allocated to Ron Griffiths had sought to emphasise the problems facing the 'Whites' in a rather stark manner. Some pessimists might have agreed with him, but hope beats eternal in the breast of the ardent football follower. The loyal were not about to give up, and letters from the public flowed in to the *Post*. Among them were several which urged the selection of prominent Athletic players, like Viv Davies and Bernard Lloyd, and, for his part, Ron Griffiths argued that it was time for concerted action.

As far as the players were concerned that action was taken on the very day the discussion column was printed. On the back page of the same edition of the *Football Post*, Ron Griffiths reported on a fine Swansea victory at Blackheath. Despite having had to play most of the game with fourteen men, the 'Whites' had won and 'stopped the rot'. The sigh of relief when the final whistle went must have roared through Swansea like a typhoon. The tone of the match report was also one of relief, and the heroes were listed. John Faull excelled in the lines-out, Prosser-Harries, until he was carried off, was sound at full-back, Bryn Edwards scored a fine try, Bryan Richards was outstanding at outside-half, and Peter Stone excelled up front. Had such a medal existed, in Soviet fashion, all fifteen would have been made 'Heroes of the Swansea Borough'. Whilst there was a long way to go, the team had begun the process of restoring the dignity of Swansea R.F.C.

When the season ended, the outcome, both in terms of match statistics and the club's financial position, was dismal. As it happened, the end of the season coincided with the death of 'Invincible' captain 'Genny' Gordon. It was almost as though the passing of the great man marked the nadir in the fortunes of the Swansea club. Twenty-one matches had been lost, whilst the club had suffered its largest deficit in terms of points scored as against conceded. Furthermore, the number of members who had joined the club during the season was significantly lower than it had been for the previous campaign. However, there was an important factor behind that statistic. Given the W.R.U. decision to deny Swansea its internationals, members at St. Helens lost their special privileges regarding tickets for the Five Nations games. Consequently, membership was less attractive.

A Barbarian – Chris Winn (England) about to bite the dust.

Notwithstanding the season's statistics, the optimists in Swansea still picked through the bones of the unhappy campaign as they sought some solace. At least, they could point to the hat-trick of victories which had been gained on the club's late tour of the West Country. They could recall the side's superb performance against Cardiff, when, though reduced to fourteen men for much of the game, the 'Taffsiders' had been matched before winning by 8 points to six. Ron Griffiths had reported that encounter as being ' the most stirring at St. Helens since the Springboks match'. They could, also cling to the hope for the future which had been provided by newcomers like J. E. Jenkins, Islwyn Hopkins and Eiros Bowen. Furthermore, all supporters could hold their heads up high, for the players had given their all. No one could question the spirit in the side. All that could be done now was to draw a line under May 1955 and prepare a clean sheet to begin in September. Surely, the ball would not bounce as unkindly for the team for two seasons in succession?

Chapter Eighteen

ROMANIANS AGAIN

1955-56

DURING THE PREVIOUS SEASON, at the end of the 'Whites' tour to Romania, Clem Thomas had presented a book written by the South African, Danie Craven, to the home union. When they arrived for their return visit, the skipper of the combined Bucharest team informed the press that, as a result of reading the book, his team had altered its style of play. Given the fact that the combined team – virtually an international side at the time – defeated the 'Whites' by 19 points to 3, Clem must have wondered whether he had done the right thing in presenting the gift?

Whatever he thought, from the point of view of the Swansea public, that defeat was disappointing. Prior to the game, there had been much in the press about the players undergoing special training. Furthermore, there was said to be 'a grim determination to improve upon the record of the previous season', and 'to regain prestige and a revive a waning interest in the town'. The signals which these comments sent to the Swansea public were such that the largest 'gate' for some time – 15,000 people – came to St. Helens expecting great things of the men in white. It was a major opportunity to encourage the stay-away supporters to return. The defeat meant that that opportunity had been missed, for, whatever they might say, the Swansea sporting public likes to follow a winning side. Yet, that judgement was harsh. The Romanians were a fine team, and the 'Whites' learnt valuable lessons from the experience. One indication of that was the side's performance against 'Ranji' Walker's XV, when the R.A.F. team came to Swansea. The 'Whites', it was reported, 'played with renewed spirit and purpose'. Five points up in as many minutes they 'ran the game', to win by a convincing margin. In that match Bryan Richards did well at centre, Raymond Jones had a fine game at outside-half, whilst Teifion Williams scored a fine try. When Neath were defeated on a day when the Swansea pack excelled, the press were unanimous in praising the play of the team as a whole. While it was too early in the season to make predictions, even the pessimist in the Swansea camp felt that there were encouraging signs. Ron Griffiths wrote of the Neath game, that 'seldom has a Swansea pack played with such sustained vigour and intelligence. Even Roy John was overshadowed'. Since, at that time, Billy Williams and Clem Thomas were both playing their rugby for the Lions in South Africa, that was praise indeed! When Bristol were well beaten in the next match, the *Western Mail* reported that 'Swansea are on the comeback trail'. Certainly, in comparing the results with those of the previous season, it was a come-back, for leaving aside the Romanian match, the Bristol victory was the sixth in succession.

In October, though, it was announced that Terry Davies had asked for a transfer to Bynea, whilst Bryan Richards had gone up to Cambridge. Both were to be missed. Whilst Richards was to return, Davies was to play many outstanding games for Llanelli and Wales. Another star

Swansea R.F.C. 1955-56.
Back Row: R. Bolch, D. Thomas, E. J. Rees, N. G. Davies, C. Johnson, J. Jeffries.
Second Row: T. J. V. Davies (Committee), R. J. Dobbs (Trainer), J. Llewellyn, A. Prosser-Harris, E. Burns, I. Hopkins, B. Ford, G. Lewis, D. P. Price (Hon. Sec.), T. Davies (Committee).
Seated: B. Mullins, R. C. C. Thomas, I. Bruce Barter (Committee), W. O. Williams (Capt.), Judge Rowe Harding (Committee), T. Williams, D. Rowlands.

was slipping through Swansea fingers. There was a further departure, too. The club lost its domestic unbeaten record, when Halifax, with Greenwood and Horrocks-Taylor in their side, won by 8 points to 6. There were extenuating circumstances, though. With Gwyn Williams off the field with a cut head, the 'Whites' played for the whole of the second-half with fourteen men. They were far from disgraced! Another 'departure' during the month was of a different kind. George Bateman, former player and trainer, and lately baggageman, 'called it a day'. George, burly, dressed in a raincoat and a Keir Hardie cap, was a familiar figure to all 'Whites' watchers. He was held in great affection by all concerned and retired with honour.

After Cross Keys had been beaten by 21 points to 0, when Billy Williams, newly returned from South Africa, led his team out onto the Arms Park for a game against Cardiff, there was an air of confidence about the side. And, on the day, that confidence was not misplaced. The 'Taff-siders' were outplayed by a 'spirited Swansea pack,' Ray Jones scored a try, John Faull kicked a penalty, and Gerald Roberts dropped a goal. At 'no side', the grin on Billy Williams's face lit up the evening sky; but, within two days the popular skipper was in hospital. He was reported to have been 'rushed in' with appendicitis, and, at the time, it was expected that he would be absent for six to eight weeks. Horace Phillips took over as captain.

After losing to the 'Quins at Twickenham, Horace also saw his side go down at home to Aberavon. Perhaps it was the fact that the newly-opened Briton Ferry Bridge had reduced the visitors' travelling time which did the trick. Whatever it was, the 'Wizards' 'laid a six year bogie' when they scored a last-minute try to win the game. Next, whilst Blackheath were defeated as a result of a brace of tries by Glen Evans, 'slip shod work' let in London Welsh at Herne Hill. As a result of the two defeats the pessimists emerged again, and there was much discussion about what were thought to be weaknesses in the side. Four scrum-halves had been tried since the season started, and a fifth, John Hopkins of Crynant, was next on the scene. In a game against Coventry he partnered Teifion Williams and was part of a victorious side which fought back in the second-half to win by 19 points to 18. In that fight-back, the pack were superb, whilst Gwynne Lawrence scored a brace of tries. That win, plus the return of Billy Williams and Clem Thomas, gave Swansea supporters new heart.

Meantime, at St. Helens, no announcement has been made regarding the appointment of a successor to T. C. Prosser, who was to resign at the end of the season because of indifferent health. Cliff Prosser was only the 6th secretary of the club in the period since its inception. He had taken over at a difficult time, and had been instrumental in setting the club back on its feet after the war, and in making the tour arrangements, which had broken new ground. He had made a fine contribution to its affairs.

As ever, the Christmas holiday matches provided Swansea supporters with their annual dose of exciting rugby. First, Watsonians were hit by a wave of 'carefree rugby', conceding 31 points whilst scoring only 3. Then London Welsh and the U.A.U. both succumbed without scoring. In all, the side scored fifty-three points in three games, with only a single penalty being conceded. In keeping with 'the gay holiday mood of the players', the selectors had given everyone a game. Among 'everyone' was Terry Davies, back from Bynea (whom he had represented in a Welsh trial), and Bryan Richards, home on vacation. In all three games the pack was outstanding. Whilst Billy Williams and Clem Thomas were to the fore, Eddie Burns, Peter Stone, Mansel Edwards, Elwyn Jenkins and John Llewellyn had all attracted special mention. Behind the scrum, it was said that Bryan Richards 'added a touch of colour and class' to the Swansea back division. Indeed, writing of Richards, the *Post* reported that 'few players in recent times have created such an impression'. With 1956 beckoning, Swansea's stock was soaring!

In his end-of-season review, Ron Griffiths was in expansive mood. Whilst 15 matches had been lost, twenty had been won, and many of them in fine style. The *Post*-man felt that, at last, Swansea had a team which promised to be a real force in Welsh rugby. However, there was a caveat. Billy Williams was needed to lead the side again for the coming season. The point behind the concern was that, in March, 'Stoker' had announced that he was going to retire from the game at the end of the season. Furthermore, he was quoted as having said – 'When I pack up, I pack up for good'. Happily for Swansea football, Billy decided not to 'pack up', and his many admirers were able to enjoy several more seasons of top class front-row play from the popular forward.

Meantime it had been decided to appoint David Price as the 7th secretary of Swansea Cricket and Football Club. As the young man began a period in office which was to set yet another record for loyal service to the St. Helens club, the *Post* described the appointment as a 'wise and popular choice'. As far as Billy Williams was concerned, when he contemplated the campaign ahead, he knew that he had to manage his affairs without Bryan Richards, who was joining the R.A.F., Terry Davies, who had moved to Llanelli, and Dai Parkhouse, who had, also requested a transfer. In addition, that great club servant, Trevor Petherbridge, had announced his retirement. However, Alan Prosser-Harris had been in fine form since his arrival, whilst John Hopkins had settled well into the scrum half position. Gwynne Lawrence, was an exciting prospect, as were Billy Davies (Penclawdd) and Teifion Williams, John Faull, who had had a 'top class season' during the previous campaign, along with Peter Stone and Gwyn Lewis were to provide the backbone of the pack. For his part, Billy's 'Lions' colleague, Clem Thomas, could be expected to use his talent and international experience to the benefit of the side. All in all, since the previous season had been one of the most entertaining since the war, the captain expressed himself reasonably confident that, in the season to come, the side could 'put on a show' again. One disappointment during the previous season had been the level of support through the turnstiles. Yet, Billy believed that a good start to the new campaign might well result in that problem being solved. Billy Bancroft, then eighty-five years of age, was enthusiastic about the emerging talent. Nonetheless, in general, as far as the game of rugby was concerned, he was 'unimpressed by the modern spectacle'. In his view, 'the game was being spoilt by the winging forwards'. He didn't mention Fred Scrine.

1956–57

Swansea the Mecca

Having broken new ground by establishing relationships behind the Iron Curtain and in France, the club administrators added to their international experience when the 'Whites' entertained, first, a German XV, and, subsequently, one from Italy. After both games, spokesmen from each of the tourist camps expressed their delight at having played on the famous St. Helens ground. As far as their play was concerned, the Germans gave a good account of themselves. Whilst they lost to a Swansea side playing in hooped jerseys, the *Post* thought that the *Deutschlanders* had 'stolen the show'. Swansea could, however, claim that, so early in the season, they were not properly prepared for such a game. The point was that they had not been able to train as they would have liked. However, by the time the Italian tourists arrived, several matches had been played, thus the 'Whites' were into their stride and better prepared to take on a side which included twelve internationals. Nonetheless, on that occasion, the lively Italians were leading at half-time by five points to nil, but were not able to contain a Swansea fight-back which resulted in the visitors conceding 13 point without scoring themselves. Prominent for the 'Whites' in that game were Hopkins and Richards at half-back, Dai Parkhouse in the centre (he had withdrawn his transfer request), Clem Thomas and Brian Mullins. Despite their defeat, the Italians said that they had enjoyed their visit immensely. They enjoyed, too, some additional hospitality. One of Swansea's Italian community, Giuseppe Rabaiotti, entertained the tourists at his Burling ton Restaurant. That, too, was greatly appreciated.

At the end of the first month of the season, Billy Williams could look back on a reasonably successful start. Whilst Gwynne Lawrence's unexpected retirement had given the captain a problem at centre, Horace Phillips was back in training, Teifion Williams was due for demob, and there was an embarrassing surfeit of first-class wing-forwards. Among them were Glyn Davies, Eiros Bowen and, of course, Clem Thomas. In addition, Gordon Morris had joined the club from Newport and was to prove to be an excellent acquisition, Dai Parkhouse had had some fine games, whilst Brian Mullins was doing well on the wing. But then, as if on cue, came the, almost traditional, Swansea poor spell.

As far as results were concerned, Cardiff, Neath and Pontypridd made October an unhappy month for the 'Whites'. Even so, a sympathetic observer might have commented that when the team lost, they lost with some style. Nonetheless, when the month came to an end, Ron Griffiths, now established as the people's 'Whites'-watcher and chronicler, was mildly critical.

Versus Harlequins – W. P. C. Davies stopped by Teifion Williams.

'It is not easy to censure a side', he wrote, 'which believes ... that the game comes first and the result second ... Entertaining rugby is all very well, provided that you have the backs capable of producing it.' Yet, as ever, when Lady Luck ceases to smile on a team which is finding things difficult, its problems tend to be exacerbated. Among others, Clem Thomas was injured in a 'missionary' game at Crynant.

In response to the run of poor results, the selectors shuffled their pack again and again. As it happened, the hand which they dealt for a game at Blackheath turned up trumps. The home team was defeated in a match in which Wyn Bratton converted a Rhys Thomas try, and Teifion Williams had a sound game at outside-half. Against London Welsh, however, the hand was one card short. Trainer Dickie Dobbs had to play because of a late second-row withdrawal. And, to the chagrin of the Swansea men, the winning 'Welsh' try was scored by exile Haydn Mainwaring. There followed an 8-8 draw with Coventry, when, remarkably, Bryan Richards was picked to play for both sides. In the end, Richards, then at R.A.F. Bridgwater elected to play in white. Furthermore, he brought with him added encouragement for the Swansea selectors. His C.O. had given permission for him to turn out for the 'Whites' in Saturday games when he was not needed for R.A.F. representative sides. Whilst it was not recorded whether the C.O. had Welsh connections, all at St. Helens were grateful for the R.A.F.'s largesse.

After that period results of games were, more often than not, in Swansea's favour, and the bullish pre-season view of the club's potential was shown to have been justified. In recording wins over Aberavon (the 'Wizard's ground record was taken in the process), the U.A.U. and London Welsh, Ron Griffiths was appealing to the stay-away supporters to come back to St.

Helens and enjoy the fare. In addition, he recorded the retirement of two Swansea stalwarts. Horace Phillips and Glyn Davies had both decided to hang up their boots. The *Post*-man placed on record his thanks, on behalf of Swansea rugby supporters for the quality of service which had been given to the club by both men.

Given that the 'Whites' had lost only two matches since the end of October, at the beginning of January there was disappointment when the team lost to the visiting R.A.F. side. Rugby League international, Mike Sullivan did the damage in that match, though there were only three points separating the sides.That game was played in muddy conditions, and there was mud, wind and rain for the next match, too, when a strong Newport side held the men in white to a draw, (though Clem Thomas almost snatched a victory in the last five minutes of the game). One talking point at that time was the fact that, unusually, the 'Whites' had fielded two former Newport players on the day; Billy Davies and Gordon Morris.

Thereafter, there were losses to the touring South African Universities side – the 'Sables' – Llanelli and Bristol, and a draw with Coventry. But there was also a new enemy at St. Helens; mud. For the first time in the club's history at St. Helens it was suffering from a problem it had known well at the old Bryn-y-Môr Field. Water was not draining away quickly from the playing surface and, as a consequence, given the heavy rain which fell at the time, several games were played in thick mud. This might be acceptable at the Arms Park, but it was not so at St. Helens. The popular theory was that the drains were clogged, but, of course, solving that problem would need to wait until the season ended. Despite this unattractive development, the wags could not be contained. One was reported as having said 'Now that we have the right conditions, perhaps they'll give us our internationals back'.

During this period, Billy Williams, as positive as ever, emphasised to Ron Griffiths that he felt that he had a young side of considerable potential. Apart from Clem Thomas, he cited John Faull, who was developing rapidly, Brian Ford, Alan Prosser-Harris, John Jeffreys, Billy Davies, and Jim Rees and Gordon Morris in the second-row. Nonetheless, results during February did not reflect that promise, and it was not until the beginning of March that the team 'clicked again', the 'Whites' winning at Pontypool by 19 points to 6. In that game, Roger Harding made his début at outside-half, though it was announced at the same time that Bryan Richards had been released to play for the club for the remainder of the season. And it was Richards who inspired a fine win over Wasps. The *Post* reported that the rugby played on that occasion 'gladdened the hearts of Swansea supporters'. Apart from the outside-half, Brian Mullins, Malcolm Rogers, and John Llewellyn had all been prominent in the game. They had played Swansea football at its best.

With Billy Williams absent with a strained back, his namesake, Teifion, took over as captain. Meantime, at the Vetch, Tom Kiley announced his retirement on medical advice. Whilst Tom had been an elegant, creative player with the large round ball, he had close connections with St. Helens through his cricket. As a result the six foot centre-half was soon to begin a period of service with the 'Whites' which, happily, continues at the time of writing.

Meantime, with the now-established half-back pairing of Hopkins and Richards operating effectively, results, once more, began to go the way of the 'Whites'. Aberavon were beaten in a match when Prosser-Harris took his total of points past the century mark, Neath's undefeated record was taken in a St. Helens match in which Glamorgan cricketer, Alan Rees, played for the 'Blacks', and Richards 'ran the game' versus Otley, when Teifion Williams scored a superb try.

As the end of the season approached there appeared in the sporting press news of the 'Calypso Boys', who were to tour during the cricket season. The U.K. was soon to hear a telling example of that art form featuring 'those two pals of mine Ramadhin and Valentine'. At the time, as far as Swansea rugby was concerned, the majority of the club's successful games had been played when their two 'pals' Hopkins and Richards occupied the half-back positions. However, given that the West Indian art form was little known in Wales, no one thought to write a calypso about them. But the Swansea 'pals' and their colleagues finished the season with a flourish as holiday football flowed at St. Helens. Among the victims of this surge were the 'Quins', well-beaten by a 'Whites' side which included Glyn Davies, who had come out of semi-retirement, (he had been helping 'junior club, Dunvant'). Ron Griffiths called the performance that day 'rugby at its best. It was bright, breezy and effective,' he wrote, picking out for special praise Clem Thomas and Bryan Richards. There followed a fine win over the Barbarians and a superb victory by fourteen men over Llanelli, when the whole of the depleted pack was outstanding.

In his report of that Llanelli match, Ron Griffiths was drooling. Arguing that the present side had great possibilities, he recorded that Bryan Richards, John Jeffreys, Len Davies* and Gordon Lewis had had splendid seasons. In addition, he picked out John Hopkins, Bryan Richards and Teifion Williams, all young men with considerable potential. As far as Alan Prosser-Harris was concerned, 'had it not been for the dominance of Terry Davies, he would have been sure to have been capped'.

As the posts were being taken down, Teifion Williams, elected captain for the season to come, paid tribute to his predecessor. He said that the name Williams would be on the captains' board for the third season in succession. He would do all that he could not to let the family down. Behind the smiles which greeted the comment was the understanding that the 'family' was not only the Williamses; it was also Swansea Rugby Club.

1957-58

Another curate's egg

'The biggest problem with the "Whites" is their lack of consistency.' The speaker might have been the proverbial average supporter on the Tanner Bank, a former player, or one of a dozen press-men who followed the club's fortunes. All would have agreed, for the malady had affected the club adversely since 1920. When the 1957/58 campaign came to an end, the comment was as relevant as it had ever been. Furthermore, the solution, as far as those who administered the club were concerned, had proved to be as elusive as ever.

Losing to Cross Keys at home at the beginning of the season was hardly the form expected of a side of 'great possibilities'. Yet, in the next match the side fulfilled all its promise when 'Ranji' Walker's XV, including nine internationals, was well beaten. But, then, there followed four successive defeats, including Prosser-Harris's last match before going up to Cambridge. Unfortunately, the problems caused by the dismal run included the worrying behaviour of a section of supporters in the grandstand. 'Rowdyism, belligerent attitudes were prevalent and verbal abuse was hurled at referees and some touch judges.' That was not the Swansea way, and the St. Helens

* Father of Johnathan.

Dudley Thomas, Billy Williams, John Hopkins and Gordon Morris take on Llanelli.

authorities appealed for such behaviour to stop. Ron Griffiths, in attempting to pinpoint the reasons for the poor form of the side, wrote that 'Swansea rugby is again in the doldrums'. Whilst a lack of wind might have been beneficial with regard to the 'Rowdies' in the stand, Swansea rugby followers knew exactly what the journalist meant. In the press, several reasons for the decline of the team were explored. Injuries to key players, and the debilitating effects of the Asian 'flu which had swept the county, were most commonly quoted. However, seventy-eight year old Dick Jones had his own opinion. 'It is my impression', he argued, 'that the players do not look quite fit enough.' The old international's solution to solve the problem, apart from harder training, was to recruit ex-players to pass on their knowledge to the present side. He didn't say who he had in his mind, but, before long, Ron Griffiths would be campaigning for the club to appoint a coach.

Whilst the next match was lost, reports of the game which followed suggested that progress was being made in the quest to improve matters. John Faull was the hero of that game, returning to the field after having a badly-cut ear stitched on the touchline, and defending fearlessly. According to the *Post*, the tension and excitement were 'nail-biting', whilst Brian Ford, Glyn Davies and Gordon Morris were 'in the thick of things throughout'. Having lost six matches in succession before that game, it was essential that the spirit generated by that win was retained in abundance. The point was that many of the players who had contemplated the club's position before that victory, had been in that unenviable position before. At the time, the *Post* carried a drawing of a Russian space ship which was designed to circle the Moon. However, given their concerns about ensuring that their revival in fortunes was not confined to a single match, the

Swansea players were not overly interested in space travel. However, no one was of the opinion that the men in white were reaching for the Moon. The optimists, at least, believed that it was only a matter of time before things improved.

It was a match against Halifax which proved to be the turning point in the season's fortunes. Brian Mullins started the revival by scoring a spectacular try within five minutes of the start. Thereafter, with Gordon Lewis prominent in the centre – he handed-off three players to score his try – the 'Whites', quicker thinking and more mobile than their opponents, won in some style. As Cwmfelin Steelworks closed, so another positive period in Swansea rugby history opened. Not that the selectors were without their problems. Whilst they had a surfeit of good class front- and back-row men, they were struggling to find the right blend in the three-quarters. Happily, John Faull helped to alleviate that problem by playing at centre, but that, he made clear, was not his preferred position.

The match following the Halifax victory took place at Twickenham, and was watched by the newly-arrived Wallabies. Ron Griffiths felt that in winning that game the 'Whites' had played their best rugby of the season. John Faull and Bryan Richards scored tries, John Leleu 'guested' with some purpose, whilst Billy Williams, Billy Davies and Islwyn Hopkins were all prominent. Whilst noting that Swansea had taken the Harlequins ground record, the *Western Mail* singled out Malcolm Rogers, at full-back, for special praise. He had 'impressed with calmness under pressure'. However, the watching Wallabies were not impressed by the standard of play in the game as a whole.

There followed the defeat of another English club, Blackheath, a draw with Aberavon, said to have been one of the most exciting matches played between the two clubs, and a defeat by Coventry. Prior to the match with the Midlanders, John Faull had asked to be moved back into the pack, and, in the next match, against Richmond, he kicked the 'Whites' into the lead after

Teifion Williams scores against the Australians. 11 January 1958.

five minutes to give the side the inspiration to go on and win. After that, with forty minutes each way being played quite frequently, the 'Whites' continued to enjoy success. In December they suffered only one defeat, and that was close-fought.

Meantime, the problem relating to the surfeit of back-row forwards was about to be exacerbated. Haydn Mainwaring was back in the country following his National Service. At St. Helens a new initiative was beginning to make itself felt. Policeman, Hubert Thomas (Mr. Great Britain in the bodybuilding world), was working with the players in their preparation for the Australian game. Under his instruction, part of each training session was devoted to the use of weights and chest expanders. In commenting on the innovation, the *Post* printed a photograph of a rather circumspect Clem Thomas using a pair of light weights. Given that, at the time, St. Helens could only be used for training when the weather was clement (the drains were, still, proving to be a problem), the mini-gymnasium which had been established proved to be extremely useful. Thomas, the caption under the photograph noted, was to captain Wales against the Australians. He was the first Swansea man to have that honour since Claude Davey.

The prelude to the Wallabies match at St. Helens was a fine victory over an R.A.F. side, in which 'Swansea's storming pack were the architects of victory'. Dudley Thomas, Billy Williams and Islwyn Hopkins were in fine form that day. And, as far as Billy was concerned, he had pleased his many admirers by turning down a £2,000 offer to go north. He was not interested! Meantime, the Aussies were 'doing the tourist bit' and were photographed at Pencoed Colliery, Crynant; though no one said whether they were impressed by that experience.

On the day when the tourists came to St. Helens to fulfil their real purpose, a packed St. Helens politely greeted the Australians but roared on its local heroes. Unfortunately, though, the longed-for result was not achieved. Paradoxically, the two halves of the game were won by the team playing against the wind. Sadly for the 'Whites', the tourists scored more points against the elements than did the home side. Nonetheless, Swansea's second-half fight-back thrilled the home supporters, as they clawed back the score. Teifion Wiliams and his indefatigable namesake, Billy, scored tries for the men in white, but the Aussies held on to win by 12 points to 6. Whilst the game had been more of a forward battle than a classic game of rugby, most observers felt that the 'Whites' had given a good account of themselves. Even the Australians declared themselves impressed.

The Swansea team on that occasion was:

M. Rogers, B. Mullins, J. Jeffreys, G. Lewis, T. Williams (Capt.), B. Richards, J. Hopkins; W. O. Williams, H. Pugh, D. Thomas, I. Hopkins, C. Johnson, G. Morris, J. Faull, R. C. C. Thomas.

In his comments following the game, Ron Griffiths stated that 'Patient "Whites" fans have waited a long time for a Swansea revival. It looks as though it's here at last.'

Whilst the journalist's end-of-the-season analysis of results hardly suggested that that forecast was right, everyone agreed that, at least, the Swansea style of play promised that there were better things to come. The enterprising manner in which victories had been gained impressed even the casual observer. Furthermore, in the mid-season purple patch 116 points had been scored and only 57 conceded. It was not difficult to see that one of the important factors behind that success had been that a relatively settled back division had been fielded. Rogers at full-back, Mullins and Williams on the wing, Jeffreys and Lewis in the centre, and Richards and Hopkins at half-back. It had been a long time since there had been such continuity. Then there was the pack. One feature of the Australian game had been the fire of the Swansea eight following a blatant late tackle on Bryan Richards. Most observers felt that, had that resurgence come earlier in the game, St. Helens would have been celebrating another famous victory over a major touring side. As it was, the Swansea pack had measured itself against some of the best forwards in world rugby and had not been found wanting.

Bryan Richards.

But, after the Lord Mayor's Show ... Whilst Coventry were defeated in the Midlands, Llanelli, in outstanding form, took the next game against a 'strangely lethargic Swansea side'. Thereafter, a draw with Bristol and a victory over Gloucester had the statisticians noting that the club had not been beaten in England. However, as has been illustrated on several occasions in this book, such observations appear to tempt fate. In March, a weakened 'Whites' team was 'well-beaten' by Leicester.

Meanwhile, the forecasters were having their say. A U.S. astronomical scientist stated that man could be landed on the moon by 1970, and could be on Mars by 1980. Ron Griffiths believed that 'St. Helens customers would be watching rugby under floodlights before long', and the *Western Mail* stated that the 'current problem of unsold international tickets would be solved by better organisation'.

At Easter, the Athletic had their share of the limelight. Having won all their home games during the season, the second-string entertained the intriguingly named Canadian touring side, Balmy Beach, and maintained their winning form. Furthermore, that spotlight on the reserve side served as a reminder of the significant part which it had played in supporting the success of the seniors. Meanwhile, the seniors encouraged a 15,000 crowd with a battling display against the Barbarians. The Rev. Ron Lloyd scored the Swansea try, whilst Arthur Smith and Malcolm Thomas crossed to allow the visitors to scrape home.

By the end of April, following a run of disappointing results, the mood of *Post* journalist, Ron Griffiths, had changed. He was asking 'Whither Swansea?' He went on to argue that 'one of Wales's greatest clubs ends another season at the rugby cross-roads where it has been since the war'. He pointed out that more matches had been lost than won, whilst there was a slight deficit in points conceded as against scored. Then, as postscript to the season, the club had to struggle to put together a party for the Romanian tour, where results reflected that fact. During that tour,

John Hopkins fell out of a boat into a lake, which, as some wag suggested, summed up the Swansea season. In the words of the song, in preparation for the coming season, Swansea rugby would need to pick itself up, dust itself down and start all over again. What a psychiatrist would have made of the collective Swansea psyche at the time is a matter of interesting speculation.

1958-59

Another new start

As Viv Davies took over as fixture secretary from Bert Fuge,* the new captain, Bryan Richards, said at the beginning of the '58/'59 season, that he wanted 'Wins, big wins!' And his team gave him a flying start when they rattled up 47 points against the District. With the introduction of the short penalty into the laws of the game, plus Richards's desire to play open football, Swansea supporters felt that the climate was right for 'Swansea football' to be played. Unfortunately, there was no opportunity to test this concept against tourists. At the last minute, the Romanian authorities had failed to fulfil their planned tour, thus Swansea and Cardiff agreed to play each other at Arms Park to fill the gap in their fixtures. Whilst the match ended in a draw, the 'Whites' pack was reported as having given a 'rip-roaring display', the *Post* report suggested that the performance of the team as a whole had given Swansea supporters early encouragement. But then, in keeping with what had become a Swansea pattern of inconsistency, the 'Whites' could only draw a 'missionary' game at Kidwelly.

Perhaps it was that result which gave the players a collective kick-up-the-pants, for, in the next game, Ranji-Walker's XV were 'beaten out of sight'. In its report, the *Western Mail* warned its readers, 'Watch Swansea this season!' Group Captain Walker was equally complimentary. After the match, in which his team conceded 29 points without scoring, he said that he could not recall seeing a Swansea side playing so well. Hooker, Norman Gale, controlled the set scrums, Clem Thomas was 'masterly', whilst the half-backs, Hopkins and Richards, were 'in complete control'. For Swansea supporters the result, and the comments, were to be savoured; which was more than could be said for a dull draw at Cross Keys in the following game. Even then, the optimists could point to the fact that the team held an unbeaten record, whilst there was reported to be 'a tremendous spirit at St. Helens.' In that regard, Dai Parkhouse was cited as a player who showed great club loyalty; even though he was being used as a utility back he did not complain.

As September came to an end, the *Post*, in its report of Swansea's game with Bristol, had the headline, 'A black day for the Whites'. By that they meant that the Avonside club had taken the unbeaten record of the St. Helens men. It was a black day for the town, too. As a first step towards scrapping the Mumbles Railway, the South Wales Transport Company had made an offer to buy the line.

During the previous season a Llanelli victory had provoked the *Post* headline 'A Scarlet letter day'. After the 'Whites' next game against the men from Stradey, the best the paper could do was to use 'Llanelly beaten'. Yet the 'Scarlets' were more than beaten. A spirited display by the 'Whites' forwards, with Billy Williams playing the second-half with a heavy plaster over a cut eye, and Gwyn Lewis and Gordon Morris to the fore, gave Swansea a fine platform on which to

* Bert had done the job for thirty years, another example of wonderful service at St. Helens.

build a victory. Behind the dominant home eight, Bryan Richards was 'master of all he surveyed'. The captain dropped a magnificent 35 yard goal, and started the movement from which Marsden Young scored a fine try. Sadly, that mid-week game took its toll. On the next Saturday, Newport took the Swansea ground record, and, in the course of that match, Terry Robbins injured his back and Brian Mullins broke his arm (though he played on after the incident, not knowing the extent of his injury).

With the first part of the team's fixture list completed, it looked as though yet another 'Swansea' season was developing; brilliance and victory in one game, mediocrity and defeat in the next. One thing was certain, 'Whites' supporters could never be complacent. Their seasons were full of surprises, joy and despair.

There followed a defeat by Harlequins and the news that the men from the north had struck again. 'Whites' centre, Gordon Lewis, joined Leigh for £2,500 and a managerial job. Bruce Barter said that he had heard rumours about the move and was not surprised. Nevertheless, the departure presented Swansea selectors with a problem; who could fill Lewis's place? It did not appear that there was an easy answer to that question. However, there was one new player in the side to play Llanelli at Stradey. Twenty-year-old Dewi Bebb, a Carmarthen College player, was to appear on the left-wing. No one knew then, but the youngster was to become one of the legendary players who have appeared on the wing for Swansea. As if to herald that fact, Bebb scored a breakaway try near the end of the game. Everyone was impressed.

'After the next match, a 'missionary' affair in the Rhondda, Ron Griffiths was discussing the future of young Bebb as an international. Some thought that the journalist was being premature with his judgement. Yet, as history shows, occasionally a new player appears who seems to have 'something special'. Bebb was of that ilk. The young man had many attributes, but two of them helped to make him such a success on the rugby field – scorching pace and balance. In due course he was to use them to good effect for Swansea, Wales and the British Lions. Unfortunately for Swansea, at that time, he was required to play for his college side, and was not available as frequently as the St. Helens authorities would have wished.

After beating Neath and Blackheath, the 'Whites' were next defeated by Pontypool, described by the *Post* at the time as 'Wales's newest glamour club'. Ray Prosser led Ponty to victory in that match, yet the three points margin of the win reflected just how close Swansea had come to beating one of the best sides of the day. Ron Griffiths thought that the spirit shown by the 'Whites' on that occasion was indicative of the progress which was being made by the St. Helens club. He felt that 'the credit side was a good deal brighter than it had been for several years'. Furthermore, that 'the customers had been provided with the right type of entertaining football'.

Coventry, then ranked number three among the English clubs, were next to lose to the 'Whites', and in his report of the game the *Post*-man's tail was wagging. He cited the tactical kicking of Bryan Richards, the tenacious play of Hopkins at scrum-half, the mobility and energy of the pack, and the power of the centres – Marsden Young and Cecil Roderick. When Richmond were also beaten, Ron Griffiths's rosy view of the situation gained some credence, and that view was reinforced when Aberavon became the next victims. However, the *piecè de résistance* at the time, was the defeat of Cardiff by 14 points to nil. In that game the pack won the day, with Billy Williams, Clem Thomas, Gwyn Lewis and Gordon Morris being singled out for special mention. Though, as the *Western Mail* put it, 'the Swansea eight played as an effective unit'. Behind the scrum, Dai Parkhouse had a fine match at full-back, whilst Marsden Young

'Whites' v. Cardiff.
Norman Gale about to hack on. Tony O'Brien, Perry Close and Gordon Morris back up.

'scorched over 45 yards to score'. As for Bryan Richards, 'What are the Welsh selectors thinking about?', questioned Ron Griffiths. The *Post*-man's enquiry being provoked by the fact that Richards was only selected as a reserve for the second Welsh trial following several withdrawals.

Late in January, Clem Thomas captained Wales to victory over England at the Arms Park in a game in which Dewi Bebb scored the only try of the game. Since the young man had only played a handful of first-class matches prior to being 'capped', the try and the manner in which it was scored spoke volumes for the winger's potential. He had arrived on the international field with the same aplomb as had accompanied his club début.

'Back at St. Helens, the Swansea pack, again, laid the foundations for 'exhibition football' as Cross Keys were defeated by 13 points to nil. Behind the pack, Hopkins, Richards, Young, Roderick and Bebb, were said to have been in 'scintillating form'. That followed another splendid performance at Pontypool, when the home ground record was retained by the proverbial hair's breadth. Once again, the Swansea supporters held their breath. Was this the promised revival?

In February, 'Supermac' was reported as having met Kruschev at the Kremlin. At the same time a *Post* headline announced – 'All Whites polish puts them on top'. Whilst Macmillan was seeking détente with the Russians, no olive branch was held out to the invading Saxons from Gloucester when they arrived for a St. Helens match. The Saxons were 'overrun' in a second-half which produced 'vintage Swansea rugby'. As it happened, in that game, only Dewi Bebb among the backs recorded a try; the others were scored by Swansea's 'athletic forwards, who showed exciting skills in the open'. Terry Robbins (2), Clem Thomas, and Billy Williams getting their names on the score sheet. The *Post* reported that the 'Whites' 'pleased the spectators with spectacular stuff'. And that spectacular stuff was resulting in more people coming through the turnstiles at St. Helens. As Ron Griffiths put it, 'the "Whites" were playing to entertain'. Unfor-

At the opening of the 'Memorial Gate' Supporters' Club Group including: Tom Davies, Cliff Bancroft, Eddie Rickard, Albert Davies, Wilfred Hill and Horace Leyshon.

tunately, that innate policy, whilst providing excitement, did not always result in victories. In the games which followed, fourteen Swansea men lost to Llanelli, whilst Bristol 'did the double' over the 'Whites' in a match in which the St. Helens men were 'strangely lethargic'.

In March, Swansea as a whole was in mourning. W. J. Bancroft, a giant in Swansea's history and synonymous with the club's 'Golden Era', died. He was 88 and had followed the fortunes of the club until the end of his life. Billy had played for the 'Whites' for fifteen seasons and had been captain for six. He had converted 415 tries, dropped 49 goals, kicked 59 penalties and scored 39 tries. Had the game been as littered with penalties as it is today, there is no doubt that he would have scored many more points than he did. Bancroft was the first Welshman to hold two 'Triple Crown' medals and was capped for Wales thirty-three times. Born in Waterloo Street in Swansea, Billy had gone to live with his grandfather, who was groundsman at St. Helens, at an early age. Thus he grew up on the stage where he was to entertain so many by his prowess at both rugby and cricket. He had been a giant indeed.

A second departure at the time provoked quite different emotions. Terry Robbins signed for Hunslet. When the move was announced, it transpired that the forward had played for Swansea on the previous Saturday when, unbeknown to the selectors, he had 'taken the silver' the week before. Given that Robbins was a key figure in the Swansea pack, there was disappointment at

St. Helens at the loss; and that was exacerbated by the sleight of hand which had been involved. Yet the realists understood that, given the rift between the northern code and the fifteen-a-side game, that was how things were done. Fortunately, Dai Parkhouse and Billy Williams both rejected similar offers at the same time. Nonetheless, an old Swansea concern was re-presenting itself, the northern poachers were active again.

On a happier note, it was announced that the Supporters' organisation was to pay for the erection of a pair of ornamental gates at the Gorse Lane end of the St. Helens. The committee was pleased with the proposal and looked forward to receiving further details.

It was to the great regret of Swansea supporters when the season came to an end. They would have been delighted had it continued. Ron Griffiths, putting on his positive hat again, argued that 'at no time since the War have Swansea demonstrated such enterprise as has characterised most of the matches in the last four months.' Furthermore, the general view was that that it had been a distinct pleasure to follow the fortunes of a team which, win or lose, had provided the paying public with full value for the price of admission. The *Post* scribe argued that 'the game needs more of the Swansea spirit of adventure.' Whilst few in Swansea would have disagreed with that sentiment, there was a sneaking feeling that supporters would, also, like to see the team winning more often. They would be delighted, too, if the irritating habit of inconsistency could be eradicated. Yet, there was no doubt that a tremendous atmosphere had been created at St. Helens. Apart from anything else, it was fitting that 'Swansea rugby' had been played so freely during the season in which one of the club's greatest heroes had departed this life. Had he been alive as the season closed, Billy would have had something positive to say about the matter.

Chapter Nineteen

BETTER AGAIN

1959-60

THE RESULTS OF THE GAMES which were played at the beginning of the 1959-60 season brought smiles to the faces of 'Whites' followers. The first six matches of the campaign were won, and new captain, Gordon Morris, expressed himself pleased not only with the results but with the way in which the victories were achieved. New Brighton had been beaten by 22 points to nil in a match in which Billy Williams was outstanding up front, and the Welsh Academicals conceded 42 points whilst only scoring 6. That game was not only noteworthy for the excellent tries which were scored – Morrie Evans did the 'hat-trick' – but it provided the opportunity to remember one of the all-time St. Helens 'greats'. Will Joseph had died during the previous week, and teams and supporters stood in silence to remember him.

As far as the players were concerned, they were enthusiastic about the new-style athletics programme which had been devised for them. Billy Williams, for example, reckoned that it had given him 'extra zip' which, in one match, resulted in the prop sprinting 25 yards to score. That was not what was expected of front-row men in those days. Meanwhile, Marsden Young was playing on the wing, though he preferred the centre position, whilst Haydn Mainwaring was being picked in the centre, though he wanted to play at full-back or wing-forward. Similarly, Cecil Roderick, whilst playing at centre, preferred the outside-half role. Not that the irony of all this was lost on the selectors. There were positions for which they did not have any obvious candidates, and others where there was a surfeit of skilled players. Nonetheless, since things were going so well it was difficult to deny that their selection policies were anything other than successful.

After Bristol were beaten by 22 points to 14, the *Post* headline above their match report summed up the feeling in the town. It read 'Superb, scintillating Swansea', and no one could be found who was prepared to argue with that sentiment. Then, in the next match other enviable assets were displayed by the side. Courage, conviction, and team spirit were among those noted by the press as the team overcame adversity to beat Llanelli. Dai Parkhouse had suffered a double fracture of the leg during the first minute of the game and, as a result, the 'Whites' played with fourteen men throughout and, yet, managed to win by 12 points to nil. Haydn Mainwaring played an outstanding game at full-back, Dewi Bebb moved into the centre and Warren Jenkins went to wing three-quarter. The remaining seven men in the pack excelled, with Gordon Morris, Norman Gale and Billy Williams prominent. However, according to the press, it was Bryan Richards who 'ran the game'.

In mid-October the *Post* published a photograph of the Mumbles Train terminating at Southend. The section of the railway from that station to the pier had already been closed, and the whole of the line was to be abandoned at the beginning of 1960. Whilst the 'Whites' lost their

Swansea v. Neath line-out. Billy Williams and Gordon Morris compete; Colin Johnson, Dudley Thomas and John Faull in support.

unbeaten record to Newport about that time, if anyone had suggested that the demise of the famous railway was something of an omen for the fortunes of Swansea R.F.C., all but the most immovable pessimists would have smiled. And when Neath were beaten and it was announced that a new refrigerator factory was to be built at Crumlyn Burrows, even they were heartened. In the parlance of the proponents of 1990's mass-psychology, the 'feel-good factor' in Swansea was particularly irrepressible at that time.

Phil Hopkins, however, was less than impressed with 'modern football'. Eighty-year-old Hopkins, who had played for the 'Whites' in every position behind the scrum from 1902-1913, told the press that 'the game isn't anything like as spectacular as it was'. And in keeping with many giants of those early St. Helens days he blamed wing-forwards for 'not giving the half-backs a chance'. It was a familiar criticism, but, then, that was the *raison d'etre* of the 'break-away', and it was a Swansea man who invented the role.

After ten games had been played and only one lost, the mood at St Helens was buoyant. Ron Griffiths in his weekly column wrote: 'Bang the drum ... Swansea have emerged from the backwoods to assume their rightful place among the leading clubs in Wales.' Yet, as captain Gordon Morris put it a few weeks later, no club has the right to success, even one as famous as Swansea. If the club was to be really successful, the team would need to earn it. And earn it they

Llanelly break away – John Hopkins about to tackle. Gordon Morris and Gwyn Lewis look on.

did when they played 'champagne rugby' to outclass Pontypool by 19 point to 6. Unhappily, though, there was a price to pay for that victory, scrum-half, John Hopkins, tore ligaments in his left ankle and was out of the game for six weeks. Bryan Richards, too, had sustained a rib injury during the match, though even so, he was still able to bring out the best in a scintillating three-quarter line made up of Marsden Young, Cecil Roderick, Morrie Evans, and Dewi Bebb.

By the end of November, the *Post* was asking whether this was the start of a second 'Golden Era' for the club? Even the pessimists were beginning to come around to the view that something special was happening at St. Helens. And that view was reinforced when, without the two injured players and seven others who were featuring in a Welsh trial, Blackheath were well beaten. In that match Cecil Roderick played in his favourite outside-half spot and 'didn't put a foot wrong'. Nor did Jim Clifford, who 'jumped like a stag in the lines-out'. With apparent strength in depth like that, the question in the minds of Swansea supporters and among the press was; Who can stop the 'Whites'? The answer was Richmond, who according to the *Daily Telegraph* beat 'a jaded Swansea side with something to spare'. Skipper Gordon Morris, however, pointed to one reason for the defeat. Ron Jones had been a passenger for the bulk of the match.

As so often happens when a winning sequence has been broken, the following game was also lost, and, not surprisingly, the wiseacres among the pessimists began to assert themselves. The side was missing John Hopkins; they were over-confident; and they hadn't been training as hard as they had. Gordon Morris, however, rallied his troops with the assertion, 'we'll be back!'

At the end of one decade and the beginning of another, two events off the field diverted attention from what Morris saw as a 'blip'. Memorial gates were erected at the Gorse Lane end of the ground. They had been paid for by the Supporters' Club, and were dedicated by Canon H. C. Williams, Vicar of Swansea. The second event was the closure on January 1st of the famous Mumbles Railway, thus ending 156 years of its life. The events were received with an appropriate mixture of joy and sadness. Meanwhile, at St. Helens, Swansea R.F.C. supporters were looking forward to a new year in which their favourites would regain the scintillating form which they had shown at the beginning of the season. At least that Swansea institution was still alive and well and would continue to be a focal point for the Borough which it represented. However, the glory which was hoped for was not achieved, at least not in its entirety.

When the campaign ended, and Gordon Morris, who had been a fine and popular captain, looked back on the season's results, the hyperbole of the local press was exposed for what it was. The season had not been 'the start of a second "Golden Era"', though, leaving aside that far-fetched comparison, all at St. Helens felt well-pleased with the outcome. Twenty-two matches had been won, 475 points scored, only 239 conceded and just ten matches were lost. To find a better outcome in the club's playing record, it was necessary to go back to the 1950–51 season. During the campaign, Haydn Mainwaring had amassed 130 points, whilst Dewi Bebb and Morrie Evans had crossed for 14 and 11 tries respectively. Could the side do even better in the campaign to come? It was an intriguing question, but one which 'Whites'-watchers of old would have been cautious about answering.

1960–61

Another hill to climb

With both Dai Parkhouse and Ron Jones fit for the start of the new season, it seemed that there would be 'healthy competition for places in the side'. And, not withstanding the most cautious of observers, it was generally held that the club had a good chance to do reasonably well in the season ahead. And that confidence increased following victories in early games over Abertillery, Bayonne and Maesteg. The match against the French side, won by the 'Whites' by 21 points to 6, was, however, marred by 'unseemly brawls'. Gordon Morris was 'laid out' by a French fist and, at one point, the 'Whites' were reduced to thirteen men.

Whilst Bristol won the next match, at the end of September, the men in white seemed to have set the scene for another successful season as they took Newport's unbeaten record in an 'all action' match in which the Swansea eight 'swarmed all over' the Uskside pack. John Hopkins, too, was outstanding in that game, whilst Leleu, Faull, Jenkins, Richards, Clifford and Gordon Lewis were all picked out by the *Western Mail* in its report of the game. The contest had been, the paper argued, 'the best game of the season in Wales'. Whilst nobody was brave enough to mention a second 'Golden Era', the thought must have crossed the minds of the optimists among Swansea followers.

As far as the selectors were concerned, they had to battle against a familiar set of problems. They had a surfeit of first-class players in some positions and a dearth in others. One of those problems concerned the back-row, where Warren Jenkins had been playing extremely well at blind-side. Should they replace him with Haydn Mainwaring, who was then available, or, knowing his predilections, play the versatile marine elsewhere? They had some bad news, too. Ron Jones had broken his leg for the second time in less than a year and would not play again during the season.

Meanwhile, Bryan Richards scored a 'picture try' against the 'Quins at Twickenham, 'dodging, darting and swerving past seven players'. The speedy Swansea back-row did extremely well in

A real 'Swansea' try for Wales – to the delight of the crowd, Dewi Bebb scores.

that match, too, John Leleu, ably supported by John Faull and Warren Jenkins, attacking and defending with gusto. Whilst Llanelli then won a tough match at St. Helens, Cliff Morgan announced to the press that the 'Scarlets' and the 'Whites' were the two Welsh clubs most likely to beat the 'Springboks'. But, whereas 'Sospan' remained undefeated in domestic competition, the 'Whites' reverted to the old pattern of inconsistency, though in some of the matches which were lost Lady Luck did not appear among the names in the Swansea line-up. However,no one could accuse the men in white of not giving their all. In a titanic battle in the Gnoll mud, Neath won the game in the last five minutes through a speculative dropped goal when a Swansea win seemed justified.

After that match the selectors felt that the pack was missing the influence of Billy Williams and persuaded him to come out of retirement. Since 'Stoker' was only thirty at the time, present day readers may wonder why he had retired at all? Yet the received wisdom at the time suggested that at thirty you were an old man.

In the weeks which followed, with heavy rain pouring down in south Wales, several games were called off, and amidst the gloomy weather another Swansea institution was being destroyed. The Empire Theatre was being demolished; rain did not stop that.

With the Empire simply a shell, that other institution of the old town, Swansea R.F.C., was doing its best to 'strike back', but, sadly, the team lost its third match in a row after play became possible. This, according to the *Post*, was hardly the form which augured well for the visit of the South Africans. Yet, any appraisal of the potential of a Swansea XV had to take into consideration the 'switchback' pattern of form which decades of the club's history had produced. And the games which followed demonstrated that things had not changed at St. Helens. A moral victory was won when a seven-man Swansea pack held Pontypool to a draw, and that match was followed by an outstanding win over Blackheath. That game was watched by Olaf, King of Norway. Viv Davies, Len Blyth and Dai Jones all shook the royal hand before the game. Whilst the king confessed to knowing little about the game of rugby, he was seen to be 'vigorously applauding' an archetypal Bryan Richards try. Art, after all, has few boundaries.

But that victory apart, results as the South African game approached were far from encouraging. Ron Griffiths, writing his preview of the match with the tourists, summed up the feeling in the town when he wrote: 'the odds are stacked very much in favour of South Africa'. Yet, whilst few would have disagreed with him, other factors had to be taken into account. Swansea pride, Swansea tradition, and Swansea passion would, surely, have an influence on the outcome of that match. And they did !

Before the match, Morlais Morris, a life-long supporter of the club, had arranged for wood-carver, Brinley Roberts to produce an engraved shield to commemorate the event. The centre-piece of this work depicted a springbok jumping over Swansea castle. The implications of this illustration were not lost on the pessimists among the club's followers. It's an omen, they argued. South Africa will 'jump over us'. Whilst the result of the match appeared to support the superstitious – the Springboks won by 19 points to 6 – the 'Whites' put up a magnificent fight. Despite losing Malcolm Rogers with a dislocated elbow before the interval, the fourteen men in white fought until they dropped. The press reported that the mighty tourists 'knew that they had been in a game'. Every man-Jack played his part, though there were several outstanding performances. Among those mentioned in the majority of reports of the game were Haydn Mainwaring, John Leleu, Gordon Morris, Jim Clifford, Norman Gale and Billy Williams. Dewi Bebb had the distinction of registering the first try which had been scored against the Springboks in Wales. That try was scored after the South Africans had taken the lead with a penalty, thus, at one point, the 'Whites' were on level terms with the tourists.

The heroes who wore the white jersey on that occasion were:

M. Rogers, M. Evans, H. Mainwaring, M. Young, D. Bebb, B. Richards, J. Hopkins, J. Leleu (Capt.), J. Faull, W. Jenkins, G. Morris, J. Clifford, G. Lewis, N. Gale, W. O. Williams.

With the tourist game behind it the club could concentrate upon its domestic fixture-list, and, by December, several wins had lifted morale at St. Helens, and this was enhanced when it was announced that Dai Parkhouse was to return to the side against the U.A.U. in the traditional Yuletide fixture. That match – won by the 'Whites' by 23 points to 20 – was full of Christmas spirit. Roger Harding, it seemed, had visited the circus which was then at the Rec., for, chasing a loose ball he found that it bounced up in front of him. Without hesitation he nodded it forward with his forehead and burst past two startled defenders, gathered in his stride and 'streaked away for an opportunist try.' The wags suggested that scouts from the Vetch Field had noted his expertise.

In February the papers carried news of two pending departures from the town. Kingsley Amis, author of *Lucky Jim*, was to leave the University to go to Cambridge, whilst Bryan Richards had obtained a teaching post in Portsmouth. Notwithstanding his status as a popular author, the former was to be missed by Swansea-ites far less than the latter. Meantime, work was to start on the Severn Bridge at the end of March. No one in Wales knew at the time that 'all the tolls were (to be) collected on the English side'.

Highlights of the remainder of the season included a superb win at the Arms Park, when Terry Thomas and Bryan Richards both scored superb tries, whilst John Faull and Jim Clifford were outstanding. Unfortunately, though, line out king, Clifford, tore ankle ligaments in that match and did not play again during the campaign. Then the Barbarians were deprived of their tour record in a game in which Tony O'Reilly was eclipsed, and Haydn Mainwaring played for most of the game with a damaged shoulder. He, too, was then absent for the rest of the season.

In April, the Soviets launched the first man into space. Yuri Gagarin in 'Vostok' made one orbit of the earth before returning to land. Meantime, Swansea's man-in-space, Bryan Richards, was playing his last match at St. Helens. He was said to have been in impish mood, scoring the first of four Swansea tries and having a hand in the others. At the end of the game, John Faull and Billy Williams hoisted the outside-half onto their shoulders and carried him off the field to 'warm, sustained applause'.

Thereafter, despite absences and injuries, there were some other fine wins, though when the curtain came down on the campaign, the season's statistics looked to be worse than most observers felt was justified. Fifteen games had been lost of the 44 played. However, 24 had been won – two more than during the previous season.

Nonetheless, as they contemplated the season to come, there was some disquiet among Swansea supporters. Who, they asked, was going to wear the number 6 jersey? Since Bryan Richards had dominated the outside-half spot, there did not appear to be a ready-made answer. Yet there were positive factors to encourage new captain Gwyn Lewis. Malcolm Rogers, Morrie Evans and Roger Harding had all done well at the back, as had Dewi Bebb, who finished as top try-scorer with twelve. Eiryn Lewis had taken his chance well when he replaced John Hopkins at scrum-half, and versatile Haydn Mainwaring, who had earned a 'cap' against France, had scored more points for the 'Whites' (73) than anyone else. Among the forwards, Billy Williams had shown that he still had a great deal to offer, Idwal Fisher had been a veritable giant in the lines-out, Gordon Morris had always made his presence felt, whilst Warren Jenkins, John Faull and John Leleu had played many fine games for the club. For his part, most observers felt that in another era Norman Gale would have been selected for Wales on numerous occasions.

1961-62

A slippery slope again

As the first game of the season approached, no newcomer had joined the club to replace Bryan Richards and there was much discussion as to who would wear the number 6 jersey. It was true that there were those who felt that Richards had been too much of an individualist, yet his brilliance in open play was not only greatly appreciated by crowds everywhere,but it also posed major threats to opposing sides. Debate about these matters persisted, but the true test would come when the season proper began.

After the early games had been played, the pessimists were to the fore. Ebbw Vale, Newport and Aberavon had all beaten the 'Whites', whilst Bristol had held them to a draw. After the Newport defeat, the *Post* headline read, 'Struggling Swansea back in the doldrums'. Yet, hardened 'Whites'-watchers who read the headline would have expected a reaction. They were not disappointed. Skipper Gwyn Lewis expressed himself 'more than pleased' as Pontypool were well-beaten. John Faull, Mike Thomas and Gordon Morris were prominent in that match, whilst Llandebie man, Eifion Cox, had a sound game at outside-half. Then, after a muted per-

Swansea R.F.C. 1961-62.
Back Row: G. A. Burnett (Committee), D. P. Price (Hon. Secretary), C. Roderick, J. Leleu, G. Thomas, G. Morris, J. H. Clifford, J. Faull, H. J. Mainwaring, M. Walters, M. Rogers, R. Davies, W. D. Jones (Committee), John Llewellyn (Committee).
Middle Row: L. B. Blyth (Committee), R. J. Dobbs (Trainer), A. Davies, N. Davies, Gwyn Lewis (Capt.), E. Lewis, H. Jones, Warren Jenkins. Front: M. Thomas, J. Isaacs, J. Evans, Dewi Bebb.

formance at the Gnoll, the 'Whites' surprised the pundits by outplaying Llanelli whilst giving what the *Western Mail* called a 'power-packed performance'.

As the Sunday opening poll resulted in a victory for the brewers, Swansea, like the whole of industrialised south Wales became 'wet'. The weather at the time reflected that result and a derby game at Neath was played in 'sloshing mud and a high, swirling wind'. Meantime, Alderman Percy Morris was campaigning for city-status for the old borough, though most 'Whites' supporters at the time would cheerfully have 'swapped' such potential for success on the rugby field.

By November, four players had been tried at outside-half, Norman Gale had asked for a transfer to Llanelli, and Warren Jenkins had been badly burned at work. Captain Gwyn Lewis must have wished that he could, still, express himself delighted. However, he was able to point to the consistently good form of hooker John Isaacs, whilst Eiryn Lewis had made the scrum-half position his own. Furthermore, the captain was delighted when 'Welsh rugby's great unpredictables', pulled out all the stops and held undefeated Cardiff to a draw. In that match, John Leleu 'was everywhere', Gwyn and Dudley Thomas were prominent in the front-row, while Idwal Fisher and Jim Clifford dominated the lines-out. In commenting on the match, Norman Lewis in the *Post* described Swansea as 'the Chelsea of Welsh rugby'. St. Helens customers, he argued, didn't know what to expect.

Meantime, Dewi Bebb changed his marital status, enabling the *Post* to print a photograph of bride and groom with the caption 'Dewi Bebb faces his biggest test yet'. No one said what the new Mrs Bebb thought, but, according to an adjacent advertisement, male guests at the wedding could have bought a new suit for £9.19*s*.6*d*. to allow them to celebrate the union with sartorial elegance.

The *Post*, however, increased its cover price by a halfpenny to threepence. Whilst it is not known whether the gods disapproved of that increase, the weather become so inclement that the club's two match northern tour was called off. Indeed as the freezing weather extended and south Wales was badly affected, the 'Whites' were without a game for as month. Among the casualties of this 'big freeze' was the Christmas-tide match against Watsonians which had been an institution at St. Helens since the last decade of the previous century.

Whilst skaters enjoyed themselves on Brynmill Park lake, the town's rugby players must have viewed their enforced break with mixed feelings. Though the 'sabbatical' did bring with it some good news: happily, Warren Jenkins was making a remarkable recovery from his burns, and there was every hope that he would play again in the not-too-distant future.

In January, as the bad weather eased and play was possible, a 'small pox screen' was set up in Swansea in response to an outbreak of the disease, which was said to have been centred in Bridgend. Meantime, the Americans were spending millions in competing in what was popularly known as 'the Space Race'. Present-day Swansea rugby supporters would, probably, react in a different way from contemporary readers to the *Evening Post* headline at the time. 'Moon shot', the paper trumpeted. However, since there was no mention of the 'Scarlets' in the accompanying report, no doubt they would quickly realise that the context of the story was different from that which they had in their minds.

February showed that the 'Northern Poachers' were alive and well. Dewi Bebb refused the lure of £10,000 to join Leeds, but Idwal Fisher accepted £3,000 to move to Warrington. Whilst Swansea supporters were disappointed with the departure of the line-out man, they had an event which helped to divert their attention. Actress, Mai Zetterling, was in Swansea to attend the premiere (at the Albert Hall), of the film 'Only Two Can Play'. It must have been all that the Swansea wags could do at the time to stop themselves using the film's title in a football context. Certainly things were not all that bright at St. Helens.

After a 3 points all draw at Stradey, the 'Whites' conceded 24 points to Ebbw Vale who, thus, became the first club side to score more than twenty points against the Swansea club since 1958. Gloucester were, also, victorious, but Gwyn Lewis felt that his side should have won that game. But, in typical Swansea fashion the men in white astounded their critics in the next match. Bristol suffered from the backlash. In his report of the match, Ron Griffiths used boxing parlance when he wrote that 'Swansea hauled themselves up off the canvas to produce their best form of the season'. And it was appropriate language, for Dickie Dobbs came out of retirement in an emergency to play in the game. Not only was the red-head the trainer of Swansea Rugby Club, he was also in charge of training at the Curvis gymnasium. Whilst there were no knock-outs in the game, the 'Whites' won on points, with John Faull and Cecil Roderick prominent throughout. Dewi Bebb scored a magnificent try.

As the end of the season approached, Ron Griffiths was arguing that 'Swansea's five-man selection committee will be glad to see the back of this season. It's been a nightmare.' Among the reasons for the side's indifferent form which the *Post*-scribe put forward was the difficulty of getting 100% attendance at training sessions. He argued that when they all came together, results improved. That was, certainly, the case in a match against Cardiff, when the Swansea forwards 'outlasted the Cardiff eight' to win by 9 points to nil. There followed a fine win over Aberavon, when, despite being a man short in the second-half, the 'Whites' gained an 11 points to 6 victory. Once again, the Swansea pack was magnificent in that game, whilst behind them, Eiryn Lewis and Cecil Roderick contained the opposition with 'astute kicking'. The highlight of that match, however, was a 'surging sprint by John Isaacs to cut inside and feed Clifford and Lewis for the latter to score'. The hooker must have been a regular at the training sessions.

Whilst the club's playing record at the time might well have been described as 'indifferent', an incident occurred in April which illustrated that the true spirit of rugby football in Swansea was still thriving. Despite having spent the whole of the previous night fighting a forest fire, Gordon Morris turned out for the 'Whites' in the four-match-decider against Llanelli, and played a significant part in a 'storming' performance by the Swansea pack to take a match which the Scarlets had been expected to win.

Nonetheless, despite these performances, the season ended in disappointment. Many factors had influenced results, among them departures, injuries and retirements, but all in all the outcome fell far short of what had been hoped for. A letter writer to the *Post*, however, was in no doubt as to the source of most difficulty. He suggested that 'a rule be applied to the effect that no player would be selected unless he turned up for training on Tuesdays and Thursdays'. Given that, at the time, Swansea players lived and worked in an area from Aberystwyth to Cardiff, that, perhaps was more easily proposed than enforced. The writer's final point, however, reminded supporters of the part which they had to play. He urged them to 'cheer instead of jeer, if Swansea is to achieve its rightful place'. Certainly the full-throated support of those who followed the 'Whites' was an essential ingredient of any equation concerned with successful rugby at St. Helens. The reality, though, was that success on the field generated positive support, whilst a lack of success resulted in the converse. The well-known conundrum ... which came first ...? might well have been re-written at the time to put the club's problems into the context of the support which it was attracting. Everyone knew that positive support can 'lift' players. How to promote it when things were not going well was another matter.

1962-63

Man of steel

John Faull, who worked in the family steel stockholding business, was elected captain for the new season. He said that he was under no illusions as to the extent of his task. He knew that he was starting from a less than advantageous position, and when adversity struck early in the campaign he was reminded that bad luck seems to be the companion of failure. In the game against touring side Garry Owen, Faull had to play at scrum-half following injury to two players. But, adopting a positive attitude, he was quickly heartened, when, in the next match Ebbw Vale were 'cut down to size'. The captain was elated and claimed that 'tough training' had provided the base from which the 23 points to 13 victory was won. According to the skipper, Mike Thomas was 'the best forward on the field', whilst Eiryn Lewis had had a fine game.

Meantime, Dai Parkhouse exemplified true club spirit. Although he was captain of the Athletic, he continued to play at outside-half for the first team whilst the search for a successor to Bryan Richards continued. For his part, skipper Faull gained considerable satisfaction from a match at

The 'Quins faces say it all – Dewi Bebb streaks away for a long-distance try.

Bristol, where his forwards 'foraged energetically' in a boot dominated contest. Jim Clifford, John Isaacs, and Gwyn and Dudley Thomas were outstanding on that occasion, whilst Eiryn Lewis dropped a remarkable goal from 35 yards.

Then, after three matches had been lost in a row, the team's morale was boosted by the return of Dewi Bebb for his first game since the Lions tour to South Africa. Yet, until the team gained a fine 19 points to 3 victory at Blackheath matters hardly went Swansea's way. Eiryn Lewis was out for four weeks with an arm injury and several other players missed one or two games. As a result of these emergencies the selectors were forced to experiment. John Faull, for example, started the season at centre, played full-back, moved to lock and, finally, did well in the second-row, whilst Warren Jenkins switched from wing-forward to prop, playing well at tight head.

In November, soon after returning after his arm injury, Eiryn Lewis broke a toe and, once again, found himself sidelined. John Evans, who had started well at full-back was out for six weeks, Geoff Thomas was declared unlikely to play for the rest of the season, and John Isaacs was ill at home. Coupled with the lack of seasoned players in reserve within the club, this injury list was a major problem for the hard-working Faull. The *Post* reported that nine out of fourteen games had been lost, and, as Ron Griffiths put it 'It is difficult to be anything but gloomy'. Yet Faull would not hear of it. The team were disappointed with the results but they 'were not down' and, in true Swansea fashion they came back with a fine performance at Cardiff, when the home side was fortunate to scrape home by a single point. The skipper said that he had been greatly encouraged by the performance.

There was encouragement, too, provided by the form of the Youth side which had won all twelve of the games it had played. The Youth had scored 295 points whilst conceding only 17. The leading points scorer was 16-year-old Stuart Ferguson who had amassed a century of points in just three months. Ferguson's father had been a professional soccer player at the Vetch, but the youngster declared that he wanted to make his name with the oval ball.

December brought with it the first home win since September, when Faull, well supported by Gwyn Thomas, Glan Morgan and John Leleu 'broke the spell'. Everyone at St. Helens was delighted. An unusual statistic from that game related to Dewi Bebb. He scored his first try of the domestic season which, perhaps, exemplified the difficulties facing the team. Unfortunately, thereafter, in the games which followed, matters did not improve. After losing to Aberavon in a match which was watched by Elizabeth Taylor and Richard Burton, the side found itself with a record which was less than encouraging. Only six games had been won of the eighteen played.

Then winter came with a vengeance. There was chaos on road and rail as a white blanket settled over Britain. In the Vale of Glamorgan snow drifts were recorded up to 12 foot deep and all games were postponed. At the end of January in the middle of the cold spell, the Welsh team to play Scotland was announced. After eighteen consecutive games for his country, Dewi Bebb was dropped, leaving Wales without a representative from Swansea. That had happened on only two occasions during the previous decade. The news prompted Ron Griffiths to eulogise about the winger. 'Despite receiving terrible service season after season, Bebb has remained loyal to Swansea.' The *Post*-man went on to argue that 'everyone knows that he would be better off playing for a club with more inventive backs. Yet he stays with Swansea.' Given that Bebb was working in east Wales and was an established British Lion, there was a great deal in Griffiths's argument. Comparing Bebb's stance with that of some current international players puts his great loyalty into true perspective.

By the beginning of February, when it was still impossible to play, 'the worst blizzard for twenty years hit Swansea'. At that point, postponements had extended to become ' the longest lay-off in living memory'. During this period, in order to keep the players reasonably fit, coach Glenn Barnes had obtained the use of the gymnasium at the University. At the time, he and the Swansea club expressed their gratitude to the University authorities. Had they known what was to happen when matches resumed, Swansea supporters *en masse* would also have proffered their grateful thanks to the men of the gown. That training was to pay off.

In the first 'post-hibernation' game, (at Stradey), the 'Whites' took command from the start. Eiryn Lewis and Gareth Thomas did well at half-back, Billy Upton was prominent in the centre, and Glan Morgan was said to have been 'the forward of the match', whilst John Isaacs, the hooker, was back in harness. Gloucester were the next to be beaten by the rejuvenated Swansea, even though Eiryn Lewis was a passenger for the bulk of the match. After another fine performance against Bristol at St. Helens, a wag was reported as pointing out that the 'Whites' were unbeaten in 1963. Whilst skipper, Faull, may have smiled at the humour, he could do so with some satisfaction. Whilst his side might not have been the best ever fielded by the Swansea club, the spirit and determination of the players and their *esprit de corps* had been major factors in the change of fortune. Dewi Bebb was enjoying the change as much as anyone. In a match against Aberavon the winger took a pass from Howard Rees on the right-hand touchline, then, 'an exhilarating fifty yard sprint took him over the try line near the posts. Not a hand was laid on him.'

Thereafter, victories over Bath, Llanelli, Cross Keys and London Welsh lifted the spirits of the team and supporters alike. In the end though, tiredness took its toll as the club attempted to play off most of its postponed matches. In one week, for example, four matches were played and, during this period, John Faull sat in the stand with an injured knee and could only watch his brave side as they battled to retain a winning momentum. Their battling spirit was typified by their performance against the Barbarians, when even though they played with fourteen men for most of the drama-packed match, the men in white were only defeated in injury time.

As a wave of emotion swept over the club after that game, the players were unanimous in asking John Faull to continue as captain. However, Faull, who had played his first game since February against the Barbarians, was concerned about his fitness. Whilst a decision was not made at that time, whoever was to be captain would represent a club with greater security of tenure. The estates committee of Swansea Corporation had approved the club's request for a further twenty-one year lease.

Chapter Twenty

A DAWN OF PROMISE?

1963-64

SOME SAID THAT IT WAS ABOVE and beyond the call of duty; Mike Thomas took a couple of days off from his honeymoon to play in the opening match of the season against the Italian club, Roma. Whatever the new Mrs. Thomas thought, Mike and his colleagues enjoyed the match with the Italians, winning by 12 points to nil. Dennis Gethin, said to be a full-back in the Terry Davies mould, did well that day, as did Gareth Thomas, new captain, Dewi Bebb, and Billy Upton. Before the match, Bebb was presented with a bouquet of flowers and a pennant, by Sergio Lanfranchi, the Roma captain. It was a good start to the season.

Meanwhile, the press, in reviewing the coming campaign, noted that, whereas Swansea had many forwards who were capable of playing for Wales, they appeared to be finding it difficult to attract backs of the right quality. As a result, they argued, the selectors were forced to be 'creative' in their choice of players for certain positions. For the opening domestic game of the season, Dai Parkhouse dusted off his number one jersey and played at full-back. Furthermore, such was his enjoyment that he converted a try scored by John Isaacs to win a close- fought game against Cross Keys. Kicking, however, at least the long-range variety, presented the Swansea captain with a problem. Since John Faull had been forced into premature retirement because of his knee problems, no replacement had emerged.

There was controversy, too, as the campaign developed, regarding the experiments with the laws which had been imposed on the game by the W.R.U. during the close season. They would not, Ron Griffiths argued, suit the Swansea style of play. He noted, for example that in a 'shocking Swansea v. Aberavon match', there were 93 lines-out and 43 scrums. The Port Talbot side won by 3 points to nil on that occasion, which, according to the *Post* scribe, resulted in the crowd leaving for home 'frustrated'. Yet the paper reported that the next St. Helens game produced 'splendid entertainment'. In that match, within three minutes, 'Dewi Bebb collected a high kick at top speed ... (he) swerved outside the Bristol full-back to score an exhilarating try'. In its report of that game, the *Post* noted that it was three years since Dai Parkhouse had broken his leg, and that the player was delighted to be back in first team football. Ron Griffiths wanted to know if there was anyone else playing senior rugby with a steel pin holding his leg together? Given the cult status enjoyed by the popular player, 'Whites' supporters might well have believed that the pin was pure gold.

In October, those same supporters may have been alarmed to see a *Post* headline which read 'Two Whites arrested', only to be relieved when they noted from the accompanying account, that the item related to an incident in Birmingham, Alabama. Subsequently, they were more than relieved when Dewi Bebb (3) and David Weaver (4), scored seven out of the eight tries

Jim Clifford.

David Weaver.

recorded by a rampant Swansea side as they destroyed Halifax by 26 points to 3. However, the more thoughtful among them would have noted that only one of those tries was converted.

As Wilson Whineray's fifth 'All Blacks' arrived in the U.K., the 'Whites' were involved in some dour domestic matches, and John Faull was said to be contemplating a come-back. Meantime the 'dawn' of the Halifax result was proving to be somewhat false. Nonetheless, the statisticians among the Swansea supporters could point to the fact that their favourites had only conceded 53 points in their first thirteen matches. Training, however, was to be intensified, not only in preparation for the visit of the New Zealanders, but also to enhance domestic performance. And that preparation proved to be beneficial when the side 'stormed to an easy win' over Richmond. Swansea, the *Telegraph* noted, were 'too quick, too bright, and too tough for the London side'. In that match, David Weaver, Billy Upton and John Isaacs were among the scorers, whilst forwards, Glan Morgan, Jim Clifford and Mike Thomas caught the eye. Aberavon were the next side to be beaten, following which the 'Whites' went to Cardiff for a dress rehearsal for the 'All Blacks' match. In the event, though, the game did not prove to be much of a rehearsal. Both sides were depleted by Welsh trial calls, and Cardiff won. The press reaction was uniform. Swansea did not look like being ready to face the New Zealanders. Yet, when the day came, ready they were!

On the day of the match, the *Post* reported that there was 'a crowd in excess of 30,000 people packed into the ground'. Before the kick off they stood bare-headed, in silence, as they honoured Edryd Jones, a member of the Swansea side which defeated the 1935 'All Blacks'. Edryd had died during the previous week.

Given that the 'All Blacks' were leading by eight points to nil with just twenty minutes of the game gone, Edryd must have looked down with some concern. Was the press corps to be proved right? Yet he, and the bulk of the enthusiastic crowd need not have worried. Apart from anyone else, there was the pint-sized Dai Parkhouse, who not only tackled like a demon, but kicked with precision, despite being 'laid out' as a result of grappling with a New Zealander twice his size. Indeed, Dai scored all of Swansea's points, and the legend of the golden pin must have been enhanced. Parkhouse personified the passion of the Swansea players who, until minutes before the final whistle were within two points of the mighty 'All Blacks' total. In the end, whilst they had to settle for a 16 points to 9 defeat, all of Swansea went home that day with heads held high. Despite the pessimism of the press, Swansea *had* been prepared.

The Swansea men who gave their all on that day were:
D. Parkhouse, D. Weaver, J. Simonson, W. Upton, D. Bebb (Capt.), G. Thomas, E. Lewis; W. Jenkins. J. Isaacs, G. Thomas, J.Clifford, G. Morgan, M. Evans, R. Jones, M. Thomas.

Following that fine performance, the 'Whites' seemed to be inspired. Despite having to play four matches in five days they won three and drew the fourth. Billy Upton, John Isaacs and Morrie Evans were picked out by the press during this spate of matches, but everyone agreed that, since the New Zealand game, the whole team was playing with greater conviction. Not only was that conviction present in the next match, but, when the R.A.F. were grounded by 27 points to 3 in a 'thrilling game', Ron Griffiths wrote of 'old time flair' as the 'Whites' ran in six tries. One proud man among the scorers was John Isaacs, who crossed for his seventh try of the season. Isaacs, who had hooked well against the New Zealanders, said that that experience had given him new-found confidence.

When Newport were defeated in the next match, the optimists were beginning to believe that the 'All Whites' had discovered a powerful new elixir. The Welsh selectors must have thought so, too, for both wingers, Dewi Bebb and David Weaver, were picked to play for their country in the same match. No one could remember whether Swansea had ever provided both wings for a Welsh side before that date. However, in the Newport match it had been the Swansea pack which had dominated. All eight were said to have been magnificent, whilst the ebullient Dai Parkhouse was described by the *Post* as a 'sort of full-back-cum three-quarter-cum fly-half, brimming over with ideas.' Since the Usksiders had not lost a match since Christmas (scoring a century of points in the process) the Swansea revival was placed in context. And on that evidence, all the early season controversy about law changes faded into the background. The 'Whites' were playing typical Swansea football again.

By beating Coventry in the Midlands – Brian Thomas (Neath) 'guested' for the 'Whites' – the momentum was maintained. But, then, there was a hiccough. In the language of the time the *Post* headline announced that 'Too gay Swansea pay the penalty'. That penalty was applied by Bridgend, who became the first side to defeat Swansea since the 'All Blacks'. The pundits put the loss down to over-confidence, as the 'Asylum Men' defended like heroes before the break, and took advantage of Swansea's frustration in the second period. There followed a fourteen-man victory over Llanelli, and a draw with Gloucester, when Peter Hamer had to withdraw after fracturing his shoulder.

Thus it was that, at the end of February, Ron Griffiths could point out that the 'Whites' had scored 28 tries since the 'All Blacks' match – two more than the side had registered in the whole of the previous season. Furthermore, the press as a whole was applauding the Swansea renaissance. The general feeling was summed-up in the *Post* statement that 'after years of mediocrity, Swansea have now found the backs to support the hard work of their forwards'. Gareth Thomas, most agreed, had proved to be one of the shrewdest outside-halves in Welsh rugby. Unfortunately, in the period which followed, the club's revival was threatened by a spate of injuries. As the *Post* noted at the end of March, Swansea had finished with a full side on only two occasions in the ten previous matches.

Nonetheless, in the next game, against Bath, Dai Parkhouse took his points total to 102 as fourteen-man Swansea (again) scored thirty-six points whilst conceding only three. In the end, though, the injuries took their toll, and, when the curtain came down on what had been an eventful and exciting campaign, the match statistics showed that the side had 'fallen away' in the latter part of the season. Yet, there was much to encourage all at St. Helens. Surely, the argument went, with a clean bill of health, and one or two effective newcomers, supporters could look forward to a more successful campaign next time. Meanwhile, congratulations were offered to Mike Thomas, who managed the rare feat of playing in forty matches.

As each of the leading 'Great Train Robbers' was sentenced to thirty years in jail, Swansea supporters were wishing that their heroes could break free from past inconsistencies and release them from their confinement as the 'Chelsea of Welsh Rugby'.

1964–65

Bebb again

Since the 1964–65 season was the Swansea club's 90th, at the beginning of September, the St. Helens authorities had arranged a special match in celebration. On that occasion the 'Whites' locked horns with 'An International XV', when both sides played open football with 'some panache'. In keeping with the predominant sentiment, the birthday-boys won by 22 points to 17. The try which won the game was scored near the end by Mike Thomas, though the move was started by Billy Upton, who had been hobbling around the field for most of the game after damaging his knee. Such was the gusto with which the game was played that the press could hardly contain itself. The *Post* toasted the victory with the hope that the 'birthday atmosphere might last throughout the season.' Of course, it was too much to ask, yet, when the final whistle blew at the end of the first domestic match, the optimists must have charged their glasses with confidence. Ebbw Vale had been 'beaten out of sight' by an 'incisive, alert, direct-runing' 'All Whites' team. Dewi Bebb scored a brace of tries, Stuart Davies one, whilst Dai Parkhouse and Gareth Thomas had shared the kicking. Like Weaver's Flour Mill, photographed in the *Post*, Ebbw Vale had been demolished.

As the optimists gave vent to their confidence, the Swansea club could point to its latest infrastructure development. The club's new floodlights were almost ready to be switched on. To inaugurate these lights a match had been arranged with Dewi Bebb's XV, and another feast of running rugby was envisaged. At the time, administrators throughout the Welsh game believed that floodlit football was going to be an important development in rugby, and a new competition was designed to take advantage of that fact. As ever, in Swansea, the wags were ready with a merry quip. At least Dai Parkhouse was. The full-back was reported as having said to his captain, 'If we win the toss, let's play with the moon in the first half'.

Meantime, the 'All Whites' continued their 'victorious march', Cross Keys being beaten by 19 points to 3. At this time, Swansea supporters were beginning to count their chickens. After all, their side had scored 64 points in winning three games and had conceded only 23. Yet, dazzled by many previous false dawns, they should have shown greater caution. Without three regulars, and with Gareth Thomas and Eiryn Lewis nursing injuries during the game, the 'Whites' lost their unbeaten record to Bristol. But the side seemed to bounce back in the match which followed. Newport were 'run ragged', under the club's £15,000 floodlights, as the 'Whites' won by 17 points to 3. Clearly, the moon posed no problems to the 'Whites' players, particularly Jim Clifford, who 'jumped like a stag in the lines-out'.

But then, the traditional Swansea script was unfolded. With Sir Adrian Boult in Swansea for the Music Festival, the 'Whites' were in need of an effective conductor themselves. In the absence of such a maestro, results fluctuated from brilliant victories to frustrating defeats. Those defeats, though, were often suffered when the side was depleted through injury. The 'Quins', for example, won by 24 points to 9, scoring the majority of their points in the second half when the 'Whites' were reduced to fourteen men. However, whilst defeats were suffered, no one could say other than that the players had given of their all in Swansea's interests. Mike Thomas, in that 'Quins' match, for example, 'tackling everything that moved', in defending the Swansea line. The 'Quins, who had scored 153 points in their previous five matches, were generous in their praise.

As the season wore on, the side continued to try to play 'Swansea rugby', and in a victory over Leicester, the extent of the players' bubbling enthusiasm was exemplified by an extraordinary *Post* photograph. It showed Mike Thomas carrying the ball towards the Leicester line accompanied by Warren Jenkins, Tony Macdonald, Dewi Bebb and Glan Morgan. Not a Leicester player was in the camera's viewfinder. Whilst that home victory was comfortable (19 points to nil), the press levelled a critical finger at the 'Whites'. They were, according to the *Western Mail*, 'too flighty in the first-half'. Whilst that language might have been more suitable to describe the behaviour of a girls' hockey team, 'Whites' supporters knew exactly what the paper meant. After a tremendous start, it was said that, in some games, the side was losing its concentration. If the team was to be consistently successful, it was felt that they would need to take a less cavalier approach to their football.

At the end of October, though, no one seemed to be concerned about 'flighty play'. The 'Whites' and the Dewi Bebb XV played an invigorating match, with the home side winning by the odd point in twenty-nine. As someone said at the time, the pace of the game seemed to have been enhanced by the floodlights under which it was played. It was a fine, open, contest, enjoyed by all who saw it, including the Mayor, Cllr. A. Willis Pile, who kicked off.

Thereafter, further injuries and another northern defection disrupted things. However, results when games were lost were often extremely close, as Swansea, usually, it seemed, with fourteen men, battled to hold their own. During this period, Neath and Aberavon were beaten, whilst, on their own pitch, Blackheath were the victors by a single point. Meantime, John Isaacs had surprised everyone at St. Helens by signing for Swinton for £2,000 plus a £20 per week job. The authorities at the Swansea club had had no inkling of the approach, thus the defection came as a body blow, for the player had been a key figure in the side. Isaacs was to be missed.

As Isaacs left Swansea, so did the last official steam passenger train chug out of Swansea High Street station. In due course, special steam excursions would help to satisfy the nostalgia of the steam enthusiasts. Isaacs, however, at least as far as the union game was concerned, was gone for ever.

There was another departure, too. In December, Dickie Dobbs, only the third trainer in fifty years of the club's history, 'called it a day'. Pressure of work, he declared, was too great to allow him to do the job properly. The red-head left his post with the grateful thanks of all at the Swansea club. There was, though, the selectors' concern as to where they were going to find a last minute replacement should such an emergency arise in the future.

At the turn of the year, as the club struggled with another spate of injuries – at one point seven first team men were sidelined – the men from the north struck again. Warren Jenkins joined Swinton for a fee of £3,000. It was another blow to the selectors, for, as Len Blyth put it, 'Warren was a fine club man and an outstanding tight-head prop'.

Given the overall situation at St. Helens at that time, as the papers carried accounts of the funeral of Sir Winston Churchill, the 'Whites' could have done with some of the former-Prime Minister's rhetoric. Since St. Helens had been constructed on a base of sand, the great man's rallying cry about fighting on the beaches would have been apposite. As it was, after defeats by Pontypool, Coventry, and Llanelli, the selectors strove to field a side which would restore earlier confidence. Yet the injuries and defections to the paid ranks had taken their toll and the task was far from easy.

One initiative, widely applauded, was to bring eighteen-year-old Stuart Ferguson into the side. Ferguson, who had played all his rugby on the wing for the Youth, was selected at full-back. The young man responded well to the challenge, kicking seven of the nineteen points scored against Abertillery as the'Whites' registered a welcome win. There followed a further victory, as the side opened up in the second-half to defeat Gloucester. In that match, Jim Clifford finished off a memorable movement to score near the posts. Dewi Bebb had sprinted from left to right, and following a series of passes, David Weaver carried on the movement to feed the lofty Clifford. Dai Rowlands and Morrie Evans also scored in that match, whilst John Campodonic supported Clifford well in the lines-out.

Following that victory the club announced that Gwyn Lewis had been appointed as coach. Lewis argued that the results which had been achieved by the team had not reflected the effort which had been put into preparation. Furthermore, 'injuries and departures to Rugby League had hit our plans'. The new coach must have thought that the fates were conspiring against him as, during the next game (at Bristol) the 'Whites' suffered three casualties. But, as he said at the time, he was not downhearted, and there was much to build on. His optimism was to be seen to be justified as, following a March snow fall, a series of positive results boosted the morale of everyone at St. Helens.

Early in the month Llanelli were beaten by 16 points to 3 as the 'Whites' called the tune, Cardiff succumbed by 12 points to 8, even though Swansea had to play with fourteen men for the whole of the second half, and Bath, on their own pitch, lost by 12 points to 8. In those games, the back-row of Thomas, Evans and Dyer excelled, Jim Clifford and Glan Morgan were also prominent, as was young Ferguson, who was kicking like a veteran. Not surprisingly, the young man was having to learn his trade as a full-back and, occasionally, was tempted out of position. He was to improve in that regard through experience and would go on to set club records with his kicking.

There followed the club's biggest victory over a club side for more than a decade (44 points to 8). Whilst opponents, Pontypool lost two players in the fiftieth minute, the 'Whites' played outstanding football in that match and had it won by half time. Noel Thomas, Billy Upton, Morrie Evans, and Eiryn Lewis all exploited openings to score.

After that, however, results followed a typical Swansea pattern, though, prior to the end of the season, supporters were treated to two tremendous matches at St. Helens. In the first, the Harlequins were leading 13-0 at the interval, though there were few in the crowd who were downhearted. After all, a 'gale force wind' and a heavier pack had been dealt with effectively during the first period. Whilst the wind abated somewhat when the teams turned around, following two Ieuan Jones penalties, tries by Billy Upton, Dai Rowlands, Malcolm Lloyd and Dewi Bebb clinched the match for Swansea.

There was an even better result next, when fourteen Swansea men did battle for most of the game with a Barbarians side which included eleven internationals. During that game, Noel Thomas was carried off after twenty minutes, and five minutes later Ieuan Jones went off with a cut head. By then the Barbarians were leading by 8 points to 3 and even the most positive thinkers among the Swansea faithful were beginning to feel that all was lost. But the Swansea men stuck to their task, and tries by Billy Upton and Clive Dyer, and a dropped goal by Eiryn Lewis took the 'Whites' into the lead. The seven-man Swansea pack then worked like demons, and with the St. Helens faithful holding their collective breath, the men in white held on to win by 9 points to 8. For Swansea supporters the match had been among the most stirring of the season.

When the ink was dry on the season's statistics, supporters would have found that the club had played a record number of games (49), had scored more than five hundred points for the first time since 1929-30, and had won 26 matches. However, with twenty games having been lost, it had been, as Ron Griffiths put it, 'a season in which the only consistent feature had been the team's inconsistency'. Nonetheless, as the optimists looked at the data, they comforted themselves with the thought that, surely, injuries would not be such a problem in the season ahead. In addition, Stuart Ferguson was maturing nicely and would be joined by John Davies, another highly promising player from the Youth side. Mike Thomas, the pack leader, and Dewi Bebb, with fourteen each, were the leading try scorers, which allowed coach Gwyn Lewis to point out that the side could attack from the front or the back. Notwithstanding the criticism concerning the side's inconsistency, no one could fault the effort which the players had made during the campaign. If they had thought of Churchill's words at the time of his death, then they responded accordingly. Away from the 'beach', however, they had been less successful, winning only three matches. Clearly, the team's away form was something to be pondered by the coach and selectors. Maybe a different approach away from St. Helens was called for. Time would tell.

1965-66

A curate's egg again

Even before the new season started there were further problems. Stuart and John Davies were both injured in the club's final trial, while prop, Dave Bowen, was absent with a mysterious illness. Nonetheless, the opening match against Cross Keys was won with something to spare. Morrie Evans, the new captain, was pleased with the start even though it had been a scrappy game. The boot ruled, and that of Stuart Ferguson ruled supreme. The young man won the game with a 35-yard penalty almost on the stroke of time.

As mortgage holders reeled at the news that an interest rate of 7% was to be applied to their

Swansea R.F.C. 1965-66.
Back Row: G. Rees (Committee), D. Weaver, D. Harris, J. Trott (Trainer), N. Thomas, Dan Jones, M. Lloyd, P. Hayward, D. H. Davies, E. Lewis, W. Upton, D. P. Price (Hon. Secretary), L. G. Blyth (Chairman Selection Committee), Gwyn Lewis (Coach).
Middle Row: J. Llewellyn (Committee), G. Morgan, R. Bowen, S. Davies, Morrie Evans (Capt.), D. Bowen, J. C. Dyer, S. Ferguson. Front: M. Thomas, P. Borthwick, E. Rickard (Assistant Trainer).

loans, Swansea's rugby progress was steady rather than spectacular. Newbridge, the top club of the previous season, were held to a draw on their own pitch, and the honours were shared with Halifax. Throughout this period, Stuart Ferguson was kicking well, whilst Morrie Evans led by example and Jim Clifford dominated the lines-out. Most observers felt that the side was showing promise, and that promise seemed assured as Aberavon succumbed by 19 points to 5.

In the middle of what had developed into an unbeaten run, it was announced that the club would try again to fix a close season tour to Prague (the previous attempt having failed). Having been the first club to tour behind the Iron Curtain, Swansea was anxious to extend its influence whilst providing its players with valuable touring experience.

When Bristol came to St. Helens for the next domestic game, they did so without their kit. It had been left at Newport along with their baggage man, when they had changed trains. As a consequence a taxi (fare £6.10s) had to be hired and the baggage man arrived breathless. Eventually, when the match started it was the West Country men who were breathless as the 'Whites' scored three times in ten minutes. Dewi Bebb, scrum-half Lewis, and forward Ron Jones scoring. As the Bristol players applauded the 'Whites' from the pitch at the end of the game, the homesters looking at the scoreboard would have been pleased to read Swansea 21 Bristol 8. It had been a most satisfactory victory.

When September came to an end, Morrie Evans expressed himself 'delighted'. Despite a heavy crop of injuries his side was unbeaten and the captain's infectious enthusiasm was rubbing off on all concerned. Given the results, Ron Griffiths questioned whether the team might be able to set a post-war record? Long-time 'Whites' followers who read the journalist's comments would probably have preferred that he had kept his thoughts to himself. The next match was lost! The fates had been tempted again. Llanelli took the club's unbeaten record in a match in which their young fly-half, Barry John, excelled. 'Surely', opined Griffiths, 'John will be given a Welsh trial this season'! Barry John apart, though, the 'Whites' were handicapped for most of the second-half due to the absence of hooker Rowlands. On that occasion, fourteen men were not enough to win.

When the next match was also lost, the selectors switched David Weaver to outside-half, and the young man responded by running 65 yards to score, (against New Brighton). It was, however, a 'winger's try' and Weaver was replaced by Gareth Thomas for the next game. In that match the side suffered a damaging blow. Jim Clifford, the key ball provider from the lines-out, broke his nose and was added to the growing list of walking wounded at St. Helens.

Then, after Ebbw Vale had been beaten on their own ground, Garryowen came to St. Helens. At half time, the Irishmen were trailing by 8 points to 3, but, in the second-half, the 'Whites' were inspired. Dewi Bebb scored a hat-trick of tries, Billy Upton 'passed beautifully', and the forwards, notably, Bowen, Farthing, Lloyd, Evans and Thomas were outstanding. For his part, Stuart Ferguson had something of a field day kicking all seven conversions. For the first time for many years Swansea had a prodigious goal-kicker.

Despite that emphatic victory, the selectors were still concerned about certain positions in the team. They were missing Jim Clifford's towering presence in the lines-out, and ex-B.P. man, Barrie Davies, who had been brought in to deputise, was also sidelined. Yet, as successive sets of selectors have found to this day, big, athletic second-row men are few and far between.

After narrow defeats by Neath and Leicester, there followed a 'romp' against Cardiff Training College, when eight tries were run in. Peter Rowe did well at outside-half in that match, and skipper Morrie Evans was outstanding. Whilst the quality of the opposition had left something to be desired, the match proved to be a useful workout for the team.

Thereafter, as Rhodesia declared U.D.I., the Swansea selectors must have wished that the club was not quite as independent as it was. So bad was the position regarding injuries, that, for a match against Llanelli, the selectors delayed announcing their side until the Thursday before the game. Apart from illnesses and injuries, Eiryn Lewis had been sent by his employers to Dagenham for a month's training course. Whilst the scrum-half volunteered to travel home each weekend, clearly he could not attend training sessions during the week.

Given the circumstances, it was not surprising that three games were, then, lost in succession, and when both Dai Rowlands and Jim Clifford announced their retirement, there were some worried frowns on the faces of the selectors. Yet they need only have looked back on the history of Swansea Rugby Club since the war to realise that, sometimes, the darkest clouds had silver linings. Once again, Swansea rugby's only consistent feature was to prove to be its inconsistency.

In December, with 18-year-old Peter Rowe at outside-half, Ebbw Vale must have wondered what had hit them? Rowe, 'assured beyond his years', was the catalyst for many fine moves during the game; Mike Thomas (3 tries) ran and handled like a three-quarter, Billy Upton 'played like an international', whilst Stuart Ferguson, again, kicked every conversion. There was encouragement from the front-row, too, Alan Mages gained steady possession.

Subsequently, the weather took a hand, and, following torrential rain in south Wales and a severe frost, many games were called off. One Swansea match which survived, however, was the traditional Watsonians game, played, for the first time under lights on Christmas Eve. The 'Whites' won that by 21 points to nil, and, thus, 1966 beckoned with the spirit in the Swansea camp suitably enhanced. Whilst most people felt good about things, the treasurer was somewhat subdued. Two money-spinning Christmas games (against the U.A.U. and London Welsh) had been cancelled, and, as he pointed out, this had not been unusual in recent years. Indeed, on only two occasions since 1959 had Swansea been able to play all three of its scheduled Christmas games. The weather in the recent winter, however, had been particularly inclement. For example, it had been one of the wettest Decembers on record, twelve inches of rain having fallen during the month. An interesting feature of the game against Watsonians, which had somehow survived, was the reappearance in Swansea colours of two former 'All Whites'. Bryan Richards and Dai Rowland had come out of retirement to help the club. Start Ferguson, meanwhile, took his points total for the season to 133. In reaching that total he had demolished the previous post-war record.

Unfortunately, the New Year brought with it little joy for the Swansea club. During the January-February period, the 'Whites' won only two of the ten matches played. Prior to the February game against Llanelli at St. Helens, there, was also something of a drama. During the previous night, intruders had entered the ground and sawn off the goal posts at the Mumbles end, and new posts had to be erected before the game could be played. For their part, Llanelli had their own drama to contend with. The students at Trinity College, Carmarthen, demanded £15 for their rag fund in return for the release of Barry John. Given the way the game went at St. Helens, there might have been those among the Swansea following who would have doubled that money in order to ensure that the outside-half wasn't released.

As Llanelli council passed a resolution regarding the spelling of the town's name, the passing of St. David's Day brought with it some encouragement for the St. Helens faithful. A fine display against Bridgend was followed by an excellent 21 points to 3 win over Bath. In that match, Geoff Atherton made his presence felt in the back-row, as did Jim Lamb at scrum-half. In the pack, Mike Thomas was said to have been the outstanding player of the match, with Morrie Evans, Dai Davies and Ron Bowen not far behind.

But, when the season ended supporters could only look back on yet another campaign of mixed fortunes. Almost half the domestic games had been won, but that was somewhat disappointing after the tremendous start which had been made to the season. Nonetheless, since there had been something of a mini-revival during the last weeks of the campaign, there was enough in the air to sustain the optimists. Apart from anything else, Stuart Ferguson had set a new post-war record as a result of scoring 195 points. Since only nine points were scored by other kickers, it was a tremendous record for a teenager. Glyn Morgan, with thirty points, was the next highest scorer in the club.

Whilst the domestic season had finished there was, still, the matter of the trip to Prague which, by then, had been confirmed. There the 'Whites', playing with some style, beat Spartak AZKG by 22 points to 6, and Prague District by 34 points to 19. The party enjoyed themselves immensely, with Gareth Thomas being nominated as Swansea's 'best attacker'. Ferguson, the boot, weighed in with another 17 points.

1966-67

A new record

As the new season approached, there were at least two pieces of good news for the Swansea selectors. Jim Clifford had decided that he would play again, and former Welsh captain, Clive Rowlands, had joined the club. Actually, the two matters were inter-related, for the big second row had been influential in persuading the scrum-half to don the white shirt.

The season started with a return match against the Czech team, Spartak, which the 'Whites' won comfortably. There followed a draw with Cross Keys at Pandy Park – Peter Rowe dropped a goal, and the opening of the Severn Bridge by the Queen (Toll 2*s*. 6*d*.). Not that the 'Whites' had to use the bridge for their next match, it was at Bridgend. Unfortunately, though, the team did not travel well and the home side were the victors by 12 points to nil. However, three Swansea men were off the field at various times during the match.

For the next game, the selectors switched Peter Rowe to centre and brought back Peter Borthwick at outside-half. With Clive Rowlands ' turning it on' against his old side, Pontypool could not contain the thrusting 'Whites'. David Weaver scored a try within five minutes, and, thereafter, the men in white dominated in both tight and open, whilst Stuart Ferguson kicked prodigiously. Among others, he kicked a forty-five yard penalty with at least ten yards to spare, and converted a corner flag try with some ease. Swansea supporters perked-up at this result, but, after a 'scrappy' win over Aberavon, Bristol won an 'uninspiring match'. Once again, it seemed, Swansea supporters were destined to follow an inconsistent team. However, at least there was some encouragement. In the pack, 19-year-old Phil Llewellyn had made his presence felt on his début and promised much for the future.

There was a sad passing, too, from Swansea's ranks of former giants. Phil Hopkins (Pontardawe) died. Phil was one of seven Swansea players who were part of the famous Welsh side which, in 1909, had beaten England, Scotland, Ireland, France and Australia. Like the others, he had been awarded a silver cup, which, at the time, the press called 'a cup in a million'. In addition, Phil was an all-round athlete. An even timer, he won numerous athletic cups up to and including the long sprint, was a scratch golfer (though he did not start to play until he was well into his forties) and was, even, offered a soccer trial by Wales.

At the beginning of October, Phil Hopkins would have looked down proudly on the side which represented Swansea against the Harlequins. Coach, Gwyn Lewis, estimated that the average age of the team was 22 – one of the youngest in the history of the club. With John Davies establishing himself in the centre, Stuart Ferguson consolidating his position at full-back, and Peter Rowe 'oozing class' at outside-half, the backs looked to have outstanding promise. Indeed, during the first twenty-five minutes of the Harlequins match they converted that promise into reality. A David Weaver try was indicative of the flair, excitement and pace which the youngsters brought to the game. Peter Rowe carved out an opening, it was carried on by John Davies, following which the ball passed through several hands before Weaver sprinted over for the try. Whilst, in the end, the Harlequins were able to take advantage of the inexperience of the side to register a victory, Swansea supporters had seen enough to give them real hope. If only the team could be kept together to mature! Sadly, the fates were to rule otherwise.

At the same time as the Lewis Lewis Department Store was celebrating its centenary, the northern poachers struck again. The exciting new outside-half 'hope', Peter Rowe, joined

A presentation to Dewi Bebb en route for Lions Tour to New Zealand.

Wigan for £2,000. Since the young man had played so little first-class football, it was an audacious signing by the League men. 'Whites' supporters were stunned, as was Parliament when the grave news was announced that there were a half a million people unemployed in the U.K. It was, said the opposition, a national scandal. Then, just as the 'Whites' were boosted by the return of Dewi Bebb following his Lions tour, the whole country was devastated by the Aberfan disaster. For weeks, the terrible anguish and pathos engendered by the disaster drowned all other concerns. Yet life had to go on, and, as it had done with previous disasters, sport played its part as a soothing balm.

At St. Helens, with the game against the 'Wallabies' only a month away, the selectors were still searching for their best side. Unfortunately, results were not going their way, for a victory over Leicester at St. Helens ended a five-week period without a win. And, given the results of earlier games, it was not surprising that that victory was achieved as a result of 'controlled kicking'. There were, though, tries from Dewi Bebb and John Davies, and encouraging performances from Jim Clifford, Roy Thomas and Doug Jones. At outside-half, Brian Diment was said to be 'blossoming' whilst being nursed by Clive Rowlands. But results remained as mixed as ever. Sound victories were followed by inept displays and, as had happened so often before, injuries began to disrupt the best efforts of the selectors. For example, in a match against Llanelli, Brian Diment and Byron Mainwaring were both taken from the field. With the 'Wallabies' game just two weeks away, that was a blow for the selectors, though, at least, the victory over Llanelli, described as 'courageous and thrilling', did much to lift St. Helens spirits. The pack were magnificent in that 'Scarlets' game, particularly when reduced to six men, as they were at one point. It was Clive Rowlands's best game for the club, whilst Phil Bennett, on his début for Llanelli, had had a torrid time as a result of the attentions of the Swansea back-row. As had so often happened at St. Helens, hope emerged from adversity. The question now being asked was, whether the men in white could earn another famous victory over a major touring side? Whilst the question, was responded to in the negative by most objective commentators, it struck a chord among the optimists. Though in truth, even their most positive assessment was, 'You never know with the "Whites"'.

Such was the 'market' situation, that the St. Helens authorities announced that field entrance for the Australian game would be on a pay-as-you-enter basis. The stand, on the other hand, would be all ticket. As the players ran out on the day, the observant among the crowd would have noted that the Swansea men were sporting special stockings. The design of this hose incorporated the green and gold of Australia and the black and white of Swansea. Two former Swansea captains who had led their teams against previous Wallabies were present at the match. Len Davies (1947-48) and Teifion Williams (1957-58) would not have dwelt on the stockings. They would have looked into the eyes of the fifteen Swansea men who were following in their footsteps. If they were searching for resolve, then they would not have been disappointed.

In the game, Mike Thomas led his pack with verve and skill, whilst Clive Rowlands, drawing upon all his experience, controlled matters behind. However, following early exchanges the tourists took the lead and, with alarm bells ringing, the 'Whites' were forced on the defensive. But then, with the pack being used as the major attacking force, captain, Mike Thomas, hurled himself over the line to score a morale-boosting try. St Helens went wild. After twenty minutes, however, after finding himself at the bottom of a 'savage ruck', the gallant Thomas was carried off and did not return until ten minutes later. Meantime, the seven-man Swansea pack fought like Trojans and did not let up despite the best efforts of the men in green and gold. In due course, Brian Diment, receiving a pass some thirty yards out, dropped a goal with great aplomb and, when Stuart Ferguson kicked a 40 yard penalty to take the 'Whites' into the lead, the whole of St. Helens erupted. It was only then that the Australians began running the ball, but the Swansea defence was immense. When the whistle blew for no-side, Swansea had gained another historic victory over a touring side.

Every Swansea man was a hero, but the press singled out 'the storming back-row' of Atherton, Evans and Thomas, the generalship of Rowlands, the fine defence of John Davies and Ferguson, and the solid front-row of Mainwaring, Thomas and Jones. In truth, though, it was unfair not to include every player who wore the white jersey that day. Swansea, as the *Post* put it, 'could start crowing again'.

The men who gained that memorable victory were:

S. Ferguson, D.Weaver, S. Davies, J. Davies, D. Bebb, C. Rowlands and B. Diment; B. Mainwaring, R. Thomas, D. Jones, J. Clifford, D. Davies, G. Atherton, M. Evans and M. Thomas (Capt.).

However, as the domestic fixture list exposed the weaknesses of the side, crowing was hardly a pastime to be indulged in at Swansea. With injuries again taking their toll, by Christmas the club's playing record left a great deal to be desired. Once again, letters to the *Post* complained of 'chopping and changing', yet, in the circumstances in which they found themselves, the selectors had little choice.

In January, both Brian Diment and Peter Borthwick left the club, whilst key men, Jim Clifford and John and Stuart Davies, were all injured. Despite the best efforts of all concerned, confidence began to slip and matches continued to be lost. By the end of February, Ron Griffiths was pointing out that the side could only boast one win in the last twelve matches, and that ten players had been tried at outside-half during the previous season and a further four during the current campaign. Then, as ever, the 'Whites' surprised their critics. With Godfrey Davies at

Dewi Bebb scores against Barbarians.

outside-half and Jim Clifford back dominating the lines-out, Gloucester were well-beaten in a thrilling game. There followed a fine win over Bristol, played on a Saturday night to avoid the televised England v. France match. In the Bristol match, both David Weaver and Dewi Bebb scored tries, and, in so doing, responded positively to numerous letters in the *Post* demanding a return to 'running rugby'. There was an attractive spin-off from that floodlit game, too. The sum of £85.00 was taken at the gate. Furthermore, since Bristol included Redwood and Sharp in their side, the Swansea victory was put into encouraging context.

Sadly, the March winds brought with them a further series of defeats, all of which brought a down-in-the-mouth response from Ron Griffiths in the *Post*. 'Swansea rugby', he wrote, 'is at a low ebb.' The club, he thought, was at a 'crisis point'. However, hardly had the ink dried on his pronouncement, when the side found its feet again. With firmer grounds beneath their feet, the players ran with purpose, and, following a narrow victory over Aberavon, in which new full-back Doug Rees did well, and Gareth Thomas, restored at outside-half, provided the 'zip', there were notable victories on the northern tour. The quality of the victory over Halifax was particularly encouraging, for the home side had lost only five games out of thirty-eight played throughout the season. That match was also a personal milestone for Stuart Ferguson. The young man kicked two superb long-range penalties and scored a try to register all Swansea's points. With Otley also being beaten, with Stuart Davies outstanding, captain Mike Thomas and his men made their way home to Swansea with smiles on their faces. They had done much during the final weeks of the season to eradicate the gloom which had settled over St. Helens in more dismal times.

As far as the season's statistics were concerned, despite being in a side which lost twenty-six of its forty-seven matches, Stuart Ferguson had set another impressive mark. He had scored 209 points. David Weaver, with twelve tries, was second top scorer.

As the players turned their thoughts to summer pursuits, they did so with the ringing tones of new skipper, Clive Rowlands, in their ears. Taking on the captaincy of such a famous club was, he said, an exciting challenge. He wanted to restore a sense of pride and create a pool of twenty or so players for the first team. Meantime, others were calling for the appointment of a 'Rugby director'. It was to be many years before that call was heeded.

Chapter Twenty-One

HWYL

1967-68

HAVING PLAYED IN THE SIDE which had lost fifty-five per cent of its matches during the previous season, new captain, Clive Rowlands, announced that the team would do better in the campaign ahead. Nor was that an idle boast. Rowlands, who was to make a name for himself as coach of the National side, was an archetypal motivator of the Welsh school. Typical Rowlands team talks before a match consisted of *hwyl* mixed with astute observation of the opposing side's strengths and weaknesses. The wag who was to suggest that Clive was the 'coach with the cauliflower palm', left the listener to that description with a clear image of the Rowlands balled fist rising and falling as it slammed into the palm of his other hand. During the season ahead, the ears of the Swansea players were going to be assailed by a tireless torrent of words and supporting non-verbal signals, all designed to lift their spirits and boost their confidence. The team would do better, or else!

One by-product of the Rowlands philosophy, was the exacting target which he set his charges during August 1967; to win the first six matches on the fixture list. Had there been a sports psychologist at St. Helens during the period of Rowlands's captaincy, his analysis would have highlighted the main threads of the captain's approach: positive thinking, pride, togetherness, and a recognition that winning (or losing) can become a habit. However, whilst recognising the potential supremacy of mind over matter, Clive Rowlands knew that he could not make bricks without straw. The tactics which his teams were to follow would need to be tailored to the strengths of the players he had available.

Having beaten Cork Constitutional by 16 points to 3, the positive thinkers among Swansea supporters might have said, one down, five to go. However, had they been at the match against the Irish side (which included Noel Murphy), they might also have been confused, for the 'Whites' turned out in a scarlet strip. Whatever the reason for this sartorial variegation, the colour might have helped the Swansea players at 'lemon time'. Then, Rowlands's tongue was given lively exercise as he urged his troops to greater effort. With Llewellyn and Mainwaring doing well in the lines-out, it came as no surprise to knowledgeable supporters that the captain's boot was much in evidence. Whilst the kind of rugby which ensued may not have been to the taste of the purists, the objective was clear! Swansea was to win the first six matches and, in the Rowlands philosophy there was no question of falling at the first fence. The artistic stuff would have to wait.

As far as the Irishmen were concerned, it was fortunate that they took the boat back to Cork when they did, for, on 5 September 1967, hurricane winds (gusting up to 82 m.p.h.) hit Swansea. Most of Langland's beach huts were flattened, the sea at Mumbles resembled a 'graveyard of battered boats', and trees were blown down in many parts of Swansea. The following day,

'T.C.' outfoxes four from Bridgend.

Dewi Bebb announced his retirement, and Stuart Ferguson was diagnosed as having broken his collar bone. Whilst skipper Rowlands was set on developing his own wind of change, the hurricane's aftermath left Swansea bereft of two key players. 'T.C.' could have done without that!

In due course, Ferguson was to return, but the loss of Dewi Bebb was something else. Over eight seasons, Dewi had been 'capped' 34 times, and he had gone on Lions tours to South Africa and New Zealand (where he scored 14 tries during the tour). As far as Swansea rugby was concerned, the north Walian had been exceedingly loyal to the club. He had played 225 games and scored 87 tries for the 'Whites', despite the fact that he had worked in Cardiff for the last four years of his career, and that in many Swansea matches he saw little of the ball. Dewi was the ideal club man! When Bebb's retirement was announced, Secretary, David Price said that he could not speak too highly of the flying winger, nor of the service which Dewi had given to the 'Whites' on and off the field of play. Dewi Bebb was to be missed, but his massive contribution to Swansea rugby would remain a matter of record.

In the weeks which followed, captain Rowlands must have wondered if the gods were plotting against him. Apart from the loss of Bebb, and the injured Ferguson, there were three props and several backs on the injury list. As a consequence the selection committee had to draft newcomers and reserves into the side, though that process was not without its advantages. For example, in the absence of the prolific Ferguson, Doug Rees (Penclawdd) at full-back was kicking well. Furthermore, despite the injuries and absences, Rowlands's side not only achieved their six win target, they suffered just one defeat in their first nine matches. Clearly, setting the initial goal before the season started had proved to be a master stroke. The players and the supporters were beginning to think positively again.

By mid-November, though, even the optimists could have developed the argument that Clive Rowlands had a personal gremlin. The captain broke his hand when playing for West Wales against the Kiwis. As a consequence, his brand of brand of Cymric motivation was missed on the field, though Eiryn Lewis was proving to be a capable deputy, and there was good news in that Stuart Ferguson made his 'come-back' in a match against Coventry. In that match, the 'Whites' scored 22 points against 9. Doug Rees 'looked like an international', and Stuart Davies and Phil Llewellyn both scored fine tries.

Whilst a foot-and-mouth outbreak in Gower resulted in Clyne golf course being closed, the 'Whites' may have wished that they could have the opportunity to put their feet up. During that period the side won only one match in an eight game sequence. However, in the last of them, Clive Rowlands made his 'come-back'. Whilst understandably disappointed with the results of the games in his absence, the captain said that he had been pleased with the play of several of the youngsters. The big problem, he thought, was in the size of the pack, and the committee were continuing their search for big men.

Happily, December provided Swansea supporters with some encouragement, Penarth, the U.A.U., and Neath were beaten. In those matches, Brian and Phil Llewellyn did well at lock, Clive Dyer was the 'outstanding forward' in two of the matches, whilst, behind the scrum, Doug Rees and Stuart Ferguson were singled out as having 'caught the eye'.

At the turn of the year, Ron Griffiths, whilst acknowledging the improved form of the side since the captain had returned, argued that 'The club has been in the doldrums for several years, occasionally picking itself up by its bootstraps, then the old inconsistency creeps in again'. Whilst they could only accept that the criticism was valid, at least the captain and the committee could maintain that, at half-time, the 'Whites' had a far better record than they had had in the previous season.

Subsequently, as the first nuclear power station in Wales was opened at Trawsfynydd, skipper Rowlands was reported as 'being in his element' as his seven-man pack 'overwhelmed' the Cross Keys eight. Morrie Evans had left the field after thirty minutes of the match, following which the captain cajoled, encouraged and bullied his septet of forwards as they 'ploughed through the mud'. According to the *Western Mail*, the result of that match – Cross Keys 5 Swansea 8 – hardly reflected Swansea's dominance. Indeed, had Stuart Ferguson not had one of his rare 'off-days' with the boot, the score would have been much more in keeping with the pattern of play.

By the end of January when the 'Whites' beat Coventry, their sixth win in seven matches, coach Ron Trimnell felt moved to comment: 'Suddenly there are hopes of a Swansea revival'. Whilst the coach's words were music to the optimists years, the 'revival' was built around the skill and tactical brain of Clive Rowlands, the boots of Rees and Ferguson, and a 'storming pack'. What, someone might have asked, if you take away one of these elements?

A week later, Clive Rowlands announced that he was going to 'hang up his boots' at the end of the season, and Doug Rees was selected by Wales. Doug, who was the first Swansea 'round-the-corner' kicker, was sharing kicking duties with Stuart Ferguson, who, in order to accommodate Rees, was operating on the wing. In the defeats of Llanelli, Gloucester and Bristol, which followed, the pair successfully shared the kicking. However, there was a persistent rumour circulating in Swansea at the time, to the effect that Ferguson was looking for another club. Whilst secretary, David Price, denied all knowledge of this, it was well-known that Stuart preferred playing at full-back rather than on the wing.

Meanwhile, Clive Rowlands's pre-match team talks were taking on legendary proportions.

Prior to a match against Bristol, for example, he was said to have locked his men in the dressing room for over thirty minutes. Whatever he said, it worked! The West Countrymen 'folded' before a sustained bout of Swansea pressure, and in the second-half the men in white dominated, with a 'storming' Stuart Davies try being the highlight of the afternoon.

In March, whilst Swansea's Victoria Station was being demolished, the 'Whites' sequence of victories continued. Indeed, following a ten match unbeaten run, it was not until the middle of the month that they were defeated. Even then, there was little in it, and most press observers preferred to focus, not upon the defeat, but upon the make-up of the side. As the *Post* pointed out, eight former Youth players were in the 'Whites' team which defeated Llanelli. Stuart Ferguson, Terry Greenslade, Derek Rogers, John and Roger Davies, Morrie Evans, Geoff Atherton, and Phil Llewellyn had all come by that route. Meanwhile, in the face of the impressive run of victories, Ron Griffiths was arguing that 'Skipper Rowlands and coach Ron Trimnell have performed a pretty remarkable resuscitation job'. At least he refrained from writing 'resurrection'.

During the remainder of the season, fine wins over Cardiff, Racing Club de France, and a wonderful match with the Barbarians, were the highlights. The Barbarian match, in particular, had the rugby purists drooling. Then, seven tries were scored, four by Swansea, though the visitors won the game through the contributions of the French pair, Claude Lacaze, and Jean Gachassin. Lacaze was the star of the match, dropping a remarkable goal from over fifty yards. For the 'Whites', Geoff Atherton scored a brace of tries, whilst Llewellyn, Jones, Mainwaring and James did well in the home pack. There was, also, a wonderful 'game of old-fashioned rugby' at Garryowen. There, the 'Whites' scored seven tries, six of which were 'beauties'. Centres Terry Greenslade and John Davies were said to have been 'deadly', lock, Phil Llewellyn, and wing, Wayne Lewis 'outstanding', whilst Mel James 'dominated in the lines- out'. The Irish supporters were loud in their praise of the young men in white. For their part, Swansea's followers basked in the glory of the victory and in the manner in which it was achieved. They appreciated, too, the significant improvement in the team's playing record compared with that of the previous campaign. A straw poll taken at the time, would have shown that Swansea supporters felt that they could look forward to the next campaign with renewed confidence. Yet, the man who was, arguably, the catalyst behind the improvement in the club's fortunes, would not be available in the season to come. Most supporters preferred not to think about the implications of that.

1968-69

Down the snake again

In August 1968, had they been able to see into the future, 'Whites' supporters would have been astounded to find that, during the new campaign, their favourites would lose more games than any previous Swansea side had done. Having climbed the ladder so successfully during the previous season, their fate was to slide down to an even lower point. Certainly, new captain, Clive Dyer, would have been nonplussed. Apart from anything else, the new experimental law which allowed kicking direct into touch only from within a team's twenty-five, appeared to favour back play. Given the form of the 'Whites' towards the end of the previous season, that change was thought to be of benefit to the young men of Swansea.

And that appeared to be the case, when visitors, Otley were 'thrashed' by 53 points to 6 in an opening game, which represented a post-war scoring record in a first-class fixture. The euphoria affected everyone at the club. Eleven tries were scored during the match, four by Geoff Atherton, while Mike Thomas and Terry Greenslade each scored twice. Captain Dyer, whilst being delighted with the victory, warned about 'going overboard' regarding the win. He had to repeat the message again, when the District League succumbed by fifty-four points to nil. Yet, he would not have been human if, secretly, he did not contemplate a successful and exciting season.

Meantime, Len Blyth, commenting on the need for a first team 'squad' of twenty-two or three players, pointed out that, with two matches per week up until Christmas, every member of the group would be guaranteed regular games. Everyone agreed that it was a good idea. However, one member of the 'squad' was not available. Stuart Ferguson was in Argentina with the Welsh team, understudying J. P. R. Williams. When he returned, at the beginning of October, he must have been taken aback to find a side which had lost four games in a row and with that, a great deal of confidence. According to Ron Griffiths, this run, coupled with a spate of injuries to leading players, resulted in morale being low at St. Helens. After Llanelli and Neath had each beaten the 'Whites' with some ease, the press as a whole ventilated the problems which the Swansea selectors had to face. As the *Western Mail* put it after a further defeat by Leicester, 'Swansea have lost nine of their last eleven games'. When Ebbw Vale were also victorious in the next match, the size of the 'gate' reflected the feelings of supporters. That Floodlit Alliance match was watched by a mere four hundred people, and Treasurer, Gwyn White's rueful comment that, 'It only goes to show that you have to win these days to attract spectators', was indicative of the concern of the club's officials. Also nonplussed were the selectors. With the series of defeats came a lack of confidence throughout the side, and that problem was exacerbated by an unusual number of injuries. Doug Rees, for example, had missed two months of the season with a troublesome knee injury, and Geoff Atherton had had to have an operation.

Nonetheless, in November, the *Post* reported that, in matches with Llanelli and Blackheath the 'Whites' had 'fought with great resolution'. At the same time, Chairman, Len Blyth told the press that he was confident that 'Swansea can haul themselves out of trouble'. In the next match the young men showed that Chairman Blyth was right. Cross Keys were beaten by 23 points to 15, with Stuart Ferguson in fine kicking form. Next, whilst the side lost to a powerful Coventry outfit, the margin was a mere two points, and most observers felt that the 'Whites' had deserved to win. The optimists were beginning to smile again.

And those smiles were more in evidence following a 'St. Helens mud bath'. In what were described as 'appalling conditions', the young side played fine rugby 'despite the mud and torrential rain'. At outside-half that day was 18-year-old Roger Blyth who had a 'sound match', and those with long memories might have noted that, by donning the white strip, 'young Blyth' had confirmed the soothsayer qualities of his father's statement on the day when he was born.

Whilst the next match was lost in a game in which Malcolm Henwood broke his arm, 'The Magnificent Seven', which was the depleted Swansea pack, and the hard tackling 'Whites' backs were holding Cardiff to a draw with five minutes to go. Then, Stuart Ferguson struck a penalty from forty-five yards to win the game. Beaming, skipper Clive Dyer confessed, 'We needed that!'

As the Post Code was being introduced by the Post Office (with the slogan; 'It's easier to find'), the Swansea selectors might have wished that it would help them in their search for players. Notwithstanding the problems which they faced with injuries, over the Christmas period the club had to play six matches in twelve days. In the event, victories over Watsonians and Capetown University (including a player called de Villiers) raised spirits, though London Welsh and the U.A.U. both defeated the 'Whites'. There followed defeats by Newport and Pontypool, though, in each case the press commented on Swansea's fighting spirit. With captain Clive Dyer required by the Police, the acting skipper against the 'Usksiders', when the 'Whites' led by 6 points to 0 until midway through the second-half, was Roger Blyth. Given the fact that Newport had lost just two of their matches up to that stage of the season (scoring 489 points in the process), Swansea could feel proud of its young men.

With new detached homes in Derwen Fawr being sold for £8,750, the young 'Whites' showed their resilience when they defeated the R.A.F. In a match influenced by a swirling, biting wind, Arwel Morgan, Roger Blyth and Stuart Davies each scored a try. Obviously exuberant, Ron Griffiths,above his report of the game, flung caution to the winds. His headline was, 'Swansea backs are running again'. According to the *Post*-man, John and Stuart Davies, and wingers Ferguson and Lewis were benefiting from the service they were receiving from 'young Blyth'. However, in his next match report, as the headline for his piece demonstrated, he was subdued. 'Coventry shatter Whites confidence.' That had an altogether different ring about it. Though, since Coventry had a powerful side at the time, and the score was only 11 points to 3, he might have been overstating his case. Indeed, had they taken their chances the 'Whites' could have won the match.

Then, as if to demonstrate that point, in the game which followed (versus Penarth), the young men did take their chances. The 'Seasiders' conceded 38 points as, to use the old time phrase, 'the leather was given the air' by the men in white. A week later that air was full of snow. Swansea suffered its worst blizzard for many years, and the sea froze at Blackpill. As a result, the 'Whites' did not play again for three weeks, when Bristol provided the opposition. Unhappily, the lay-off seemed to have affected the Swansea men more than their opponents, and the *Western Mail* described the Swansea performance as 'disjointed'.

The following week, however, after coach, Ron Trimnell had resigned, the 'Whites' outplayed Llanelli despite losing Clive Dyer after eighteen minutes of the match. The *Post* headline gladdened the hearts of Swansea supporters, 'Whites shock rivals and lift sagging morale'. Furthermore, both home tries were scored when the side was one short, one by Wayne Lewis and the other, 'a cheeky interception' by Stuart Ferguson.

Further fine tries were scored in the next match, against Bath, as 'exciting Swansea overwhelmed the visitors'. Mike James, Phil Llewellyn, Dai Bowen and Stuart Ferguson's scores 'excited the crowd', whilst the 'deadly boot of Stuart Ferguson 'converted the tries and took advantage of penalty opportunities'. After struggling for so long, no one could understand why the young men were suddenly running into the form which they had shown in the previous season. After all, they were, largely, the same young men who had set the pulses racing under Clive Rowlands, and they had a season's extra experience behind them.

But then, with the 'Whites' 'reverting to type', Cardiff, Racing Club de France and Pontypool all beat them. Neath, however, found themselves beaten by 'smart Swansea outfit'. The 'Whites' won by 19 points to 6, and scrum-half, Arwel Morgan scored a hat-trick of tries. During this period came the sad news of the death of Dai Parkhouse, the man with a heart as big as Mumbles Head. Dai, who was only thirty-three at the time of his death, remains, to this day, one of the most loved players (and the term is appropriate) ever to have worn the white jersey.

When the posts were hauled down, Chairman, Len Blyth, in his post-season comments, spoke of the lack of consistency, the need for additional quality players, and for big men in the pack. For his part, Ron Griffiths suggested that 'Swansea need to take a long hard look at their affairs'. Why, he asked, is it necessary to have a management committee of upwards of forty men? Meantime, Stuart Davies, elected as captain for the season to come, rallied his troops in Agincourt style. 'Take heart! Next season will see improvement in the performance record!'. New coach, Morrie Evans, nodded in agreement.

Morrie Evans.

1969-70

Further down the snake

During the summer of 1969 there had been a great deal of discussion in Welsh rugby circles about the possibility of a cup competition. Sixteen clubs were to take part, and, naturally, there was the expectancy that the 'Whites' would be involved in the competition. The question of a national (dare one use the word?), league was another matter.

After Ebbw Vale had been beaten in Swansea's opening match, Morrie Evans was at pains to put the victory into perspective. 'It was an encouraging start', he said, 'but I'm not kidding myself that we are out of the wood yet!' His caution was to prove to have been prudent. In the match which followed, Roger Blyth broke his collar bone, and whilst 'they fought like tigers', the fourteen men 'Whites' were beaten by Bristol. In addition, following the Blyth mishap, the 'injury bug' struck again. After scoring a hat-trick of tries against the League, Wayne Lewis was injured, whilst big second-row man, Mike James was out with torn ligaments. To add insult to injury, James had suffered his injury on a building site and not on the field of play.

There followed a 'second-half thumping by Newport', who took the score from 9 points to 5 at the interval to 35 points to 8. In that match, after a fighting performance in the first-half, the 'Whites' had the 'wind taken out of their sails by a giveaway try of monstrous proportions'. Whilst John Davies scored a consolation try near the end, as a competition, the match was over long before then.

At the end of September, Ron Griffiths, reviewing the first month of the season, argued that Swansea had many problems. According to the *Post*-man, 'the most glaring was at forward, where, again, the pack lacks weight.' Griffiths continued with his campaign during the following week, when he wrote, 'The extent of Swansea's rugby problems were graphically illustrated today, when most of the selectors did not bother to travel to see the team in action against the Harlequins'. The *Post*-scribe went on to argue that urgent action should be taken to strengthen the side for the match with the South African tourists. Whilst most of the press reports of the 'Quins match spoke of a brave showing by the Swansea men, the general opinion was that bravery would not be enough against the Springboks.

That bravery was evident again in matches against Neath and Llanelli, though, given results at the time, morale was at a low point at the Cricket Field. When Wayne Lewis asked for a transfer, Ron Griffiths, clearly concerned about the overall situation, wrote, '... despondency has spread through the club like a prairie fire, the outlook is bleak, and, sadly, there does not appear to be very much hope of better things in the future'. It was a dismal pronouncement, and the *Post*-man should have known better.

Stuart Davies.

Once again, the phoenix rose from the ashes. Blackheath, according to the *Western Mail*, 'were stunned by an outstanding Swansea side'. With the Mountain Ash pair, Hylton Bowen and Tom Pullman at half-back, the 'Whites', losing by six points at half-time, 'turned it on' to beat the London side by 32 points to 15. The pessimists were stunned. Could this be the side which had performed so badly in recent matches? The optimists, however, permitted themselves a covert smile as they savoured tries by John Davies (2), Stuart Davies, and Dave Morgan. Whilst Morgan joked that he had raced all of two yards to score, the three Davies tries were right out of the top drawer.

Whilst the next match was lost, the *Post* reported on 'an encouraging defensive performance by Swansea.' Opponents Llanelli, with Phil Bennett outstanding, were seeking their fourteenth consecutive win. In that context the Swansea performance was encouraging. Indeed, Ron Griffiths, now taking on a positive attitude, felt that, 'On this performance Swansea can be confident of providing the Springboks with worthy opposition'. For the first time for months, Swansea rugby was beginning to have some belief in itself again.

When the day of the South African match dawned, the expected problems with anti-apartheid demonstrators manifested themselves in scuffles in and around St. Helens. The police, who were out in force, were obliged to clear the area by carrying protesters away. For the first time in its long history, St. Helens witnessed a significant police presence, and happenings which were foreign to rugby football arenas. However, when the game got under way, the Swansea men rose to the occasion. They 'tackled everything that moved', and, when the final whistle was blown, the Springboks, whilst victorious, 'knew that they had been in a game'. Furthermore, since the 12-0 scoreline at half-time was unchanged at the end, most observers felt that, in the second period, the Swansea defence had been outstanding. Afterwards, Chairman, Gordon Morris, expressed himself 'immensely encouraged' by the performance that day, and by that against Llanelli. He felt that the 'side was beginning to find faith in itself.' The *Western Mail*, was in agreement, and in its report on the Springboks match, was of the opinion that in Alan Rutherford and Dai Bowen, the 'Whites' had two powerful props, that hooker, Roy Thomas had 'forced himself to the forefront of Welsh hookers', and Stuart Ferguson, at full-back had 'grown in stature'. All in all, given these comments and other opinions expressed in the media, the St. Helens authorities must have felt quietly confident that the corner had been turned.

The Swansea side which attracted positive comments that day was:
S. Ferguson, J. Davies, D. M. Morgan, S. Davies (Capt.), L. Jones, H. Bowen, T. Pullman, A. Rutherford, R. Thomas, D. Bowen, M. James, J. Joseph, C. Dyer, M. Henwood, D. Winslett.

Unhappily, the last match in November resulted in another defeat. Despite the fact that Mel and Mike James had 'dominated the lines-out', the 'Whites' were well beaten by Richmond. Stuart Ferguson scored all Swansea's points via his boot, and, sad to say, they were the last points scored by the player in a Swansea jersey. Leigh, the Rugby League side, paid Ferguson £6,000 to join them. It was, he said, too good an offer to refuse. At St. Helens, the committee could only shake their heads sadly, swallow hard, and get on with trying to improve the fortunes of Swansea R.F.C. Naturally, they would miss the young man with the big boot, for he had topped the club's scoring list for three campaigns, and, up to that stage in the season, he had already passed a century of points. Yet, as time was to show, when one door closes ...

As the old borough of Swansea was enjoying city status for the first time, results did not go the way of the 'Whites'. Nonetheless, there were some encouraging signs to give comfort to all who loved Swansea rugby. Nineteen-year-old language student, Roger Blyth was drafted in to replace the departed Ferguson, and quickly made his mark. The player had served his apprenticeship by playing in every position behind the scrum, with the exception of inside-half. That experience was to stand him in good stead, though several seasons were to elapse before he consolidated himself in the number 15 jersey. Another young man, Arwel Rees, made his début against Cardiff, and although he finished on the losing side, most people were impressed with his performance. The 'Forwards Union' had cause to remember that game, too. Big Mike James, following up a Dai Bowen kick ahead, unsettled the Cardiff full-back, gathered the ball and crashed over for a try.

At the end of the month, there was a further, and as it turned out, significant change at St. Helens. Ieuan Evans took over as coach. In the history of the 'All Whites', that appointment may come to be seen as a watershed. Whilst the new coach's regime was also to have its ups-and-downs, it is generally accepted that the Evans brought order, control and vision to the St. Helens club. He was the fifth coach to take charge at the Cricket Field in as many years. Consequently he felt it necessary to make an impression at the start. The *Post* noted that 'He will begin with a face-to-face meeting with the players ...' Whatever was said then must have helped to provide the firm basis from which the coach was to influence Swansea rugby's renaissance.

When the year ended, the Motor Manufacturers' Association announced that it had been a bad twelve months for car sales – the poorest since 1963. In Swansea, at the end of the season, all who loved the game of rugby must have ruefully observed that, like the car men, their season had been the worst for some time. Indeed, statistically, the outcome for the 'Whites' had been the worst ever. Thirty-two games had been lost; sixty-two per cent of those played. The pessimists were in their element. Ieuan Evans, however, would have none of it. He said, 'I have faith in Swansea rugby ... That faith remains undiminished ... this club can still reach the top!' Swansea supporters must have looked hard at themselves. Whilst the new messiah had faith, Whites followers, after years of uncertainty, were looking for something more concrete. Nevertheless, as the future was to show, Old Moore would have had great difficulty in improving upon Evans's forecast.

1970-71

Up the ladder

Trevor Evans.

During the close season, a former 'All White', Ivor Morgan hung up his whistle after fifteen years of refereeing. Ivor had played at fly-half for the 'Whites' and for the 'Scarlets'. Meanwhile, at St. Helens, Stuart Davies was not required to retire from the captaincy; he was elected for a second season. His position on the field, however, was different from that which he had occupied at the start of his career with Swansea. Reluctantly at first, he was converted into a wing three-quarter, where he had considerable success. Against Bristol, for example, for the first time in his career, he scored four tries in a match, and, according to Ron Griffiths, they were all 'sizzlers'. Subsequently, on the Yorkshire tour, he repeated the feat against Halifax. As the *Post* had it then, 'with pace, side-step and body swerve he has blossomed into a wing of outstanding ability'. The captain was also an important element in Ieuan Evans's planning. *Esprit de corps*, as Napoleon suggested, is a key factor in ensuring success in any campaign. The coach knew that Stuart Davies's personality and approach to the game would be invaluable in that regard.

Training for the new season started early, and, among those who trained twice per week from early July, was a flank forward called Trevor Evans. Pacey, 6'2" and fifteen stone, the young man's attributes were to stand him and the 'Whites' in good stead in the seasons ahead. Indeed, he made an impact immediately. In a runaway win for the 'Whites' against Cross Keys, the *Post* reported that 'Evans is a real find'. This opinion was exemplified by the paper's description of a try scored by Jeff Thomas. 'Trevor Evans was, twice, involved in the movement ... (he) powered along the touchline, linked up with Stuart Davies, took a return pass from the skipper and fed Jeff Thomas, who scored.' Following that victory, whilst the less inhibited among the Swansea committee might have felt like whooping with delight, they contained themselves to cautious smiles. No one could blame them for their caution. As the old adage has it, once bitten, twice shy. In Swansea's case, however, the old saw could be modified to read, many times bitten ...

Meanwhile, coach Evans's ideas and planning were having an impact on several aspects of the organisation at St. Helens. Among other things, a decision was taken to 'trim' the number of selectors from 'an unwieldy seven to three'. No doubt, the chapel-going supporters of Swansea rugby would have wished that the trio would be as wise as those who travelled to Bethlehem. Furthermore, in carrying the metaphor forward, they would have yearned for the resurrection of Swansea rugby.

After the spectacular victory over Cross Keys, against Pontypool and Bristol the 'Whites' found things to be much more difficult. At Pontypool, Mel James scored two tries, as the 'Whites' won by 14 points to 3, which was indicative of the pattern of a match which was, largely contained among the forwards. At Bristol, it was said that the side 'failed to match the power up-front'. Nonetheless, whilst they were defeated, the team's second-half performance gave everyone greater heart. At that stage, coach Evans let it be known that whilst he was reasonably pleased with the way things had developed, there was still a long way to go; however, there were encouraging signs. Many people commented on the change of 'atmosphere' at the club. Among them was Roger Davies, who had left the 'Whites' during the previous season but had returned to the club to 'plug the gap at full-back'. He told the *Post*' There is such a vast difference in outlook ... you can sense the mood of confidence as soon as you enter the dressing room.' Happily, that confidence was reinforced in the next match.

At half-time in that game, the ever-popular Leicester team was leading by 3 points to nil. When the whistle went for no-side, the 'Whites' had amassed twenty-one points, whilst the 'Tigers' had failed to score again. Swansea tries were scored that day by Roger Blyth, Trevor Evans (2), Stuart Davies (2) and John Evans. According to the *Post*, all but one had been 'superlative'.

Following another victory (over Penarth), as he commented on the situation, Ron Griffiths fairly bubbled. He thought that 'The change in Swansea rugby fortunes was something of a miracle'. Redhead, Trevor Evans was 'proving to be the best flanker since Clem Thomas', whilst the team as a whole was 'beginning to believe in itself'. The *Post*-man was even more effusive when the 'Whites' won, comfortably at Blackheath. The headline above his match report on that occasion said it all: 'Adventurous Swansea overwhelm Blackheath'. In fairness to Griffiths, it *was* remarkable stuff. In three consecutive matches, the men in white had amassed 73 points whilst conceding only 15.

By then, not surprisingly, the optimists were to the fore. Comparisons were being made with the great Swansea sides of the past, and the general opinion was that the pack was the strongest for years. The 'Whites' were back! Not only were they back, but they were young enough to promise even better rugby in the future. Thirteen of the regular fifteen were on the right side of twenty-five. To many, the future seemed assured. Only the timid pessimists were not caught up in the euphoria. Their understandable, 'ah, buts' would have reminded those who wore rose-coloured glasses that, in the history of the club since the war, there had been several false dawns. The optimists tried to blank out such thoughts. They wanted to enjoy the renaissance.

An unexpected defeat at Coventry ensued, and the St. Helens men were 'brought down to earth with a bump'. The Midlanders won by 19 points to 6, and the defeat provided a lesson which was well learnt. As Ieuan Evans put it, 'There is a difference between being cocky and being confident'. The slap on the wrist served the young men well.

In the matches which followed, Richmond were beaten, after a 'jittery start', as were Cardiff. It was true that Gareth Edwards went off during the second-half of the game with the 'Blue and Blacks', but by then, the 'Whites' were well on top. The scorers in that match were Roger Hyndman, who crossed for two fine tries, and flanker, Trevor Evans, who 'scored with panache'. Another player making his mark at that time was full-back, Dennis Lewis who, soon after, passed his first century of points for the club.

Not surprisingly, the improved form and the winning run brought more spectators to St. Helens. There was a £750 'gate' for the Cardiff match, whilst £1,000 was taken on the day that London Welsh appeared. According to treasurer, Gwyn White, the 'Welsh' gate was the best for a decade. In addition, the delighted White noted that the number of patrons and members had also increased. Whilst the success of rugby clubs for most followers is reflected in points scored as against those conceded, and in the thrills and excitement which are generated at matches, a businessman would argue that the true test would be the level of income generated. If that was true, Swansea was 'on the march again!'

After beating Pontypool with a much-changed side, the 'Whites' then lost two matches in succession. Coach Evans, however, took the defeats philosophically. 'They are a young team. They are still developing', he said. Furthermore, he believed that each of the defeats had its plus point. Whilst injuries and absences had disrupted selection, it had forced the committee to experiment. Two newcomers had shown up well through this process. A young, former soccer player called Wheel had done well on his début, as had Stefan James (an Oxford 'Blue'). Then Geoff Atherton, on being recalled, had 'reminded the selectors what a useful footballer he was'. Ieuan Evans also spoke highly of the spirit in the 'squad', citing Mike James's blind-side try against Pontypool, when the backs smilingly applauded the big man.

For a variety of reasons, January came and went with the side playing only two games. Yet, despite this lack of match practice, the young team continued to play well. In February, Bridgend, on their own pitch, were the victims of the young 'Whites', which was noteworthy, since Swansea had not won on the Brewery Field for three seasons. In that match, Stuart Davies scored an outstanding try, sprinting 60 yards to touch down. According to the *Western Mail*, the captain 'was applauded by his own team, the Bridgend supporters and,even, some of the home team'. Surging speed, body swerve and side-step were all used by the captain to make that score possible.

By the beginning of March, Swansea supporters were starting to relax. Ieuan Evans, making good use of the press, was pointing to the number of youth players who were coming to St. Helens. He was, also, commenting on the new men who were beginning to establish themselves. Geoff Wheel, he thought, was 'certain to make the grade'. Nor did he forget his regulars. He cited Gordon Davies and Mike James as examples of dedicated clubmen. The big men had appeared in over two thirds of the matches. That, he said was 'commitment'.

Before the season ended, the young men were taught another lesson. They were 'swamped' by London Welsh (41 points to 6). Whilst smarting at the extent of that defeat, the men in white could look back on a season in which the side had improved significantly upon the previous season's outcome. The 'Whites' had won thirty-three matches, the highest total in the club's history, though, at that point in time no one commented on that fact. Furthermore, they lost only twelve games, twenty less than in the previous campaign, and scored 650 points, the highest total since 1898-99. In addition, as coach Ieuan Evans stated, the young players all had another season's experience under their belts and should be better players for that.

Dennis Lewis had set a new points scoring record (244) in his first season, Roger Hyndman, with 15 had set a post-war try scoring record for a forward, while scrum-half Alwyn Gittins was not far behind with 14. Then, to put the icing on the cake, it was stated that Mervyn Davies would like to come back to Swansea to teach. At that time, had someone thought of raising a petition to find Davies a post in Swansea, the City's education department would have been submerged under a ton of paper.

Sadly, amidst all the positive factors which had stemmed from the season which had just finished, there was a sad note. Watsonians, a Christmas fixture for more than half a century, would not appear again on the Swansea list. Nor would the District League, another long-standing fixture; their place would be taken by a combined west Wales side. Whilst change is inevitable, without those matches, things would never be quite the same again.

Chapter Twenty-Two

THROUGH ANOTHER TRAP DOOR

1971-72

Phil Llewellyn leads out the 'Whites'.

HAVING BEEN RELATIVELY SUCCESSFUL during the previous season, all at St. Helens, in looking forward to the new campaign, felt reasonably confident that the club would continue to improve its performances. Certainly, Phil Llewellyn, the new captain, was. He told the press that the spirit in the club 'was great', and he felt sure that the 'Whites' would do well in the season ahead. No one challenged that view, for it reflected the collective opinion of the management team, the players, and the majority of supporters. The press, too, was of the same opinion, with Ron Griffiths exemplifying the view of the media men. He wrote: 'Swansea stand on the threshold of the new season with their prospects just about the rosiest for a decade. Optimism ... is at an all-time high, and there is a welcome surge in membership.'

In the event, the patient, which coach Ieuan Evans and the management team had nursed back to health, had an unexpected relapse. Far from improving upon the performance of the previous season, the 'Whites' lost more games than they had done in all but three campaigns since the War. It followed that, given the level of pre-season confidence in the Swansea camp, the 1971-72 campaign came as a shock to the system.

No one seemed able to explain what had gone wrong. Ieuan Evans, for example, said that he could not put his finger on the reason. Nonetheless, despite the disappointing outcome, he remained confident. He reminded his listeners that the 'Whites' were a young side, and even went as far as confidently forecasting that 'the best is yet to come!' In an upbeat statement, which contrasted sharply with the mood of that moment, he cited the promise of several young players who were developing well. In particular, he forecast that Geoff Wheel would be 'capped' before he was twenty-five.

At the beginning of the season none of the problems which were going to affect the team were apparent. Consequently, rugby talk in Swansea took place in a confident setting. Rumours were circulating about new players who were coming to St. Helens, and the most seductive of these concerned Mervyn Davies. According to 'the best sources', the Welsh number 8 had obtained a teaching post in the city, which, of course, meant that, in the near future, he would be playing his rugby in a white jersey. The rumours became so persistent that the press were searching the smoke to find the fire. In due course, they confronted Secretary, David Price, who tried to put the matter to rest. He told the press that he would have been delighted to have been able to confirm the rumour, but he had no knowledge of the matter. In due course Merve-the-swerve would be coming back to St. Helens; the rumour was to prove to be reality; but not at that time.

Just before the new season started, there was a surprise departure from the club. Hooker, Alan Mages left St. Helens. Whatever was the reason for his departure, it was a blow which the selectors could have done without. He was the only experienced number 2 in the Swansea squad, and given his striking ability, and his play in both the tight and loose, he was not an easy man to replace. In addition to losing Mages, by the end of the first 'proper' game, the injury list at St. Helens was too long for comfort. Among those who were unfit were Mike James, who was out for a month with a dislocated elbow, and new captain Phil Llewellyn, who left the field in a match against Cross Keys.

By the end of September, the *Western Mail*, in commenting on an 'All Whites' defeat (at Newport), argued that 'Swansea, voted the most improved side in Wales last season, are slipping'. Ron Griffiths, in attempting to pin-point the reasons for the side's poor showing, thought that the balance of the team had been disrupted by the spate of injuries. Whether that was right or not, the facts in the *Post*-man's article were unpalatable as far as Swansea rugbyites were concerned. The team had conceded 57 points in two matches. The cynics were having a field day. According to them, the previous season's results were a flash-in-the-pan. Swansea rugby was back to its old inconsistent self.

When October ended, in supporting Ieuan Evans's view that 'We'll be back', Chairman, Gordon Morris, put on a brave face. Nonetheless he had to admit that he was bemused by the situation. We know that the boys can play, he said, and went on to stress that it was 'inconceivable that a team which had played as well as the 'Whites' had, should suddenly lose its grip'. As it happened, Morris's statement was made on the day before the men in white earned their first victory in ten matches. That day, the collective sigh of relief from St. Helens at the outcome of that match must have been audible on Kilvey Hill. Sadly, the win did not come soon enough to change the mind of record points scorer Dennis Lewis. According to the press, the series of defeats had damaged morale to such a degree that there was unrest in the Swansea camp. Thus it was that Lewis also left the club, which meant that the 'Whites' did not have either a recognised hooker or an experienced place kicker. Ieuan Evans was well aware that he had to stop that rot, whilst restoring confidence within the squad.

Blackheath were the visitors for the next match, and at no-side, there were cautious smiles at St. Helens as the visitors trooped off having been beaten by 16 points to 6. Roger Hyndman scored two tries on that occasion, and was the outstanding forward on view. Given that the victory was the second in succession, the optimists at St. Helens must have hoped that they could see the beginnings of a revival. Whilst that did not prove to be the case, at least it heralded a period in the season when more games were won than lost.

As Saunders Lewis was nominated for the Nobel Prize for literature, and the Driver and Vehicle Licensing centre was opened in Swansea, Ron Griffiths could not have been accused of poetic licence as he castigated the W.R.U. He had the whole of Swansea's rugby fraternity behind him. The controversy concerned the visit of the New Zealand tourists. A press leak had suggested that Swansea was not going to be included in the Kiwis' itinerary, but would have to join with Neath to provide a combined XV. At the time, the Union would not comment, other than to say that no decision had been made as to which clubs would face the tourists. Clearly, the W.R.U. had been taking lessons from politicians in the 'vague-speak' language. Griffiths,

Roger Hyndman – determined try scorer.

rejecting that statement, argued that it was disgusting that the Union had arrived at such a decision without even consulting the Swansea club. In Swansea there was talk of raising a petition and sending a delegation to Cardiff. The truth, though, as the future was to show, was that eastern minds had been made up. Swansea would either combine or not be involved in the tour. All the arguments about tradition and the standing of the Swansea club came to nought. It was a veritable slap in the face for the stalwarts at St. Helens, and the management there felt that they had no alternative other than to decide not to combine.

Meantime, there was a further departure from St. Helens. John Davies, a Welsh trialist centre, moved to Stradey Park. On top of that, injuries continued to mount, which resulted in the club having to field 'patchwork sides'. Not that they, necessarily, performed badly. Despite the problems, victories over Coventry and Richmond lifted morale, as did newspaper comment that flankers, Roger Hyndman and Trevor Evans were worthy of consideration by the national selectors. In addition there was better news regarding the injured. Skipper, Phil Llewellyn and lock, Mike James came back from injury for the game at Richmond, whilst other casualties were said to be on the mend. All in all, the situation appeared to be improving, and Swansea heads were held higher than they had been for some time. Once again, Ieuan Evans used the press to boost the confidence of his charges. He was delighted, he told the media, that there was tremendous competition for places in the pack.

Perhaps that pronouncement struck a collective chord, for, in the next match, Christmas came early to St. Helens. The *Post* noted that 'everyone clicked' as the 'Whites' scored fifty points in a 'ten try spectacular'. In that match, wing, Martin Davies, scored a hat-trick of tries in the second-half, Clive Roderick's distribution was said to have been outstanding, and Trevor Jones, Roger Blyth, Roger Hyndman, John Roberts and Morrie Evans all crossed to score. The Swansea dressing room was jubilant that day, though the more thoughtful may have stopped to wonder what makes such days possible? Why does it only happen occasionally? What is it that makes fifteen men combine with dreamlike simplicity on one occasion, yet stumble and stutter on another? If any reader can supply the answer, the author will be pleased to bottle the product and market it (carefully) only to sides which are not on the Swansea fixture list.

At the turn of the year, Mervyn Davies, who had played for the 'Whites' over the Christmas period, denied that he was homesick for Swansea; the club was continuing its fight to be included in the itinerary for the visit of the New Zealanders; and Trevor Evans was selected for the Probables in the first Welsh trial. As far as results were concerned, they were disappointing, with both Christmas games and that on New Year's Day being lost. As the *Post* put it, 'The only Christmas cheer at St. Helens was the £1,400 "gate" derived from the London Welsh match'. The crowd that day was the largest recorded at St. Helens since the Romanian game in 1953.

Thereafter, the 'Whites' proved to be as inconsistent as ever. A five match winning run was followed by three consecutive defeats, and two wins 'on the trot' by four successive losses. Yet there were highlights which would have graced any season. Among them was a cliff-hanging triumph over the Barbarians, and an excellent 22 points to 0 victory over Neath. Progress in the Challenge Cup, however, was halted at the Quarter Final stage by a determined Llanelli side. Consequently, with nothing to show for all the effort which had been expended to improve matters, the season's record was disappointing. Almost half the games which had been played had been lost.

Nonetheless, whilst that was true, the 'atmosphere' at St. Helens was surprisingly positive. There appeared to be collective phlegmatic view that, like the popular song, it had been just one of those things. Ancient adages about water under the bridge were quoted widely, and the general view was that the effort should be put into improving things for the future rather than worrying about the past. Whilst neither of these options is mutually exclusive, with the Centenary Year in view, the St. Helens management did not have time to mope. Apart from anything else, Bruce Barter's steering committee had its hands full in planning the many events which were scheduled for the special season. As far as the players were concerned, Ieuan Evans made sure that the press noted his pleasure at the development of some of the younger men. Among those mentioned by the coach was Geoff Wheel who, as he gained in experience, was maturing into a fine forward. David Protheroe was another, and many sound judges believed that he would become and international. Indeed, Swansea's own Clem Thomas went so far as to say that the young man was 'the best fly-half at Swansea since Bryan Richards'.

1972-73

The patient responds

When, at the end of September, the 'Whites' remained unbeaten in the new campaign, Ieuan Evans was delighted. Not only were his charges undefeated, they had won all eight matches played, scoring 264 points in the process and conceding only 53. Among the defeated teams were Internationale Roma, and Frescati, clubs which the 'Whites' had met on their short Italian tour. Unfortunately, though, whilst the party was in Italy, matters off the field attracted greater attention than those on. Indeed, after a fracas involving a gang of Italian youths, the Roman police were involved. Happily, however, the party returned home with a full complement of players and, in due course, following an enquiry, the members of the 'Whites' party were exonerated. Seventeen year old David Richards, who had been taken on the tour for experience, must have wondered whether that was the kind of thing his mentors had in mind?

Mervyn Davies – ready to 'Swerve'.

Notwithstanding the impact of that contretemps on the men in white, plus a demanding travel itinerary and two hard matches, the 'Whites' returned home in sufficient shape to beat both a strong Newport side and Ebbw Vale. Swansea's supporters could hardly believe their eyes; not only were their favourites consistent, they were consistently good. The management were delighted. Indeed, had Vivian Davies, the new Chairman, been a cat he would have been purring loudly. All else apart, when he looked at the team sheet for a 'Whites' match, he saw the name T. M. Davies at number 8. Mervyn was home! Rumour had become reality. The player had secured a post in Swansea and, like his father before him, he was available to play for his home city. Not surprisingly, Mervyn's arrival gave additional impetus to everything that was going on at St. Helens. He was a world-class player, and, as the chairman of the city's soccer club pointed out when it was announced that 'The Swerve' was coming home, had he been a footballer he would have cost £400,000 (the top soccer transfer fee at the time).

Apart from the more conspicuous Davies, another of the ilk had returned to St. Helens from Llanelli, and a new second-row, Barry Clegg had thrown in his lot with the Swansea club. As the old saw has it, success breeds success, and with Mervyn Davies at St. Helens it was more likely that other talented players would wish to become part of a winning squad.

Not surprisingly, at the end of the first week in October, the 'Whites' sat proudly at the top of the Merit Table. At the time nothing seemed to be impossible and the optimists, at least, dreamed about a successful campaign and silverware in the St. Helens display cabinet.

There was one weakness, though. Place kicking was a problem. In the emergency, scrum-half Robert Dyer had been coerced into undertaking the kicking duties, even though he argued that it was not his forte. On 12 October he had to be persuaded to undertake other duties, too. Mel James, to use the old phrase, 'took the bribers gold' and went north. That was a blow for the Swansea club, for James was an outstanding forward who would go on to achieve a great deal in the professional game. Had he stayed in Swansea, who knows what the class of '72 might have achieved? In his absence, Dyer became captain and Mervyn Davies his vice.

Two days after James had left, and in the absence of Mervyn Davies, the 'Whites' lost their unbeaten record. It was a close run thing, though. Playing at Stradey, and with less than two minutes to go, the men in white looked as though they were going to win yet again. John Roberts had just crossed for a try which gave the 'Whites' the lead. The referee had looked at his watch, when there was an infringement which resulted in the 'Scarlets' being given a penalty. Unfortunately for the Swansea men, Gwyn Ashby sent the ball sailing between the uprights. The scoreboard registered Llanelli 13 Abertawe 11. Swansea were no longer unbeaten.

Back at St. Helens, Vivian Davies thanked the Supporters' Club for their generosity in providing the team with a srummaging machine. As the Chairman put it, given the strength and ability of the 'Whites' pack, the machine would allow them to hone their skills to an even greater degree.

By the middle of November, when Cross Keys were beaten in the first round of the Challenge Cup by 28 points to 7, the lack of an effective place kicker in the side was apparent to everyone. In that match with the 'Keys', the 'Whites' scored six tries, none of which were converted, and were awarded five penalties, all of which were missed. Whilst the weakness did not affect the result of that match, it was the reason why the next game (against Coventry) was lost.

Nonetheless, up to that point, despite this problem, the match statistics for the season made happy reading for all at St. Helens. The side had played 19 matches, won 14 drawn 1 and lost 4, and the points count stood at: for 461, against 196. Furthermore, the club was still in the Cup, seemed likely to progress to the final of the Floodlight Alliance competition, and was well-placed in the Merit Table. Consequently, the positive thinkers were arguing that, at the end of the campaign, the 'Whites' were going to bring some silverware to St. Helens.

Apart from the satisfaction which such thoughts brought to the Swansea committee, they were delighted to note the splendid progress being made by people like Geoff Wheel, and the dedication of hooker, Alan Mages, who had missed only two of the matches played by the club up to that point in the season. Apart from his hooking, Mages was proving to be a lively forward in maul and ruck, and about the field. He was in his element against Richmond, when he took three strikes against the head, all of which resulted in tries. Indeed, the hooker was on hand to take a Mark Keyworth pass and score one of them himself.

In what the *Post* called 'Ieuan Evans's New Year Message', the coach built upon the positive noises which had been coming from St. Helens as the season progressed. 'My aim' he said, 'is to get the ball moving by using the wings to stretch defences ... I'm sure that this can be done and that we shall end the season on a positive note'. At that, Dick Jones, Billy Trew and Dickie Owen must have joined in the heavenly chorus of approval as they relished the thought of 'Swansea football' being played.

In the first month of the new year, after 42 points had been scored against the Police, Newport came to St. Helens for a third round cup tie. At half-time, with the 'Usksiders' leading by 3 points to nil, there were those who doubted the practicability, in a cup game, of fulfilling the coach's desires. Furthermore, their doubts would have been reinforced when Arwel Rees was carried off. Yet, Swansea's fourteen men had other ideas. Robert Dyer kicked an equalising penalty five minutes into the second period, then Darryl Cole broke through a gap in the Newport defence to feed Phil Llewellyn, who scored a fine try. After that, the game took on a new complexion, and the 'Whites' played a more expansive game, which resulted in their increasing the points total to 24. The 'Whites' were in the fourth round of the Cup! Furthermore, the Newport match had given the Swansea committee an unexpected bonus. Robert Dyer had made a mockery of the so-called 'Whites' Achilles heel; he was successful with most of the place kicks, even one from the 'wrong' touch line.

In the year of the 'Oil Crisis', a February highlight for the 'Whites' was a 'storming victory' over Gloucester. The *Observer* reported that 'Gloucester reeled before the onslaught of a rampant Swansea pack'. All eight were in form, but the outstanding trio among them was the rampant back-row of Mark Keyworth, Mervyn Davies and Trevor Evans. Among the backs Robert Dyer and David Protheroe flourished behind a winning eight and, as if to show that Ieuan Evans's plan was not just a pipe-dream, wings, Steve Thornton (4) and Hywel Griffiths (3) ran in all the tries of the day. Next Bristol conceded 23 points and Llanelli 14, as the 'Whites' flourished during this winning streak. Then in March, the men-in-white took Neath's ground record. With the club in the semi-final of the Welsh Cup, reasonably well-placed in the Merit Table, and with an interest in the Floodlight Alliance final, at that time nothing seemed to be impossible.

Not surprisingly, the players were growing in confidence. Barry Clegg out-jumped the great Delme Thomas when Llanelli were defeated at St. Helens, Phil Llewewllyn was 'capped' against Ireland, Robert Dyer was ' playing well enough to take anybody on', and Roger Blyth's performances at full-back were 'being applauded in many quarters'. Dyer, the stand-in captain, Ieuan Evans and the committee, must have thought that the world was their oyster.

Unfortunately, at Aberavon in the semi-final of the Welsh Cup, no pearl was found in the opened mollusc. Cardiff, clearly not having read the St. Helens script, won a bruising match by 12 points to 8. Swansea supporters consoled themselves with the thought that had the 'rub-of-the-green' favoured the 'Whites', then they would have won the tie. But fortune remains an active ingredient in the chemistry of most games. Thus it was that, in the parlance of soccer managers, from then on, the 'Whites' could concentrate on winning the Merit Table and the final of the Floodlight Alliance competition. The majority of the St. Helens management (and the press, for that matter) were confident that Swansea's name would be etched on at least one of these trophies.

Unfortunately, in due course, that confidence was shown to have been misplaced. The 'Whites' lost to Llanelli in the final of the Floodlight Alliance, and were 'pipped at the post' in the Merit Table competition. Nonetheless, despite these disappointments, there was an air of quiet satisfaction at the Cricket Field. The side had won more matches than ever before (34), had scored more than double the points which they conceded, new young players coming through had justified their potential, and, then, there was the mouth-watering prospect of David Richards, the schoolboy outside-half. Many astute judges had said that he was 'going to be something special'. Robert Dyer had scored 162 points, whilst Darryl Cole headed the try scorers (with 16). The dwindling number of pessimists in the Swansea camp were lost for words. The best they could do was to question the longevity of the Swansea revival. Had they put their thoughts into words, they would have asked, is this another false dawn? Would the patient have a relapse during the next campaign? The point was, that, as a result of the Swansea club's post-war history, 'Whites' supporters had become inured to an expectation of inconsistency and broken dreams. The increasing band of optimists, though, pushed such thoughts to the back of their minds. This time it would be different! Surely!

1973-74

100 not out – on merit

Prior to the start of the new season, Bruce Barter and his colleagues outlined their plans for the many events which were going to be enjoyed during the Centenary season. The list was impressive, and all connected with the club looked forward to participating in the hundredth birthday celebrations. Meantime, Ieuan Evans and his committee knew that they were expected to deliver success to the club's supporters in keeping with what was going on off the field. Given that opposing teams would be doing their best to ensure that the 'Whites' were not successful, theirs was the more complex task. The desired outcome, though, could have been described by any Swansea supporter in few words. Swansea R.F.C. would be successful on and off the field. The objective was easily understood. The task of achieving it was much more difficult.

On the field, the first major match was that against the Fijians on 8 September 1973. Those who were there saw the tourists 'cut loose' in the second-half to win comfortably. Despite the fact that the 'Whites' were defeated, the crowd enjoyed the flowing play of the islanders and, at the end of the match, showed their appreciation with warm applause. As a matter of record, the Swansea men that day were no longer clad in all white. The team turned out in a smart narrow-hooped jersey in the club's colours greyish white (to approximate silver), blue and red, with the Centenary symbol on the chest. Chairman, Viv Davies explained that the symbol – an osprey - had been chosen because of its speed, grace, commitment and beauty in flight – a pictorial metaphor for Swansea's brand of rugby.

At outside-half for that game against the Fijians was David Richards, who, after playing superbly for the Welsh Secondary Schools, had been likened by the press to a young Barry John. Ieuan Evans did all he could to defuse that particular situation, for it was a ridiculous burden to place on such young shoulders. Richards, however, showed that he was mature enough not to let the comparison bother him. Against the Fijians, Cross Keys and Bristol he played intelligent football and, indeed, scored a fine try against the West Countrymen. The committee, players and supporters liked what they saw. Leaving Barry John aside, the knowledgeable were convinced that they had been watching a player of exceptional ability.

In early October, when playing the 'Quins at the Stoop', the 'Whites' maintained their unbeaten away record in a match in which Roger Blyth made his mark as a place kicker. The highlight of that match, though, was a fine Alan Lewis try, which involved the player side-stepping three would- be tacklers to plunge over. After that match, the club's playing record read: P.9 W.6 D.1 L.2. Whilst not quite as good as at the same stage in the previous campaign, it was sound enough to give supporters the 'feel good factor' so sought-after by modern-day poli-

The 1973-74 side in Centenary colours.

ticians. As it transpired, that was achieved when, after losing to Bristol in mid-September, the side went thirteen matches without defeat. Among those matches was a fine 9 points-all draw with the touring Australians.

On that occasion in front of a 15,000 crowd, the Swansea pack was outstanding. Indeed, such was their power that, when the third minute of injury time had been played, the home side led by 9 points to 6. Sadly, a minute later, a Swansea man offended, and Jeff McLean kicked his third penalty of the match to put his side level. It had been a close-run-thing for the men from 'Down-under'. When the final whistle sounded the scoreboard registered a draw. As far as the Swansea supporters were concerned, though, as they made their way home, they made the case to their own satisfaction, that the homesters had won the match. At least, the argument went, the Swansea boys had won a moral victory! Whilst all the Australian points had come from penalties, the 'Whites' had crossed the tourists line for a fine try.

That try was worth recalling! From a scrum just inside the Australian half, Dyer broke right and passed to Protheroe. The outside-half turned inside two would-be tacklers and slipped a beautifully timed pass to Mike Yandle, who burst through the cover to score under the posts. Roger Blyth converted and, subsequently, kicked a 35 yard penalty to give Swansea the lead. Had the final whistle blown then, the 'Whites' would have added a further tourist scalp to their belt. In the event, McLean's intervention ensured that the fairy tale did not have such a happy ending.

The Swansea men who represented the new city on that proud day were:
R. Blyth, G. Jones, D. Cole, M. Yandle, G. Higgins; D. Protheroe, R. Dyer (Capt.), P. D. Llewellyn, A. Mages, N. Webb, B. Clegg, G. Wheel, M. Keyworth, T. M. Davies and T. Evans.

The result of that match meant that the overall record of games with the Australian touring sides was evenly balanced. It read: P.5 W.2 L.2 D.1 F.38 A.40

The next two domestic matches, in the W.R.U. Cup and the Floodlight Alliance, were both won comfortably, but, thereafter there were mixed fortunes until the Christmas period. At that time, because of the oil crisis, the traditional U.A.U. match was cancelled, but, subsequently, 1974 began with a sequence of five consecutive wins. Among them was a 27 points to 19 victory over Neath (to do the 'double'). That game was a triumph for Alan Mages, who had a hand in all four tries, scoring two himself. On that occasion the press was fulsome in its praise of the Swansea pack, and behind them, of Yandle, Morgan, Gerwyn Jones and Blyth.

Meanwhile, off the field, in conjunction with the Centenary celebrations Bruce Barter and his committee mounted several events. Among them was one which was to result in a much-envied organisation being established. Horace Phillips was given the task of bringing together former Swansea players. It was a task which necessitated the detective skills of a Sherlock Holmes and the tenacity of a bull terrier. After a great deal of effort, Horace arranged an inaugural dinner, in the Patti Pavilion, of what was to become the Swansea 'Former Players' Association. For the first time, players of different eras, linked together by the fact that they had all pulled on Swansea's first team jersey, gathered together. It was a special night in the annals of the St. Helens club. Unfortunately, though, the energetic Phillips, after all his hard work, was struck down with tonsillitis and was unable to attend. He missed a remarkable night. Since that time, under the energetic stewardship of Dil Johnson, the Association has been the means by which former players are kept in touch with matters St. Helens.

Happily, at the time of that first dinner, the 'Whites' were sitting proudly at the top of the Merit Table. In that competition their record was enviable. Of the nine matches played they had won eight and drawn the other. C. C. (Charlie) Chambers, Fred Meager and the rest of the club's pioneers must have looked down proudly at their successors. The St. Helens management team was, also, more than pleased. Surely, the argument went, at the end of this campaign we shall have some silverware in our showcase to celebrate the centenary in style!

1974 saw a change to local government boundaries which would put an end to one perennial schoolboy quiz question. No longer would Monmouthshire players be able to choose whether to be English or Welsh for international rugby purposes. Newport now found itself in Gwent – a Welsh county. The 'Whites' were also relocated. They were, now, residents of West Glamorgan. Thus, when the Newport side came to St. Helens on 12 January to compete with Swansea in the third round of the Welsh cup, both teams were representing new counties. Unfortunately for the men from Gwent, they found the 'Whites' in tenacious form. In particular, the home back-row of Evans, Davies and Hyndman was outstanding in that game, Clegg dominated the lines-out, and young David Richards showed that the tackling aspect of his game was on a par with his flair and distribution. It was Robert Dyer, however, who scored the winning points, kicking a penalty five minutes after the start and another five minutes before the final whistle. As the 6 points to 0 score suggested, it had been a hard-fought match and the 'Whites' had demonstrated their steel as well as their supportive organisation.

The win caused some Swansea supporters to dream about winning the Cup. For the more romantic it was right and proper that, in their centenary year, their favourites should do just that. Unfortunately, despite having Roger Blyth back from injury, Cardiff, the 'Whites' quarter final opponents, had ideas of their own. The 'Blue and Blacks' won a hard-fought match, though the Swansea supporters, searching for comfort from the outcome, could point to an injury to prop, Neil Webb in the first ten minutes of the match as one factor. After that, Webb, gamely, remained on the pitch but spent the match hobbling from one scrum to the next. Ieuan Evans, however, would have no truck with excuses. He said, 'We were not good enough on the day'. Swansea rugbyites had to accept that, whilst there would be other days in which the side might make amends, the 'Whites' would not be in the final of that season's Welsh Cup competition.

Yet, the supporters could savour the quality of some of the players in the Swansea side. Geoff Wheel, for example, was in tremendous form, ripping the ball out of mauls with an alacrity which made him one of the most feared forwards in the game. Nor was this ability lost on the Welsh selectors. They selected him to play against Ireland (joining Phil Llewellyn and Mervyn Davies). It was another accolade for the St. Helens club, another indication of the improvements which had been wrought, and a positive comment on the quality of the Swansea squad. Laughingly, coach, Ieuan Evans noted that he had been a couple of seasons out with his forecast about when the soccer convert would be 'capped'. 'He's come on faster than I dared hope.'

Before the season ended there were several matches in which, as Ron Griffiths put it, 'The 'Whites' clicked'. Indeed, they must have clicked like a set of castanets, for, following the cup defeat, the side lost only five matches of the seventeen which were played. Among – the days when the 'clicking' was most apparent was one in March, when Bath were overrun by an outstanding 'Whites' XV. The men in white scored 36 points – all with a flourish – as they brushed aside the Avonsiders. Most of Swansea's seven tries were notable that day. Gerwyn Jones helped himself to a hat-trick and was involved in others, whilst Protheroe, at outside-half, and centre, Cole both featured in several of the 'expansive tries' that were scored. It was vintage 'Swansea stuff' and, if the old ground could have spoken, as the players left the field, it would have joined in the sustained applause. Whilst the backs 'grabbed the glory that day, the victory was based upon a 'majestic pack' with an outstanding back-row of Evans, Davies and Hyndman. Uninhibited, Ron Griffiths called them 'world-class'.

Another crowd-pleasing performance was given in the match against the New Zealand club, Ponsonby (also celebrating its centenary). On that occasion, 46 points were shared in an 'end-to-end contest which was hugely enjoyed by the crowd'. From the Swansea point of view, a home victory by six points was 'just what the doctor ordered'. Then there was the match against the W.R.U. President's XV in which the Swansea men, in their centenary garb, scored half a century of points in some style.

Towards the end of the season, a fixture pile-up (due to postponements) provided the St. Helens committee with problems. As a result, the last two matches on the Centenary calendar had to be played in early May. Happily, at that time the 'Whites' stood at the top of the Merit Table, a position which was confirmed as a result of the side winning the last two games. Swansea had won the accolade by playing all Merit Table teams twice. Thus it was that their championship was undisputed. No contrived, single special game this, the competition had been won on merit!

At the club's A.G.M. in June 1974, coach, Ieuan Evans praised the players for their efforts during the previous season. He congratulated them on their 'tremendous team spirit' and the fact that they 'had come a long way together'. His next statement, though, was the one which captured the attention of supporters of Swansea rugby. 'With a little luck we can outshine the best in Britain. Next year will see the zenith of our efforts.'

Had the coach been a seasoned politician, he might not have made such a statement. As specialists in that field are taught from an early age, concrete promises, more often than not, become hostages to fortune. Of course, Evans did say 'the zenith of our efforts'. He did not mention results, *per se*. However, there were those there that day with selective hearing. They would have focused upon the first sentence rather than the last. 'We can outshine the best in Britain!' That was what they wanted to hear! Had they noted the second sentence, it is probable that they would have taken 'Zenith' as meaning 'the tops'.

1974–75

A slight hiccough

Alan Mages, elected captain for the season ahead, was expansive as he contemplated the campaign. He enthused about the club's internationals, including Roger Blyth, who had set a new record by scoring 252 points during the previous season. David Richards, he thought, would wear the red shirt of Wales in the not-too-distant future, whilst the younger men in the pack, like Geoff Wheel and Barry Clegg would 'go a long way'. He was to be proved right on several counts.

During the close season, Mervyn Davies had toured with the Lions and was not available for the early matches of the new term. Not that that seemed to have affected the 'Whites'. After the first four matches, all won in style, the points record read: F.104 A.39. It was as if the 'Golden Era' had returned. Even the pessimists began to think that Ieuan Evans's 'zenith' might be achievable. However, the outcome of a visit to Bristol put the earlier results into perspective. Not surprisingly, the team found that other sides, aware of the Swansea record during the previous season as well as the side's reputation, 'lifted' their game when they played the 'Whites'. In Bristol's case they did that so well that the 'Whites' were beaten by 22 points to 12. It was a salutary lesson for the young side. They were to learn from it.

In the middle of October, if they hadn't learnt the lesson then they were to have further opportunities to do so. Fine wins against Penarth, Newport and the Harlequins were interspersed with defeats by Bridgend and Llanelli, both of which were hard-fought. There was a close-run-thing too in a St. Helens match with Leicester, when Roger Blyth kicked a match-winning penalty ten minutes from no-side. Prior to that kick, the 'Tigers' had defended their line in a manner in keeping with their nickname. Conversely, the 'Whites' confronted with such an effective defence, made errors born of their frustration. At least, though, the home ground record was safe.

At that stage in the season, the selectors were faced with a mounting injury list. In a victory over Neath, the side finished with thirteen men. Gerwyn Jones broke a collar bone, and John Morgan came off with a damaged leg. Furthermore, both Phil Llewellyn and Mark Keyworth were 'in the wars', and Barry Clegg was in Morriston Hospital with a back problem. One result of this was that Mike James was asked to come out of retirement to help fill the gap at a time when his business activities were calling for more of his attention.

Notwithstanding these problems, there were some fine winning sequences during this period. Indeed, seven consecutive wins were recorded. Among the notable victories was a magnificent win at Blackheath, where the home side were beaten by 21 points to 7. It was the second-half performance which caught the eye that day. Among the tries which were scored was one which

Mike James about to pounce?

the *Post* referred to as 'memorable'. It came after Hopkins and Tyrrell had worked a scissors move and then fed Dyer. The scrum-half drew his man before serving Protheroe, who side-stepped the full-back to score. It was a try straight out of the Swansea manual. Against Llanelli 'injury-hit Swansea showed sterling character as fourteen men won a rousing match'. Roger Blyth was 'king of the scorers' that day, scoring 19 of the 21 points recorded by the 'Whites'. After that game, skipper Mages praised his men for their outstanding team spirit and for their quality rugby. Indeed, had Napoleon been at St. Helens on that memorable day, he could have rested his case concerning *esprit de corps* and successful armies, by citing that Swansea victory.

After a successful Christmas period, when London Welsh, Percy Park and Glamorgan Wanderers were defeated, the side travelled to Scotland for a New Year's Day match with old adversaries, 'Watsonians'. Perhaps it was a match too far. The 'Whites' were beaten by 34 points to 9. Nevertheless, in domestic football, after beating Newbridge in the middle of December, the side strengthened its grip on the first place in the Merit Table. Among those most prominent during a sequence of ten wins, were skipper, Alan Mages, Mervyn Davies and David Richards – who was available during the Christmas vacation, and was maturing 'faster than Swansea had dared hope'.

Robert Dyer, protected by Trevor Evans, v. Pyle (W.R.U. Cup).

Unfortunately, mid-January saw the 'Whites' being beaten at Pontypool (when 'everyone thought that they would win'), and losing to Newport, at Rodney Parade in the third round of the Welsh cup competition. The *Post* reported that 'Swansea were shattered by these defeats, and now face the task of picking themselves up and recharging their batteries'.

At that stage, the general consensus of opinion had it that the 'Whites' had a slight chance of retaining their Merit Table title. The truth was, though, that even the optimists had a diminished view of what was meant by 'slight'. Furthermore, despite the buoyant leadership of Mages, and the positive attitude of the coach, it appeared that the spirit in the Swansea camp was 'lower than it has been for some time'. Some said that 'personalities' were at odds there, but, whatever the cause, in a surprisingly short time, sweetness and light had been replaced by something less attractive. Thus it was that, when a powerful Coventry side came to St. Helens at the end of January, the expectations of the loyal Swansea following were, to say the least, modest.

In the event, when half-time arrived in that match with a nil-nil scoreboard, not even the most rabid optimist could have foreseen what was about to happen. Within two minutes of the restart, David Protheroe scored a fine 'solo' try. Minutes later, Robert Dyer fed David Jenkins and 'there developed a brilliant pattern of passing; at least six players were involved, some twice, before Dyer took the final pass to dive over'. At the end, 'the crowd were breathless'. Coventry were bemused, having suffered one of their heaviest defeats. The door of the home dressing room had hardly closed behind the last player off the pitch, when Ieuan Evans burst in to congratulate his charges. 'Coventry', he told the elated Swansea men, 'said that we are the best team they have met this season.'

When the 'Whites' lost their next match (at Ebbw Vale), the exciting defeat of Coventry was but a memory. The Vale won by a single penalty to nil, and left the Swansea supporters grumbling that it looked as if the players were different from those who had swamped the Midlanders. There was concern, too, in the next match, when, at half-time, according to Trevor Dargavel, 'Swansea were shaken by the 4 points to 15 deficit'. However, whatever was said at lemon-time stirred the Swansea players into action. The pack gained the ascendancy over the Neath eight, and did not lose it until no side. As a result, scrum-half, Huw Davies 'blossomed and, using his guile and strength, brought the 'Whites' backs into play'. In that second-half he was inspirational, bringing the Swansea supporters to their feet as he charged down a clearance kick, ran cleverly, drew his man and sent Mark Keyworth over to score. When the final whistle had been blown, the 'Whites' had scored 22 points in that second period while the 'All Blacks' did not add to their half-time total.

After losing a match at Gloucester in driving rain and clinging mud, some of the old confidence seemed to return, as, indeed did Phil Llewellyn who played his first 1975 game following his long lay off. During this period, the 'Whites' won six games in succession. Among the clubs which were beaten at this time, were Bristol and Bridgend. In the Bristol match, Phil Llewellyn, Barry Clegg and Mervyn Davies dominated the lines-out, and, at Bridgend, Mike James was carried off on a stretcher, but surprised everyone by coming back ten minutes later to hobble through the remainder of the game. It was to be the big man's last appearance in a Swansea shirt, and in keeping with his approach to the game and to the club, he kept going until the final whistle. Whilst James finished playing on that day in Bridgend, in the not-too-distant future, he was to give the club great service off the field.

In March, the Welsh selectors asked the club to play David Richards at outside-half in a match against Northampton. In that game, the young man grasped his opportunity with both hands. In a 47 points to 0 victory, he scored two tries himself and was involved in several others. His line kicking was excellent, as was his defensive work. The young man had 'arrived'. Clearly, the Welsh selectors who were present felt the same way; Richards was invited to train with the Welsh squad at Afan Lido.

Between then and the end of the season, results were mixed. The Harlequins and Cross Keys each had 28 points scored against them in games in which Geoff Wheel and Alan Mages were outstanding. Phil Llewellyn, however, not long back after injury, snapped an achilles tendon and was obliged to have his leg in plaster for eight weeks. It was the end of his season, some said of his career, and the 'Whites' were to miss him. At Cardiff, the Swansea team had what Ron Griffiths called, 'One of their off-days', whilst, at Newport the home team won a hard-fought match by a single point.

Most of the end-of-term reports in the press had a similar theme. Swansea had disappointed. The *Western Mail* pointed to the forward talent at St. Helens, and concluded that they had not fulfilled their promise. The *Post* commented on a 'disturbing inconsistency', and on a 'rumbling discontent' in the Swansea camp – among others, David Protheroe had left St. Helens. Long-time 'Whites' supporters were very familiar with that particular malady. However, Ron Griffiths, whilst recalling that 'every so often the "Whites" turn it on, and have their supporters glowing with pride', felt that, 'with five internationals in the side' the record was not good enough. Even he, though, had to agree that it had been far better than in the 'dark days of the 1960's'. All comparisons, after all, are relative.

Chapter Twenty-Three

A REGROUPING

1975-76

THE STATISTICIANS AMONG THE Swansea rugby faithful had to go back to 1962-63 to find a season during which fewer games were played by the 'Whites' than in the 1975-76 campaign. They would have noted, too, that of the forty-two which were played, forty per cent were lost, which did not compare favourably with the proportion of defeats in the previous season. Furthermore, only twenty-three games were won, the lowest total since 1969-70. Nevertheless, with the benefit of hindsight, they may well have perceived that the '75-'76 season was, what the military would call, a time of 'regrouping'. That theory suggests that, sometimes, it is necessary to retreat and re-form your resources before you advance again. Given that over the five seasons which were to follow, the 'Whites' were to achieve some long-cherished objectives, the 'officers' at St. Helens must have managed the process very effectively.

At the start of the season the 'Whites' were without five key players. New captain, Mervyn Davies, Roger Blyth, Barry Clegg, Trevor Evans and Geoff Wheel were with the Welsh side which was touring Hong Kong and Japan. In their absence, Baden Evans was to have stood in for Mervyn, but, unfortunately, Baden was a casualty before he kicked a ball in anger. Thus it was that Neil Webb took over the captaincy pending Mervyn Davies's return. Webb found himself working with a new coach for, following the resignation of Ieuan Evans, Stan Addicott took on the task. Stan, in praising the work done by his predecessor, said that he wished to build upon all the good which had been done. Not surprisingly, though, the new man brought with him his own methods and his own 'style'. In many ways, he was less prescriptive and more participative in his approach than Evans had been. As a consequence, when the 'Whites' began their preparation for the season's programme, they had a new management team and a different style of leadership. The ethos, however, remained the same; 'Swansea rugby' would be played whenever possible! No doubt, as the pundits suggested, there would be a period during which the new organisation 'bedded-down', but with so many familiar faces in the camp that was not expected to be a problem for long.

After a 'warm-up' game against Dunvant, when the 'Whites' scored 58 points, Cross Keys came to St. Helens and conceded 'a bagful of tries'. Ian Hopkins, in particular, enjoyed himself that day, scoring three tries and converting six. Whilst, at the time, Hopkins was not aware of the fact, in scoring twenty-four points in the match he had set a new club record (beating Roger Blyth's total by a point).

After the game, Neil Webb and Stan Addicott found themselves fending off the great expectations of both press and public. Both men tried to play down the victories , the manner in which they were gained and the extent of the team's superiority over their opponents. Addicott, however, joined with Webb in agreeing that the management team were quietly confident about the season ahead. Both men felt that the club had quality in depth in most positions, and had to concede that they had been 'pleased' with performances in the opening matches.

They were right to be cautious. Since the war, the 'Whites' had started several seasons with a glut of tries and exciting rugby, only to stumble when they met opponents of better quality. Indeed, it had seemed as if the team had made a habit of flattering to deceive.

September 1975 provided the cautious with a further reasons to be conservative in their expectations. Ebbw Vale, for whom the date (the 13th) must have been lucky, beat the 'Whites' and took their ground record in a game dominated by the boot of Stephen Lewis. Despite having far more possession than their opponents, the Swansea men had not been able to turn it into points. Bristol, the next visitors, were also victorious in playing against a 'Whites' side which, according to the press, was 'disjointed'. That defeat caused further doubts to emerge in the minds of Swansea supporters, for the win was Bristol's first of the season.

At the end of September, the *Western Mail*, commenting upon the side's indifferent form, argued that the absence of the quintet of internationals was a key factor. Ron Griffiths, following a similar line, suggested that when the five returned they would make a 'a huge difference' to Swansea's fortunes. Long suffering 'Whites' supporters grasped the hope which was implied in the argument with alacrity. The logic was inescapable, wasn't it? With, probably, the best third of the side unavailable it would have been surprising had the absence of these players not affected performances.

Yet doubts crept into the collective mind of Swansea supporters. As one commuting professional man put it to the author, 'At that time I'd come home from the city on Friday evening relaxed and confident and return on the Monday tense and exhausted'. The humour was not without its irony.

Happily, as if to prove the argument, when the five returned to the fold, results improved immediately. Indeed, during October and up to the match against the touring Australians, only one game was lost out of the ten which were played. That was more like it! During this period, Wayne Williams and Roy Woodward did well, whilst Roger Blyth was playing a sound game at outside-half. Whilst reluctant to move from the full-back position, Blyth realised that the club had two competent full-backs besides himself, but, in the absence of David Richards, no outside-half of similar quality. As a result, the versatile Blyth was pressed into service in the fulcrum position. Stan Addicott recognised the player's dilemma, but, as he told the press, 'The last thing we want to do is to ruin his chances of further honours at full-back, but it is difficult to know what we are to do'. Addicott, and every Swansea supporter believed the answer to the problem lay with David Richards. Unfortunately, though, his college had first call on his services. The 'Whites' would have to wait.

It was the last home match before the Australian game which provided Swansea supporters with the kind of gleeful satisfaction which matched their early season hopes. A strong Coventry side were beaten by 21 points to 16 in a St. Helens 'thriller'. That match, if it could be repeated, would not only satisfy the craving of loyal 'Whites' supporters, it was of the kind to bring back to St. Helens lapsed followers in their thousands. It was watched by both English and Welsh selectors, and what they saw must have left them with the assurance that, in the two cities which were represented that day, British rugby was alive and thriving.

In the match, Coventry took the lead, but minutes later, after good work by Richards and Williams, Woodward, tenacious as ever, surged down the left wing, kicked ahead, followed up and scored a breathless try. Whilst Preece and Duckham then gave the visitors the advantage, the 'Whites' did even better. Two John Rees penalties and a try by Trevor Evans – who barged through three attempted tackles – gave the 'homesters' the match. It had been one of the games which Ron Griffiths had written about at the end of the previous season. Swansea supporters made their way home after the match sated with memories of rugby excellence, and warmed by the glow of victory.

The game played by the 'Whites' on the Saturday before the tourist match was at Richmond, when the team maintained its 'winning streak' – just. Indeed, the press suggested that they had to hang on grimly during the last quarter of the game. Happily, Mervyn Davies rallied his men and Swansea emerged the victors.

Thus it was that, when the Australians came to Swansea they met a side which had won its previous six matches. With 'invalids' Blyth and Wheel back from their sick-beds, the team was at full strength and there was an air of quiet confidence at St. Helens. Could the club add to its impressive record against touring sides? Whilst doubt lingered at the back of their minds, many supporters felt that the team was better than that which had drawn with the 'Wallabies' on their last visit. If that was the case, the argument went, then there was a good chance that their favourites would win. Such thinking, of course, was focused only upon the Swansea team. The equation, if it was to be meaningful, required consideration of the relative strength of the Australians.

On the day, after twelve minutes Cornelsen scored a 'smart try' for the tourists, McLean converted that and followed, soon after, with a penalty. At that stage of the match, with the Australians nine points in front, it looked as if they would be comfortable winners. However, the 'Whites' had other ideas, and two John Rees penalties pulled them back to within three points of the 'Wallabies'. With the possibility of victory beckoning to both sides, the second-half of the match was hard-fought, and, at one point, Swansea supporters, delighted to see Phil Llewellyn 'crash over for a try', felt that the game had been won. However, the shake of the referee's head sent a collective sinking feeling through their bodies. There was something familiar about the script, something ominous about the scenario; the try was disallowed. As it transpired, the only points added to the half-time total were scored in injury time via the McLean boot. Consequently, the Australians trooped off the field having beaten Swansea's best. Whilst disappointed, all involved with Swansea rugby could, at least, gain some consolation from a comment by the Manager of the Australian tourists. Ross Turnbull let it be known that Swansea had given the 'Wallabies' their hardest match of the tour!

The Swansea team which did the city proud that day was:

W. R. Blyth, G. Higgins, J. Rees, W. Williams, G. Jones, D. Richards, R. Dyer, A.Lewis, A. Mages, P. D. Llewellyn, B. J. Clegg, G. A. D. Wheel, T. P. Evans, T. M. Davies (Capt.), M. Keyworth.

Soon after the Australian match, it was announced that Mark Keyworth had been selected to play for England against Wales. As result, the Swansea club could point, proudly, to the fact that they were to supply flank-forwards for both sides in an international. Not that this was a new record for the St. Helens club; Clem Thomas and Vic Roberts had done the same thing in the Fifties.

Huw Davies, Hywel Hopkins, Jeff Herdman – there's an opponent somewhere!

Whilst the 'Whites' lost the two games which followed the Australian match, subsequently, they ran into match-winning form taking the next six in succession. On the way, they played some fluent rugby, scoring 156 points in the process and conceding just 44. Among the victories were two cup ties, the second of which was a magnificent 22 points to 6 victory at the Gnoll. Not only did the 'Whites' dominate that match, they did it with Geoff Wheel limping for most of the game. In addition, David Richards left the field with a hamstring problem, but not before the young man had scored a magnificent blind-side try, handing off three would-be tacklers and scoring near the corner flag. In addition, he dropped a superb goal with, seemingly, half of Neath on his back.

Thereafter, results were mixed as the side, disrupted by injuries, made progress in the cup but disappointed in other matches. Nevertheless, as British Rail introduced its new 125 service from Swansea to Paddington, Swansea's own 'flyer', Roy Woodward was adding to his total of tries on a regular basis. Like all effective wings, Woodward had a keen eye for an opening and a built-in determination to cross the line once he saw the opportunity. Whilst it was true to say that he was not the fastest wing ever to pull on a Swansea shirt, his awareness and opportunism often gave him the space which faster men might not have enjoyed.

By the end of March, the 'Whites' had fought their way to the semi-final of the Welsh Cup. Their opponents were Pontypool, and the venue Cardiff on a Sunday. Whilst the men in white were victorious that day, as they made their way home, their joy was tinged with deep concern for their captain. Mervyn Davies had collapsed during a period of open play and had been carried off on a stretcher. Players and supporters alike held their breath in the silence which encompassed the ground. This was not a man being carried off, it was a demi-god! A man whose appeal surmounted the inter-tribal barriers which bedevil Welsh rugby.

At the time, it was not known that Mervyn's 'injury' had been a brain haemorrhage which was to incapacitate the giant for some time thereafter, and to result in his premature retirement from the game. It was to be the end of an outstanding career during which his head, swathed in a broad white band, would become a kind of personal trade mark throughout the rugby-playing world. Mervyn Davies inspired those around him. His was a combination of dedication to the task in hand and a belief in the superiority of his team. 'Merve-the swerve' led by inspiring example. Swansea, Wales, the Lions and rugby football the world over suffered a great loss that day. Few men in the annals of the modern game have made such an impact on rugby football as had T. M. Davies. He was a giant of the game in every respect. Happily, Mervyn recovered to lead a normal life, but his many fervent admirers were never to see him on the rugby field again.

Back at the National Stadium, Swansea had to reorganise. Some have said that what ensued must rank among the club's greatest performances. Apart from having lost their inspirational captain, specialist prop, Alan Lewis had to leave the field. Given the players which were available, there was no other option open to the 'Whites' than for Baden Evans to take the prop role, and for John Evans, 'all 5'6" of him', to play as a flank forward. If ever *hwyl* and the power of mind over matter won the day, it was then. 'Mervyn's men' won the match by 22 points to 14. Swansea was in the W.R.U. Cup Final for the first time.

Between that Sunday of mixed emotions and the day of the final, only one match of the six played was won by the men in white. Some said that the players had had the final on their minds, others pointed to the ill fortune brought about by injuries and the 'rub-of-the-green'. Yet, when the Barbarians were defeated in an exhilarating match by 37 points to 25, the optimists hurried out of their shelters to greet the renaissance. The boys would 'do it for Mervyn'. Surely, the fates would not decree any other outcome? Even Phil Bennett, captain of Llanelli, owned to having felt the vibes. But Dyfed witch doctors had their own brews, and they, too, were represented among the largest crowd to have seen a Cup Final since its inauguration. Whilst men were to win and lose the match, according to Ron Griffiths, as the preliminaries were being enacted, 'His (Mervyn's) absence hung like a cloud over a gala occasion – it was like a first night of a world-acclaimed play without the leading man'. Certainly, there was an emotion-filled atmosphere throughout the match.

Unfortunately for Swansea supporters, the fairy tale writers had taken the day off. Llanelli 'snuffed out Swansea's hopes via the boot of Phil Bennett'. When the final whistle was blown, the scoreboard read; Llanelli 16 points, Swansea 4. Amidst great disappointment in the Swansea camp, at least the 'Jacks' among the spectators could savour Swansea's score. It was set up by Phil Llewellyn, who, after a tapped penalty, charged towards the Llanelli line. En route, he linked up with Roger Davies who fed John Rees. Rees was 'held up illegally' and, from the resulting tapped penalty, David Richards, on the loop, went over in the corner.

When the season's dust had settled, the press summaries relating to Swansea might have been written about several campaigns since the war. There were some brilliant performances, and some which the team would wish to forget. As Ron Griffiths put it, 'It was the usual Swansea tale of inconsistency'. Acting captain, Neil Webb, was blunt in his own appraisal. 'We failed to take our chances and paid for it.' Still, there was always the season to come. At that time, hope was still beating eternal in Swansea hearts, just as it had done during each close season for the previous hundred years. Only time would tell if such hope was justified.

1976-77

A welcome improvement

Mike James, the new chairman of the selection committee, said that the short Swiss tour, which he had arranged, was part of the team-building programme which he and Stan Addicott had devised. In those terms, in particular,the tour was a great success. On their return, James said that 'the games were not difficult and the hospitality overwhelming'. There were some problems, however. The matches had been played on rutted pitches and, as a result, Lewis Dick, Roger Blyth and John Evans had all suffered leg injuries. In Blyth's case, it was to result in his playing only a handful of games in the season ahead. Those problems apart, those who noted such things, recorded another Swansea 'first'. The club had been the first to go to France, the first to play behind the Iron Curtain, and the first Welsh club to tour the land of the clocks and gnomes.

When the team returned to domestic rugby, after a 'warm-up' match against Morriston, Cross Keys were the first visitors to St. Helens. Given the results of 'Keys' games in previous seasons, the expectations of the St. Helens faithful were focused on a relatively easy match. In the event, a weakened Swansea side had to raise its game in the second-half to ensure victory. Happily, Roger Davies kicked accurately to take advantage of penalties, otherwise the Gwent side might have enjoyed a surprise victory. There followed a game with a similar pattern against Pontypool, though, on that occasion, in the second-half the side performed to its full potential. Then, an Alan Meredith try was indicative of the quality of rugby played by the 'Whites'. Meredith made a superb blind-side break, linked with Lewis Dick, who picked up a pass around his ankles, the wing, having made ground, fed inside to the supporting Meredith who dived over to score. The crowd enjoyed that try immensely, as they did another by the tenacious Woodward.

At that point in the season, in the middle of a fine run during which seven wins in succession were recorded, secretary, David Price, was delighted to announce a significant rise in membership. Numbers were twenty per cent greater than during the previous season. Most observers felt that the Cup Final appearance had caught the imagination of Swansea's rugby followers to the extent that casual supporters had been converted to regulars.

After the Pontypool match, captain Trevor Evans told the press, 'I thought that we coped rather well. They are a difficult side to play against.' When the pressmen asked if that meant that the club could look forward to a successful season, Evans was guarded. 'We could have', he said, 'but I'm not making any forecast; not yet, anyway.' Long-standing 'Whites' followers could understand his caution. The pitfalls in that path had been fallen into many times before. However, when the 'Whites', suitably inspired by a brilliant performance by fly-half, David Richards, 'overwhelmed Bristol at the Memorial Ground', Swansea smiles were more assured. Four 'spectacular' first-half tries set the scene and, at the final whistle, Swansea were 'clearer winners than the score (38 points to 21) suggested'.

Soon after that, however, the winning run came to an end when Newport adapted more effectively to the St. Helens mud. The 'Whites', though, 'bounced back' in the next match to 'destroy Penarth with a colourful brand of rugby'. The score, 43 points to 7 said it all. Since, at that stage, neither Roger Blyth nor Robert Dyer had appeared, and other injuries were affecting the squad, there was a general feeling at St. Helens that, when everyone was available, the team would be even more effective. Not, as the results implied, that the stand-ins were doing a bad job. Indeed, Roger Davies, back from Llanelli, was playing very well at full-back and, in five appearances, had amassed 53 points. Such quality in depth within the squad gave the St. Helens management considerable comfort.

Nonetheless, between the Penarth match and the Christmas period, results were mixed, though the club did win its way into the second round of the Cup. In the first round, Geoff Wheel 'led his pack with panache', and Barry Clegg was 'outstanding in the lines-out'. As a result, thirty points were scored against Pyle, even though, 'a crop of kicks had been missed'. The result of the second round match, however, cast a pall of gloom over St. Helens. Unfancied Glamorgan Wanderers won, what was for them, a famous victory. The *Post* headline said it all, 'Problems mount as Swansea hit rock-bottom'. The 'Whites' had lost the tie by 12 points to 6, and, once again, 'abysmal place kicking' had contributed to the defeat. Whether the situation was as bad as the *Post* headline suggested was a moot point, but there was little doubt that 'heads were down' at St. Helens. An early exit from the cup was the last thing that Trevor Evans had contemplated.

Certainly, the defeat was difficult to understand. Fine wins had been achieved against Richmond and Ebbw Vale by playing outstanding rugby. Jeff Herdman was doing well at hooker, the international second-row pairing of Clegg and Wheel was amongst the best in the country, Huw Davies, at scrum-half, was 'positive, creative and strong', Lewis Dick, Roy Woodward and Gerwyn Jones on the wings were 'showing up well', Alan Meredith was demonstrating his versatility by performing effectively in several positions behind the scrum, whilst David Richards, when available, was playing a brand of football which persuaded many shrewd judges of the game to forecast that the young man would 'reach the top'.

Meanwhile, at St. Helens, it was announced that, in line with other senior Welsh clubs, Swansea had 'fitted out a medical room at the cost of £3,000'. Secretary, David Price, said that what had happened to Mervyn Davies had alerted clubs to the need for emergency facilities 'on the ground'. In future the medical men would be able to undertake any urgent treatment in proper surroundings without delay.

As the season wore on, there was an announcement concerning the establishment of the Welsh Development Agency. The task of the Agency, it was said, was to bring new investment and jobs to Wales. At St. Helens, as part of *its* development programme, the club was introducing new young men into the side. Two names which were to become well-known, not only at the Cricket Field, but in world rugby, were introduced during that period. A nineteen year-old forward called Richard Moriarty joined the club from Morriston. The young man had played a game for Neath 'on permit', but said that he would prefer to play at Swansea. His was a happy decision for Swansea supporters, one which would see Moriarty become a veritable icon for Swansea rugby. The other young man, who made just one appearance during the season, was Mark Wyatt. The fact that he would go on to set significant kicking records for the club was not known at that time. However, Chairman James and his fellow selectors liked what they saw, even then.

Meanwhile, as far as results were concerned, the club having come to terms with the cup exit, enjoyed greater success. Of the twenty-one matches played in the second-half of the campaign, fifteen were won and one was drawn. Given the extent of the injury problems which afflicted the club during this period, this was encouraging. Certainly, it provided a sound basis for the management to build upon in the future. At the time, the chapel-going optimists in the club, thinking back to the *Post* headline which included the words 'rock bottom', may have brought to mind the parable about houses being built on sand and rock. Certainly, the St. Helens management were working to establish a sound foundation for future success. St. Helens might have a sandy base, theirs was rock solid.

Among the best results in the second-half of the season was what the *Post* called 'a six-try bonanza' against Neath at St. Helens. On that occasion, the 'Whites' scored 33 points without reply as Neath 'were run off their feet'. Those who did the running, included Roy Woodward, Alan Meredith, Baden Evans, Huw Davies and Gerwyn Jones. Gerwyn's try caused the greatest excitement, in that he ran 'all of sixty yards to touch down'. Alan Meredith played at full-back in that match, and Byron Mugford, another fine club man, showed his versatility by playing in the front-row. Even the Forwards' Union (the 'donkeys') had to concede that it was something special when a wing three-quarter (one of 'the girls') ventured in 'where it hurt'. In due course, Mugford was to serve the club in other capacities, thus joining a group of other former 'All Whites' who saw their involvement at St. Helens in terms of a life time of service.

Next, Abertillery suffered at Swansea hands. In that match, an 'explosive opening brought 13 points in fifteen minutes'. Alun Donovan, at outside-half, was 'in the pink' that day, whilst Gareth Jenkins, Baden Evans and Lewis Dick ran in the tries. Subsequently, despite a lengthening injury list, Bedford were beaten by the odd point in thirty-three, and Bridgend lost by 27 points to 12, in a match which saw the return of Barry Clegg and captain, Trevor Evans from injury. On that occasion, the half-back partnership of Huw ('Spider') Davies and David Richards blossomed. At Easter, the Harlequins and the Barbarians were both defeated, with Steve Bater, who finished as the club's leading points scorer, registering thirteen of Swansea's twenty-three points in the 'Quins game.

All in all, as the St. Helens management team looked back on the season, they must have been encouraged, for injuries, international calls (Trevor Evans and Geoff Wheel were 'capped') and the fact that some players were not always available, provided the selectors with many problems. Mike James in an end-of-the-season discussion with Ron Griffiths, was confident enough to forecast that 'Swansea will make a greater impact upon the Welsh rugby scene next season'. James said that his optimism was based upon 'the crop of quality youngsters at the club, and the maturity of the internationals within the squad'. Huw Davies, Huw Rees, David Richards, Alan Meredith, Richard Moriarty, and Jeff Herdman were all mentioned. And when these 'youngsters' were lined up alongside internationals like Trevor Evans, Geoff Wheel, Roger Blyth and Mark Keyworth, the future, all the optimists agreed, was to be relished.

1977-78

Cup glory

Alan Meredith, who had been the leading scorer during the previous season, was elected as captain for the new campaign. The new skipper, faced with an enquiry from a reporter as to where he was going to play, shook his head. 'I don't know', he said, 'All I know is that it will not be at scrum-half.' During the previous season, the versatile Donovan had played in most positions behind the scrum. Whilst he had his preferences, like the great club-man he was, he played wherever there was a need. It was the kind of selfless service which separates some special players from others. Meredith, however, was positive about one thing. He was delighted that Phil Davies, who had played more matches (41) than anyone else during the previous campaign, had decided to stay at St. Helens. The player had been linked with Llanelli, but, after a long discussion with Mike James, he said that he was staying with Swansea.

In September there was a further accolade for the Swansea club. David Richards was chosen by the Barbarians, along with Alan Meredith and Geoff Wheel, to play against the British Lions side in the Silver Jubilee match at Twickenham. Someone was marking the young man's card and no one at St. Helens was surprised. Among those who were delighted with the news was Stuart Davies. Stuart had taken over the coaching duties from Stan Addicott whilst the established coach was in the U.S. for a four-week course.

When the season started, the Swansea selection committee must have wondered if the fates were conspiring against them. Once again there was a long injury list, and, with three men playing in the Jubilee match, the 'Whites' lost their unbeaten tag at the second hurdle. After Cross Keys had been defeated, Moseley, on their own ground, emerged as victors. Whilst there was disappointment at such an early setback, one young man retained fond memories of the game for several years after. Richard Moriarty, 'put his head back and ran twenty yards to score'. He was delighted!

There followed a fine win at Bristol, with Alun Donovan at outside-half and Geoff Wheel leading the side in the absence of Alan Meredith. There were some fine tries among the thirty-three points scored by the Swansea men, and an excellent dropped-goal by Donovan. Geoff Wheel, for his part, out to prove his fitness following his withdrawal from the Lions summer tour, was virtually ever-present during the club's first nine matches. When the season ended, however, because of international and other calls, he was tenth in the Swansea appearance list. Jeff Herdman was top with 34 matches, whilst Phil Llewellyn, Richard Moriarty and Mark Keyworth made it a triple tie for second place. With the appearance list including four other players with twenty-eight or more games, the importance of continuity in a team game was underscored.

Yet there were problems for the selectors relating to certain positions. For example there were five wings, Gwynfor Higgins, Gerwyn Jones, Roy Woodward, Lewis Dick, and Mike Langdon, yet, of course, only two could play in any one match. As it transpired, the heavy injury list which affected the club early in the season 'the heaviest in the club's history' – helped to alleviate the problem. Among the 'wounded' were Baden Evans, Barry Clegg, David Richards and Roger Blyth. For Blyth, who had missed most of the previous season a second injury was frustrating.

In mid-October it was 'Swansea's day and no doubt', as Neath were beaten at the Gnoll. Then, with Geoff Wheel 'dominant', and his pack, 'winning most of the ball', the 'Whites' 'coasted to victory' and, in the process took Neath's long standing ground record. Gwynfor Higgins scored a fine try on that occasion. Playing in the centre, he combined with Gerwyn Jones to score. From then up until the first round of the Cup, the 'Whites' won eight matches out of nine played, despite further injuries to Huw Rees, Alan Meredith, and Geoff Wheel.

The club's first opponents in the Cup were Burry Port, who included Dennis Lewis, the former Swansea record points scorer, in their line-up. As the day of the match approached, there was much talk in Swansea about taking the game seriously. The defeat by Glamorgan Wanderers in the previous season flashed like a warning signal in Swansea minds. Phil Davies, doing well at number 8 and said to be 'attracting the attention of the Welsh selectors', played an important part in the match when it took place, as did Roger Blyth, which was just as well. In the first-half, Dennis Lewis's boot had put the west Wales side in the 'driving seat' before two Blyth penalties and an extra-time try by Gareth Jenkins won the match for the 'Whites'. It had been a close-run thing.

After that match, there was a request by Baden Evans for a transfer. Baden felt that the pool of players at St. Helens was too large, and he wanted to play more regular first-team football. No one at St. Helens complained, for the player had given the club several seasons of loyal service, and his request was understandable. With a pool of flankers like Trevor Evans, Mark Keyworth, Gareth Roberts and Phil Jones, the selectors had problems knowing which to choose. Soon after, Robert Dyer joined Pontypridd. Once again, the management at St. Helens understood the player's dilemma. With Huw Davies doing so well, the former-captain was not getting enough games to satisfy his needs.

A week later, the selectors and all at St. Helens were shocked to learn of the tragic death of Phil Davies, who was killed in a car crash. Phil, who never spared himself on or off the field, had been a popular figure at St. Helens, and several sound judges had predicted that he would gain international honours. Whilst Phil Davies the player was to be missed, Phil the man was an even greater loss.

By the turn of the year the team was on course for a satisfactory season. They had won 19 of the 24 games which had been played during 1977, and were due to meet Newbridge at home in the W.R.U. Cup. Whilst the 'Whites' were the favourites to win that game, the psychological pressure brought to bear as a result of the previous season's early exit had not been exorcised. As a result, the play of the 'Whites' was described as 'stuttering'. Indeed, had Roger Blyth left his kicking boots at home, Newbridge might have won the game. But Swansea were the victors, which the sentimentalists would have argued, was right and proper, for, before the kick-off, there had been a minute's silence in memory of the club's president, Bruce Barter. Bruce, who had been a great club servant on and off the field, had, among many other things, been the architect of the celebration arrangements for the Centenary Year. Like that other noted architect, Clough Williams-Ellis, who died soon after, his service to the club would be remembered.

In the period before the next round of the cup, some exciting rugby was played at St. Helens. In reporting on a match with Coventry the *Post*'s headline read, 'Blyth leads points spectacular'. The full-back, forgotten by the Welsh selectors since he lost a season through injury, scored three tries, converted four and kicked a penalty. In all that day, he scored 23 points out of the 43 registered by Swansea. Lewis Dick, Jeff Herdman, and skipper, Alan Meredith were the other Swansea try scorers. In that match, and in several others during the remainder of the season, Richard Moriarty was playing second-row. Stan Addicott felt that playing at lock would help to harden the young man, and, in view of the longevity of Moriarty's career, the process must have been extremely effective.

Meantime, Huw Davies, who broke a bone in his hand playing against the Welsh Academicals, was hoping to be fit for the fourth round of the Cup. The opponents were to be Bedwas, so, once again, there was the expectancy that the 'Whites' would win comfortably. After all, after scoring eight tries against top English side, Coventry, the Swansea coach had said, 'We put it all together'. However, the coach, digging into his bag of clichés, warned, 'We cannot be complacent. One swallow doesn't make a summer'.

Summer it was not. After the spring-like majesty of the Coventry victory, 'the big freeze' arrived. Indeed, such was the extent of the wintry weather, that the 'Whites' did not play again for four weeks. Then, as fate determined, the first match to be played after the lay-off was the cup game at Bedwas. After the long gap between games, the freezing weather, heavy rain and thick mud in the Valley town were hardly conducive to the playing of attractive rugby. As a consequence, the match turned out to be a trial of strength and stamina on a gluepot of a pitch which was made worse by 'constant torrential rain'. As the thirty warriors trooped off at the end of the game, covered with mud and indistinguishable one from the other, the cheers were for Swansea. Gallant Bedwas had been beaten by 20 points to 12. The three tries scored by the inappropriately named "Whites", were credited to Barry Clegg, Lewis Dick and Gerwyn Jones. Since the names of both wings were on the score sheet, the win was a testimony for coach Addicott's instruction to his men to 'get the ball wide whenever possible'. However, there was a rider to the instruction, 'only after the forwards have taken control'. For the second time, Swansea found itself in the semi-final of the W.R.U. Cup. The silverware, so keenly desired by Swansea followers, beckoned.

Prior to that match, however, the club had a better opportunity to prepare. There were six matches on the fixture list which were to be played before the semi-final. Consequently, the selectors had the opportunity to establish the most effective side, and to prepare the players for the challenge physically and mentally. Mike James, chairman of the selectors, said at the time: 'Ideally we would have liked to have had a settled side by now, but we've had so many problems'. For his part, Ron Griffiths in the *Post* was buoyant. Unsaddling his old hobby horse he argued that 'Swansea began the season seeking that level of consistency which has eluded them in the past ... Now, at last, they are putting things right !'

As if to demonstrate the accuracy of that statement, Bath were 'swept aside' by 45 points to 0; and the Harlequins (semi-finalists in the English cup) were 'thoroughly defeated by a Swansea side which played as a complete unit'. That win, however, resulted in further problems for the selection committee. Roy Woodward, Gareth Roberts and Gareth Jenkins were all injured in the game. After that, a 45 points to 0 win over Penarth and the defeat of the Barbarians by 36 points to 15 concluded the pre-semi-final fixture list. Five wins out of six, and a bagful of points made up the kind of winning run which coaches dream about. Not surprisingly, the confidence level at St. Helens was 'sky high'. Whilst this atmosphere was to be enjoyed, it provided the coach with the task of controlling the level of that confidence. Consequently, the old adage of 'confident but not cocky' became the order of the day.

Aberavon was the neutral venue chosen for the 'Whites' to play the 'Blue and Blacks'. Prior to the game, the press made Cardiff slight favourites which, as Stan Addicott said, suited the St. Helens camp. On the day, with Alan Meredith at full-back (Roger Blyth could not play), the 'Whites' soon held an advantage as a result of superb work by the pack. Even though the east Wales men kicked a penalty to take the lead, Swansea supporters felt that their team was still in control. Soon after, Dai Richards was head-butted, and the resulting penalty restored parity. Then, five minutes before half-time,the outside-half scored a superb try to put the St. Helens men in front. Herdman struck against the head, Huw Davies flashed the ball out to Richards who, 'set off on a thrilling run, side-stepping one way and then the other, to go over in the corner'. The timing of that score, provided the 'Whites' with a powerful psychological boost. When Evans and Herdman added further tries in the second period, it was Swansea's day. For the second time in three seasons the 'Whites' were in the Cup Final. St. Helens was aglow with satisfaction. This time, the supporters argued, Swansea will win.

A week later there was a further boost to Swansea morale. Barry Clegg, David Richards and Geoff Wheel had been chosen to go to Australia with Wales. Roger Blyth was named as a 'stand-by' which, considering that he had missed the bulk of the previous season, was an accolade itself.

Results during the run-up to the Cup Final, however, caused some concern in Swansea, for three of the five matches played were lost. However, the management team held a different view. It was important, they said, to rest senior players prior to the Final, and they had taken the opportunity to do that. No one was rested, however, for the penultimate match of the season. Then, the team 'lit up St. Helens with a thoroughly convincing display'. Herdman and Meredith each scored a brace of tries in that match, Huw Davies added another and the reliable Roger Blyth kicked nineteen points. As a 'warm-up' game it had everything; forward control, creative back play, thrusting work by the three-quarters and, when it was necessary, solid defence. The score, thirty-three points to three, put the victory into perspective. The Final would be another kettle of fish, but the win and the manner in which it had been achieved significantly increased the proportion of optimists in the Swansea camp. The scene was set.

Newport, long-standing opponents of the Swansea club, were a well-organised side. The bookmakers, however, made the 'Whites' favourites, and, as so often happens, their judgment proved to be impeccable. Nonetheless, as the *Western Mail* had it, 'Swansea had to work hard for their victory'. And that was true! No try-bonanza this. Indeed, the only try resulted from a piece of Herdman opportunism. David Richards, however, dropped a 'classical' goal with the aplomb of a seasoned international. Clegg won the line out ball, Llewellyn took it on, slipped to Meredith, who kicked to the posts. With Blyth through on him, a Newport player fumbled, and Davies somehow 'scrambled the ball out to Richards who, calmly, dropped a goal'. The response from the Swansea support was far from calm. In due course, their cheers reached fever pitch as Gareth Jenkins, forty yards from the Newport posts, 'struck the ball sweetly and it sailed through the uprights to push Swansea further ahead'. Given the distance, that was a dropped goal of which the legendary Billy Bancroft would have been proud.

At the end, the general consensus of opinion was that the 'Whites' had well deserved their victory.The team, the management and supporters were all delighted. There was silverware in the Swansea display cabinet at last ! And quite right, too!

Since this was Swansea's first Cup Final victory of modern times, it is right that we should list here the team which wore the famous colours that day. It was a formidable XV, not only with outstanding players, but with a collective sense of purpose.

W. R. Blyth, H. Rees, A. R. Meredith (Capt.), G. Jenkins, A. J. Donovan; D. Richards, H. Davies, H. Hopkins, J. N. Herdman, P. D. Llewellyn, G. A. D. Wheel, B. J. Clegg, T. Evans, R. Moriarty, M. Keyworth.

The *Sporting Post* was exuberant that Saturday night, for on that day, the 'Whites' had won the Cup and the 'Swans' had clinched promotion. Faced with the dilemma as to which story should be covered on the front page of the paper, the editor took a creative approach. He split the old Broadsheet front page into two and ran the stories side by side. It was a momentous day for the city of Swansea.

At St. Helens, the smiles would have melted the polar ice cap. Silverware had been obtained, seventy-five per cent of the club's matches had been won, and the team was growing in maturity even though it was a relatively young side. Roger Blyth (with 233) headed the list of points scorers and the try scorers (15), with Gerwyn Jones (14) and Alan Meredith (13) not far behind in the try table. There was one departure though. Lewis Dick, having found employment in Cheltenham, felt that he could not give the time required in travelling to Swansea. However, the Scot let it be known that he had 'greatly enjoyed his time at St. Helens'.

1978–1979

Marking time

As the new season approached, one of the problems which the selection committee believed they had to face concerned Alun Donovan. Donovan had returned from the Welsh tour of Australia with an enhanced reputation, yet the 'Whites' had Roger Blyth at full-back, and David Richards at outside-half, the two positions which were most favoured by the player. In the event, that and related problems concerning the abundance of talent at St. Helens, came to nought, as Donovan's injury kept him on the sidelines for the bulk of the season, and a spate of other injuries adversely affected the balance of the side. Indeed, at the beginning of February, the *Post* reported that, 'Swansea's enviable record ... has suddenly run into a nightmare in the shape of an extensive injury situation ... almost without parallel in the club's history.' Such was the position, that, at one stage, the club had to cancel an Athletic fixture because that side had been decimated by the withdrawal of men to play for the senior side. Yet, notwithstanding these problems, the 1978/79 season was not without its excitement nor its successes. Indeed, as far as results were concerned, it was not until late October that the side lost its unbeaten record.

After a victory over Cross Keys in the opening match of the season, the 'Whites' went on to win the next seven games. Memorable among them was a 26 points to 3 victory in Bristol, a 50 points to 6 defeat of Abertillery, and a 35 points to 15 win over the Harlequins. There was, also, an excellent victory over Neath when the *Post* reported that 'Swansea showed their best form of the season.' In that match Mike Langdon scored a fine solo try, and, battling scrum-half, Huw Davies, crossed twice. During the Abertillery game, David Richards helped himself to a hat-trick of tries, whilst other 'Whites' scored six others during the game. The best of those was, again, scored by Langdon. Gareth Roberts, who played an outstanding match at flanker, led the break-out, and an exciting move developed during which Huw Davies and Trevor Cheeseman were involved twice before the winger 'stretched his legs to score'.

There was a fine performance, too, in a St. Helens fixture with Cardiff. Then, what Ron Griffiths called 'a patchwork side', played thrilling rugby to outgun the 'Blue and Blacks'. The 'Whites' took the lead when Gareth Davies was indecisive, and Alan Meredith intercepted his attempted pass to sprint over. A second try was even more spectacular. From a quick heel, David Richards was released, made ground, missed out his co-centre to give to Mark Wyatt, who came into the line from full-back. Wyatt cut inside then came off his left leg to feed winger Langdon who went over in the corner. *That* was a real Swansea try!

Gareth Edwards pounces in vain.

It was the weather which then took a hand. Before the Devolution Referendum was undertaken, snow and ice brought chaos to south Wales. In retrospect, had there been the opportunity, the St. Helens men would not have voted for the break in fixtures which resulted from this 'freeze'. Results subsequent to the disruption being far poorer than they had been before. It was as though the side had lost its winning momentum. Before the snow, the 'Whites' had lost just 18% of their matches. Afterwards, the proportion lost in the final period of the season, increased to 46%. Yet, paradoxically, the break had given several of the 'invalids' the opportunity to recover from their injuries, though not all the players were fit or available for every match.

For example, for the third round Schweppes Cup game, neither Geoff Wheel nor Phil Llewellyn were able to play, though Barry Clegg and David Richards did. The opponents in that match were Ebbw Vale and, on the day, the 'Whites' were favourites. However, after three minutes of the match, Richard Moriarty had to leave the field, and, thereafter, the Swansea men did not seem to be 'firing on all cylinders'. Indeed, at half-time, the 'Whites' were trailing by 12 points to 3, the only Swansea points coming from a Gareth Roberts penalty. In the second-half, the men in white began to 'put their game together', though it was not until the final minutes of the match that a fine move involving Gareth Jenkins, David Richards and Alan Meredith gave the latter the chance to accelerate through a gap in the opposing defence to regain the lead. It

No stopping Jeff Herdman.

had been too close for comfort! Yet a win is a win, and the 'Whites' found themselves in the fourth round once again, and, in that round, they were drawn at home. The opponents were to be Llanelli, a tough nut to crack at the best of times; but, as the received wisdom has it, home advantage in the cup is coveted by all teams.

Because the snow and ice had disrupted the fixture lists, the Whites' found themselves having to play the Llanelli cup match just seven days after the previous round. In its report of the match, the *Western Mail* called the contest 'a titanic struggle', and so it was. The Swansea pack was outstanding that day and, had the television people developed their technology at that time to show possession ratios, then white would have dominated red. Unfortunately, though, the cultured boot of Phil Bennett pushed the Swansea men back time and again. The tremendous work of the pack, and, in particular Barry Clegg and Trevor Cheeseman, was to no avail. The final whistle saw the 'Scarlets' exuberant and the 'Whites' disappointed. The scoreboard was indicative of the closeness of the match; Swansea 3 points, Llanelli 4. The 'Sospan' line had not been crossed. All the home side had to show for all their effort was a Roger Blyth penalty. Thus it was that the curtain fell on Swansea's cup progress for the 1978/79 season.

At the end of the campaign, the Swansea captain, Alan Meredith, blamed 'an unusually heavy crop of injuries for our slide this season. We were never able to field a constant side, and the confidence drained away.' Meredith felt that, after the cup exit, injuries mounted and attendances at training sessions fell away. The captain believed that, with the cup exit went the kind of interest which keeps players keyed-up. Had there been a sports psychologist at St. Helens at that time, he would have tried to re-focus the players' minds, and to agree new targets with them to re-establish positive thinking. As it was, Alan Meredith said that he would not like to have to go through such a season again. 'There were times', he said, 'when we picked a team on Monday, changed it on Wednesday, and, by the time Saturday came around, had to change it again.'

Whilst the captain's reaction was understandable, with the benefit of hindsight, and being insulated by time from the emotion which typically colours Celtic disappointment, the season can be seen in another light. It is possible, for example, to see the 1978/79 campaign as an interim base camp used by climbers as they tackle the likes of Everest. After the effort of climbing one section of the mountain, they stop and gather strength in order to allow them to progress further up the side of the mountain. It's possible, too, to perceive of the season as one with many positive aspects. For example, the 'pre-freeze' performance of the side had been enviable. Only five matches were lost out of the twenty-seven which had been played. Barry Clegg and David Richards had been 'capped' by Wales, thus adding to the growing list of internationals in the Swansea squad. One of those internationals, Trevor Evans, had come back late in the season, after being absent injured for more than six months. Alun Donovan, who struggled to regain fitness throughout the season, had set his sights on a fresh start at the beginning of the next campaign, and Roger Blyth was back to full fitness which would, in due course, see him regaining his place in the Welsh team. Less obvious at the time, was the début of a young man called Mark Wyatt who was, also, to become an international.

Roger Blyth topped the scoring list again with 152 points, whilst Mike Langdon was leading try scorer with fifteen. All in all there had been many positive aspects to reflect upon, and, as if to underline that fact, for the first time, the 'Whites' were the winners of the Welsh National Sevens tournament. Seven, say some, is a lucky number. Would that influence the club's fortunes in the season ahead? Only time would tell.

Chapter Twenty-Four

AS GOOD AS GOLD

1979-80

IF A PERIOD IN THE LIFE AND TIMES of Swansea R.F.C. had to be selected as the nearest, in terms of achievement, to the days of the 'Golden Era', many St. Helens *aficionados* would pick the seasons 1979-80 and 1980-81. It was during this period that all the hard work of coach Stan Addicott, his team, and the St. Helens management came to fruition. It was the first time since the end of the Great War that Swansea was not bedevilled by inconsistency, and it was a period during which an outstanding squad of players, functioning as a team, had great success. In addition, it was a period during which new club records were set, and one in which several Swansea men represented Wales and the 'British Lions'.

Whilst, in September 1979, the optimists were to the fore, few of them expected that the season ahead would turn out as it did. Certainly, there was little in the pre-season musings of the media men which even hinted at the level of that success. Swansea, after all, had flattered to deceive on so many occasions that even the positive thinkers half expected inconsistency and disappointment. Consequently, when the 'Whites' party returned, unbeaten, from their pre-season tour, there was still an element of doubt in Swansea minds as the coming season was contemplated.

Chairman, Gordon Morris, in explaining that the tour had been arranged to help foster team spirit, expressed the hope that the benefits achieved in that regard, would be maintained throughout the campaign. He was reasonably confident that they would. In addition, he was pleased to announce, that the 'British Lion' loose-head prop forward, Clive Williams, had joined the club. Williams, according to Morris, was one of the best exponents of his art in world rugby. Had the chairman known what was to transpire, he might, also, have taken time to talk about a twenty-year-old wing who used to play for Fylde, who had joined the Swansea camp. Appropriately for a wing, the young man's name was Swift. Whilst Alun Donovan was immobilised as a result of an injury sustained in Australia, there were more positive rather than negative things for the chairman to talk about. Notwithstanding the relative disappointment of the previous campaign, and the usual nagging doubts, in the weeks before the new season started there was an air of quiet confidence at St. Helens.

The opening match on the Swansea fixture list was against Cross Keys at St. Helens, and whilst the 24 points to 3 victory was appreciated by supporters, what really caught their eye was the play of young Swift. He scored three tries that day, which, immediately endeared him to the supporters. In his report of the match, Ron Griffiths noted that the new man, 'has pace, knows his way to the line, and has encouraging confidence in his own ability'. Roger Blyth crossed for a brace of tries in that match, whilst Richard Moriarty and Clive Williams (also a débutant) ensured that the front eight was represented on the scoring list.

'All Whites' off on a Far East tour, 10 August 1979.

After a 'flag showing' game against Brecon in which Malcolm Dacey ('one of Wales' most exciting newcomers'), made his début, the team travelled to Moseley. There, with Dacey at outside-half and David Richards playing in the centre, the home side was defeated by 23 points to 9, though the performance of the side in the first-half of the game hardly suggested such an outcome. However, whatever was said at 'lemon time', transformed the team's approach to the game. Once again, the name Swift was on the score sheet, this time courtesy of a tremendous break by Huw Davies who, skillfully, made space for the wingman.

After the Police had been 'swamped' by 41 points to 9, when the 'Whites' took on Bristol, they played their second home match of the season. Clearly, the half-time talk from the previous game had had a lasting effect. The 'Whites', playing well from the start, won by 26 points to 3, which, according to the *Western Mail,* did not flatter the men in white. Swansea, the paper reported, were in 'an enterprising, dominant mood'. Since, prior to that match, the visitors had remained unbeaten for a remarkable 21 games, the victory was put into context. The atmosphere in the ground that day was electric, as, according to the *Post*, 'Swansea gave a performance of the highest, crowd pleasing quality'. To win against an unbeaten team was one thing. To win in some style was another!

By the beginning of December, the club's record was outstanding. Of the eighteen matches played, seventeen had been won, 447 points had been scored and only 143 conceded. Press com-

'All Whites' 1979-80.

ment on that performance focused around the collective work of the side, the commanding presence of Clive Williams, the inspiring captaincy of Geoff Wheel, the outstanding performances of Richard Moriarty, Barry Clegg and, newcomer, Trevor Cheeseman. Wheel's pre-season target about developing an effective front eight combination had been heeded. Furthermore, to the captain's delight, the contribution of the Swansea pack was being recognised. Nonetheless, as has always been the case, the backs, thriving on the quantity of good ball received, had been able to parade their exciting talents, to the delight of supporters. Players like, Huw Davies, David Richards, Roger Blyth, Tony Swift, and Malcolm Dacey, blossomed in the process. As far as Ron Griffiths was concerned, he found it difficult to contain himself. *Post* readers could almost hear the chuckle in his voice as he recounted the deeds of his white warriors. Despite all his previous disappointments, Griffiths found himself being carried away with the euphoria of the situation. The best he could do was to temper his joy. Even then, he wrote: 'It will be surprising if a trophy or two does not end up among the Swansea clubhouse silverware.'

Among the outstanding results in the October of that season was a 61 points to 9 'demolition' of Blackheath. In that match, Roger Blyth scored 25 points, and flying wing, Tony Swift, scored another 'hat-trick' of tries. Other outstanding performances included a 26 points to 18 defeat of Neath at the Gnoll to take the 'All Blacks' ground record, a 27 points to 12 victory over Leicester, and a 35 points to 6 win at Richmond. It was heady stuff. No wonder Ron Griffiths was getting carried away!

During that period, Roy Woodward, the stalwart wing of the previous campaign, announced his retirement from the game, and Alan Donovan said that it would not be long before he was able to play again. Meantime, Geoff Wheel, when asked what his ambition was for the club, said, 'It must be to win the Schweppes Cup'. And, by that time, he and his team mates were making steady progress in that regard. In the first round, Pencoed were defeated by 40 points to 0, with Tony Swift scoring four tries, and 'revenge' was gained over Glamorgan Wanderers in the second round, the 'Whites ' scored nine tries that day.

Not surprisingly, the St. Helens faithful became caught up in the euphoria, and, even when the 'Whites' lost for only the second time that season (in early December), the supporters shrugged that off. Cardiff had scored their winning try deep into injury time, and, as every schoolboy knows, referees watches are rarely accurate, and are never so when the other side wins a match by scoring in extra-time. Anyway, they may have reasoned, Gordon Morris knows what he is talking about, and he had said that 'the present squad is the best at St. Helens during my long association with the club'. They enjoyed Ron Griffiths's 'half-term report' too. Griffiths had written, 'Geoff Wheel can sit back and reflect on four months of rugby activity which has earned Swansea glory, and lifted them to the pinnacle of British clubs'. What more was there to say?

With four 'Whites' – Roger Blyth, David Richards, Clive Williams and Geoff Wheel in the Welsh side to play France, and with Neath being beaten decisively at the Gnoll in the third round of the Cup, for Swansea supporters, the new year started with a smile on its face. Mark Wyatt must have thought so, too; he scored eleven of the fifteen points conceded by Neath. Yet another Swansea gem had been unearthed.

By February, the *Western Mail* was eulogising about the Swansea record, whilst the *Post* was moved to declare that the 'Whites' had a playing record 'unequalled by any other British club'. Was this, supporters were asking, the start of a second 'Golden Era'? Roger Blyth may have thought so, as in a 38 points to 3 'rout of Neath', he broke his own aggregate points record. Commenting on this new mark, Ron Griffiths felt that, with ten weeks of the season to be played, the full-back was in line to set 'a record which would take some beating'. Tony Swift also reached a milestone in that match, equalling John Jenkins' post-war try count. The 'All White' steamroller seemed to have gathered a momentum of its own.

Next, Gloucester were defeated at Kingsholm, no mean feat at the time, Bedwas fell in the fourth round of the Cup, and Coventry, the Police, and South Glamorgan Institute had a total of 109 points scored against them. By now, there was a growing self-belief in the Swansea camp which was being matched by results. Indeed, by the end of March, when the cup semi-final was to be played, the 'Whites' had lost only three of the thirty-eight matches played, and had won thirty-four. Whilst the semi-final was to be played against Newport, a more than competent side, at the time, the mood in the Swansea camp discounted defeat. Gordon Morris put that 'atmosphere' into perspective when he said, 'We're not over confident, just confident. We've lost sufficient games to keep our feet on the ground!'

Among those who were keeping their feet on the ground was Bernard Cajot. Bernard, a scrum-half in the Fifties, contrasted the heady atmosphere of the time with that which applied when he was playing. Since then, Cajot, who was acting as trainer, had served the club selflessly in true 'All White' fashion. Now, he recalled the time when 'we struggled to find a team'. That, however, was not the case on 29 March 1980. Then, on the Arms Park, the 'Whites' came from behind to beat the 'Amber and Blackings' by 23 points to 13 in the semi-final of the cup. It had been a fine display of 'thinking-man's' rugby. In the process, the team increased its points tally beyond the one thousand mark, whilst Roger Blyth pushed his new record past three hundred points.

Thereafter, whilst the 'Blue and Blacks' took the St. Helens ground record, the 'Whites' scored heavily against Cross Keys, the 'Quins, the Barbarians, and Aberavon, recording a total of 161 points in the four games. Thus it was that the side travelled to Cardiff to meet Bridgend in the final of the Cup, in a confident mood. Unfortunately, they went without David Richards and Clive Williams, who had withdrawn from the side because of the imminent 'Lions' tour.

Prior to the final, the 'Whites' found themselves boosted by opinions from many corners. For example, the *Western Mail*, in discussing Swansea's overall season, argued that, 'Consistency brings the title (the *Western Mail* Championship) to Swansea'. Generations of Swansea supporters had waited many years to read such words. If they had been pinching themselves to ensure that Swansea's consistently outstanding performances were not the product of a dream, then this comment would have provided reassurance.

Having travelled, boosted by such remarks, and with a positive mind set, Swansea supporters were disappointed to return home without the cup which had been coveted by Geoff Wheel. Whilst David Richards and Clive Williams were absent, the 'Whites' had taken the field with a strong, experienced XV. Indeed, seven of the Swansea side were playing in their third Cup Final. All in all, the strength of the forwards and the skill and panache of the backs, were believed to have given the 'Whites' an advantage. In the event, Bridgend's game-plan stifled Swansea's flair and frustrated the St. Helens men. Gerald Davies, writing in the *Times*, reflected the view of many who were there that day, when he wrote: 'The two most exciting Welsh teams played out a duel of barren, unenterprising rugby'. The 'Whites' found it difficult 'to get out of second gear', and Bridgend, under the influence of Steve Fenwick's boot, bided their time, keeping the ball close among the forwards and grinding their way forward. The old adage that a team can only play as well as its opponents allow, was shown to be valid that day. It was one of those matches which cry out for someone to utilise individual skill and outrageous flair to break the negative mould. Sadly, none was forthcoming, and Bridgend, more effective at the grinding game, ran out the winners.

Despite their disappointment at not obtaining the cup 'scalp', all who loved Swansea rugby could look back on the club's most successful season since the First World War. Indeed, since the side had played thirty per cent more matches than their 'Golden Era' predecessors, it could be argued that the season's outcome was superior to all but a handful of performances since the Club was formed. Played 46, won 40, drawn 1, lost 5; points for 1,196, against 334, had, been an outstanding outcome. Furthermore, whilst the statistics confirmed that the team had been extremely successful, peer opinions and those of the British rugby fraternity as a whole, underlined the qualitative aspects of the team's performance. There were titles, too. The 'Whites' were winners of the Unofficial *Western Mail* Championship; of the *Daily Mail* Anglo-Welsh Championship; of the *Sunday Telegraph* Anglo-Welsh Championship; Runners-up in the Schweppes W.R.U. Cup; Runners-up in the Whitbread Merit Table; and they were the *Sunday Telegraph* Team-of-the-Season. Roger Blyth's 348 points during the season had set a new Swansea record, and Tony Swift's try count (29) was the best post-war total. It was little wonder that those who believed in such things were sure that the halls of Valhalla were ringing out with triumphant choruses as Bancroft, Trew, Jones, and Owen and their like celebrated a magnificent season of Swansea rugby.

1980-81

Another nugget

Having enjoyed such success in the previous campaign, the 'Whites', the St. Helens management, and their euphoric supporters, could hardly wait for the new season to begin. As far as the squad itself was concerned, they 'limbered up' for the season proper by undertaking another short tour, this time to France. There, one of their opponents was Bayonne, a club which had had links with St. Helens over many years. The touring party, however, did not include Brynmor Williams, David Richards, or Gareth Roberts, while Alun Donovan, Huw Rees and Mike Langdon were nursing knee injuries.

On the party's return, tour manager, Mike James, was able, once again, to tell the *Post* that the venture had been a success. He said that it had been enjoyed by the players, and that morale in the Swansea camp was at a high level. Nonetheless, despite all the positive signs, the old Swansea doubt lurked in the background like a prowling wolf. The unspoken questions were; can we do as well this season as we did in the last? Will the old malady of inconsistency return?

When Cross Keys were defeated in the opening game of the season proper, the wolf retreated. In that match, Brynmor Williams, Jeff Herdman, Richard Moriarty, and Alun Donovan all scored tries. Since the press reports of the match suggested that the 'Keys' were a 'tougher nut to crack' than had been the case, the 29 points to 10 victory gave all at St. Helens considerable comfort. The optimists took the win as an indicator that another successful campaign was in prospect. Soon after, Swansea morale was boosted even further, when David Richards, 'killed the rumour that he was going to Cardiff'. Richards was reported to have said, 'I started with Swansea and that's where I intend to stay'. His words were music in the Swansea loyalists' ears. Not that the young man was going anywhere (in the rugby sense) for a while. He had come home from South Africa with a dislocated shoulder, and the injury was taking time to mend.

Meanwhile, David's half-back partner, Brynmor Williams, had been chosen to play for a Wales XV against an Overseas side. He was joined by three other Swansea men, Roger Blyth, Clive Williams, and Geoff Wheel. 'Whites' supporters saw in those selections further evidence, if it was needed, of the standing of their favourites. At that, the wolf retired even further.

In the next home match, against Moseley, it was Geoff Wheel who earned 'the loudest cheer of the day'. Picking up a loose ball on the visitors '22', Wheel, 'charged through a packed defence', to score. Together with a brace of tries by Tony Swift and one each by Mark Davies and Mark Keyworth, that try earned the team a convincing victory. Apart from the happy outcome of the match, the day was special in another respect. Before the kick-off, the captain had been presented with the '*Daily Mail*' pennant which had been won by the club in the previous season. The 'warm applause' which greeted the award, no doubt, disguised the attitude of the ultra-positive thinkers among 'Whites' followers, which encompassed the thought, 'thank you, we'll see you again next year!'

Brynmor Williams – determined kick.

Roger Blyth tackles Bernie Frazer (N.Z.).

By the end of September, Spencer Feeney, writing in the *Post*, observed that, 'It looks as though Swansea will again be the club that everyone wants to beat'. And, given the collective human nature which team sports invoke, few would have disagreed with the journalist's observation. It is a fact of sporting life that lesser teams often 'raise their game' when facing champions. Because that is so, it necessitates a response from the premier team which ensures that the quality and effectiveness of its play are superior to those of its challengers.

One side which mounted such a challenge was Newport. In the first-half of that match the Uskside club did very well and, at half-time, the scoreboard read Swansea 7 Newport 3. Indeed, had it not been for Swansea's excellent defensive work, the score might have been closer than that. The second-half, however, was a different matter. By then, the Swansea pack had gained the ascendancy and three excellent tries were scored as the 'Whites' dominated the game. One of those tries was illustrative of the brand of fifteen man rugby which Swansea played during that second period. Jenkins burst through the Newport cover, fed Swift, who was upended near the posts. The ball ran loose and Roberts 'scooped it up' to send Clegg over for the try. Blyth converted.

As the New Zealand match approached, the general consensus of opinion in Swansea was that Richard Moriarty 'must get a cap'. Mervyn Davies was one of those who argued Moriarty's case. With half an eye on the young man's 'energetic' early style, Mervyn argued that 'Richard is now more controlled and reads the game well'. In due course, when the selectors ignored the Swansea pleas, the St. Helens camp was disappointed. Mike James, however, remained convinced of Moriarty's potential and told the *Western Mail* that, 'He has missed-out this time, but if he continues working at his game they will have to pick him'. In addition, James and his committee were confident that Tony Swift would be 'capped' by England, whilst Malcolm Dacey's selection for the Wales 'B' side was indicative of the potential of that young player. Clearly, at the time, the St. Helens stable was packed with young thoroughbreds.

With Swansea's match against New Zealand beckoning, the club's supporters were disappointed to see Llanelli take the 'Whites' unbeaten record (ten matches without defeat), but the following week, the side 'bounced back' to beat the Welsh 'All Blacks' convincingly. The *Post* headline above the report of that match 'Swansea Stunner', was greatly enjoyed by 'Whites' supporters, and the soothsayers saw the victory of white over black as being an omen for the following Saturday. Even those who were less certain of such things allowed the second-half performance of their favourites to colour their judgment. Four tries had been scored during that period, as Neath were 'swamped in a dress rehearsal for Saturday'. Unfortunately, as the future was to show, whilst the opponents at the Gnoll were dressed in black, the bodies which would fill the New Zealanders' kit were somewhat different. It was as though understudies had taken the roles in the dress rehearsal, and when the stars had replaced them they gave a level of performance which was on another plane.

On the day of the New Zealand match, before the kick off, the surviving members of Swansea's 1935 side which had beaten the New Zealanders, and those of the 1953 team which had earned a draw with the tourists, were introduced to the crowd. The 25,000 who were there that day showed their appreciation of those Swansea heroes with great warmth. Some said that the old 'Whites' had been paraded to counter the effect of the New Zealanders' 'War chant'. If that had been the case, sadly, it didn't work. After the match, coach, Stan Addicott said that he was 'shattered'. Captain, Geoff Wheel, generous in his appreciation of the formidable 'All Black' performance, said 'It was country versus club. This time, the country taught us a lesson.'

The tourists won the match by 32 points to nil, which was considered to have been a ' thumping' at the time. However, given that Wales were defeated by 23 points to 3 soon after, Swansea's performance can be viewed in a different light. Nonetheless, everyone at St. Helens was disappointed that day. After all, the 'Whites' team was a fine combination which was a third of the way through another highly successful season. In retrospect, though, the New Zealand performance may be seen as being a precursor of that country's dominance of the world rugby scene in the decade ahead. Whilst beaten, no one could fault the Swansea men for their effort that October day in 1980.

The team was:

W. R. Blyth*, A. H. Swift*, G. Jenkins, M. Dacey*, A. D. Meredith, D. S. Richards*, D. B. Williams*, C. Williams*, J. N. Herdman, G. John, B. Clegg*, G. A. D. Wheel* (Capt.), M. Keyworth*, R. D. Moriarty*, M. Davies*.

To demonstrate the quality of that team, eleven of the side (marked with an asterisk) were, or would be, Internationals.

Mark Davies – with Mike Ruddock in support.

When the 'Whites' returned to domestic rugby, Blackheath were beaten by 12 points to 9, the Police 'shipped 70 points', and the defeat by the 'Scarlets' was avenged. At half-time in the Sospan game, both sides had scored six points. The press, to a man, described the first period as 'thoroughly depressing', littered with penalties and 'continually punctuated by the 'peep' of the referee's whistle'. It was hardly a typical 'Scarlets' versus 'Whites' match. The second-half, however, was quite different. Two tries were scored by the Swansea men in a five minute period, which, together with a Mark Wyatt penalty ensured a victory for the 'Whites'.

When the first round of the Cup was played, Jeff Herdman led the pack superbly as the Swansea front eight dominated the match with Hendy. Whilst the result was as expected, given past experience, the possibility of a minnow winning was always at the back of the mind. That, after all, is the so-called 'Romance of the Cup'. That win was followed by a 42 points to nil 'nine-try spree', when Richmond were the victims. Tony Swift (4) and David Richards (3) headed the try-scorers that day, and, as someone pointed out, the London club were 'no minnows'.

Thereafter, the 'Whites' ran into devastating form. In the second round of the cup, Ystrad Rhondda's line was crossed ten times in a 61 points to 9 rout, and London Welsh were beaten by 41 points to nil. By then, the 'Whites' had a record which compared favourably with the previous season's. Of the twenty five matches played, including the 'All Blacks' game, twenty had been won and another drawn. Unbeknown to anyone at that time, the team's performance in the second-half of the campaign was to be even more impressive.

After beating Aberavon at St. Helens, the team had to travel to Ystradgynlais for a third round cup tie. Since two other smaller clubs had been disposed of with ease in the earlier rounds, the 'Whites' travelled up the Valley in a confident mood. After fifteen minutes of the game, however, a 'fracas' resulted in a Swansea man being sent off. For the rest of the match, in less than attractive conditions, both sides, like First World War troops, fought for every inch of ground. In the end, the 'Whites' were pleased to come away with a 3 points to nil victory, courtesy of the Blyth boot.

With a nineteen-year-old called Bleddyn Bowen back training at St. Helens after a knee injury, two other newcomers – a wing by the name of Arthur Emyr and a flank-forward, who, according to the *Post*, was called Mike Ruddick – turned out in a 58 points to 9 'demolition' of Sheffield. Both scored on their débuts and would go on to play a significant part in the St. Helens story.

In the weeks following that match, the 'Whites' scored 38 points against Abertillery, Penarth conceded 62, Pontypridd were beaten by 21 points to nil, Neath by 21 points to 3, whilst Gloucester conceded 20 points whilst scoring 7. Since the Gloucester match provided the 'Whites' with their thirteenth win in succession, the pedigree of the Swansea club was even more firmly established. Not only was the club extremely successful, it was one where the *esprit de corps* was second to none. An Athletic game at Llantwit Major in January 1981 provided powerful evidence of that fact. Among the second string side were three internationals, Mark Keyworth (England), and Alun Donovan and Phil Llewellyn (Wales). As had been the case in the previous season, only nine players in the first team squad had not played for the Athletic by the time the season ended. That, surely, was a litmus test of team spirit during one of the most successful periods in the club's history.

In February David Richards showed his versatility by appearing on the wing for Wales, while Geoff Wheel (the 'Ripper'), had established himself as a fixture in the Welsh pack. Meanwhile, at St. Helens, the richness of the team spirit was demonstrated, yet again, when Roger Blyth, the leading points scorer for the previous three seasons, agreed to share full-back duties with Mark Wyatt. The older man was demonstrating archetypal Swansea club spirit, which he would endorse later in his life when he became a key member of the St. Helens management team.

After Newbridge had been defeated in the fourth round of the cup, the Swansea camp faced up to the problem of picking the side for the semi-final against Cardiff. As Gordon Morris put it, 'We have a terribly difficult task in choosing the side to play against Cardiff'. The chairman went on to say that it was inevitable that many talented players would have to be left out of the side. As he put it, 'they are bound to be disappointed and we shall be disappointed for them'.

When Ebbw Vale were 'crushed' by 37 points to 6 at St. Helens in the match before the semi-final, Morris said that the task was even more difficult. After that match, Morris spoke about 'the authority of the team'. Indeed, given that a victory which followed took their run of consecutive victories to fifteen, it was not surprising that the side should have an imperious look about it. Where in the U.K. was there another first-class club with such a record? The question remained unanswered.

Thus it was that, when the 'Whites' travelled to neutral Bridgend to compete with the 'Blue and Blacks', they were confident and in good spirits. Sadly, they found the Brewery Field pitch to be thick with mud, and, as the match unfolded, Cardiff adapted themselves to the conditions more effectively. With players 'aquaplaning' on parts of the ground, and the mud clinging to boots and ball, Gareth Davies's boot 'ruled the roost'. Not for the first time, the 'Whites' fell at the penultimate fence, as their hugely talented side failed to play to its potential.

In the middle of April the 'Whites' avenged themselves for that defeat by beating the Cardiff-

David Richards about to deliver a coaching manual pass.

ians on their own ground. Whilst that victory was enjoyed, in both financial and prestige terms, it was small consolation for the semi-final defeat. Nonetheless, that win and a final victory at Aberavon, ensured that the 'Whites' became Merit Table Champions. It was a proud moment for skipper, Geoff Wheel, and just reward for the attention he had given to, and the effort he had put in to captaining the club over two seasons.

At the end of the season, when in conversation with Ron Griffiths, secretary, David Price spoke about the tradition of service at St. Helens. Apart from his own 25 years of service as secretary, two other St. Helens men personified that service ethic. Vivian Davies had been fixture secretary for 24 years, and Gwyn White, treasurer for 14. Many others, named and unnamed in this book, have dedicated themselves in a similar way. Rhodes might have said that of such men are empires made. Any chronicler of the life of the St. Helens club, like the author, would come to the conclusion that, of such men are great rugby clubs made! At least, it applied to the club at the Cricket Field.

After winning the National Sevens tournament again, the Swansea party flew to California for an end-of-the-season tour. They went as Champions, and with rich memories of an extremely successful season. The statistics for the campaign showed that Mark Wyatt had replaced Roger Blyth as the leading points scorer (243), whilst Tony Swift (28) headed the try-scoring list. Buried in the figures was another noteworthy record. Young Richard Moriarty had played more games (42) than anyone else. Clearly, the Protestant work ethic was alive and well in Morriston. The man infected with that spirit was to replicate that level of service for many years to come.

1981-82

Not quite so good

Before the new season began, there was a strong rumour circulating in Swansea to the effect that Alun Donovan was going to join Bridgend. Happily for Swansea folk, it was a rumour without foundation. Alun remained at St. Helens, and went on to gain further 'caps'. However, whilst the Donovan story proved to be a rumour, there were facts to be absorbed by supporters regarding the fitness of certain players. As the season began, Huw Rees had had a problem with his knee whilst on the club's U.S. tour, and Tony Swift, Gareth Roberts, and Mark Davies were all nursing injuries. However, according to Ron Griffiths, Huw Rees apart, the injuries were not serious. Consequently, after two extremely successful seasons, and with the bulk of men who played then still available, prospects for the 1981-82 campaign appeared to be bright.

After the first two fixtures, there were those who thought that 'bright' was an understatement. Following a 'loosener' at Gorseinon, the 'Whites' entertained Cross Keys, and, to the delight of home supporters, 'won the match by a mile'. The racing analogy was apposite, for the 'Whites', who scored 73 points without reply, 'ran away with the game'. After that, Moseley and Ebbw Vale were among the side's victims before the Swansea men registered their sixth win in succession by beating Bristol. It was another fine start, and the St. Helens management, the squad, and supporters, seeing that the season was unfolding in a manner which mirrored the two previous campaigns, exuded confidence. Even the pessimists dropped their guard. Newport didn't, however, and for the first time since 1977 the 'Whites' lost to the 'Usksiders' on their own ground. The defeat was disappointing, for Swansea had enjoyed the greater share of possession, but two tries from Huw Rees and a Wyatt penalty were not enough. Newport won the game by 18 points to 14. When Pontypool took the next match by an even bigger margin (22 points to 13), there were concerned frowns at the Cricket Field. After the outstanding performances of the previous two seasons, two losses in succession caused the old nagging doubts to return. The wolf approached, again.

Fortunately, the third away match in succession did not result in another defeat. On Twickenham's wide-open spaces, the 'Whites' recovered something of their early season form to defeat the Harlequins. Not only had the 'rot been stopped', the match proved to be the precursor of a fine run during which eleven matches were won in succession. Noteable among those victories was the defeat of Llanelli. Playing on a Friday night under the St. Helens lights and in wretched conditions, the 'Scarlets' succumbed to Swansea's strength, flair and organisation. Malcolm Dacey was said to have had a 'performance of skill and maturity' behind a dominant pack, whilst his partner, Brynmor Williams was singled out for praise for the quality of his service from the base of the scrum. Dacey scored the first of Swansea's four tries, and had a hand in another, as the 'Whites' ended Llanelli's ten-match unbeaten run in 'half a gale, with the rain lashing down'. One of the scorers in that game was pleased to see that the papers had spelled his name correctly in their match reports. Mike Ruddock, who played a significant part in subduing the 'Scarlet' forwards and half-backs, scored a fine try.

With the Bridgend bypass on the M4 being opened during the previous week, the Brewery Field men found that their journey time to St. Helens was shorter than it had been. Unfortunately for them, however, the 'Whites' by-passed their defenders with some ease, to win rather more comfortably than the 19 points to 7 result suggested. It was the next match which caught the eye, though. With Bleddyn Bowen at outside-half, the 'Whites' produced a 'power-packed performance to swamp Neath'. The side scored six tries that day, with Bowen and Tony Swift each getting a brace.

On 28 November, Australia were due to come to St. Helens to face a 'Whites' side which, by then, had lost just twice in nineteen matches. Before that day, however, there were several victories of note which served to boost the confidence of the Swansea camp. By then, too, Mark Wyatt was 'harvesting points like an adding machine', whilst new flank forward, Mike Ruddock, was 'catching the eye', and Brynmor Williams was proving to be a 'brilliant opportunist'. Unfortunately, though, in beating the Police in the first round of the W.R.U. Cup (the match immediately before the 'Wallabies' came to St. Helens), both David Richards and Tony Swift pulled hamstrings. Neither was able to recover in time to face the tourists, and the 'Whites' side which represented the City that day was:

M. Wyatt, H. Rees, A. Donovan, G. Jenkins, A. Meredith, M. Dacey, B. Williams, C. Williams, S. Davies, G. John, B.Clegg (Capt.), R. Moriarty, M. Davies, T. Cheeseman, M. Ruddock.

Given the level of confidence present in the home side, it came as no surprise to faithful 'Whites' followers that their heroes turned around at half-time holding a 3 points to 0 lead. The points had been registered by Malcolm Dacey, who dropped a fine goal. The Australians, who had paid the 'Whites' the compliment of making just three changes from the side which had beaten Ireland on the previous Saturday, had struggled to impress in the first period. Frustrated by Swansea's tactics (the game plan focused upon the 'Whites' pack) the match became ill-tempered. Unfortunately for the St. Helens men, Barry Clegg (a pinched nerve in the neck), and Mike Ruddock (a broken nose) had to leave the field during the third quarter of the match. It was after that that the 'Wallabies' began to take control of the game, and, in due course, they 'cut loose in a seven minute spell to score three tries'. Despite the heroic efforts of the men in white, thereafter, the blanket defence of the tourists nullified all Swansea's attacks. At the final whistle, Australia had beaten Swansea by 12 points to 3. A week later, however, four 'Whites', Alun Donovan, Geoff Wheel, Richard Moriarty and Mark Davies, avenged the defeat when, as members of the Welsh side which played the 'Wallabies' they helped beat the men from 'Oz'.

After the Australian match, because of snow and ice, no rugby was played for four weeks. Then, in quick succession, Glamorgan Wanderers, and London Welsh were beaten by 33 points to 3 and 47 points to 8 respectively. In both matches, the 'Whites' played with 'confidence, panache and enterprise'. If we are to accept that newspaper comment, since the first Enterprise Zone to be created in Britain was established in Swansea around that time, the side's initiative was apposite.

Wrexham were the next to be beaten (in the 2nd round of the cup), when the 'Whites' replicated their Yuletide form to run in six tries in a 36 points to 12 victory. Following this success, several rugby writers commented on the fact that the side was, again, playing the fluent, penetrative Swansea style of football, which had been so much enjoyed during the previous season. While, in the next match, Newbridge (and the elements) managed partially to nullify that flair, when Ebbw Vale came to St. Helens four days before the next cup round was to be played, the 'Whites' cut loose, scoring 54 points while conceding only 3.

In the days before the third round tie was played, the general consensus of opinion in the press suggested that the 'Whites' would beat 'Pooler', their opponents, with something to spare. However, on the day, and not having read the script, the Pontypool pack battled its way into the ascendancy. Playing effective eight-man rugby, with Eddie Butler, Steve Sutton and Jeff Squires 'inspirational', Pooler won the day. Whilst Swansea folk could point to the fact that Geoff Wheel's nose had been broken, and his contribution missed, 'Pooler' did score three tries to win the match. The *Western Mail* described the Swansea side as being 'shell-shocked'. Not for the first time, Pontypool had shown that they were a difficult side to play against.

Whilst during the remainder of the season the 'Whites' scored some fine victories – notably, beating Bath by 41 points to nil, and Newport by 31 points to 6 – following the cup defeat, the 'spark' seemed to have gone out of the Swansea side. It is true that a number of key injuries adversely affected the team throughout the campaign – David Richards, for example missed much of the season. However, the psychological implications of the cup defeat seemed to have had the greatest negative effect.

In typical Celtic fashion, in the face of a relatively small number of defeats, supporters and the media dredged through the St. Helens despond to find plausible reasons for the relative decline of the team. Ron Griffiths, for example, concluded that, 'It has been a disappointing by the standards Swansea have set themselves over the last two seasons ... the side did not match up to expectations ... and lacked consistency.'

Whilst the *Post*-man and Swansea supporters, in their relative gloom, focused upon the negatives, the truth was that, winning 32 games out of the 43 played would have satisfied the followers of most clubs. (Indeed it would have pleased those of Swansea in most campaigns since the War). It was true that the team did not perform as effectively as it had during the previous campaign. Furthermore, during the second-half of the season, the Swansea patient had a relapse with respect to that much-disliked malady, inconsistency. It was also true that the team lost to both the Barbarians and the 'Quins for the first time since 1968, whilst the Harlequins victory had been the first by an English club at St. Helens since 1976. Yet there was much for the optimists to feed upon. As far as results were concerned, performances up to the Pontypool match had matched those of the two previous seasons. The defeat of Cardiff at St. Helens late in the season had been achieved by 'a brand of positive, attacking rugby that was almost breathtaking'. In addition, in new young players like Emyr and Ruddock, the club's management believed they had men of great potential. Then, once injuries healed, men such as David Richards, Tony Swift and Geoff Wheel would be available to lend their talent and experience to the Swansea cause. Despite his absences through injury, Tony Swift showed his ability once again by topping the try getting list (15), and, relative newcomer, Mark Wyatt had scored 310 points in 30 appearances.

As the players headed for Zimbabwe for their close-season tour, optimists and pessimists among the 'Whites' supporters were pondering on the season which had passed, and contemplating the campaign to come. To quote the old saw, more believed that the cup was half empty rather than half full, a typical Celtic trait. As the Chief Executive of a multi-national corporation once told the author, 'I never put a Welshman in charge of corporate planning, they are influenced to too great an extent by the mood of the moment'. Whilst it is said that 'all generalisations are false', Welsh readers will be able to compare their own experience with the statement of that chief executive. But then, we Welsh have other talents. At St. Helens the planning was of a shorter-term nature. Playing skills, team-work, *esprit de corps*, and fitness, all matters of greater immediacy, were those upon which the focus of management was concentrated.

1982-83

More silverware

On his return from the Zimbabwe tour, Alun Meredith announced his retirement. Alun had been a fine servant to the club, starting out at scrum-half and, subsequently, playing at full-back, wing and centre. Not only did that say a great deal about the player's versatility, it also spoke volumes about his willingness to play where the club had a need. And that was greatly appreciated by the selectors on numerous occasions. Alun retired with the warmest wishes of all at St. Helens. Another versatile stalwart, Roger Blyth, told the *Post* that he had also intended to retire, but, persuaded by Mike James, and finding that he still enjoyed the game, he was going to 'semi-retire'. In view of the length of the remainder of the Blyth career, some semi-retirement that proved to be!

As far as David Richards was concerned, the captain had no thoughts about retiring. Indeed, now fully fit, he was hoping that he would avoid the kind of injuries which had disrupted his first season at the helm. David found himself working with a new coach, Ian Hall, and both men told the *Post* that they were 'reasonably confident' about the season ahead, and felt that they would achieve a 'measure of success'. Any student of politicians 'vague-speak' would have recognised the beauty of the statements. They could be interpreted by pessimists or optimists in which ever way satisfied their predilections. In view of what was going to happen during the season ahead, had there been an examination, the optimists' 'translation' would have gained most marks.

After a 'warm-up' match at Skewen, the 'Whites' played their first senior match of the season against Gloucester at Kingsholm with Malcolm Dacey at fly-half and David Richards in the centre, the 'Whites' took the game to the home side, but found themselves in arrears when the half-time whistle sounded. In the second period, however, the St. Helens men 'put their game together'. New centre, Kevin Hopkins scored a fine try, as did another newcomer, Paul Gallagher, on the wing. At the end the 'Whites' left the field winners by 23 points to 16, which, given the strength of Gloucester at the time, was an encouraging early-season win for the men in white.

There was further encouragement for the St. Helens loyalists in the next two matches. Cross Keys conceded 31 points while scoring 12, and Moseley succumbed by 31 points to 13. Since Moseley and Gloucester had been joint winners of the English John Player Cup competition in the previous season, the win completed a unique double for the men in white. Not only were the English cup finalists beaten, the victory was achieved in true Swansea style. As Ron Griffiths reported, 'It was a demonstration of Swansea class which left Moseley clutching at straws'. One 'breathtaking' try was illustrative of the Swansea class that day. Gareth Roberts collected a drop out, made ground, found Huw Davies at his shoulder, Huw passed to David Richards who made a half-break before transferring to Mark Wyatt to carry the movement forward. Wyatt

Swansea R.F.C. 1982-83.
Rear Row (standing) left to right: L. M. Evans (Football Match Committee), Dickie Dobbs (Linesman), Stuart Evans, Gareth Roberts, Clive Williams, Mike Ruddock, Barry Clegg, Garry John, Malcolm Dacey, Huw Gilson, Gareth Jenkins, Roger Blyth, Bernard Cajot (Trainer), M. J. James (Chairman Selection Committee).
Front Row (seated) left to right: Trevor Cheeseman, Tony Swift, Huw Davies, Jeff Herdman, Ian Hall (Coach), David Richards (Capt.), Norman Blyth (Club Chairman), Mark Davies, Paul Gallagher, Mark Wyatt, Kevin Hopkins, Keith Colclough, Arthur Emyr, Eddie Rickard (Baggage Master).

drew his man, then fed Kevin Hopkins, who turned inside to score. They enjoyed that in the stand and on the 'Tanner Bank'. That was a real Swansea try!

By the end of September the side had won all ten of its matches, scoring 238 points in the process whilst conceding 120. Given that clubs of the stature of Bristol, Pontypool and Newport were among those beaten during that period, Ian Hall's verdict that he was 'pleased with the progress which had been made' was nicely understated. However, the coach did admit that he was particularly pleased with the side's performance against Pontypool (a 33 points to 9 victory), when, he felt, 'We put it all together'. Since after 'stuttering to victory' in an earlier game, against Maesteg, David Richards had said that 'We are not firing on all cylinders yet', the St. Helens engine must have had a thorough overhaul by the time the Pontypool match was played.

The next match, however, brought the unbeaten run to an end, the Harlequins winning in London. Then, after a victory over Llanelli, Bridgend became the first Welsh club to beat the 'Whites'. However, these proved to be minor setbacks. After the Bridgend game, another winning run developed during which no fewer than seventeen matches were won in succession. It was an impressive record, one of which the giants of the Golden Era would have been proud. No wonder that St. Helens smiles were lighting up Swansea bay. Indeed, there were those with a poetic inclination who believed that, if the Swansea faithful could have guaranteed the continuance of such illumination, it might have resulted in the demise of the lighthouse at Mumbles.

During this impressive run, Llanelli's own twenty-one match record was 'besmirched', when, on a damp Stradey afternoon, Mark Wyatt kicked the winning penalty seven minutes from the end. Malcolm Dacey, who impressed Phil Bennett by his play in the match, scored a try and 'ran the game with authority'. Another Swansea man who caught the Bennett eye at that time was Richard Moriarty. 'Benny' was unequivocal in his praise. 'Richard Moriarty', he wrote, 'is the best forward I have seen this season, quick about the field, a ball-winner in lines-out and elsewhere, and tremendously mobile'. Even in the partisan jungle of Welsh rugby, whilst some would have wished to replace 'is' with 'one of', Phil Bennett's opinion was widely shared.

A match at Leicester, towards the end of October, provided 'Whites' supporters with a warm glow of satisfaction. Several 'Swansea' tries were scored in a 'rousing second-half against a top English side'. Then the touring Maoris were beaten in a 'bruising St. Helens match'. Since that was the first defeat suffered by the tourists, the triumph was appreciated even more. Mark Wyatt enjoyed that match, kicking five penalties, three of which were from 45 yards or more.

The triumphant Swansea side that day was:

M. Wyatt, A. Swift, D. Richards (Capt.), H. Rees, A. Emyr, M. Dacey, H. Davies, C. Williams, S. Davies, G. John, T. Cheeseman, R. Moriarty, G. Roberts, M. Davies, M. Ruddock.

After another outstanding display against Blackheath, when several papers reported that Malcolm Dacey had boosted his claim for the Welsh fly-half position, the young man found himself in the national side to play the tourists. He was not the only Swansea player in the team; Mark Wyatt, David Richards, Richard Moriarty and Mark Davies also wore the red shirt that day. Indeed, Dacey's selection took the number of internationals in the Swansea squad at the time into double figures. However, soon after, one of them, Brynmor Williams, joined the long list of 'Whites' who had left the club for the Rugby League. This time, though, the player went east instead of north. He joined the newly-formed Cardiff Blue Dragons, leaving Swansea with just one experienced scrum-half, Huw Davies. Happily, Davies was in fine form and carried the burden of the position throughout the remainder of the season when lesser men might have wilted.

As the season unfolded, Ron Griffiths, in the *Post*, was relishing his task as official 'Whites'-watcher. He reported that, 'Swansea believe that they could go all the way in the cup this season'. Later he indulged himself with a reflection of the power of the Swansea squad. 'The club', he wrote, 'has so many outstanding players that they must be the envy of every club in the country'. The *Post*-man went on to congratulate the St. Helens management on their 'diplomacy' in keeping the players 'happy and employed'. Griffiths was right about the richness of the squad, but as far as diplomacy was concerned, the management had a different view. Mike James, chairman of selectors, called it a 'happy problem', and emphasised the team spirit which permeated the club, and which enabled his committee to deal with their selection problems effectively. That, certainly, was an enviable strength!

Among the many examples of such team spirit was the way in which the full-back position was being handled. Roger Blyth, an international, and club points record-holder had welcomed the development of Mark Wyatt. He argued that he and Mark were not rivals for the position, rather, he would 'fit in when required'. At least in respect of the number 15 spot, it followed that 'negative' competition was a problem which did not exist.

The end of 1982 arrived with the 'Whites' having won their way through to the third Round of the cup. In addition they had won several outstanding victories. Richmond 'succumbed to a rampaging Swansea', scored just six point while the 'Whites' amassed thirty-one. In that match, Roger Blyth brought his points total to 100 points for the eighth time in ten seasons, whilst Ruddock, Swift and Emyr crossed for tries. Equally savoured, was a victory over Cardiff by the 'Whites' after they had been trailing at half-time. There was a new name to note in the Swansea side that day. Keith Colclough, who was understudying the, seemingly ever-present Clive Williams, had a fine game against an experienced opponent. In addition, Glamorgan Wanderers had their 'comeuppance' in a 49 points to 9 St. Helens 'avalanche', and London Welsh conceded 39 points in a 'thrilling exhibition of all that is good about Swansea rugby'.

Early in January, there took place what the *Western Mail* called a 'dress rehearsal for the third round of the W.R.U. Cup'. On that occasion, on a rain-soaked pitch, the 'Whites' always had the edge on the 'Amber and Blacks'. One of the tries scored by Swansea on that wet Rodney Parade surface was an example of the Dacey talent. Receiving the ball just outside his own '22', Malcolm 'jinked his way through three would-be tackles', drew another man and slipped a neat pass to the ever-supporting Jeff Herdman who crashed over with a Newport man on his back.

As it turned out that victory was the seventeenth and last in the winning sequence, for, in the next match, Llanelli avenged themselves of the defeat suffered earlier in the season. Then as had often happened before, a second match was lost. Coventry on their own ground, snatching victory in the dying minutes of a hard-fought game. After such a wonderful winning run, two defeats in succession immediately before the next cup round, was hardly the outcome desired by coach, Ian Hall. The antennae of the pessimists began to twitch.

They were exercising their twitches during the next two games as well. Whilst Newport were beaten by 12 points to 9, Mark Wyatt had pulled the chestnuts out of the fire by kicking the winning penalty deep into injury time. Even the optimists were concerned, for the home pack was pushed around in embarrassing fashion by the bigger Newport eight. The next performance also left a great deal to be desired. This time the side 'scraped home unconvincingly by scoring in the eighth minute of injury time'. Unless there was an improvement, popular opinion suggested, the team's prospects against Llanelli were less than good.

So concerned was Ian Hall that he was said to have been 'planning a rehabilitation exercise for the pack'. During a radio interview, he continued with the motoring analogy. He said, 'We have been looking like an engine in need of a tune-up'. In the week that followed, the coach continued with this line of comment, talking down Swansea's chances in the coming game. Llanelli, however, would have none of it. Indeed, had Shakespeare been working for the *Llanelli Star*, he might have written, 'Methinks that Swansea doth protest too much'. Yet, at St. Helens, the problems were thought to be far from illusory. Ron Griffiths, adopting the motoring analogy wrote: 'Swansea have such a demanding fixture list that they have been stale since Christmas. Their batteries have run down.'

In the days before the Stradey game, whatever was said or done at St. Helens, by the time the 'Whites' ran out onto the Stradey pitch, their engine must have been purring powerfully. The much maligned 'Whites' pack produced 'a fine disciplined performance 'to sweep into the semi-final'. The defeat was the first cup round to be lost by Llanelli on their own pitch, which put into context the performance of Swansea that day. In dreadful, conditions, the Swansea backs flourished behind the platform provided by their dominant pack. Tony Swift crossed twice, whilst, given the conditions, Mark Wyatt's kicking was outstanding.

Progress in the cup, and the club heading the Whitbread Merit Table, resulted in an increase in the optimists and a decrease in pessimists. Engines, batteries, tune-ups, and the like were forgotten. The 'Whites', it seemed, had caught their second breath.

Unhappily, in a match at Bridgend two weeks before the semi-final tie, captain, David Richards broke his collar bone. Thus it was that the 'Whites' went into that penultimate round led by Mark Davies. As it happened, Richards had waited until the week before his accident before naming his number two. On making the announcement the captain had said that 'because of the large number of excellent candidates, he had bided his time'. Mark, according to Richards, had been selected because he 'reads the game well, leads by example, and has all-round ability'.

Having lost heavily at Bath on the Saturday before the semi-final, the old doubts began to creep back. However, the fates had not finished with supporting the men in white. Opponents, Newbridge were well-beaten, as 'Swansea sparkled their way to the final ... as they turned-back the clock to recapture their pre-Christmas form'. Huw Davies, Arthur Emyr, and Mark Davies were the 'Whites' scorers in a match which was 'won in some style'.

Now that they were in the final of the cup competition, the ideal scenario would have had the Swansea men winning each match with ease. Instead, that old malady 'inconsistency' was present again at the Cricket Ground. After beating the 'Quins', the 'Whites' took on the Barbarians, who had drawn 32 point all with Cardiff two days earlier. The result of that game was received with incredulity by the press men who telephoned to obtain the final score. The man in the Swansea office who provided the information was asked by two enquirers, 'Are you sure that's right?' The result, Swansea 58 Barbarians 6. It reverberated around the rugby world. The press used words like 'crushed', and 'overwhelmed', as they reported on the Swansea win of a quality 'which coaches dream about but seldom achieve'. Yet, later that week, the 'Whites' suffered their heaviest defeat of the season as Cardiff dominated the game.

With Roger Blyth injured, Mark Wyatt out with a broken collar bone, David Richards sidelined and Malcolm Dacey having to undertake a fitness test, as the date of the final approached, there were concerns in the Swansea camp. In the event, Blyth and Dacey both played in what turned out to be a disappointing Swansea performance. The 'Pooler' pack, playing their traditional game, 'ground down' the 'Whites' eight, to set up an 18 points to 6 victory. Roger Blyth's two penalties were all that the St. Helens men could show for their afternoon's work.

Disappointed as they were, Swansea supporters, looking back over the season as a whole, had much to savour. 40 matches of the 47 played had been won, Roger Blyth and Mark Wyatt both topped the 200 points mark, while Arthur Emyr and Tony Swift each scored 25 tries. Once again, the club were Winners of the Whitbread Merit Table, of the *Western Mail* Unofficial Welsh Championship, of the *Daily Mail* Anglo-Welsh Championship, they were the *Sunday Telegraph* Team of the Season, finalists in the W.R.U. Challenge Cup and winners of the Snelling Sevens Tournament. Furthermore, if they ignored all that, who among them could forget that marvellous victory over the Barbarians? Most were convinced that the team would do even better in the season ahead, and there were those who, on seeing the new Welsh one pound coin with its inscription 'Pleidiol wyf i'm Gwlad', would have appreciated a version which carried a modified inscription, where 'Gwynion' replaced 'Gwlad', for the 'Whites' have never been without a strong band of devotees.

Chapter Twenty-Five

MORE MATCHES, LESS SUCCESS

1983–84

ONLY IN ONE SEASON SINCE THE inception of the club had more games been played than during the 1983/84 campaign. During that season, fifty-one matches were played as against forty-seven in the previous one. The most telling statistic, however, was that the 'games lost' column showed that the 'Whites' had been beaten nineteen times. This represented the largest number of defeats for a decade, and showed a disappointing decline from the previous season, when the team had been beaten on only seven occasions. Yet, when the season started, the general opinion among the media men and supporters alike gave good reason to expect a continuance of the form shown in the 1982/83 campaign. Furthermore, the season's early results were such as to confirm that opinion.

First, a 'warm-up' game at Gowerton was won 'with something to spare', and, then, in a St. Helens match against Gloucester, the side ran in nine tries. Furthermore, the general consensus of press opinion after that match, suggested that the men in white were far from flattered by the 46 points to 16 victory. Indeed, had the 'Whites' not 'taken their collective foot off the accelerator after leading 30 points to nil, the visitors might never have claimed a brace of tries late in the game. In the match, Huw Davies scored two tries, and was closely involved in several others, as did Tony Swift. The try of the game, however, was that scored by Kevin Hopkins who, according to the *Post*, 'provided the spectators with the 'thrill of the afternoon'. Receiving just outside his own '22', 'his brilliant side-stepping run took him through the Gloucester defence'. Another report vested the score with supernatural trappings. 'Such was the mesmeric quality of the try', the paper reported, 'that the spectators might have been forgiven for assuming that Hopkins had beaten sixteen men in scoring'. At that try, the result of the match, and the fluency of the 'Whites' football, the optimists smacked their lips. Even those who saw the world through gloomy spectacles relaxed somewhat. Swansea teas in Swansea homes that day would have been graced with smiling husbands, and wives who sensed that the time had come to mention some desired purchase. Meantime, the ladies who had been at the game were, themselves, open to largesse of unusual proportions.

There followed a win against Cross Keys which bemused the supporters. In that midweek match, the Gwent men frustrated the 'Whites' to such a degree that it was only as a result of a David Richards try late in the game that the side was able to salvage something from the evening's work. Was this, questioned the pessimists, the start of another season of inconsistency? Three days later, the optimists showed similar concern. 'Moseley', according to the *Daily Telegraph*, 'handed out a lesson to the Welshmen'. Whilst the score (6 points to 14), hardly suggested a rout, the paper's report implied that the 'Whites' had been out-thought by the home side. At that, with the memory of the Gloucester game still fresh, doubts about inconsistent form began to

Swansea R.F.C. 1983-84.
Rear Row, standing (left to right): L. M. Evans (Match Committee), R. J. Dobbs (Touch Judge), Gethin Thomas (Asst. Coach), S. Evans, C. Williams, M. Davies, J. Williams, M. Griffiths, T. Cheeseman, R. Blyth, M. Wyatt, K. Colclough, D. Williams, A. Meredith (Match Committee), S. Davies (Match Committee), M. J. James (Match Committee).
Front Row (left to right): B. Cajot (Trainer), H. Gilson, G. Jenkins, T. Swift, I. Morgan (Chairman), D. Richards (Capt.), C. Hitchins, J. Herdman, H. Davies.
Seated on Ground (left to right): A. Williams, M. Dacey, R. Jones, E. Rickard (Team Attendant).

seep into even the most optimistic supporter's mind. In two of the four matches played, the side's form had fallen below that which had been demonstrated during the previous campaign.

Nevertheless, when Bristol came to St. Helens in the middle of September, the 'Whites' had massaged their collective ego as a result of a match against Bonymaen. Whilst the score, 42 points to 4, had to be considered in the light of the standing of the opposition, a win was a win! In addition, the match had been won in some style. At the time, had there been a sports psychologist at St. Helens he would have spoken about 'positive imaging', and impressed upon the players the need for them to focus their minds upon successful application of the moves worked out in training. As it was, the side went into the game with the Bristolians with a spring in its collective step. Happily, the outcome of the match was all that could have been desired. The *Post* headline said it all: 'Swansea storm back to form'. The pack was singled out for praise that day, with forwards scoring three of Swansea's five tries, though Jeff Herdman, who scored one of them, was, at the time, operating as an emergency wing. Flanker, Mike Ruddock, however, scored a brace of tries following two excellent back-row moves.

Newport, on their own ground, were the next side to be beaten, but a run of four successive defeats followed thereafter. One of them, by Llanelli, also resulted in the 'Whites' ground record being taken in a 'raw and physical encounter'. That defeat was particularly disappointing, for, prior to the kick-off, David Richards had been presented with the *Daily Mail* Pennant, which was one of the trophies which had marked the success of the previous season's side. Then, as if to confound the supporters, the next match resulted in a fine 44 points to six victory over Halifax – when 'the visitors were overwhelmed'. Whilst that win gave heart to Swansea supporters, the three defeats which followed were said to have 'knocked the stuffing out of the team's confidence'. At that, even the most positively myopic Swansea supporter had to accept that the old malady, 'inconsistency' had re-established itself at the Cricket Ground.

By the end of December 1983, the supporters, looking back on the first-half of season, must have thought about the curate's egg. Whilst all three Yule-tide matches had been won, the club's record at that time read: P. 28, W. 17, L. 11. In his half-term report in the *Post*, Spencer Feeney sought an explanation for the side's disappointing showing. Despite the promise of the early games, the team was not thought to be 'firing on all cylinders'. Geoff Wheel's strength

Three Swansea boys – line astern – v. All Blacks. Roger Blyth, Richard Moriarty and David Richards.

'Embrace me' – Mike Ruddock 'clobbers' a Llanelli wing.

was being missed, and a 'spate of injuries' had disrupted selection. Among the injured were David Richards, out with a neck problem, Arthur Emyr, with hamstring trouble, and Tony Swift, with a damaged knee. The *Post* felt that the pack's work in 'rucking, mauling and scrummaging, was not what it was', which, according to the paper, did not allow the backs to shine as they had. Yet, given the talent which was at St. Helens at the time, there was universal puzzlement at the side's relatively poor showing. For example, the team contained players of the quality of Mark Wyatt, Kevin Hopkins, Malcolm Dacey, and Mark Davies, all of whom had been selected to play for Wales against Japan. Furthermore, there was 'semi-retired' Roger Blyth who was proving to be an able deputy for Mark Wyatt at full-back. At least, in their darkest hours, as they contemplated the rest of the season, the optimists could parade this galaxy of stars in their mind's eye. Perhaps, they may have reasoned, the new year would provide the team with a fresh, winning, start.

Unfortunately, when January ended, such hope was seen to be ill-founded. Two matches out of the four played during the month had been lost, and the club had been beaten in the third round of the Cup. Yet. one victory, gained in front of the T.V. cameras, had given hope to everyone at St. Helens. Ron Griffiths called it 'A Swansea rugby oratorio'. For the first time that season, he believed, 'all the pieces had slotted together'. He noted that the forwards had been quicker to the breakdown, and 'had won a great deal of possession in the tight and in the loose'. As the *Post*-man's readers considered these words, they would have brought to mind the players of quality who comprised the Swansea front eight. Clive Williams, Trevor Cheeseman, Richard and Paul Moriarty, Jeff Herdman, Gareth Roberts, Mike Ruddock and Mark Davies among them. And behind the front eight were internationals like Wyatt, Blyth, Swift, Richards and Dacey, and excellent footballers such as Huw Rees, the promising nineteen-year-old Aled Williams and Robert Jones, who was one year junior to the outside-half. Few clubs could match the quality of that roll call! Yet!

Sadly, the cup defeat which might have 'kept the season alive' coincided with the demise of Swansea's Mettoy factory. Given that, in the future, that company's famous die-cast models would be produced in China, the closure was a blow to the city's economy. In giving reasons for the closure of the plant, a Mettoy spokesman cited poor yields, inconsistent quality, and poor returns on capital employed. Swansea rugby supporters found that, as far as the St. Helens club was concerned, they could identify with two of those reasons. When 'all the pieces were put together' the quality was superb, whilst the yield of 'points for' was often abundant. At other times, however, the converse was true. Unfortunately, 'other times' were too common.

In February, 'a torrential hail storm' resulted in a match at Penarth being abandoned after thirty-five minutes. Whilst the match was thus a non-event, it did provide a pointer to the future, though no one at the Penarth ground that night could have known. The team was led that evening by flanker, Mike Ruddock. Within a decade the young man was to be involved in leadership at St. Helens which encompassed a far wider brief.

Meantime, despite the indifferent form of the team, the Welsh selectors 'kept tabs' on Swansea's internationals. For example, in a match at the Brewery Field, four of the 'Big Five' were present to check on 'the duel between Mark Wyatt and Bridgend's Howell Davies'. After the match, however, they were said to have been very impressed by several of the Swansea players. Among those mentioned were the Moriarty brothers, who had 'dominated the lines-out'.

The Moriarty brothers.

As the season wore on, inconsistency continued to affect the side. Fine wins were followed by defeats, sometimes at the hands of sides which, at least on paper, should not have troubled the men in white. Conversely, some of their victories showed the team at its brilliant best, which, at least, gave frustrated supporters hope as well as enjoyment. For example, Exeter were defeated by 78 points to 4 in a match when, 'the fluidity of Swansea's passing was a joy to behold', and 33 points and 34 respectively, were registered against Sale and Ebbw Vale with 'exciting tries' being scored on each occasion. In early March, according to the *Post*, 'for forty-five minutes Swansea

Trevor Cheeseman awaits developments.

rugby sparkled like a Christmas tree'. No Swansea supporter was concerned about the unseasonal analogy, as Swift, Emyr, Dacey, and Williams scored tries 'with a flourish', and Wyatt's trusty boot converted them and kicked the penalties. Sydney, the unfortunate visitors, looked to be heading for a thrashing as the 'Whites' turned about sitting on a 22 points to 6 lead. However, early in the second-half, in trying to stop an Australian scoring, Huw Davies broke his leg. That accident seemed to have had a depressing effect on the Swansea men, and the second-half was relatively nondescript.

At the end of March, Trevor Cheeseman, who had played twenty-six successive matches, was given, what the *Post* called, 'a well-earned rest'. Trevor had demonstrated, yet again, the kind of service which dedicated 'All Whites' have given to the Club from its inception. In part, this book is a celebration of such dedication, which has been particularly noticeable at times when the side has been less than successful. After all, it is not difficult to maintain enthusiasm when the team is winning; to do so when there have been a series of depressing results, calls for a superior level of loyalty and dedication. Cheeseman demonstrated such qualities in abundance.

When the time came to consider the season's statistics, despite the disappointing outcome to the campaign as a whole, Swansea supporters could, at least, savour the form of their favourites in the season's final matches: played 7, won 6, lost 1, for 159 points, against 111, augured well for the season to come. Furthermore, among the matches which were won was one against the club's arch rivals, Cardiff. Whilst the 'Whites' only won by a single point (15 to 14), it was the tenacity of the side and the quality of its team work which enabled the victory to be gained. In addition, the game provided a glimpse of the future in the shape of the accuracy, speed and length of passing of the club's youthful scrum-half. For example, in the Cardiff match, Robert Jones, 'flung out a bullet-like pass to Malcolm Dacey. Dacey made ground, transferred to Williams, who fed Richards. The captain changed direction to improve the angle of attack, and made space before passing to Swift, who, on finding his path to the line blocked, fed the supporting Emyr who hurtled across for a try'. As they contemplated the score, 'breathless' was the collective term which fitted players and spectators alike. It was a 'Swansea try' of immense proportions. Had he been there, Dickie Owen would have congratulated the teenager who started the movement. Indeed, he might have wished to transfer his sobriquet to the young man from Trebanos.

A glance at some of the season's statistics would, also, have given supporters greater heart. Mark Wyatt led the points scoring list, again, with 294, while Roger Blyth – semi-retired – had amassed 163. The top try-scorer was Tony Swift with 21, whilst the Forwards' Union had reason to feel pleased with flanker, Mike Ruddock, who had scored 16 tries to put him into second place. Finally, the club's total of points scored (1,229) had been beaten in only one previous season. At that, an objective statistician might have pointed to the changes in scoring value, to the number of games played, and to the points which had been conceded. However, at the time, as Swansea supporters searched for comfort among the statistics, it was not surprising that selective myopia was a common complaint among them. Indeed, it would have been surprising had they not given Mr. Magoo a run for his money. Certainly, they were disinclined to dwell too long on the negative. Hope was still beating eternal in the collective heart of those who frequented the Cricket Field during the rugby season. Next season, they believed, *would* be better.

1984–85

Black-out and an improvement

In July 1984, the strongest earthquake ever recorded in Wales (5.4 on the Richter scale) shook the northern part of the Principality. In the south, as the Swansea players prepared themselves for the coming season, their supporters hoped that their favourites had shaken off the inconsistency which had marred the previous campaign. Mark Davies, the new captain, expressed himself 'reasonably confident' that his side would do well. Apart from anything else, he believed that 'the spirit in the camp is better than it has been for some time'. The captain did not elaborate on that comment, but the media, in reviewing the prospects for the season ahead, seemed to be united in their caution. The pressmen noted that there were few new faces at the club, which, given the previous season's inconsistency, they took to mean that the outcome for the 'Whites' could well be similar to that of the '83/'84 campaign.

Mark Davies.

As it happened, press and supporters alike were given an early indication of the potential quality of the St. Helens side, as the club's official fixture list was opened by a match at Kingsholm. It seemed that the traditional 'loosener' had been abandoned and, as the *Post* put it before the game, 'the team will face a stern challenge on Saturday'. In the event, the 'Whites', without Wyatt, Emyr, and Gareth John, were involved in a nail-biter which they won by the odd point in thirty-nine. During the match, fortunes fluctuated as the Swansea men were confronted by a determined Gloucester side. However, the 'Whites' held on to the slender lead which they had gained early in the final quarter. Two 'Swansea tries' were scored that day. The first by 'teenage scrum-half', Robert Jones, who, in the tenth minute of the match 'beat the cover on the blind-side to score'. The second of these tries drew warm applause from the home supporters. John Thomas and Mark Davies made the initial break on the narrow side, the movement was continued by the diminutive Jones, who, in turn, fed Malcolm Dacey. Dacey drew his man and, from there, the ball 'sped to Jenkins, then to Swift, before the wingman sent Mark Thomas over in the corner'. That try, and the general play of the Swansea men was greatly appreciated by their supporters, as was the tenacity of the team when, in the final quarter of the game, they were forced to defend as Gloucester did all in their power to gain the ascendancy.

There followed a 'showcase' match against Ystalyfera, and a fine victory in the first home match of the season, when Moseley were beaten by 28 points to 18. In that match against the Midlanders, the veteran, Trevor Cheeseman, was outstanding, whilst the pack as a whole gave a powerful display. Among the backs, Roger Blyth had a fine day with the boot, kicking two forty-yard penalties and converting each try scored.

After beating Cross Keys in the next match, the 'Whites' travelled to Bristol, with 'four wins under their belts and 122 points in the bag'. It was an impressive start. Meanwhile in the face of an overabundance of back-row specialists, Gareth Roberts left St. Helens to seek more regular first team football. For his part, Tony Swift, having completed his accountancy studies was also said to be leaving the club. In the event, the wingman was persuaded to delay his departure, which was just as well, for Arthur Emyr was 'struggling to regain fitness after a nasty hamstring problem'. Swift, who had appreciated the opportunity which had been provided for him at St. Helens, opened his account in the match against Bristol. Unfortunately, though, it was not enough. The West Countrymen took Swansea's unbeaten record in winning by 19 points to 12. In the process, they broke a six year losing sequence against the 'Whites'.

After that setback, three more matches were won, including one against Newport, when Malcolm Dacey dropped a fine goal in injury time. By the end of September 1984 the club's playing record would have satisfied the sternest critic. P. 8, W. 7, L. 1, F. 204, A. 110, was, to say the least, encouraging. Furthermore, Paul and Richard Moriarty were back from Australia and were available for selection, which, according to the *Western Mail* would add another dimension to the play of the Swansea pack.

In October, Huw Davies (28 + V.A.T.) told Ron Griffiths that reports that he had retired from first-class rugby were premature. He was, he said, working hard to regain fitness after breaking his leg. Davies, however, took the opportunity to comment on the young man who was wearing the Swansea number 9 shirt at the time. 'For a lad of his age he has a tremendous amount of skill. I haven't seen anyone with such a full range of talents at such an age'. Huw Davies was not alone in his judgment. Meantime, David Richards, himself a former 'teenage prodigy', found that his rugby future was in doubt. The former captain had dislocated a shoulder playing against Lansdowne, in what was described as 'a match which never reached any heights but managed to plumb a few depths'. In that game the referee had to be replaced ten minutes from the end, which prompted the inevitable Swansea wag to declare that the official had 'had enough'. At that point in time, it seemed that David Richards felt the same way.

By the time the Australian tourists came to St. Helens, the 'Whites' met them boosted by a record which showed that only three matches had been lost of the fourteen they had played. With teenagers Aled Williams and Robert Jones at half-back for the 'Whites', romantic Swansea followers hearkened back to pre-war days when another young pair had been in those positions in a side which had beaten a team from the Antipodes. Romance, however, makes relatively few appearances on the rugby stage. On the day, an efficient 'Wallabies' side took a six points lead after just six minutes. Whilst the 'Whites' fought back to overturn that lead as a result of a 35 yard sprint by Arthur Emyr, and a Mark Wyatt penalty, the Aussies were undaunted and scored twice more before half-time. In the second-half the tourists increased their lead, and things looked black for the men in white. Two minutes after Codey had stretched the Australian lead even further, things were even blacker. The St. Helens floodlights failed and the game had to be abandoned.

The Swansea men who did battle with the Australians that evening were:

M. Wyatt, A. Swift, I. Jeffreys, G. Jenkins, A. Emyr, A.Williams, R. Jones, C. Williams, H. Gilson, S.Evans, T. Cheeseman, J. Williams, P. Moriarty, J. Thomas, M. Davies (Capt.) (replaced by B. Clegg, 60 mins).

Before the end of 1984, the 'Whites' were involved in several stirring matches. Prominent among them was a 13 points-all draw with Cardiff at St. Helens, when the conversion of a Mark Davies try, scored in injury time, 'squared the scores'. In that match, Richard Moriarty, after six weeks absence, 'strode about the field like a Colossus'. The game was played in dreadful conditions, yet both sides managed to provide high quality entertainment, which said a great deal about the playing philosophies of the two clubs.

Later, Pontypridd were beaten by 40 points to 3, whilst Newbridge were the victors on their own ground. After that, the 'Whites' went on to win four matches in a row to bring down the curtain on Orwell's year with a 'more than respectable record'. At that stage, only six matches had been lost of the twenty-eight played. At least as far as Swansea rugby was concerned, Orwellian gloom was not on the agenda.

The new year started with a whimper. No rugby was played until 26 January, when the 'Whites' met Ebbw Vale in the third round of the Cup. The three weeks' respite before that day proved to be beneficial for the Swansea injured. Among others, Arthur Emyr was back to fitness, and showed it by scoring some fine tries. As far as the cup game was concerned, as the *Post* had it, 'Swansea made untroubled progress into the quarter-final, beating Ebbw Vale by 25 points to 6'. Meantime, Spencer Feeney, contemplating the remainder of the season, felt that 'After a difficult and frustrating first-half, Swansea can look forward to an extremely successful new year'. Whilst the season's final record was to show that the journalist's confidence was somewhat misplaced, the outcome was to be an improvement on the previous campaign.

After convincing wins over Glamorgan Wanderers and Bedford, the latter conceding 48 points in a 'fluid match', the 'Whites' lost a match at the Gnoll by 19 points to 12. However, since that defeat followed a run of seven successive victories, as the quarter-final cup match approached, there were more optimists than pessimists at St. Helens. The opponents for that tie were Pontypool, which promised 'a battle up front'. Unfortunately for the 'Whites', on that day the 'mean machine' of the Gwent men ground its way to victory. Nevertheless, the game was not without its thrills; Arthur Emyr ensured that that was the case. The wing intercepted a

Arthur Emyr in full stride.

Bishop pass 'only yards from his own line, and careered down field for 90 yards to score with the entire Pontypool side in pursuit'. Whilst the number of pursers was somewhat exaggerated, the distance and the manner in which it was covered would have allowed the most colourful reporter to dig deep into his lexicon. Sadly, the Emyr try was insufficient to win the game and, once again, the 'Whites' could forget the Cup for another season.

When the season ended, the 'Whites' found themselves in third place in the Merit Table. When all things were considered, it was a reasonable outcome, though captain Mark Davies had hoped for better things. Nonetheless, there were several positive factors for 'Whites'-watchers to consider as they contemplated the future. Robert Jones, after little more than a season in senior football, had been invited to play for the Crawshay's squad in the Hong Kong Sevens; Mark Wyatt had set a new points scoring record for the club with 376; Arthur Emyr, despite starting late in the season had crossed for 21 tries, whilst forwards, Paul Moriarty and Mark Davies, had raised the standard for the Forwards' Union by scoring 13 and 12 tries respectively. Aled Williams, at outside-half, had forged a fruitful relationship with Robert Jones, and had also done well in the centre. Williams had played 26 matches, scoring 51 points, whilst Malcolm Dacey had contributed another 26 points. John Williams, with 37 appearances, topped the list for the number of matches played, followed by Paul Moriarty, Mark Davies, Mark Wyatt, and Trevor Cheeseman. A careful statistician would also have noted, deep in David Price's records, that 'semi-retired' in relation to Roger Blyth appeared to be justified. The full-back had played just six matches during the season. No one could be found, however, who was prepared to bet that this fact signalled the end of the former points record holder's career in the game. Which was just as well. The veteran was to be needed far more frequently in the season to come.

1985-86

Enter the young Turks

Tony Swift.

As the new season approached, Mark Davies said that he was pleased to have been given the captaincy again. He believed that useful lessons had been learnt during the previous campaign which would stand the team in good stead in the season ahead. Furthermore, promising young players like Robert Jones and Aled Williams, had a good season's experience under their belts, whilst most of the 1984/85 squad was still available. He believed that provided key players could steer clear of injury, there was no reason why the club could not improve upon the previous season's outcome. The captain was also pleased to welcome a new wing, Mark Titley, a timely replacement for the departed Tony Swift. For Titley, it was the start of a decade at St. Helens during which he would provide Cricket Field *aficionados* with performances which provoked a special brand of excitement.

After a 'loosener' against Resolven, the team started its season proper with a 'bang'; Gloucester were beaten by 44 points to 3, whilst the next visitors to St. Helens, Cross Keys, conceded one more point while scoring just 4. It followed that, at that stage of the season, the club had scored 122 points in three matches whilst conceding only 10. It was vintage stuff. When Moseley were also beaten in the next match, Swansea optimists were beginning to count their chickens. Inconsistency? they might have asked. What is that? If they did, however, they were soon to remember. Pembroke County took the side's unbeaten record in the next match. At that, the sanguine put the defeat down to over-confidence and an unrepresentative team, though neither excuse, on being examined closely, could have been dignified by being called a reason. While following that defeat, the official line was that it was as well to get such a performance out of the way early in the season, it is probable that 'wrists were slapped'.

Whatever was said and done then, at the end of the St. Helens match which followed, Swansea smiles seemed to indicate that the 'hiccough' was no more than that. In that game, visitors Bristol, faced with torrential rain and a spirited Swansea side, did well with the elements at their backs. However, when the teams turned around, the West Countrymen 'crumbled in the face of a second-half Swansea barrage'. In that second-half, with the wind and rain at their backs, the 'Whites' stormed forward at every opportunity. Furthermore, despite the conditions, the team contrived to play remarkable football, with Swansea's handling and passing being described as 'outstanding'. One try exemplified the skills which were on show that dismal day. Robert Jones broke wide from a scrum and, with two Bristol men about to smother him, he sent a 'long, raking pass' to Arthur Emyr. Emyr, with the benefit of space within which to work, ran powerfully down the line, moving inside as he was about to be tackled. As he fell, the wing fed the supporting Wyatt, who 'skipped through a couple of tackles' to score. Given the conditions, it was indeed a remarkable try.

With just one match lost out of the six played, that victory was, for many, another indicator that the season ahead would prove to be successful. Furthermore, given that the 50th anniversary of the famous triumph over the 'All Blacks' was approaching (the 'Whites' being the first club side to beat the New Zealanders), the superstitious donned rosy-coloured glasses. Unfortunately, on that day, with a certain J. Callard at full-back, Newport 'pipped the St. Helens men in a rousing finish'. The Rodney Parade side which had led by 13 points to 0 at half-time, scored only 4 more in the second period, but it was enough to give to give them victory by a single point despite a spirited Swansea fight-back. Whilst Newport had been the first senior side to lower the Swansea colours, it had only been by one point. Furthermore, as the players made their way down the M4, they could encourage themselves by replaying 'the try of the game' on their mental videos. It had started near the Swansea line. Newport put down a pass and 'Moriarty scooped it up and went racing away'. The big man passed to Emyr on the wing, who surged into the Newport half. As Callard came across to tackle him, the north Walian found Robert Jones at his shoulder and the diminutive half-back, taking the winger's pass, sped over the line to score.'

Despite this defeat, the Swansea club's record was more than respectable, but after the side lost a second match (to Pontypool), the papers began to question the quality of the St. Helens squad. The *Post*, for example, felt that 'Swansea still have to reach their potential', and the *Western Mail*, following a similar line noted that, 'flashes of brilliance have been followed by frustrating matches studded with mistakes'. Not that the St. Helens management needed to be made aware of these facts. They were as frustrated as anyone, and could only point to a growing injury list as one of the reasons for the side's relatively poor showing in the second-half of September. Among others, Mark Wyatt had been missing from the team since the Gloucester match, whilst Richard Moriarty had broken a hand.

With the touring Fijians due to play at St. Helens in the middle of October, all at the Cricket Field were striving to ensure that the club did itself justice in that game. The general opinion was that a return to the side's early season form would ensure that the visitors were given a run for their money. And, in the games which took place before the match with Fiji, it seemed that the Swansea men were on course to ensure that this would be the outcome. The 'Quins were defeated on their own ground, and Llanelli beaten at St. Helens. Whilst the optimists read more into these victories than may have been justified, objective onlookers felt that the side was still not as cohesive as it had been at the start of the campaign. The reality was that that mysterious alchemy which team coaches seek throughout their careers had not been entrenched at the Cricket Field at that time. As a result, it was not sufficiently secure to keep the threat of inconsistency at bay.

Nonetheless, given that, in the early part of their tour, the Fijians had been themselves struggling to blend into an effective unit, most commentators felt that the 'Whites' ought to give a good account of themselves on the day. Unfortunately, the converse was true. The team did not do itself justice, particularly in the second-half after Huw Davies had had to leave the field. Even though the 'Whites' scored the 'try of the game', Malcolm Dacey crossing within ten minutes of the kick-off, the tourists won the match by 23 points to 14. The St. Helens camp was disappointed. They believed that they should have won the game.

The side which faced the Fijians that day was:

M. Thomas, M. Titley, D. Richards, K. Hopkins, I. Jeffreys, M. Dacey, H. Davies (replaced K.Williams), K. Colclough, H. Gilson, S. Evans, M. Colclough, J. Williams, M. Davies (Capt.), T. Cheeseman, R. Moriarty.

After that defeat, as the season unfolded in a frustrating way, commentators, professional and amateur were ready with advice for the Swansea selection committee. Prominent among the critics were the 'Bloggs for Snodgrass' brigade, as were the 'My team would be' lobby. As far as the selectors were concerned, they found themselves attempting to solve problems similar to those which their predecessors had had to face many times since the War. As the Chairman of selectors put it, 'We are prepared to go to any lengths to recruit new forwards'. One aspect of the problem facing the selectors was that, whilst there were several back-row men at St. Helens, there were relatively few front and second-row specialists. For example, at the time, the Club had just two specialists props in the squad. One of these, Clive Williams, was thirty-six, and the other was Keith Colclough, who had been required to operate on both sides of the scrum.

Paradoxically, there followed a run of six matches without defeat, which must have put the concerns of the selectors into a different context. However, if this sequence resulted in any complacency at St. Helens, it would have been dispelled by the three defeats which followed. Among those defeats was one by Maesteg at St. Helens, which the *Western Mail* called 'one of the shocks of the season'. Still, as they sought for reassurance, Swansea supporters could focus on a victory over Newbridge (33 points to 4) and success in the second round of the Cup. Apart from the results, in the Newbridge match, the Swansea faithful were thrilled by a seventy-yard run by Mark Titley for a try, and a hat-trick of scores from Paul Moriarty. After that match, as the Swansea faithful made their way home, they must have shaken their collective heads in disbelief. How, they might have asked, could a side which could play such convincing rugby have lost so many matches?

In the new year, it was announced that nineteen-year-old Robert Jones had gained his first cap, a tremendous achievement for a young man so new to the game. Robert's selection was noteworthy not only because of his age, but also for the fact that he was playing in only his second season in senior football. Still, the young man with the bullet-like pass had a pedigree which spoke well for his future. He had captained the Welsh Schools side at Under 15, Under 16, and Under 18 levels. In due course he would also captain his country, but in the meantime, there was his first 'cap' to savour.

After losing to Aberavon, the team, as if to demonstrate its true ability, won four matches in succession. Among those defeated was Ebbw Vale, in the third round of the Cup. Whilst the east Walians had made the 'Whites' fight all the way for their win, in the second-half, in particular, the Swansea men dominated. During the match, after a Maurice Colclough 'forwards try', the crowd were treated to thrilling scores by Paul Moriarty and Mark Titley. It was a win of noble proportions, after which, the press reported, there was a buoyancy in the Swansea camp. Days later, it had all evaporated. Ron Griffiths, in his report of a game at Penarth, stated that 'the Swansea players sat shamefaced in their dressing room'. They had lost to Penarth for the first time since 1974. Admittedly, the 'Whites' had fielded a 'patchwork side', but the defeat was a blow to morale at the club. Unfortunately, in the match which followed, the 'Whites' were, to quote the *Post*, 'booted out of the cup'. Such was the atmosphere at the Cricket Field at that time that St Helens officials felt it necessary to apologise to supporters for 'lack of commitment. We have lost games which we should have won!'

In the meantime, supporters were aghast to learn that flanker, Mike Ruddock, had met with an horrific accident. Mike had been working on a telegraph pole when a passing lorry became entangled with the cable. This resulted in him being dragged thirty feet to the ground. Such were the young man's injuries, that it was estimated that a man who was less fit might have died from them. Sadly, Mike was never to play again, yet, the circumstances which contrived to end his playing career, served to bring forward his entry into the coaching side of the game. In the years ahead, the popular Ruddock was to return to St. Helens in that role. Then, his name would be writ large on the unfolding canvas upon which the life and times of Swansea Rugby Club are portrayed.

At the time, over and above the club's concern for the player, Mike Ruddock's accident exacerbated the problems facing the selection committee. Nonetheless, despite all the setbacks which the club had had to face, coach Jeff Herdman refused to be despondent. He pointed to the number of internationals at the club, and said that he had been particularly pleased that Paul Moriarty had joined his brother in the Welsh side. He spoke, too, of the potential within the team. Kevin Hopkins, for example, had shown his attacking skills in beating five men in a St. Helens match and sending Mark Davies over for a try. He enthused about Mark Titley, and recalled Ian Jeffreys's try against Moseley, when the player ran seventy-five yards to score. Any sports psychologist listening to the former hooker would have applauded the emphasis on the positive in what he had to say.

Some said that it was the return of Richard Moriarty after twelve weeks' absence, together with the Herdman 'harangue', which was the catalyst for the improvement in the club's fortunes in the final stages of the season. Whatever it was, it had a remarkable effect. Of the final eleven domestic matches only one was lost, and a new sparkle was evident in the form of the players. With Paul Moriarty scoring tries at such a rate that the Three-quarters' Union was thinking of tabling an objection, and the three Youth 'Caps' (Anthony Clement, David Young and Richard Webster) making exciting and telling débuts, smiles were returning to St. Helens faces. In the Easter matches, the Barbarians were beaten by 48 points to 13, the 'Quins by 29 points to 19, and Cross Keys conceded 41 points whilst scoring only 8. The *pièce de résistance*, however, was the victory over Cardiff in mid-April. As the *Post* had it, 'Cardiff are run ragged'.

Among the Swansea scorers in that Cardiff match was Paul Moriarty, who finished the season with 25 tries, a new record for a forward. As far as the Youth Caps were concerned, even on their débuts they gave the impression that they were mature senior players. Since the Cardiff match was David Richards's final game, and semi-retired, Roger Blyth, was finally to hang up his boots, the emergence of the youngsters delighted the Swansea faithful. Ron Griffiths, though, believed that Dai Richards was retiring before his time. He wrote, 'After watching David Richards destroy the Cardiff mid-field with another exhibition of running, I think that it is a major tragedy that he is retiring'. Richards, however, had made up his mind, and it had to be sufficient for the Swansea faithful to remember his silky skills, his vision, and his pace. A thinking man's rugby player, David, having analysed his situation, had come to the conclusion that he would 'move over and make way for the young rising stars in the side'.

When the season ended, the press and the St. Helens public looked back on a campaign which had promised so much, but, the last weeks of the season apart, had flattered to deceive. Mike James, seeking to build upon the side's end-of-season form, praised Mark Davies for his efforts, both as captain and as a player. 'No one', said James, 'could have worked harder in the interests of Swansea rugby'. For its part, the *Post* announced that Paul Moriarty was the 'player of the year', not only because of the flanker's tries, but 'because he displayed the kind of aggressive back-row play of the "All Black" type'. Arthur Emyr, with twenty tries was the top scoring back, whilst John Williams (35) and Paul Moriarty (34) had made the most appearances during the season. Whilst overall, eighteen matches had been lost of the forty-nine played, the successful end-of-season run served as a ready stimulus for the optimists. Indeed, even the pessimists were less gloomy.

When Mark Davies decided not to stand again, it came as no surprise that Richard Moriarty was elected captain for the 1986/87 campaign. According to the *Post*, the big man had fine leadership qualities, and a 'total dedication to the Swansea cause'. As the paper pointed out, 'he rarely misses a training session'. The paper also made the point that the new captain 'would add missing steel to Swansea's play'. With those words as a reference, and with 'St. Helens brimming over with talent again', eager 'Whites' supporters must have looked forward to the new season throughout the summer months. Surely, that pool of talent, and that leadership would ensure that successful, Swansea football would be played. As ever, the supporters wanted to enjoy the thrills of the open game whilst seeing their team winning. It was a tough combination of objectives for any team to achieve, as, indeed, was the task of banishing the virus which infected St. Helens with inconsistency. Yet, all three objectives had been achieved before. Surely, it was not too much for long-suffering 'Whites'-watchers to ask? Jeff Herdman, Mike James and the selection committee, Richard Moriarty and the players knew what they had to do. Furthermore, they were confident of the quality of the squad available to them. In the relative calm of the close season their confidence grew.

1986–87

Cup finalists

In August 1986, Aled Williams, whom the St. Helens management had been grooming to replace David Richards as a centre, left the club to join Bridgend, where he was to be used as an outside-half. It was a disappointing development for all at St. Helens, for the young man was held in high regard. However, with Tony Clement and Malcolm Dacey available for the outside-half position at the Cricket Field, and favouring the number 10 shirt, Aled felt that the move would be beneficial to him. As it happened, in the longer term it was to prove to be beneficial to the 'Whites' as well.

As usual, the first senior match on the club's fixture list was against Gloucester. This time it was at Kingsholm, and proved to be a dour, tough game, which the 'Whites' won by six points to four. Since all of Swansea's points came from the boot of Mark Wyatt, there were no thrilling tries for the press to report. Nonetheless, the team had shown itself to be an effective unit, at least defensively, as the determined Gloucester men were repulsed. At least, it was a victory. In the 'Whites' first home match, however, the St. Helens faithful were treated to a feast of running rugby, as Cross Keys were defeated by a remarkable 70 points to 6. During that match, thirteen tries were scored by the 'Whites', though there was a cost. Such was the club's injury list after the three opening games that the selectors found that they had just one specialist centre available for the next match (against Moseley).

Meantime, there was much discussion in the press about the demands which were being made on players who were in the Welsh squad. Swansea with six: Kevin Hopkins, Arthur Emyr, Malcolm Dacey, Robert Jones, and Richard and Paul Moriarty, were affected more than most. The concerns being aired by the journalists reflected those of the clubs involved. These concerns were not only about the claims being made on players' time, but, also the impact on their bodies of what was described as 'over training'. Some said that these demands lay behind one of the reasons why modern players seemed to be more prone to injury than their predecessors had been. Nonetheless, for most players, the appeal and honour associated with playing for Wales were such that there was never a shortage of men prepared to accept the demands which were placed on them by club and country.

In the next St. Helens match, Moseley were well-beaten by a Swansea side which dominated the game from the first minute. Consequently, at the end of the third week of the season, the Cricket Field faithful were well pleased with the state of affairs at Swansea R.F.C. In that Moseley match, a 'maiden try' was scored by young number eight, Stuart Davies. Other scorers were Robert Jones and Paul Moriarty, whilst the Wyatt boot was, again, 'swinging clinically'.

After a draw at Bristol's Memorial Ground – when the 'Whites' dominated but failed to take advantage of their opportunities – the last match in September provided Swansea supporters with another outstanding result. The 'Whites', as the *Post* put it, 'put on the style', crushing the 'Amber and Blacks' by 51 points to 12. The Swansea pack was outstanding that day, controlling matters in the tight and the loose and providing the kind of platform which running backs dream of. Not surprisingly, given the talent in the Swansea back division, they were not slow to take advantage of the situation. With Bleddyn Taylor at full-back, and Tony Clement at outside-half, the game flowed like Niagara in flood. Arthur Emyr crossed for a hat-trick of tries, Paul Moriarty and Kevin Hopkins each scored two, whilst Richard Webster and Mark Titley also crossed. At that stage in the season, St. Helens was bubbling! In seven matches the 'Whites' had scored 200 points, whilst only 54 had been conceded. Whilst the record was not quite as good as the best of the 'Golden Era', for modern followers of the game at St. Helens, it was difficult to conceive of anything better.

The 'winning streak' was extended by the result of the next match, when Tony Clement fulfilled many a Welsh schoolboy's dream by scoring at Twickenham. Indeed, the young man scored twice, which along with a try by hooker, Hugh Gilson, and fine kicking by Mark Wyatt, defeated the 'Quins on their own patch. As far as Wyatt was concerned, his accuracy that day was such that he showed himself to be untroubled by the swirling winds, which the received wisdom in rugby football at the time suggested impaired goal kicking at 'H.Q.'. Swansea supporters were willing the Welsh selectors to note that fact.

The next day, a Swansea XV lost to Lansdowne on their own turf, then, after a fine win over 'Sospan', and a high-scoring draw (22 points all) with Bridgend, Neath surprised the rugby world by winning a St. Helens match by 22 points to 10. After the quality of the team's football in the opening games, this defeat knocked Swansea supporters back on their heels. Surprisingly, the 'Whites' pack had lost out to the Neath eight. Whilst Tony Clement put Paul Thorburn under pressure and 'stole' the ball to score a fine try, it wasn't enough. Neath were the victors, and in winning, took the St. Helens ground record, and became the first Welsh side to beat the 'Whites' during the campaign.

That weekend, in the *Sporting Post*, Phil Bennett, in his column, commented on two Swansea players who had caught his eye. Phil stated that, in the defeat of Llanelli, Malcolm Dacey had played his best match for two years, whilst Richard Webster was 'the best young flanker in Wales'. Another Swansea player who was attracting press comment was another Richard, Moriarty. 'Dickie' had come back from the Welsh tour of the South Seas with useful experience behind him. After David Pickering had been invalided home, Richard was made captain. The responsibility, he said, was such that it helped him focus on personal discipline. As the *Post* put it, 'every time he takes the field he thinks about discipline'. As a consequence, the argument continued, whereas, in the past, he allowed himself to be goaded, the converse was now true. Now, his aggression was channelled to winning the ball and setting up opportunities for his team-mates to score.

As 1986 drew to a close, Swansea-ites could look back on 'a pretty successful first-half'. Of the twenty-seven matches which had been played, seven had been lost, two drawn, and among the victories were some outstanding performances. At Christmas, for example, the St. Helens crowd had been treated to vintage football, as 59 points were scored against 'The Welsh'. Then, on New Year's Eve, Llanelli were the victims in a 33 points to 12 victory. Coupled with the high scoring matches with which the season had been opened, had the phrase 'feel-good factor' been coined at the time, it would have been recognisable at St. Helens. It was true that certain of the seven defeats which the side had suffered had been unwelcome. Ebbw Vale, Newbridge, and Glamorgan Wanderers, for example, had won when the form book suggested that they had 'no chance'. Still, the club was through to the third round of the Cup, when they were to meet Maesteg. Furthermore, there were far more positive than negative factors to consider in the first-half record. Given the prevailing spirit at St. Helens, the general consensus of opinion was that, in 1987, the team would build on the successes of the season so far.

Unfortunately, the second-half record proved to be far less successful than the first. Of the eighteen matches played in the period from January until May, ten were lost. Furthermore, only one match of the last seven was won – the Easter game against the Barbarians. But, none of that was known as the new year began. Consequently, when Aberavon came to St. Helens on 1 January 1987, confidence was at a high level. Apart from anything else, the previous day the 'Whites' had beaten the men from 'Sospan', and the Port Talbot side was not thought to be in the same league as the 'Scarlets'. In the event, however, 'Bravon' surprised the 'Whites' by coming from behind to take the game and register a rare victory at St. Helens. Once again, the lack of strength in depth in the St. Helens squad was quoted in the press as a major factor in what was seen as 'typical Swansea inconsistency'. The absence of captain Richard Moriarty (he had had an operation on his shoulder) hardly helped matters, but Richard apart, at the time, there was a shortage of quality front-five men at the Cricket Field.

As if to emphasise the capriciousness of their form, the 'Whites' raised their game in the third round of the Cup. Prior to the match, Jeff Herdman had said that 'We are not going up the Llynfi valley bubbling with confidence'. Not, he emphasised, that this meant that the side lacked confidence. Rather, that the players recognised that the lack of consistency, which was plaguing the club again, served to make them 'realistic'. The coach, however, believed that his charges would win. And win they did, giving a 'battling performance' in the first period, and scoring twenty-four points in the second. The pack was outstanding that day, and among the try scorers was John Thomas, who had not played during the two previous seasons, and Maurice Colclough, who, it was said, did not train in case he used up his energy. Another noteworthy feature of the game at Maesteg, was the captaincy of young Robert Jones, who 'called the shots'. The fourth round beckoned.

Before the fourth round match (against the 'Police'), Penarth, and Abertillery were 'well-beaten', conceding 46 and 35 points respectively, but the 'Whites' lost a 'tough match' at the

Clive Williams.

Gnoll by 13 points to 9. Prior to the game with the 'Police', the bookmakers showed their confidence in the 'Whites', by making them favourites. Jeff Herdman, however, in trying to achieve that delicate balance in the minds of his charges between confidence and cockiness, repeated a version of the message he had delivered before the Maesteg round. And, at half-time, it seemed as though his caution was justified. The 'Whites', with both regular props unavailable, had Clive Williams 'come out of semi-retirement' to fill one of the spots. It was his contribution as a veritable icon which was said to have given the Swansea pack new heart. In the second period, the pack came into their own, outplayed their 'Blue Lamp' rivals and set the backs running. Tries by Arthur Emyr and Richard Webster won the match for the 'Whites', whilst the Wyatt boot 'swung with ready precision', to convert tries and penalties. Now that they were in the semi-final, and were, no longer, in contention for the Merit Table championship, Swansea eyes began to focus upon the Cup. Could this, the question was asked, be the 'Whites' year to win the trophy again?

With Mark Wyatt, Robert Jones, Paul Moriarty and Kevin Hopkins playing for Wales, no one doubted the quality of the players in the Swansea squad. However, the perennial problem still remained unanswered. How can it be that, with such a galaxy of stars at St. Helens, the team could be so unpredictable? Ron Griffiths, long time 'Whites'-watcher, clearly, felt bemused by the matter. He wrote: 'Swansea have proved to be so thoroughly inconsistent that many believe that they are lucky to have reached the semi-final. They climb mountains one week, and are down the pit the next'. At that, the optimists would have noted that there were far fewer pits than mountains in Wales, and have asked, as more of the latter were closed, did that suggest that things would improve in the future? Meantime, the pessimists polished their Davey lamps.

Unfortunately, no one at St. Helens could contradict the *Post*-man's comments. Furthermore, they were at a loss to explain why there was such inconsistency. Whilst one man doesn't make a team, some have greater influence on matches than others. One such player was still absent. Richard Moriarty was 'fighting back to fitness'. Many believed that things would be better when he returned.

If, as Ron Griffiths suggested, there were those who felt that the 'Whites' were lucky to be in the last four of the Cup, there were very few, if any, who did not give the team the credit for having controlled the semi-final match from beginning to end. Swansea, according to Gareth Roberts, writing in the *Post*, were in charge from the beginning. Once again, the pack was on top of its game, and with Robert Jones giving an outstanding display of 'scrum-worker' rugby behind them, Newbridge were 'thoroughly beaten'. Tries were scored by Paul Moriarty and Maurice Colclough, whilst Mark Wyatt's boot registered three penalties and a dropped goal for the 'Whites'. Thus it was that, for the fifth time since the inception of the competition, the 'Whites' found themselves in the final of the Cup.

Not surprisingly, given their position in the Merit Table, in the four weeks before it was played, the Cup Final dominated the thinking of Swansea supporters. Since Cardiff were to be the opponents in the Final, when the 'Whites' travelled to the Arms Park on 11 April for a Merit Table match, their supporters and the press were looking at that game as a 'dress rehearsal' for the big match tie. Cardiff won and stopped the 'Whites' from scoring for the first time that season (indeed, no. one could remember when that had happened before), the setback brought the gloom-mongers out in force. Jeff Herdman, however, would have none of it. He told Swansea supporters to forget that defeat! 'The Final', he said, 'would be a different matter!' Yet, for the Swansea loyalists that was easier said than done, particularly when the Barbarians and Sale were, both, comfortable winners in the games immediately before the National Stadium date.

As a result, on the day of the Final, Swansea supporters who made their way to Cardiff for the game, travelled with little expectation. The media agreed. The 'Blue and Blacks' were 'solid favourites'! Paradoxically, this proved to be of greater benefit to the men in white than to their opponents. In the Swansea dressing room it was decided that the 'Whites' would play an expansive game. As Jeff Herdman told his men, 'we have everything to gain and nothing to lose by playing to our strengths'. That proved to be true.

Whilst at no-side, Cardiff had won the match (by 16 points to 15) the 'Whites', their supporters and most neutrals believed that the Swansea men had deserved to win. Brilliantly led by Richard Moriarty, who 'kept Swansea on the boil throughout', the men in white played expansive, entertaining rugby. Whilst most commentators felt that they had done enough to win, fate, which has the greater say in such matters, decreed otherwise. On the day, Tony Clement gave a display of astonishing maturity for one so young, and earned the 'Man of the match' award. Swansea's enterprise throughout the match was said to have been 'thoroughly refreshing' and many commented on the exciting potential which existed at St. Helens. Without doubt, the 'Whites' scored the try of the match. Robert Jones, Tony Clement (playing at outside-half), and Mark Wyatt combined in a 'flowing movement which ripped the heart out of the Cardiff defence', to release Kevin Hopkins who crossed for the try. Whilst Cardiff were the victors by a single point, Swansea, according to most neutrals had gained a moral victory. Indeed, most 'Whites' supporters believed that had Maurice Colclough not retired at half-time with a back problem, Swansea would have held on to win. At this distance the cold statistics give no hint of this truth. Those who were in Cardiff that day, however, perhaps on reading this, will feel again that warm glow of pride which surged through Swansea bodies that day. That was 'Swansea football', even if there were no winners' medals to celebrate the fact.

In the days after that match, as the Swansea touring party made their way to Zimbabwe and Kenya, they may have contemplated the season which had finished with a question in their minds. They might have asked, what could have been achieved had we played like that throughout the campaign? Whilst no one could answer the question, the thought processes involved may have helped to boost confidence, team spirit and pride at being a Swansea player. The next season would give them another opportunity to fulfil the massive promise which lay within the Swansea squad. Surely something would have been learnt from another, rather disappointing outcome.

Chapter Twenty-Six

A SEASON OF DISAPPOINTMENT

1987-88

As Richard Moriarty contemplated the season ahead, he did so in the knowledge that it was probable that he was to have the twin responsibility of captaining both Swansea and his country. It was a signal honour for the Morriston boy who had worked so hard at his game and his approach to it. Whilst he was not the first Swansea man to captain club and country, the honour spoke volumes of the effort Moriarty had made in order to progress from raw youth to world-class forward. To several of the young players at the club who at the time were seeking to make their way in the game, 'Dickie' must have been an inspiration. Certainly, he was an example of what could be achieved by dedication, hard work and focused self-control.

Two of those youngsters were approaching the '87/88 campaign having begun their own development programme. Back-row forward, Richard Webster told Ron Griffiths that he felt that the previous season had seen his progression from boy to man. Webster had played in the Welsh Cup Final team, gone to Australia, where he was called into the Welsh squad, and earned his first full 'cap' in the play-off game for third place in the World Cup competition. The youngster said that it had 'all been unbelievable'. For his part, with Malcolm Dacey having decided to join Cardiff, Anthony Clement found himself to be Swansea's number one specialist outside-half. Clement had been playing in Wellington during the close season, and had found that to be 'a tremendous experience.'

Prior to the start of the new campaign, in surveying the Swansea scene, the press in general, considered the club's prospects to be promising. Much was made of the young talent throughout the side, and of the spirit at the club. Unfortunately, after a 'warm-up' game against Mumbles, the opening match proper provided Swansea-ites and the media men with something of a shock. The *Post's* headline writer could only re-work one of his efforts from the previous campaign. 'Another "Whites" Grey Day', he wrote. Gloucester, who were said to have given the 'Whites' the 'runaround', defeated the Swansea men (on their own pitch) more easily than the 6 points to 19 score suggested. In one fell swoop, the 'Whites' had lost their unbeaten record and their ground record. There were other negatives for the St. Helens men to ponder, too. Richard Webster and John Rawlins were both carried off injured during the match.

Whilst this defeat rocked the Swansea squad back on its collective heels, there were skill and spirit enough at St. Helens to ensure that the match which followed was won. As far as the Swansea players were concerned, it had been unnecessary to emphasise the importance of winning that match. Their pride had been hurt. Cross Keys, the opponents in question, were never in the game. Thereafter, the four matches which followed gave 'Whites' supporters and the media reason to believe that pre-season forecasts of a successful campaign at the Cricket Field had not been the product of a misplaced confidence. First, Moseley were beaten on their own ground, though it took late tries by Mark Titley and Tony Clement to gain the win, and again, in the following match, it took two 'barnstorming' tries by Arthur Emyr late in the contest to defeat Bristol at St. Helens. As the *Western Mail* pointed out at the time, 'At least this gives lie to the notion that Swansea are a forty-minute team'. There followed a fine win at Rodney Parade, when full-back, Adrian Stewart, kicked fourteen points and Stuart Parfitt scored an opportunist try. After that match, the Swansea record read, played 7 won 6. At that, the superstitious among the Swansea faithful probably tried hard not to dwell on such data. They had crossed that particular bridge too many times. Unfortunately, it seemed that too many had rejoiced. In keeping with what had seemed to have become an enduring Swansea tradition, the next two matches were lost, though the 'Quins, one of the victors, themselves had won as a result of a final minute penalty after tries by Arthur Emyr and Paul Moriarty had given the 'Whites' the lead.

By the middle of October, coach Jeff Herdman was bemoaning the fact that Swansea's injury list was, already, lengthy. Captain, Richard Moriarty, David Jones, Ian Brown, John Thomas and Richard Webster were among those who were sidelined. By then, five matches out of the twelve which had been played had been lost, but, not before 'everything had come together at the same time' as the 'Whites' thrashed the 'Scarlets' by 43 points to 9. Swansea supporters who were there that day must have wondered why a team, so brilliant on that occasion, could have such an indifferent playing record. According to the *Post*, Llanelli were 'shattered'. During what the paper said could only 'be described as a virtuoso performance', Mark Wyatt collected 23 points, whilst Paul Moriarty, Tony Clement, Keith Colclough, Arthur Emyr and Ian Davies – who was said to have had a tremendous match – scored tries. For his part, Maurice Colclough, who had been brought into the side even though he had not trained, declared, 'at 34 I'm against training on principle.'

Later, after having to report on two further defeats in succession, Ron Griffiths wrote, 'One of these days, one of these years, Swansea may find the consistency that other clubs with fewer top players, achieve'. The evening after the victory over Llanelli, however, was for assuming that that time had come. Such days were to be savoured, and savoured, and savoured again. Like a camel in the desert retaining its stock of water, at the time, Swansea supporters needed to store up the good times in their collective memories so as to help them over the barren periods when results were less favourable.

Prior to the third round of the Cup, coach, Herdman suffered another unwanted blow. Thrusting wingman, Arthur Emyr had his leg in plaster. However, as if the gods were intent on boosting morale at the Cricket Field, days later, it was announced that Robert Jones had been voted the 'Outstanding European player' in the previous season's World Cup. This was an accolade without precedent for Welsh rugby, the Swansea club, and for its popular acting-captain. Yet, in the months ahead, the award would be seen to have failed to stem the petty-minded parochialism prevalent in south Wales rugby. Arrant prejudice would seep from the pens of some so-called Welsh rugby supporters as they sought to decry the talent of the young man from Trebanos through their letters to the press. According to these one-eyed correspondents (depending upon which club they supported), players X, Y, or Z were far superior to the Swansea man. The expert opinions of those who had made the World Cup award were as nothing compared to the credentials of some of those scribes whose rugby pedigree had peaked

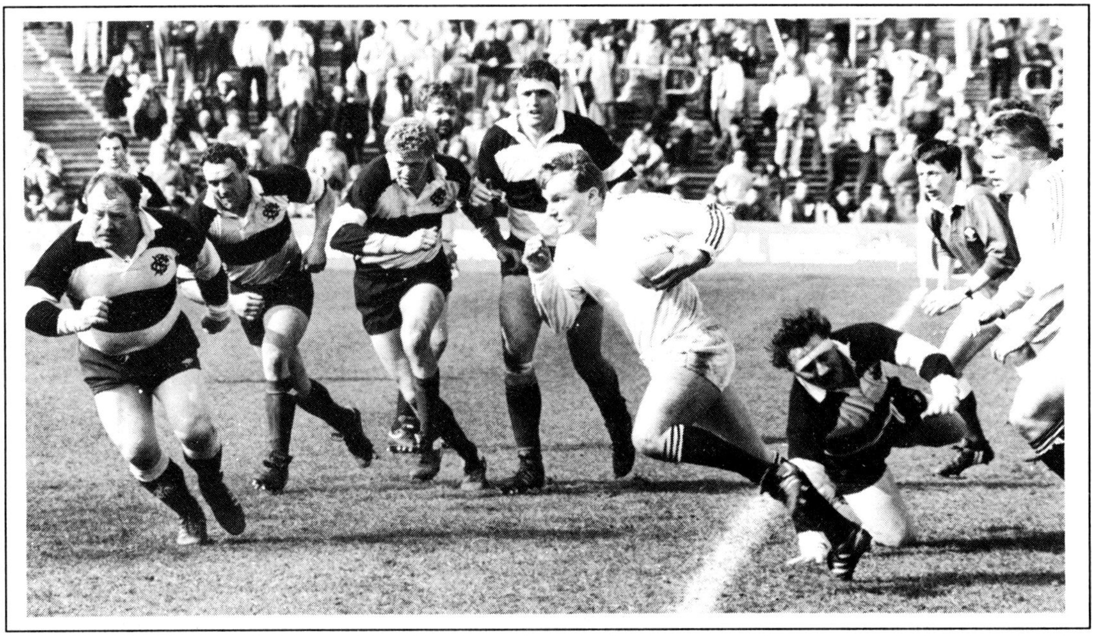

'Determined' – Bleddyn Taylor 'en route' for the line.

when they made their débuts for Cwmscwt Fourth XV. Yet, as the future was to show, over many years, as Robert Jones continued to attract praise and acclaim from around the world, criticism of the player continued whilst parochial pretenders were replaced, even in their club sides, year on year.

When 1987 ended, the injury list in the Swansea camp continued to give coach and selectors concern. Richard Webster was out with his knee injury, and Richard Moriarty, after a brief 'come-back', had dislocated his shoulder for the third time. Whatever frustration the Swansea camp felt at the absence of these key men, for the players concerned it must have paled into insignificance. Both men had been out for many months, whilst Moriarty was not only missing the opportunity to lead his club side, his absence from the international scene meant that someone else was being given the opportunity to establish himself at the helm of the Welsh XV.

Nonetheless, as far as the St. Helens faithful were concerned, 1988 started with a smile on its face. Despite incessant rain – Aberavon, for example, were said to have had more than two thousand gallons of water pumped off their pitch to enable a match with the 'Whites' to proceed – the Swansea men played fine football in beating Newport (by 37 points to 6), Glamorgan Wanderers (by 18 points to 0) and in drawing with the 'Wizards'. Indeed, at the time, such was the side's form, that when a journalist suggested to Jeff Herdman that in travelling to Pontypool for the fifth round of the Cup, Swansea were setting out on 'Mission Impossible', he would have none of it. The coach quoted the former Pontypool wing, Bleddyn Taylor, as saying that the 'Whites' were in 'with a chance'.

Unfortunately, when the day came, in awful conditions which favoured 'Poolers' eight man game rather than Swansea's more expansive approach,the home team won the day. Nonetheless, at half-time, the 'Whites' led by 12 points to 10, through a Wyatt penalty and a penalty try, awarded, ironically, for obstruction on Bleddyn Taylor. Thereafter, however, the Pontypool pack gained the ascendancy to wipe out the slim Swansea lead and win the match for the homesters. Among the Swansea men who trooped off that mud-patch on that gloomy day, was Richard Moriarty. Not only had the captain recovered sufficiently from his shoulder injury to enable him to play, he had 'got up from his sick bed' (he had 'flu) to lead his side. Not surprisingly, he was 'not his usual self', and there were those who attributed Pontypool's ability to 'come back' in the second-half to the sapping of Moriarty's strength by his first-half exertion. Whatever the reason, to borrow 'soccer-speak', for another season, the 'Whites' could concentrate upon the Merit Table challenge.

As the remainder of the season unfolded, the club's playing record was impressive. Whilst doing well against Merit Table opponents, the 'Whites' won every match played during the period 30 January to 2 March, scoring 156 points and conceding only 58 in the process. Nevertheless, the press was muted in its praise. For example, in its account of a 31 points to 10 victory over Penarth, the *Post* reported that 'Swansea displayed all their usual traits ... creative brilliance at its best, and an uncanny ability to go off the boil at the precise moment when better things are expected'. And a seven-try, 40 points to 13 victory over London Welsh – with Bleddyn Taylor crossing for a hat-trick according to the *Western Mail* was 'not entirely convincing'.

As it transpired, the results of the remaining fixtures of the season appeared to confirm the growing caution of the press. Seven of the remaining eleven matches were lost, and, while the club finished in second place in the Merit Table competition, the St. Helens men and their loyal supporters must have been disappointed as they looked back on yet another season of inconsistency. Nevertheless as seems to have been ever the case at the Cricket Ground, there were positive factors for the optimists to contemplate as they chewed over the carcass of another rugby campaign. Robert Jones, David Young and Paul Moriarty, all young men, were established in the Welsh international side, as was Richard Moriarty. Arthur Emyr was beginning his 'come-back', nineteen-year-old Paul Arnold, who had graduated through the Youth and Athletic sides, was being hailed as a future international, and centre, Tim Michael, only twenty, had scored ten tries in just thirteen matches. Bleddyn Taylor, with eighteen headed the list of try scorers, whilst Mark Wyatt (244 points) and Adrian Stewart (135) were the leading points scorers for the club. Keith Colclough and Mark Titley (37 each) had played most matches, whilst Ian Davies (with 35) was in third place.

''Smine!' – Paul Arnold breaks through.

Nevertheless, at the time, words of cautionary advice in the *Post* were typical of those being offered to the St. Helens management. 'Swansea, today, acknowledged that the season had been disappointing ... in the closing weeks of the season the show fell apart ... clearly, the time is ripe for a rethink at St. Helens ... Swansea have enough talent to make an impact on the Welsh scene every season ... It could start happening in September'. The word from St. Helens was that they 'were glad to see the back of the 1987/88 season', which some saw as an indication of the collective state of mind in the Swansea club. Surely, the patient Swansea followers must have thought, with the talent available, the invalids returned to fitness, and a new face or two, performances in the campaign ahead must be an improvement on the season which had just ended. Yet the bookmakers were hardly troubled by those who adopted this point of view as their own.

1988-89

Change for the better

The close season brought several changes in the St. Helens organisation, one of which was the arrival of a new coach in the person of Trevor James. The bearded schoolmaster from Pembrokeshire had, it seemed, a reputation as a disciplinarian. It was said that he demanded 100 per cent attendances at training sessions and 'no slacking'. James was to be assisted by Alun Donovan, who was to concentrate on working with the backs. There was a shock departure, too. Much to the chagrin of the St. Helens club, David Young joined Cardiff. Why did he go? The question was asked repeatedly, but no one could provide a satisfactory answer. Meantime, news of Richard Webster's progress back to fitness was also disappointing. It seemed that he would not be available until Christmas at the earliest. Thus, for the first part of the season at least, the Swansea pack would be shorn of two young internationals. Other pre-season injuries were to exacerbate the problems facing the new coaching team.

The report in the *Sporting Post* of the opening game of the season, described a 'Whites' defeat with the headline 'Injury ravaged Swansea swamped by powerful Gloucester'. According to the report, there was no doubting the completeness of the Gloucester victory. Rarely had a 'Whites' side been beaten so badly at Kingsholm. Furthermore, the *Western Mail* report suggested that, had it not been for a Bleddyn Taylor try late in the game, the score (35 points to 13) would have provided a better reflection of the superiority of the Gloucester men.

Fortunately, on the following Saturday, the match against Lansdowne at St. Helens enabled the 'Whites' to chalk up their first victory. Flanker Alan Reynolds crossed for two of Swansea's five tries of the day. This time, it was the Irish side's turn to make the score more respectable by scoring late in the game. However, that was of little concern to the St. Helens faithful as they enjoyed the tries scored by Reynolds, Tim Michael, Mark Bernard and Tony Clement. Furthermore, they had the début of new centre, Bleddyn Bowen, to look forward to. Bowen had transferred from the 'Police' and, had he not sprained an ankle in training would have played against the Irishmen. As it was, he was obliged to wait a further fortnight, when, as ill-luck would have it, he injured a knee in his initial game.

Whilst that match, against Newport, was won as a result of a Tony Clement dropped goal ten minutes from the end, three other matches in that sequence resulted in defeats. At that, Ron Griffiths, in conversation with coach, Trevor James and Roger Blyth, found himself following a familiar line of questioning. Weren't they disappointed with the start? What could be done about the inconsistency which had bedevilled Swansea for so many years? Blyth could only agree that everyone at the club was disappointed in the results which had been achieved. For his part, the coach felt that he needed about three months before his influence would really begin to have an effect. Whilst that was a reasonable statement, it hardly provided the loyal Swansea

A typical Bleddyn Bowen break.

supporters with the kind of comfort which they needed at the time. Meantime, all they could do was to hope for better things. Happily, the next result provided some solace.

Playing at Twickenham, the 'Whites' showed what they were capable of, not only as far as skill, talent, flair and teamwork were concerned, but also spirit. The *hwyl* demonstrated that day would have done justice to the archers at Agincourt. Paul Arnold, to the delight of the Forwards' Union, dumped the ball over the 'Quins try line to open the score, and Alan Williams, who had worked like a proverbial Trojan, scored a second try from a five-metre scrum. Whilst the next match was lost, there followed four consecutive victories which did much to lift the spirits at St. Helens, on the pitch, in the stand, and on the bank. The clubhouse and a few of the near by hostelries were not excluded, either.

Among those victories was a tremendous win over Leicester, which attracted the *Post* headline, 'Super Whites tame Tigers'. Among the Tiger-tamers were two of the young stars who were making their presence felt at the Cricket Ground at that time – Paul Moriarty and Tony Clement. With Clement playing at full-back, Paul Arnold at Number 8, Bleddyn Bowen kicking fifteen points, and Alan Williams and Tim Michael both getting tries in the defeat of the men of letters, the sun shone brightly in Swansea that Saturday.

After the four consecutive victories had resulted in a renewed level of expectancy at St. Helens, the old malady resurfaced when Llanelli won there. Worse was to follow, for the 'Whites' were dispatched from the Schweppes Cup competition at the first hurdle by Glamorgan Wanderers. With all due respect to the 'Wanderers', they had no business winning, and at the Cricket Ground at that!

To say that the whole of Swansea's rugby community was stunned would have been understating the case; 'devastated' would have been more apt.

In its coverage of the game, the media could only fall back on cliches about the 'magic of the Cup'. Whilst spokesmen for the Swansea club saw little magical in the situation, they, too, were bemused. Where, asked the papers, was Swansea's commitment on the day? What is wrong at St. Helens? As far as Ron Griffiths was concerned, it seemed to be an excellent time to undertake his, almost annual 'psychoanalysis' of his Cricket Ground patient, though he could only trot out words which had become familiar to his readers over more than a decade. 'One of the big mysteries of Welsh rugby', he wrote, 'is that Swansea sides, often brimming with Internationals, fall down so frequently'. The questions were as old as the 'reasons' which were said to be behind the problems, and the remedies being prescribed to overcome them. The new coaches expressed themselves as mystified as anyone. They complained, 'We don't seem to gell as a team. One week it's the backs who flop, and the next week it's the turn of the forwards'. The players, equally bemused, were, nonetheless determined. Paul Moriarty, speaking for his colleagues, told the *Post*, 'We are determined to lift Swansea ... The players are fitter now than they have been for a number of seasons ... it's up to us to put it right!' The words must have come as sweet music to the puzzled coaches. After all, in the end, any coach can only influence through his philosophies, his methods and his leadership qualities. Once his side steps over the white touchline, only players can 'make it happen'. Given that no one doubted the extent and the quality of the talent available at St. Helens, it was reasonable to argue that it was the attitude of the players, or the way in which they organised themselves which was the root cause of the problems which the club was facing. If that was true, the impassioned statement which had been made by Paul Moriarty on behalf of the players, could be taken as implying that the 'attitude' aspect of the formula was being addressed.

In the aftermath of the Newbridge defeat, the St. Helens men took the opportunity to show their mettle. Clearly, the quality of the opposition has to be taken into account when assessing the performance of any side. However, at the time, the quality of play of the 'Whites' in several games which were played in succession, could only be described as outstanding. Penarth, 'faced with the pace and spirit of an effervescent Swansea side', were 'taken apart'. That day, the St. Helens faithful saw their favourites put sixty points on the board. Then Moseley were beaten by 29 points to 10, the 'Whites' avenged their defeat by Glamorgan Wanderers in a 23 points to 3 'runaround', and Tredegar, whilst scoring 19 points, conceded 53.

Thus it was that 1988 ended with four consecutive victories and a host of morale boosting points (for supporters as well as the team). As the older men in the Swansea stand on New Year's Day 1989 remembered the days when they pocketed bronze threepenny-pieces for knocking doors with New Year greetings (in English or Welsh, as appropriate), they must have wished that the year ahead would be happy as far as their favourites were concerned. Happily, whilst the results of the first two matches of 1989 might have been taken as suggesting that insufficient dark men had crossed Swansea thresholds at the last stroke of midnight, what happened thereafter implied that the converse was true. Indeed, after losing to Llanelli and Aberavon, the 'Whites' were defeated on just three other occasions during the remainder of the season. Given the results at the turn of the year, though, those who noted such things, may have remembered that Trevor James had said that he needed three months to make his influence felt.

Swansea's successful run began at Rodney Parade on 14 January 1989. Robert Jones played a major role in the defeat of the 'Amber and Blackings', as did the returning Arthur Emyr, who scored a brace of tries. Other scorers were, Tony Clement, with a thirty yard penalty, Paul

Moriarty, Stuart Parfitt, Bleddyn Taylor, and Robert Jones, all of whom crossed for tries. London Welsh were the next to feel the Swansea lash as the 'Whites' scored 38 points, following which, Ebbw Vale shipped 53 points whilst scoring 10.

But then, just when everything in the Swansea garden appeared to be blooming, W.R.U. decision-making dealt the club a severe blow. Coach, Trevor James, having enjoyed his work at St. Helens and having begun to get to grips with the changes which he believed to be essential, decided that he would make a career change. The W.R.U. wished to appoint three Regional Development Officers. James, having been attracted by the job specification, applied for one of the posts under the assumption that, had he been successful, he could have continued with his job at St. Helens. However, after resigning from his teaching job and commencing the W.R.U. work, Trevor found that the 'powers that be' at the Union required him to resign from his Swansea post. At the time, among the many confusing statements that were made was one which related to amateur and professional status of rugby coaches, and which implied that the James must now be regarded as professional. Whilst the Pembrokeshire man stated at the time that, had he known, he would not have applied for the W.R.U. post, matters had progressed too far. One result of this was that James resigned from St. Helens and, once again, the club there found itself without a chief coach.

Days later, an announcement from the Cricket Field confirmed that, in the short term, Trevor Cheeseman, Alun Donovan and Neil Jones – each of whom had been working with James, would continue as a coaching team. The club, it was said, did not intend 'rushing in to name a new supremo'.

In March, as the 'Whites' scored points with regular frequency, and one of the men responsible for crossing for some of the most spectacular tries gained his first 'cap' Among the first people to congratulate the player, Arthur Emyr on his selection, was fellow north-Walian and former 'White', Dewi Bebb. Bangor had another famous son! Meantime, at St. Helens, whilst other Swansea wingmen, Bleddyn Taylor and Mark Titley, were scoring tries with even greater frequency than Emyr, there was still concern about the pack. With Richard Moriarty absent with a back injury suffered during the middle of March, there was, according to the *Post*, 'a selection crisis at St. Helens'. It seemed that only two locks of sufficient calibre, Paul Arnold and Steve Williams, were available for consideration. Given fitness and experience factors, this resulted, in some matches, in Paul Moriarty being played out of position in the second-row. The younger Moriarty, whilst responding to the request of the selectors, let it be known that he did not enjoy playing there. He was unhappy, too, with regard to the position in which he found himself with the Welsh selectors ever since a new coach had been appointed. Since that event, despite the fact that the back-row which had been selected by Wales was hardly performing as an effective unit, the big Swansea man had been ignored. He was not even given the encouragement of being selected among the replacements. This presented the player with 'a double signal of rejection'. Consequently, when Widnes, who had long admired the Swansea man's play, 'read the tea leaves', they offered Moriarty what was then a record fee for a forward – £100,000 – to join them. It was as a result of that sequence of events that the Swansea selectors found themselves without another top-class forward, when their need for big men was apparent. Roger Blyth, chairman of the 'Whites' selection committee, was scathing in his comments, 'Swansea, Wales, and the Union game have lost a fine forward ... they (the W.R.U.) treated him diabolically ... he leaves a massive hole in the Swansea pack'. Whilst, at the time, the contract offer involved was a significant incentive for the young man to 'take the northern silver', the general opinion at the Cricket Field was that, had Moriarty felt that he was under consideration to be restored to the Welsh side, he might well have elected to remain in the Union game. Such considerations, of course, involve conjecture. However, what is not in doubt, is that the men from Rugby League clubs have their antennae beamed in on the Welsh Union scene. Not surprisingly, over the years, they have found that a good time to approach a would-be acquisition is when, for whatever reason, the player is disappointed or disgruntled with his lot. Certainly, from their point of view they struck at the right time as far as the big Morriston man was concerned, and the wrong time for Swansea rugby.

Meanwhile, notwithstanding the selectors' concerns about the constitution of the Swansea pack, the 'Whites' continued to win in fine style. Whilst the opposition in one of the next three games may not have been 'top class', the men in white scored sixty-four points on that occasion, and they registered more than forty on each of the other two. Among those who suffered were the 'Welsh' at Old Deer Park, where the 'Whites' were have said to have run in forty-two 'breathtaking points'. Bleddyn Taylor opened the account within ten minutes, and, whilst points were added steadily throughout the game, in the last quarter the 'Whites' cut loose in 'true Swansea style'. After a thirty-yard run by Tony Clement, Tim Michael took over to score. Then Bleddyn Taylor hurtled through a tackle and ran thirty-five yards to dive over. It was one of those matches when the home crowd wanted the referee to blow up with ten minutes to go.

To the joy of the Swansea faithful, from then until the end of the season the 'Whites' continued to 'serve up superlative rugby'. Some said that the play was a throw back to the days of the 'Golden Era'. Whilst that may have been a claim too far, there was no doubting the strength and talent of the backs. It was plain for all to see. What, Swansea supporters asked themselves, might we have done had we been able to field a pack to complement such brilliance? Had Paul Moriarty remained at St. Helens and had his brother, Richard, and Richard Webster been available, surely, the argument went, results would have been even better! Despite the inevitable implications of conjecture which were contained in the discussion, no one at St. Helens was prepared to take that side in the debate which argued the case that the availability of these men would not have changed things for the better. In any event, debating logic has no place in rugby club dreaming. Each season, up and down the country, when the next season's potential performance is considered, blind eyes are turned on the 'downside' factors. Robert Jones, appointed captain for the coming term at St. Helens, was no different in his assessment. His comments to the press were, what the P.R. men call 'up-beat'. After the success of the season which had recently ended he was confident. 'There is a tremendous amount of talent at St. Helens ... it is time that the club's potential was realised! ... With Richard (Moriarty) back in the pack, I am sure that it will make a world of difference to our prospects.'

When the final curtain fell, it was reported that 'there will be no summer break for the Swansea players'. Roger Blyth let it be known that the coaching team wanted to ensure a level of fitness far in advance of what the players have reached up to the present. Consequently 'they will train twice a week, in the short-term in preparation for the visit of the "All Blacks", and in the longer term to help to put this club back where it belongs'. Swansea supporters were impressed. Was this the outcome of consulting the philosopher's stone? And would the initiative result in inconsistency being banished from the Cricket Field for ever? Blyth emphasised that, after Trevor James left, the coaching team of Alun Donovan, Trevor Cheeseman and Neil Jones had 'done a fine job'. Without doubt, said the chairman of selectors,' team spirit has improved considerably ... but we are not kidding ourselves, there is still much to do!' Yet, much had also been achieved. Bleddyn Taylor had scored 20 tries, Mark Titley and Alan Williams 16 each, and Mark Wyatt, once again, headed the points scoring list, with 168. With 30 matches having been won in an exciting season, and 1,110 points being scored whilst 691 were conceded, as the faithful looked back there was much to savour. Furthermore, the side had not only been successful, it had played attractive, crowd-pleasing football. For the Swansea faithful, that was at least as important!

1989-90

Brave, brave, Swansea and a new coach

At St. Helens, during the busy close season, rumour still persisted in permeating the conversations of Cricket Field *aficionados*. Mark Wyatt was said to be pondering his future as a player, and, given that no formal announcement had been made about coaching staff, various names were being mentioned as potential 'Supremos'. The press, not surprisingly, was also involved. The *Post*, for example, reported that 'Swansea are anxious to involve more of their former players, which could be one of the reasons why Mike Ruddock was among the interested spectators at one of the games at the end of last season'. Ron Griffiths, sensing more than casual interest in the former flanker's presence at St. Helens, reminded his readers of Ruddock's pedigree. 'Since his premature retirement he has taken up coaching at Cross Keys ... his influence was evident in the performance of the "Keys" pack in the match against the "Whites" last season'. Whilst the *Post*-man was somewhat premature as regards the potential date of arrival of the likeable Ruddock at St. Helens, no doubt it was his journalist's nose which smelt in the Cricket Field air at the time, the potential that a meaningful relationship might develop. Like a doting parent, the journalist was always on the look out for a 'suitable' partner for his beloved 'child'. It is possible, however, that he might have misread the signals. As Mike Ruddock was to show, he is a man dedicated to improving his knowledge and understanding of the game of Rugby Football. There were few casual visits in the Ruddock diary. The majority have a specific purpose.

Meanwhile, the individual fitness programme which had been launched at St. Helens was said to have 'already made a difference', and the news from Australia delighted all at St. Helens. The club captain for the coming season was reported to have played, magnificently, for the Lions in all three Tests. In mid-August came the news that 'a tough, uncompromising coach, Alan Lewis' was to take the helm at St. Helens. Lewis, who had spent four seasons with the Swansea club in the mid-Seventies, had clear objectives in his mind. 'It's my job to get forward commitment ... to make everyone who wears the Swansea shirt, proud'. The words were hardly new. 'Whites' followers had heard similar phrases before on the appointment of other new coaches. Yet, there was a ring about the new man's comments which suggested that if tenacity was an ingredient in the elixir which he proposed, then success would be assured.

On reading Ron Griffiths's comments on the season ahead, it is probable that the new coach would have nodded his head in agreement. 'If Swansea are to scale any heights they will need to change their attitude ... rugby today is an amateur game which demands a professional approach'. No longer could the Corinthian spirit which had been a central element in the Swansea

Mark Wyatt – record holder – head steady, follow through.

ethos for many decades, be allowed to flourish unfettered. Whilst, deep in the hearts of old St. Helens-ites, such a transition may not have been welcomed, the reality of the environment in which the modern game was being played decreed that either the club embraced the new philosophy or ceased to be an influential institution within it. The thinking among the St. Helens rugby population would have recognised that there was no alternative. The rest would have to be led to such understanding.

Given that the approaching season was to be the last before a league system was embraced by clubs in Wales, apart from the new man at the helm at St. Helens, change was at the back of the mind of all those who contemplated the future. Since the previous campaign had ended with such high promise, as they filed onto the 'Tanner Bank' for the opening match of the new season, 'Whites' supporters were filled with hope. For the first time since it was built, they gazed across the pitch at an empty stand (which was closed on the day for safety reasons). From their unfamiliar vantage point, the romantic among season ticket holders, along with dreamers who regularly stood in the open, may have thought of the unpopulated stand as a silent backcloth to the demise of traditional rugby at St. Helens. How fitting on that day, would have been a Swansea victory of old-time proportions and style! And why not? It was hardly too much to ask following a season of achievement which had underscored the potential at St. Helens.

Alas, at the end of the match, against Gloucester, dreamers and the pragmatic alike would have been jolted back to reality as the powerful visitors defeated their favourites by 32 points to 17. At the end, searching for solace among the ashes upon which the ancient bank had been built, the St. Helens faithful may have reasoned that, at least, late tries (by Arnold and Emyr) showed that the much-trumpeted pre-season training had helped to improve stamina. And that conclusion may have been seen to be confirmed by those who saw the next match (at Lansdowne), when, on a lovely day 'old fashioned rugby at its best' was played. Then, on Irish turf, the 'Whites' ran in 'a late flurry of tries', to win a 'satisfying contest' by twenty-five points to ten. Among the 'delightful' tries which were scored in that late flurry, was one by Stuart Parfitt. Mark Titley started the move by beating the cover on his own '22'. Titley passed to Parfitt at half way, and the centre out-paced the home defence to touch down. In keeping with the sentiment of the day, 'warm applause' was said to have 'rippled around the ground as the generous Irish showed their appreciation'.

In the *Sporting Post* for that September Saturday night, whilst the report on the victory over Lansdowne would have been read eagerly by the St. Helens faithful, they would, also, have noted Ron Griffiths's comments on the inside of the paper. Referring to the 'prophets of gloom' among the Cricket Field following, the *Post*-man reported that 'Since Swansea lost their opening game ... they (the doomsters) are already predicting that nothing has changed ... it's the same old pattern, drifting from game to game'. Obviously in disagreement with the pessimists, Griffiths quoted Clive Rowlands as one of the many knowledgeable people in the game who 'endorsed Alan Lewis and Alun Donovan as coaches'. A week later, the journalist was to build upon his positive outlook as Bristol were beaten by the 'Whites'.

Notwithstanding the criticism which some had levelled at the St. Helens management, the *Post's* report of the game with the West Countrymen was illustrative of how good coaching and appropriate tactics can make a virtue out of necessity. As the *Western Mail* put it, 'Swansea were inspired by a lively pack'. The *Post*, following the same theme, reported that 'Swansea's lighter but livelier forwards came from behind to outscore Bristol'. With Robert Jones and Tony Clement back in the side, the 'Whites' were said to have 'demonstrated mobility, team-work and opportunism. Two of Swansea's scores were illustrative of these qualities. First, a quickly-taken tapped penalty caught the Bristol men on their heels. The ball travelled to Kevin Hopkins, who, seeing an appropriate gap raced through to score. In the second-half, the returning Tony Clement demonstrated his speed and strength. Gathering on the blind-side after a set scrum, the full-back drove powerfully towards the line, thrusting off two, would-be tacklers en route. Five yards from the Bristol line, Swansea forwards arrived in support, to force the full-back over despite the massed defence of the Bristolians. Later that day, Clement said that he was delighted to learn that Richard Webster, who had been selected by Wales for the 1991 World Cup squad, was making good progress back to fitness. No doubt, had he been playing against Bristol, the Webster shoulder would have been placed firmly behind the Clement rear end as the full-back was propelled over the line.

Without doubt, for the Swansea club and its supporters the visit of the New Zealanders was to be the highlight of the first quarter of the season. The special training having 'gone well', coaches Lewis and Donovan were 'reasonably confident' that the outcome would be favourable. Not surprisingly, there were concerns. One of the most important related to the middle of the line-out, a position of significant importance in the modern game. Everyone was hoping that Richard Moriarty would be able to appear, though, given the length of his absence, the informed regarded this as doubtful.

The match to be played immediately before the 'Kiwis' came to St. Helens, was that against Llanelli, which, since they had won all but the first game of the season before that Saturday, was viewed with some confidence by the Swansea men. Whilst the 'Whites' went into the 'Sospan' match without Bleddyn Bowen – who had a leg in plaster – there were few pessimists at St. Helens that day. At half-time, the 'Whites' were leading by 13 points to 7 as a result of tries by Bleddyn Taylor and Arthur Emyr. At that stage, the Merit Table Champions from the previous season looked likely to be beaten. However, in the last quarter of the match the 'Scarlets' gained the ascendancy, and clinched victory in the last fifteen minutes. As a result, Swansea went into the match with the 'All Blacks' on the back of a defeat. Whilst that, and the absence through injury of two key players were not helpful to the Swansea cause, that day in October 1989, the 'Whites' were to give their all. The *Post* headline, 'Brave, Brave, Try, Whites' was pertinent. With Botica outstanding for the New Zealanders, they took an early lead when the player kicked a fifty-five yard penalty. Thereafter, despite the best efforts of the Swansea men, New Zealand ground their way into the ascendancy. By half-time, the 'Whites' had to contemplate a scoreboard which showed 21 point to 3 deficit, with a Mark Wyatt penalty being all the homesters could show for their effort.

However, that afternoon, the juice of the Swansea lemons must have been particularly potent. In the first five minutes of the second period the 'Whites' scored twice. Mark Wyatt struck a second penalty with typical precision, and then a massive Tony Clement kick created a platform for a try. Gathering as the New Zealand cover closed, Robert Jones dummied then offloaded to the supporting Ian Davies who charged over to score. The roar which greeted the try was said to have brought the traffic in Morriston to a halt. 'Yan', having sorted himself out from the bevy of New Zealanders who were lying on top of him, rose to a hero's acclaim. It was said that he looked quite pleased.

As the home cheers continued to reverberate around the historic field, the St. Helens faithful scented a famous victory. Sadly, it was not to be. Stung into reaction, the 'All Blacks', digging into their reserves, forced their way back into the 'driving seat'. At no side, they left the field the winners by 37 points to 22. Given that, two weeks later, Wales suffered a 34 points to 9 defeat, the pride of the Swansea faithful in the performance of their heroes against the 'All Blacks' on that memorable day may be seen to have been more than justified.

Swansea's 'Brave, Brave, heroes' that day were:

M. Wyatt, A. Titley, S. Parfitt, K. Hopkins, A. Emyr, A. Clement, R. Jones, I. Buckett, B. James, M. Morgan, S. Williams, P. Arnold, I. Davies, S. D. Davies, A. Reynolds.

The response from many quarters to that performance by the 'Whites' kept the pride warm in Swansea bosoms long after the event. Among those who enthused was, former coach, Trevor James, who forecast that 'in a year, maybe two, Swansea will have a side capable of going places'. Radio and T.V. pundits concurred, though, there was always the proviso, implied if not stated, that a side 'capable of' might not always achieve its potential. Nonetheless, the young pack (average age 23) was praised as much as the backs, and, even a commentator who, in Swansea was famed for his 'Anti-White' views, was fulsome in his praise of the team as a whole. Billy James, at thirty-three the only experienced player in the pack, added his note to the rhapsody of congratulations which was showered on the young side. Discounting the significant contribution which he had made in the New Zealand match, the hooker said, 'they are the most talented bunch I have ever played with.'

By the end of December, the 'Whites' had made 'comfortable progress' in the Cup, beaten Cardiff in a memorable Arms Park clash (by 29 points to 7), Newbridge by 41 points to 19, with Mark Titley scoring a hat-trick of tries, and Bath by 17 points to 9. Arthur Emyr scored twice and Stuart Parfitt once against the English champions. All in all, as the old decade ended and the new began, the team could look back on an encouraging first-half. Despite a series of unfortunate injuries, and the special physical and psychological pressures which stemmed from preparing for and playing the match against New Zealand, seventeen of the twenty-three matches played by the club had been won. Happily, those who had started the season with concern about the effectiveness of the pack, could gain confidence from considering the consistent performances of the front eight. Front-row men like Buckett and Morgan, locks Arnold and Williams, all encouraged, tutored and cajoled by the veteran, Billy James, and the burgeoning back-row men, Ian and Stuart Davies and Alan Reynolds. In an ideal world, there is no doubt that most would have benefited from additional inches and pounds, but their all-round footballing skills, their verve and dedication to the Swansea cause, and the speed with which they were 'learning their trades', were unquestioned. 'Mumbles' Davies, Fred Scrine and the old giants would have been proud of them.

The new decade

After the first match of the new decade was lost, the side put together a sequence of six victories. Among them were: a 'seven try bonanza' when Newport were the victims, (Mike Morgan scored twice in that match, whilst Stuart Davies, who came on as a substitute, scored another), a 34 points to 3 victory over Abertillery, and a 78 points to 3 'demolition' of Penarth. That match was a triumph for Steffan Jones, for the young man scored four tries and kicked nine conversions during the eighty minutes to set a new mark in the Swansea record books – 34 points in a game by a single player.

With Nelson Mandela being freed in South Africa – one of several initiatives which were to result in the 'Springboks' being restored to the World rugby family – Swansea's 'Whites' were enjoying some freedom of their own. One hundred and ninety points were scored by the side in seven matches, often as a result of playing open, 'Swansea' football.

Among this set of victories was a cup win over Glamorgan Wanderers, which helped to assuage the pain which, in Swansea, was associated with the memory of the defeat of the 'Whites' by the 'Wanderers' in the same competition in 1988. That victory took Swansea into the sixth round of the cup, when they were drawn to play Newport at St. Helens. Having beaten the Gwent club five weeks earlier, the 'Whites' were considered to be favourites to win the encounter; and win they did. However, in order to do so they had to claw themselves back into the game after trailing by 10 points to 3 at half-time. In the second-half, the Swansea pack wrested control from the opposing eight, and appropriately, the three tries scored in that second period all came from 'Whites' forwards. Messrs. Arnold, Buckett and Reynolds each crossing to score.

Having beaten Newport, the 'Whites' found themselves in the semi-final of the cup competition, when they were to meet Neath. As it happened, prior to that match, the 'Whites' ran into form, performing well against Bridgend, Ebbw Vale, and Cardiff and scoring 112 points in the process. As a consequence players and supporters travelled with confidence. In the event, in front of a 20,000 crowd, Neath sealed victory by dropping a goal in the last minute of the match. Prior to that score, the 'Whites' had stormed the Neath line, and threatened time and again to take the match themselves. Whilst the men in black held out, they, and the body of media men who were there that day, expressed themselves surprised by the 'steel' in Swansea's play. Another put it in simpler language, 'They gave as good as they got.'

With the Cup no longer a concern, the 'Whites' ended the season with a flourish. In the four matches which brought down the curtain on the campaign, they lost to the Barbarians, but beat Rosslyn Park by 40 points to 3 (the 'Park's' heaviest defeat of the season), won against Aberavon by 39 points to 21, and against Pontypool by 43 points to 33. It was old fashioned 'holiday' football at its best.

With hindsight, it is interesting to look back on that Pontypool match as the final act of 'traditional' rugby on the historic field. The season to come was to involve the inauguration of the new Heineken League system, which was to result in playing methods and philosophies being developed which would focus upon what the coaches called 'a more controlled game'. That day, however, was for Corinthians, though Pontypool started as if they had not received St. Paul's letter. With self-interest in their hearts, they tore into the 'Whites', 'rocking them back on their heels'. At one stage in the match, with the St. Helens scoreboard registering Swansea 11 Pontypool 31, it appeared that 'Pooler' were in sight of a comfortable victory. The Swansea men, however, had other ideas, and, in the final third of the game, the 'Whites' played football filled with grit, determination and not a little talent and flair. When Richard Webster 'stormed over for the winning try', the crowd as a whole rose not only to applaud the score, but to acclaim the festival of football which had preceded it. In the circumstances, the romantic among the Swansea crowd may have thought that it was entirely appropriate that the ancient field had witnessed a match brimming with such vitality as to be eminently suitable to serve as a celebration of pre-League rugby.

With the squad going to Florida for an inter-season 'warm-up' – at least the weather would have been appropriate – Billy James let it be known that he was to join the party, Whilst making the announcement he enthused about the position in which the Swansea club found itself. He said 'We have everything ... a crop of fine young forwards who can only get better, a pair of forward-looking coaches and a first-class club structure'. James was not alone in his views. In his end-of-the-season comments, Ron Griffiths reflected the confidence which emanated from the Cricket Field. He wrote, 'After years of trying, Swansea think that they have got the recipe right ... the public, too, are aware of the greater levels of fitness and skill at St. Helens ... Last season's record – 27 wins in 41 matches, plus the emergence of young players who are going to be around St. Helens for years, suggests a fine future for the club'. Since the Welsh rugby fraternity had awarded Swansea men awards for 'Player of the Year' and 'Most promising player' (Arthur Emyr and Steve Williams), it was clear that others were also impressed with the St. Helens set-up. This time, surely, there was no question of a false dawn! Or was there?

1990–91

Coming to grips with league football

With the first League match (Cardiff away), not scheduled until 22 September, the 'Whites' began the initial season of the new decade with a winning visit to Kingsholm. Not only was the victory impressive, it was gained by a side which was depleted as a result of injury. The highlight of the match was a superb Arthur Emyr try after fine interplay with Mark Titley. In keeping with the requirements, the 'Whites' squad for the season was announced early in September. Among those listed was Malcolm Dacey, back from Cardiff; Billy James and Lloyd Isaac, were to share hooking duties. On seeing the full list, however, there were those who asked, who is going to do the kicking? With Mark Wyatt only scheduled to help out and offer advice, it was apparent that the squad did not contain a specialist place-kicker. Other news included the fact that Richard Moriarty would not be able to start the season in view of the fact that his broken arm was taking longer to heal than had been expected.

Malcolm Dacey – eyes an opening.

Nevertheless, with pre-season confidence boosted by further victories (over Lansdowne and Bristol), the St. Helens men approached the first League match in the club's history with as much confident expectancy as their supporters. Sadly, Cardiff, on their own ground, dispelled much of that confidence with alacrity. Worse was to follow. The club's first home match in the League was also lost. After that defeat, the comments of media pundits reflected doubt about Swansea's style being suited to league football. Alun Donovan, reacting to this criticism, argued that, 'We're still learning how to cope ... we began to play in an expansive style ... but leagues have increased the focus

Tony Clement and Arthur Emyr – about to leap at Kiwi throats.

on defence ... to win you have to adapt, and the rugby can be pretty dull'. In a fraction of the time it had taken to build up, pre-season confidence seeped from the minds of the optimists and fairly gushed out of those of the pessimists. In its place, the voice of the resident St. Helens gremlin echoed the old doubts. New set-up, inconsistency banished, who's kidding whom? (Clearly, given his understanding of the niceties of language, the gremlin must have been a Dynevor boy).

Fortunately, following wins in two club matches, as one media man put it, 'away from the strictures of league football', the defeat of Newbridge at St. Helens provided the club with its first league points. And that total was doubled when the 'Whites' went to the Brewery Field and beat Bridgend as a result of an injury-time try by Bleddyn Taylor. Not only did the win provide valuable league points for the St. Helens men, they also took the Bridgend ground and unbeaten records in the process. In addition, the winning try was of 'Swansea' proportions. Clement, collecting deep in his own half, ran strongly towards the right touch line. Drawing his man, he passed to Titley, outside him, who surged forward in his inimitable style before passing to the supporting Hopkins. Hopkins shipped the ball to Parfitt, who off-loaded to Dacey, who made ground before feeding Taylor who surged over the line to score. During that movement an illusion was created that there were more Swansea men on the field than homesters. It was an illusion which coaches Donovan and Lewis would like to have been able to replicate. Bridgend and the home crowd were stunned. The 'Whites' had recovered from a half-time score of 6 points to 21, to win the match by the odd point in 43. It had been a remarkable performance! The optimists asked, who said that league football had to be dull and boring? For their part, the coaches, studying their action-replay videos, sought ways to stop such attacks.

Nonetheless, with the evidence of the Bridgend victory behind them, Swansea optimists began to regroup. They were arguing that the victory illustrated the quality of the squad, which, leagues or no leagues would show through in the play of their favourites. Surely, their case suggested, it was simply a matter of adapting to the strictures of league football! Unfortunately, there was more to it than that, and, when the final matches of the competition had been played, the records showed that the 'Whites' were eighth in the table, having won half the games played whilst scoring 353 points and conceding 306. The outcome was disappointing, but there were extenuating circumstances which did not help the Swansea cause. Among them was the resignation of coach Alan Lewis early in January. At that time, Lewis believed that he did not have the confidence of the players, and felt that it would be best if he resigned. He was sad, he said, because 'Swansea means a great deal to me'. Whatever the rights and wrongs of the situation, there was no doubt about Lewis's sincerity in that regard. Roger Blyth demonstrated that the club recognised that, when he said that the coach had 'made a tremendous contribution to Swansea rugby. It is sad to see him go'. That aside, though, the disruption to the organisation of the team in the second-half of the season as a result of Lewis's departure did not help matters at St. Helens. What it did do, however, was to accelerate the plans concerned with the recruitment of a new supremo.

In undertaking that task, the management at St. Helens believed that the strength of the club's squad and its potential would be one of the factors which would help them find the right man. For example, notwithstanding the disappointing outcome of the season, the result of several league matches gave cause for encouragement. Among the clubs which had been defeated by the 'Whites', were Cardiff (23 points to 15), Bridgend (30 points to 15), and Pontypool who conceded a remarkable 63 points whilst scoring only 3. The performance of the Swansea side against 'Pooler' that December day must rank among the best ever seen at St. Helens. Ron Griffiths called it 'rather special'. It had been, he said, 'wonderful entertainment and skill provided by a back division which, with the exception of Bleddyn Taylor, was all-international'. All the pieces were put into place on that bitterly cold, windy, winter's day, when all who were there managed to forget the conditions as they were warmed by movements of outstanding Swansea proportion.

Interestingly, when David Price compiled his season's records, the leading points scorer was captain, Robert Jones, who, in the absence of a specialist had undertaken the bulk of the place kicking himself. Mark Titley (15) led the try scorers, followed by Bleddyn Taylor (14), and the two Davies's, Simon and Ian, on 13. Having scored a total of 998 points, the statisticians among the faithful may have noted that, for the first time in twelve seasons the club had failed to register a four-figure total. Not that that bald fact was of great import. In the second League season when the 'Whites' became champions, despite an increase in try value, even fewer points were scored.

After the curtain had fallen on the 1990/91 season, rugby conversations in south Wales were dominated by concepts such as tackle counts, and by analysis of the tactics which were being adopted by club coaches. There was, too, much discussion about the impact of league football on 'club' matches and, in Swansea, of the likelihood that the traditional Easter match with the Barbarians was no longer what it had been. As has ever been the case, change brings with it facets which are often unattractive to those imbued with the values of previous cultures. The reality, though, is, that those who have to manage any organisation which has to be effective in an environment which has embraced change, can rarely preserve all of the cherished features which were enjoyed under earlier circumstances.

At the Cricket Field, this was to result in structural and cultural changes which, as time was to show, were an essential element in the organisational development of Swansea Rugby Club. In the future, interested historians may perceive that 1990 was something of a watershed in the history of the club at the Cricket Field. Certainly, they may be assured that none of those charged with the management of the far-reaching changes which were made at the time, were enjoying sinecures. Every person involved in developing the new structure at the club had to contribute. No longer would there be a place for the proverbial archetypical Welsh rugby committeeman who is purported to have attempted to justify his presence on a decision-making body by saying, 'I'm here to find out what's going on'.

Chapter Twenty-Seven

ORGANISATIONAL CHANGE AND A NEW COACH

DURING THE FINAL WEEKS of the 1990/91 season and throughout the summer which followed, a new organisational structure was being developed at St. Helens. The prime-mover in this process was Mike James, who had been appointed as Club chairman after serving for 15 years on the rugby selection committee. A tough, uncompromising forward in his playing days, James was to bring these attributes plus vision and tenacity to his new role. In addition, he and his board colleagues (Geoff Atherton, Roger Blyth and Byron Mugford) realised that they should utilise the talent which was at their disposal within the wider organisation. As has ever been the case at St. Helens, a variety of professional people, with great affection for their club, were willing to make a contribution to its life. Consequently, in developing the new constitution, which was a necessary element in the overall process, Mike James drew upon expertise inside and outside the club. Treasurer, Brian Simpson, Prof. John Beynon, and Rosemary Morgan of the club's honorary solicitors, Morgan Bruce, produced numerous drafts of the constitution before it was presented to the club for consideration.

Clearly, this work was of considerable importance as far as management and members were concerned. The club as a whole had to be satisfied that the changes which were proposed were to its benefit, and that its democratic processes were unimpaired by them. As it transpired, when the chairman and his like-minded allies began the process of enacting the changes involved in the new constitution, they found themselves pushing at a half-open door – at least as far as the majority of Swansea committee members were concerned. These members, having attempted for many years to manage the club through structures and communication systems which had been designed to meet the needs of a more leisurely bygone age, had become increasingly aware of the many deficiencies of such methods. Yet, inertia, plus a desire not to offend loyal committee people who, in many cases, had given years of service to the club, resulted in decisions concerned with major change being avoided or postponed.

Having arrived at the final chapters of this book, the reader will have sympathy with this last concern. He or she may be aware, from personal experience as well as from the present narrative, of the outstanding service which, over the years, has been given to the Swansea club by a veritable host of individuals. Indeed, the implications of such service form an important part of the institution which is Swansea Rugby Club. Nonetheless, effective management has to concern itself with broader issues. In the process, and in recognising the contribution made by such service in an organisation primarily run by people who give their time and talent without monetary reward, such dedication is to be encouraged. What is necessary, however, is to ensure that the potency of such loyalty is not dissipated, but that it is channelled, marshalled and focused more appropriately. Where this is done successfully, the benefits associated with dedicated service make a greater contribution to enriching the life of the club, are of greater reward to individuals, and make a greater contribution to the achievement of 'corporate' objectives.

However, in situations where change is being implemented, as they strive to protect the *status quo*, some dedicated individuals fail to grasp this wider perception. At St. Helens at the time, as would have been the case in any situation involving substantial organisational change, some people came to accept the need for change later than others. They were, however, in the minority. Furthermore, since then, the successes which have been achieved as a result of implementing the new management structure and systems, have won over all but a tiny minority among the club's membership. With the benefit of the club as their prime consideration, an objective of Mike James and his 'board' was to ensure that that process continued.

In this they were assisted by the new structure which had been developed. For example, the new board itself was indicative of the far-reaching changes which had been made at St. Helens, in that it comprised just seven people. Previously, its work was being undertaken by two committees which had a combined membership of forty-five; clearly, far too large a body for effective decision-making. And, at the time that the organisational changes were first mooted, effective, timely decision-making was essential to the continuance of first-class rugby at St. Helens.

For example, in considering the club's position, the members of the board had perceived both threats and opportunities in the developments which had occurred in world rugby. Among other things, the *de facto* professionalism inherent in the approach of some countries to the 1987 and 1991 World Cup competitions, and the establishment of the Heineken League system in Wales, had changed the face of rugby irreversibly. As a consequence, those whose task it was to manage the affairs of the St. Helens club realised that the key decisions which they would be taking in the short and medium term would have a significant impact upon the future of Swansea Rugby Football Club.

Notwithstanding the foregoing, as far as most members of a sporting organisation are concerned, the true test of its success is not how effectively the 'business management' system works, but rather, how successful the club's team is on the field of play. Messrs James, Atherton, Blyth and Mugford, whilst acknowledging such an objective as their prime concern, recognised that, in the exacting economic climate of the nineties, such success can only be achieved when an effective business and organisational structure is in place. Not that the business structure is sufficient in itself; it can only be part of the whole. In parallel, they had to find a leader, a man who would evolve and manage effective processes concerned with player recruitment, individual and team development, playing policies, tactics and the many other issues associated with the game of rugby football today. And, not to put too fine a point on it, like every club member, they sought someone who would be successful.

There was another issue, too. They recognised that the job specification which they had in mind for this important post, would not fit the profile of the 'spare-time' appointment usually associated with the traditional coach in Rugby Union football. Instead, as those who managed other leading clubs were beginning to recognise, they had come to accept that the post should be filled by a full-time professional.

As a result, once again, the St. Helens management found themselves having to take a decision which 'flew in the face' of past philosophies regarding how the club was managed. In that regard, however, they were supported by what politicians had come to call 'market forces'; other rugby clubs in the U.K. were following the same logic. And, as the prevailing received wisdom had it, 'if you don't join them then you will be left behind.' In addition, given that the subject of professional coaches was being discussed *ad nauseam* in clubs up and down the land, few members at St. Helens were unaware of the perceived implications of such decision-making. It followed that, since they wanted their team to be successful, and given the threats to such success which were inherent in not embracing the professional coach philosophy, most sup porters were in favour of paying the right man. From that position, it was not too difficult to recognise that the organisational changes which were being made at St. Helens were appropriate enabling measures. As a consequence, Mike James and his colleagues found considerable support among the membership. Meantime, they recognised that the next decision which they had to make was crucial to the effective implementation of their strategy. Who should become the club's first professional coach/manager?

In April 1991, feathers were ruffled at the Neath club when it was announced that the Swansea men had been talking to Brian Thomas, the long-time Castell-Nedd stalwart. Whilst Thomas was sometimes a controversial figure, James and his colleagues saw in him a man with the experience and ability to fill the post which they had envisaged. Thomas, admitting that he was flattered by the approach and excited by the challenge, promised to consider the offer very carefully. In the event, after initially accepting the job, he withdrew. He said that the emotion which inevitably surrounded his long association with the Gnoll club, had been too much of an influence on him. He was staying at Neath. At the time, cynics suggested that Brian Thomas had used the Swansea offer to elicit a similar proposal from the Neath club. At St. Helens, however, those who were involved in the several conversations which took place before Thomas made his decision, held other views. As they perceived it, Brian Thomas had arrived at his decision primarily as a result of the emotions concerned with his long association with the Gnoll. Furthermore, in all discussions he had displayed frankness and sincerity in keeping with such a stance. Put in the vernacular of the two clubs involved, Brian Thomas was too black to become white!

Not having succeeded in their initial quest to recruit a highly experienced coach with an impressive track record, the board turned their attention to other candidates. Among them was a young man who had played in the Swansea strip.

In retrospect, Ron Griffiths's comments in the *Post* two years earlier, regarding Mike Ruddock and the club, had been nearer the mark than the journalist might have realised. For several seasons, the St. Helens management had been monitoring Ruddock's progress as a coach. Apart from the fact that they liked what they had learnt, Mike Ruddock had what many believed to be a built-in advantage. Whilst he hailed from the eastern valleys of the Principality, having played for the 'Whites', and having come to love the club, he was a *de facto* Swansea-ite, at least far as rugby football was concerned. Whilst his track record as a coach was limited, in their conversations with the former flanker, and drawing upon their experience of him as a player, they became convinced that Ruddock was the man to take Swansea forward. As a result, after appropriate discussions, Mike Ruddock was appointed as Director of Coaching.

The press, keen to get to know the new man and his ideas, asked him what he expected to achieve in his first year at St. Helens? The new coach was cautious. Not surprisingly, he said that he had to get to know the players, and to really assess their strengths and weaknesses before he decided how he was going to develop his playing squad. When asked about the objectives which he had set himself, he told the media men that his first objective was to improve the club's position in the Heineken League. And,when pressed to say what that meant in terms of where the 'Whites' would finish the season in the championship table, he said 'fourth'. It was a sensible statement. In the event, though, he was to surprise himself and them!

1991-92

Champions

In the July before beginning his first season in charge at St. Helens, Mike Ruddock was able to enjoy watching his new charges winning the Snelling Sevens. Whilst the joys of this version of the rugby game are different from fifteen-a-side, at least the new coach was able to assess the skills of those who played. And given that many of those skills are applicable to the rugby game proper, it was not surprising that he liked what he saw. In addition, of course, it did no harm to start the season with a trophy in the cupboard. Winning, like losing, can become a matter of habit.

With Heineken League football not beginning until November, (because of the 1991 World Cup) Ruddock had the opportunity to work with his players for some nine weeks whilst they played 'club' matches. Given his relatively late arrival at St. Helens, this was to prove to be advantageous, particularly since the first match in the club calendar – against Shannon – was lost. That was not how the script was supposed to unfold, yet, as the future was to show, effective management can gain advantage from the lessons learnt from adversity. In Mike Ruddock, the St. Helens club had a man who believed in this process. As a result, Swansea Rugby Football Club was to benefit in many respects.

At the time, such benefits were clear for all to see as the side enjoyed a run of six matches without defeat. Nonetheless, it is fair to say that the press remained largely unimpressed by what they saw. The *Daily Telegraph*, for example, reported that 'Swansea are playing their rugby in fits and starts'. At that, Mike Ruddock might have evoked the old maxim of the beleaguered business – 'We can do the impossible straight away; miracles take a little longer'.

In addition, whatever was said by the media, the side was winning; and, if the press criticism was to be accepted, there was always the age old sporting response – if a side can win when it is not playing well that augurs well for the day when 'it puts its game together'. And, as far as the loyal Swansea followers were concerned, whilst yearning for flowing football, exciting tries and spirited teamwork, they could be more patient whilst their side was winning. Furthermore,whatever the press said, already there had been matches to enjoy.

Against Moseley, in dreadful weather, the 'Whites' 'stormed to victory'. In the process they scored six tries whilst conceding just one. Then, after being 'run ragged' by a fine Bristol side in the first-half of a St. Helens match, they 'turned the tables' in the second period to win by 26 points to 16. Steffan Jones, Tim Michael, Alan Williams and Simon Davies were try scorers that day, whilst, in the absence of skipper Kevin Hopkins, Stuart Davies captained the side. In the future, that experience was to prove to be of benefit to the storming back-row man.

Meantime, at the *Evening Post*, a new scribe took up the task of reporting on matters 'Whites'. Ron Griffiths, faithful correspondent for some three decades, retired and was replaced by

Graham Thomas. Ron Griffiths, like 'Pendragon', and 'Argus' before him, brought a special brand of dedication to the job of covering Swansea rugby matters for the city's evening paper. That dedication reflected his origins. A Fforestfach boy, he had grown up with the 'Whites' as his team, though, as it transpired, his first *Post* assignment was to cover Neath's matches. As far as he was concerned, though, when the opportunity came to report on St. Helens matters he was delighted. With every due respect to his friends at the Gnoll, covering Swansea games was a special task for the Old Dy'vorian. Such was his passion that, throughout the period during which he reported on the St. Helens scene it was possible to detect an ongoing yearning for his team to do well. Like the club's supporters, over many seasons he had been frustrated by the dreaded malady, inconsistency. Sadly, Ron Griffiths was not to live long after his retirement, and thus did not enjoy even the beginning of the period when the age old problem was addressed more effectively. Ron Griffiths left behind a lasting impression of a professional journalist who was dedicated to his task, and would be missed by his many friends.

During the weeks immediately before the first Heineken League match was to be played, the 'Whites' warmed up with two confidence-boosting victories. Whilst, subsequently, a weakened side lost at Rosslyn Park, by then the concept of focusing attention on specific games was well-developed within the Swansea camp. The focus for Saturday 9 November 1991 was on the match against Cardiff. Having won the corresponding game during the previous season, the 'Blue and Blacks' came to St. Helens as favourites. They were a good side. After the match, however, as the *Post* headline boasted 'Five try feast refreshes the fans', the implication was that the 'Whites' were better.

The *Post*'s headline writer's play on the popular advertisement for the Dutch beer, merely reinforced the Swansea smiles which were in place that day. With Tony Clement back after a hip injury, the 'Whites' were said to have 'blossomed on the back of an impressive forward display'. After ten minutes, however, that possibility was being held in rein. By then Cardiff had scored six points as a result of two penalty kicks, but they were not to hold their lead for long. Tries by Kevin Hopkins and Mark Titley in the first-half and by Stuart Davies, Bleddyn Taylor and Richard Webster in the second, sealed victory for the 'Whites'. It was an impressive start to the season's League campaign and, apart from anything else, demonstrated that the men in white could attack from the front and the back. Two tries had been scored by forwards.

After losing the next League fixture to the boys from the Gnoll, a 'highly efficient, powerful Swansea pack', once again, laid the foundation for a fine victory. This time Newbridge, on their own ground, were the victims of outstanding 'Swansea' football. A feature of that victory was a remarkable try by Tony Clement, when he grounded the ball over the line even though it appeared that he had been held by two defenders. In addition, the 'Whites' scored one of those special tries which the St. Helens faithful were to enjoy in abundance as the season progressed. Not surprisingly, Mark Titley and Simon Davies were involved, and style, speed and panache exuded from them as they orchestrated the score.

Following another fine victory – over Bridgend – Phil Bennett felt moved to revise his pre-season forecast concerning the 'Whites'. He wrote, 'I said that Swansea would struggle this season ... but from what I have seen at St. Helens recently, it is clear that Mike Ruddock has started to turn things around'. Since, at that stage in the season, the Swansea men found themselves in first place in the embryo league table, the optimists in Swansea may have accused the Llanelli man of understatement. Furthermore, whilst the more prudent among Swansea's supporters recognised that there was, still, a long way to go, as Pontypridd and Maesteg were well-beaten in successive matches, even they were being tempted to speculate about championships. In the match against the Llynfi Valley side, a 'Blitz of tries' were scored, nine in all. Ian Davies (4), Alan Reynolds, Simon Davies, Kevin Hopkins, Mark Titley, and Bleddyn Taylor crossing for tries, several of which were of the 'Swansea' variety. Played 6, won 5, 10 points ... top, made happy reading for the St. Helens faithful. The acid test, however, was to come in the next match. The 'Scarlets', who were second in the table were playing well, and had an unblemished home record.

Mark Titley ... has them guessing.

Prior to that match, St. Helens welcomed back one of its former players. Aled Williams, who was to play an influential part in the Swansea campaign in the months ahead, was back 'home'. Aled, who had left Swansea so that he might play regularly at outside-half, was to do that in the white jersey of Swansea. Mike Ruddock had long-admired the silky skills which Williams brought to his game. An outside-half in the traditional Welsh mould, there was the added benefit that he could kick penalties and conversions. Among the players whom Aled met on his return was Garin Jenkins. By then, the hooker had settled well at St. Helens, and, as the months ahead were to demonstrate, his strength and tenacity, his hooking skills, his pace about the field, his accuracy in throwing in from the line, and his unquenchable spirit were to make him a key member of the Swansea squad. Wales was to have the advantage of those attributes too.

Aled Williams.

As the *Western Mail* noted at the time, 'Ruddock's squad building is proceeding at a pace'. However, whilst the introduction of some new faces was important in that process, so was the work being undertaken with the established members of the Swansea squad. The talk at St. Helens was of individual fitness programmes, and, even, of using people called 'sports psychologists'. At the news of the latter, reactionary lips curled in contempt, though, as time and success were to demonstrate, such attitudes were to be amended. As the Swansea coach and his specialist assistants recognised, the impact of mind-set on the performance of individuals and teams is often significant. They reasoned that if it was possible to have greater control over this aspect of team performance, then there would be benefit in pursuing the matter. They recognised, too, that if mental procedures which enhanced performance existed, then they would need to ensure that the 'treatment' was ongoing. Dai Gremlin, lurking in the innermost reaches of individual and collective minds, is ever ready to permeate them with doubt and to erode self-belief. Ask any Saturday golfer! The coaches found that the position of the 'mind men' was, that certain techniques could be used to engender and reinforce confidence. In the months ahead, those theories were to be applied in testing conditions.

The first such test came after the 11 points to 6 defeat of the 'Whites' at Stradey which resulted in the Sospan men gaining top place in the league table. For the moment, Llanelli, who, later in the season, were to dash Swansea hopes in another competition, stood proud. For the first time during the season the 'Scarlets' looked down on the 'Whites'. However, by the turn of the year, as a result of fine wins over Neath, Newport and Cardiff, the 'Whites' had regained 'top spot'. By then, Swansea, under the new Ruddock regime, had won the respect of their peers. If nothing else, they had 'done the double' over the 'Blue and Blacks' of Cardiff. At that, an outbreak of mild hysteria was diagnosed among Swansea supporters. Swansea Rugby Club was on the march again, and the Welsh rugby community could not help but note that fact. Nor was the resulting aura lost on players from other clubs. Scott Gibbs, for example, perceiving a squad, system, and ethos at St. Helens which he felt would match his own burgeoning talent, signed for the 'Whites'.

Meantime, one of the longer-established members of the Swansea squad demonstrated that try-scoring is not the exclusive prerogative of the backs. Keith Colclough scored twice in a 'Six try 6th round cup victory' over the 'Police'. In scoring those tries, Keith, an archetypal front-row man of significant longevity, showed an awareness and opportunism which emphasised the quality of his all-round game.

Having said that, the mysteries of front-row play as far as the average spectator is concerned are as those of Samarkand or the Bermuda Triangle. Because this is so, the proponents of this art are less frequently credited with the quality of their contribution to a game than are players in other, more 'visible' positions. In including this paragraph here, the author wishes to demonstrate that, whilst as mystified as many about such matters, the recent protestations of two members of the Front-Row Union ('All Whites' branch) about the press coverage of their playing activities, may not be taken as applying to this book. Furthermore, as far as the press corps is concerned, the author is willing to list the dark Swansea alleys which, in order to preserve their health, rugby journalists should avoid. Reciprocal favours may be negotiated at the time the information is provided.

By mid-March, the level of confidence among Swansea supporters, the St. Helens management, and in the minds of those who wrote about Welsh rugby, was such that there was talk of a Swansea 'Cup and League double'. And this, despite the fact that the side was unexpectedly defeated at the Brewery Field. That result brought Bridgend level on points with the 'Whites' in the Heineken table. At that stage in the season, both sides had played thirteen games and won nine, whilst Llanelli, who were third were still in contention with seventeen points, just one less than the leaders. The 'Whites' however, had a superior try-count. It was clear, however, that, if the growing confidence was to be maintained, the side needed to win its next match, and if possible, add to the total of tries which they had scored during the campaign.

Keith Colclough and friends – from a tapped penalty.

As it transpired, Swansea's performance in the following match made a significant contribution to their try-count and to their confidence. It also added two points to their cumulative total. Pontypridd was the side to be hit by 'A Swansea blizzard'. As the *Post* had it, 'the awesome "Whites", after leading by a single point at half-time, ripped the "Ponty" defence apart in the second period'.

In that match, Tony Clement crossed for a brilliant 'hat-trick' of tries, each of which demonstrated his athleticism, strength and pace. Simon Davies scored twice, and Aled Williams kicked penalties and conversions with clockwork precision. To cap his day with the boot, the outside-half also dropped a fine goal.

Following that match, Richard Moriarty, who was enjoying the success which had come to St. Helens as much as anyone, declared that (at 34) he was not ready to think about retirement. Indeed, as far as the supporters could tell, the big man was as fit and able as he had ever been. As those readers who have struggled with *anno domini* at any level of the game will testify, continuing success can add wings to tired limbs. It can also change an individual's view of an approaching match or training session, (particularly in wintry conditions) from stoic acceptance to schoolboy expectancy. Perhaps 'Dickie' was enjoying such an elixir.

The victory over Pontypridd heralded a run of six successive victories in cup and league, which took the club to the final of the cup competition and to the Heineken League title. That title, to the great joy of the ebullient St. Helens faithful, was won with one match in hand. Furthermore, among the sides which were beaten during the final, triumphant winning run, was Llanelli. Since the 'Scarlets' were the opponents which the Swansea men were to meet in the final of the Cup, the thoughts of 'the double' were rarely far from Swansea minds. The citizens of the 'Tinopolis', however, had ideas of their own. The cup, as they say, 'is a one-off'; it's a sprint rather than a marathon; and the outcome of league matches may have little bearing on a cup result.

In the meantime, however, the 'huge, travelling, Swansea support' greatly enjoyed the victory at Newport which secured the championship for Swansea. In the first-half of that momentous match – at Rodney Parade – Scott Gibbs had shown his pace and strength to 'crash over for a thrilling try'. When Robert Jones added a second, whilst Newport could only convert two penalties, the 'Whites' began the second-half with a 10 points to 6 advantage. Whilst not decisive, the lead gave the Swansea men a basis for building a winning margin in the second period. And build they did. Early in the second-half the Abertawe contingent roared their approval of a try of 'Swansea' proportions. A Newport player chipped ahead but was beaten to the ball by Robert Jones. Jones, side-stepping a second Newport man 'threw out a scorching pass' to the supporting Tony Clement, who, changing gear, surged towards the Newport line. With Simon Davies,in full flight, at his shoulder, the full-back turned outside, straightened, then fed the wing, who sprinted across. It was a 'breathless' try, and the applause was deafening, as it was when Kevin Hopkins, surrounded by a joyous host of Swansea supporters, received the Heineken Trophy.

Afterwards, the press was universal in its praise of the Swansea squad and of Mike Ruddock. The coach, as one paper put it, had injected steel and self-belief into Swansea flair. As far as the St. Helens faithful were concerned, what they believed in their partisan hearts turned out to be true. The neutral, Phil Bennett, wrote, 'Swansea have simply the best club side in Wales by a mile!' 'Of course', the Swansea support chorused, 'we knew it all along.'

The problem was, though, that Llanelli men also read the *Evening Post*. With the Cup Final imminent, they would have something to say, both to Swansea and to their fellow townsman. Other mental lessons were about to be learnt. Do not believe your own publicity! Take care not to motivate your opponents with your pronouncements! Whilst no one in Swansea was responsible for what Phil Bennettt said, the alarm bells should have rung if they had asked, 'What are the 'Sospan' men going to make of this?' 'Cocky "Whites"; we'll show them', might have been a polite translation of what was said and thought at that time in the old tinplate town.

On the day of the final, the 'Scarlets' were 'hyped-up', whilst the Swansea men were strangely subdued. Llanelli, inspired by a typical Ieuan Evans try, took the cup back to Stradey. Understandably, after the match, the Swansea camp and their huge support were disappointed. The players knew that they had failed to perform to their potential, and felt that they had let themselves down as well as their loyal supporters. Yet, the lessons to be learnt from that day were not lost on Mike Ruddock nor the squad. They would be of benefit on a future occasion.

Afterwards, the press, as if orchestrated by a common conductor, let it be known that, as far as the cup competition was concerned, Swansea were under-achievers. One win in 23 years of trying, it was said, was indicative of an inherent weakness in the Swansea psyche. Mike

It's ours lads! Kevin Hopkins with the Heineken Trophy.
(Messrs Arnold and Davies act as a chair).

Ruddock, already planning for the following season, read and listened to such comments with interest. A mind reader who happened to be passing St. Helens during the following week, might have received the words 'We shall see', as the coach considered his response. One thing was certain, in due course, that response would be made on the field.

Whilst it was natural that there was some disappointment at St. Helens as a result of the outcome of the final, there was also great satisfaction. Winning the Championship and making such significant strides within the club as a whole, had changed expectations at St. Helens. Furthermore, the season had been memorable in several respects. Everything else apart, at the start of the campaign, only a supreme optimist would have dreamt of the possibility of the 'Whites' winning the League Championship, reaching the Cup Final, and gaining the *Western Mail* trophy as the side which scored more tries than any other in all divisions of the Heineken League.

There was, also, the fact that all these things had been achieved whilst six Swansea men had been 'capped' during the campaign. All in all, the outcome was, to say the least, most satisfactory! Mike Ruddock and his team of coaches could be pleased with the progress which had been made. And, as someone might have asked of Mike at the time; how do you spell fourth?

Meantime, the press in summarising the outstanding Swansea season fuelled a level of euphoria in the Old Borough which must have matched that of the 'Golden Era'. Garin Jenkins, Scott Gibbs, Robert Jones, Tony Clement, Paul Arnold, Alan Reynolds, Stuart, Simon and Ian Davies, Richard Webster, Mark Titley and, captain, Kevin Hopkins were most mentioned. One player, however, who attracted special comment was Richard Moriarty. 'Dickie' had been ever-present during the League campaign, had had a considerable influence on the outcome of many games and on the play of the young men around him. For his part, Richard praised the work of fitness coach, Trevor Cheeseman in helping him maintain the necessary standards during a gruelling season.

As the St. Helens faithful put away their old season tickets, there was a rare collective satisfaction abroad. Yet, born of many years of uncertainty, there was always Dai Gremlin lurking in the shadows. Was it all a one-season-wonder, or could the exacting standards be maintained? Only time would tell.

1992–93

Wallabies walloped

Having been so successful during the previous campaign, the St. Helens camp and its buoyant supporters contemplated the season ahead with something more than quiet confidence. Whilst they recognised that it might be too much to expect the side to replicate the level of success which had been achieved during the 1991/92 season, most observers felt that, during the new campaign,the 'Whites' would be a force to be reckoned with. There was much comment, too, from press and supporters alike regarding the November match with the touring Australians. How well would the 'Welsh Champions' perform against the 'World Champions'?

As that match approached, nonagenarians throughout Swansea searched their attics diligently for banners which they had saved from the days of the 'Golden Era'. Swansea, Champions of the world! And why not?

Meanwhile, the news of the appointment of a new President at St. Helens was received warmly. After a remarkable thirty-seven years of uninterrupted service as honorary secretary, David Price was made President of Swansea Cricket and Football Club. David's hosts of friends were delighted! Over almost four decades, the new President had earned universal respect, not only for his meticulous work as secretary and for his detailed record keeping,but also for his integrity and good humour. The man appointed to replace the new President was Byron Mugford. Like David Price, Byron had played his senior rugby at St. Helens, and, in the process had proved himself to be an outstanding clubman. He was to demonstrate that those qualities were still extant through his work as secretary.

During the close season, the 'Whites' had travelled to Canada to play a short series of matches,

Garin Jenkins – speed and strength.

and there was genuine pleasure at St. Helens concerning both the outcome of the games and of the tour itself. The games had provided the players with useful practice, whilst the tour enabled the coaches to monitor the progress of the fitness programme. Mike Ruddock said that he was extremely pleased with what had been achieved. He was delighted, too, with the comments of the club's Canadian hosts. The 'Whites' were complimented on their attitude on and off the field, and on the manner in which they had established good relationships wherever they went. The Canadians let it be known that the members of Swansea Rugby Club had been excellent ambassadors for their home city and for Wales.

On the squad's return there was a new face among them. University College Swansea student, Chris Clark, described by the press as a 'good prospect' arrived at St. Helens, whilst Dai Joseph left and Ian Buckett was making plans to go to Oxford. Young Clark did not know it at the time, but, within weeks he was to play in one of the biggest games of his life.

Like other squads which were assembling at the time, in the season ahead, the Swansea men would find themselves having to face over twenty changes in the laws. Given that the potential impact of these changes on individual and team performance was so great, Mike Ruddock had arranged for referee, Robert Davies, to come to St. Helens to discuss them with the players. The sessions were appreciated, though, as has ever been the case, wherever rugby players gather the wags have their day. After the first meeting, one player, referring to a colleague, said that, since he didn't understand the old law in the first place, the change was unlikely to affect his game.

Whilst Newbridge were beaten, at St. Helens, in the initial league match of the new season, some media men emphasised that the team had had to 'come from behind to win'. At this, Tony Clement, whilst accepting the observation, remained confident. He said 'we will do well! Mental strength is the name of the game.' Clearly, the sports psychologists had made their mark with one of the physically fittest men in the Swansea camp. It seemed that, as the jargon has it, the player was taking a 'holistic' approach to his rugby fitness programme – fitness in mind and body. Whilst no doubt, there were still cynics at St. Helens regarding the work of the 'mind men', up to that point in time, at least, no one could argue other than their work appeared to be having a positive influence on the Swansea squad. Where this conclusion was accepted, given the long history of inconsistency at St. Helens, older supporters must have wondered whether the 'mental training' work being undertaken at the Cricket Ground was the element which had been missing in the past? Nothing in the complex world of human behaviour is quite so simple; yet the conclusion that it was, was gaining credence by the day. *Post hoc, ergo proptor hoc?*

During the next match, with a side which showed seven changes from that which had been used in the opening game, the 'Whites' were 'a joy to behold as they scored five tries in eighteen minutes'. The match in question, against Maesteg on their own ground, was won by 35 points to 6, with Stuart Davies, the club's new captain, in charge for the first time. Next, the 'Police' conceded 74 points, when the Swansea men scored eleven tries, (including a hat-trick by P.C. Simon Davies), and by then, the received wisdom among 'Whites' supporters suggested that the reason for the early-season raggedness was tiredness after the Canadian tour. From now on, the argument continued, we shall see proper Swansea performances.

And, indeed, from there on, the 'Whites' appeared not to be able to put a foot wrong. Llanelli were beaten at Stradey, 'for the first time in years', Neath were defeated at St. Helens, when 'Ice-cool Aled kept the "Whites" in contention', and Newport, Pontypool, Pontypridd and Bridgend all succumbed to Swansea's 'power and flair'. After the Pontypridd match, won, as it was by a 'last gasp try 'the "Whites" were two points clear at the top of the Heineken First Division. Their record, as the old timers used to say was 'unbesmirched', and was a remarkable testimony to their fitness and teamwork as much as to their individual flair and skill. Since the 'Ponty' match was played on 31 October 1992, it was the last before the men in white took on the Australian tourists. Because of this, three players had been rested for the Sardis Road game, and it was left to Garin Jenkins to score the winning try there. Four days later, Garin was to replicate that effort by scoring against the 'Wallabies'.

On the grey, misty November day, when the 'Whites' appeared in the tunnel to take on the Australians, it seemed that the whole of Swansea was there to greet them. The men in white had not only won the Heineken League championship at the end of the previous season, they had won every one of their nine matches to date in the current campaign. It was a formidable record! As a result, it was little wonder that as the players emerged onto the field, they were met by a wall of supportive noise, and an atmosphere steeped in an all-pervading *Cymric* confidence. No one had seen Dai Gremlin, and there was a rumour that, in his despair, he had jumped off Worms Head at high tide.

Immediately prior to the match, the Australian management who, unlike the 'Whites', had not had the opportunity of being reminded of the adage about not motivating your opponents with your pronouncements to the press, fuelled that very fire! Noticing that Keith Colclough was the only player in the Swansea side without representative honours, whilst Chris Clark was an unknown youngster, the 'Wallabies' manager said that he felt that the Swansea front-row was its weak spot. Colclough, already sensitive about the lack of opportunity which had come his way to gain representative selection, was incensed. Afterwards, Keith said that he believed that Mike Ruddock had deliberately fed the information about him to the Australians in order that he would be 'needled'. Ruddock, of course, merely turned up the corners of his mouth in an enigmatic smile when the suggestion was made. However, whatever the source of the information, the end product was the same. The Swansea front-row, and in particular Keith Colclough, went out to face the Australians fired-up with determination; some said, sheer, naked *hwyl*. Weak spot? We shall see!

'Dickie' Moriarty – playing outside-half!

When the first scrum was called in the shadow of the grandstand, as Colclough and his opposite number, Ryan collided, the Australian 'popped out like a champagne cork'. As Mike Ruddock was to say afterwards, from that moment on the Australian prop was 'finished'. Furthermore, the Swansea man's ascendancy inspired those around him, and they responded appropriately. Kearns, who, according to the rugby ratings was the best hooker in the world, was outplayed by Garin Jenkins, whilst young Clark performed as if he was a seasoned international. Nor were the Swansea second-row dominated. Whilst the line-out count was shown to be in favour of the tourists by a massive 27-9, they were hardly able to deliver a good ball throughout the afternoon. Richard Moriarty and Paul Arnold stuck to their task and successfully disrupted much Australian work. Indeed, it was from a line-out when Aussie ball was spoilt, that Garin Jenkins pounced on an awkward tap-back to score a try for the 'Whites'. But that was in the second-half.

During the first period, Scott Gibbs crossed for the first Swansea try following tremendous work by the home eight, and an outstanding release from

Stuart Davies ... on the charge.

Robert Jones. At this, the Australians looked dumbstruck, and as Swansea retained the ascendancy for long periods, the only 'Wallaby' scores came from the boot of full-back Kelaher. When the whistle sounded for no-side, Swansea had added to their glorious record against major touring sides by beating, decisively, the World Champions. There was a further accolade for the men in white, too. Swansea was the first side for nineteen matches to prevent the 'Wallabies' from crossing their line.

After the match, the Australian coach, Bob Dwyer, delighted Swansea followers by saying, 'that was as good a performance as I can remember by a Welsh side'. And, of course, the performance had to be put into context by remembering that, only fifteen months earlier, Wales had crashed to New South Wales by 71 points, and to Australia by 63 points. It had been a victory of monumental proportions. A victory for planning, flair, passion and self-belief. As they looked down, the Swansea old timers must have been delighted!

Not surprisingly, Mike Ruddock was also delighted. Like skipper, Stuart Davies, he heaped praise upon his warriors. All fifteen, he said, had made a fine contribution. The front-row had 'played the game of their lives', the second-row had 'never given up', whilst Richard Moriarty had given a display of 'masterclass dimensions'. As far as the back-row was concerned, they were 'fearless and tireless in defence and attack'. Behind them, the half-back pairing gave 'world class displays', Robert Jones had 'orchestrated matters' whilst Aled Williams, with a personal toll of two penalties, a conversion and a dropped goal, 'gave the Welsh selectors another demonstration of his outstanding ability'. Then, as far as the back five were concerned, their uncrossed try line was a testimony to their defensive work, whilst all five, particularly Scott Gibbs, 'always posed a threat'.

In the *Post*, Richard Thomas wrote, 'To win the Heineken League Championship in style is one thing, but to completely tame the World Champions is something on a much higher plane'. It was surprising that, on reading Thomas's comment, none of Swansea's nonagenarians who had found their 'Swansea – World champions' banners, bothered to write to the journalist. Their argument, after all, was simple. If you beat the so-called World Champions, doesn't that mean that you have the title?

Such was the atmosphere at St. Helens that memorable day, that long after the ground was deserted, the field seemed, still, to reverberate with the noise and passion of the match. As they made their way home, even undemonstrative spectators found themselves to be drained of emotion. Later, following justified celebration, and after the adrenalin had ceased to pump around their bodies, the players, too, were similarly drained. It had been a magical day; one of the greatest in the history of the Swansea club! It was a day to be enjoyed deep into the night. Next day, Swansea workplaces of all kinds were peopled by folk who, having a match of special significance to remember, found themselves somewhat distracted.

In 1884, when E. S. Richards stood on the steps of the Workingmens' Club, and realised for the first time that Swansea Football Club was an institution, he could have had little idea of the scale of interest and devotion which, in the future, the 'Whites' would arouse in the city. The pride engendered by a 'famous' victory must have multiplied in the intervening years, if only as a result of the increase in population. Furthermore, Swansea was 'in the spotlight' throughout the rugby-playing world. If the City Fathers ever needed a positive indication of the benefits which the Old Borough derived from the success of its sporting organisations, the win over the Australians provided it. Only major multi-national companies could contemplate advertising expenditure of the size necessary to achieve such 'corporate recognition' as was Swansea's at that time.

The triumphant Swansea side which played in that famous game was:

A. Clement; M. Titley, K. Hopkins, S. Gibbs, Simon Davies, A. Williams, R. Jones, C. Clark, G. Jenkins, K. Colclough, R. Moriarty, P. Arnold, A. Reynolds, Stuart Davies (Capt.), R. Webster.

After the victory over the Australians, there were those who suggested that there would be a negative reaction in league matches immediately subsequent to the big day. The argument was that the 'boys have taken too much out of themselves'. In the event, in the games which followed, that did not prove to be the case. Reaction was to come later. First there was a 'club match' victory over the 'Wasps', after which the 'Police' and the 'Wizards' were both defeated to extend the club's consecutive winning run in all matches to an impressive thirteen. At that, most pessimists were voting for the other party. Dai Gremlin, however, bloodied but not defeated, was biding his time. That came in the next match. Cardiff took the 'Whites' unbeaten record as a result of a Steve Ford 'injury time try'. The score, Swansea 6 points, Cardiff 8, was indicative of what had been an extremely close match. The outcome however was that the

Swansea men had shown themselves to be fallible for the first time during the 1992/93 campaign. The defeat, despite the efforts of the management team and the squad, was to prove to be the first rotten apple in the barrel.

Nonetheless, by the end of the year, after freezing conditions had disrupted the rugby programme, the 'Whites' had regained first place in the developing league table, although, in terms of points gained, they were equal with Cardiff. Newbridge had been defeated by 28 points to 0, (Aled Williams scored two tries and a total of 23 points), and Abercynon, in the cup, were given a '75 points to 0 thrashing'. Twelve tries were scored in that cup match, with Simon Davies (playing at full-back) registering three, and acting skipper, Mark Titley scoring twice.

When matches resumed after the 'freeze', many people felt that the 'Whites' would have benefited from the enforced break. However, just as some matches are quite different in the second-half from the first, so Swansea's momentum seemed to have been disrupted. Llanelli, playing against fourteen 'Whites' for much of the match, won, at St. Helens by 15 points to 10. Apart from losing the match, and the points, the St. Helens management were to find that they were going to have to do without Garin Jenkins for a long period.

Nevertheless, following the Llanelli match, the 'Whites', having gained the same number of points as leaders Cardiff, were second on try-count. Llanelli lurked in third place. Thereafter, however, the St. Helens men won four league matches in succession, and the optimists were arguing that 'the "Whites" would go on to retain their Championship title'. The problem was, though, that both Llanelli and Cardiff had done as well as the Swansea boys over this period. Any one of the three sides, provided that they continued winning, could take the title. It was a tight, three-horse race.

Whether Dai Gremlin had any friends in the virus business or not is not known, but what happened during the first week in April smacked of his interference. A 'flu epidemic hit the Swansea squad. Such was its impact, that when the Swansea men travelled to Pontypridd for an important league match, six men who were to play that day had only reported back two days previously, whilst four other regular first team men were in their beds at home. Not surprisingly, the impact on the team's performance of the absences was considerable, as was the fact that the men who had recovered were, hardly, in the pink of condition. Pontypridd were held to a 10 points to 9 lead at half-time, but, in the second period, as the Swansea men tired, Ponty 'ran away with things', to register a 35 points to 12 victory. No one offered the 'flu problem as an excuse, yet, in retrospect, given the closeness of the title battle, one wonders whether it was fair to ask the 'Whites' to play on that occasion?

Whatever the rights and wrongs of that argument, the Pontypridd match was not, in itself, that which resulted in the 'Whites' failing to retain the Heineken title. As if impaired by their change in fortune, the St. Helens men lost the two remaining games in their league schedule. In addition, the 'Whites' were beaten, at Cardiff, by Llanelli in the semi-final of the Cup. To all intents and purposes, Swansea's season ended that day. After the final league matches had been played, the 'Whites' were third in the Heineken table. That fact, plus having been cup semi-finalists would have satisfied the supporters of many clubs. For the newly expectant Swansea supporters, however, the outcome had a strangely deflating effect.

Mike Ruddock, though, was unperturbed. In announcing that he was going to New Zealand on a five week fact-finding mission, he said that 'the "Whites" would be back in contention'. He agreed that the side had 'peaked' (for the Australian match) too early, and that they had missed

Garin Jenkins. Yet, the coach might have said, look what we have achieved! Whilst Mike Ruddock did not list the club's achievements, those who checked on such things would have found that, apart from the cup semi-final spot and third position in the league, the side had put together a thirteen match unbeaten run during the first months of the season, and they had beaten the Australians. The season took on a new look when those things were considered. Certainly, the time was inappropriate for introspection.

Nevertheless, Mike Ruddock did concede that he had been disappointed about the season in one respect. It would have been nice to have won something for Kevin Hopkins's sake. The former captain retired after the match with Cardiff and received the best wishes of all at St. Helens and those of the many supporters who had been privileged to have seen him play.

Chapter Twenty-Eight

CHAMPIONS AGAIN

1993–94

AT THE END OF THE 1993–94 CAMPAIGN, as the mud-covered players enjoyed the tremendous reception which was being given to them by the St. Helens faithful, Mike Ruddock and his coaching team must have looked back over the season with a mixture of wonder and relief. The 'Whites' had won the Heineken First Division title by four clear points, by winning twenty of the twenty-two matches played. Yet the bald statistics indicated nothing of the drama which had unfolded at the Cricket Field as the season progressed. Within weeks of the start of the season, Richard Webster had signed professional forms for Salford, the influential Scott Gibbs had been badly injured whilst playing for the Barbarians against New Zealand, and, soon after regaining fitness, joined St. Helens in the Rugby League. Aled Williams, another influential performer had been unavailable for six weeks after having his cheekbone fractured by a blow to the face, and captain, Stuart Davies had missed eight or nine weeks of the season. And that said nothing of injuries which kept other key players on the sidelines for several weeks at a time. Furthermore, following their Lions tour, Mike Ruddock had suggested that Tony Clement, Scott Gibbs, and Robert Jones should rest for several weeks. Richard Webster, although given the same option, wanted to start immediately the season began.

Robert Jones.

In many respects, the fact that the 'Whites' had done so well despite these absences, was a testimony to the squad of players and to the systems which had been developed during the Ruddock regime. As one paper put it, even when teams had been 'cobbled together', they performed to a higher level than many of the clubs which they opposed. Nevertheless, some might have asked, what could have been achieved had all the squad been fit and available throughout the season? Yet, such questions are futile. Few teams become champions having won ninety-one per cent of matches played during a season, however strong they are on paper, and the 'Whites' had done that. Furthermore, there were benefits which would emerge in the longer term which had been triggered by the emergencies which the selectors had faced.

The League programme started with a 15 points to 11 win at Newbridge, though, in order to seal the victory, it was necessary for the 'Whites' to score two 'Swansea' tries in the last three minutes of the game. Meanwhile, at St. Helens, Baden Evans, another great club servant, was appointed as team administrator, and Scott Gibbs announced that he was staying in Welsh rugby. Careful listeners, though, would have noted that the gifted centre had given no indication as to the length of that stay.

After Dunvant had been beaten in the second match of the league campaign, Cross Keys surprised the 'Whites' with a spirited display before the Swansea men seized the initiative to win the match. Ian Davies's try late in that game, which was converted by Aled Williams, ensured the victory and a further two points. There followed an excellent win over Llanelli – by 22 points to 12 – when the scoring of the 'Sospan' men was confined to penalties. For Swansea, who dominated the second-half, Aled Williams kicked superbly, landing two penalties from over forty metres, but it was a 'Swansea' try which set the afternoon alight as far as the 'Whites' supporters were concerned. The try was created by Robert Jones, who, picking up from a retreating scrum inside the Llanelli '22', drove down the blind side. The scrum-half then found Titley backing up, the wingman straightened and took two defenders with him before feeding Richard Webster, who, from the distance involved, was 'unstoppable'. So, unfortunately, as his subsequent defection to the Rugby League was to show, was his desire to take the northern silver.

In the week before the Llanelli match, rumours persisted that Webster was going north. Since no attempt was made by the player to issue a strong denial, there was a cloak of inevitability thrown over St. Helens. The loss of such a fine player was hardly welcomed at the Cricket Ground. An international, a Lion, and a superb club footballer, he was the kind of man which coaches are delighted to have in their squads, whilst other sides view them with apprehension. When rumour became reality, Mike Ruddock and his cohorts had no option other than to manage without the big man. Plan 'B' had to be put into place.

Paradoxically, *sans* Webster, October produced three fine victories for the 'All Whites'. Pontypool were beaten by 30 points to 10, Bridgend by 20 points to 16, and Newport by 30 points to 3. Apart from the benefit of league points which ensued from these victories, they all contributed generously to the Swansea try count. Since, if the season finished with two or more teams having the same number of points, the club with the highest number of tries would be adjudged the winners, it was important to score as many as possible during the campaign.

In all three matches Aled Williams was outstanding. Against Pontypool he scored a total of thirty points and 'ran the game', but the turning point of the match came when Aled made a superb break. Thrusting off one leg, he looped around a 'Ponty' flanker, and exchanged passes with Scott Gibbs before making forty yards and then sending out a prodigious pass to Tony Clement, who 'stormed over for the try'. The outside-half kicked four penalties and a dropped goal. Even the Pontypool supporters joined in the chorus, 'Why the devil isn't he playing for Wales?'

At that stage of the season, the league competition looked as if it was developing into a three

Alan Reynolds – on his way.

horse race. Neath were at the top of the table, having won seven and drawn one of their eight matches, whilst Llanelli and the 'Whites' were joint second with fourteen points. Both sides had lost one match. That in which the St. Helens men had been defeated had been against Neath at the Gnoll. At the time, the side selected by Swansea had aroused controversy, for it was said to have lacked certain key players. After the 'Whites' had been beaten, amateur selectors throughout Swansea criticised the St. Helens selection committee for their choice of side. Yet, whatever their motives at that time, at the end of the campaign, the Swansea selectors could point to the Championship table and mutter clichés about 'marathons, not sprints'. The objective among the early season critics, might also have noted a subsequent statement by Mike Ruddock, when he pointed out that it was better to make your experiments early in a season. If they came off then you were aware of other options open to you. Conversely, if they failed, then there was still ample time to make up ground. The coach might have said, too, that the approach was in keeping with Swansea's long-standing tradition of 'blooding' young players in tough matches.

When October ended, notwithstanding the fact that the 'Whites' were 'in the championship frame', and had just demolished Newport with a points ratio of 10:1, the players were not entirely satisfied with their performances. Alan Reynolds felt moved to say that the side had someway to go before it reached its potential. He put the matter in perspective when he said, 'As a team we haven't clicked yet – but we're working hard at it!' 'Santa's' pronouncement, made on behalf of the players, was encouraging for the loyal St. Helens support. There was another factor, too, which the Cricket Field faithful noted. The remainder of the New Zealand tourists, Tony Clement, Scott Gibbs and Robert Jones would soon be back. When they were again available for selection, the argument went, there would be no doubt that the boys would 'click'. Then the 'Whites' would be an effective unit 'in no time!'. Yet, whilst there was an immediate improvement in teamwork when the tourists returned, in the next match Dai Gremlin, (last seen on a bus at Reynoldston) struck again. During a match which attracted the headline 'Grim victory in the mud', Stuart Davies injured his knee. Such was the extent of the injury, that the captain did not return to the side until three months had passed. Clearly, it was another blow to Mike Ruddock's planning. Not only had he lost a powerful and effective back-row forward, his side was to be deprived of an inspirational, dynamic leader for an important part of the championship campaign. With Richard Webster having 'gone north', the coach had lost two thirds of his first choice back-row.

Nevertheless, despite the absence of the captain, the 'Whites' certainly 'clicked' in the match which followed. Cardiff, the visitors, were 'comprehensively outplayed'. The final score was 22 points to 6, although most neutrals felt that it did not reflect the extent of Swansea's superiority. Apart from the fact that the points scored by the 'Blue and Blacks' were accounted for by two penalties, the Jones, Williams, Gibbs triangle 'mesmerised' the Cardiffians. The trio were at the heart of all three Swansea tries. Happily for the St. Helens men, the victory took them back to the top of the league table, though their lead over the second and third teams was only slight. Neath had one point less, with a game in hand, whilst Llanelli were two points behind. There was no room for complacency.

Because that was so, the victories over Newbridge and Dunvant, which followed, were welcomed in the St. Helens camp, even though the latter match was won by just a single point in 27. In addition, the homesters complained that one Swansea score should have been disallowed. No such problem arose in the next match, however. Fifteen tries were scored by the 'Whites' against Cross Keys which produced a Heineken League record. That performance can only be described as having been a *tour de force*. Tries seemed to have been run in from every part of the field and, whilst feeling sympathy for the 'underdog being whipped', the Swansea faithful allowed themselves to be sated. In the event it proved to be a rather pleasant indulgence.

At the time that that victory was reported in the press, Scott Gibbs was contributing a column to the *Sporting Post* called 'In a league of his own'. Presumably, the title reflected the fact that the player had stated that he had turned his back on the offers which he had received from League clubs in the north. At the same time, in order to support his stance, the management at St. Helens was doing everything, in accordance with W.R.U. rules, to help satisfy the player's ambitions off the field. Gibbs had stated that he wanted to develop a career outside the game, and a computer company in Swansea was interested in employing him on that basis. In addition, the possibility of the player following a personal management development programme was being investigated. All parties involved assumed that Scott Gibbs would take advantage of the opportunities which were being made available to him. However, as the various discussions were developing, the player, whilst appearing for the Barbarians against New Zealand, suffered a serious injury.

In due course, as he was convalescing, discussions regarding his career planning were to continue. In retrospect, however, it is interesting to reflect on the fact that, during this period, the player did not pursue the various discussions with any vigour. Had he, even then, decided that, once fit, he would go north? If that was true, then an argument could be constructed along the lines that, on suffering the injury, Scott Gibbs had become acutely aware that his rugby career could end in similar circumstances. If that was so, he may have concluded that he ought to take the northern signing-on fee as his security. However reasonable such a conclusion was from the player's viewpoint, the manner of his leaving caused much disappointment at St. Helens. In addition, the company concerned with Gibbs in his career discussions, and several professional people who worked with the young man to satisfy his needs outside rugby, were, understandably aggrieved, not so much by his going, but by the manner in which he left.

Meantime, however, the 'Whites' assault on the championship continued apace. They maintained first place in the table throughout January and February, though Cardiff, Neath and Pontypridd remained in contention. There was no question of relaxed progress to the title, and, furthermore, given the defection of Gibbs and Webster and the absences of other senior players from the from the Swansea squad, there were those who were expecting the 'Whites' to stumble, and allow one or more of the pursuing pack to bypass them. Mike Ruddock and his colleagues, however, ensured that that would not happen by marshalling their available resources in an effective way. And, as the coach was to say when the season ended, the tremendous team spirit in the side had helped to carry them through.

Whilst the league campaign continued, progress was also being made in the cup competition. Ebbw Vale and Seven Sisters were disposed of in the early rounds, but, unfortunately, a strangely lack-lustre 'Whites' were well-beaten in the sixth round by Pontypridd. Sardis Road is hardly the most popular of venues for any side, yet the Swansea men had travelled to the ground that day 'reasonably confident of victory'. In the event, they were 'out-fought and out-kicked' as one paper put it. After the match, as the Swansea contingent made its way home, both the weather and their spirits were gloomy. Dai Gremlin, up to his old tricks was sowing his seeds of doubt with abandon. They'll stumble in the league now. You'll see, just like they did last season! Mike Ruddock, however, well aware of the tactics of the insidious Gremlin, hit back immediately. 'That will not happen this time!' There was no doubt in the statement. Some 'Ah but's' on the bus kept their counsel. The remainder, the majority, straightened in their seats. Ruddock's statement was hardly a Churchillian rallying cry to the nation; yet it was to have the same effect at St. Helens.

Now free of cup concerns, the 'Whites' focused upon their remaining league matches. There were six to play at that stage, and after beating Bridgend via 'another last gasp comeback', Swansea's lead at the top of the first division had been increased to three points. Cardiff were second, though they had played one game more than the 'Whites', whilst Neath lurked in third place. The Neath threat, though, diminished somewhat when the men in white defeated them by 15 points to nil. That victory over Neath was notable in that the game was played in atrocious conditions. It involved magnificent defensive play by the 'Whites', as they played into the teeth of a gale. After that match, the proportion of doubters at St. Helens was reducing by the day. Mike Ruddock's version of 'We shall fight them on the beaches ...' having produced the desired results. Furthermore, that conclusion was reinforced when Newport were beaten and the cup defeat by Pontypridd was avenged.

The next match, at Rodney Parade, against Newport, attracted a large contingent of Swansea supporters. Happily, the script writers who control such things, combined well with Mike Ruddock and his players so as to ensure that Swansea were the victors (by 27 points to 22). The match was of old fashioned dimensions, and several thrilling tries were scored by both teams. However, two of those by 'All Whites' stood out. The first came at a crucial time. Newport were leading at that point in the match by 11 points to 0, and it was important that the men in white should get back into the game. Then Mark Titley took a hand in the proceedings. Forty metres out from the Newport line, the winger collected the ball and darted forward. Faced with a line of 'Usksiders', he chose to chip over their heads and continued his run to collect his own kick. From that point on it was 'no contest'. He sold a 'dummy' to the Newport full-back and scorched over for a fine individual try. Given that the crowd-pleaser to cap all others was to leave St. Helens at the end of the season, it was fitting that he left his devoted 'fans' (no other word will suffice) with a mental picture of yet another 'Titers' special. Furthermore, as he had done on so many occasions since coming to the Cricket Field, he inspired his colleagues with his score. Another try was rather special, too. Following a superb threequarter movement (straight out of a 1938 version of the *Boys' Own*, 'How to play rugby football'), when ten pairs of hands were in contact with the ball, Steve Barclay was hauled down within a yard of the line. Newport, however, had reckoned without the Swansea forwards who, also having read the manual, were up in support. Between them, Robin McBryde and Stuart Davies, first to the breakdown, won the ball and fed an unlikely 'centre' in Paul Arnold, who took the pass well to plunge over. The smile on the lock's face lit up Newport from the Transporter Bridge to Usk. At no-side, the 'Whites' left the field with another two points added to their league total. It had been a fine win!

With Aled Williams, back in the side for the first time for six weeks, the 'Whites' took the field for their penultimate league match – against the 'Wizards', knowing that if they won they would become champions that day. Eighty minutes later, the delirious Swansea supporters were cheering their heroes, who, for the second time in three seasons had clinched the Heineken title. Furthermore, they had seen their favourites 'do the job in style', scoring 32 points whilst Aberavon managed only 3. Inevitably, the contented 'Whites' watchers had seen a 'Swansea' try. Simon Davies, perhaps realising that in the season to come he was going to have to undertake the 'Titers' role, took matters into his own hands. Collecting near his own '22', he scorched down the line and handed-off one challenge before selling a superb dummy to the 'Bravon full-back and scoring under the posts.

Naturally, winning the championship again gave everyone at St. Helens tremendous satisfaction. Not only had the crown been won in some style and with a match to spare, it had been achieved despite the fact that key players had not been available for long periods during the campaign, and that, Richard Webster and Scott Gibbs, two influential internationals and British lions, had 'gone north'. In many respects, given the circumstances, winning the title then was a greater achievement for the Swansea management and players than it had been two seasons earlier. As Mike Ruddock put it, 'the absence of big names forced us to give young players their opportunity, whilst the side's pattern of play had to be adapted to take advantage of differing talents'. The coach said that he was pleased with the progress which had been made by players like David Weatherley, Dale McIntosh, Chris Loader and Andy Moore, all of

David Weatherley – poise and balance.

Captain Stuart and fellow 'Greys' take the Heineken for the second time.

whom had 'emerged' during this period. New resources, players with many seasons in front of them, had appeared out of necessity. There was an additional benefit in all of this, each of these men, and others who were being nurtured within the club's systems, were not there by accident. Clearly, the club's development system was working.

When he first came to Swansea, Mike Ruddock had developed a medium-term plan. His idea at the time was that the plan should cover a three year period. Speaking after the Aberavon victory, the coach said that, during the first three year period, he would have been contented with one Heineken League title, or a cup win. Given Swansea's inconsistency at the time he arrived, even that was a demanding goal. Happily, he said, 'the boys have done better than I had hoped'. Of course, after three years at the helm and after having developed coaching and training structures which were, by then, well honed, he admitted that he had held a different view at the beginning of the campaign which had just finished. Furthermore, the benefits of earlier planning were beginning to be enjoyed. Consequently, the burden of the coach's message was that the club should strive for continuing improvement. As far as he was concerned, Ruddock intended to develop his planning process to face up to that challenge. As the jargon has it, his three-year plan was 'rolling'. As year one becomes history, so year four is added. Thus, as the mud-spattered 'Whites' collected their trophies that April day in 1994, season 1996-97 was being integrated into the St. Helens planning process, at least in the Ruddock mind. Soon he would be beginning to contemplate the season ahead and, beyond that the three year planning horizon. It was of little wonder that the senior management at St. Helens had decided that their coach should be appointed on a full-time professional basis. Moves, scrummaging, passing the ball and kicking were now only one element in the coach's job profile. And his input to the club's 'corporate planning' process was crucial to its success.

Meanwhile, with his Heineken League trophy in his pocket, Robert Jones was about to leave for South Africa, where he was to play for Western Province in the Currie Cup competition. Before he left, though, club chairman, Mike James, presented the popular scrum-half with another award. During the 'Golden Era' at St. Helens, 'Caps' were awarded to players on the same basis as county cricketers receive theirs today. The chairman announced that the idea had been revived at St. Helens, and that Robert Jones was to be the first recipient. The award, the chairman said, was for 'outstanding service and loyalty to the "All Whites" over many years'. Everyone present said 'amen' to that.

1994-95

Despondent and jubilant

Having won the Heineken League championship for the second time at the end of the previous season, the 'Whites' were among the clubs which, according to the bookmakers, would do well in the campaign ahead. Not surprisingly, Swansea followers were pleased with that expectation, and with the squad of players which Mike Ruddock had at his disposal, though they were sad to see Mark Titley leave St. Helens for fresh pastures. The supporters were happy, too, that they could look forward to the visit of the 'Springboks' at the end of October. With memories of the defeat of the Australians still fresh in their minds, the general conclusion was that, at worst, the South Africans would be 'run close'.

In the first place, though, there was the question of defending the club's Heineken title, and, there was some consternation at the Cricket Field when the 'Whites' were defeated by 35 points to 23 at Stradey in the opening match, and by a single point, against Pontypool in the third. Furthermore, whilst Treorchy were well beaten in the second League match, the press was arguing that the Swansea side was not as convincing as it had been expected to be. But then, perhaps stung by the criticism, the 'Whites' put their game together to defeat the 'Blue and Blacks' of Cardiff. It was a timely result in many respects.

As the season developed so matters improved and, by the end of October the team had won ten of the fourteen matches which it had played, scoring 395 points in the process whilst conceding 239. There followed substantial wins over Bridgend and Newbridge and a rather 'stut-

Footnote: Among the elements in the original plan was a development programme for schools, which was evidence of the long-term thinking of the coach and the board at St. Helens. Despite the costs involved (in 1994/95 this cost £38,000) this initiative continues.

tering' defeat of Newport. By then, the general opinion in the press was that, whilst they were doing reasonably well, the 'Whites' would need to raise their game 'several notches' if they were to trouble the South Africans. Not that these comments created too much concern amongst the Swansea faithful. Apart from anything else, the 'Whites' had an enviable record against major touring sides, and appeared, always, to be able to lift their game against such visitors. Furthermore, having observed the patterns of Mike Ruddock's management, the supporters were of the opinion that 'the boys will be focused on the day'. There was the comfort, too, that five of the team which was expected to play against the 'Springboks' had been in the Swansea sides which faced the New Zealand and Australian tourists. In consequence, the quintet formed a phalanx of experience and skill which few clubs could replicate. There was another issue for Swansea supporters, too. Since the Welsh selectors had not, in their opinion, picked enough of their favourites for the Wales 'A' match against the tourists, the St. Helens contest would provide a platform for those not 'capped' to shown their worth. Thus it was that, in the week before the match, Cricket Field optimists and pessimists were united in the belief that Swansea's record against touring sides would be enhanced yet again.

After playing on a Neath mud patch in the mid week before the St. Helens match, the South Africans warmly welcomed a near perfect playing pitch for the game against the 'Whites'. The visitors fielded a strong side which, from the kick-off made its presence felt. In particular, the pack demonstrated typical South African mobility and pace and put pressure on the Swansea eight. Later, adjectives like 'Awesome' were used to describe the play of the men in green and gold, whilst full-back, Joubert, was to be feted for his immense contribution to the match. For twenty minutes, though, all that was but a South African day-dream. Indeed, with Swansea looking to move the ball whenever the opportunity arose, the 'Springboks' had concerns of their own. Furthermore, after twenty minutes, the 'Whites' scored a try which was indicative of their potential.

Tony Clement came in from full-back to combine with the 'Whites' back-row. Aled Williams, receiving on the right, off loaded to Boobyer, who burst through a South African tackle, swerved around Joubert and passed to Simon Davies who scored. At that, the Swansea faithful began to relax in readiness for another famous victory over a major touring side. And, as if to emphasise that possibility, within minutes, the wing was again sprinting for the 'Springboks' line in splendid isolation. Unfortunately, he was called back by the referee and, in retrospect, that may be seen as the moment in the match when the pendulum swung into the green and gold sector. Nevertheless, the South Africans lead at half-time was, from the point of view of the home side, only marginal. Lemon time, the St. Helens faithful probably thought, would give Mike Ruddock the chance to lift his men. Unfortunately, the break proved to be of greater benefit to the visitors than to the 'Whites'. In the second-half the 'Springboks' 'ran riot'. In all, they ran in a dozen tries, of which Joubert scored four and converted nine. Throughout this devastating period, the stunned Swansea supporters could only bravely, try to appreciate the skill, pace and tenacity of the touring backs, and the dominance of their forwards. Whilst it is easy for a supporter to be a sportsman when his side is winning, faced with a humiliating defeat, it is necessary to dig deep for such inspiration. The collective emotion at St. Helens that dark day involved a contradictory cocktail of pain, concern, pity, and admiration of outstanding rugby football. Despite their chagrin, the massed crowd behaved with great dignity. As did the Swansea players and Mike Ruddock, who, when the final whistle went, sought to support his

Simon says – it's a try – the South Africans look on.

players. Later, in the naked glare of a television camera, the coach must have faced the most difficult moments of his rugby career. Yet, faced with that challenge, he showed courage and humility as he praised the play of the tourists and sought to deflect any criticism of his team's performance towards himself.

Throughout this book, in the appropriate chapter, all the sides which have represented Swansea Rugby Club against major touring sides have been listed. Some might argue that, given the outcome of the game with South Africa, it would have been prudent not to include the names of the team here. However, given the outcome of this, the final season described in this book, there is another, more appealing view. That is that, subsequently, in achieving what they did, the men in question demonstrated outstanding qualities of character. After receiving such a physical and psychological 'drubbing' it says much of the individuals and the squad as a whole that they were able to fight back to win a major trophy during the same campaign. In all this, quite rightly, the players would wish to point to the part played by Mike Ruddock and his management team, and it would be foolish not to accept that argument. Yet, the seventeen men who are listed in the panel opposite were those who had to cross that psychological Rubicon which must have seemed to them, on that traumatic October day in 1994, as a bottomless chasm. No one could cross for them. Whatever help they received could only facilitate that progression. It follows that there is more than a little pride involved in listing the following team.

The Swansea men were:

A. Clement (Capt.), S. Davies, R. Boobyer, D. Weatherley, S. Marshall, A. Williams, R. Jones; I. Buckett, G. Jenkins, K. Colclough, P. Arnold, R. Moriarty (M. Evans), A. Reynolds, I. Davies, R. Appleyard (Stuart Davies).

In the aftermath of the 'Springboks' match, Mike Ruddock and his team, supported by all at St. Helens, searched among the ashes of the defeat for elements which would provide the spark of revival. And, given the position at the time, that word was apposite. At that stage, cynics in south Wales rugby, plus the previously latent pessimists at St. Helens, emerged to write off Swansea's season. Yet, from what was, without doubt, a nadir in the club's history, the Swansea men began the task, the outcome of which would have given great pleasure to the young Phoenix.

Yet, that work had to begin 'on the hoof', whilst the club sought to maintain a challenging presence in the league competition. There was no question of the players retiring to some convenient sheltered spot in order to lick their collective wounds. If ever there was a challenge to the concept of mental toughness, those days in November 1994 provided them for the players. In the short term, two of the top sides had to be faced in succession. When Pontypridd won by 32 points to 10 at Sardis Road, and Neath by 27 points to 19 at St. Helens, some Swansea *aficionados* feared the worst. To many of the Cricket field faithful, it appeared that the club was floundering on the back the 'Springbok' aftermath.

Throughout this period, however, much work was being done off the field in order to restore confidence, and to build a renewed challenge. The press, for example, made much of a programme designed to build greater upper-body strength, of several 'talk-ins' with the club's sports psychologist, and of the blooding of a number of young men who were thought to be stars of the future. Given the results, though, the cynics were massing. Had St. Helens been a soccer club there might have been demonstrations demanding the manager's head, or that of the chairman. But Mike Ruddock was undeterred. Showing the steel which was personified by his game when playing for the 'Whites', he stuck to his task. Following sound military principles, he, his team of coaches and the squad regrouped and reconsidered their objectives. As the old adage has it, the water had gone under the bridge. It was time to look to the future.

Recognising that there was, by then, a very slim chance of retaining the Heineken title, apart from achieving a respectable place in the table, there was just one other objective available which was concerned with winning a trophy. With the 'sudden death' aspect of cup football providing a different challenge from that of the league, it enabled the St. Helens men to re-focus, taking each match as one element and building from there. Having 'scraped through' the fourth round of the cup, and having scored 58 points whilst conceding 24 in the fifth, the real tests of the squad's resolve came at the next stage. The 'Whites' were required to play Neath at the Gnoll.

In retrospect, the outcome of this match may be seen to have been the watershed in the recovery process. Neath, always a difficult side to take on at the Gnoll, were recognised favourites to win. Indeed, there were even those among the Swansea followers who, like politicians approaching a threatening by-election, were rationalising their thinking in case the 'Whites' were

Captain 'Boot' – Tony Clement finds a 'monster' touch.

defeated. In the event, those who were there, travelled home convinced that the revival was in motion.

Subsequent to the two point Swansea victory (forty-two were scored on the day) much was made in the press about the 'Whites' decision to appear as the 'Blues', Neath, thus, being obliged to play in a peculiar pastel shade of turquoise, were said to have been 'put off their game by the change in Swansea garb'. However, against the backcloth of something akin to a minor outcry invoking Swansea gamesmanship, most objective commentators noted that the victory had been gained as a result of a renewed spirit in the Swansea side. In addition, they perceived an effective combination which demonstrated that the views held at the beginning of the season concerning the quality of the Swansea squad were not flawed. Indeed, at least at St. Helens, the general consensus of opinion was that the Swansea men should have won by a larger margin, Meantime, Garin Jenkins, said by the press to have been the architect of Swansea's sartorial transformation, merely smiled. There was the implied question which asked, were those who were complaining about the change, now saying that 'all this mental stuff had something going for it?'. And, if so, were they the same people who had previously ridiculed the whole business? Those who have had to respond in games of rugby to the strength and technique of the Jenkins challenge, would be aware that his throw away line, 'handbags at dawn' simply put the matter of shirt colour into perspective.

Thereafter, as the team's challenge for a respectable position in the league table continued, there came the news that, having beaten Newbridge in the quarter final of the cup, the 'Whites' were drawn to play against Cardiff at the penultimate stage. Cardiff, the bookmakers' favourites, not to say that of the bulk of the media, were able to field a side boasting eleven men who had been selected for the Welsh World Cup squad. Swansea could field just five. The match was scheduled to be played at the Gnoll, but, in the event, at the last minute, it was switched to Stradey Park. In retrospect, the romantic among the Swansea followers argued that that was an omen. For whatever reason, many 'Taffsiders' supporters chose not to travel to the Tinopolis, which, given that many more from Swansea did, provided the 'Whites' with an added vocal benefit.

At this point in the narrative, it is important to record another accolade for the St. Helens club and for its coach. Following the dismal performance of Welsh sides in the Five Nations championship, the then national coaching team resigned en bloc. As a result, and given the proximity of the World Cup competition, the W.R.U., moving with admirable speed, appointed a new coaching team. One of the three names which was announced was Swansea's Mike Ruddock. In noting that appointment, the press as a whole, in profiling the man agreed that he was respected throughout Welsh rugby as an outstanding coach. When Mike Ruddock accepted that challenge, he brought further honour to the Swansea club as well as to himself. In so doing he must have reflected on the vagaries of rugby coaching and of the measures which had restored his previous level of self-belief. Given his predilection for analysis and improvement, having come through a considerable crisis earlier in the season, he was, at the time of his appointment, even more effective as a leader. He had gained, in typical Ruddock fashion from adversity. As it transpired, he was to learn, too, from his working with the Welsh squad, for Alec Evans, the Cardiff supremo, was the senior in the new triumvirate.

Leaving aside their collaboration in the Welsh cause, Evans and Ruddock were to pit their wits against each other in preparation for the match at Llanelli. In itself, that was an intriguing tustle. That which took place on the pitch, however, was to prove to be of even greater moment. Typical of the Swansea coach, he picked Alan Harris for the Stradey match. Despite the fact that the young wing had played a mere handful of senior rugby matches, Ruddock saw him as a potential match winner. Though, of course, Harris would need to defend, too. Cup semi-finals rarely provide the opportunity for flowing, running rugby. That day at Stradey was to be no different.

Meantime, prior to the Cardiff match, the club's performances in the league seemed to have ensured that the 'Whites' would finish in a respectable place in the table. Pontypridd, the club placed second behind 'double favourites' Cardiff, were 'crushed' by 22 points to 6, whilst Neath were beaten by 25 points to 22 on their own ground. By then, the Swansea men were fifth in the table with a match in hand.

On the day of the semi-final clash, the weather was far from appealing. In the first-half in particular, a strong wind drove fine rain from one goal to another of the type of which mam used to say, 'will make you soaking wet through'. The 'Whites' came out like greyhounds out of a trap and, for a third of the game, dominated proceedings. Within four minutes, Aled Williams had kicked a penalty (after Taylor had obstructed Weatherley). After twenty minutes, Aled repeated his success, and the 'Whites', becoming greyer by the minute, found themselves with a six point cushion. Soon after, however, the Cardiff men began to claw their way back into the game. Not via the line-out, though. In that aspect of the game, and to the delight of the Swansea contingent, Paul Arnold outjumped the skyscraping Derwyn Jones and Stuart Roy time and again. As Arnold said later, he'd had 'a little help from his friends'. And, quite apart from judicious support, that included throwing in of pin-point accuracy by Garin Jenkins. By half-time, though, despite missing other kickable penalties, Adrian Davies's boot had brought his side level with the Swansea men.

After the break, Cardiff began where they had left off, and soon, via the Davies boot, (a dropped goal on this occasion), the 'Taffsiders' were in front. Furthermore, they were building threatening attacks through their forwards, and, for many 'Whites' followers there was the feeling that the game was slipping away from their favourites. But, then came what many were to say was the turning point of the match. The Cardiff outside-half missed a kickable penalty which might have won the game for the 'Blue and Blacks', and, from then on Cardiff heads began to drop. When Aled Williams kicked his third penalty to bring the sides level again, the tension at Stradey could have been cut with a knife. For twenty minutes the teams grappled with each other in a bid to find a way through the opposing defence. Then, to the surprise of many, the final whistle was blown. Given that few people have intimate knowledge of the specific laws dealing with extra time in Welsh rugby cup matches, many in the crowd were bemused. Bids from a half an hour each way, to two fifteen minute halves, were made. The referee, however, knew that the allocated time was just ten minutes each way. Furthermore, he restarted the match whilst people were still debating the time allocation. And it was the 'Whites' who took advantage of surprise.

A tackle by Cardiff's Ford had prevented a try on the left, but the Swansea men kept the ball alive. Aled Williams, taking the ball slightly to the left of centre field, dipped his shoulder and made a half break before feeding the supporting Roddy Boobyer on his right. Boobyer, finding himself in space surged for the line to score. The 'Whites' were, then, five points in front, and, after Aled Williams had kicked an awkward conversion – a pressure kick if ever there was one –

the scoreboard read Abertawe 16 Caerdydd 9. Thereafter, for Swansea supporters time passed more quickly than they had dared hope. The 'Whites' were in the Cup Final again! Stuart Davies, Paul Arnold, Rob Appleyard and Aled Williams were outstanding that day, but, as Mike Ruddock put it 'Everyone of them was a hero'. As they absorbed the delight of the day, the Swansea supporters must have struggled to put out of their minds the label which had long been carried by their favourites. 'They can't perform when they get to the final'. Eradicating that absurd generalisation was a task for Mike Ruddock and his sports psychologist colleagues. Mere Swansea supporters, though, had to manage on their own.

After the semi-final, there were two league matches to play. The first was in mid week at Treorchy. Given the intensity of the previous match, the decision was taken to rest all but one of the winning side. The Rhondda side took advantage of that situation as well as the points. That left one league match before the final. The visitors to St. Helens were Abertillery, a side which had to win to retain its place in Division One of the Heineken competition. Inexplicably, after building up a comfortable lead, the 'Whites' 'took their foot off the throttle'. Abertillery, however, fired by the emotional challenge of the afternoon, did the opposite and overturned the Swansea lead to win the match.

Following that disappointing defeat, as the day of the cup final approached, the pressure on the Swansea club was greater than many appreciated. Had the 'Whites' won the match against Abertillery they would have finished third in the league. Apart from the prize money which that win would have attracted, third place would have ensured that St. Helens would be one of the grounds to be visited by the Fijians during their Welsh tour. Apart from the prestige of that event, 'gate' money alone would have run into five figures. Furthermore, and in many respects more significant than the all-pervading financial issues, there was the question of the perceived status of the Swansea club in the eyes of the rugby world. In particular, in much of the discussion in the media concerning 'European Leagues', there had been an almost universal acceptance that Swansea would be among the Welsh clubs involved. As far as the architects of such an event were concerned, though, there was no question of automatic involvement. Third in the league and, at worst, runners-up in the cup would have met the 'status' requirements rather well. Having finished outside the first four in the league, if the Swansea club was to maintain its status then the team had to win the cup.

Nonetheless, whilst none of this was lost on the players, their mindset was rather different. Whatever had been the reason for the Abertillery defeat, the players were determined to restore their self-respect, and to show a wider audience what they were capable of doing on the rugby field. Then there was the matter of Swansea pride, and the fact that it had been in 1978 that the side, coached by Stan Addicott, had last won the cup. No other Swansea team had been able to emulate that feat. In consequence, the players did not need any incentive to give their all for the club and for the city of Swansea. Not surprisingly, Mike Ruddock, aware of these strong feelings within his squad, set out to reinforce them. He reminded the players that, as had happened in previous weeks, when the cup was won by the 'Whites', they had beaten Neath and Cardiff *en route*. At that, some objective outsider might have argued that this was little more than coincidence. However, the thinking of sportsmen who, as a breed have a strong collective folk memory of the veracity of such things, is affected by such comparisons. In 'Soccer-speak', they might say 'our name is on the cup'. However, irrational, such matters do affect confidence! In addition, in order to add credence to the comparison, Ruddock asked Stan Addicott to speak to the squad. Addicott, probably the longest-serving coach to have worked at St. Helens, was the ideal man for the situation. It had been his team which had last won the cup, and his participative style reinforced his message. He told the players that his cup-winning side had contained fewer internationals than the present team; by implication, therefore, they should do better. Putting aside any comparison between the strength of the opponents on the two Saturdays, none of this was lost on the players. Not that they were over-confident. The outcome of the Abertillery match had seen to that, and there was always, the threat of the Neil Jenkins boot.

The Final

Since the cricket season had started, it was apposite that, on the day of the cup final, the weather was more appropriate for the summer sport than for rugby. As one match report had it, it was a 'broiling day'. At kick off, with just a sliver of shade protecting the Pontypridd line there were few places in the arena that day where the thirty gladiators could hide from the scorching sun. As a result, as the match progressed, the milkman-like carriers who provided liquid for the players made frequent incursions onto the field. Old men in the stands, thought back to their playing days, when the received wisdom was that a player didn't take liquid during a match. The thirty men on the field that day must have blessed the person who demonstrated the fallacy of that 'rule'.

At half-time, despite not insignificant pressure from the men in white, and a lung-bursting break by Roddy Boobyer, the 'Whites' found themselves with a seven point deficit. A rush of blood had presented Pontypridd with a gift try, and the Swansea men had not been able to convert their efforts into points. There was a bonus though. Happily for the Swansea men, the player some wag had dubbed the 'Metrognome' in recognition of the clockwork precision of his kicking, was affected by the emotion of the day. He missed three kicks which, on another day, he would have put over in his carpet slippers. Had he kicked to his form, the 'Whites' would have turned around with far more than a single score deficit to make up. Had that been the case, the outcome might have been different. Though, if your name is on the cup ...

In the second period, the strength of the Swansea forwards began to erode that of the Pontypridd eight. Brilliantly marshalled by Stuart Davies, who gave an outstanding display, the Swansea pack gained the initiative. With Paul Arnold (Man of the match), controlling the lines-out, a 'Whites' score seemed to be inevitable, and all Swansea thought that it had come following a surging run by Alan Harris. Unfortunately, the touch judge, brandishing his callipers, indicated that the wing had strayed onto the line. The gods, though, had seen enough. The 'Whites' were going to win!

Soon after, Aled Williams, after converting a penalty to close the points gap to four points, demonstrated the silky skills around which his game is built. From a set scrum midway into the Pontypridd half, Robert Jones peeled to the right. Stuart Davies, acting scrum-half, fed Jones, who transferred to Williams on his left. The outside-half side-stepped past a defender and fed Rob Appleyard who, with a drive reminiscent of Stuart Davies, dived over the line to score. The Williams boot was unerring. Swansea led Pontypridd by 10 points to 7.

As the match wore on, with Paul Arnold still dominating the line-out and the Swansea eight controlling matters in the tight and loose, another try seemed to be inevitable. From a line-out, Arnold gathered and set up a maul. With the Pontypridd men visibly tiring, the drive forward gained new impetus in its second stage. Then Stuart Davies fell to the ground and, as the maul progressed, he regained his feet to gather the ball as it emerged. Surging left through a group of would-be tacklers he seemed to stumble but regained his feet and drove over to touch down. The conversion was a formality. The match was won and lost. For only the second time in the club's history, the 'Whites' had won the W.R.U. Cup.

Later, whilst inevitably the media highlighted the play of certain individuals, everyone in the Swansea camp spoke of a magnificent team effort. Every Swansea man had played an important part in the victory! They had shown that they were better organised than their opponents, fitter, and with a greater belief in themselves. It had been a great day!

The men who won the cup for:

A. Clement (Capt.), A. Harris, R. Boobyer, D. Weatherley, Simon Davies; A. Williams, R. Jones; C. Loader, G. Jenkins, K. Colclough, P. Arnold, A. Moore, A. Reynolds, Stuart Davies, R. Appleyard.

When the triumphant supporters returned to St. Helens, it was entirely appropriate that they were able to look out at the historic arena and see the Swansea club doing battle with another with willow and leather. After all, as will be seen from the early chapters of this book, had it not been for the cricketers seeking something to do in the winter, there might never have been a rugby club at St. Helens. As the club's title implies, cricket came before football. Whilst this book is intended as a celebration of over 120 years of rugby football in Swansea, at its end it is proper to remind ourselves of the source of the life of the institution which is Swansea Rugby Club. Without those cricketers of the early 1870's, the fascinating story which is contained within these pages might never have unfolded. Had that been the case, generations of Swansea-ites would have been deprived of the enjoyment provided them by the men in white, who, for so long, have strode across the St. Helens stage. Gods and geniuses, 'craftsmen' and 'labourers', fast and slow, internationals and administrators, remembered and long forgotten, committee-men and supporters, all those who have worn the famous white jersey, and all those who have supported them, have played their part in the life and times of Swansea Rugby Club. Each of them, some more so than others, should be thanked for their contribution to this story, to rugby football and to the life of the Old Borough. Diolch yn fawr iawn!

P.S.

(Perennial Service)

THE *SHORTER OXFORD DICTIONARY* defines P.S. (the accepted abbreviation for postscript) as 'an additional sentence or paragraph at the end of a letter'. However, in the present case, whilst this item may be regarded as a postscript to the main text, given its subject, a more apt title is that which is included in brackets above. The subject is that greatly loved St. Helens stalwart, BERNARD CAJOT, which, for many 'All Whites', players, administrators and supporters will put the subtitle into context.

Whilst speaking at the 1995 Patrons' Dinner, the theme chosen by Clive Rowlands allowed him to draw upon the long list of outstanding players who have worn the white jersey. In the process, Clive mentioned a veritable galaxy of men who are well-known not only at St Helens, but to the rugby world at large. Men who, individually and collectively may be best described by the single word 'famous'. Yet among those referred to (with typical Clive Rowlands fervour), was Bernard Cajot, a man who, according to a St. Helens contemporary was 'just a good honest player'. Whilst the warmth of the tone used by the speaker in giving this description is lost in the printed word, the phrase, in the view of many long-standing St. Helens men, 'fits the bill'.

If that is the case, an uninformed visitor might ask, why was Bernard Cajot mentioned in the Rowlands speech? The simple answer to that question is that Bernard *is* a great 'All White'. It is just that he epitomises another aspect of greatness; one which is bound up in the selfless service which he has given to Swansea Rugby Club for more than forty-seven years. He stands as an outstanding example of people who, throughout the one hundred and twenty years of the life of Swansea Rugby Club, have given loyal, loving, continuing service to the institution which is known as the 'All Whites'. Bernard Cajot, like Bob Dowdle and George Bateman before him, has given a significant amount of his time, talent and energy for the benefit of his club. To the casual observer such service is 'anonymous'. It is lost among the myriad of activities which go to make up any living organisation. Yet, for the informed, it is as essential an element in the life of the St. Helens club as any other.

Those who know Bernard Cajot will vouch for the fact that the service which he provides is performed without thought of recognition or reward, other than knowing the satisfaction which is obtained from a job well done. He provides his service because there is a need, and because, in its own way, it contributes to the greater good of the St. Helens club. That service plays its part in enabling the fifteen men who wear our club colours to perform effectively, to give great enjoyment to many people, and to provide those special moments of pure joy when Swansea triumphs over some famous foe and St. Helens basks in the glory of it all.

Bernard would argue that behind the façade of the playing field with its potential of glory and recognition for those who take part, stand many other 'backroom boys' who, like him, give great service to the Swansea club. And, whilst that is true, everyone of them would say that the extent and quality of Bernard Cajot's service to Swansea Rugby Club is without equal in recent times. It is probable, too, that his friends and colleagues would be happy to regard Bernard as the personification of all who serve the Club in whatever capacity.

This, then, is a tribute, not only to Bernard, but to the anonymous corps of volunteers who serve the club in many ways, year in, year out . All would agree, however, that among them Bernard Cajot stands tall, which more than justifies the inclusion of this tribute to the special service which *he* has provided to the 'All Whites'. Furthermore, it is difficult to conceive of a more fitting postscript to this celebration of the life and times of Swansea Rugby Club. Service, after all, has been at the heart of this famous institution from its inception !

As the host of that famous old T.V. show would say at the conclusion of the programme, 'Bernard Cajot, player, trainer, kitman, confidant to many hundreds of "All Whites". This is your life".' All who, knowingly or unknowingly have gained from the years of service which you have given to Swansea R.F.C. are pleased to place on record this tribute to, and our gratitude for that special service!

Author's Note

It is typical of the man that I have not been able to find a photograph of Bernard Cajot. I am told that whenever team photographs were taken Bernard was somewhere in the background. However, his smiling face is included in this book at page 319. This seems to have been one of the few occasions when he was captured by the camera.

THE WHITE LIONS

Vernon Rees Davies

ENTER FROM BRYN ROAD the hallowed portals of St. Helens Pavilion, turn right up the stairs, go slowly and thoughtfully because you are now treading the revered ground where, without exception, every distinguished personality in the history of cricket and rugby has trodden before you. Turning left at the top of the stairs proceed towards the St. Helens Lounge and there you will see an Honours board naming the Swansea 'All Whites' who have toured with the British Lions dating back to 1904.

The first International British Rugby Union touring team was in 1888 to Australia and New Zealand and trips to South African followed in 1891 and 1896. Australia was the venue in 1899 and a tour of South Africa took place in 1903.

Our story begins in 1904 when seven Welsh players were picked for another trip to Australia and New Zealand. The party included two Swansea players, Fred Jowett, a wing three-quarter, and T. S. Bevan, a front-row forward. Both had been previously capped by Wales. Fred Jowett, a schoolmaster, who took over the wing from the outstanding 'Genny' Gordon, scored 42 tries for Swansea in season 1902/3, an all time record; nearest, with 34, would be Harold M. Powell, 1937/38, and Tony Swift with 29 in 1980/81. Fred Jowett disappeared from the Swansea scene and re-emerged playing Rugby League for Hull Kingston Rovers.

Jowett and Bevan left for Australia and New Zealand with the British team on 11th May, 1904, and returned on 28th October, 1904, five and a half months away by boat and train to play 14 matches in Australia (all won) and five in New Zealand (won two, lost two, drawn one). Sid Bevan played in all four Test matches, three versus Australia (all won) and one versus New Zealand (lost).

The five and a half months' trip explains why so many legendary Swansea players of that era, like W. J. Trew (29 Welsh caps), the 'Dancing Dicks', Dickie Owen and Dick Jones, W. J. Bancroft, Will Joseph and so many others, found it impossible to be away on such long tours when there were severe employment problems at home in south Wales. On the 25th March, 1912, both Owen and Trew withdrew from the Wales team to play France preferring to go on Swansea's Devon tour!

The next tour was in 1908 and Anglo-Welsh only in selection. Nine games were played in Australia, winning seven but losing seven and drawing one out of seventeen played in New Zealand. Swansea's only representative was mining engineer Edgar Morgan, a strong, robust hooker from Pontardawe. Capped for Wales four times in 1914, he was later commissioned as an Army Officer (Captain, Royal Engineers) during World War 1. He was a member of the legendary Welsh pack of forwards who were dubbed 'The Terrible Eight', (terrible – meaning awesome rather than unbearable!) and led by the Reverend Alban Davies. Edgar played in two of the three Tests against New Zealand.

In 1910 and 1924 there were visits to South Africa but many leading British players declared themselves unavailable for long breaks from their professions and jobs.

Carrying the 'All Whites' banner to South Africa in 1924 was the young Cambridge University wing, Rowe Harding. He played in three out of the four Tests. Later he played seventeen times for Wales, sometimes as captain. Members of the British team on that tour were bedevilled by injuries and heavy tackling on the hard South African grounds. Much later, as Judge Rowe Harding, he became President of the Swansea Cricket and Football Club and devoted a lifetime of service to his beloved 'All Whites'.

In 1930 the popular David Stuart Parker who was later to become a councillor and respected landlord of the famous Cricketers' Hotel outside St. Helens where he presided over many jovial reunion parties. Of striking personality, Dai was a leading goal-kicker and hooker and storyteller of world renown in rugby circles. He played in twenty one games in New Zealand and seven in Australia. Dai was included in all the Test matches.

The British had regarded the early tours in the 1880s and 90s as exercises to spread the gospel of rugby football. Between 1910 and 1938, however, the impression clearly emerged that the pupils were becoming the masters.

It was in 1930 that the British Touring team became the 'British Lions', the party carrying a supply of gold-plated 'Lions' brooches to hand out to friends on tour. The 'Lions' wore blue jerseys bearing a badge of three gold lions. Today they wear red jerseys.

Police Constable Eddie Morgan, native of Abercrave and an outstanding front-row scrummager for Swansea and Wales in the 1930s, was chosen for the 'Lions' tour of South Africa in 1938. Eddie played fourteen matches for the 'Lions' holding his own against the mighty Louw brothers. He was to have been 'All Whites' captain in 1939 but Adolf Hitler had other ideas for that particular year.

With Eddie Morgan on the 1938 trip to South Africa was former Gowerton schoolboy prodigy, Haydn Tanner, scrum-half in the unforgettable schoolboy half-back combination of Tanner and Willie Davies who starred in Swansea's greatest ever victory over the New Zealand 'All Blacks' in 1935 at St. Helens. Haydn collected 25 caps for Wales and one wonders how many he would have gained had there not been a war in the middle of his career.

The 'Lions' of 1950, although including fourteen Welsh players, could not find room for one 'All White', which might explain why they failed to win a single Test!

Two of the most impressive post war 'All Whites' were R. C. C. (Clem) Thomas and W. O. (Stoker) Williams. Clem, with 26 Welsh caps, and Billy, with 22, went to South Africa as 'Lions' in 1955. They were part of the team described by the doyen of South African rugby, Dr Danie Craven, as the finest touring team ever to visit South Africa. The four Tests were shared, two apiece.

In December, 1953, the 'Whites' played young John Faull, a well-built reserve centre carrying 15 stone and standing six feet three inches, against the touring New Zealand 'All Blacks'. Two huge 50 yard penalty goals by Faull gave Swansea a draw. Later, John was converted into a No. 8 forward, where he represented Wales and the 1959 Lions in Australia and New Zealand. Faull played in four of the six Tests and was said to have performed like a Titan in the victory over New Zealand at Aukland in the fourth Test.

The standard of British rugby deteriorated during the 1960s. Not one of the twelve Tests against South Africa and New Zealand, played in 1962, 1966 and 1968, was won. Only one 'All White', the great wing three-quarter, Dewi Bebb, was included amongst the 'Lions' in both 1962 and 1966. Dewi was the salient Welsh wing of the period and played in Tests against New Zealand, South Africa and Australia. He also played 34 times for Wales between 1959 and 1967.

1971 to 1977 has been described as the 'Lions' golden era but Swansea was not represented in the magnificent 1971 team which lost only twice on the tour of Australia and New Zealand. Swansea boy, Mervyn Davies, was a conspicuous member of the team but at the time he was officially a London Welsh player.

In 1974, when Mervyn was such a power at No. 8 in the 'Lions' pack in South Africa, he returned to play for the 'Whites' at St. Helens. Mervyn is very proud to have been in the only 'Lions' team ever to come home with an unbeaten record.

Trevor Evans, our dynamic International flanker of the late 70s, became a 'Lion' in 1977, touring New Zealand and playing against Fiji on the way home. After losing only four matches out of 25 in New Zealand it was a shock to lose, 25 pts to 21, in Fiji.

The 'Lions' of 1977 also named, in the original selection, G. A. D. Wheel, the renowned Swansea and Wales lock-forward who received a shattering blow when, on the eve of departure for New Zealand, he failed to pass the customary medical test. A 'Lions' squad was selected in 1986 to celebrate the Centenary of the Game's ruling body. One of the games, 'British Lions' versus Overseas Unions, was played at Cardiff Arms Park. One of the 'Lions' replacements was the Swansea and Wales outside-half, Malcolm Dacey, who, during the course of the game, replaced the injured Rutherford of Scotland and uniquely became a 'Lion' without having taken part in a 'Lions' overseas tour.

Bill Beaumont of England led the 1980 'Lions' in South Africa. Included in the side were centre, David Richards (17 Welsh caps), and prop, Clive Williams (8 Welsh Caps). David, one of Swansea's all time greats, had to return from South Africa upon the death of his popular father, Glynn. David played in the first Test only but Clive played in all four and scored a try in the last Test at Pretoria to bring the 'Lions' their only Test victory.

The 'Whites' were not favoured by the 1983 'Lions' selection committee for the New Zealand tour which was not a conspicuous success, all four Tests being lost.

In the 1989 'Lions' party for Australia was Swansea's Robert Jones as first choice scrum-half and he was later joined by the up-and-coming Anthony Clement who came into the party as a replacement. Robert played in all three Tests successfully partnering, in the last two, Robert Andrew of England. It was reported that the new 'Lions' halves were instrumental in the subsequent British victories.

It is interesting to note that both the 1980 and 1981 teams included that great English lock forward, Maurice Colclough, who spent the twilight of his career with the 'All Whites' but was not a White 'Lion'. Brynmor Williams was another who became a 'Lion' before joining Swansea. Terry Davies (1959), Alun Thomas (1955 as a player and 1974 as Team Manager) and David Young who served their apprenticeships in first-class rugby with Swansea later became 'Lions' after joining other Clubs.

The 1993 tour to New Zealand found England supplying no fewer than 16 of the 30 selected 'Lions'. This equalled the Welsh dominance in 1977 when 16 Welsh players went to New Zealand. In 1993 just five Welsh players found favour. Ieuan Evans of Llanelli, the Welsh captain, was joined by Robert Jones, Anthony Clement and new 'Lions', Richard Webster and Scott Gibbs, all from Swansea. With the Test matches standing at one victory apiece, the stage was set for a dramatic last Test with a distinct possibility of a 'Lions' victory. Unfortunately, this was not achieved.

Current comment is that the 1993 'Lions' could be the last. With rugby football surging ahead in popularity world-wide and International Rugby Unions already complaining about their calendars being full, the future of the 'British Lions' is vulnerable. It is regrettable, but possible, that becoming a 'Lion', once a rugby player's pinnacle of attainment, could be sacrificed for short, inter-country tours during the close season and the World Cup commitment every four years.

Cliff Morgan* writes, 'I am seldom provoked to anger but there is a paranoid species today who are making an outrageous suggestion that this (1993) summer's Lions Tour to New Zealand could be the last. A curse, I say, on those with dubious motives who have the audacity to meddle with a tradition in the game which will out-last time or gold plated trophies or those who zig-zag their way through the jungle of modern sport creating bigger concrete stadiums and hideous multi-colour jerseys.'

Acknowledgement

The author is grateful to John Griffiths, rugby statistician, for permission to use information from his book entitled 'British Lions' which was first published in 1990 by The Crowood Press, Swindon, Wiltshire.

* Lion to South Africa 1955.

Appendix 1

'ALL WHITES' SINCE THE CLUB'S INCEPTION

WHEN THIS BOOK WAS IN THE planning stage, it was decided that a list of the men who have worn the club's first team jersey should be included as an appendix. However, the statistics for the period 1874–1955 were not comprehensively recorded, or have been lost which meant that it was necessary to build that part of the list from newspaper reports and whatever other sources proved to be available. Unfortunately, particularly during the club's early days, the press did not always list the teams in match reports, and little was found from 'other sources'. It follows that, whilst every effort has been made to trace the names of all men who have played for the 'Whites', it is possible that others, not included in the following list, may have worn the jersey. Nevertheless, a list which includes over 1,200 names was developed and is included here as the best record which is available at the present time.

As far as the period from 1956 is concerned, the meticulous records compiled by David Price enable us to feel more confident about the more recent years in the club's history. Nonetheless, even then, we cannot guarantee that every man involved is included. However, knowing David, it is probable that very few, if any, have been omitted from the '1956 to date' listing. Given the foregoing, the following data are presented as two listings. The first (list (a)) covers the period 1874 to 1955, and the second (list (b)) from 1956 to 1995. In all over 2,000 names are included in both lists.

It will be noted that there is a date in brackets following the name of each player. This is the date, in the first list, when the individual's name was first mentioned in press reports and in the second when the players were first included in David Price's records. Given the uncertainties described above, it is also possible that the player might have appeared for the first time on an earlier date than that shown. However, the dates indicated should enable interested readers to locate a player, at least approximately, in the period in which he played at St. Helens.

As far as the listing for the period from 1956 is concerned, whilst names of players have been taken from David Price's extensive records, and may be regarded as being far more accurate than the first listing nonetheless, the proviso contained in the foregoing preamble needs to be borne in mind.

Where a player was designated in the press by his surname only, and where we have not been able to establish his initial(s), a question mark is placed before the surname.

Appendix 1a

'ALL WHITES' 1874-1955

A

A. Abberfield (1947)
R. Abbott (1936)
D. Abraham (1952)
M. Abraham (1931)
G. Addenbrooke (1945)
W. Allen (1927)
D. Alexander (1922)
E. Ambrose (1893)
L. Anthony (1946)
R. Anthony (1951)
A. Arnold (1907)
T. Arnold (1905)
W. Arnold (1903)
B. Arthur (1935)
D. Austin (1897)
J. Austin (1886)

B

Cpl. Baker (1945)
C. Ball (1926)
J. Ball (1894)
R. Ball (1881)
S. Ball (1893)
W. Ball (1894)
C. Bancroft (1937)
J. Bancroft (1905)
W. J. Bancroft (1889)
D. H. Banks (1933)
? Barratt (1923)
B. Barter (1924)
A. Bassett (1933)
D.J.Bassett (1933)
A. Basil (1888)
G. Batcup (1948)
L. Bateman (1930)
R. Bateman (1930)
R. Bateman (1952)
T. Bateman (1902)
D. Bater (1952)
C. L. Bath (1873)
? Beaugear (1907)
J. Bell (1875)
? Bennett (1889)
D.J.Bennett (1919)
H. Benson (1887)
Dr. Bertram (1924)
? Bevan (1883)
A. Bevan (1921)
D. Bevan (1920)
G. Bevan (1948)
H. Bevan (1886)
M. Bevan (1932)
S. Bevan (1897)
W. G. Bevan (1936)
B. Beynon (1903)
E. Beynon (1929)
E. Beynon (1945)
G. Beynon (1947)
G. E. Beynon (1923)
J. Beynon (1927)
J. Beynon (1948)
N. A. Beynon (1945)
P. Beynon (1927)
T. Beynon (1892)
W. Beynon (1893)
W. A. Beynon (1893)
W. G. Beynon (1933)
E. Bishop (1888)
T. Blackmore (1892)
? Blenkinsop (1878)
L. Blyth (1947)
N. Blyth (1945)
R. Bolsh (1953)
H. Bowden (1933)
E. Bowen (1926)
E. Bowen (1954)
G. Bowen (1884)
G. Bowen (1947)
H. Bowen (1889)
J. E. Bowen (1928)
M. Bowen (1928)
M. Bowen (1932)
W. Bowen (1886)
W. Bowen (1919)
V. G. Boyle (1926)
O. Brace (1951)
W. Bratton (1950)
T. Briggs (1945)
A. G. Brown (1935)
C. Brown (1875)
E. Brown (1923)
R. H. Brown (1877)
G. Bryant (1892)
? Bryant (1888)
? Bryce (1900)
L. Buckland (1877)
S. H. Buckland (1881)
E. Bull (1880)
R. Buller (1920)
L. Burchell (1877)
E. D. Burnie (1872)
? Burnie (1891)
W. Burgess (1925)
D. Burns (1922)
E. Burns (1951)

C

B. Cajot (1950)
E. Carlyle (1878)
F. Carlyle (1878)
N. Challenger (1880)
C. C. Chambers (1874)
C. Chappel (1927)

A. Charles	(1887)
E. Charles	(1889)
F. Charles	(1921)
H. Charles	(1886)
?. Chegwidden	(1892)
T. Chugg	(1935)
B. Clewer	(1921)
G. Clarke	(1953)
T. Clarke	(1875)
? Cleasier	(1920)
C. Clement	(1929)
W. Clement	(1927)
W. J. Cole	(1901)
C. Cole	(1953)
? Cobner	(1888)
D. Collins	(1951)
P. Collman	(1954)
C. S. Coke	(1890)
? Colville	(1895)
H. Colquhoun	(1887)
E. Comley	(1934)
G. Combe	(1946)
? Connick	(1903)
M. Condon	(1903)
E. Cook	(1936)
H. E. Cook (N.Z.)	(1945)
J. Cook	(1936)
D. C. Cooper	(1926)
E. Copus	(1878)
C. Cowling	(1930)
F. Crocker	(1894)
H. Crocker	(1907)
W. Crocker	(1894)
R. Croker	(1895)
S. Croker	(1895)
W. Cronin	(1887)
H. Cross	(1954)

D

Andrew Davies	(1934)
A. Davies	(1909)
A. Davies	(1922)
A. H. Davies	(1951)
Rev. Alb. Davies	(1910)
B. Davies	(1954)
Ben Davies	(1907)
B. Davies	(1934)
C. Davies	(1896)
C. Davies	(1931)
C. Davies	(1934)
C. Davies	(1937)
C. Davies	(1954)
C. M. Davies	(1934)
C. R. Davies	(1913)
D. Davies	(1887)
D. Davies	(1900)
D. Davies (Mumbles)	(1901)
D. Davies (Danygraig)	(1901)
D. Davies	(1946)
D. H. Davies	(1920)
D. M. Davies	(1955)
D. Emlyn Davies	(1931)
D. Glyn Davies	(1946)
D. Idwal Davies	(1937)
D. John Davies	(1947)
Eddie Davies	(1920)
Elwyn Davies	(1955)
E. Davies (Amman Untd.)	(1931)
E. Davies	(1906)
Emlyn Davies	(1947)
Evan Davies (Bryntawe)	(1905)
Evan Davies	(1911)
G. Davies	(1895)
Geoff Davies	(1931)
Geo Davies	(1932)
Glyn Davies	(1929)
Graham Davies (Mumbles)	(1919)
Geo Davies	(1932)
Granville Davies	(1935)
G. R. Davies	(1952)
H. Lloyd Davies	(1949)
H. Davies	(1892)
Howell Davies	(1909)
Howard Davies	(1937)
I. Davies	(1890)
Islwyn Davies	(1931)
J. Davies	(1892)
J. Davies	(1896)
J. Davies (Llandeilo)	(1900)
J. Davies (Penclawdd)	(1913)
J. Davies (Pontardawe)	(1923)
J. A. Davies	(1937)
Jack Davies	(1900)
Jack Davies	(1908)
Jack Davies	(1920)
Jack Davies	(1926)
Jack Davies	(1948)
Jim Davies	(1905)
J. L. Davies (Livingstone)	(1898)
Joe Davies	(1895)
Johnny Davies	(1921)
J. R. Davies	(1948)
L. Davies	(1898)
Leight.Davies	(1945)
Len Davies	(1945)
Les Davies	(1936)
Lewis Davies	(1907)
Llew Davies	(1906)
M. Davies	(1948)
Maurice Davies	(1937)
Mervyn Davies	(1938)
Morlais Davies	(1954)
Morris Davies	(1955)
P. Davies	(1955)
Phil Davies	(1936)
Dr. P. O. Davies	(1921)
R. Davies	(1924)
Redvers Davies	(1930)
Rees Davies	(1934)
R. H. L. Davies	(1948)
Syd Davies	(1921)
T. Davies	(1907)

T. Davies (1922)
Terry Davies (1950)
'Tit' Davies (1913)
Tom Davies (1897)
Tom Davies (1928)
(Resolven)
T. R. Davies (1946)
Trevor Davies (1913)
V. Rees Davies (1939)
V. Davies (1947)
W. Davies (1900)
W. Davies (1928)
(Amman United)
W. Davies (1945)
W. A. Davies (1912)
W. C. Davies (1935)
W. H. Davies (1933)
W. T. H. Davies (1934)
Will Davies (1929)
Will Davies (1946)
W. J. Davies (1906)
W. J. Davies (1923)
W. J. Davies (1945)
W. R. Davies (1924)
W. R. C. Davies (1955)
W. S. Davies (1929)
(Greenhill)
W. T. Davies (1935)
(Aberdare)
D. J. Daines (1949)
A. B. Daniel (1948)
? Dargavel (1913)
P. J. Dark (1931)
C. Davey (1928)
R. Dawes (1930)
T. Day (1928)
W. Deacon (1890)
? Deakin (1887)
G. Deeley (1931)
J. Dempsey (1930)
T. L. Dick (1938)
W. Dixon (1952)
R. Dobbs (1945)
R. L. Dobson (N.Z.) (1945)
J. Doggatt (1878)
W. Doggatt (1886)

E

? Eddins (1924)
(Gowerton)
? Edmunds (1892)
D. E. Edmunston (1921)
B. Edwards (1948)
D. Edwards (1875)
D. H. Edwards (1907)
G. A. L. Edwards (1926)
H. Edwards (1933)
J. Edwards (1892)
M. Edwards (1955)
R. Edwards (1990)
W. M. Edwards (1910)
O. Elias (1878)
I. Ellis (1923)
J. Ellis (1924)
A. Evans (1917)
Alwyn Evans (1954)
B. Evans (1955)
Bryn Evans (1927)
Bryn Evans (1949)
Ceri Evans (1948)
Chris Evans (1920)
D. B. Evans (1925)
D. D. Evans (1922)
D. M. Evans (1931)
D.W.Evans (1926)
Denver Evans (1945)
E. Evans (1893)
Edgar Evans (1932)
Elwyn Evans (1921)
Geo Evans (1912)
Rev. G. A. Evans (1931)
Gil Evans (1892)
Glyn Evans (1955)
Gwyn Evans (1936)
Gordon Evans (1952)
H. Evans (1909)
Islwyn Evans (1920)
Ieuan Evans (1946)
Jack Evans (1911)
(Gowerton)
J. G. Evans (1952)
Joe Evans (1906)
(Pontardawe)
Joe Evans (1929)
Lewis Evans (1932)
Llew Evans (1926)
Lyn Evans (1928)
Mort Evans (1924)
P. Evans (1923)
Phil Evans (1913)
Pross. Evans (1948)
R. Evans (1896)
R. C. Evans (1927)
Rhys Evans (1926)
T. Evans (1919)
T. J. Evans (1933)
(Tumble)
Tol. Evans (1923)
W. Rice Evans (1889)
? Everard (1875)

F

C. Farr (1880)
J. Faull (1953)
W. H. Faull (1925)
Capt. Fenning (1947)
? Firth (1886)
J. Flynn (1919)
D. Folland (1931)
B. Ford (1953)
T. Frame (1952)
? Francis (1906)
? Francis (1924)
G. Francis (1946)
W. J. Francis (1947)
A. Freer (1901)
V. Friend (1936)
B. Ford (1953)
F. Fuller (1895)
H. Fuller (1906)

G

? Gammon (1886)
M. Gange (1950)
T. Gange (1946)
L. Ganz (1948)
V. Ganz (1948)
H. Gardner (1901)
L. Gazzi (1950)
E. Gethin (1922)
J. Godfrey (1919)
E. S. Goff (1909)
S. Goldsworthy (1884)
F. Gordon (1894)
H. Gordon (1893)
W. Gordon (1893)
E. Gorman (1946)
A. Green (1874)
Llew Green (1874)
H. Greville (1948)
D. J. Grey (1919)
Evan Grey (1919)
? Grey (1894)
F. Grey (1950)
Joe Grey (1923)
W. Grey (1894)
? Griffiths (1888)
B. Griffiths (1924)
B. Griffiths (1936)
B. Griffiths (1945)
D. Griffiths (1907)
(Pontardawe)
E. Griffiths (1927)
E. Griffiths (1946)
Gwyn Griffiths (1934)
Gwyn Griffiths (1952)
H. Griffiths (1925)
H. Griffiths (1950)
J. Griffiths (1949)
J. Griffiths (1950)
L. Griffiths (1937)
Mal Griffiths (1932)
T. Griffiths (1948)
T. J. Griffiths (1950)
W. Griffiths (1893)
W. Griffiths (1919)
W. S. Griffiths (1934)
G. Grimshaw (1925)
S. Groot (1879)
C. Grove (1946)
P. Guppy (1937)
E. Guy (1931)
E. Gwiliam (1931)
? Gwilym (1878)
D. Gwynn (1878)
W. H. Gwynn (1880)
E. Gwynne (1920)

H

M. Halfpenny (1955)
T. Hallet (1952)
R. Hamblin (1955)
? Hansard (1892)
Rowe Harding (1920)
B. Harries (1945)
J. Harries (1883)
W. Harries (1930)
W. J. Harries (1925)
A. Prosser-Harris (1950)
C. Harris (1891)
D. Harris (1898)
E. Harris (1898)
Evan Harris (1927)
H. Harris (1938)
Neville Harris (1953)
T. Harris (1884)
T. Harris (1898)
Wren Harris (1927)
W. C. Harris (1931)
A. Harry (1913)
B. Harry (1948)
G. Hayward (1905)
W. Hayward (1909)
H. Head (1874)
B. Hedges (1952)
T. Henry (1905)
I. Herbert (1931)
J. Herbert (1931)
J. Heyes (1938)
H. Hiams (1905)
? Hill (1901)
R. J. Hill (1911)
T. A. Hill (1927)
W. Hill (1927)
Rev. G. Hinton (1931)
J. Hitchings (1951)
F. Holbrook (1911)
B. Hollingdale (1912)
W. Holmes (1896)
? Hombersley (1875)
Hywel Hopkin (1948)
Dan Hopkins (1922)
D. J. Hopkins (1954)
Evan Hopkins (1926)
Islwyn Hopkins (1953)
John Hopkins (1945)
M. Hopkins (1930)
Phil. Hopkins (1902)
(Pontardawe)
S. Hopkins (1955)
T. G. Hopkins (1923)
T.H.Hopkins (1905)
T. T. Hopkins (1933)
Tom Hopkins (1926)
Tom Hopkins (1946)
W. D. B. Hopkins (1929)
B. J. Howells (1886)
E. Howells (1938)
G. Howells (1951)
Ioan Howells (1886)
J. Howells (1906)
J. Howells (1924)
Lyn Howells (1924)
Syd Howells (1934)
W. Howells (1931)
W. H. Howells (1921)
W. H. Howells (1887)
'Cato' Hughes (1892)
D. J. Hughes (1922)
E. Hughes (1931)

Owen Hughes	(1924)
Owen Hughes	(1952)
R. Hughes	(1908)
Cyril Humphries	(1946)
D. Hunt	(1921)
D. O. Hunt	(1939)
H. Hunt	(1903)
J. D. Hunt	(1936)
R. Huxtable	(1913)
W. A. Hyde	(1931)

I

A. Ingram	(1874)
P. Ingram	(1874)

J

H. Jackson	(1893)
T. Jackson	(1895)
W. Jackson	(1893)
M. Jacob	(1930)
Arthur James	(1951)
B. James	(1878)
Carwyn James	(1954)
David James	(1889)
Evan James	(1889)
Geo. James	(1887)
G. James	(1923)
J. C. James	(1875)
Ken James	(1951)
Perris James	(1951)
Sam James	(1899)
T. James	(1886)
W. James	(1888)
D. Jeffreys	(1875)
G. Jeffreys	(1947)
W. J. Jeffreys	(1919)
A. M. Jenkin	(1893)
R. S. Jenkin	(1893)
A. Jenkins	(1893)
A. E. Jenkins	(1919)
A. O. Jenkins	(1919)
A. W. Jenkins	(1948)
Bryan Jenkins	(1952)
D. Jenkins	(1930)
D. Jenkins	(1936)
D. R. Jenkins	(1924)
D. K. Jenkins	(1925)
E. Jenkins	(1893)
Gwili Jenkins	(1938)
Graham Jenkins	(1950)
G. Jenkins	(1936)
H. Jenkins	(1896)
J. D. Jenkins	(1926)
J. E. Jenkins	(1954)
J. W. Jenkins	(1947)
Joe Jenkins	(1936)
K. Jenkins	(1955)
Lewis Jenkins	(1905)
Loughor Jenkins	(1922)
Oswold Jenkins	(1910)
Owen Jenkins	(1913)
Plummer Jenkins	(1928)
R. Jenkins	(1893)
R. Jenkins	(1898)
R. S. Jenkins	(1893)
Tom Jenkins	(1901)
W. Jenkins	(1893)
W. R. Jenkins	(1931)
I. Jeremiah	(1923)
S. Jerram	(1912)
Glyn John	(1947)
Howard John	(1950)
J. H. John	(1912)
Llew John	(1951)
? Johns	(1893)
W. D. Johnson	(1948)
A. Jones	(1906)
Alan Jones	(1946)
Alan Jones (Gorseinon)	(1956)
Dr. A. Jones	(1948)
Ben Jones	(1924)
Brian Jones	(1936)
C. Jones	(1919)
C. Jones	(1931)
Chris Jones	(1955)
Cliff Jones	(1935)
D. Jones	(1927)
D. Jones	(1938)
Dai Jones	(1931)
Dai Jones	(1945)
Dan Jones	(1919)
D. H. Jones	(1948)
D. J. Jones	(1912)
Denzil Jones	(1947)
Doug Jones	(1947)
E. Jones	(1928)
E. A. H. Jones	(1924)
Edgar Jones	(1933)
Elvet Jones	(1945)
Elwyn Jones (Tumble)	(1953)
Emrys Jones	(1912)
E. M. Jones	(1875)
E. R. Jones	(1951)
F. C. Jones	(1878)
G. Jones	(1925)
G. C. Jones	(1955)
Gilbert Jones	(1936)
Glyn Jones	(1930)
Gough Jones	(1949)
Dr. Graham Jones	(1946)
Guy Jones	(1948)
Gwynn Jones	(1950)
G. C. Jones	(1955)
H. Jones	(1946)
Harold Jones	(1923)
H. C. Jones	(1879)
Howard Jones (Abercrave)	(1946)
Howie Jones	(1930)
H. Prosser-Jones	(1948)
Ian Jones	(1954)
J. Jones	(1950)
Jack Jones	(1925)
Jim Jones	(1919)
Jim Jones	(1927)
Joe Jones	(1923)
Johnny Jones	(1925)
K. Jones	(1948)

Lewis Jones (1921)
Llew Jones (1920)
Malc. Jones (1935)
Mars. Jones (1919)
M. F. Jones (1877)
Mog Jones (1922)
M. S. Jones (1875)
M. T. Jones (1878)
Nort. Jones (1934)
Paul Jones (1892)
R. Jones (1899)
Ray Jones (1954)
Reg Jones (1933)
Roy Jones (1924)
Stan Jones (1931)
S. L. Jones (1936)
T. Jones (1899)
T. Jones (1922)
Terry Jones (1948)
T. L. Jones (1895)
Tom Jones (1925)
Tom Jones (1952)
(Glynneath)
W. Jones (1882)
W. E. Jones (1936)
W. H. Jones (1887)
Wilf Jones (1948)
Will Jones (1919)
W. J. Jones (1931)
W. O. Jones (1925)
W. R. Jones (1930)
Fred Joseph (1907)
Lando Joseph (1950)
Will Joseph (1899)

K

J. Kelman (1886)
F. Kendell (1877)
W. Kift (1907)
T. Kingdom (1936)
J. Kingdom (1936)
? Kneath (1881)
H. R. Knill (1874)

L

? Lancey (1905)
G. Lande (1910)
W. Lang (1936)
J. Lang (1936)
R. Lang (1953)
T. Langley (1933)
F. Lavis (1907)
C. D. Lawrence (1953)
C. G. S. Lawrence (1953)
D. S. Leigh (1934)
J. Leleu (1952)
D. Lenihan (1919)
H. B. Letcher (1888)
Albert Lewis (1924)
Alf Lewis (1891)
Arthur Lewis (1891)
B. Lewis (1909)
D. Lewis (1947)
F. Lewis (1908)
Gwyn Lewis (1930)
Gwyn Lewis (1953)
H. Lewis (1910)
I. Lewis (1947)
I. D. Lewis (1948)
J. Lewis (1911)
J. Lewis (1951)
J. E. P. Lewis (1886)
J. H. Lewis (1875)
J. W. Lewis (1911)
K. W. Lewis (1950)
P. Lewis (1948)
R. Lewis (1923)
Ron Lewis (1948)
R. J. Lewis (1936)
Tom Lewis (1923)
Trevor Lewis (1945)
W. Lewis (1886)
W. Lewis (1923)
W. Lewis (1930)
W. Lewis (1945)
W. Lewis (1953)
W. A. T. Lewis (1931)
Windsor Lewis (1927)
W. J. Lewis (1911)
Rowland Ley (1948)
(Llansamlet)
R. Ling (1926)
J. Littlejohn (1939)
B. Livingstone (1893)
R. Livingstone (1892)
D. Llewellyn (1945)
J. Llewellyn (1950)
B. Lloyd (1954)
E. Lloyd (1953)
H. Lloyd (1947)
H. L. Lloyd (1946)
O. Lloyd (1934)
P. Lloyd (N.O.R.) (1924)
J. Lockyer (1905)
A. Lodwick (1947)
Edgar Long (1925)
N. Long (1948)
J. Longdon (1889)
D. Lowe (1878)
? Ludlow (1886)
? Luly (1886)

M

T. Mabbett (1924)
A. Mainwaring (1951)
D. Mainwaring (1892)
H. Mainwaring (1952)
D. P. Manley (1926)
A. W. Marchant (1931)
J. Marker (1953)
L. Marker (1948)
P. Martin (1954)
? Mathews (1920)
A. Matthews (1887)
D. Matthews (1936)
E. Matthews (1946)
H. Matthews (1888)
H. Matthews (1934)
I. Matthews (1925)
F. F. Meager (1875)

J. Meredith (1886)
R. Messer (1894)
C. Michael (1931)
G. Michael (1921)
L. V. Michael (1931)
W. Midet (1920)
F. Mills (1892)
? Mitchell (1919)
D. Moran (1946)
C. Morgan (1875)
D. Morgan (1884)
D. Morgan (1937)
Dan Morgan (1905)
E. Morgan (1891)
E. Morgan (1937)
Edgar Morgan (Pontardawe) (1907)
F. Morgan (1895)
F. Morgan (1936)
Geo Morgan (1930)
Glyn Morgan (1948)
Goronwy Morgan (1951)
Guy Morgan (1926)
Herbie Morgan (1907)
Ivor Morgan (1905)
J. Morgan (1886)
J. Morgan (1937)
J. Norwyn Morgan (1953)
Jonah Morgan (1893)
J. P. Morgan (1928)
Leonid Morgan (1948)
L. C. Morgan (1945)
N. R. Morgan (1946)
R. L. Morgan (1930)
Sam Morgan (1927)
Steve Morgan (1934)
T. Morgan (1907)
Dr. Teddy Morgan (1908)
Tom Morgan (1892)
Tom Morgan (1936)
W. Morgan (1878)
W. H. Morgan (1937)
W. R. Morgan (1934)
A. Morris (1936)
Arwyn Morris (1950)
D. Morris (1936)
G. E. Morris (1882)
G. L. Morris (1878)
I. Morris (1888)
I. Morris (Hendy) (1921)
Ivor Morris (1920)
J. Morris (1879)
J. Morris (1913)
P. Morris (1895)
R. R. Morris (1930)
Y. Morris (1924)
? Morrison (1877)
G. Morse (1946)
O. Morse (1947)
H. Moulton (1909)
?. Moxham (1875)
A. Moxham (1893)
B. Mullins (1954)
H. P. Murphy (1953)
W. P. Murphy (1937)

N

? Nettall (1899)
? Nicholas (1878)
Tom Nicholas (1906)
W. Nicholas (1937)
? Norman (1888)
F. Nurse (1919)
T. Nurse (1937)

O

Tony O'Connor (1953)
R. Oldham (1893)
J. Orrin (1886)
Bruno Orsi (1952)
Albert Owen (1923)
'Dodger' Owen (1912)
G. Owen (1931)
P. Owen (1909)
R. Owen (1899)
S. Owen (1892)
W. H. Owen (1926)

P

? Paddison (1908)
D. J. Paddock (1936)
Bert Palmer (1920)
Frank Palmer (1919)
Fred Palmer (1923)
L. Palmer (1917)
R. Palmer (1950)
Tom Palmer (1920)
A. Pape (1946)
A. Parker (1923)
Dai Parker (1923)
C. Parker (1925)
S. Parker (1919)
T. Parker (1934)
Tom Parker (1913)
W. Parker (1893)
D. Parkhouse (1955)
W. G. A. Parkhouse (1948)
W. Parkyn (1886)
J. Parry (1938)
L. Parry (1938)
G. Payne (1881)
Harry Payne (1931)
Harry Payne (Skewen) (1952)
R. Peachey (1953)
? Pearce (1889)
L. Pearce (1948)
? Percival (1913)
? Pedrick (1923)
A. L. B. Percival (1924)
W. H. Perrett (1936)
H. C. Perry (1927)
? Peters (1877)
Bryn Peters (1923)
T. Petherbridge (1945)
E. Peterson (1875)
Bryn Phillips (1952)
D. Phillips (1878)

D. Phillips	(1938)
Elvet Phillips	(1945)
G. Phillips	(1879)
G. Phillips	(1931)
Horace Phillips	(1950)
J. Phillips	(1946)
John Phillips	(1936)
O. Phillips	(1947)
P. Phillips	(1888)
R. N. Phillips	(1886)
S. Phillips	(1925)
T. Phillips	(1922)
? Pike	(1906)
Harold Powell	(1937)
J. Prescott	(1892)
F. Presley	(1930)
? Price	(1907)
D. Price	(1923)
D. Price	(1950)
Edgar Price	(1925)
E. D. Price ('Iago')	(1936)
S. Price	(1923)
G. Prior	(1936)
? Pritchard	(1875)
E. Prothero-Thomas	(1930)
D. R. Prosser	(1930)
?. Pugsley	(1887)
T. Pugsley	(1911)
N. Pugh	(1931)

Q

M. Quirk	(1951)

R

J. Randall	(1946)
? Rapsey	(1903)
J. Rapsey	(1908)
H. Rawlings	(1919)
Aubrey Rees	(1935)
A. M. Rees	(1935)
'Billo' Rees	(1920)
B. G. Rees	(1951)
Dan Rees	(1898)
Denver Rees	(1928)
D. G. Rees	(1948)
Elvet Rees	(1924)
Elvet Rees	(1950)
Elvet Rees	(1955)
E. J. Rees	(1952)
F. Rees	(1922)
Fred Rees	(1906)
Fred Rees	(1926)
Geo Rees	(1930)
Gerwyn Rees	(1948)
Glyn Rees	(1948)
G. J. Rees	(1949)
Gwynfil Rees	(1938)
H. Rees (Skewen)	(1927)
Hubert Rees	(1923)
D. Idwal Rees	(1928)
Ivor Rees	(1919)
Jack Rees	(1926)
Jack Rees	(1930)
Jim Rees	(1955)
Joe Rees	(1919)
Mog Rees	(1919)
Owen Rees	(1922)
R.Rees	(1951)
Ray Rees	(1936)
Rhys Rees	(1902)
T. F. Rees	(1936)
Tom Rees	(1925)
Tom Rees	(1945)
Vic Rees	(1935)
W. Rees	(1886)
W. P. Rees	(1919)
E.Reid	(1886)
? Reynolds	(1898)
Sam Rice	(1892)
P. C. M. Rice	(1925)
B. Richards	(1955)
C. Richards	(1887)
E. S. Richards	(1884)
Handel Richards	(1909)
H. Richards	(1951)
I. Richards	(1946)
Ken Richards	(1952)
Ron Richards	(1934)
W. Richards	(1895)
Will Richards	(1927)
W. Richards	(1922)
A Richardson	(1875)
H. Richardson	(1908)
Chas. Riches	(1875)
Cuthbert Riches	(1875)
T. Roach	(1926)
D. Roach	(1926)
A. Roberts	(1909)
E. Roberts	(1890)
Gerald Roberts	(1954)
Glyn Roberts (Skewen)	(1927)
J. Roberts	(1955)
T. Roberts	(1879)
T. Roberts	(1892)
V. W. Roberts	(1950)
Will Roberts	(1926)
W. H. Roberts	(1934)
? Robertson	(1877)
?. Robinson	(1895)
H. Robinson	(1877)
J. Roderick	(1937)
D. Rogers	(1946)
M. Rogers	(1955)
? Romans	(1899)
? Rosser	(1878)
Ivor Rowlands (Skewen)	(1954)
J. R. Rowland	(1946)
W. Rowland	(1946)
C. F. Rowlands	(1951)
P. Rowlands	(1920)
T. Russell	(1892)

S

K. Sage	(1947)
Denzil Sambrook	(1946)
Glyn Samuel	(1935)
Dai Samuel	(1890)
Jack Samuel	(1890)
W. J. Samuel	(1947)

D. Sanders (1951)
I. B. Sanders (1946)
? Saunders (1887)
? Saunders (1909)
Odo Saunders (1928)
Owen Saunders (1921)
C. K. Saxton (N.Z.) (1945)
F. Scale (1905)
Fred Scrine (1895)
Dr. M. Shapiro (1937)
L. J. Shaw (1947)
P. Shefford (1908)
J. Shepherd (1911)
R. Shepherd (1912)
L. Shipton (1924)
W. E. Shugg (1881)
? Sims 1896)
T. Slattery (1933)
Aubrey Smith (1900)
C. Smith (1892)
D. Smith (1896)
Edgar Smith (1911)
J. Smith (1892)
J. A. S. Smith (1904)
Ted Smith (1892)
W. (Bill) Smith (1892)
W. R. Smith (1924)
R. Smitham (1921)
M. Snipper (1930)
N. Sparrow (1946)
W. Stanton (1921)
? Stephens (1878)
G. Stephens (1950)
Rhys Stephens (1952)
? Stevens (1877)
P. Stone (1954)
R. Stone (1925)
W. Stone (1925)
? Stroud (1899)
P. Studdart (1883)
T. Sullivan (1936)
C. S. Sutton (1875)
H. E. Sutton (1875)
Roy Sutton (1948)
D. G. Swain (1947)
E. Sweet (1881)
W. Symonds (1901)

T

C. Tanner (1893)
H. Tanner (1934)
I. Tanner (1945)
W. Tanner (1920)
D. Tarr (1933)
E. J. Tarr (1934)
D. H. Taylor (1934)
G. H.Taylor (1933)
W. J. Taylor (1933)
Abel Thomas (1948)
A. C. Thomas (1948)
Alf Thomas (1913)
Alun Thomas (1946)
B. Thomas (1893)
B. Thomas (1934)
C. Thomas (1898)
D. Thomas (1909)
(Pontardawe)
D. Thomas (1927)
(Danygraig)
Dorian Thomas (1938)
Dan Thomas (1934)
D. F. Thomas (1930)
D. H. Thomas (1930)
Dorian Thomas (1938)
D. J. Thomas (1901)
(Dunvant)
Dudley Thomas (1951)
D. Edgar Thomas (1930)
D. Bruce Thomas (1953)
E. Thomas (1913)
(Gowerton)
E.Thomas (1931)
Emrys Thomas (1923)
Glyn Thomas (1926)
Gwyn Thomas (1934)
Glyn Thomas (1936)
H. Thomas (1900)
H. Thomas (1921)
(Gowerton)
Hadyn Thomas (1934)
Harold Thomas (1901)
Harold Thomas (1923)
Harvey Thomas (1908)
Herbert Thomas (1948)
Idris Thomas (1930)
Ivor Thomas (1924)
J. Thomas (1886)
J. Thomas (1908)
J. D. Thomas (1930)
J. W. Thomas (1878)
L. Thomas (1954)
L. G.Thomas (1938)
M.Thomas (1948)
Ned Thomas (1950)
Percy Thomas (1950)
R. (Bob) Thomas (1892)
R. Thomas (1946)
R. C. C. Thomas (1948)
R. H. Thomas (1937)
S. Thomas (1937)
T. Thomas (1922)
(Skewen)
T. L.Thomas (1936)
T. R.Thomas (1919)
V. Thomas (1955)
W. Thomas (1874)
Watcyn Thomas (1928)
Willie Thomas (1906)
W. H. Thomas (1928)
W. L.Thomas (1936)
E. Thorogood (1886)
H. Thorogood (1882)
C. Tickfield (1874)
H. Toft (1906)
J. Toft (1906)
W. H. Towers (1887)
V. Tossell (1936)
G. Tregidon (1953)
G. Treharne (1950)
? Trevellion (1875)
Harry Trew (1909)
J. B. Trew (1882)
Vic Trew (1952)
W. J. Trew (1898)

W. J. Trew Jnr	(1927)
? Trick	(1891)
A. Trosei	(1946)
D. Troy	(1927)
John Troy	(1928)
? Tubb	(1877)
E. Tucker	(1937)
H. Tucker	(1893)
W. Tucker	(1922)
J. P. Tyler	(1930)
? Tyrell	(1920)

V

E. Vincent	(1954)

W

T. Walkey	(1946)
T. T. Walsh	(1878)
L. Walsh	(1878)
Maurice Walsh	(1907)
C. F. Walters	(1926)
H. Walters	(1936)
Hopkin Walters	(1945)
Ron Walters	(1938)
T. Walters	(1945)
W. Walters	(1945)
Stan Walter	(1948)
? Ward	(1877)
C. Ward	(1928)
W. Ward	(1886)
W. D. Ward	(1945)
P. Warren	(1874)
A. Waters	(1911)
J. Elwyn Watkins	(1927)
Jack Watkins	(1927)
? Webber	(1913)
? Wedge	(1880)
T. G. Wells	(1937)
A. Whapham	(1886)
H. Whapham	(1892)
A. Wheeler	(1919)
D. White	(1934)
G. White	(1931)
Geo White	(1923)
Joe White	(1930)
P. White	(1945)
T. White	(1897)
G. Whitton	(1934)
B. J. Wilkie	(1921)
G.Wilkie	(1930)
J. Wilcox	(1892)
Tom Wilkins	(1921)
? Williams (Dunvant)	(1901)
? Williams (Llansamlet)	(1920)
Albert Williams	(1905)
Albert Williams	(1923)
A. Williams	(1874)
Ben Williams	(1912)
Ben Williams	(1933)
C. Williams	(1886)
Clive Williams	(1934)
Colin Williams	(1936)
D. Williams	(1875)
D. Williams	(1894)
Dai Williams	(1913)
D. F. Williams	(1926)
D. M. Williams	(1927)
Doug Williams	(1930)
D. J. Williams	(1907)
Eddie Williams	(1922)
Ernie Williams	(1922)
E. Williams	(1938)
E. Williams	(1948)
Ernest Williams	(1949)
Frank Williams	(1910)
Frank Williams	(1947)
Glan Williams	(1937)
Glyn Williams	(1922)
Glyn Williams	(1930)
G. R. Williams	(1933)
Gwyn Williams	(1924)
Dr. Gwyn Williams	(1948)
Gwyn Williams	(1955)
H. Williams	(1906)
H Williams	(1895)
Howel Williams	(1910)
Ike Williams	(1908)
Jack Williams	(1893)
John Williams	(1938)
J. H. Williams	(1896)
Ken Williams	(1948)
Ken Williams	(1956)
Peter Williams	(1950)
Phil Williams	(1921)
R. (Dick) Williams	(1907)
Ron Williams	(1931)
Rees Williams	(1934)
Rhys Williams	(1936)
R. Williams	(1945)
Stan Williams	(1913)
S. Williams	(1948)
T. (Canary) Williams	(1886)
T. Williams	(1890)
Tom Williams	(1909)
T. R. Williams	(1938)
Teifion Williams	(1951)
Tudor Williams	(1920)
Tudor Williams	(1951)
W. Williams	(1886)
W. Williams	(1933)
W. B. Williams	(1901)
W. D. Williams	(1934)
W. D. Williams	(1948)
W. J. Williams	(1895)
W. J. Williams	(1937)
W. O. Williams	(1949)
? Witts	(1888)
A. J. Wolfe	(1886)
W. Wolfe	(1886)
? Wylie	(1979)
I. Wynne	(1952)

Y

E. G. Yates	(1953)
E. Youatt	(1931)
D. H. E. Young	(1953)
G. W. Young	(1953)

Appendix 1(b)

'ALL WHITES' 1956–1995

A

Mark Adams (1991)
W. Alexander (1958)
Ogwen Alexander (1968)
H. Allen (1965)
Chris Anthony (1994)
Roy Anthony (1957)
Robin Appleyard (1992)
Mark Arnal (1977)
Mark Arnold (1972)
Paul Arnold (1987)
Gwyn Ashby (1972)
Geoff Atherton (1965)

B

Doug Baker (1960)
Jason Ball (1992)
David Banner (1974)
Stephen Barclay (1992)
Colin Basey (1970)
Ron Bateman (1965)
Norman Bater (1962)
Steve Bater (1976)
Geoff Bayliss (1962)
K. Beal (1969)
Dewi Bebb (1958)
Mark Bennett (1990)
B. Beresford (1980)
Ian Bernard (1974)
M. Bernard (1988)
Phil Bessant (1968)
F. Bevan (1962)
H. Bevan (1986)
R. Bevan (1984)
J. Beynon (1971)
R. Beynon (1973)
Meirion Bishop (1971)
L. Blackmore (1984)
Terry Bluck (N.Z.) (1988)
John Blyth (1981)
Roger Blyth (1968)
Roddy Boobyer (1994)
Chris Boker (1984)
Andrew Booth (1993)
Peter Borthwick (1962)
D. Bourne (1964)
A. Bowen (1964)
B. Bowen (1980)
Bleddyn Bowen (1988)
D. Bowen (1964)
Hylton Bowen (1969)
Ron Bowen (1965)
J. Boyle (1981)
Chris Bradshaw (1988)
Keith Bradshaw (1966)
Ian Brown (1986)
J. Brown (Bonymaen) (1982)
Ken Brown (1961)
Simon Bryant (1984)
Ian Buckett (1988)
T. Bunce (1987)
Jeff Butt (1961)
John Butt (1962)

C

Adrian Cambriani (1979)
Philip Came (1975)
John Campodonic (1963)
K. Charles (1974)
C. Charvis (1994)
Trevor Cheeseman (1975)
Ben Childs (1988)
David Churchill (1991)
Chris Clarke (1992)
Rody Clarke (1960)
Nigel Clarke (1976)
Steward Clarke (1971)
Barry Clegg (1972)
Anthony Clement (1985)
John Clement (1968)
Mike Clement (1985)
Paul Clement (1972)
Jim Clifford (1959)
Perry Close (1958)
Darryl Cole (1966)
D. Coles (1988)
Keith Colclough (1978)
Maurice Colclough (1984)
Jeremy Cooper (1981)
B. Cornelius (1978)
C. Coslett (1980)
K. Coslett (1974)
Mark Cotton (1985)
Ron Cowan (1960)
P. Cowle (1963)
Eifion Cox (1961)

Brian Creswell (1958)
D. Cross (1967)

D

Malcolm Dacey (1978)
M. David (1994)
Adrian Davies (1991)
Brian Davies (1965)
Colin Davies (Amman) (1971)
David Davies (1956)
Dai Davies (1961)
D. L. Davies (1958)
Don Davies (1970)
E. Davies (1995)
Eddie Davies (1961)
Gareth Davies (1994)
Geraint Davies (1990)
Geoff Davies (1967)
Geoff Davies (1982)
Gerald Davies (1963)
Godfrey Davies (1966)
Gordon Davies (1970)
Graham Davies (1981)
H. Davies (1988)
H. Davies (1977)
Huw Davies (1967)
Ian Davies (1976)
Ian Davies (Amman) (1987)
James Davies (1970)
Jeff Davies (1980)
Jeffrey Davies (1970)
John Davies (Cwmgorse) (1970)
John Davies (Llanelli) (1972)
John Davies (Narberth) (1973)
John Davies (1964)
J. M. Davies (Trebanos) (1971)
Ken Davies (1958)
Kevin Davies (1994)
Lee Davies (1993)
Len Davies (Trimsaran) (1956)
Mervyn Davies (1972)
Mark Davies (1979)
Martin Davies (1967)
Martyn Davies (Dunvant) (1967)
Mike Davies (Tumble) (1971)
M. Davies (1983)
Nick Davies (1981)
N. Davies (1987)
N. Davies (1994)
Norman Davies (1961)
N. G. Davies (1956)
Paul Davies (1969)
Peter Davies (1962)
Phil Davies (Carmarthen) (1963)
Phil Davies (1974)
R. Davies (1975)
Ray Davies (1961)
Roger Davies (1967)
Rowland Davies (1985)
Simon Davies (1988)
Steve Davies (1979)
Stewart Davies (1972)
Stuart Davies (1963)
Stuart Davies (1985)
Tony Davies (1967)
Viv Davies (1965)
W. J. Davies (1969)
W. Davies (1966)
Brendan Dawson (1987)
Howard Delve (1977)
Nick Devonald (1982)
Lewis Dick (1976)
Brian Diment (1966)
Alan Dobbins (1965)
Alun Donovan (1976)
Carl Douglas (1981)
Clive Dyer (1962)
David Dyer (Carms.) (1971)
Robert Dyer (1970)

E

J. Ebsworth (1957)
D. Edwards (1988)
Don Edwards (1963)
Mansel Edwards (1961)
Mel Edwards (1961)
Neil Edwards (1979)
John Elias (1972)
Vernon Ellias (1957)
Paul Elliott (1976)
Bryn Ellis (1960)
Arthur Emyr (1980)
Garmon Emyr (1988)
Chris England (N.Z.) (1988)
Adrian Evans (1974)
Baden Evans (1971)
Brian Evans (Vardre) (1971)
Bryan Evans (1960)
Bryn Evans (Gorseinon) (1959)
David Evans (1959)
David Evans (1994)
Euros Evans (1989)
Gareth Evans (1969)
Gethin Evans (1981)
Huw Evans (1970)
Iestyn Evans (1991)
Jeremy Evans (1984)
John Evans (Cwmllynfell) (1961)
John Evans (Brynamman) (1969)
John Evans (1974)
Jonathan Evans (1990)
Justin Evans (Glais) (1993)
Loy Evans (1974)
Mark Evans (1993)

Mike Evans (1968)
Morrie Evans (1958)
P. Evans (1959)
Raymond Evans (1969)
Ray Evans (Aberystwyth) (1974)
Richard Evans (1990)
Robert Evans (Gowerton) (1961)
Roy Evans (1961)
Stuart Evans (1982)
Trevor Evans (1970)

F

Alan Fall (1966)
Tony Farthing (1963)
Stuart Ferguson (1964)
D. Ferrant (1960)
Idwal Fisher (1960)
Clive Ford (1972)
Michael Ford (N.Z.) (1984)
Jason Forster (1993)
Steve Forster (1985)
Lyndon Frame (1962)
Tony Francis (1968)

G

Norman Gale (1957)
Paul Gallaher (1982)
E. Gardiner (Cwmavon) (1962)
Kevin George (1985)
P. George (1994)
Leighton Gerrard (1988)
Denis Gethin (1963)
Scott Gibbs (1990)
Colin Gibson (1991)
John Gibson (1972)
Huw Gilson (1982)
Alwyn Gittings (1965)
T. Gootridge (1978)
M. Greaves (1988)
Jon Greenslade (1993)
Terry Greenslade (1966)
Brynmor Grey (1966)
Peter Griffin (1958)
B. H. Griffiths (1957)
Howell Griffiths (1972)
L. Griffiths (1980)
Lyn Griffiths (1993)
Michael Griffiths (1971)
M. Griffiths (1983)
Royston Griffiths (1963)
Simon Griffiths (1991)
John Grise (1984)
D. Gronow (1963)
Ken Guard (1961)

H

Ian Hall (1981)
Peter Hamer (1962)
Roger Harding (1957)
A. Harris (1986)
A. Harris (1995)
David Harris (1963)
D. Harrison (1980)
Len Hartland (1958)
Robin Harvard (1984)
Clive Haste (1984)
David Hawkins (1961)
David Hawkins (1994)
Malcolm Henwood (1968)
Jeff Herdman (1971)
A. Hewson (1980)
P. Heywood (1964)
J. Hicks (1976)
Gwynfor Higgins (1973)
Chris Higgs (1967)
Andy Hill (1971)
Colin Hillman (1985)
John Hinton (1969)
C. Hodges (1966)
Mike Holding (1991)
D. Holland (1992)
A. Hopkins (1986)
Cellan Hopkins (1994)
Gerard Hopkins (1969)
Hywel Hopkins (1976)
Ian Hopkins (1970)
I. Hopkins (1975)
John Hopkins (1956)
Kevin Hopkins (1982)
Norman Hopkins (1964)
R. Hopkins (1967)
R. Hopkins (1978)
A. Horseford (1987)
B. Howells (1977)
B. Howells (1992)
Brian Howells (1957)
Don Howells (1969)
J. Howells (1968)
M. Howells (1965)
Odwyn Howells (1970)
John Hudson (1985)
Brynmor Hughes (1976)
D. Hughes (1963)
J. Hughes (1966)
Ken Hughes (1962)
P. Hughes (1986)
Richard Hughes (1974)
Bill Hullin (1962)
Peter Hunt (1968)
S Hurley (1988)
Chris Hutchings (1982)
Roger Hyndman (1969)

I

Howard Iles (1976)
Lloyd Isaac (1990)
John Isaacs (1961)
Ken Isaacs (1982)

J

D. Jacka (1961)
D. Jacobs (1994)
B. James (1988)
D. James (1973)

D. James (1986)
David James (1964)
David James (1975)
John James (1963)
Kevin James (1981)
Mel James (1967)
Mike James (1968)
Nick James (1991)
Rhys James (1978)
Steffan James (1968)
Trevor James (1971)
Viv James (1958)
Charles Janczewski (1972)
G Jarvis (1971)
Ian Jeffries (1984)
John Jeffries (1957)
Alan Jenkins (1971)
Billy Jenkins (1972)
Colin Jenkins (1969)
Craig Jenkins (1992)
D. Jenkins (1977)
Danny Jenkins (1975)
David Jenkins (1973)
(Neath)
G. Jenkins (1986)
Garin Jenkins (1990)
Gareth Jenkins (1975)
Harry Jenkins (1966)
Huw Jenkins (1968)
(Morriston)
John Jenkins (1985)
K. Jenkins (1976)
Peter Jenkins (1965)
Steffan Jenkins (1991)
Warren Jenkins (1958)
Gareth John (1957)
Gareth John (1969)
Gareth John (1978)
(Skewen)
Gareth John (1979)
(Waunarlwydd)
John John (1965)
R. John (1981)
Colin Johnson (1956)
P. Johnson (1988)
A. Jones (1988)
Alan Jones (1958)
B. Jones (1986)
Brian Jones (1966)
Brian Jones (1968)
(Cwmllynfell)
Christopher Jones (1986)
Dan Jones (1965)
Darryl Jones (1963)
David Jones (1982)
Douglas Jones (1963)
D. Jones (1986)
Elfan Jones (1961)
Eric Jones (1967)
G. Jones (1978)
Gareth Jones (1968)
(Llanelli)
Gerwyn Jones (1970)
Huw Jones (1959)
Ian Jones (1957)
Ieuan Jones (1964)
Ieuan Jones (1976)
Iwan Jones (1993)
(Llanelli)
Keiron Jones (1980)
Kevin Jones (1984)
Lyndon Jones (1969)
M. Jones (1956)
Mark Jones (1987)
Martyn Jones (1967)
(Bryncoch)
Mike Jones (1971)
(Vardre)
Morlais Jones (1960)
Neil Jones (1976)
Omri Jones (1969)
Philip Jones (1975)
(Bryncoch)
Ray Jones (1969)
Rhodri Jones (1992)
Robert N. Jones (1983)
Robbie Jones (1991)
Robin Jones (1990)
Ron Jones (1967)
Ron Jones (1957)
(Crynant)
Ron Jones (1963)
(Penclawdd)
Roy Jones (1969)
(Penclawdd)
S. Jones (1988)
Steffan Jones (1990)
Timothy Jones (1977)
Viv Jones (1961)
W. Jones (1987)
David Joseph (1990)
John Joseph (1969)

K

Matthew Kehoe (1990)
Mark Keyworth (1972)
J. Kinsay (1991)

L

Jim Lamb (1964)
A. Lane (1980)
N. Lancett (1977)
Mike Langdon (1977)
Andrew Langford (1985)
P. Langford (1974)
James Langworth (1985)
D. O. Lawrence (1965)
Warren Leach (1992)
David Lee (1967)
Byron Lee (1968)
Alan Lewis (1973)
Guy Leleu (1980)
John Leleu (1957)
C. Lemon (1960)
Derek Leonard (1958)
Alan Lewis (1976)
(Llanelli)
Brian Lewis (1960)
David Lewis (1958)
Dennis Lewis (1970)

Eiryn Lewis (1960)
Gordon Lewis (1958)
Iestyn Lewis (1993)
Jamie Lewis (1992)
John Lewis (1959)
L. Lewis (1966)
Lindsay Lewis (1970)
M. Lewis (1988)
Mike Lewis (1977)
R. Lewis (1980)
Ron Lewis (1979)
Roy Lewis (1971)
Selwyn Lewis (1971)
Terry Lewis (1968)
(Resolven)
Wayne Lewis (1966)
B. Light (1975)
Barrie Llewellyn (1966)
Brian Llewellyn (1966)
Phil Llewellyn (1966)
Del Lloyd (1959)
Dewi Lloyd (1960)
Malcolm Lloyd (1964)
Rev. Ron Lloyd (1957)
Chris Loader (1992)
D. Lotter (1979)
N. Lucas (1973)
(Bonymaen)
J. Lythcoe (1991)

M

Andrew Macdonald (1963)
Tony Macdonald (1962)
P. Macgarry (1988)
J. Maclean (1957)
Jeff McAvoy (1982)
(Llandybie)
Robin McBryde (1990)
Chris McDonald (1994)
Sean McIntosh (1993)
S. McWilliams (1982)
P. Maddocks (1964)
Allan Mages (1963)
Benny Mainwaring (1966)
K. Markey (1966)
A. Marriott (1978)
David Marsden (1971)
Sean Marshal (1993)
Dean Mason (1980)
A Mathews (1956)
Bernard Matthews (1966)
Wayne Matthews (1991)
Alan Meredith (1971)
S. Meredith (1985)
Andrew Metcalfe (1992)
Tim Michael (1987)
B. Miers (1963)
Gilbert Miles (1964)
Andrew Moore (1993)
Carl Moore (1981)
Stephen Moore (1991)
Arwel Morgan (1968)
Brian Morgan (1961)
Brian Morgan (1976)
Christopher Morgan (1993)
David Morgan (1969)
David Morgan (1972)
(Cardiff)
David Morgan (1991)
Glan Morgan (1961)
Glyn Morgan (1964)
(Gowerton)
Glyn Morgan (1965)
(Brecon)
Glyn Morgan (1969)
Huw Morgan (1971)
John Morgan (1972)
(Gorseinon)
Mike Morgan (1987)
Paul Morgan (1984)
Ron Morgan (1993)
(Abercynon)
Stuart Morgan (1993)
Terry Morgan (1962)
Tony Morgan (1974)
Paul Moriarty (1983)
Richard Moriarty (1976)
Aubrey Morris (1961)
(Lampeter)
G. Morris (1962)
Glyn Morris (1969)
Gordon Morris (1956)
Graham Morris (1974)
Jackie Morris (1957)
John Morris (1960)
John Morris (1968)
(Resolven)
Lyn Morris (1974)
(Tumble)
Paul Morris (1984)
Wynford Morris (1964)
John Mudgeway (1986)
Byron Mugford (1968)
R Mynott (1992)

N

David Nehemiah (1960)
D. Neils (1979)
Philip Noble (1972)

O

Anthony O'Brien (1958)
D. Osborne (1962)
Bernard O'Shea (1956)
Craig Owen (1993)
D. Owen (1962)
G. Owen (1966)
R. Owen (1973)
(Abercrave)

P

Stuart Pardoe (1991)
Stuart Parfitt (1986)
D. Parker (1992)
Stuart Parker (1962)
G. Parry (1975)
Eric Patterson (1968)
Nigel Payne (1985)

Geoff Pearce (1969)
Graham Phennah (1982)
Hadyn Phillips (1956)
Howell Phillips (1992)
J. O. Phillips (1965)
Meirion Phillips (1960)
Phil Phillips (1965)
Simon Phillips (1988)
Andy Powell (1969)
Lyn Powell (1962)
Roger Powell (1973)
Roger Powell (1980)
Mike Power (1971)
Andrew Price (1991)
Colin Price (1964)
Gareth Price (1968)
K. Price (1986)
Kevin Price (1990)
Malcolm Price (1958)
Nigel Price (1977)
David Protheroe (1973)
Gerald Protheroe (1962)
Gerrard Protheroe (1969)
Michael Provis (1977)
Eifion Pugh (1975)
Hadyn Pugh (1957)
Jeremy Pugh (1985)
Ken Pugh (1961)
R. Pugh (1965)
W. Pugh (1988)
David Pullin (N.Z.) (1972)
Tommy Pullman (1969)

R

K. Rapson (1991)
J. Rawlings (1987)
A. Redmond (1992)
P. Reed (1991)
Alan Rees (1971)
Arwel Rees (1969)
David Rees (Bridgend) (1981)
Doug Rees (1966)
E. J. Rees (1956)
Gareth Rees (1969)
Greg Rees (1973)
H. Rees (1977)
Howard Rees (1961)
Howard Rees (1969)
Hugh Rees (Abercrave) (1976)
Jason Rees (1975)
Jason Rees (1992)
John Rees (Brynamman) (1973)
John Rees (1993)
Norman Rees (1969)
Ray Rees (1961)
Tony Rees (1965)
Alan Reynolds (1989)
C. Richards (1980)
D. Richards (1972)
J. Richards (1989)
Brian Roberts (1991)
D Roberts (1986)
Gareth Roberts (1977)
Gerald Roberts (Amman) (1956)
John Roberts (1962)
Keith Roberts (1976)
Terry Robbins (1958)
J. Robinson (1991)
R. Robinson (1977)
Cecil Roderick (1958)
Clive Roderick (1970)
Steve Rodliff (1984)
Derek Rogers (1963)
Alan Roper (1981)
Terry Rowan (1971)
Peter Rowe (1965)
Clive Rowlands (1966)
D. Rowlands (1957)
Keith Rowlands (1960)
Mike Ruddock (1980)
Alan Rutherford (1962)
Les Rutherford (1988)
Colin Rylance (1971)

S

Iestyn Samuel (1984)
Robert Sandry (1969)
M. Scheffler (1978)
John Selway (1962)
Dominic Setaro (1983)
Richard Shaw (1993)
M. Shepherd (1993)
Terry Sherrard (1967)
John Shore (1967)
John Simonson (1961)
C. Smart (1962)
Carl Smith (1969)
J. Smith (1980)
Malcolm Smith (1959)
S. Smith (1966)
Grayson Spurlock (1984)
R. Squibb (1971)
C. Stephens (1969)
Robert Stephens (1971)
Jeff Stevenson (1984)
Adrian Stewart (1987)
Greg Stirunt (1985)
Robert Subbiani (1985)
H. Summers (1992)
Andrew Sutton (1992)
R. Sweetman (1962)
Tony Swift (1979)

T

Neil Tashara (1979)
Bleddyn Taylor (1986)
Adrian Thomas (1971)
Andrew Thomas (1994)
Arwel Thomas (1993)
B. Thomas (1975)
Brian Thomas (Neath) (1958)
Brian Thomas (1959)
Brian Thomas (Vardre) (1971)
Brian Thomas (1984)

C. Thomas	(1961)
Christopher Thomas	(1977)
Christopher Thomas	(1993)
Chris Thomas	(1985)
Colin Thomas	(1970)
Colin Thomas	(1974)
Dai Thomas	(1958)
D. Thomas	(1962)
D. Thomas	(1978)
David Thomas	(1980)
Dean Thomas	(1994)
Dick Thomas	(1971)
Eifion Thomas	(1960)
Gareth Thomas	(1962)
Gareth Thomas (Llanelli)	(1960)
Geoff Thomas (Amman)	(1962)
Geoff Thomas	(1971)
Greg Thomas	(1984)
Gwyn Thomas	(1960)
Hugh Thomas (Llangennech)	(1968)
Huw Thomas	(1962)
Ian Thomas	(1993)
Iestyn Thomas	(1971)
J. Thomas	(1988)
John Thomas (Maesteg)	(1984)
D. King Thomas	(1964)
Lyn Thomas	(1964)
L. Thomas	(1988)
M. Thomas (Tondu)	(1982)
Marcus Thomas	(1994)
Mark Thomas	(1982)
Mike Thomas	(1960)
Myrddin Thomas	(1962)
Neil Thomas	(1984)
Noel Thomas	(1963)
Paul Thomas (Llandybie)	(1977)
Paul Thomas	(1984)
Peter Thomas	(1969)
Peter Thomas	(1974)
Randel Thomas	(1960)
Ray Thomas	(1956)
Rhydian Thomas	(1963)
Rhys Thomas (Crynant)	(1957)
Roy Thomas (Penclawdd)	(1965)
Terry Thomas	(1960)
Ken Thompson	(1981)
Steve Thornton	(1972)
Raymond Tilley	(1973)
Mark Titley	(1985)
Brian Toms	(1973)
D. Townsend	(1971)
Harry Trew	(1957)
Jeff Trotman	(1985)
J. Trott	(1957)
Mike Truman	(1973)
M. Truslove	(1988)
Ian Tyrell	(1969)
J. Tyrell	(1975)

U

Billy Upton	(1962)
Adrian Uren	(1966)

V

John Vaughan	(1969)
Richard Vaughan	(1963)

W

Andrew Walters	(1984)
G. Walters	(1977)
John Walters	(1973)
Lyn Wlaters	(1958)
Morley Walters	(1961)
Anthony Wake	(1992)
Stephen Ware	(1974)
Howard Watkins (Clydach)	(1963)
Hugh Watkins	(1984)
Ian Watkins	(1992)
K. Watkins	(1968)
Paul Watkins	(1984)
Ray Watkins	(1968)
Mark Waygood	(1984)
David Weatherley	(1994)
David Weaver	(1962)
John Weaver	(1959)
Neil Webb	(1972)
Richard Webster	(1985)
John Weidenbach	(1992)
Geoff Wheel	(1970)
Ken Wheelan	(1966)
Peter White	(1976)
Steve White	(1987)
Geoff Whitson	(1958)
David Wigley	(1985)
J. Willcoxson	(1960)
Adrian Wiliams (Abercrave)	(1987)
Alan Williams (Amman)	(1985)
Alan Williams (Kidwelly)	(1971)
Aled Williams	(1983)
B. Williams	(1977)
Barrie Williams	(1969)
Brynmor Williams	(1959)
Brynmor Williams	(1979)
Clem Williams	(1960)
Clive Williams	(1979)
Daniel Williams	(1983)
D. Williams	(1987)
Danny Williams	(1957)
Derek Williams	(1968)
E. Williams	(1974)
Elgar Williams	(1961)
Eurfyl Williams	(1959)
G. Williams	(1957)
G. Williams	(1975)
Gwynfor Williams	(1982)
Gwyn Williams	(1963)
Huw Williams	(1968)

Huw Williams (1987)
John Williams (1984)
(Ebbw Vale)
J. H. Williams (1961)
Ken Williams (1956)
K. Willliams (1979)
(Pontardawe)
Keith Williams (1978)
(N.D.S.)
Keith Williams (1984)
Kevin Williams (1976)
Lyn Williams (1965)
N. Williams (1986)
Paul Williams (1990)
Ray Williams (1958)
R. Williams (1988)
R. Williams (1982)
(Aberystwyth)
R. E. Williams (1985)
Rhodri Williams (1987)
Robert Williams (1990)
(Amman)
R. Williams (1966)
Steve Williams (1988)
Terry Williams (1962)
Wayne Williams (1974)
(Llanelli Wdrs.)
B. Willis (1964)
Leighton Winder (1993)
David Winslett (1969)
Phil Withers (1993)
M. Woods (1987)
Roy Woodward (1975)
Graham Wyatt (1971)
Mark Wyatt (1976)
Phil Wyntle (1993)

Y

Mike Yandle (1973)
Carl Yates (1985)
(Vardre)
David Young (1985)
Marsden Young (1958)

Appendix 2

SWANSEA RUGBY FOOTBALL CLUB PLAYING RECORDS SEASON BY SEASON

					Points		
Season	*P*	*W*	*D*	*L*	*For*	*Against*	*Honours*
1874/75							
1875/76	11	3	6	2			
1877/78							Cup Winners
1879/80							Cup Winners
1880/81	10	7	2	1			
1882/83							Cup Winners
1886/87							Cup Winners
1887/88	26	17	4	5	247	62	
1888/89	28	13	6	9	183	145	
1889/90	29	22	3	4	240	56	'Premiers'
1890/91	29	26	1	2	419	71	
1891/92	32	22	5	5	328	70	
1892/93	31	16	3	12	202	127	
1893/94	35	16	8	11	213	131	
1894/95	28	16	5	7	172	85	
1895/96	30	15	8	7	172	80	
1896/97	34	23	3	8	528	101	
1897/98	31	23	2	6	392	82	
1898/99	35	29	2	4	732	47	Champions
1899/00	32	31	0	1	586	57	Champions
1900/01	32	28	2	2	467	81	Champions
1901/02	32	25	4	3	503	62	Champions
1902/03	28	24	0	4	619	68	Runners-up
1903/04	32	30	1	1	571	38	Champions
1904/05	31	27	4	0	525	51	'Invincibles'
1905/06	32	22	2	8	275	109	
1906/07	30	24	3	3	304	63	
1907/08	32	28	1	3	373	65	

Season	P	W	D	L	Points For	Points Against	Honours
1908/09	33	2	2	4	368	97	Runners-up
1909/10	34	26	4	4	418	64	
1910/11							
1911/12	35	19	6	10			
1912/13	37	29	6	2	457	82	Champions
1913/14	36	24	5	7	326	111	
First World War							
1919/20	40	23	5	12	318	183	
1920/21	44	24	10	10			
1921/22	47	27	9	11	437	205	
1922/23	40	15	6	19	286	244	
1923/24	40	21	4	15	280	224	
1924/25	37	16	4	17	330	337	
1925/26	43	27	1	15	508	324	
1926/27	43	22	1	20	431	381	
1927/28	43	27	1	15	508	324	
1928/29	42	29	3	10	554	267	Welsh Champ. R.-Up
1929/30	41	30	3	8	589	215	Welsh Champ. R.-Up
1930/31	38	20	2	16	383	336	
1931/32	39	26	5	8	400	208	Welsh Champ. R.-Up
1932/33	39	19	6	14	427	229	
1933/34	39	21	1	15	364	214	
1934/35	42	26	5	11	426	238	
1935/36	37	22	1	14	341	196	
1936/37	35	17	4	14	321	228	
1937/38	37	24	0	13	440	221	
1938/39	38	19	5	14	312	230	
Second World War							
1946/47	35	19	3	13	354	235	
1947/48	43	27	3	13	394	190	
1948/49	42	29	4	9	439	248	
1949/50	43	29	3	11	476	226	
1950/51	38	24	4	10	334	183	
1951/52	37	18	6	13	327	297	
1952/53	40	22	4	14	304	243	
1953/54	42	20	7	15	380	328	
1954/55	38	14	3	21	249	290	
1955/56	39	20	4	15	353	285	
1956/57	46	25	13	8	403	309	

Season	P	W	D	L	*Points* For	Against	Honours
1957/58	40	17	4	19	333	322	
1958/59	39	21	6	12	427	256	
1959/60	38	22	6	10	475	239	
1960/61	45	25	5	15	482	325	
1961/62	41	14	7	20	307	245	
1962/63	39	19	3	17	313	291	
1963/64	44	24	4	16	464	292	
1964/65	49	26	3	20	557	457	
1965/66	44	21	4	19	450	301	
1966/67	48	18	4	26	414	440	
1967/68	50	29	5	16	554	417	
1968/69	48	17	4	27	599	545	
1969/70	52	17	3	32	512	646	
1970/71	46	33	1	12	650	414	
1971/72	50	24	4	24	796	705	
1972/73*	48	34	2	12	963	445	
1973/74	47	31	4	12	728	445	Merit Table Champs
1974/75	47	31	1	15	896	486	
1975/76	42	23	2	17	755	586	WRU Cup Finalists
1976/77	44	30	1	13	827	507	
1977/78	41	31	0	10	870	447	WRU Cup Winners
1978/79	40	27	2	11	693	381	WRU Cup Finalists
1979/80	46	40	1	5	1196	384	Welsh Champs., etc.
1980/81	47	41	1	5	1242	399	Merit Table Champs.
1981/82	43	32	1	10	1082	446	
1982/83	47	40	0	7	1131	577	Anglo-Welsh Champs., etc.
1983/84	51	32	0	19	1229	751	
1984/85	45	31	2	12	1102	638	
1985/86	49	30	1	18	1024	654	
1986/87	45	26	2	17	1032	654	WRU Cup Finalists
1987/88	47	29	1	17	1028	672	
1988/89	44	30	0	14	1110	691	
1989/90	44	30	1	13	1237	771	
1990/91	43	30	0	13	998	634	Hein'kn Champs. etc.
1991/92+	44	31	1	12	928	582	WRU Cup Finalists
1992/93	35	25	2	8	875	547	
1993/94	40	36	1	3	1185	552	Hein'ken Champs.
1994/95	41	27	0	14	948	747	WRU Cup Winners

* Try value increased to four points

+ Try value increased to five points

Notes.
Despite searching every avenue, it has not been possible to establish club records for the majority of seasons from 1874/75 to 1887/88. All those which have been found are included in the above listing. The number of points scored and conceded for those early years are not included for the same reason. In addition, no attempt has been made to unravel the mysteries of scoring values for the earliest seasons. As Smith and Williams[1] point out, the values varied with confusing frequency.

In modern times, the changes in try values were introduced in seasons 1972/73 (to 4 points), and 1991/92 (to 5 points). The foregoing records need to be read with those changes in mind.

Appendix 2(a)

THE HEINEKEN LEAGUE

The foregoing records relate to all games played, which in recent years, has included Schweppes or SWALEC cup matches, 'Club' matches, and those played in the Heineken League. Given the importance of the league competition in modern rugby, the 'Whites' record in the Heineken League since its inception is included in the following table.

HEINEKEN LEAGUE PERFORMANCE SEASON BY SEASON

SEASON	*P*	*W*	*D*	*L*	*F*	*A*	*Pts*	*League Position*
1990-91	18	9	0	9	353	309	18	8th
1991-92	18	13	1	4	393	205	26	1st – Champs
1992-93	22	17	0	5	548	326	34	3rd
1993-94	22	20	0	2	549	264	40	1st – Champs
1994-95	22	12	0	10	475	400	24	6th

1. *Fields of Praise* – D. Smith & G. Williams – the Official History of W.R.U.

Appendix 3

SWANSEA CLUB CAPTAINS

1874/75	C. C. Chambers
1875/76	C. C. Chambers
1876/77	F. F . Meager
1877/78	F .F . Meager
1878/79	F. F. Meager
1879/80	A. Richardson
1880/81	F. F. Meager
1881/82	G. L. Morris
1882/83	G. L. Morris
1883/84	E. S. Richards
1884/85	W. H. Gwynn
1885/86	W. H. Gwynn
1886/87	E. S. Richards
1887/88	E. S. Richards
1888/89	W. H. Towers
1889/90	W. Bowen
1890/91	W. Bowen
1891/92	W. Bowen
1892/93	S. Coke
1893/94	W. J. Bancroft
1894/95	E. Thorogood
1895/96	A. M. Jenkin
1896/97	W. J. Bancroft
1897/98	W. J. Bancroft
1898/99	W. J. Bancroft
1899/00	W. J. Bancroft
1900/01	W. J. Bancroft
1901/02	F. J. Gordon
1902/03	F. J. Gordon
1903/04	W. Parker
1904/05	F. J. Gordon
1905/06	F. J. Gordon
1906/07	W. J. Trew
1907/08	W. J. Trew
1908/09	W. J. Trew
1909/10	W. J. Trew
1910/11	W. J. Trew
1911/12	R. M. Owen
1912/13	W. J. Trew
1913/14	D. J. Thomas

First World War

1919/20	H. Lewis
1920/21	T. Parker
1921/22	R. Huxtable
1922/23	J. (Joe) Rees
1923/24	F. Palmer
1914/25	J. H. John
1925/26	J. E. Watkins
1926/27	J. E. Watkins
1927/28	D. S. Parker
1928/29	W. Rowe Harding
1929/30	R. Jones
1930/31	W. J. Trew (Jnr)
1931/32	J. (Jack) Rees
1932/33	B. Evans
1933/34	T. Day
1934/35	D.Thomas
1935/36	E. Long
1936/37	R. (Ronnie) Williams
1937/38	H. Payne
1938/39	W. E. Harris
1939/40	E. Morgan

Second World War

1946/47	D. J. Davies
1947/48	R. (Rees) Williams
1948/49	L. Davies
1949/50	B. Evans
1950/51	B. Evans
1951/52	L. Blyth
1952/53	R. Sutton
1953/54	W. D. Johnson
1954/55	R. C. C. Thomas
1955/56	W. O. Williams
1956/57	W. O. Williams
1957/58	T. (Teifion) Williams
1958/59	B. Richards
1959/60	G. Morris
1960/61	J. Leleu
1961/62	G. Lewis
1962/63	J. Faull
1963/64	D. Bebb
1964/65	D. Bebb
1965/66	M. Evans
1966/67	M. Thomas
1967/68	D. C. T. Rowlands
1968/69	C. Dyer
1969/70	S. Davies
1970/71	S. Davies
1971/72	P. Llewellyn
1972/73	M. (Mel) James
1973/74	R. Dyer
1974/75	A. Mages
1975/76	T. M. Davies
1976/77	T. Evans
1977/78	A. Meredith
1978/79	A. Meredith
1979/80	G. Wheel
1980/81	G. Wheel
1981/82	D. S. Richards
1982/83	D. S. Richards
1983/84	D. S. Richards
1984/85	M. (Mark) Davies
1985/86	M. (Mark) Davies
1986/87	R. Moriarty
1987/88	R. Moriarty
1988/89	R. Moriarty
1989/90	R. (Robert) Jones
1990/91	R. (Robert) Jones
1991/92	K. Hopkins
1992/93	S. (Stuart) Davies
1993/94	S. (Stuart) Davies
1994/95	A. Clement

Appendix 4

SWANSEA'S INTERNATIONALS

The list which follows includes all players who have been 'capped' whilst at St. Helens up to and including the domestic season 1994/95. Thus, the World Cup (South Africa) appearances are not included. The date in brackets, following the player's name, is the year when he was 'capped' for the first time. In all, 140 players have been honoured by their countries whilst at St. Helens.

'Capped' by Wales

ANDREWS, F. G.	(1884)
ARNOLD, P.	(1990)
BANCROFT, J.	(1909)
BANCROFT, W. J.	(1890)
BEBB, D.	(1959)
BEVAN, S.	(1904)
BEYNON, B.	(1920)
BEYNON, E.	(1925)
BISHOP, E.H.	(1889)
BLYTH, L.G.	(1951)
BLYTH, W.R.	(1974)
BOWEN, G.E.	(1887)
BOWEN, W.	(1921)
BOWEN, W.	(1886)
CLEGG, B.	(1979)
CLEMENT, A.	(1987)
DACEY, M.	(1983)
DAVEY, C.	(1930)
DAVIES, Rev. A.	(1913)
DAVIES, D. I.	(1939)
DAVIES, G.	(1900)
DAVIES, H.	(1898)
DAVIES, H.	(1939)
DAVIES, L.	(1939)
DAVIES, M.	(1981)
DAVIES, S.	(1992)
DAVIES, T.	(1953)
DAVIES, T. M.	(1969)
DAVIES, W.	(1931)
DAVIES, W. T. H.	(1936)
DAY, T.	(1931)
DEACON, T.	(1891)
DONOVAN, A.	(1978)
EMYR, A.	(1989)
EVANS, B.	(1933)
EVANS, D. B.	(1926)
EVANS, I.	(1922)
EVANS, S.	(1985)
EVANS, T. P.	(1975)
EVANS, T.	(1924)
EVANS, W. Rice	(1890)
FAULL, J.	(1957)
GALE , N. R.	(1960)
GIBBS, S.	(1991)
GOLDSWORTHY, S.	(1884)
GWYNN, D.	(1882)
GWYNN, W. H.	(1884)
HARDING, R.	(1923)
HAYWARD, G.	(1908)
HIAMS, H.	(1912)
HOLLINGDALE, B.	(1912)
HOPKINS, K.	(1985)
HOPKINS, P.	(1908)
HOPKINS, T.	(1926)
HOWELLS, W. H.	(1888)
HUXTABLE, R.	(1920)
JACKSON, T. H.	(1895)

JAMES, D.	(1891)
JAMES, E.	(1890)
JENKIN, A. M.	(1895)
JENKINS, D. R.	(1927)
JENKINS, G.	(1991)
JOHN, J. H.	(1926)
JOHNSON, W. D.	(1953)
JONES, D.	(1947)
JONES, H.	(1930)
JONES, J.	(1924)
JONES, R.	(1901)
JONES, R. N.	(1986)
JONES, R.	(1927)
JOSEPH, W.	(1902)
JOWETT, W. F.	(1903)
LANG, J.	(1931)
LELEU, J.	(1959)
LEWIS, B.	(1912)
LEWIS, H.	(1913)
LLEWELLYN, P. D.	(1973)
LONG, E.	(1936)
MAINWARING, H. J.	(1961)
McCUTCHEON, W.	(1891)
MEREDITH, J.	(1888)
MICHAEL, G.	(1923)
MILLS F,.	(1892)
MORGAN, D.	(1885)
MORGAN, E.	(1938)
MORGAN, E.	(1914)
MORGAN, I.	(1908)
MORGAN, W. G.	(1927)
MORIARTY, P.	(1986)
MORIARTY, R. D.	(1981)
MORRIS, G. L.	(1882)
MORRIS, I.	(1924)
MORRIS, R. R.	(1933)
OWEN, A.	(1924)
OWEN, R. M.	(1901)
PALMER, F.	(1922)
PARFITT, S.	(1990)
PARKER, D. S.	(1924)
PARKER, T.	(1919)
PARKER, W.	(1899)
PAYNE, H.	(1935)
PHILLIPS, H. D.	(1952)
REES, D.	(1968)
REES, D.	(1900)
REES, E. B.	(1919)
REES, J. I.	(1934)
REES, J.	(1920)
REYNOLDS, A.	(1990)
RICHARDS, B. R.	(1960)
RICHARDS, D. S.	(1979)
RICHARDS, E. S.	(1885)
SAMUEL, D.	(1891)
SAMUEL, J.	(1891)
SCRINE F.	(1899)
TANNER, H.	(1935)
TARR, D. J.	(1935)
THOMAS, D.	(1930)
THOMAS, D. J.	(1904)
THOMAS, R.	(1900)
THOMAS, R. C. C.	(1949)
THOMAS, W. H.	(1912)
THOMAS, Watcyn	(1927)
TITLEY, M.	(1983)
TOWERS, W. H.	(1887)
TREW, W. J.	(1900)
WEAVER, D.	(1964)
WEBSTER, R.	(1987)
WHEEL, G. A. D.	(1974)
WILLIAMS, C.	(1977)
WILLIAMS, D. B.	(1978)
WILLIAMS, T.	(1888)
WILLIAMS, T.	(1912)
WILLIAMS, T.	(1921)
WILLIAMS, W. O.	(1951)
WYATT, M.	(1983)
YOUNG, D.	(1987)

'Capped' by England

KEYWORTH, M.	(1976)
ROBERTS, V. G.	(1947)
SWIFT, A.H.	(1981)

'Capped' by Scotland

DICK, L. G.	(1972)

Appendix 5

SWANSEA MEN WHO HAVE CAPTAINED WALES

The following players captained Wales whilst playing for Swansea:

William Bowen
W. J. Bancroft
R. M. Owen
W. J. Trew
Jack Bancroft
Rev. Alban Davies
Tom Parker
Joe Rees
W. Rowe Harding
Watcyn Thomas
R.C. C. Thomas
T. M. Davies
R. D. Moriarty
R. N. Jones

In addition, several 'All Whites' captained Wales whilst playing for other clubs. They are:

Guy W. Morgan	–	London Welsh
E. C. Davey	–	Sale
J. I. Rees	–	Edinburgh Wanderers
Terry Davies	–	Llanelli
Bleddyn Bowen	–	South Wales Police
W. J. James	–	Aberavon
Haydn Tanner	–	Cardiff

Appendix 6

SWANSEA'S BRITISH LIONS

NZA	–	1904	T. J. Bevan
NZA	–	1904	W. F. Jowett
NZA	–	1908	E. Morgan
SA	–	1924	R. Harding
NZA	–	1930	D. Parker
SA	–	1938	E. Morgan
SA	–	1938	H. Tanner
SA	–	1955	R. C. C. Thomas
SA	–	1955	W. O. Williams
NZA	–	1959	J. Faull
SA	–	1962	D. Bebb
NZA	–	1966	D. Bebb
NZA	–	1971	T. M. Davies
SA	–	1974	T. M. Davies
NZA	–	1977	T. P. Evans
NZA	–	1977	C. Williams
SA	–	1980	C. Williams
SA	–	1980	D. S. Richards
World XV	–	1986	M. Dacey
AUS	–	1989	R. N. Jones
AUS	–	1989	A. Clement
NZ	–	1993	R. N. Jones
NZ	–	1993	A. Clement
NZ	–	1993	R. Webster
NZ	–	1993	S. Gibbs

Appendix 7

SWANSEA MEN, THE W.R.U. AND I.R.F.B.

Presidents

1881	C. C. Chambers – The first President
1885-1906	Sir J. T. D. Llewellyn
1953-54	E. Davies
1962-63	J. W. Faull
1966-67	T. C. Prosser.

Secretary

1892-96	W. H. Gwynn – The first paid secretary.

International Rugby Football Board Representatives

1892-95	W. H. Gwynn
1958-61	J. W. Faull

Appendix 8

SWANSEA'S W.R.U. CUP RECORD SEASON BY SEASON SINCE 1971-72

Year	*Reached*
1971/72	Round 4
1972/73	Semi-Final
1973/74	Round 4
1974/75	Round 3
1975/76	Final - Runners-up
1976/77	Round 2
1977/78	Final – Winners
1978/79	Round 4
1979/80	Final - Runners-up
1980/81	Semi-Final
1981/82	Round 3
1982/83	Final - Runners-up
1983/84	Round 3
1984/85	Round 4
1985/86	Round 4
1986/87	Final - Runners-up
1987/88	Found 5
1988/89	Round 3
1989/90	Semi-Final
1990/91	Semi-Final
1991/92	Final - Runners-up
1992/93	Semi-Final
1993/94	Round 3
1994/95	Final – Winners

Appendix 9

MAJOR TOURIST MATCHES – IN DATE ORDER

Date			*Versus*	*Score*		*Won/Lost Draw*
December	24	1888	'Maoris'	Swansea 0 pts	'Maoris' 11	L
December	30	1905	New Zealand	Swansea 3 pts	New Zealand 4	L
December	26	1908	Australia	Swansea 6 pts	Australia 0	W
December	26	1912	South Africa	Swansea 3 pts	South Africa 0	W
September	27	1924	New Zealand	Swansea 3 pts	New Zealand 39	L
October	23	1926	'Maoris'	Swansea 6 pts	'Maoris' 11	L
October	10	1931	South Africa	Swansea 3 pts	South Africa 10	L
September	28	1935	New Zealand	Swansea 11 pts	New Zealand 3	W
December	13	1947	Australia	Swansea 8 pts	Australia 11	L
December	15	1951	South Africa	Swansea 3 pts	South Africa 11	L
December	12	1953	New Zealand	Swansea 6 pts	New Zealand 6	D
January	11	1958	Australia	Swansea 6 pts	Australia 12	L
November	26	1960	South Africa	Swansea 3 pts	South Africa 19	L
December	14	1963	New Zealand	Swansea 9 pts	New Zealand 16	L
November	26	1966	Australia	Swansea 9 pts	Australia 8	W
November	15	1969	South Africa	Swansea 0 pts	South Africa 12	L
November	3	1973	Australia	Swansea 9 pts	Australia 9	D
November	29	1975	Australia	Swansea 6 pts	Australia 12	L
October	25	1980	New Zealand	Swansea 0 pts	New Zealand 32	L
November	28	1981	Australia	Swansea 3 pts	Australia 12	L
October	30	1982	'Maoris'	Swansea 15 pts	'Maoris' 12	W
October	30	1984	Australia	Swansea 7 pts	Australia 17	L
October	16	1985	Fiji	Swansea 14 pts	Fiji 23	L
October	21	1989	New Zealand	Swansea 22 pts	New Zealand 37	L
November	4	1992	Australia	Swansea 21 pts	Australia 6	W
November	5	1994	South Africa	Swansea 7 pts	South Africa 78	L

Appendix 10

LEADING TRY AND POINTS SCORERS SEASON BY SEASON

As WILL HAVE BEEN NOTED FROM Appendix 1, available information concerning the early days of Swansea Rugby Club is, to say the least, sparse. In particular, the penchant of observers to produce statistics about a game did not affect rugby football for some time after it began to attract public interest on a significant scale. As a consequence, the following data commences some thirteen seasons after the club began to play rugby. Even then, in some cases, it has not been possible to find some data. Where this is the case, the column concerned has been left blank so as to enable the reader, should he or she wish, to add the information when and if it becomes available. It should be noted, too, that during the first decade of the following listing, whilst it was possible, in most cases, to establish the tally of the leading try scorer, that associated with leading points scorer was not always as clear. Nonetheless, the data which is included is a best approximation of the total for each season. The leading points scorer, where listed, is not in question.

Season	*Leading Try Scorer*	*Leading Points Scorer*	
1887-88	W. H. Jones – 9	D. Gwynn	55
1888-89	W. H. Jones, W. H. Towers, A. Whapham – 6	W. J. Bancroft	56
1889-90	J. Meredith – 9	W. J. Bancroft	54
1890-91	D. James – 20	W. J. Bancroft	72
1891-92	C. S. Coke – 19	W. J. Bancroft	67
1892-93	H. Whapham, C. S. Coke – 8	W. J. Bancroft	40
1893-94	C. S. Coke – 7	W. J. Bancroft	47
1894-95			
1895-96	R. Messer – 7	W. J. Bancroft	37
1896-97	G. Davies – 13	W. J. Bancroft	59
1897-98	F. Gordon – 15	G. Davies	61
1898-99	W. J. Trew – 33	W. J. Bancroft	191
1899-1900	W. J. Trew – 31	W. J. Bancroft	93
		W. J. Trew	93

Season	*Leading Try Scorer*	*Leading Points Scorer*	
1900-01	D. Rees – 20	W. J. Bancroft	82
1901-02	D. Rees – 20	W. J. Bancroft	86
1902-03	W. F. Jowett – 42 +	W. F. Jowett	126
1903-04	W. F. Jowett, W. J. Trew – 29	W. J. Trew	128
1904-05	D. Rees – 30		
1905-06	W. J. Trew – 16	W. J. Trew	52
1906-07	W. J. Trew – 13	Jack Bancroft	81
1907-08	W. J. Trew – 14	Jack Bancroft	66
1908-09	I. Morgan – 18*	Jack Bancroft	101
1909-10	W. J. Trew – 10	Jack Bancroft	77
1910-11	H. Evans – 28	Jack Bancroft	88
1911-12	F. Holbrook – 18	Jack Bancroft	48
1912-13	F. Holbrook – 15	Jack Bancroft	60
1913-14	B. Lewis – 15	Jack Bancroft	49
GREAT WAR			
1919-20	B. Beynon – 9	B. Beynon	47
1920-21		W. Bowen	56
1921-22	Rowe Harding, I. Evans – 15	J. Rees	63
1922-23	Rowe Harding – 10		
1923-24	J. Jones – 11	J. Jones	44
1924-25		Dr. Bertram	51
1925-26	J. E. Watkins – 13	D. Parker	63
1926-27	R. Jones – 16	D. Parker	49
1927-28	D. P. Manley – 21	D. Parker	164
1928-29	D. P. Manley – 25	D. Parker	173
1929-30	D. P. Manley – 29	D. Parker	157
1930-31	H. Jones – 18	H. Jones	54
1931-32	D. Folland – 10		
1932-33	D. Folland – 15	R. R. Morris	62
1933-34	H. M. Powell – 11	G. Davies	65
1934-35	H. M. Powell – 24	H. M. Powell	72
1935-36		E. Long	48
1936-37		G. Jenkins	73
1937-38	H. M. Powell – 34**	H. M. Powell	102
1938-39	H. M. Powell – 26	H. M. Powell	78

SECOND WORLD WAR

* = Record number of tries scored by a forward at that time.
+ = All time record.
** = Post 1st World War record.

Season	*Leading Try Scorer*	*Leading Points Scorer*	
1945-46	G. Addenbrooke – 19	G. Addenbrooke	59
1946-47	G. Addenbrooke – 19	G. Addenbrooke	57
1947-48	G. Beynon – 9	A. Thomas	94
1948-49	J. W. Jenkins – 20	L. Davies	88
1949-50	W. D. Johnson – 14	L. Davies	71
1950-51	H. Thomas – 11	L. Davies	65
1951-52	H. D. Phillips – 11	W. Jones	66
1952-53	W. D. Johnson – 10	Arwyn Morris	58
1953-54	T. Williams – 17	J. Faull	52
1954-55	T. Williams, H. D. Phillips – 9	A. Prosser-Harries	55
1955-56	G. Lawrence – 13	A. Prosser-Harries	76
1956-57	T. Williams – 11	A. Prosser-Harries	119
1957-58	T. Williams – 10	J. Faull	50
1958-59	M. Evans – 12	D. Parkhouse	88
1959-60	D. Bebb – 14	H. Mainwaring	131
1960-61	D. Bebb – 12	H. Mainwaring	73
1961-62	D. Bebb – 8	J. Faull	81
1962-63	M. Thomas – 9	Gareth Thomas	79
1963-64	D. Bebb – 13	D. Parkhouse	85
1964-65	D. Bebb, M. Thomas – 14	Gareth Thomas	59
1965-66	G. Morgan – 10	S. Ferguson	195
1966-67		S. Ferguson	214
1967-68	D. Rogers – 14	S. Ferguson	145
1968-69	S. Ferguson – 9	S. Ferguson	184
1969-70	Stuart Davies – 21	S. Ferguson	107
1970-71	J. Evans, R. Hyndman – 15	D. Lewis	244
1971-72	M. Davies – 13	C. Roderick	84
1972-73	D. Coles – 16	R. Dyer	162
1973-74	R. Blyth, G. Higgins – 15	R. Blyth	251
1974-75	R. Blyth – 14	R. Blyth	254
1975-76	R. Woodward – 20	John Rees	116
1976-77	A. Meredith – 15	S. Bater	93
1977-78	R. Blyth – 15	R. Blyth	233
1978-79	M. Langdon – 15	R. Blyth	152
1979-80	A. Swift – 29 +	R. Blyth	348
1980-81	A. Swift – 28	M. Wyatt	243
1981-82	A. Swift – 15	M. Wyatt	310
1982-83	A. Emyr, A. Swift – 25	R. Blyth	211
1983-84	A. Swift – 21	M. Wyatt	294

+ = Post 2nd World War record.

1984–85	A. Emyr – 21	M. Wyatt	376 #
1985–86	P. Moriarty – 25 *	R. Bevan	111
1986–87	A. Emyr – 25	M. Wyatt	290
1987–88	B. Taylor – 18	M. Wyatt	244
1988–89	B. Taylor – 20	M. Wyatt	168
1989–90	M. Titley – 26	M. Wyatt	256
1990–91	M. Titley – 15	R. Jones	137
1991–92	M. Titley, S. Davies – 17	A. Williams	131
1992–93	Simon Davies – 15	A. Williams	247
1993–94	Simon Davies – 17	A. Williams	256
1994–95	D. Weatherly – 12	A. Williams	271

* = All time record for a forward. # = All time record.

Appendix 11

SOME SWANSEA R.F.C. RECORDS

Note. Given the relatively few matches played by the club in its earliest seasons, the data for that period was not considered for inclusion in the following section.

1. *Least and Most; Highest and Lowest*

(a)

Most matches won in a season:	41	season 1980/81
Most matches lost in a season:	32	season 1969/70
Least matches lost in a season:	0	season 1904/05
Least matches won in a season:	14	seasons 1954/55 and 1961/62

(b) *Points:* The following statistics are influenced by the value attributed to a try at the time in question. Consequently, the data are presented in three sub-sections:

(i) When a try was worth three points
(ii) When a try was worth four points, and
(iii) When a try was worth five points

Most points scored in a season :

(i) 796 points – season 1971/72
(ii) 1242 points – season 1980/81
(iii) 1185 points – season 1993/94

Least points conceded in a season:

(i) 38 points – season 1903/04
(ii) 381 points – season 1978/79
(iii) 547 points – season 1992/93

Least points scored in a season:

(i) 171 points – season 1892/93
(ii) 693 points – season 1978/79
(iii) 875 points – season 1992/93

Most points conceded in a season:

(i) 705 points – season 1971/72
(ii) 771 points – season 1989/90
(iii) 634 points – season 1990/91

(c) *Percentages*

(i) highest percentage of matches played which were won:
83.74% – season 1903/04

(ii) Lowest percentage of matches played which were won:
34.15% – season 1961/62

(d) *Record victory/defeat*

Record victory: 95 points to 22 v. Cross Keys, 4/12/93
Record defeat: 3 points to 79 v. Bath, 9/2/93

(e) The following section relates only to the period 1956–1995.
Most wins in succession: 17 – season 1982/83
Most losses in succession: 10 – season 1954/55

(f) *Some individual records*

(i) *Most matches played by an individual* in a career at St. Helens (still ongoing at the time of writing):
Richard Moriarty, 463 (to the end of season 1994/95)

(ii) *Most matches played by an individual in a season:*
Stuart Ferguson, played 47 out of 48 matches – season 1966/67

(iii) *Most points scored by an individual in a career at St. Helens:*
Mark Wyatt, 2,679 points

(iv) *Most points scored by an individual in a season:*
Mark Wyatt, 376 points – season 1984/85

(v) *Most tries scored by an individual in a career at St.Helens:*
Arthur Emyr, 143 – seasons 1980-1991

(vi) *Most tries scored by an individual in a season:*
Fred Jowett, 42 – season 1902/03

(vii) *Most tries scored in a season by a forward:*
Paul Moriarty, 25 – season 1985/86

(viii) *Most points scored by an individual in a match.*
Steffan Jones, 34 points v. Penarth – season 1989/90

(ix) *Most tries scored by an indivdual in a match for the 'Whites':*
Harold Powell, 6 tries v. United Services – season 1938/39

SOME INTERESTING FACTS

1. Six Swansea players appeared in the Wales XV during season 1907/08 and 1991/92.
2. St. Helens (The new Cricket Ground) was opened on Whit Monday 1875, for the traditional Cricket Club athletics meeting.
3. The first cricket match played on the ground took place on 21 April 1876.
4. The first rugby match played on the ground took place on 13 October 1876.
5. The first International rugby match on Welsh soil took place at St. Helens on 15 December

1882 . England were the opponents, and two Swansea men, D. Gwynn and G. L. Morris, were in the Welsh team.

6. Among more than a half dozen grounds which were 'opened' with a match being played against the 'Whites' were :
   Morriston R.F.C.; 19 September 1891
   Llanelli R.F.C. – The New Stradey; 1904/05 season
   Devonport Albions – 3/10/1896.
7. For a match at Newport on 2 February 1897, the 'Whites' fielded a side which included five men with the surname Davies, (including the whole of the three-quarter line), The half-backs were both called James (Evan and David), whilst two men called Williams, a Jones and a Thomas, played in the pack. One obvious foreigner played at full-back. He was W. J. Bancroft!
8. During the 1983/84 season, Roger Blyth scored more than a century of points for the ninth time in eleven seasons.
9. During the 1982/83 season, when the 'Whites' beat Llanelli at Stradey Park in the W.R.U. Cup, it was the first time that the 'Scarlets' had lost a home cup tie since the inception of the modern competition.
10. During the early part of the 1982/83 season, the 'Whites' beat Moseley and Gloucester in successive matches. Since the two English sides had been the joint-winners of the John Player cup at the end of the previous season, the victories formed a unique 'double'.
11. For the 1964 Five Nations match against England, the 'Whites' supplied both wings : Dewi Bebb and David Weaver.
12. Swansea's first 'round-the-corner' kicker was Doug Rees (1967/68).
13. For the 1976 International, England v. Wales, the 'Whites' provided a flank forward for each side. (Mark Keyworth and Trevor Evans). However, this was not the first occasion when Swansea wing-forwards played for both sides in an England v. Wales international. Twenty years earlier, Clem Thomas and Vic Roberts had set the same mark.
14. The first Swansea match in which both sides wore numbers was that against Aberavon during the 1928/29 season.
15. The first match in which the Swansea men wore white shirts and white shorts (to become genuinely all-white for the first time) took place on 10 January 1925 when the side met Penarth at St. Helens.
16. When W. J. Trew (Jnr.) was elected captain for the 1930/31 campaign, it was the first time that a father and son had captained the club.
17. In the 1906 England v. Wales match, Dickie Owen was the Wales scrum-half, whilst D. R. Gent occupied the position for the English. Whilst Gent was English, he had been brought up in Swansea and educated at Swansea Grammar School. Another unusual Swansea 'double'.
18. During the spring of 1892, the 'Whites' did not concede a single point in matches played over a two month period.
19. Two Swansea men, Rowe Harding and Gwilym Michael, were chosen to play for the combined England/Wales side for the 'Centenary' match at Rugby School (during the 1923/24 season).
20. The first try scored for the South Wales Football Club (the predecessor of the W.R.U.) was registered by A. H. Richardson – a Swansea player – (versus Hereford).

21. The first county game to have been played in Wales took place at St. Helens in November 1881, when Glamorgan opposed Monmouthshire.
22. The 'Whites' won the *Snelling Sevens* in 1982,1989, and 1991, and the *Welsh National Sevens* in 1979 and 1980.
23. The following players have two things in comon. They have all (a) captained Swansea R.F.C., and (b) played against the three major touring sides (S.A., N.Z., Australia):

    (i) Dil Johnson, (ii) Billy Williams, (iii) Clem Thomas, (iv) Teifion Williams, (v) Richard Moriarty, (vi) Robert Jones, (vii) Tony Clement.

    These seven men are further examples of outstanding club loyalty and committment at St. Helens.
24. When they defeated New Zealand on 28 September 1935 the 'Whites' became the first club to have beaten the three major touring sides.
25. During the 1982/83 season, the club scored 173 tries to set a new record.
26. During the period 1957/78, the 'Whites' failed to score during a match on only five occasions. Opponents, during the same period, were unable to register any points on forty occasions.
27. The 'Whites' were:
    Welsh Merit Table Champions 1973/74, 1980/81 and 1982/83.
    Schweppes or *SWALEC* Cup winners 1977/78 and 1994/95.
    Western Mail Welsh Champions 1979/80, 1982/83.
    Sunday Telegraph Team of the Season, 1979/80, 1980/81.
    Dail Mail Anglo-Welsh Champions, 1979/80.
    Anglo-Welsh Chapions 1982/83.
    Heineken 1st. Division Champions, 1991/92 and 1993/94.
28. Prior to the World Cup competition in South Africa in 1995, Robert Jones had played for Wales on 52 occasions. As such he is the most 'capped' 'All White' of all time.
29. During the period 1898/99 to 1904/05, the 'Whites' won the Welsh Championship on six occasions out of seven and they were runners-up at the end of the seventh season.
30 During the season 1903/04, the side conceded a total of only 38 points in 32 games (whilst scoring 571), a remarkable defensive records, equal to just 1.19 points per game.
31. Over thirteen seasons, Mark Wyatt scored an average of 207 points per campaign whilst playing for the 'Whites'. Apart from one season (when he was absent for a great deal of time) and his first and last campaigns, his points total was always a three figure number. Mark scored more than three hundred points on two occasions and was only six points short at the end of a third season.
32. During the 1995 World Cup in South Africa, Robert Jones became the most-capped Welsh scrum-half of all time (54).

INDEX

C

I

J

N

O

Y

Z

LIST OF SUBSCRIBERS

The list which follows identifies the individuals and concerns who supported the publication of this book as a result of subscribing to the special limited edition of 275 copies of this title. The number alongside the name of the subscriber is that which was allocated to the individual copy in the name of the subscriber, and which was inscribed on a certificate printed in the book.

In presenting this list, Swansea Rugby Football Club, and the author and publisher wish to place on record our appreciation of the support provided by all who subscribed. Without that support, and that provided by the BJ Group plc, it would not have been possible to produce such an extensive history; a slimmer volume would have ensued at proportionately greater cost.

ADDICOTT, Stan 201
ALCOA MANUFACTURING (GB) LTD. 267
ALCOA MANUFACTURING (GB) LTD. 268
ALCOA MANUFACTURING (GB) LTD. 269
ALCOA MANUFACTURING (GB) LTD. 270
ALEXANDER, Bill 156
ATHERTON, Geoff, *BSc C.Eng., FIEE* 64
AYLESBURY, Alan, *OBE* 165
BATER, Des 212
BEBB, Dewi 257
BEYNON, Prof. J. H., *FRS* 135
BIRKS, Rhys 55
BLYTH, John L. 100
BLYTH, Len 72
BLYTH, W. R. 99
BLYTH, W. N. 101
BOND, David 56
BOOTH, J. W., *MA* 171
BOWEN, Aubrey, *BSc* 248
BOWEN, E. W. M. 151
BOWEN, H. G., *MB Bch* 183
BOWEN, H. G., *MB Bch* 184
BRATTON, W. 137
CHEESEMAN, Trevor C. 126
CLARK, Lady Marjorie 134
CLIFFORD, Jim 174
CONIBEAR, R. J. 133
DACEY, Malcolm 237
DANCE, Craig, *BA (Hons.)* 145
DAVIES, Andrew Richard 10
DAVIES, Anthony P. 29
DAVIES, C. D. 265
DAVIES, D. Cliff 98
DAVIES, Dr. T. Maldwyn 79
DAVIES, Gerald 138
DAVIES, Heather A. 74
DAVIES, Huw 97
DAVIES, Michael Robert, *BSc (Hons.)* 28
DAVIES, N., *ACCA* 108
DAVIES, R. J. 7
DAVIES, Robert J. Ll. 19
DAVIES, Stephen 57
DAVIES, Stuart, *BSc, C.Eng, MICE* 143
DAVIES, T. J. V., *BA* 104
DAVIES, T. H., *LVO BSc (Econ.)* 88
DAVIES, Timothy J., *DipFD, HND* 69
DAVIES, Vernon Rees 105
DAY, Graham Manton, *FCA* 189
DAY, T. H. 38
DENHAM, Leonard Patrick 106
DEVONALD, Alan 209
DOWNES, E. Malcolm, *MB, BCH, FRCS* 49
DURBAN, Ioan H., *CIPD, FIMgt* 40
DYER, Clive 172
EDNEY, Neil, *B.D.S.* 186
EDWARDS, A.V., *BA (Hons.), Adv.DipEd* 48
EDWARDS, John 160
ELLIS, Glyn 226
ELLIS, Gwyn 93
EMYR, Arthur 77
EVANS, Baden 232
EVANS, Brian 39
EVANS, Bryn 177
EVANS, D. Anthony, QC 17
EVANS, D. E. 266
EVANS, D. Tal 25
EVANS, Dr. Mark 90
EVANS, Dr. Richard G., 117
EVANS, Glyn, *JP* 144
FALVEY, M. W. A. 111
FARMER, D. G. 1
FARMER, E. R., *MSc, FCCA* 129
FARMER, Prof. D. H., *MSc, PhD* 255
FARMER, T. J. 2
FAULL, I. T. 80
FIELDING, C. B., *BA* 159
FISH, Roger, *ACII* 188
FRANCIS, Donald & Phyllis 11
FRANCIS, Nicholas Alexander Benjamin 5

STEAD, Peter 158
STEVENS, D. P., *ISO* 258
SUFF, C. G., *BA FRSA* 91
SUMMERFIELD, David 164
TANNER, H., *BSc, FRIC* 224
THOMAS, Alun 175
THOMAS, Chris R. C. 14
THOMAS, Clem 230
THOMAS, Dudley 241
THOMAS, Gerry, *MPS* 85
THOMAS, Gethin 81
THOMAS, Gregory 169
THOMAS, Gwyn, *MSc, PhD* 173
THOMAS, Mike 227
THOMAS, P. L. 102
THOMAS, R. H. V. 199
THOMAS, R. J. 253
THOMAS, Robert E. 136
THOMAS, Roger, *MBII* 83
TOWNS, J. M. 203
TREW, Victor Thomas, *JP* 205
TROLLOPE, G. H. 24
UREN, Paul R. 181
WALTERS, John 220
WALTERS, Morley T. 149
WATKINS, Philip R. V. 60
WEAVER, David 217
WEAVER, Elvet 127
WEBB, Neil William 180
WHITE, D. Percy 141
WHITE, Gwyn 153
WIGLEY, Bob 67
WILLIAMS, B. C. 264
WILLIAMS, Clive 182
WILLIAMS, Clive 233
WILLIAMS, E. B. 166
WILLIAMS, Frank 37
WILLIAMS, Michael A. H., *BA (Law) Hons.* 89
WILLIAMS, Sir Glanmor 4
WILLIAMS, R. A. G. 154
WILLIAMS, Roy 114
WILLIAMS, S. G., *BSc (Econ.) M.R.T.P.I.* 21
WILLIAMS, Teifion, *BA* 42
YOUNG, Howard, *BA DipEd* 41